Religion, Morality & the "New Right"

Religion, Morality & the "New Right"

Edited by Melinda Maidens

Facts On File, Inc.
460 Park Avenue South, New York, N.Y. 10016

Religion, Morality & the "New Right"

Published by Facts On File, Inc.
460 Park Avenue South, New York, N.Y. 10016
© Copyright 1982 by Facts On File, Inc.

Library of Congress Cataloging in Publication Data

Maidens, Melinda.
    Religion, morality, and the "new right".

    Includes index.
     1. United States — Moral conditions.   2. Conservatism — United States.   3. United States — Religion. I. Title.
HN59.2.M34   306'.0973   82-2333
ISBN 0-87196-639-5   AACR2

International Standard Book Number: 0-87196-639-5
Library of Congress Catalog Card Number: 82-2333
9 8 7 6 5 4 3 2 1
PRINTED IN THE UNITED STATES OF AMERICA

Contents

Preface

Religion has been a part of American life since the Pilgrims landed on Plymouth Rock in 1620. Fleeing religious persecution, they sought to create a society governed by Biblical strictures and embodying true Christian virtue. In a modified form, their fundamental concepts of Judeo-Christian morality have been accepted for many years as national values.

In the past 20 years, these values were questioned by many and rejected by some. America experienced an enormous upheaval in the 1960s, and its effects have not worn off. The divorce rate has climbed, sex roles have changed and the younger generation has openly split with parents on the question of new "lifestyles."

A reaction to the turbulent 1960s had to be expected, and it came during the late 1970s. In the form of the Moral Majority and other "New Right" elements, this reaction struck a responsive chord in millions of Americans. They were the ones who had watched the developments of the 1960s and early 1970s with profound distaste yet had felt helpless to strike back. Their frustrations provided the energy for the emergence of the "New Right." When people heard television and radio preachers unafraid to express beliefs that had been scorned as "old-fashioned," they took heart. Religion became respectable once more upon the election of "born-again" Baptist Jimmy Carter as president in 1980. People found that their religious convictions made a strong impression upon politicians when combined with the ballot box.

Anxiety over the implications of the "New Right" movement is not confined to 1960s "revolutionaries" and liberals. Religious leaders of all faiths are worried by the prospect of a revivalist tidal wave that might sweep aside tolerance and make a mockery of America's cherished freedoms. Their fears may turn out to be as unfounded as the conservatives' fear of the destruction of the Republic by the long-haired youth of the 1960s (some of whom are now wearing three-piece suits). America has an unusual capacity to absorb all kinds of fringe movements without damaging its basic commitment to individual rights.

It is important to examine closely the "New Right's" goals, the reason for its rapid growth and the movement's intentions for the future of America. The "New Right" is not simply a group of "middle Americans" yearning for a past depicted by Norman Rockwell. Their actions are geared toward the present and future, and they have already had lasting effects, from local school boards to the halls of Congress.

The "New Right's" concerns—abortion, women's rights, family life and public education—are topics of intense controversy even in the calmest of discussions. With the "New Right's" religious fervor, these topics fairly crackle with emotion. The "New Right" has provided editorial writers with a choice supply of topics for lively discussion, and the editorials in this book, gathered from all 50 states, contain plenty of controversy. They were not chosen to favor or condemn any viewpoint, since the public debate on our national values should be open to all.

March, 1982   Melinda Maidens

Part I: Politics

"Congress shall make no law respecting an establishment of religion, or prohibiting the free exercise thereof; or abridging the freedom of speech, or of the press; or the right of the people peaceably to assemble, and to petition the Government for a redress of grievances." So runs the all-important First Amendment to the Constitution. It is the basis of America's most valued liberties. Sometimes, though, these liberties conflict with each other in ways that our Founding Fathers could not have foreseen. Freedom of religion may involve a suppression of freedom of speech, and vice versa. The government must maneuver delicately through a maze of conflicting public demands.

This maneuvering between religion and politics is not new in American history. Religious groups have combatted slavery, lobbied for social services for the poor and taken positions on government actions from "blue laws" to the Vietnam War. This interaction is all the more lively because America is one of the few Western countries without an official church. Almost every country in Western Europe has an established church, which is supported by state taxes and affected by state laws.

Despite our firm commitment to separation of church and state, Americans demand that religion be a basis of public morality. Judeo-Christian principles of justice and compassion are supposed to guide government policy, and Judeo-Christian moral standards are expected of government officials. The problem is that Americans are not limited to Jews and Christians. There are many other faiths, and what should be the relationship of religious morality to a society that seeks to accommodate people of all faiths?

Conservative Trend Noted; Significance Debated

The term "New Right" made a gradual appearance on the American political scene during the late 1970s. A number of events had taken place in 1978 that indicated a growing conservatism in the public's political and social attitudes and a new resolve to change the country's policies. The most dramatic illustration of this trend was the so-called "tax revolt" given shape by Howard A. Jarvis, a California realtor who sponsored a state ballot initiative to limit property taxes. The measure, Proposition 13, was passed by an overwhelming margin in the June 1978 primary, signaling the start of a grass-roots movement to cut taxes and reduce government operations. The success of the tax-reducing ballot initiatives symbolized a general disillusionment with "big government," usually defined by opponents as excessive business regulations, intrusive integration programs and overgenerous welfare payments. In foreign affairs, too, America was becoming more conservative. There was a new public willingness to increase defense spending and reassert American power around the world. The conservative trend was most apparent in contributions to lobbying groups during the 1978 congressional elections. Heading the list of the largest national money-raisers were three conservative political action committees: Ronald Reagan's Citizens for the Republic, which raised $2.1 million, the National Conservative Political Action Committee, which raised $2 million, and the Committee for the Survival of a Free Congress, which raised $1.5 million.

THE MILWAUKEE JOURNAL
Milwaukee, Wisc., February 13, 1978

It's known as the "New Right," but there's something awfully old about it. The latest incarnation of the right wing isn't much newer than the Know-Nothing Party of the 19th century, the American Independent Party of the 1960s or the various other ultraconservative movements that have cropped up along the fringes of politics.

Like its predecessors, the New Right is more interested in raising issues that will exploit voters' fears and frustrations than in talking about major questions of government policy. For the Know-Nothings, the pressing needs were to keep Catholics out of politics and clamp down on immigration. In the '60s, rightists played up racial tensions and "law and order." The New Right has latched onto gun control, the Panama Canal treaty dispute, abortion and instant voter registration.

It isn't that the New Right has a monopoly on any of these subjects; mainstream Republicans and Democrats debate them, too. The difference is that the rightists employ emotional issues to almost completely camouflage their ultraconservative economic views. Apparently they know they can't win many elections if they fly their true colors.

The New Right (which includes the Committee for the Survival of a Free Congress and the National Conservative Political Action Committee) hopes to oust progressive Republicans and Democrats in this year's congressional primaries and general election. Perhaps the greatest danger is that the threat from the right may scare moderate Republicans into taking a more conservative stance.

However, a much sounder course for mainstream politicians is to concentrate on central policy questions and trust that the voters will discover the emptiness of a political movement that offers no coherent program — just a bundle of emotional appeals.

Richmond Times-Dispatch
Richmond, Va., July 4, 1978

Sociologists and other experts offer differing interpretations of the new mood of America, as manifested by the spreading taxpayers' revolt and other such expressions of discontent, but optimists might view it as a renascence of the spirit of Boston Harbor. In essence, the people who vote to curtail taxes, who resist enactment of the Equal Rights Amendment and who fight such legislative proposals as the aborted labor reform act appear to be venting the same resentment of oppressive and meddlesome government that motivated those outraged patriots who dumped the East India Company's subsidized tea into the water in 1773.

Explaining the attitude of colonial Americans at that defiant period, Edmund Burke observed:

"They augur misgovernment at a distance, and snuff the approach of tyranny in every tainted breeze."

This is an appropriate description of the mood of America as it celebrates the 202nd anniversary of the Declaration of Independence. Throughout the land, from ocean to ocean, people are growing acutely aware of the distressing fact that they are victims of misgovernment — of governmental extravagance, governmental waste and governmental inefficiency. Nearly every breeze from Washington brings the whiff of new federal tyranny in the form of legislative or bureaucratic edicts that restrict individual freedom and rights.

It is almost as if King George III had been resurrected and placed firmly in command in Washington. Consider this particular grievance that the Declaration of Independence expressed against him:

"He has erected a multitude of new offices, and sent hither swarms of officers to harrass our people, and eat out their substance."

Could there be a more accurate characterization of the federal government today? Its offices are multitudinous, and it has swarms of officers out harrassing the people — dictating their choice of schools for their children, regulating the recreational activities of school boys and girls, advising farmers on the safe use of ladders, complicating the operations of businesses large and small and substituting their arrogant judgment for the free will of the people in myriad other offensive ways. As for the people's "substance," the government gnaws at that steadily with exorbitant taxes and with inflationary policies that larcenously erode the purchasing power of paychecks.

And so people are reacting, at last, by voting to curb taxes and by resisting such needless expansions of governmental power as that represented by the ERA.

It is a welcome and wholesome mood. For too long, middle America has been quiescent in the face of growing governmental power, submitting too placidly to pernicious policies that mock the founding spirit of the republic. It was the hope of the men who breathed life into this nation two centuries ago to create a political entity that would minimize governmental power and maximize individual freedom and responsibility. But we have become, through the persistent efforts of liberal statists, an entity that is doing precisely the opposite. If the new spirit of Boston Harbor lingers and grows, however, this disastrous trend can be reversed.

It is an encouraging note on which to celebrate today.

St. Louis Globe-Democrat
St. Louis, Mo., February 22, 1978

Time and again pollsters, who should know better, make the mistake of asking an individual what he considers himself from a general political point of view.

For an accurate evaluation of political philosophy, the questions should be directed at determining specifically where an individual stands on issues.

The question of rating one's self as conservative, middle-of-the-road or liberal was asked recently by the Harris Survey. No conclusions can be drawn from such a grossly unscientific approach. The final results of this type of survey do not contain sufficient fodder to qualify as a light conversation piece.

The poll reported that there had been "little real change" in how Americans see themselves in the past 10 years. This year's survey puts 32 percent of the respondents into the conservative catagory, 41 percent in the middle and only 18 percent claiming to be liberal.

A decade ago expressing conservative views didn't rank No. 1 on the public hit parade. "But now it is beginning to be intellectually respectable," according to Paul W. McCracken, who served as chairman of the Council of Economic Advisers in the Nixon Administration and now is on the economics faculty at the University of Michigan.

The transition has even pierced adademic circles. A recent survey showed that professors overwhelmingly preferred private rather than public funds for research because of the governmental controls that accompany the grants, McCracken said.

Now that the trace of stigma is disappearing, conservative views are espoused by vast numbers of people who still identify themselves as middle-of-the-roaders. Some liberal congressmen are well aware of that fact of political life and go out of their way to hide their voting record from public view and the electorate's close scrutiny.

How different the percentages in the Harris Survey would have been if the pollsters had concentrated on the issues rather than on misleading lables. An examination of stands dear to the hearts of conservatives provides strong evidence of a nation moving to the right and away from the fallacies and broken promises of the liberal left.

A growing concern is seen over massive budget deficits and the soaring national debt. The cry against governmental overregulation and control is getting louder. Wasteful spending and callous disregard for taxpayer revenues is denounced.

The increasing acceptance of these stands, long embraced by conservatives, is an indication of changing times. Perhaps the truths of conservatism are being adopted as their own by many middle-of-the-roaders. The nation is the winner because it is not the label but the basis political philosophy that makes the big difference.

ARKANSAS DEMOCRAT
Little Rock, Ark., July 4, 1978

That famous New York Times-CBS Poll that purported to deny the existence of the "New Right" last January has been shown up as a fraud—by another poll that was run to prove that any polls constructed like these two are invalid.

That sounds complex. What happened was this: The New York Times-CBS poll, which reported that conservatives were turning liberal, focused on three questions. Should government help people get medical care, and jobs and see to it that blacks get fair treatment in jobs and housing?

Large positive majorities (81, 74 and 68 per cent) said yes to all three questions; big majorities of the conservatives included in the poll (79, 70 and 64 per cent) agreed. The "New Right," the pollsters concluded, was a myth—there was no new outburst of conservatism.

Along came the North American Newspaper Alliance four months later to test out the truth of these findings. NANA decided to duplicate the previous poll questions—but also to substitute "private enterprise" for "government" in a second poll taken simultaneously among other respondents. To make a long story short, the duplicate poll run by NANA produced much the same percentages as the Times-CBS poll. However, NANA's second poll (asking whether free enterprise should help people get medical care and jobs and promote black interests) drew majority percentages of 71, 70 and 56 per cent—not all that far off the responses given when the Times-CBS poll asked its sample whether government should do these things.

Confusion confounded? No, according to Opinion Research, which conducted the two NANA polls, both the January Times-CBS poll and the May NANA polls were invalid. They supplied or suggested the agency that should concern itself with health, jobs and civil rights. In such situations, says Opinion Research, people tend to say yes.

Maybe that'll teach us all a lesson about polling: it can be used to prove anything.

ST. LOUIS POST-DISPATCH
St. Louis, Mo., May 1, 1978

A test of what is called the "new" or "reinvigorated" right in American politics may be offered this week as voters choose congressional candidates in primaries in Indiana, North Carolina and Texas. The states involved, however, sometimes have conservative tendencies, and any test of the right wing is difficult because its tactics have changed and its successes are hard to measure.

The new right receives a kind of compliment in the form of a warning from the Americans for Democratic Action on the other side of the political spectrum. An ADA report notes that several new right-wing groups have appeared in recent years, that they are not bound by conventional conservative rhetoric but will exploit any issue that broadens their constituency, that they seek their constituency in both parties, that they have a great deal of money to spend—and that they have "begun to win."

Among their victories, the ADA lists defeats of a new federal voter registration measure, public financing of elections and the consumer protection agency. On top of that, *Group Research Report* credits the new right with having helped substantially in the election of conservative congressmen in four of five special elections last year.

Perhaps so, but this year the symbolic issue chosen by the right as a rallying point for future progress was that of the Panama Canal treaties. The American Conservative Union, 300,000 strong, alone spent $1.1 million trying to persuade or bring pressure on senators to vote against those treaties. Other rightist groups added to the spending total, to the lobbying and to the anti-treaty literature. And they lost. Or did they? Even in losing in the Senate, they undoubtedly attracted attention to their cause and possibly interest in allied causes.

Still, they could not persuade even one-third of the senators on whom they concentrated, and it may be questioned whether the emotional Panama Canal issue can be translated into equal conservatism on other issues, except among devout conservatives. The middle-road quality of American politics has not allowed for many vigorous swings far away from the center. While there seems to be a conservative trend in the country, a good deal more evidence is needed before concluding that the drift is as conservative as the new right itself.

The Sun Reporter
San Francisco, Calif., September 14, 1978

We hear a lot these days about the resurgence of the "new right" in American politics and the fact that the liberals seem to be in disarray. The trouble with this kind of talk is that it can become self-fulfilling prophecy if it isn't checked in time. The careers of men like Richard Nixon, Ronald Reagan, and Howard Jarvis testify to the ability of politicians to bluff themselves into high office and influence mainly by convincing people that large numbers of other people take their harebrained ideas seriously.

For minorities and others accustomed to receiving the short end of the political-social-economic stick in this country, the results of this kind of public opinion steamroller can be disastrous, as the nationwide climate of stinginess that followed Proposition 13 clearly shows. The people who make our laws and chart our national agenda are, in the main, prosperous whites. They tend to act on behalf of racial minorities and people less prosperous than themselves only in response to pressure from their constituents. Therefore, when the climate of national opinion is perceived to be predominantly liberal, progressive legislation tends to be the order of the day, whether it would benefit the lawmakers personally or not. But these same progressives can be expected to pull in the carpet at the slightest sign that the public is leaning toward the right.

The important thing to understand is that it doesn't require an actual change in the way large numbers of Americans are thinking—merely the appearance of a change broadcast flamboyantly enough by those who stand to gain the most from ignoring the needs of the poor and the powerless. Therefore, suggestions that conservatism is on the rise, liberalism is in decline, and the like should be met by quick and effective resistance from Blacks and seriously progressive Americans. If not, we can expect to see the quick erosion of the gains we fought so hard for.

Division Begins to Blur Between Church & State

The "New Right" differed significantly from the "old right" in its approach to religion. The conservative trend that developed in the late 1970s had a religious background. President Jimmy Carter's "born again" Christianity was perhaps the most famous example of religion in public life, and he was followed by others. Religion suddenly became a useful motive for policy decisions. The "New Right" made religion the very heart of its political program and acknowledged Christianity as the basis for its stance on political issues. Unlike the "old right," which generally was uncomfortable about combining religious beliefs and U.S. statutes, the "New Right" did not hesitate to introduce Biblical precepts into law. The opening phrase of the First Amendment: "Congress shall make no law respecting an establishment of religion, or prohibiting the free exercise thereof. . . ." was cited by both sides of the church-state argument. Should—or can—a politician keep his religious convictions separate from lawmaking? Can churches, in turn, claim immunity from legal obligations?

Los Angeles Times
Los Angeles, Calif., October 15, 1979

In this country, church and state are supposed to keep their distance from each other.

The principle has been settled since the First Amendment said that "Congress shall make no law respecting the establishment of religion or prohibiting the free exercise thereof."

That is a simple enough standard, except that it is not. It might have been once. It no longer is, nor has it been for many years. Society has become too complex, and the issue keeps recurring in various forms.

Often in the past the government has been accused of encroaching on the practice of religion, and judges have taken a wary look at any government action that tends in that direction.

One celebrated case arose in 1943 when Jehovah's Witnesses challenged, on the grounds of religious freedom, a board of education requirement that public-school students in West Virginia salute the American flag. The U.S. Supreme Court agreed, and the majority opinion by Justice Robert H. Jackson has been quoted frequently since: "If there is any fixed star in our constitutional constellation, it is that no official, high or petty, can prescribe what shall be orthodox in politics, nationalism, religion or other matters of opinion or force citizens to confess by word or act their faith therein."

But lately, as a Times Washington correspondent, Jim Mann, reports, conflict between church and state has arisen over the secular activities of religious groups, which argue that the First Amendment extends to their conduct even in that sphere.

The Worldwide Church of God challenged in a Los Angeles court the right of the state attorney general to use public funds to investigate the financial affairs of the church. The court ruled against the church. A few days before, the U.S. Supreme Court refused to intervene in a dispute over the appointment of a temporary receiver to administer the finances of the Worldwide Church. The church maintained that, because of the receivership, "the religion clauses of the First Amendment are a dead letter."

The United Methodist Church claims that it cannot be sued for breach of contract related to the bankruptcy of Pacific Homes, a church-connected chain of retirement homes. A California court found otherwise, stating that the use of the courts to resolve such charges "cannot be foreclosed . . . because one of the named defendants is a religious body."

In New York, a grand jury sought to question a former New York City council member, who is also a priest, about his conversations with a prison inmate and prison officials. The priest said the questions would both breach the relationship between priest and penitent and violate his right to the free exercise of religion. The courts agreed that the priest could not be questioned about his conversations with the prisoner, but ruled that he had no similar protection against disclosing his conversations with prison officials.

The sharp increase in such conflicts between church groups and government may suggest a novel development: an encroachment, perhaps, by church into the realm of the state rather than the historic encroachment by state into the realm of the church.

Justice Jackson's words 36 years ago have lost none of their significance. The state must remain powerless to prescribe any orthodoxy in matters of belief, but it must follow that religious beliefs cannot be a shield for illegal conduct.

When either church or state crosses the line into the other's sphere is not always easy to determine. Courts themselves frequently divide on the issue, but the principle of separation is as sound now as it was two centuries ago. In a pluralistic society, it is not only sound, it is also imperative. ☐

St. Louis Review
St. Louis, Mo., October 26, 1979

As the United States nears an election year an underlying question is once again raised: should a public official's religious convictions have implications for his positions on national issues?

Last Sunday, Governor Joseph Teasdale gave his personal endorsement to the principles enunciated at the Pro-Life Convention held in St. Louis.

Governor Teasdale's stand in behalf of human life has drawn criticism from pro-abortionists as an infringement on church-state separation. In this, they are wrong. Our Constitution does not require our elected officials to be secular humanists. In fact it is our courts which are violating the Constitution by enshrining secular humanism as the national religion.

Our Constitution assumes that there will be an interplay of attitudes among our legislators and elected officials which arise from their individual religious convictions and commitment.

Unfortunately, there are Catholic office-holders who try to separate religious convictions from public service. This schizophrenic approach to public service is not required by the Constitution. We are neither surprised nor offended that Senator Jacob Javits can be counted on to espouse the agenda of the Jewish community in the U.S. By contrast, Catholics are dismayed that a Jesuit priest, Representative Robert F. Drinan, can be counted on to vote for extension of federal funding for abortions. Representative Drinan complains that the pro-life movement "has become politicized over this one issue as if it would solve all our problems . . ." He is wrong in his assessment of the pro-life movement, and he fails to convince us that there can be any other secure rights in our land, if the very right-to-life is denied.

If there were not courageous political leaders in our historic past animated by strong religious commitment, slavery would still be the law of our land. If there had been courageous and moral political leaders in Germany in the Hitler era, perhaps the right-to-life in that country would not have been abrogated.

We applaud Governor Teasdale for his recognition that politicians do not have to take a hands-off stand in their approach to politics having their root in moral judgments.

Conservative Preachers Becoming a Political Force

The 1980 presidential campaign saw the emergence of evangelical Christians, an estimated 30 million to 65 million Americans, as an interest group with strong potential for affecting the outcome of political races across the country. Fundamentalist Christian groups had only recently begun to take part in politics as a group, abandoning a long tradition of shunning organized political action. Much of the impetus to organize came from television preachers, whose sermons reached millions of viewers in the South and West. The most influential figure was Rev. Jerry Falwell, who founded the Moral Majority in June 1979 and urged his followers to vote for candidates who took "Christian" stands on public issues. The Moral Majority and other evangelical political groups formed the core of the ultraconservative "New Right," which many observers took to be a backlash against the social liberalism that had characterized much of American life since the 1960s. The Moral Majority opposed abortion, the Equal Rights Amendment, homosexual rights and the strategic arms limitation treaty and supported prayer in public schools and increased defense spending.

Organized religion clashed with politics for the first time in Massachusetts Sept. 14 when Humberto Cardinal Medeiros, the archbishop of Boston, warned Roman Catholics not to vote for candidates who favored abortion. His warning came in a pastoral letter that was read in hundreds of churches throughout his diocese. His message did not name particular candidates, but it was clearly directed against two candidates in Democratic primaries for the state and federal legislatures. Despite his letter, the two Democrats won nomination.

The Chattanooga Times
Chattanooga, Tenn., October 2, 1980

In much the same manner as when he argued last February for a sensible form of gun control before a roomful of New Hampshire voters opposed to it, Rep. John Anderson this week went before a meeting of the National Religious Broadcasters Association to spell out his differences with the so-called "fundamentalists" who he said are advocating "nothing less than an American version of religious intolerance."

Mr. Anderson probably garnered no support for his independent presidential candidacy but he said a couple of things worth remembering in a campaign where efforts by religious groups seem to be polarizing attitudes.

He pledged himself to defend freedom of speech for radio and televisions devoted primarily to religious programming but warned that when such broadcasters "get into partisan politics, they jeopardize" their tax-exempt status and "invite the very thing you fear . . . some constriction of freedom." And he added: "In the long run, religion can retain its spiritual authority only if it keeps its distance from partisan politics. When a preacher becomes a politician, he diminishes the independent prophetic quality of his message. . . ."

It's still an open question how much effect the highly visible preachers will have on the presidential election; we noticed the other day that Pat Robertson, host of the popular "700 Club," has resigned from the Religious Roundtable with the comment that it was becoming too political. Mr. Anderson's comments underscore the importance of church members exercising sufficient care to ensure they are not led astray by persons and groups operating with ulterior motives.

San Francisco Chronicle
San Francisco, Calif., September 22, 1980

POLITICS AND RELIGION have repeatedly made a deadly mixture, a fact not lost upon the founding fathers nor on millions of victims both before and after the founding fathers put their hands to paper. The political ideal, at least for Western democracies, involves the art of compromise and finding acceptance. Religion is based upon moral absolutism.

We ruminate with some not very original themes at this time because the thinly drawn line between church and state is obviously being trespassed. In this election year, a whole new evangelical-political movement is busy at the hustings, not so much seeking to save souls but to see that ballots are cast for the true believers.

The well-publicized and vigorous emergence of the Moral Majority and other like-minded groups into a place of consequence in American politics is troubling to us for several reasons. Principal among them, as we have noted, is that separation of church and state is being transgressed. The intent of the new movement is not, of course, establishment of a mandated state religion but, rather, to install only the subscribers of the faith in office.

THE FACT THAT candidates for public office must pass a loyalty test of adherence to win support of these groups gives us further pause. The loyalty test involves opposition to all abortion, opposition to limits upon strategic arms and opposition to the Equal Rights Amendment. It involves support for restoring prayer in public schools, support for a larger defense budget and support for major tax cuts, to cite only a few issues. We do not believe that narrow interpretations of the Old and New Testament should be the sole guide in arriving at decisions in matters of such magnitude and complexity.

The evangelical-political movement has, however, already achieved some successes, having played a significant role in the Republican senatorial primary in Oklahoma and assuring the defeat of an Alabama member of the House who did not align himself quickly enough in favor of school prayers.

The intrusion of clergymen into politics has not been limited to fundamentalist Protestants. And we were encouraged last week with evidence that pulpit politics may be overrating its strength. Humberto Cardinal Medeiros, archbishop of Boston, issued a pastoral letter to all parishes two days before the Massachusetts Congressinal primary election. Two Democratic candidates favored abortion. The cardinal's letter warned that support of such candidates involved any Catholic inseparably with "that guilt which accompanies this horrendous crime and deadly sin." The candidates won anyway and some believe the letter encouraged the turnout of their supporters in heavily Catholic precincts.

THE FAILURE OF the cardinal was a success for independent judgment and a comfort for those of us who fear the potential when state and church are intertwined.

RENO EVENING GAZETTE

Reno, Nev., September 26, 1980

Recent events have thrust the issue of religion and politics squarely in front of us again.

Two days before the Massachusetts congressional primary, Humberto Cardinal Medeiros, archbishop of Boston, issued a pastoral letter opposing two Democratic candidates who favor abortion. The archbishop urged their defeat, and told parishioners that support of them would involve any Catholic with "that guilt which accompanies this horrendous crime and deadly sin." While the parishioners were not threatened with excommunication, they were certainly warned that their souls would be placed in immortal danger.

Then, during the Reagan-Anderson debate, one reporter asked the two presidential candidates their views on the political involvement of the archbishop and other religious leaders. Ronald Reagan defended their right to persuade others to their views within the political process. Anderson, conceding their right to speak, said they should not tell people how to vote.

Immediately following the debate, on the television program "60 Minutes," Dan Rather took us on his own tour of far right evangelical leaders active in politics. Though Rather refrained from outwardly voicing an opinion, his implications were clear: these men are bigoted, narrow-minded, and ready to damn all who disagree with them in the least iota. Woe betide those who fail their so-called "loyalty tests" on abortion, ERA, prayer in the schools, defense budgets, and tax cuts.

It must be said that Rather's presentation appeared somewhat slanted. For instance, it offered a leading liberal senator's views about the evangelicals, but offered no supportive statements from other officials of equal stature. Rather's report also seemed bluntly political, coming immediately after the Reagan-Anderson debate and linking some of Reagan's advisors with the evangelical political movement.

Slanted or not, however, the Rather report did highlight a major phenomenon which has troubled many. Opponents accuse religious leaders of endangering the survival of the republic through their moral absolutism and transgression of the constitutional separation of church and state. On the other hand, proponents often see their opposition as morally bankrupt and endangering the survival of the republic through their immorality.

The issue is more complex than this. For instance, let us consider the opposition of the Roman Catholic Church to abortion. If this is not a moral issue, what is? If a church cannot concern itself with moral matters, what can it concern itself with? One would think, almost nothing. And inasmuch as Christian theology relates the final destination of the soul to its owners' moral character, the church would seem well within its domain in warning of the fate awaiting transgressors.

Much of the far right movement, including its evangelical components, has its roots in a deep-seated fear for the future of a society in which moral character is disintegrating. Employee thefts, soaring crime rates, corruption in government and business, the glorification of self over the welfare of the community — these factors and others speak loudly of the reality of that concern. Should evangelical leaders not be involved in these matters? Of course they should — and politically if they wish.

We cannot take liberal opposition to their political involvement too seriously — not if we remember the great pleasure with which liberals welcomed church support of their social causes of the 60s.

But at the same time, we cannot ignore those who fear the loss of liberty if religion gains a hold over government. History tells us all too clearly the abuses of religions when they are able to enforce their moral absolutes through law; the Inquisition of the Roman Catholic Church is fresh in our minds; so is the chaos and suffering in Iran, caused in large part by the uncompromising absolutism of its religious leaders.

Nor have we forgotten the unhappy legacy of Prohibition, a moralism run awry that left us a legacy of bootleggers become organized mobsters.

At the same time, however, absolutism and tyranny are not unknown in secular government: witness Soviet Russia and a thousand other tyrannies over the centuries. Governments are far from perfect, whether religious or secular.

It is true that bigotry exists among some far-right proponents. But in a democracy dedicated to the free flow of ideas, how can we deny them the right to express those views? And, going one step further, how can we deny them the right to engage in the political process, even so far as encouraging voting habits, either individually or in groups? We can't, if we are to remain true to the democratic process.

This is a difficult choice, to be sure. The majority of Americans would not care to see any one religious group, or affiliates of that group, gain control of the nation. (Evangelists say they have no wish to run government but, obviously, power gained will be power used, whether directly or indirectly.) The separation of church and state is not an outmoded fancy, but a still-pertinent attempt to (1) leave churches free from governmental persecution but at the same time (2) prevent adherents of any one religion from gaining such a political ascendancy that they may, in the fashion of religions, dictate their views to all others. Violation of either protection endangers the freedom of all.

Nevertheless, for generations religious groups and their adherents have played a role, sometimes larger, sometimes smaller, in our political lives without endangering the democracy. The views of the current religious revivalists — whether we agree with them or not — must be a part of the flow of ideas, and that includes organizational efforts to promote those ideas. To deny them this right — even under the authority of the Constitution — would be a dangerous undertaking.

The Charlotte Observer

Charlotte, N.C., September 25, 1980

The Mecklenburg Presbytery, governing board of Presbyterian churches in Mecklenburg, Stanly, Union and Anson counties, met a serious and difficult responsibility head-on last week when it condemned the political activities of some so-called "fundamentalist" organizations.

The problem with these "New Christian Right" groups is *not* that they're trying to influence political decisions; that is everyone's right. The problem is *not* that their beliefs strike many other Christians as narrow and mean-spirited; what they believe is their business.

The problem is that in claiming an exclusive right to proclaim the truth concerning issues on which many Christians disagree, they wrap their pursuit of political power in the banner of Christianity, unrestrained by concerns about the separation of church and state.

Their disregard for religious freedom is a matter of concern for Americans of all religions or of no religion. But their claim of omniscient leadership in the name of Christianity should be of special and serious concern to other Christians.

The resolution passed Wednesday by the Mecklenburg Presbytery reflects that concern: "While it is appropriate for Christians to form organizations for political action," it says, "it is pretentious for any organization or individual to claim to have 'the' Christian, or 'the' moral, or 'the' Biblical position on any given issue."

It is not easy for professing Christians to take issue with organizations that affirm "moral" and "Biblical" positions, particularly when some of those positions are consistent with generally accepted Christian beliefs. There is a tendency not to want to undercut others who claim — perhaps sincerely — to be serving the same God and proclaiming the same Gospel.

But Christian leaders who see the danger of this movement must speak out, as the presbytery did Wednesday. They should not leave it to the right-wing fringe to define the meaning of Christian citizenship in a free and religiously diverse society.

the Charleston Gazette

Charleston, W.Va., October 2, 1980

THE SAGINAW NEWS

Saginaw, Mich., September 11, 1980

A new lobbying group calling itself the "Moral Majority," presumably to make sure Congress understands where that leaves anyone with different views, has been set up in Washington.

It has seized upon some sure-fire issues: Homosexual teachers, abortion, pornography, the lack of prayer in public schools, the SALT II treaty. Send your dollars now, its first mailing pleads, or watch "our grand old flag" go down the drain.

Oddly, the appeal speaks in terms of freedom, yet opposes issues many Americans would define as elements of freedom, whether absolute or within certain limits.

Still, that's not what bothers us most about the "Moral Majority." Citizens can reasonably disagree on the kind of America they would prefer. Any group has the right to promote its own definition.

But the organizer of the "Moral Majority" is not content to rest his case on civil liberties.

He is Dr. Jerry Falwell, one of the better-known of the television preachers. And Falwell claims not just righteousness as his inspiration. He says he is entering politics as the agent of God.

"In recent months God has been calling me to do more than just preach — He has called me to take action," Falwell declares. "I have a divine mandate to go right into the halls of Congress and fight for laws tha save America."

Lacking Falwell's direct personal connections, we cannot confirm or deny his report of where God stands on such questions as the SALT II arms-limitation treaty. Certainly one very prominent born-again Christian might differ with Falwell's definition of morality on that point.

We do know what we think of the idea of our national laws being written, or the nation being run, by anyone who professes his political opinions and actions as divinely mandated.

Many well-meaning, sincere, worried Americans will disagree with our view of Falwell's political activities. That is their right under laws, and a Constitution, written to recognize and make room for the enormous variety of viewpoints represented among 220-plus million Americans.

Falwell, too, has the right to speak out. But Americans who respect and honor diversity in our society will be frightened by his representation that there is only one correct view, and he is its spokesman.

We need only look at what has happened in an existing theocracy, one where a particular set of religious beliefs has gained and asserted absolute power and claimed possession of all morality, to know that we want no part of it in the U.S.

IT IS somewhat surprising to hear from the lips of William F. Buckley and other conservative intellectuals a defense of Moral Majority, a fundamentalist pressure group that counts as religious issues the national budget, taxes and defense capability.

Because the Far Right for so long has done so poorly at the polls, it is probable that the intellectuals of the Right are willing to sacrifice reputations for sensibility in the pursuit of victory. In any event, we savor our vision of Buckley dining with the Rev. Jerry Falwell.

Mr. Falwell is a fundamentalist preacher who exercises great influence through the "electronic church." His broadcasts from Lynchburg, Va., are carried on 681 television stations. Last summer he showed up in Detroit and, astonishingly, was given a large hand in writing the Republican platform. As the leader of Moral Majority he has become so celebrated that he became a *Newsweek* cover story in which, lounging beside his swimming pool, he explained that the Lord rewards the faithful with material riches.

Although Moral Majority generally supports Republican candidates, a *New York Times* survey shows, curiously, that Jimmy Carter can count on more fundamentalist votes than Ronald Reagan can. Possibly that is why Ronald Reagan courts the Evangelical Right by giving the theory of evolution the back of his hand recently in Dallas.

If Carter can count on the rank-and-file True Believer, Reagan has the support of the leadership of Moral Majority leaders. Whether any kind of Moral Majority support is desirable is yet to be established.

In Kanawha County, candidates backed by Moral Majority did not fare well in the primary. And the polls suggest that the handful of Moral Majority-backed winners in the primary are facing tough sledding in the general election.

At the national level, Moral Majority has boasted of defeating Rep. John Buchanan of Alabama, a conservative who apparently wasn't conservative enough. Moral Majority claims credit, too, for ousting Mike Gravel of Alaska from the Senate. These successes, if indeed they are Moral Majority successes, don't amount to much when compared with conspicuous defeats, to wit:

Moral Majority tried hard, but failed to beat Sen. Frank Church of Idaho. Likewise Sen. George McGovern of South Dakota and Sen. Birch Bayh of Indiana. All three were advertised as being on the Moral Majority hit list. Church was especially vulnerable as a liberal with a conservative constituency.

To find the real impact of Moral Majority it may be necessary to go to Holy Writ which, Reagan assured his Dallas listeners, contains the answers to complex political questions.

ST. LOUIS POST-DISPATCH

St. Louis, Mo., September 26, 1980

"We are talking," said a consultant for the fundamentalist right, "about Christianizing America." That should be news to millions of Christians, not to mention Americans of other faiths, who simply would not agree that the nation requires the political faith of the far right.

Yet the political invasion of the fundamentalists is a phenomenon of the 1980 campaign. While traditional churches have struggled to maintain memberships, evangelical movements have grown. About 30 million Americans consider themselves strict Bible believers; another 20 million are "born again" Christians, and they are being courted for political reasons by organizations such as the Moral Majority and the Religious Roundtable, which plans a meeting in St. Louis Oct. 10. The political fundamentalist alliance has strong ties with secular conservative groups, and widespread influence through the "electronic church." Broadcasts by the Moral Majority leader, the Rev. Jerry Falwell of Lynchberg, Va., are carried on 681 TV and radio stations.

The rightness of the political fundamentalists, of which they seem assured, is far to the right. They assert themselves not only for school prayers and against abortion and the Equal Rights Amendment, but also attempt to make moral issues out of supporting a balanced budget, tax cuts and world superiority in defense while opposing arms limitation, a Department of Education and abrogation of the security treaty with Taiwan.

It is true that many churches take public positions on some issues, but religion generally has not placed a moral value on a balanced budget. It is also true that some church leaders have, quite mistakenly, intervened in political campaigns. On the abortion issue Cardinal Humberto Medeiros of Boston recently warned against voting for two congressional candidates, yet both won in Catholic districts.

Perhaps the fundamentalist politicians' interference will not have much more success. They did boast of the primary defeat of Sen. Mike Gravel in Alaska and, strangely enough, of defeating a conservative Republican Baptist minister, Rep. John Hall Buchanan of Alabama, because he was not conservative enough. But they did not oust Sens. McGovern of South Dakota, Culver of Idaho, Bayh of Indiana and Church of Idaho, and these men remain on their "Christian" hit lists. Yet political evangelism may not even speak for a majority of fundamentalists. A Gallup poll found that among strict Bible believers, responses on political issues, except for abortions and school prayers, were not very distinct from those of most Americans.

Nevertheless, Ronald Reagan is pursuing support from the political fundamentalists. He told them in Dallas that the Bible held ansers to complex political questions, that if evolution is taught then the biblical story of creation ought to taught with it, and that the First Amendment was written not to protect people from religious values "but to protect those values from government tyranny."

That is a misreading of American history and the First Amendment. The Constitution was intended not only to protect religious values from government but equally to protect the body politic from sectarian domination. And what the fundamentalist right is doing is to inject allegedly religious tests for political issues in a nation where both have been diverse and largely separate. It is one thing to believe that God created the earth in seven days and another to write it into law for all to heed. America was founded on religious as well as political principles, but it was not founded on principles such as that.

St. Petersburg Times

St. Petersburg, Fla., September 21, 1980

Cloaking themselves in old-time religion, bands of new-fangled fanatics are threatening America with a grim and perilous future.

Their tactics include the technologies of television and computers. Their strategy is the destruction of dissent. Their goal is minority rule.

How, indeed, can anyone presume to defy the "Moral Majority?"

CALL IT the "Moral Monopoly" instead.

The "Moral Majority" faction, which recently put down roots in St. Petersburg, undertakes to rate politicians as more moral if they favor the death penalty and reductions in government spending but less moral if they favor ratification of the Equal Rights Amendment and the SALT II treaty.

Some of its issues, such as abortion, are relevant to religious belief, leaving aside the propriety of impugning the morality of those who disagree. But whatever has SALT II to do with one's being more or less moral? What makes welfare reform immoral? Is it immoral to oppose the death penalty? According to the New Testament, even Jesus of Nazareth may have been of mixed mind about that; he prevented a legal execution.

Many good-hearted people have subscribed to Moral Majority in the belief that if they vote as it teaches they will be doing right. But they would also be delivering America into the hands of a few men: the television evangelists and right-wing fund-raisers who have invented Moral Majority and like-minded national movements and who command them as if they were private armies of the Lord.

"WE ARE no longer working to preserve the status quo," boasts Paul Weyrich, one of the founders of Moral Majority and director of the ultraconservative Committee for the Survival of a Free Congress. "We are radicals, working to overturn the present power structure in this country."

Here is an example.

U.S. Rep. John H. Buchanan, R-Ala., is also an ordained Baptist clergyman who favors voluntary prayer in schools. But when Buchanan hesitated at signing a petition that would force the House to vote on a dubious bill denying authority to the courts in that regard, Moral Majority marked him, and he was defeated in his primary. "I'd say they did a rather thorough job of beating my brains out with Christian love," he said.

IRONIES abound. Christian Voice, another of these groups, rated all members of Congress on 14 so-called "key moral issues." Four ordained clergymen got the lowest marks; a thrice-married representative since implicated in Abscam was rated 100 percent.

In the eyes of Christian Voice, it was immoral not to pledge to support Taiwan "from an attack by Godless communist China." It was moral, however, to vote against the new federal Department of Education.

Religion is in the heart of the believer, and nothing can prevent political power-seekers from trying to misuse it. In St. Petersburg, happily, there are prominent clergy willing to point out the difference. It was an important event when 14 clergy members of Religions United for Action in the Community (RUAC), an interfaith group, confronted the Moral Majority at a meeting earlier this month.

They told the Moral Majority that it speaks only for itself. " ... What I object to is including me when you say that your opinion represents all Christian people or the entire Judeo-Christian faith," said the Rev. Daniel Horn, RUAC's president.

IF RIGHT-WING radicals succeed in seizing power in the name of religion, say farewell to the separation of church and state, which protects each from the other, and to a lot of the blessings of liberty that the founding fathers thought they had secured for themselves and their posterity.

What happens when church usurps state? History has examples. The Inquisition littered Europe with tortured corpses and suppressed science under pain of death. Now, across the water, behold that modern moral monstrosity, the Ayatollah Khomeini.

Let it never happen here.

ARKANSAS DEMOCRAT

Little Rock, Ark., September 29, 1980

The church militant – politically militant Christian fundamentalists – are going to have a say in this presidential election, and to hear the assorted moral censors tell it, it's a terrible thing to see American politics profaned and our freedoms threatened by this crowd.

What's happening is that "pulpit politicians," Jerry Falwell and others, are applying religious-moral standards to the presidential and congressional candidates – judging them by both their votes and their views – and reporting the results to fundamentalist followers who put up money for advertising campaigns against reelection of those on the hit list.

Some call this mixing church and state. That line's just for the ignorant. Religious groups are as free to politick as anybody else. What burns the opposition is that the Falwells & Co. are mixing bedrock Protestantism and conservative politics.

The critics are already down on them for pursuing issues that brought their movement to birth – opposition to abortion, homosexuality, federalization of the family and an all-invading government. Whether the fundamentalists cite Scripture or conscience, it's all one to the people (fundamentalists call them Humanists) who think it isn't valid politics to oppose the social gospel that ratifies all these practices as proper.

But it's the inclusion of what is said to be purely political issues in the fundamentalist portfolio that really outrages the opposition. How, they ask, can these people call for the B1 bomber or the neutron bomb in the name of Christianity?

Well, it is hard at first blush to make a religious case for the B1 bomber. But if you're fiercely anti-Communist, as fundamentalists are, and if you also believe that Jimmy Carter has neglected defense, then it follows that letting godless Communists threaten or get the best of us is both irreligious and immoral.

If the fundamentalists insist on moralizing their politics, it's only what a lot of other people are already doing anyway.

Nor are fundamentalists' political hit lists different from anybody else's. Politicians regularly live (and die) by the ratings that watchdog groups like the Americans for Democratic Action, Americans for Constitutional Action and the AFL-CIO put out yearly. The point for politicians is that it's no use hollering that the indices the fundamentalists judge you by are politically invalid. If those issues can beat or elect you, they're sure enough political. Learn to cope.

Finally, there's the argument that if the moral fundamentalists elect enough of their people and defeat enough of the other fellow's, we'll end up in a society like the ayatollah's – a sort of church-state ruled by Christian fundamentalist fanatics. Well, it would be completely constitutional and democratic if that did happen – it would merely mean that a majority of Americans had come over to the moral fundamentalists' candidates. That, in fact, is what the majoritarians hope happens.

It won't, of course; the country is too diverse. Leaders are talking of four or five million fundamentalist votes this fall, at most. But the "pulpit political movement" is one to be reckoned with, now and in future.

Chicago Defender

Chicago, Ill., August 18, 1980

We now have three born-again Christians running for the Presidency: Carter, Reagan and Anderson. All three are fighting for the same fundamentalist religious vote.

In a time when politics and economics are the number one consideration in the minds of most voters, it should seem strange to the electorate that the candidates are so busy thumping religious drums.

The fact is that the religious vote is a big one in the country. Also, the fact is that the one Catholic contender, Kennedy, is out of it. And no one thinks seriously about a Black, a woman or a Jew as a Presidential possibility.

Maybe all three of these men should be running for pastor of the church, with headquarters in Washington.

AKRON BEACON JOURNAL

Arkon, Ohio, September 24, 1980

IN THIS ELECTION year, preachers across the country are using the pulpit for political purposes. Many of them, connected through what they call the Moral Majority, hold deep convictions that the answers to complex national or international issues can be found in American churches, in the Bible, and in the beliefs of those who minister to their congregations.

Just last week, for example, Harry Cook, the respected religion writer for the Detroit Free Press, wrote that the leader of the Moral Majority movement, the Rev. Jerry Falwell, "will have a larger impact on the 1980 political races than any religious leader ever has had in this country's 200-year history."

America was founded on the notion and the constitutional doctrine of freedom of expression and freedom of individual opinion. Mr. Falwell and his fellow preachers associated with him in the Moral Majority movement have as much right to their opinions as anyone else. It should not be otherwise in a free society.

Citizens protected

Even so, there is something disturbing about what is happening.

In addition to protecting religious beliefs, the Constitution of the United States also protects Americans from religious coercion, as so many early settlers knew it when they fled Europe. The First Amendment to the Constitution says: "Congress shall make no law respecting an establishment of religion, or prohibiting the free exercise thereof. . . ."

Separation of church and state is engrained in the American ethic. For 200 years, Americans have been free to hold whatever religious beliefs they wish, and free from the establishment of any organized religious movement that would dictate political beliefs or the conduct of the people's government.

It is on this basis that churches and many church-related activities and properties have long been held to be exempt from taxation.

Twenty years ago, the fear was that John F. Kennedy's Catholicism would play a role in his potential presidency. He effectively defused that concern in his appearance before the Protestant ministers in Dallas.

In this election year, there is cause for concern as to whether religion in an organized, established fashion is going too far in its approach to politics, and is devoting unwarranted attention to issues that cannot be resolved simply by clerical dogma.

For example, here in the Akron area, candidates running in the November election for a wide variety of local public offices, including county recorder, treasurer, and the new county council have received a questionnaire from the local branch of the Moral Majority movement.

The questionnaire seeks to learn the candidates' views on many questions. Signed by the Rev. George Crawford of Atwater, the cover letter says, "I appreciate your time and effort in helping to inform us on these very important moral issues."

Each American is, of course, entitled to his own view as to what is moral and what is not. The questionnaire, however, has almost no relationship to any of the important local offices the candidates seek, and in part deals with questions for which it requires strained logic to equate the general concept of morality.

One question asks, "What is your position on SALT II?" Since what a county treasurer does in office has no relationship to the framing of American foreign policy, it is hard to fathom how one could intelligently decide for whom to vote in the county treasurer's contest based on such a question. Secondly, is one's view pro or con SALT II a matter of morality?

The questionnaire itself is reprinted below. Clearly, it asks many questions on which many Americans hold firm views, and about which there are complex legal and legislative issues.

It is hardly possible to respond to many of the questions asked with the short, simple responses that seem to be desired.

For example, if one truly believes in the separation of church and state (Question 17), how does one react to the idea of "voluntary prayer and Bible reading in public schools" (Question 23)?

How to judge?

And what judgment is to be made of candidates who do respond? Is one who gives short, simplistic answers on such complex issues to be favored from the pulpits by ministers of a particular faith as being more moral than an opponent who attempts to explore and discuss the various facets of the issues?

Should we judge people's capabilities and potential value to American society on the basis of one person's or one group's religious views that seek to reduce all issues to that group's concepts of morality?

Religious freedom in America does not exist for one religion, or for one denomination, or for one particular set of beliefs within a denomination.

And, while every American is entitled to individual opinion, both religious and political opinion, it is difficult to comprehend the lasting value of religious/political movements that seek to adjust that individuality of opinion to simplistic political standards thrust forth from the pulpits of some churches.

Of course, ministers are free to put whatever questions they wish to those who seek public office. And, candidates receiving such questionnaires are, of course, totally free to respond to them in any manner they wish. They are also free not to respond if that appears to be the best way to react to those who believe that the decisions of voters should be made on narrow ground that is often irrelevant to the offices being filled.

Oregon *Journal*

Portland, Ore., October 4, 1979

One worrisome aspect of the movement that combines religious fundamentalism with right-wing politics could be read between the lines of a letter that recently appeared on this page.

It would have the reader believe that this movement is Christianity and those who are concerned about it are actually opposed to Christians in politics.

But the truth is that the adherents of the cause are not representative of Christians generally, either Protestant or Catholic, any more than they are representative of the American political system in its entirety.

They are representative only of themselves, both religiously and politically, and are rather unusual in trying to combine both.

If they would recognize as much, their movement into American politics would be much more honorable. But since their theme seems to be that they alone stand for Christianity, they are likely to take just as absolute a view of their political convictions.

Such a position defies the American tradition of vastly diverse political ideas, each respecting the others as it competes with them to shape public policy.

The political and religious mixture at least borders on violating the doctrine of separation of church and state for the combination by its very nature would seem to advocate establishment of a religion.

It is not that the fundamentalists are not welcome in politics. It is rather that they should recognize there may be other legitimate political ideas which are not necessarily immoral just because they do not subscribe to them. Apart from other religions, many other Christians would appreciate it if they would not presume to represent all of Christianity in American politics.

THE MILWAUKEE JOURNAL

Milwaukee, Wisc., September 25, 1980

Is the principle of church-state separation violated when a pastor tells church members how to vote?

Independent presidential candidate John Anderson says "yes." We think he overstates the case, but we still believe that some religious leaders are becoming much too dogmatic and heavy handed in their political activity.

As a constitutional concept, the principle of separation requires that the government "make no law respecting an establishment of religion or prohibiting the free exercise thereof." That does not forbid religious leaders to engage in political action. A minister, priest or rabbi has just as much right as a union leader or Rotarian to endorse candidates and take part in political campaigns.

However, like anyone else who ventures into the political briar patch, members of the clergy can expect some scratches. Some voters will regard them simply as political combatants, not as agents of divine guidance.

The farther they reach beyond traditional concern for ethics and morals, entering secular controversies, the more likely they are to invite criticism or skepticism. For example, many voters probably see no religious angle in the demand of politically conservative church leaders for more military spending and in their opposition to the Equal Rights Amendment.

Similarly, when leftist clerics supported the then-violent Black Panther movement or sponsored armed revolution in foreign countries, many persons suspected that political bias transcended spiritual considerations.

Theoretically, at least, religious groups can jeopardize their special tax privileges if they become too purely political in their activities.

Most disturbing of all, however, is the fact that some religionists seem insensitive to the tradition of religious freedom that allowed them to thrive in the first place. For example, they demand state-prescribed prayers in the public schools, an unconstitutional imposition on people who do not share their religious views. That would be a clear violation — not just in principle but in practice — of church-state separation.

Los Angeles Times

Los Angeles, Calif., October 3, 1980

The preachers are coming, the alarm bells are ringing, and cries about separation of church and state are heard in the land.

It is a phenomenon that has caught public attention in a year when religious feelings and convictions have been injected into various elections around the country and may have influence in deciding who will be the next President.

Most of the thunder is coming from fundamentalist Christian leaders whose political views tend to range from conservative to far right.

Their most prominent spokesman for the moment is the Rev. Jerry Falwell, whose "Old-Time Gospel Hour" reaches millions of television viewers each week. He explained in these pages recently the purposes of Moral Majority Inc., which he organized last year to "provide leadership in establishing an effective coalition of morally active citizens."

His words reflect the tenor and temper of the movement: "First, we take a pro-life position . . . Since 1973, more than 6 million unborn babies have been legally murdered in America. Second, we are pro-family. Government legislation is becoming the No. 1 force for the destruction of the family. And we are pro-morality. Humanism, with its emphasis on moral relativism and amorality, challenges every principle on which America was founded."

Somehow he managed to include in these moral concerns a defense of the free-enterprise system and an argument for greater military spending.

The response was impassioned and predictable.

One reader replied, "I totally reject Falwell's implied suggestion that God is an untraconservative Republican who wants a balanced budget, the abolition of social-welfare programs and who demands we tax the poor to support an insane nuclear arms race that is taking us hell-bent into the flames of Armageddon . . . ."

Another reader objected that Falwell "has no right to goad his Moral Majority into taking away the rights of all of us by imposing their particular brand of Christian intolerance onto the private lives of the rest of us."

In Boston, Cardinal Humberto Medeiros found himself under a similar attack after he sent off the following letter to his flock: "Those who make abortions possible by law—such as legislators and those who promote, defend and elect these same lawmakers—cannot separate themselves totally from that guilt which accompanies this horrendous crime and deadly sin."

But is it clerical intervention in the political arena that is causing the uproar, or is it the nature of the substantive positions of conservative clergymen that is stirring up the controversy?

Intervention by clergymen in public affairs—if intervention is the word that applies—is nothing new in this country's history. Clergymen were the leaders in the civil-rights movement of the 1960s, many were outspoken in their opposition to the Vietnam War, and they framed their arguments in moral terms.

Just recently, Sen. George McGovern, defending himself from attack by fundamentalists, offered his own interpretation of religious values. He accused the evangelicals of "threatening the humane and progressive tradition of the social gospel"—that is, of course, the gospel as he interprets it.

What is nevertheless troubling about many leaders of the fundamentalist movement is their strident tone, their intolerance of opposing views. (This failing is not exclusive to them. Many of their secular critics seem to feel that any mention of "moral concerns" is at best quaint and amusing, and at worst meretricious.) One conservative minister recently shouted, "I'm sick and tired of hearing about all the radicals and perverts and liberals and leftists coming out of the closet. It is time for God's people to come out of the closet . . . and change America." There was little Christian charity in that pronouncement.

What is also disturbing about the evangelicals is their insistence that a "Christian" vote is a conservative vote, their tendency to convert strictly political issues into moral issues, and their inclination to suggest that they have a morally superior view of what this society should be.

Yet we believe that the democratic political process can maintain its balance, and that the voters can sort out the issues. Medeiros' pastoral letter was an effort to defeat two congressional candidates who favored abortion rights. The two candidates won their elections. The fundamentalists may lobby their constituencies, but their followers are free to make their own choices in the voting booth.

The trends may shift one way or another temporarily, but the free play of forces in a democracy are always at work to restore an equilibrium between opposing factions.

The Oregonian

Portland, Ore., October 1, 1980

Religion in politics, per se, is not an abuse of the constitutional doctrine separating church from state. Nor is a minister's political advice to a congregation, in support of a church's moral principles, wrong or much different from the political recommendations of a labor leader to union members.

However, in mixing church theology with political ideology, ministers have an obligation to plumb facts as well as conscience in presenting political views from the pulpit. That a group of Portland evangelical ministers urged defeat of some Oregon political candidates in the May primary because of their support for gay rights was abusive to the degree that the targeted candidates were not thoroughly examined to determine what their positions actually were on gay rights. In short, political endorsement functions, for churches as well as newspapers or special-interest groups, require accountability to truth and responsibility for research.

In addition to the Portland example of increased clerical involvement in politics is the national example of the Moral Majority's entry into presidential politics.

The danger inherent in the Moral Majority crusade nationally is not that churches are becoming more politically involved, but that ministers may be using their spiritual tools irresponsibly.

Presidential candidate John B. Anderson was wrong when he said, "To try to tell the parishioners of any church of any denomination how they should vote or for whom they should vote violates the principles of separation of church and state." Anderson would have been right to say that ministers who make political endorsements in the name of God are practicing spiritual extortion on their congregation members by leaving the impression that a vote against the church's political endorsement may constitute a sin.

Most responsible ministries, in advocating political choices as a method to advance a church's moral imperatives, do not threaten — directly or by innuendo — parishioners with everlasting hell-fire and damnation should they exercise their political freedom to disregard the church's political endorsements.

The danger, then, occurs with the ministries that approach political issues and candidates with an overzealous strategy, as if the political endorsements were branded into stone from the fire of a burning bush.

Citizens concerned with the burgeoning conflict between a church's moral mission and political affairs of state should respect the former's constitutional right to pursue policy change through the political process. But they should be wary of rigid moral crusades that promise severe spiritual consequences for parishioners whose personal ballot conflicts with one recommended by the church.

Moreover, before falling victim to religious blackmail, a parishioner should question a minister's political advice just as he or she would question the advice of a special-interest organization, a newspaper or a neighbor. Indeed, almost every informed vote involves multiple, often competing crises of conscience.

The test, of course, is this: If a parishioner who disobeys a church's political advice feels he or she has committed a sin, the ministry of that church probably has argued the case too forcefully, thereby stepping over the thin line between the affairs of church and state.

WORCESTER TELEGRAM.

Worcester, Mass., September 13, 1980

Although the United States has a long, constitutional tradition of keeping government separate from organized religion, it has an equally long constitutional tradition that any American citizen can speak his mind on political matters for any reason whatever, moral, political, personal or whatnot.

In the current political campaign, we are seeing an intense involvement of ministers, priests, bishops and cardinals. Some people are nonplussed by this. But those religious are citizens just like everyone else — no more and no less. As far as the Constitution is concerned, they have every right to engage in the political process, including running for office if they are so inclined.

The wisdom of religious intervention into politics is something else. History suggests that it sometimes backfires. When clergymen try to impose strict religious and moral stands on what others see as essentially medical and personal issues, there should be no surprise if there is disagreement and even resentment.

Abortion is a prime example. Many think that abortion, under any circumstances, is an unmitigated evil and that it would be a sin to support anyone who condones it.

But many others see abortion as sometimes a medical necessity — as when a mother's life would be endangered — and otherwise an individual moral issue. They think it outrageous — even immoral — for the government to intrude in such a personal, private decision.

The steady heating up of the abortion controversy across the country shows that it isn't going to go away. It is the sort of confrontation where compromise seems well nigh impossible, at least among those who hold strongly to either side of the argument.

Perhaps it is not too much to hope that the partisans on both sides will eventually come to see that those who oppose them are not hopelessly mired in ignorance, immorality and callousness. There are thoughtful, concerned people on both sides of the matter. Those who oppose abortion are acting out of anguish for the rights of the unborn. Those who think that women have the ultimate responsibility in this matter are deeply concerned about individual rights and humanity.

Although abortion is not the sort of thing that lends itself to political compromise, it has become deeply entangled in current political campaigning. Voters will have to deal with it as best they can in the privacy of the voting booth. It is one factor among many that will influence the results next week and in November.

The Des Moines Register

Des Moines, Iowa, September 19, 1980

The debate about mixing religion with politics has focused mainly on the "new Christian rightists," largely Protestant evangelicals and fundamentalists. But last week the Roman Catholic archbishop of Boston, Cardinal Humberto Medeiros, sparked a controversy that will reach beyond Bay State politics, already simmering over a Vatican directive that scratched Representative Robert Drinan, a Jesuit priest, from his re-election race this year.

The issue is abortion, which has mobilized numerous Catholics for political warfare in recent years. It is a subject many Catholic bishops discuss with a measured defensiveness, coupling it with church social concerns to offset criticism of one-issue myopia. Medeiros, however, issued a pastoral letter, read Sunday in many churches, calling upon Catholics to vote against candidates who favor the use of federal Medicaid funds to pay for abortions for the poor.

The letter put the religious question in the middle of two hotly contested Democratic primary races in which candidates favoring Medicaid abortions faced anti-abortion rivals. Medeiros didn't mention names, but his targets were obvious: State Representative Barney Frank, who hopes to fill the Fourth District seat Drinan is giving up, and incumbent James Shannon in the Fifth District.

Frank and Shannon won in Tuesday's primaries, and Medeiros and his aides may well be wondering if the pastoral letter backfired. Drinan didn't let up in his campaigning for Frank, and Senator Edward Kennedy urged voters to "reject the politics of negativism."

What bothered some Catholics (Shannon is one) and offended many Jews (Frank is one) and Protestants was the archbishop's heavy-handed intrusion. Catholic teaching against abortion is hardly a secret, but critics compared Medeiros' action unfavorably with that of his predecessor, Cardinal Richard Cushing, who in 1965 steered the church clear of a legislative controversy over legalizing birth-control devices. Cushing observed that "it does not seem reasonable to me to forbid in civil law a practice that can be considered a matter of private morality."

The difference in attitudes is important. Medeiros wants laws that will reinforce Catholic teachings, although non-Catholics may disagree with those teachings. Cushing refrained from risking Catholic moral influence in political battles that most likely would result in civil laws reflecting the compromises needed to satisfy opposing views within society.

Cushing's stance showed respect not only for the national tradition of church-state separation but also for the religious pluralism that has evolved in American culture. His example is worthy of emulation this year by overly pious politicians as well as church leaders who fancy themselves political manipulators.

Religious pluralism is an American strength that is sure to be weakened if religious leaders begin clamoring to legislate morality as a quick fix for a multitude of public vexations.

CHICAGO Sun-Times

Chicago, Ill., September 24, 1980

We had hoped, after last week's primary in Massachusetts, that the issue of church-state separation had been firmly settled for a while. Voters there wisely upheld that principle. They nominated two congressional candidates whom the archbishop of Boston, Cardinal Humberto Medeiros, had indirectly attacked because of their views on abortion.

But in Sunday's presidential debate, one of Ronald Reagan's comments about the role of the church in politics indicated that Reagan doesn't understand that constitutional separation any more than Medeiros does.

The question was asked, "Do you approve of the church's action" in Boston and "should a president be guided by organized religion on issues like abortion. . . ?"

With basic freedoms at stake, including religion and conscience, Reagan should have said no. Instead he implied approval. He said too many churches "have been too reluctant to speak up" for what they believe.

That isn't the issue. Churches *do* have the right to speak on moral matters, as they did on civil rights in the '60s. But Medeiros sought to tell his flock how to vote—and to oppose candidates whose views he opposed.

He—and Reagan—should heed Medeiros' predecessor, Cardinal Richard Cushing, who once said of birth control that "it does not seem reasonable to me to forbid in civil law a practice that can be considered a matter of private morality." That says it well.

We hope the country is listening.

THE LOUISVILLE TIMES

Louisville, Ky., September 18, 1980

One-issue politics suffered a setback in Tuesday's Massachusetts primary. Unfortunately, it came at the expense of ecumenism and only after the fine line separating church and state was severely bruised.

Doing the bruising was the archbishop of Boston, Humberto Cardinal Medeiros, with a last-minute warning to Roman Catholic voters not to support pro-abortion candidates. Ironically, the archbishop's political venture was aimed directly at the race for the seat being vacated by Rep. Robert Drinan, a Roman Catholic priest leaving office in obedience to Pope John Paul II's order that clergymen not mix in politics. Also affected was U.S. Rep. James Shannon, 28, a Roman Catholic who when elected in 1978 was the youngest member of Congress.

Both Rep. Shannon and Barney Frank, the major target of Cardinal Medeiros, won their Democratic primaries. Both candidates took stands in favor of a woman's right to choose to have an abortion and both advocated federal funding for abortions for women who cannot afford them.

In a last-minute pastoral letter last week, Cardinal Medeiros made abortion the paramount issue in their races by informing his flock that "those who make abortions possible by law — such as legislators and those who promote, defend and elect those same lawmakers — cannot separate themselves totally from that guilt which accompanies this horrendous crime and deadly sin." He urged Roman Catholics to vote in the primary "to save our children born and unborn."

It was an uncalled-for intrusion of the church in secular affairs, made all the worse by the fact that it occurred in the home state of John F. Kennedy. All the questions about the separation of church and state that he did so much to answer will surely resurface, despite his brother Edward's quick and highly visible support for the cardinal's victims.

Even in its timing the archbishop's message was unfortunate. It was issued while Mr. Frank, a Jew, had retired from the campaign temporarily to observe Rosh Hashanah and thus could not reply immediately.

If there is a bright spot, it is that voters have once again shown that they will not be dictated to. In that, all clergymen might find a reminder that there's a difference between preaching and meddling.

The Boston Globe

Boston, Mass., September 25, 1980

Humberto Cardinal Medeiros' intervention in two Massachusetts congressional races has made national news. The role of religion in politics was the last and strongest question in the League of Women Voters' debate. A Globe editorial has drawn over 120 letters from readers. Clearly this issue divides Americans and it goes beyond the question in Massachusetts.

Ours is a nation that was founded on freedom of religion, that believes in freedom of speech and thought. It is also a nation whose founders were fugitives from religious oppression, whose defined principles include separation of church and state, side by side with free speech.

How can the two principles be reconciled?

Is there a distinction between freedom of speech and freedom of religion? Is it possible to draw a line between politics and morality? Such a distinction was suggested by the two candidates in last Sunday's debate: Ronald Reagan urged the church to "speak up." John Anderson worried about an attempt "to sway votes."

In times of national unease, individuals draw together behind the banners of tradition and faith. Today, Jews are worried about Israel and they are tending to band together to exert political pressure in its defense, against what many see as a retreat by President Carter. Fundamentalist Protestants, frightened by a changing society, are expressing that fear in political terms, targeting specific candidates like George McGovern, Frank Church and John Culver for defeat at the polls because of their "liberal" stands on particular social issues.

Those efforts — often highly practical and much better organized than the intervention by Cardinal Medeiros — are entirely valid within the doctrine of free speech. But, even if they do not violate the letter of church-state separation, they are also offensive to many Americans.

It is not a matter of law, but a matter of propriety. Invoking God for one cause to the exclusion of all others demeans religion. It also demeans the political process. It's a reversal of the constitutional prohibition against Congress' establishing a religion; this is religion's attempt to establish a Congress.

The Globe's Ellen Goodman expressed it well this week. "The churches are becoming the new Tammany Hall of the 1980s," she said. Their crusades, besides being explicit in terms of candidates, are increasingly narrow in terms of morality. That tactic, particularly when cloaked with the weight of religion and accompanied by the fear of punishment for sin as defined by a clergyman, is at odds with the doctrine of individual conscience. It reduces morality as a whole to an issue in particular. And it smacks of zealotry.

Churchmen of every persuasion have a right and a duty to speak up on matters of principle and, in terms of forum and timing, to do it as effectively as possible. But they must expect disagreement.

Churchmen have a right to single out issues and candidates. But, to the degree they narrow their view and attack individuals, they must expect criticism. As Patricia Harris noted before a student debating society at Princeton on Tuesday, "moral absolutism" of the kind we are seeing today poses a threat to the pluralism and tolerance of American democracy. That is why any church is at risk when it tries to mix politics with morality.

THE CHRISTIAN SCIENCE MONITOR

Boston, Mass., October 27, 1980

Seldom in recent history has the question of morality come so strongly to the fore. The moral and spiritual fiber of the United States is being severely tested on matters as private as abortion, sexual conduct, and family life — and as public as justice for blacks, women, minorities; compassion for the world's poor; noninterference in the internal affairs of other nations; and the fostering of human rights for peoples everywhere. It is widely recognized that America must have a strong moral and spiritual foundation. Without such a foundation, society grows lawless and stagnant; it loses its compass.

But morality must be built within the thoughts and lives of individuals and then translated into the nation's laws and policies through the democratic process. It cannot be imposed by the state either on individuals or on nations. And it is not Christian morality that lapses into bigotry, self-righteousness, or pious preachiness.

This election year finds Americans pondering these issues because of the emergence of religion as a political force. Significantly, perhaps, it is not only the Islamic world that is witnessing a resurgence of religious fundamentalism, with the difficulties this poses for democratic government. In the US, too, we see the merging of the Christian "new right" with the political right into a theocratic force that seeks to dominate the political process. The trend is worrisome.

Let us say at the outset that we understand the reasons for the religious revival. Many Americans feel deeply the need for a national moral awakening, for a turning back from what is seen to be a more and more permissive society. The fears are not unfounded. No one of the Judeo-Christian faith can fail to be concerned about the widespread immorality, the rise in out-of-wedlock births, the increased use of hard drugs by the young, the growth of pornography, the indecency portrayed in novels, on television, and even flaunted in the news magazines. America indeed needs to be shaken out of its unthinking tolerance of these trends. To the extent that Christian fundamentalists bring these issues to public notice, their efforts have value. An aroused public is a necessary prelude to constructive reform.

It is the method of correction which must be watched, however. All too often religious activism is narrowly and simplistically bound up with one issue, such as abortion or the Equal Rights Amendment. Some Christian groups go so far as to use "moral scorecards" to rate the performance of public figures on such unrelated issues as school prayer, the defense treaty with Taiwan, and the formation of a Department of Education. When self-appointed groups set out to decide who is moral and what a "Christian position" is, they risk practicing moral zealotry and destroying good public servants. The results can be incongruous, and often hardly moral in themselves. Such an able senator as John Glenn, for instance, who is an elder in the Presbyterian church, is rated zero by one ultra-conservative organization. Congressman Richard Kelly, implicated in the Abscam bribery investigation, merits 100.

What is needed for righteous government is not to elect those who supposedly hold the right view on a single or even several issues. It is, in the words of an editorial in Christianity Today, "to secure responsible political leaders of intelligence, deep moral commitment, political wisdom and administrative skills." Leaders, in other words, of probity who have the ability to govern.

It must be remembered that America is an increasingly pluralistic society, an amalgam of different races, cultures, nationalities, religions. Even the dominant Judeo-Christian religious groups differ as to their interpretation of biblical teaching and the practice of Christianity. In these conditions Americans can only be grateful for the Constitution's wisdom of erecting a wall of separation between church and state and leaving religious practice to individual conscience. For one group to insist on formal public prayer in school, for instance, smacks of dictating religion to those who may pray differently or not at all. Similarly, to provide tax aid for religious schools, as Ronald Reagan advocates, would put the government in the business of supporting religion. Surely religious tolerance is best safeguarded when the state injects itself the least.

This is not to say that government has to be morally neutral or that Christian religious groups should play no part in the political process. Few would argue that church groups should go so far as to tell citizens how to vote. But they have every right to speak out on social and political issues if they wish, to participate in national debate, to point to unethical behavior in or out of government. Christians of all denominations in fact need to weigh in more in the democratic process if laws, court decisions, and public policies are to reflect the highest standards of morality. Religious tolerance must not mean tolerance of drugs, pornography, antifamily laws — all of which cry out for public indictment. It is simply the single-issue moral absolutism and parochialism we deplore.

A moral America encompasses more than an obligation to protect human life — and abortion is a practice we oppose but which involves such complex issues as to be best left to individual conscience and choice. Morality involves the whole tone of society — the integrity of government leaders, the ethics of corporate business, and the sensitivity of schools, universities, news media, and the arts and entertainment industry to purifying the nation's cultural as well as physical environment. It means addressing such problems as justice for blacks and other minorities, equal rights for women (recognized even by many opponents of ERA), and training of the unemployed. Is it morally tolerable that millions of people cannot find work, that joblessness among black youth, in particular, runs a high 40 percent?

Looking abroad, few would deny that America should stand for principle in the conduct of its affairs. Toward this end, reform efforts must continue to assure that US policy remains free of such undemocratic practices of the past as interfering in other countries' electoral processes.

President Carter's early focus on human rights did much to lend a moral dimension to foreign policy, but in execution the policy often left the US seeming merely moralistic and naive. We would have the US continue to hold high the banner of universal human rights and to use every prudent means to promote them. To neglect this matter would be to abandon the country's traditional ideals — and the very things on which millions of people around the world look to the US for example and leadership.

But there must be the maturity to know that it is a nation's practice rather than its words which ultimately carry weight. For example, can Americans accept that, at a time when there is a rising world demand and competition for energy and other resources, they are often wasteful and inefficient in their own consumption of these resources? Surely out of a sense of justice and of compassion for the less fortunate they can do more to foster economic growth in the third world, and to help husband the earth's bounty in a way that embraces and blesses all.

In the end, too, America's influence for good will depend on what kind of society it is and what it chooses to present to the world as worthy of emulation. In terms of its freedoms, its opportunities, its creativity and innovation, it is still the most revolutionary land on the globe. Yet the US image abroad is at times undercut by practices which tend to obscure positive American contributions. This happens, for instance, when some Americans overseas show off the worst aspects of their culture — tawdry movies and magazines, vulgar music, a materialistic way of life — or when some US business firms export foods, chemicals, and other products which are declared unsafe for domestic use. Those representing the US should respect the cultural and physical environment of other nations as well as their religious and other traditions.

This is not to fail to appreciate the enormous cultural, economic, and political benefits which America has shared and continues to share with those willing to accept them — but merely to point to the need for cultivating moral and spiritual sensitivity in an age of growing global interdependence. The great underlying test of a nation's integrity, after all, lies not only in the virtues of its society but in its demonstrated love for mankind, in doing unto others as it would have others do unto it. This is the ideal for which the people — and their leaders — must unceasingly strive.

THE INDIANAPOLIS STAR

Indianapolis, Ind., November 2, 1980

Fundamentalist ministers' interest in the 1980 election has aroused hostility among those who see it as a threat to the constitutional separation of church and state.

The First Amendment, which deals with that issue, prohibits Congress from making any law "respecting an establishment of religion."

The amendment does not bar churchgoers or clergymen from political activity. If it did, it would give atheists a monopoly on politics. That is not its intent. Its intent is to prevent establishment of a state religion.

Liberal hostility to the fundamentalist role is easy to understand. The fundamentalists are conservatives.

Religious groups have been active in politics for years. They have promoted a host of causes and candidates. Liberal clergy have run for public office. One, Father Robert F. Drinan, was elected to Congress by Massachusetts Democrats.

The people who are bothered today by the "Moral Majority" and other conservative religious groups, did not consider that a violation of the principle of separation of church and state.

Also, a clergyman, the Rev. Donald Harrington, heads the Liberal Party in New York. In 1976 a clergyman, the Rev. James Wall, managing editor of Christian Century, headed Jimmy Carter's campaign in Illinois. A clergyman, the Rev. Bob Maddox, serves on President Jimmy Carter's White House Staff.

The furor raised over conservative church interest in the political process is built on a double standard.

Church people on one side of the political spectrum have as much right to express their views and back candidates of their choice as church people on the other side. At least they do in a free country. No one should have a monopoly on the political process.

THE COMMERCIAL APPEAL

Memphis, Tenn., June 1, 1980

THE LATE JUSTICE Hugo L. Black wrote in a 1947 Supreme Court opinion, "The First Amendment has erected a wall between church and state. That wall must be kept high and impregnable. We could not approve the slightest breach."

But men like Rev. Jerry Falwell of Virginia and the national electronic church are saying, "What can you do from the pulpit? You can register people to vote. You can explain issues to them. And you can endorse candidates, right there in church on Sunday morning."

And men like Dr. Adrian P. Rogers of Bellevue Baptist Church in Memphis are saying, "We will see more and more evangelicals taking definite stands for political issues and for persons who are running for office, and I think they should."

And men like E. E. McAteer of The Religious Roundtable are saying that political power "is being able to set the agenda for debate. The agenda for debate is the Bible."

And men like V. Lance Tarrance, a political pollster, are saying, "If (Ronald Reagan) can halve the born-again vote, he can do wonders."

The Reagan campaign and the "preachers-into-politics" movement detailed in The Commercial Appeal recently by reporter Michael Clark seem to be merging, perhaps toward the kind of union of church and state which the framers of the Bill of Rights forbade, lest their new nation fall into the same institutionalized religious persecution which had brought them to this land.

THE QUESTION IS: Which side will the American people take? The people are the bedrock of Justice Black's "wall," and they must decide finally whether it will be breached by forms of exclusionary religious practice and exclusionary politics which are so contrary to the Constitution and so foreign to our form of government.

Heresy has not yet become an issue in the current national political campaign but aren't we dangerously close when evangelist James Robison declares that the President of the United States fails the test of Christianity, and therefore political leadership, because he "has sought the counsel of the ungodly"? Or when Falwell founds something called the Moral Majority, which suggests, at least, that those who do not belong are without moral or democratic credentials?

There is little chance that this nation ever will have or even consider a Buddhist, a Mohammedan or a Taoist as a candidate for president. But are we to say that members of such faiths are ineligible for political office? Not if any semblance of democracy is to survive.

Certainly we cannot and will not tolerate any preachment which would deny a Jew access to public office in this country because he is not a "born-again Christian."

THERE IS, OF COURSE, nothing sinister about spiritual revivalism in this country. It goes deep into our history and is part of our strength. Revivalist Charles G. Finney and his converts led great reform movements in the 1830s and '40s. Dwight L. Moody and imitators like William A. 'Billy' Sunday fought what they saw as paganism in the fast-growing cities of the United States through the turn of the 20th Century.

They and the many who followed them have continually renewed this country's proud and essential Judeo-Christian ethic and given rise to the great church denominations which support it.

But we have also had excursions into political bigotry by Christian fundamentalists before. The Know-Nothing movement of the mid-19th Century is not a memorable chapter in American history. We should countenance no recurrence of that, no matter how well intended.

To the extent that today's revivalists and evangelicals are retesting America's spiritual fiber, they are a force for good. But to the extent that they are testing the seductive powers of television, money and political influence, they are a potential force for harm to free democratic action and free religious belief.

A loose coalition is forming between religious fundamentalists like Falwell's Moral Majority, Rogers' 13.3-million-member Southern Baptist Convention, McAteer's Roundtable, Bill Bright's Campus Crusade for Christ, Jim Bakker's PTL Club, the National Association of Evangelicals, the National Religious Broadcasters and political fundamentalists like Richard Viguerie, publisher of the Conservative Digest and operator of a huge direct-mail fund-raising business; Phyllis Schlafly of the anti-ERA forces; the Committee for the Survival of a Free Congress and the Conservative Caucus.

AS INDIVIDUALS AND individual groups they are entitled to their points of view and respect for them. As a coalition for a singular view of a single issue — American morality — they blur the lines that separate church and state and begin to offer not reform but revolution.

It is not a long step from building toward one political creed to building toward one religious creed. Or is there much doubt that a coalition born of the idea to "train evangelicals for places of leadership in government," as McAteer has advocated, would move also to try to place evangelicals in every pulpit?

Rogers said, "Now, where is the point where a man ceases to be a minister of the gospel and becomes a political animal? That's a good question."

Indeed.

It should tell us something about the direction of this movement when national political campaigns look past the best of its intentions and reduce it to pure vote strategy.

Richard Wirthlin, poll-taker for Reagan, said last weekend that his candidate intended to keep President Carter from "cornering the market" on born-again Protestants. Wirthlin included in an April poll for Reagan the question, "Was there ever a time in your life when you made a special personal commitment to Christ that changed your life?" One-third said yes, and in a Monday campaign stop at a meeting of California gospel singers Reagan declared, "This nation is hungry for a spiritual revival."

AMERICA IS HUNGRY, too, for political leadership more interested in what it takes to govern than what it takes to win and competent to deal with vast social and economic problems in a pluralistic nation and a complex world. That and spiritual revival are not, and were never intended to be, one and the same thing.

Nevada State Journal

Reno, Nev., October 2, 1980

Secretary of Health and Human Services Patricia Roberts Harris, in a speech to Princeton University students the other day, attacked the conservative religious groups which have become politically active lately as being "dangerous to democracy."

She is as far off base in this statement as she was earlier when she professed to see the white sheets of the Ku Klux Klan behind the Ronald Reagan campaign for the presidency, and thus touched off the recent flap over the injection of "racism" claims in the race between Carter and Reagan.

The new religious-political movements being headed by such as television evangelist Jerry Falwell can perhaps be criticized for being too narrow in their political interests, for being too shrill at times and too able to browbeat government. This is true of most political special interest groups, including those within Ms. Harris' constituency.

But, in the aggregate they are good, for they are drawing Americans into the political process, getting them to register, and getting them to vote.

And that is a great contribution, given today's political climate in which more and more Americans are being turned away from politics. It is estimated that only about half of eligible Americans are registered to vote and it is the rare election when half of the registered actually vote.

That is a dangerous trend in a "participatory democracy" for, without adequate participation, we could wake up one day without any democracy, at all.

At the very least, such apathy is causing some unfortunate political results, most notably a federal government that often does not seem in the least responsive to the sentiments of mainstream America.

This is possibly that minority of citizens who do vote tend to be better-educated and more liberal in their views than the man on the street, and that the people they elect represent their attitudes.

Thus, anything that helps to turn the average American who has dropped out of political interest back into participation is doing the nation a favor.

This is certainly not the ideal approach to encouraging the exercise of this citizen responsibility, but it is one of the few that is working, and people like Ms. Harris should not knock it.

It would explain, too, why the special interest group has been gaining in popularity, for such groups do listen to their members and represent their thinking, and they are gaining the power to be heard.

And these groups do have the political clout that can gain the ear of political figures who often seem deaf to the wishes of the individual.

The Knickerbocker News

Albany, N.Y., October 27, 1980

Religion has traditionally played a role in American politics, sometimes subliminal, sometimes overt.

Candidates have often been portrayed as "good, church-going, God-fearing men." Religion was obviously important in the 1928 presidential race, when Al Smith's campaign train traveled the countryside and burning crosses lined the tracks in some counties. The religous undercurrent has occasionally bubbled to the surface of our national political consciousness and taken over — Prohibition may be the prime example — but for the most part, personal beliefs in God and organized religion have remained in the background.

Not so this year: The evangelical-fundamentalists are on the move, shouting from the streetcorners and waving banners. Their organizations have names like Moral Majority and Christian Voice, and they're making a lot of politicians (and a lot of non-politicians) very uncomfortable.

We see nothing wrong in what these groups are doing, in its purest form. Taking a moral stand, then working for politicians who share your views, is a valid and effective political tactic.

These political and religious conservatives have apparently been provoked beyond endurance by the sin and wrongheadedness they believe surrounds them. We share many of their concerns: Television, for instance, is welcomed into virtually every home and is too often filled with sexual innuendo and bloody violence. Pornography, particularly the sadistic, violent type that objectifies and victimizes women and children, is rampant. Sin, by many standards, is on a spree.

These people seem to feel their environment is out of their control, that they cannot dent the public conscience from their traditional pulpits and proselytizing missions. So they have taken to the airwaves and the streets to speak out for what they believe.

We cannot question their right to speak or their motive. But just because one religious group takes a position doesn't mean its view is good or correct or reflective of the entire spectrum of "Christian" position on any issue.

God, they believe, is on the side of the ultraconservatives — specifically Ronald Reagan and, for the most part, the Republican platform, though their support for specific candidates is only implied. Most of these organizations cannot endorse a particular candidate without jeopardizing their tax exempt status.

The Moral Majority, in rating candidates, listed 14 criteria upon which to judge a Christian candidate. Candidates must support the Kemp-Roth tax cut bill to get a perfect "Christian" rating. Kemp-Roth a matter of morality? Here and in their disregard for other issues — among them poverty and discrimination — we begin to differ.

The United States has, by history and strong belief, been a nation of diversity, where those of all religions are free to worship and vote. The diversity is also political; left to right, it would be hard to find a nation whose people span a wider spectrum, or argue about it more vehemently. While the religious right can claim to own God's political sympathies if they wish, we — and most other Americans — prefer to believe otherwise.

The evangelical-fundamentalists have a right to their views of politics, and so do the rest of us.

OKLAHOMA CITY TIMES

Oklahoma City, Okla., October 24, 1980

THOSE who have tried for years to shape American thought and morals into a liberal mode suddenly are finding their turf invaded from the right, and they are reacting desperately to it.

A group called "People for the American Way" is sponsoring a series of television commercials designed to counteract exhortations by "fundamentalist" preachers for their congregations to base their votes this fall on conservative principles. The new group of lay and religious leaders has a willing helping hand in Norman Lear, TV producer whose shows, stretching the bounds of good taste, probably did the most to shock and stir hostile reaction from conservative Americans.

Lear and his theological friends contend it is not right to inject religion into politics, to persuade people to cast their ballot for or against a candidate on the basis of whether he holds a "Christian position" on the issues.

Much of the debate over this new phenomenon has focused on terms that are too loosely defined, such as "born-again Christian" and "fundamentalist." These have become buzz words that trigger simplistic images, either favorable or unfavorable. What should be the criterion is whether preachers who profess Christianity have departed from their mission to preach the Gospel and wandered over the line into partisan politics. In such cases, criticism is justified.

But groups like Lear's obviously fail to perceive their own inconsistency. They don't understand that people clinging to conservative religious views have suffered too long in silence and that their present rising voice is a natural response to the excesses of the religious left. The latter did not hesitate in the 1960s and 1970s to utilize the pulpit to air *their* political views. Now they find it uncomfortable sharing the roost with those chickens coming home.

Roanoke Times & World-News

Roanoke, Va., October 26, 1980

It takes some pondering to figure out why fundamentalist Christians should now be so criticized for doing what other Christian groups have been doing for decades, even centuries: taking stands on political issues. The World Council of Churches and, at the next level, the National Council of Churches regularly issue pronunciamentos on economic and political questions. The Vatican has not been reluctant to issue papal bulls and other papers on economic and political questions. The leadership of Methodists, Episcopalians and Presbyterians — usually much more liberal than the members at home in the churches — has even made contributions to political groups. Much rage has resulted among those who fill the collection plates.

Why, then, is it suddenly so wrong for fundamentalist Christians, in their own organizations, to take stands for or against candidates in relation to their own views of abortion, family life, homosexualism, pornography and other issues which concern, or vex, them?

Fifteen years ago some young clergymen in the so-called mainstream churches didn't feel they were with it unless they marched the streets taking a stand on the Vietnam war, racial equality, poverty or some other issue. Should they now point fingers at — or cast the second stone at — fundamentalists who want to express their views on abortion by voting?

There is no excuse, in our opinion, for the lack of tolerance by those who pride themselves on their liberality and tolerance. There is, however, a difference in the two behaviors which has put the fundamentalists at a disadvantage in popular opinion. The extremists among them — especially in that wing we call the electronic clergy — has laid claim to exclusiveness. God, we hear, listens to them and to them alone.

It is one thing for an individual, a church or a group of churches to set forth a position applying a particular morality or religion to a political issue. It is another thing to draw a circle and declare, in public and over the air waves, that they and they alone have access to the only truth. Within the confines of a seminary, perhaps a stern theology will lead to a claim for exclusivenesss; in a pluralistic society and outside the church walls, such claims create resentment. Insisting upon them has created a backlash the fundamentalists do not deserve: They have the same right to express their opinion in public as anybody else.

The Birmingham News

Birmingham, Ala., December 7, 1980

Was the Reagan landslide a temporary convulsion, a political aberration, or does it portend that a conservative viewpoint will grow deeper and broader during the next several decades in the United States?

The answer depends in small measure on the performance of the incoming Republican administration and on the Republican majority in the U.S. Senate. If the GOP leadership in concert with conservative Democrats in the House is successful in slowing inflation, reducing the tax burden and in creating policies which nurture business and industry to create new jobs and reduce unemployment, the answer is undoubtedly yes.

But even if the new leadership is only partially successful during the next four years, the trend toward conservatism is likely to continue for at least the remainder of this century, if not longer. That assumption is based on several factors now visible in the body politic. Foremost is the self-correcting mechanism that is unique to our society, guided as it is by a constitution, by a long experience of freedom (especially in decision-making) and with an underlying historic and pragmatic distrust of governmental power.

As the public becomes more conversant with conservative principles and arguments regarding specific issues — such as income transfer, nonproductive regulation, schooling, etc. — an even larger percentage of voters will realize that their thinking on the issues is more compatible with stated conservative positions than with those of liberals.

Liberals who have dominated government, the media and the culture for the past 50 years — since the early '30s — have attempted of late to depict ascendant conservatism as something new. The conservative leadership has been called the New Right, Neo-conservatives, Radical Right and even fascists. The historic truth is that conservatism has a long and honorable tradition that goes back to and beyond colonial days in America. It is not a new movement, but the resurgence of a consciousness and a viewpoint that is as old or older than the nation itself.

One should note also that conservatism and liberalism transcend political party boundaries. While most Republicans are conservatives, some subscribe to liberal viewpoints, and Democrats have always had a tough core of conservatives to deal with in Congress, especially.

Although infrequently discussed in these terms, American society is composed of three systems which also transcend party boundaries. They are an economic system, a political system and a moral-cultural system. While their outlines are not always distinct, even in the case of government, the three systems under democratic capitalism are relatively independent and serve to keep any one of the systems from acquiring too much power at the expense of the remaining two.

The role of the economic system is to create wealth; that is, to provide food, shelter, clothing, transportation and creature comforts. The economic system also furnishes the wherewithal to operate government and to sustain the moral-cultural system. The working contract among the three systems is the Constitution. It is also an instrument with which to measure government's performance and power. When the power of the public sector becomes a threat, as it has during various times in our history, it is the job of the economic system to check that power, first with votes and then with purse.

The role of the political system — of which government is the center — is to tend to the safety of individuals and keep the country secure from internal and external threats — from criminals at home and hostile foreign forces. The political system's regulatory function is justifiable only in preserving equity among equals and as it looks to the general welfare of all the people. It is the responsibility of the political system also to put only those constraints on the economic and moral-cultural systems that serve the interests of all society.

The moral-cultural system's mission is to attend society's moral, psychic and spiritual needs and to provide guidance in such areas through mediating structures such as churches, schools, news media, theater, the arts and books and to create forums where ideas and knowledge may be offered and exchanged. The moral-cultural system also has a dynamic role in helping society resist the concentration of power in government.

The conservative sees government as necessary, since neither society nor the individual is perfectable by their own means, a sharp departure from current liberal views. The conservative acknowledges that the economic system is not perfect and neither are the political system nor the moral-cultural system. That being the case, society must turn to a power greater than itself — to the Creator — for guidance in the adjudication of wrongs and disputes as well as for ultimate justice.

The conservative generally believes that the Creator addresses all three systems, but most effectively passes His wisdom to society through the minds and feelings of free men and women rather than through governmental departments or through self-appointed overseers.

Where the conservative and liberal plainly fall out is over the role of government. Conservatives believe in government that is strictly limited by the Constitution and by the power of the people which only voluntarily flows to government through the political system. Liberals — the term is really a misnomer in the case of the present leadership; it is really statist or socialist in viewpoint — believe the role of government, the state, is to make decisions for the entire society that affect the most intimate aspects of an individual's life, from what to do with his money to his health and to how to rear his children. Liberals would not only have government control the economic system, but they would have government form compacts with the moral-cultural system to enhance government power.

The recent presidential election did not trigger a conservative flood as some suggest. On the contrary, the election outcome was the result of a flood of conservative opinion which has been building for at least 20 years in the United States, due in part to the failure of liberal remedies. The election, therefore, was a symptom rather than a dynamic cause.

If the conservative mood is not checked by international developments, such as world war, Americans should witness a sharp de-emphasis of government's role in society. We should see political policies which enhance personal freedom in terms of decision-making at many levels gradually exchanged for those that now restrict personal decisions. We should also see policies that free up the economic system so the countless ideas — the real currency of the economic system — of the millions of men and women engaged in business and industry can be transformed into diverse kinds of wealth and service for society at every level.

A lot of knots must be untied before either the economic system or the moral-cultural system can recover in relative freedom from the crude restraints emplaced by the political system. But one would be hard put to deny that Americans as individuals and as a society want a restrained and limited government with less power to encroach on their freedom to make the decisions which are best for them and their families.

Therein lies the first and best reason why the country will continue in a conservative mode for some time to come. And once Americans taste the fruits of that greater freedom in terms of material, moral and spiritual benefits, they are likely to remain on a steady course.

The Hartford Courant

Hartford, Conn., November 13, 1980

James J. Kilpatrick and Garry Wills recently suggested in their columns on this page that the Rev. Jerry Falwell and his Moral Majority are just another special interest group, no better or no worse than any other such alliance that picks political favorites for an election.

The reaction to Mr. Falwell in intellectual circles — especially in the Northeast — may have been a bit extreme, prompted in part by the natural suspicion of evangelical religion in a region that sees so little of it. But we must differ with our columnists when they suggest that the Moral Majority suffers merely from not being trendy. That conservative alliance operates under a banner that says "God," and such a claim smacks of false advertising that merits some pointed criticism and rebuttal.

The Moral Majority chooses to tell America that the Good Lord has an opinion on the merits of the Panama Canal Treaties and the effectiveness of arms control agreements. As individuals of whatever political and religious persuasion, the Moral Majority enthusiasts are free to analyze candidates as they see fit, but they must be prepared to suffer some legitimate scorn when their morality index excludes all but the most narrow range of right-wing ideologues seeking election.

The Moral Majority movement, given the sociology of a state like Connecticut, had little, if any, direct political impact in the Northeast, but the main-line Protestantism and Catholicism and Judaism of the region have a special obligation to counter a religious movement that does not speak their language.

As the main-line faiths know all too well, evangelicals were long excluded from the airwaves of America, in favor of more "proper" religious radio and television programming. In response, conservative preachers such as Mr. Falwell bought their way into the electronic media. They deliver their message with an effectiveness that is the envy of churches and public relations agencies alike.

With their success on Nov. 4 has come a certain muddying of religious identities that makes their political arguments all the more necessary to rebut. All Baptists are not independent, fundamentalist Baptists; all conservative Protestants with an evangelical sympathy are not enthusiastic about right-wing politics; and all Christians are certainly not card-carrying members of the Moral Majority. The Moral Majority's intermingling of politics and religion hints at a unity of political platform and theology that is rarely true.

In colonial Massachusetts, loose-tongued Congregationalists were fined five pounds for disparaging their preacher or his sermon. Today, there is more than one preacher, more than one sermon, and a federal government that keeps a careful distance from the tenets of any faith.

The Moral Majority had chosen to target certain politicians for defeat at the polls, with an arbitrary fervor that brings to mind the lament of William Penn: "Were some as Christian as they boast themselves to be, it would save us all the labor we bestow in rendering persecution so unchristian as it most truly is."

The Moral Majority strains the concept of morality, in the search of a political end. The Moral Majority does not represent any religious majority, beyond its own narrow confines. And while the Moral Majorty has as legitimate a right to its religious inclinations as any other alliance of true believers, Americans need not feel guilty about finding the group's tactics and mission potentially dangerous.

THE SACRAMENTO BEE

Sacramento, Calif., April 27, 1980

There have been growing indications in recent months that religious groups and cults are becoming increasingly active in electoral politics. Just a week ago, The Bee disclosed that Mormons in California had raised substantial funds to defeat an Equal Rights Amendment referendum and to elect anti-ERA legislators in Florida. Since then, we have learned that a conservative religious group called Christian Voice has begun to issue annual "Christian-moral" ratings of all members of Congress which, the group hopes, "will have a dynamic effect toward influencing how Christians will vote in the November elections." Those developments come on top of growing evidence that conservative religious voices — in the pulpit, on the platform and on the television screen — are becoming increasingly vocal in their expressions of overtly political views.

Capping all those activities is "Washington for Jesus," a rally scheduled in the nation's capital Tuesday which, though billed as a non-political event, will almost certainly be devoted to attacks on abortion and welfare, calls for voluntary school prayers and the teaching of creation on a par with Darwinian evolution, and the articulation of conservative political views in general. A draft declaration produced by One Nation Under God, the organization sponsoring the rally, calls on legislators to "frame laws, statutes and ordinances that are in harmony with God's word" and to "repeal those ... which have offended him." The sponsors hope to have 1 million people in Washington for the rally.

All those groups have a right to their views — have a right to preach or speak in favor of any practice or policy they regard as consistent with their beliefs, against any that is not. Nonetheless, when the expression of views begins to move into overtly political activity, it becomes dangerous stuff — dangerous not only because there is no compromising on something that is elevated to a moral issue, but also because a religious assault on government inevitably involves government intrusion on religion. The minute one religious group succeeds in influencing government policy on behalf of its own sectarian or moral views, that policy is likely to infringe upon the sectarian and moral views of others.

As the record of the past decade makes clear, there is more than one "Christian" position even on something as relatively specific as abortion. It's for that reason that the state must allow as much latitude for individual choice and individual conscience as the circumstances permit.

The framers of the Constitution and the Bill of Rights understood those principles all too well, which is why they prohibit both a government establishment of religion and any law forbidding "the free exercise thereof." One is obviously unattainable without the other. For that reason also, it should be evident not only to the civil libertarian but to every member of a religious group that caution and self-restraint must be paramount in the use of religious organizations, religious symbols and religious criteria in the realm of secular politics. When the barrier between church and state is broken, the breach runs in both directions.

THE BILLINGS GAZETTE

Billings, Mont., October 6, 1980

Quite a fuss is being made this year over the involvement of religion in politics.

The envangelicals and fundamentalists are making the most noise with their New Morality and broadcasting evangelists who fear the nation is doomed to go to hell unless we all embrace their form of salvation.

We can't help but feel some of these zealots have gotten their hands and hog-calling voices into a good deal and are going to make the most of it. If they can preach salavation and make a few bucks at the same time, well, it's good for their business.

These are the same yahoos who would oppose giving a nickel to Catholic schools under the principle of separation of church and state, yet they want to run the state according to their concept of the Lord's guidance.

What's behind it all bothers us. No, not the belief in the Creation of the Biblical writers or that the foot washers, snake handlers or dunkers pursue a given path to the hereafter. Let anyone be born again who so chooses.

That's the point. Let each choose for himself, choose in a manner which does not inflict his belief on others.

This nation was founded by men who were God-fearing enough but also saw the dangers of allowing those who controlled the state to impose their ideas of how to pursue eternal salvation on others.

That's what is meant by separation of church and state. It doesn't say that a student can't say a prayer to himself before school, a test or an athletic contest. He can. What it does mean is that no school board, administrator or teacher can require the recitation or reading of a prescribed prayer which suits the religious fancy of those in charge.

Those who fear intrusion of church on state are on firm historical ground. History is replete with instances of followers of one particular brand of religion coming into power and then forcing their beliefs and customs on all others.

To think it would be different in the United States of America is foolish.

Arkansas Gazette.

Little Rock, Ark., October 25, 1980

A self-appointed judge of America's sins and foibles is on safe ground when he argues that a "majority" of the citizens can be considered "moral." With equal logic, he could argue that the "majority" is "immoral" because, as it is written, "all have sinned."

Everything is a matter of degree in the judgment of those who qualify for some measure of morality. Reverend Jerry Falwell, who presumably is a student of the New Testament, might even grant that ultimate salvation is "by grace" and "not of works, lest any man should boast."

Understanding, as he must, the weaknesses of mortals, Mr. Falwell invited a close scrutiny of his organization when he described his followers as the "Moral Majority." If he had been content with the lower case (merely "moral majority") he could have argued that the behavioral standards of Americans had risen to a point where half the citizens, plus one, were virtuous. By capitalizing the term and identifying the membership, Mr. Falwell invited a scrutiny of his followers that could become a bit of an embarrassment.

Those who belong have an obligation to be "Moral" in all things. Since membership, so far as can be determined, is open to all who embrace Mr. Falwell's views on the subject (and, presumably, make their donations and pay their vows), there is always the danger that the rolls of the Moral Majority will include ordinary sinners.

Conceivably, there are those who believe some segment of the school day should be dedicated to public prayer (a Falwell litmus test) but who also would put away their wives in divorce or admit to lusting after women.

In another part of the world — say Boston or Cleveland — there may be those who are "against forced busing" of their children but who might, in another context, violate the commandment that says "Thou shalt not steal" or the one that forbids covetousness. In this imperfect world, each sins in his own way.

How, then, can we decide who is moral and who is immoral? For Mr. Falwell, the task of separating the sheep from the goats is simple. Those who accept his role as shepherd are sheep.

He may say, with the Master, that there are other sheep "which are not of this fold." When, on the other hand, he capitalizes his organization and calls it the "Moral Majority," he asserts that his flock contains no goats. All are pure.

The obligation, then, is to show that his following actually is a "majority" of the citizens. Otherwise, the name is a fraud on its face. If his rolls contain the names of 1,000,000 or 2,000,000, which would be a highly-inflated figure, the herd would be impressive — but this is a country of 220,000,000-plus people. Mr. Falwell's "cloud of witnesses" definitely is a minority, regardless of who makes the count. Any contrary claim becomes a bit absurd.

Article V of Mr. Falwell's 10-article "Christian Bill of Rights, says, "We believe that all students enrolled in public schools should have the right to voluntary prayer and Bible reading."

Just about everyone believes in that "right" but some substantial part of the population believes the schools are forbidden by the Constitution to conduct these prayers and Bible readings — regardless of whether the ceremonies are directed by Christians, Jews, Moslems, or followers of one of the other religions. The Supreme Court agrees.

This matter must be decided on legal, rather than theological, grounds. The High Court has spoken.

Now if someone should wish to challenge Mr. Falwell in the theological arena, he might start with the quotation:

"When thou prayest, thou shalt not be as the hypocrits are: They love to pray standing in the synagogues and in the corners of streets that they may be seen of men. Verily I say unto you, they have their reward."

Mr. Falwell's prayers and fulminations are not limited to the street corners and churches. He reaches (and is seen and heard by) quite a few people and his reward, according to reports, is considerable.

Religion is, among other things, an emotional experience of the believers. It does not work as a system of government and history is replete with examples of its failures.

On the screen of current events, we have ample proof that the fervor of spiritual leaders can be dangerous when it is permitted to influence unduly the policies of civilian authorities. Lest we imagine the hazards are exemplified only in Iran, dominated by a strange religion and an even stranger high priest, we might glance at Ireland where Christians have been killing Christians for lo these many decades.

Those who gain high office by reason of perceived divine grace often are tempted to spread the Gospel by whatever means are needed — including force. For this purpose, the rack and the wheel were invented; for this reason, millions of God's Children have sizzled at the stake, torched by sheep of a different fold.

The Kansas City Times

Kansas City, Mo., October 11, 1980

Nervous tremors strummed by the deep interest this year of electronic evangelists and leaders of fundamentalist sects in the election are understandable and well-founded. Religion and politics always are a volatile mix. But it is natural for preachers and religious groups to be concerned with the shaping and function of government, for government is all-pervasive. The collision is the norm; it is a dominant theme through the history of western civilization.

There is nothing improper or unconstitutional for persons of strong religious convictions to try to apply their beliefs to government. It is only when government becomes a part of that pressure that the church-state question becomes an issue. What the preachers say on the airways and what they do with money collected through ostensibly religious programs and resulting questions of tax exemption most definitely are legitimate areas of inquiry. The dangers of church-state violations seem obvious.

In the long run, in a democracy, ecclesiastical interference in the process tends to be self-correcting. This is so even under (or maybe especially under) authoritarian regimes associated with a state religion. Anti-clericalism has a long and often honorable tradition, both within and without organized religion.

It is the nature of ecclesiastics to attempt to enforce the ritual, dogma and rules as would the authorities of any organization. The essence of a society is the determination and enforcement of a behavior or discipline that requires at least a measure of self-sacrifice, if not as revealed wisdom then for the greater good of all. In a free society, transgressors against religious codes are punished by a denial of benefits or even banishment from the flock. Those who will not follow church law can be denied sacraments, or the comforts of the group, or be told that they will burn in Hell.

The problem always arises when religious moralists try to burn sinners here on Earth.

In a modern democratic society, politics and elections determine the law. And when religionists seek to shape the law according to their beliefs, then fundamental freedoms may be in danger. Those who have been saved often cannot understand why everyone may not wish to be saved in precisely the same manner.

It is one thing to accept a faith and through it do good works and find salvation. It is something else to try to impose a faith on others through the law which ultimately is enforced by the police power and the threat of legal violence. That is to spread faith by the sword.

The law, if it is written through a blend of politics and religion, can be a mighty sword.

THE BLADE

Toledo, Ohio, October 11, 1980

THE furor over whether fundamentalist religious groups should play a role in this year's presidential and congressional elections generally misses the point. It is not whether a television preacher or a self-styled leader of the "moral majority" has a right to speak out for or against candidates or issues. He certainly does have that right, just as clergymen in the 1960s and 1970s spoke out and demonstrated for civil rights or against the Vietnam war.

Rather the question is whether some of these self-righteous guardians of public morality are sailing under false colors. There is no question of their potency. Candidate Ronald Reagan has seen fit to appear twice before gatherings of fundamentalist religious leaders. But there are some rather respectable dissenters, too. A group of religious leaders, representing Jewish, Catholic, Lutheran, and Southern Baptist groups, recently denounced the political activity of the "New Right evangelicals" as a threat to both church and state.

One spokesman, Charles Bergstrom of the office for governmental affairs of the Lutheran Council in the U.S.A., added: "It is arrogant to assert that one's position on a political issue is 'Christian' and that all others are 'un-Christian,' 'immoral,' or 'sinful'."

This is particularly so when one takes note of the fact that the right-wing Christian groups have based their political evaluations of officeholders in part on such secular issues as government spending and the Panama Canal treaties. Or when one notes that one of the darlings of the new religious rightist movement, Rep. Robert Bauman of Maryland, recently was allowed to plea bargain his way out of a morals charge only by fuzzing the episode over with a claim that he was an alcoholic and by agreeing to undergo treatment.

There is something unappetizing, too, about the way the new pietists gang up on unwary politicians who displease them — sometimes with deadly effect. Eight-term Alabama Congressman John Buchanan, a Baptist minister, lost his seat last month as a result of such tactics. He said later: "They beat my brains out with Christian love." But some of the intended targets are fighting back, and sometimes with good effect.

Piety along the Potomac for political purposes is not a new phenomenon in American life. The church-going habits of American presidents have been noted in the press for years, even though the Constitution flatly states that "no religious test shall ever be required as a qualification to any office or public trust under the United States."

The term "born-again Christian," long familiar in religious circles, gained currency in political parlance with a vengeance four years ago when candidate Jimmy Carter saw political advantage in being so described. He even continued to teach Sunday school classes for a time after becoming President.

But piety is a two-edged sword, one that can be used by anybody with a loud voice or, better yet, an electronic pulpit from which to enunciate ideas and plead for various causes. Fortunately, the history of religious humbug being what it is, sooner or later the public will tire of such cant and turn the more blatant of these television-spawned religio-political evangelists off — quite literally.

Moral Majority's Fervor Attracts Adherents, Anxiety

The election of Ronald Reagan as president in 1980 appeared to confirm America's conservative trend. The "New Right" took particular satisfaction in Reagan's victory, since it had been instrumental in pressuring the Republican Party to abandon its traditional support for the Equal Rights Amendment to the Constitution and adopt a strong anti-abortion posture during the campaign. The Moral Majority stepped up its political efforts in light of the conservative electoral success. Rev. Jerry Falwell turned his fundraising efforts into a multimillion-dollar empire, Moral Majority, Inc., which mounted an intense voter-registration drive for adherents and contributed to the campaigns of local, state and federal supporters. The group's success worried opponents, who charged it with forcing its moral standards on the American public. Even the Rev. Billy Graham, the country's foremost mainstream evangelist, expressed concern over the Moral Majority's tactics. At a convention of religious broadcasters in Washington, D.C. in January, 1981, he warned that the television preachers were vulnerable to egotism and reliance on "worldly methods." He said he was pleased at the recent rise of evangelism, but he preferred Christians to be more reserved in their political activity. He reminded his audience that there were other problems besides abortion and pornography "which demand our attention as Christians," such as halting the arms race. (Most of the militant evangelical groups, including the Moral Majority, supported U.S. military superiority.)

The Charlotte Observer
Charlotte, N.C., January 6, 1981

The emergence of the Christian conservative movement as a highly publicized political force has put the spotlight on a number of sensitive issues, including parental rights, homosexual rights, children's rights, prayer in public schools and abortion.

Those are among the issues raised in a bill known as the Family Protection Act, introduced in the U.S. Senate last year by Paul Laxalt, the Nevada Republican who is one of President-elect Reagan's closest friends.

Among other provisions, it would deny U.S. Supreme Court jurisdiction in cases involving state laws on prayer in schools; require notification of parents when a minor requests an abortion or contraceptives or venereal disease treatment; allow employers to fire employees for being homosexual.

People who shudder at some of those proposals, as we do, nevertheless should welcome the opportunity for a focused national debate on these issues. They involve matters of deep concern to many Americans — too deep for elected officials to ignore.

Some of the bill's provisions appear to be blatantly unconstitutional. Others, such as tax changes to encourage stability, responsibility and self-reliance within families, may be worth serious consideration. Instead of an instinctive negative reaction, those of us who rarely find common ground with the so-called fundamentalists ought to look at each proposal on its merit, and look for ways to deal with some of these concerns without trampling on constitutional rights.

There can be no compromise, of course, with people who want the government to prohibit certain kinds of behavior simply because it offends them; or who would have our society ignore, in the name of parental rights, the problems of abused children; or who would sanction, under a "pro-family" banner, discrimination on the basis of sex; or who would give states the authority to approve or disapprove religious beliefs and practices.

But within the limits of legislative authority, under the protections of the Constitution, there may be some room to maneuver in ways that reflect the reasonable concerns of people who believe social progress and the expansion of freedoms are undermining the family and some cherished — and useful — traditional values.

THE COMMERCIAL APPEAL
Memphis, Tenn., September 9, 1981

IF THE THUNDER on the Right seems to have toned down a decibel or two, do not be misled. It is only the calm before the storm over the "social agenda," that set of issues encompassing abortion, family "protection," school busing and school prayer, to name but a few.

These matters are of paramount importance to the New and Christian Right, which are not about to be put off any longer or let the President of the United States and the Congress forget who helped put them in power.

The coalition's role in that election may have been minor, indeed — but not to hear the Far Right tell it. It proclaims its self-importance loudly and with the same certainty it uses to expound its beliefs — beliefs it would impose on all Americans, whether or not they agree.

Will its voice alone be heard? Will it dictate the law of our land?

The President is under pressure to honor a Republican platform, in which New Right craftsmanship plainly showed in the so-called "moral" planks. The rumblings of discontent heard last week in Dallas by The Commercial Appeal's religion editor, Michael Clark, are only the latest reminders of the President's promises and are bound to echo in the White House.

The halls of Congress will reverberate, too, and Congress could yield if it thinks the administration has surrendered. If Reagan is already committed, some legislators will say, what's the purpose of putting up a fight? When constitutional amendments can be laid off on the states and when any law Congress passes will be subject to review by the nation's courts, why make an issue of the "social" issues?

THUS, IT IS politically tempting to yield to the New-Christian Right, but the President and Congress should not. They should be aware that this is a minority speaking, amplifying its voice to say that it is not. But the majority of Americans must speak up if their elected representatives are to see how small this group really is.

In poll after poll, the majority of Americans has repeatedly opposed strict laws or amendments against abortion. The majority of Americans appears to favor sex education in the schools, the teaching of evolution and the Equal Rights Amendment as never before. Most Americans report that religion is important in their lives, although they don't hold with those who claim that they, alone, understand divine will and can interpret it for the good of the Republic.

The majority of Americans also seems to be sticking by the President and Congress despite increasing doubts about the economic package and despite the fact the program is starting to hit home.

How long that support will last is anyone's guess, but there's no question about it if the social agenda is pushed on this nation. Most Americans won't stand for it, and neither should their government.

The TENNESSEAN
Nashville, Tenn., May 31, 1981

MEMBERS of the New Right have taken Senate Majority Leader Howard Baker to task for not scheduling a greater number of social and moral issues for Senate action.

The Reagan administration and the congressional leadership are more interested in getting the President's budget and tax package out of the way before getting bogged down in fights over moral issues and so the leadership has pushed these issues to the back burner.

Senator Baker, who has been trying to lead the Senate back to the times when it had some reputation as a debating society, has promised the New Right he will set aside time to debate social and moral issues without any relevant legislation being considered.

The New Right, which also wants to go back but in a different direction from Senator Baker, is having none of this. It's not interested in debate; it wants votes on such issues as abortion, school prayer, busing, the death penalty, and others.

Senator Baker, a longtime advocate of school prayer, is no backslider on moral issues in politics. But he is not aggressive enough to suit the fanatical evangelists of the New Right and the Moral Majority.

Apparently these groups will not be satisfied until everyone has been forced to adopt their puritanical code of morality.

The Birmingham News
Birmingham, Ala., September 6, 1981

As detailed in a recent *Birmingham News* series of reports, there appears now to be a surge of activity among organizations of what might be called the "militant right." Such groups as the various fragments of the Ku Klux Klan, the several varieties of American Nazis and the relatively new "Christian Patriots" are assuming a higher profile and may even be moving toward some sort of consolidation of views, if not of forces.

It is important to keep such activity within perspective, it should go without saying. The membership of these organizations is numbered in scant thousands, even when membership rolls are expanded on a national basis and given the benefit of a doubt. Compared to the great mass of the American public, this "militant right" constitutes what can properly be called a fringe of the body politic, even if its collective activities and the long shadow of such names as "Klan" and "Nazi" invite notoriety.

Yet, as much as it would be a mistake to overestimate the significance of the "militant right," it would as well be remiss to undervalue the forces within the society which have given life to this visible movement.

Indeed, the extent to which at least some of the activities and philosophies of this "militant right" are mirrored in other segments of the society is uncomfortably apparent. For instance, the emphasis on self-protection and stockpiling of food and supplies now seen among the established organizations bears remarkable similarity to the "survivalist" craze, whose enthusiasts predict a coming Armageddon against which the wise will prepare themselves. Similarly, the "militant right's" practice firing ranges and weapons training bears at least a passing resemblance to the decision by many private individuals to carry firearms and know how to use them.

To what degree these trends can be compared is of course open to debate, but it would seem reasonable to assume that they share like origins. It further would seem reasonable to conclude that a large part of this impetus is simple fear.

Fear, of course, is a basic human emotion, shared by us all. Yet it would seem clear that an increased and active fear of a future marked by any number of possible calamities — nuclear war, race riots, food shortages — is at the heart of the "militant right" and the corollary forces which can be perceived at work in "normal" society. Indeed, the fear itself need not be of Armageddon: Fear of being mugged, or of losing one's job, or simply of a loss of pride (even if that pride unfortunately involves the need for one group to feel "superiority" over another) is quite enough to inspire any number of "militant" activities.

How to control such fears is, of course, another matter, and it should be quickly admitted that all such fears are not entirely groundless. The regular issuance of reports reflecting increased crime, the cloud of nuclear war, economic pressures and the host of uncertainties which accompany modern life are only real enough, and feed the fears of many citizens.

Yet it is equally clear that a society prey to fear — and when "militancy" occurs, fear only redoubles — cannot function as it should. A loss of faith in the future corrupts the present and can become a prophecy which self-fulfills. Violence begot of "militancy" only begets more violence, with the greatest violence of all done to the fragile fabric of the society itself.

Taken as a symptom of national problems and not merely a discrete phenomenon, the "militant right" emphasizes the necessity for both government and private citizens to rededicate themselves to improving our national life so that the midnight fears of the moment are reduced and the future again becomes something to anticipate eagerly, not a subject of despair.

The ways of going about this are as numerous as the problems involved, but the principal thing is that the attempt be made, and for citizens to be given constructive channels to work through their fears toward a better tomorrow.

As easy as it would be to dismiss the "militant right" as a lunatic fringe — and while it is certain that certain of its members are in fact lunatic, and will remain in any case at the fringe of American life — it would profit us all to listen to the cry of fear which such a momement represents and to work toward resolutions of our common fears before fear itself defeats us.

The Virginian-Pilot
Norfolk, Va., October 19, 1981

Various Christians who would like to distance themselves from the Rev. Jerry Falwell's Moral Majority and also make a political difference held an organizational meeting recently in Chicago. They adopted a four-page statement, and so, from now on, you can expect . . . what?

Not much. The statement finessed a number of salient issues, like abortion and capital punishment. It had trouble, bred from fear of "alienating homosexuals," in saying what a family is. This is not surprising, inasmuch as the idea in organizing the group was to make it as ecumenically Christian as possible. These days there probably is no better formula for political vapidity.

Moral Majority, by contrast, suffers from no such organizational defect. It is a political group, and its political goals determine its membership. To the degree it is religiously ecumenical, it is so not by any special design.

It so happens, of course, that there isn't much religious (or Christian) diversity in its membership, since most of those allied with Moral Majority are in theological agreement with the Reverend Falwell. But as there are still *some* members of Moral Majority who are not Falwellists when it comes to religion, the point remains that it is is allegiance to common political goals that defines Moral Majority.

The group that met in Chicago was certainly right to say that Christians can conscientiously hold differing views on moral and political issues. But if it or any other similar group would seek to do more than merely to stand in opposition to the Reverend Falwell—if it would seek to make a political impact of its own—it will have to articulate certain political goals, and then it will have to seek out whichever churchmen (and others) might be interested in jointly pursuing them. Church people who would make a difference cannot let their political light hide under a bushel.

the Charleston Gazette

Charleston, W.Va., July 24, 1981

WE ARE puzzled by the determination of so many Americans, including the editors of the *Charleston Daily Mail* to jettison the tradition of separation of church and state. We are amused by their desperate production of evidence to show that the First Amendment is not really what the courts have held it to be.

The separation of church and state has never been strict. Our coins bear a religious motto. Military chaplains are paid from the public purse. Ministers who offer prayers to the Congress are similarly remunerated. Various services to parochial schools are supplied with tax funds. Evangelists speak in public auditoriums. Examples abound. Nobody cares except Madalyn Murray O'Hair.

Whatever the Founding Fathers intended, "separation" has come to mean not absolute divorcement but a reasonable apartness. The tradition has served the people well in that it has spared them from taxation for the direct support of religion. A Catholic would be upset, we have always assumed, if he were forced to pay directly for the proliferation of Presbyterianism.

The collapse of the tradition of separation inevitably would make government responsive to the most influential denomination. The history of man has shown that the religion favored by government does not hesitate to use its advantage to promote its own dogma. Contemplate, please, the picture of a Jerry Falwell regulating conduct with the support of the state.

A scramble for government favor demeans religion and we are pleased to observe that leaders of most of the more readily recognized faiths in America are quite happy with the principle of separation. It is not the religious leaders of America but the editorial writers of the *Daily Mail* who yearn for a marriage of church and state.

Some months ago, the afternoon paper produced an apologia for a state church, clearly the high point of a relentless campaign against Thomas Jefferson. Less remarkable but no less vigorous is a newer argument resting upon these points: (1) Separation of church and state is a fairly recent concept and (2) the 1789 Northwest Ordinance is evidence that the First Amendment does not bar religion from a role in government.

We are delighted to be able to agree on the first point. Separation of church and state is, indeed, a fairly recent concept, as is, for instance, the concept of romantic love. We don't know why the point was made, but secure in the knowledge that novelty does not mean mischief, we agree.

On the second point, the afternoon paper observes that the ordinance reads "Religion, morality, and knowledge being necessary to good government and the happiness of mankind, schools and the means of learning shall forever be encouraged."

Let us say immediately that we are as attached to religion and morality as the next newspaper. But how does a congresional affirmation of the common virtues show a desire for a church-state partnership? If an early Congress desired such a partnership, why didn't it simply establish it? We believe we sense a suggestion that the Founding Fathers decided, in an impish mood, to strew about obscure cles to be discovered in 1981 by editorial writers.

The Idaho STATESMAN

Boise, Idaho, February 4, 1981

Evangelist Billy Graham hit the nail on the head the other day when he warned Christians against joining the rush to mix politics and religion.

"Liberals organized in the '60s, and conservatives certainly have a right to organize in the '80s," Graham said. "But it would disturb me if there was a wedding between the religious fundamentalists and the political right. The hard right has no interest in religion except to manipulate it."

Graham, no liberal himself, makes sense. Christians have the right to vote for candidates who reflect their moral, ethical values. That's what everyone does. But people should beware of religious leaders who are too eager to jump into the political arena and tell the congregation which candidates are right or wrong.

Voters who want officeholders to reflect their moral values would do better to gather information on candidates from neutral sources and then make judgments accordingly. Putting too much faith in anybody immersed in politics, even evangelists, can be dangerous.

THE INDIANAPOLIS NEWS

Indianapolis, Ind., December 19, 1981

Church-state separation is producing ironic contrasts these days.

The problem is not what the Founding Fathers had in mind when they wrote: "Congress shall make no law respecting an establishment of religion, or prohibiting the free exercise thereof."

What's happened in recent years is that the Supreme Court and others have developed an odd interpretation that has little to do with the intent of the Constitution. Now we are told that all government institutions must be neutral toward all religion and do absolutely nothing to advance it. That's an impossible task since all of life involves essentially religious issues.

But the practical result is that student groups can meet voluntarily in school rooms for all sorts of purposes — military training, athletics, economic discussions, protest. But they cannot meet for prayer. Does anyone seriously think that's what the authors of the Constitution meant?

Terry Eastland answers with a resounding no in a Commentary magazine article, "In Defense of Religious America," earlier this year. "The intention of the framers of the First Amendment was not to effect an absolute neutrality on the part of government toward religion on the one hand and irreligion on the other. The neutrality the framers sought was rather among the sects, the various denominations.

The misinterpretation of the First Amendment church-state clause has had practical and ironic effects in other areas as well — school newspapers. Student editors have asserted their First Amendment free press rights in a recent controversy at DePaul University. University officials confiscated copies of The DePaulia this fall when the editors printed a story on the rape of a student, despite a school administration order not to print the story. The order to confiscate the newspaper was rescinded, and editor Vince Kellen proudly declared: "Universities cannot carelessly walk around First Amendment rights. When they do, as DePaul did, they attract more attention than they bargained for."

Then at the Daily Reveille at Louisiana State University, university officials have censored an advertisement for contraceptives. The ad, placed by a nearby drugstore, pictured two wine glasses and male contraceptives with the words: "The perfect nightcap."

"The blatant actions of the university in bowing to pressure and exercising censorship are unacceptable," student editors declared in an editorial.

Meanwhile, at Arizona State University, student leaders and some faculty members have been complaining about the State Press editorial page, which some think has too much religion on it. A graduate student, Ben Sanders, wrote two essays on the weakness of modern value-free relativism and its dominating impact in several academic fields. "The dogmatic relativism of the social sciences, which rejects all truth as such, is bankrupt," he wrote. "Thus, let us affirm those truths and values articulated by the great philosophers of the past — such as Aristotle and Augustine — as well as by extraordinary thinkers of the present age — C.S. Lewis and Alexander Solzhenitsyn. In that affirmation of true values, we will be turning toward that which has brought hope, life and meaning to people."

Other writers have been expressing similar views, generally defending a Christian philosophical perspective, much to the chagrin of some readers. Some are just complaining, asking for more balance on the editorial page. But Rose Wertz, a sociology teacher, said she was planning to contact the American Civil Liberties Union for a possible lawsuit against the student newspaper. The potential crime: Violating church-state separation by publishing religious views in a state university newspaper.

That's the irony. Rape stories are all right — freedom of the press. But a Christian world view violates the Constitution.

What is needed, beginning with the U.S. Supreme Court, is a new interpretation of the church-state clause, more consistent with what the Founding Fathers had in mind. And those who want to confine religious expression to the churches and synagogues should perhaps submit a constitutional amendment to that effect.

Democrat [and] Chronicle

Rochester, N.Y., September 14, 1981

IT'S HARD to disagree with many of the professed goals and concerns of the members of The Moral Majority. For example, they put a high value on patriotism and family life. They want greater reverence for life itself, they believe deeply in God, they want to raise the standards of personal conduct, and they put private enterprise far above state control.

Many other Americans also hold these things dear. What they find repugnant, however, is the insistence of the Moral Majority followers that theirs is the only way, that there may be no disagreement without penalty.

There is in fact great danger in denial of the right to differ, for this is a nation that was founded in dissent, and we continue to believe that differentness is central to our vitality.

Timely, then, was the strong warning given by A. Bartlett Giamatti, president of Yale University, in a speech prepared recently for delivery to incoming freshmen. He sees in the intimidating tactics of The Moral Majority a threat to free minds everywhere:

"ANGRY at change, rigid in the application of chauvinistic slogans, absolutistic in morality, they threaten through political pressure or public denunciation whoever dares to disagree with their authoritarian positions. Using television, direct mail and economic boycott, they would sweep before them anyone who holds a different opinion.

"From the maw of this 'morality' come those who presume to know what justice for all is; come those who presume to know which books are fit to read, which television programs are fit to watch, which textbooks will serve for all the young; come spilling those who presume to know what God alone knows, which is when human life begins. From the maw of this 'morality' rise the tax-exempt Savonarolas who believe they, and they alone, possess the truth. There is no debate, no discussion, no dissent. They know."

THOSE are strong words, but they needed saying. The kind of fundamentalism that nourishes The Moral Majority erodes the traditions of freedom.

Chicago Tribune

Chicago, Ill., September 27, 1981

Every major religion preaches peace and brotherhood and mercy, yet some of the cruellest and most intolerant repressions in history have been committed in the name of God.

This is the paradoxical threat that arises whenever a revivalist religious group seeks to extend its influence beyond parochial boundaries and to establish itself as an organized force in the world of politics. It is why many Americans worry about the ambitions and influence of groups like Moral Majority even though they may share most if not all of its concerns. It is The Tribune's response to those of our readers who wonder why a normally conservative paper like this should be so critical of people who are a bit more conservative than we.

Throughout history people have turned to religion when they feel that they have lost their bearings in a rapidly changing society. There is abundant reason today to wonder what has happened to the old time values—to family unity, to the work ethic, to self-reliance, to fiscal prudence, and the like.

But there is also reason to worry when religious zeal turns into self-righteousness and intolerance and is used to cloak activities that are essentially self-serving or political. Consider some examples of history:

● The Crusades. Though billed as an effort to restore Christian control of the Holy Land, the leading roles were played by opportunists who proclaimed their loyalty to the Pope, recruited troops in the name of the Lord, and set off in the hope of winning their own principalities and a share of the fabled riches of the Orient—or, in the case of the Venetians, to set up trading offices. Whatever conquests these princes achieved dissolved in bickering among themselves (at least one, Conrad of Montferrat, was assassinated in the process). The stage was thus set for a new Crusade. This went on for two centuries until Europe and the church were in such disarray that the Mohammedans were able to retaliate by conquering most of southeastern Europe.

● The Inquisition. For centuries, the Catholic Church tried to deal with dissent within its ranks (called heresy) by means of an inquisition, a sort of grand jury investigation that often led to confiscation of property. But in 1478 Ferdinand and Isabella of Spain, seeking to consolidate their power, prevailed on Pope Sixtus IV to let them handle inquisitions, ostensibly as a service to the church. They and the "Most Catholic Majesties"

who succeeded them used it viciously—not against Catholic dissenters but against anybody who threatened the power of the monarchy, particularly Jews. Spain made the inquisition a political tool and gave it its notorious reputation for cruelty. Not until 1816 was the Vatican able to abolish torture by the Spanish inquisitors.

● The Puritans. The Puritans came over from England in search of religious freedom. But having established themselves as the dominant power in Massachusetts Bay Colony, they proceeded to convert the colony into an intolerant theocracy from which dissenters like Roger Williams were banished. A final orgy of fanaticism led to the Salem witch trials in the early 1690s; but by then the government had made so many enemies that the king of England revoked its charter and established a more liberal government

● The mullahs. True to the pattern of history, rapid social changes in the Middle East have brought a Moslem revivalist or fundamentalist movement dedicated originally to a restoration of traditional Moslem values. It has appeared as a religious movement in many countries, but in Iran it was harnessed by enemies of the shah and has led to a vicious Islamic Republic in which the mullahs praise Allah, recite the Koran (in which brotherhood and mercy figure even more prominently than in the Bible), and then order the execution of a dozen political enemies. More recently, the Moslem fundamentalists have appeared as a political faction in Egypt, leftist in ideology and bitterly opposed to President Sadat. They have demonstrated under banners carrying such unbrotherly messages as "Believers do not take the Christians and Jews as friends."

● Israel. In recent months the Begin government has been challenged by extreme Orthodox Jews who have become influential in small political parties, who make such religious demands as stricter observance of the Sabbath (no El Al flights, for example), but who have also become an obstacle to the quest for peace—a sort of mirror reflection of the "Moslem Associations" in the Arab world.

The list could go on, but the message is clear. We're not suggesting that the Rev. Jerry Falwell is about to become Chief Inquisitor for the U.S. But when religious zeal is diverted to political ends, it loses its religion and all too often becomes a vehicle for intolerance and divisiveness leading ultimately to the destruction of its own original goals.

WORCESTER TELEGRAM.

Worcester, Mass., July 8, 1981

When the Rev. Jerry Falwell and his colleagues took the name Moral Majority for their movement, they plunged the country into a semantic briar patch that has ensnared most everybody.

■ Falwell's mixture of Biblical fundamentalism, political conservativism and anti-science theology probably appeals so far to only a minority of the American people. However, according to a major survey funded by Connecticut Mutual Life, although only about 26 percent of Americans are "highly religious," religion is at least a latent force in the lives of 75 percent. And, according to the study, this religious feeling does carry over into moral convictions about various issues.

In that sense, at least, there is a "moral majority" out there.

The Connecticut General study makes some interesting findings, including: "It is via religious commitment that some Americans have been able to retain their faith in family, community, work, and in the American political process." and "Today it is moral issues that have, via religion, vaulted to the forefront of the political dialogue." and "It is the level of our religious commitment which, in the early part of the 80s, is a stronger determinant of our values than whether we are rich or poor, young or old, male or female, black or white, liberal or conservative."

But this moral majority differs from the views of some in the formal Moral Majority. It does not seek to impose its views on others. It is more tolerant of personal behavior that does not conform to the old strictures. For example, most of the people interviewed for the Connecticut General study did not think sex between two single people or sex before marriage is immoral. And, while only 29 percent expressed a preference for a traditional marriage "in which the husband is responsible for providing for the family and the wife for the home and taking care of the children," 63 percent supported the idea of "an equal marriage of shared responsibility in which the husband and wife cooperate on working, homemaking and child-raising."

Religion and morality, as ever, are intertwined in the minds of most Americans. But individual attitudes and beliefs still vary widely, even though there is a general consensus on some basic things.

That is the way it must be in this country, where freedom of all beliefs, or of no beliefs, is engraved in the Constitution and the many judicial rulings down the generations.

DAYTON DAILY NEWS

Dayton, Ohio, March 20, 1981

For persons capable of clearing away the wool that has been pulled over their eyes, it is now clear that the Moral Majority is interested in politics first, with "morality" only a means to that end. The source of this not-very-surprising information is the Moral Majority itself.

The fundamentalist organization headed by the Rev. Jerry Falwell has issued a statement in which it officially says it cares more about the political positions that public officials take than it cares about their morality.

Cal Thomas, the group's vice president for communications, says that as far as the Moral Majority is concerned, public officials can be boozers and womanizers (or, presumably, manizers) so long as they have the right positions on legislation — against abortion and pornography, for husband-wife relationships and strong national defense.

The spark for the Moral Majority's remarkable honesty in the cause of hypocrisy was a rumor in Washington that the group is fighting the appointment of Anne Gorsuch as head of the Environmental Protection Agency. The *Denver Post* recently reported that Mrs. Gorsuch and Bob Burford, nominated to head the federal Bureau of Land Management, developed a "close personal association" when they served together in the Colorado legislature. Both are divorcing.

The fact that Mrs. Gorsuch and Mr. Burford bring anti-environmental records to their jobs as protectors of the environment is good enough for the Moral Majority.

Mr. Thomas says of Mrs. Gorsuch, "As far as her conservative credentials are conerned, it would seem she has them together. Her living arrangements, we would say, would be irrelevant..."

Such elasticity is common in politics and would be welcome if it signaled a new, humane tolerance in the Moral Majority. But the Moral Majority has tried until now to pass itself off as essentially religious rather than political, and it emphatically is not tolerant. It seeks, for example, sexually repressive legislation with which to enforce intolerance, and never mind if the sponsors of the legislation personally violate its objectives in their own lives.

Bemused observers of the volatile mix of fundamentalist religion and rightwing politics have wondered for some time why the Moral Majority has not seemed embarrassed that some of its coziest political bedfellows have been exposed as grafters, predatory homosexuals and all-around sleazes.

It is now clear from the Moral Majority's own statement that it simply does not care if political crooks and creeps Bible-thump under its banner. By its own self-definition, the Moral Majority joins the familiar old American hustle of wrapping wolves, not in sheep's but in shepherd's clothing.

Oregon *Journal*

Portland, Ore., February 16, 1981

The Moral Majority says it is going to save Oregon from all those godless politicians. But those candidates who climb in bed with the righteous right should be warned that they will face a loss of freedom, for there is no deviation from the path proclaimed by the self-appointed moralists.

Mike Gass, Oregon chairman of the Moral Majority, says the Medford-based group plans to expand throughout Oregon. By 1984, according to a news report, Gass hopes his group will be able to influence the votes of 300,000 Oregonians and to run a candidate against Sen. Mark Hatfield, R-Ore.

The oddity of the evangelical far-right political movement is that it shuns many moral and religious elected officials because they don't vote "right" on all the key issues. These key issues vary among groups.

Nationally, the list usually favors constitutional amendments to ban abortion and permit voluntary prayer in schools, killing the Equal Rights Amendment, backing stiffer penalties for pornography and drug abuse and opposition to sex education and gay rights.

Christian Voice, a California-based group, prepares a "report card" on Congress which goes beyond the usual list of issues. The group has opposed sanctions against Rhodesia, supported Taiwan and decided creation of the U. S. Department of Education was immoral. Five of six clergymen in Congress last year scored less than 50 percent on the moral report card.

Jimmy Carter and Mark Hatfield, despite their deep and unchallenged fundamentalist religious convictions, have been opposed by the religious right because they strayed on the issues. Last year Rep. John Buchanan, a Baptist minister and moderate Republican from Alabama, lost the so-called "Christian" support and was denounced as "un-Christian" by the head of Alabama's Moral Majority chapter.

A fight over a school prayer bill last year brought criticism by the Christian right of Rep. Mickey Edwards, R-Okla., a staunch conservative who a Moral Majority member said "is with us 90 percent of the time."

It's apparently difficult to be a Democrat and win support of the Christian right. But it's not enough to be a Republican and a conservative. One must be undeviating on the issues, a virtual captive of small groups that make their own judgments on what's moral and what isn't. Those political candidates who bow to that kind of pressure may find that the cost of agreeing with these groups means that they must compromise common sense to be listed as voting "right" by the moralists. And that cost is too great.

Roanoke Times & World-News

Roanoke, Va., September 24, 1981

The relationship between church and state is a delicate one in this country. The founding fathers appealed to a divine creator in the Declaration of Independence, but wrote into the Constitution an amendment proscribing state-established religion.

Americans historically have seen themselves as a God-fearing nation, but the separation of church and state has been a basic principle by which we have governed ourselves. The recent rise of the religious right has led many Americans to fear God in a new way — as the center of an absolutist movement intent upon defining morality and enforcing it on its own terms.

The politicizing of the pulpit has thus become a prime topic in America. It was the theme of a conference on church-state relations attended by 125 people in Richmond recently. The Virginia Council of Churches sponsored it. There were lively differences of opinion.

"The electronic preachers of the Moral Majority are doing what every citizen and group of citizens has a right and duty to do," declared the Rev. Dean Kelley, an officer in the National Council of Churches. "It is the business of the church to meddle in politics."

Whether churches have a "duty" to meddle in politics is a matter of individual opinion. That they have a right to enter the political arena should be beyond dispute.

If a preacher wants to inveigh against the Equal Rights Amendment and for a school-prayer amendment, that's between him and his flock. If he wants to endorse a candidate for political office from the pulpit, that's between him and his flock. If he wants to advocate repeal of the First Amendment and establishment of a national priesthood, that's between him and his flock.

But what the ministers must realize is that when they enter the political arena, they must expect punches to be thrown. When they get into secular battles, they cannot expect their clerical robes to protect them.

As Meyera E. Oberndorf, a Virginia Beach city councilwoman who is a devout Jew, observed: "Churches and organized religion have to be sensitized enough to know that zoning laws cannot be waived because they beat their breasts and say I represent God."

Pat Robertson of Virginia Beach, founder of the Christian Broadcasting Network and host of the 700 Club, a religious TV show with a national audience, raises another caveat: "Once the church becomes part of the power structure, it participates in wrong if wrong is being done. It can no longer withdraw dispassionately." He adds, "When the church wins a power struggle, it becomes the vehicle for secular power. People without faith enter the church to gain secular power and wealth ... We don't want any camp followers."

Robertson nevertheless gave his blessing to those who, under divine prodding, give their political endorsements.

Dr. Robert Alley, professor of humanities at the University of Richmond, charged, though, that Dr. Robertson and other electronic evangelists give only lip-service to a pluralistic society. They would be pleased, he said, "to assume the role of national priest" and do not accept differing religious and social views.

If that is true, that is their right. And those who fear the threat of a religious invasion of the political arena have every right to oppose them at every step, not pulling their punches just because the adversary wears a clerical collar. When one steps from the pulpit into the political arena, he must be expected to be treated like a politician, not like a preacher.

Chicago Defender

Chicago, Ill., February 24, 1981

Former President Gerald R. Ford isn't heard from much these days but he did make an interesting statement a few days ago. He said he had strong concerns about the Christian fundamentalist Moral Majority getting involved in politics. This was an involvement that helped President Reagan win the White House last fall.

Ford was even a bit alarmed at the thrust of the Moral Majority. He said: "I have never believed in organized religion getting into the political arena."

It seems a sound position. If every religious bloc in the country moved into the major political parties as a bloc, the whole picture of the electoral process would soon be changed — and not for the better.

The theory of keeping the state and the church separate is still a good one. The United States has made much of its progress by holding scrupulously to this approach.

The Register

Santa Ana, Calif., December 2, 1981

The Rev. Jerry Falwell seems to be moving increasingly toward a strictly political orientation and away from the kind of concerns that gave his Moral Majority movement whatever legitimacy and attraction it may once have possessed. His recent statements on a revised Equal Rights Amendment smack of political opportunism.

At a rally in Tucson, Falwell said that once "we have buried the corpse of the Equal Rights Amendment" as it is presently written, he would support a new Equal Rights Amendment if it had a couple of extra clauses, specifically a ban on homosexual marriages and a prohibition on female soldiers in combat. Falwell spoke of the proposal as if it represented a means of reaching out to sincere feminists, but it has the scent of politics about it. It appears more like a somewhat cynical effort to develop a cause around which a movement can be organized and financed.

ERA supporters and others have discovered that proposing constitutional amendments is a marvelous way to get publicity and raise money. Such proposals can also serve as a springboard for discussion of wider areas of social policy. The ERA, whether it is passed by another three states or dies again in June, has aroused widespread discussion of feminist concerns. Falwell seems to want to take some of that energy and appropriate it to his own issues.

He has chosen some odd ones. Homosexual marriages are frankly strange, perhaps even repugnant to most people. But it's difficult to understand what public policy goal would be served by banning them. Moral objections to such arrangements are understandable, but must they be enshrined in a constitutional prohibition? Isn't God competent to enforce His laws in His own way without technical assistance from the city council or the feds?

The question of women in combat is also one that seems inappropriate for inclusion in the Constitution. It is difficult to see why it is more objectionable to send women to kill and be killed than it is to send men, from a strictly moral perspective. There are practical questions of physical characteristics, stamina, strength and cohabitation in foxholes that will probably militate against widespread use of women in combat in the foreseeable future, but is combat immoral only for women but acceptable for men? It's difficult to understand why.

Jerry Falwell and all his allies and opponents certainly have the right to make whatever comments or proposals they wish with regard to public policy. They should expect to have such comments and proposals scrutinized on their merits (if any), however, and not approved automatically because somebody is a preacher (or a public official or a Ph.D.).

Political activism carries with it certain temptations toward opportunism and demagogy. Rev. Falwell, judging by his recent actions, does not seem to be exempt from such temptations.

The Honolulu Advertiser

Honolulu, Ha., May 12, 1981

The Rev. Jerry Falwell, television evangelist and founder of the Moral Majority, will be in Honolulu later this month to preach, conduct rallies and perhaps found a local branch of his conservative political action group.

Hawaii is the only state where the 4-million-member Moral Majority is not organized and some here would like to remedy that.

AT THE SAME time a number of local groups and individuals, centered on the American Civil Liberties Union, are planning counter-demonstrations to express opposition to Falwell's views.

In a nutshell, his "return to morality" crusade is for school prayer and against abortion, the ERA, sex education in schools, homosexuality and pornography.

This should make for a lively exchange of views about what is morality and who is the majority. These issues excite strong emotions but it is hoped that no one does anything to deprive others of the right to express their views and gather support for their side.

Hawaii has been regarded as quite liberal in matters such as the ERA (it was the first state to ratify), abortion (long legal here) and working wives (a bigger percentage out of the home earlier than any other state). Tolerance has generally been the norm here, though Hawaii is not immune to the conservative trend many see sweeping the country.

IN THAT REGARD, we note the remarks of Daniel Yankelovich, a psychologist who heads the social research firm that does surveys for clients such as Time Magazine:

"We hear that America is becoming more conservative, but that's certainly not true culturally," he told Psychology Today magazine. "Despite the elections, despite pressures from the economy, I believe we are moving further and further away from a common, rigid set of personal and social values.

"Surveys and my own interviews show a widening acceptance of cultural pluralism. We are *not* going back to the old values — to the notion that working hard, getting married and having kids are the only acceptable life goals, that premarital sex is immoral, that homosexuality is intolerable, that people don't have the right to make their own, different choices about how they will live, and with whom, and for what.

"In fact, the existence of the so-called Moral Majority in a way shows the growing strength, not the weakness, of what I see as a cultural revolution-in-progress. The Moral Majoritarians are counter-revolutionaries, trying — I think futilely — to roll back what has already happened."

AND YANKELOVICH IS not alone in this view by any means. Another widely reported survey by a life insurance company on "American Values in the 80s: The Impact of Belief" found in this country "a moral current . . . a widespread religiousness that is spontaneous and diffuse, rather than part of the Moral Majority."

But the survey also noted a dramatic shift in views on marriage and the family to favor "an integrated, more egalitarian approach in which both husband and wife cooperate in working, homemaking and child-rearing."

Thus the views of Falwell's supporters may not be as firmly in accord with the majority as they would like to believe. They are entitled to those views, of course, and to live their own lives by the moral norms they believe appropriate.

It is only when members of a minority try to exert undue influence on the political system to impose restrictive views on others that they are likely to encounter a firm resistance.

Conservative Lobbyists Draw Fire for "Hit List"

The National Conservative Political Action Committee came under sharp attack late in May for a series of advertisements urging the defeat of individual senators and congressmen considered "too liberal" on foreign and domestic issues. Democrats for the 80s, a political action group formed in opposition to NCPAC, charged the conservative lobby with falsely accusing Sen. Paul S. Sarbanes (D, Md.) of having voted for a congressional pay raise in 1979. NCPAC was charged with similarly falsifying the voting records of other congressmen in its advertising efforts to reduce their voter support in the 1982 congressional elections. NCPAC had been influential in 1980 in defeating several leading liberal Democratic senators, including Frank Church of Idaho. Democrats for the 80s, which was led by Pamela Harriman, accused the conservative group of "lies and distortions" in its "negative" advertising campaigns. NCPAC director John T. Dolan charged in response that Democrats for the 80s was "vicious and personal" in its attacks on NCPAC, and he asserted that NCPAC "does not believe in lying about or distorting the record of any elected official, liberal or conservative." According to many political observers, the rise of NCPAC and Democrats for the 80s was indicative of a new phenomenon in American politics: political pressure from independent conservative and liberal lobby groups that were not tied to either parties or individual candidates.

Portland Press Herald

Portland, Maine, June 5, 1981

The trouble with many single-issue political action groups is that they are less interested in good government than in promoting their own narrow viewpoints. Accuracy frequently becomes the victim of zeal.

Such is the case with the National Pro-life Political Action Committee, which has chosen Maine Sen. George J. Mitchell to top its "hit list" of pro-abortion candidates it wants to defeat in 1982.

Mitchell cannot by any stretch of the imagination be classified as "pro-abortion." He has publicly declared his personal opposition to abortion on numerous occasions and has voted with the pro-life movement each time an abortion issue has come up in the Senate.

But that's not good enough for NPPAC, which has its own stringent litmus test in such matters. Because Mitchell has not specifically co-sponsored a constitutional amendment to ban abortions, "we consider him to be pro-abortion," the NPPAC director says.

That reasoning stands logic on its head.

The same can be said of the National Conservative Political Action Committee, which earlier this year also included Mitchell on its "hit list." In doing so the group's executive director criticized the senator for votes he never cast and otherwise grossly distorted Mitchell's record on the issues.

That kind of campaign tactic may work elsewhere, but Maine voters traditionally have rejected the politics of distortion and single-issue fanaticism. It just doesn't wash here.

Fort Worth Star-Telegram

Fort Worth, Texas, June 4, 1981

At the height of his power, the late Sen. Joseph McCarthy would tell his audience, be it members of a Senate committee or reporters at a carefully staged press conference, "I have in my possession certain facts which, if proven to be true...."

Having set the stage with that self-contradicting statement, the senator would proceed to tarnish yet another reputation, ruin yet another career with vicious accusations that often had little basis in truth.

That such tactics did not die with the senator from Wisconsin was made evident recently by the revelation that the National Conservative Political Action Committee, an organization that spent almost $7.5 million in 1979-80 trying to bring about the defeat of designated political candidates, has played fast and loose with the truth in some of its dealings.

For example, NCPAC has accused Sen. Henry Jackson, long known as one of the Pentagon's champions on Capitol Hill, of opposing increased defense spending. The charge was based on a vote Jackson cast against a 1979 budget-resolution amendment to a defense spending bill.

It turns out that the resolution in question was a minor one that had little bearing on whether defense spending would be increased or not, and it also was opposed by such well-known hawks as Sen. John Stennis of Mississippi and Sen. Barry Goldwater of Arizona. But since NCPAC isn't in the business of trying to defeat them at the polls, it singled out Sen. Jackson for its hatchet job.

And then there's the matter of the positions taken by Sens. Dennis DeConcini of Arizona and John Melcher of Montana on abortion and the Panama Canal, respectively.

According to NCPAC mailings, DeConcini supports abortion and Melcher voted "to give away the Panama Canal."

The main thing wrong with the accusations is that they are wrong. Figures kept by the National Right to Life Committee, a militantly anti-abortion group, reveal that DeConcini voted against abortion on 28 different occasions since joining the Senate. And Melcher voted against the treaties that ceded the Panama Canal to Panama.

John T. (Terry) Dolan, NCPAC's youthful director, acknowledged, once the truth had been pointed out, that mistakes had been made, but he called them "typesetting errors" and said they would be corrected in a later mail release, as if that would somehow magically wipe out the damage that had been done.

NCPAC's strategy is of the utmost importance in this area, since Sen. Lloyd Bentsen and Rep. Jim Wright both have been mentioned by Dolan as being considered for his "hit list."

Voters should be very careful to watch for "typesetting errors" in information coming from NCPAC.

And NCPAC, having conferred upon itself the awesome power of remaking the Congress in its rather narrow, inflexible image, should strive for accuracy as it goes about the task.

Corrections in subsequent mail releases are poor substitutes for the truth in the first place.

THE LINCOLN STAR

Lincoln, Neb., June 5, 1981

Understandably, some members of Congress have been disturbed by making the election hit list of the National Pro-Life Political Action Committee. The committee has "targeted" these members of Congress for defeat in their next election and will concentrate its funds and efforts in that direction.

"If we can knock off some high visible office-holders, it sends a signal to the mushy middle, as I call them," said Peter B. Gemma Jr., executive director of the group.

Well, there is nothing new in the fact of special interest groups seeking to promote their cause through the election process. But in picking up what seems to be the example being set by the moral majority groups of the hard right, the pro-lifers make no friends here.

The evil in these tactics of targeted candidates is that the action takes place on the basis of a very narrow interest base and, in the case of the pro-life group, a single issue. Additionally, the approach suggests, and in the past has included, just about any means, fair or foul, of achieving the desired end.

The actions of political action committees were out of hand in the last presidential election and show every sign of continuing in that vein in ever enlarged numbers. The "targeting" and "knocking off" of candidates, the development of "hit lists" and the insistence of total and absolute fidelity to a cause

on the part of narrow special interest groups has no democratic ring to us.

It does have a distinctly demagogic ring. And what does it do to the art of compromise? One of the candidates on the pro-life hit list has a four-out-of-five favorable voting record on one issue. Good grief, if you aren't happy winning four out of five, you are one mighty hard person to please.

If all of us become too narrow-minded, too selfish and too vindictive, none of us will end up with anything. The hard-core special interest groups need a little lesson in how to get along with the rest of the world. But don't hold your breath until it happens.

The Cincinnati Post

TIMES ⟲ STAR

Cincinnati, Ohio, May 6, 1981

Republican National Chairman Richard Richards is on the right track in trying to disassociate the party from the frenzied activities of an independent right-wing group that calls itself the National Conservative Political Action Committee.

At the moment, NCPAC is bombarding liberal Democratic Sen. Paul Sarbanes of Maryland through an extensive television and newspaper advertising campaign. It has similar crusades planned against other politicians on its hit list who are coming up for re-election in 1982.

There's a good chance that NCPAC's excesses might help Sarbanes rather than hurt him. Richards said the other day that NCPAC's campaign last year

against Democatic Sen. Frank Church of Idaho backfired and nearly enabled Church to win re-election when the vote shouldn't have been even close.

Richards has hinted that he will seek ways to curb independent political groups that can raise large sums of money and "create all kinds of mischief."

Muzzling such organizations by law may not be possible or even desirable, given the American tradition and constitutional guarantees of free speech. But Richards is right to distance the Republican Party from activities that might prove damaging to the GOP and to the Reagan administration, which needs Democratic support to get its programs through Congress.

Democrat ✦ Chronicle

Rochester, N.Y., May 21, 1981

VARIOUS OBSERVERS in recent years have spoken of the danger posed by special interest groups. But few have addressed the issue as knowledgeably and effectively as does Josph A. Califano Jr., former Secretary of Health, Education and Welfare, in his new book, *Governing America.*

"If interest groups face off against each other on only one issue, they need not worry about their adversaries tomorrow on another. They tend to see only the horns protruding from their opponents' heads and the halos floating above their own."

Too many of these groups, says Califano, are penetrating the executive and legislative branches, where they're exercising an influence greatly disproportionate to their numbers. Congress reacts by setting up bureaus and boards responsive to the special interests, with the result that it becomes increasingly difficult to deliver services efficiently to the taxpayer.

Califano understands how some special interest causes tug at the emotions. "Nothing is more appealing than helping people who are physically crippled, but the focus on the handicapped alone, like all one-dimensional views of the world, is too narrow for the formulation of broad policies in the national interest."

If national policy becomes too fragmented by the push and pull of special interests, the broad general national interest is in serious danger of being lost sight of. Califano is right to warn us all of the consequences.

THE LOUISVILLE TIMES

Louisville, Ky., June 6, 1981

The resignations of a senator and three congressmen from the advisory board of the National Pro-Life Political Action Committee should do much to expose the dishonesty of that organization, which last week identified nine members of Congress as targets for defeat in 1982.

Several of those targeted have records that would do a "pro-lifer" proud. For instance, Sen. George Mitchell of Maine has opposed federal aid for poor women's abortions on four of five roll-calls. His sin in the eyes of the committee is that he opposes an anti-abortion amendment to the U.S. Constitution, despite the fact that others who oppose abortions also reject such amendments.

The anti-abortion group's efforts may be hurt most by the loss from its committee of Rep. Henry Hyde of Illinois, one of the leading proponents of legislative restrictions on abortion. His latest "success" was passage by both houses of a measure to cut off federal Medicaid assistance for abortions unless the life of the mother is at stake. Neither rape nor incest would be a basis for providing Medicaid money for abortions. Of course, women who can pay

for them will be able to obtain abortions without any obstacles during the early months of pregnancy.

This shameful measure deserves no commendation, and Rep. Hyde's insistence that the poor should be doomed to unwanted pregnancies forced upon them by rapists is shocking.

But he and the others who resigned from the committee cannot help but be troubled by the zealotry which seeks, as in Sen. Mitchell's case, to identify only the "purest of the pure in heart." Even Rep. Hyde may fear that one day he will be branded for not doing precisely what the committee demands.

The influence of the group is not inconsequential. It plans to raise and spend $650,000 to defeat the nine incumbents — Democrats and Republicans — it has targeted.

But with influential congressional leaders absent from its ranks, it may have trouble raising all that money. Let's hope so. The mission is a fraud, and fortunately, even those who refuse to recognize the discriminatory nature of their opposition to abortions for the poor see it for what it is.

THE BLADE

Toledo, Ohio, June 7, 1981

THE latest effort by a one-issue fanatic group, the National Pro-Life Political Action Committee, to target nine congressmen for political death has drawn an appropriate response from three lawmakers on the group's advisory board. They have resigned.

Sen. Jake Garn of Utah and Reps. Henry Hyde of Illinois and Robert Young of Missouri said they did not like the practice of issuing "hit lists." A fourth congressman, Rep. Marty Russo of Illinois, also was said to be drafting a letter of resignation. Ironically, all of these members are strongly identified with the anti-abortion or pro-life cause, and one, Mr. Hyde, has been a leader in efforts to restrict the use of federal funds for abortions.

In issuing the hit list Peter Gemma, executive director of the political action group, said: "If we can knock off some highly visible officeholders, it sends a signal to the mushy middle, as I call them." To Mr. Gemma and others of his ilk it matters not what the congressmen targeted have done in other fields or how admirable their overall voting record might be. The touchstone is their stand on abortion.

But an additional factor that draws the attention of single-issue fanatics is the degree of political vulnerability of the incumbent. This is a cowardly way to approach a campaign, and it might even be counterproductive. The hit-listers would achieve more clout if they could claim credit for helping bring about the defeat of a legislator who appears to be virtually unbeatable.

There are good reasons for lawmakers like Mr. Hyde to avoid lending their names to political action groups that target members of their own party for extinction. For one thing, they might need an extra vote on an issue of importance to them some day. They are not likely to get it from a colleague they have marked for defeat. Nevertheless, the congressional members who resigned from the PAC board are to be commended for refusing to go along with these bullying tactics.

The News and Courier

Charleston, S.C., June 17, 1981

The National Conservative Political Action Committee is setting its sights on liberals these days just as the labor unions, the Americans for Democratic Action and other such groups go after Republicans or ultra-conservative Democrats. Nothing wrong there, of course. Sauce for the goose, and all that.

NCPAC, however, has been playing the game in a style neither sophisticated nor conservative. For example, in its campaign last year to unseat Sen. Thomas Eagleton of Missouri, NCPAC informed voters he had backed a big aid package for the Sandinistas in Nicaragua. Fact: Sen. Eagleton never voted for the aid bill, but openly opposed it on three occasions. NCPAC also said Sen. Eagleton voted against production of the neutron bomb. Again, untrue.

More recently, in Oklahoma, NCPAC made some insinuations about House Budget Committee Chairman James Jones' positions on defense and welfare spending that were true in respect to the Reagan budget but untrue in respect to the Carter budget, which is at issue where 1982 cuts and increases apply.

Everyone knows politics can be tough. There is good reason to believe politics is being made tougher than it has to be when NCPAC's director asserts that "a group like ours can lie through its teeth and the candidate it helps stays clean." Republican Party Chairman Richard Richards might have had NCPAC in mind when he said the other day that unaccountable political groups can "create all kinds of mischief."

Deliberate distortions and the rationalization of lying are more than mere mischief. They constitute an assault on the election process, which isn't in the best of health, anyway. Voter intelligence and integrity can be openly mocked only at risk. Sen. Eagleton's re-election should tell NCPAC that decency draws some limits, even in politics.

The Virginian-Pilot

Norfolk, Va., June 5, 1981

Senator Jake Garn, R-Utah, and Representative Henry Hyde, R-Ill., are two of the staunchest opponents of abortion in the Congress.

"Superstars in the anti-abortion movement," Washington Post reporter Bill Petersen calls them.

So why did they resign from the National Pro-Life Political Action Committee?

Well, the committee had issued a "hit" list of four senators and five representatives it planned to spend $400,000 in 1982 trying to defeat. In the mutual protection society that is the United States Congress, that proved hard to swallow.

Pro-life groups aren't the only ones with political "hit" lists. Pro-choice groups have them too. Several years back, some organizations compiled a "hit" list of the "Dirty Dozen," 12 congressmen with bad marks on the environment. Some of "the dirties"

were cleaned right out of Congress.

Whether the "hit" lists are open or subtle, they permeate our politics. Organized labor's "hit" list includes those supporting right-to-work and opposing Davis-Bacon or common situs picketing. Dairy industry "hit" lists include those opposing milk subsidies. The National Rifle Association targets those favoring gun control. Feminist groups aim at ERA opponents. Teacher organizations slate for political extinction congressmen opposing a federal Department of Education.

And on and on runs the political blacklisting of those on the wrong side of one group or the other. In federal elections, the "hit" lists are becoming effective because of artificially low levels on individual financial giving and almost limitless opportunities for groups operating independently of the formal structure of political campaigns.

"Hit-list" politics is old and lawful. If citizens feel that deeply on a particular issue, there's nothing that says they can't "hit-list" their opponents.

But the rest of us should toss these "hit" lists in the sewer. We owe public figures the decency of judging their overall performance—their general political philosophy—not one single, solitary vote.

And we owe them the civility of consideration in the round—on grounds of integrity, intelligence, vision, and compassion—qualities that can transcend party and even philosophy.

After all, how many of us want to be "hit-listed" at home or work because of a single disagreement? How many of us want to be seen by others through a one-dimensional lens?

In a time when the tides of zealotry are rising on all sides, there's more need than ever for value judgments not on single issues but on whole men.

THE MILWAUKEE JOURNAL
Milwaulkee, Wisc., June 10, 1981

We hope it was not just the survival instinct that impelled a US senator and two representatives to resign from the advisory board of the National Pro-Life Political Action Committee. We would prefer to believe that it was their abhorrence of destructive single-issue politics.

Sen. Jake Garn (R-Utah), Rep. Henry Hyde (R-Ill.) and Rep. Robert Young (D-Mo.) resigned from the board in protest after the committee had announced it would spend $650,000 in an effort to defeat nine congressmen whose views on abortion legislation are unsatisfactory to the group. A committee spokesman said the purpose of the campaign was to "knock off some highly visible officeholders" as a warning to those who are in the "mushy middle" on the abortion issue.

Apparently the committee thinks its own particular way of curbing abortion is the only one congressmen should be permitted to espouse. Among the lawmakers on the committee's "hit list" was a senator who had voted four times out of five against using federal money for abortions. The committee's objection to him was that he opposed a constitutional amendment to ban all abortions.

We do not challenge any group's right to campaign against abortion — or for it. However, all interest groups should recognize that they are part of a pluralistic society and that people honestly hold a variety of views on the subject. All congressmen cannot reasonably be expected to line up on the same side of the issue.

In order to make the democratic process work, voters should judge officeholders on the basis of their overall records. And pressure groups should work through coalitions to support or oppose politicians on the strength of a variety of policy questions, not just a single issue. After all, a politician might take the "right" position on abortion while opposing everything else that members of the groups favored. Or he could be "wrong" on abortion and "right" on all the other issues.

In short, single-issue politics is not compatible with sound, rational government. Garn, Hyde and Young had a wonderful opportunity to make that point in emphatic terms, and they almost did, but not quite.

Garn complained of "hit list" politics. Young said he did not want his name "used in this sort of tactic against other members of Congress." A spokesman for Hyde said he didn't want to lend his name to defeat fellow Republicans whose views might differ from his own.

In any event, they rebuked the committee's heavy-handed approach. That's a good start.

The Seattle Times
Seattle, Wash., June 5, 1981

ONE of the more tasteless practices of political-action groups of the so-called new right these days is to borrow from the vocabulary of organized crime in describing their political opposition.

The nation has been treated in recent months, for instance, to the publication of "hit" lists of congressmen "targeted" for defeat by organizations such as the National Conservative Political Action Committee.

Another group that likes to compile "hit" lists, this one on the abortion issue, is the National Pro-Life Political Action Committee, whose executive director wants to "knock off" nine congressmen who are in what he calls the "mushy middle."

That was too much even for Illinois Representative Henry Hyde and Representative Robert Young of Missouri, both known widely for their anti-abortion views. Neither could stomach what they called "negative campaigning"and submitted their resignations.

The gesture was entirely in order. Surely there is enough room in America for political differences without invoking images of criminal violence.

The San Diego Union
San Diego, Calif., June 4, 1981

NCPAC — the National Conservative Political Action Committee — is going after liberal candidates these days just as the labor unions, Americans for Democratic Action (ADA), COPE, and other such groups set their sights on Republicans.

Nothing wrong there. What's fair for the goose and all that. But NCPAC, being newer at this rough game than its liberal adversaries, is not as sophisticated in its play. As *The Washington Star* points out, NCPAC has been playing entirely too much hardball of late

Last year, for example, in its campaign to unseat Sen. Thomas Eagleton of Missouri, NCPAC told the voters that he had voted for a $75 million aid package for Nicaraguan Sandinistas. Actually, he never voted for this aid and openly opposed it on three separate occasions.

NCPAC also accused Sen. Eagleton of voting against production of the neutron bomb. Again, not true.

More recently in Oklahoma, NCPAC represented to the voters that House Budget Committee Chairman James Jones of Tulsa supports reduced defense spending and increased spending on social and welfare programs. These insinuations are true with respect to the Reagan budget but false in relation to the Carter budget, which is at issue where 1982 cuts and increases apply.

Politics being politics, a certain amount of rough house might be written off to exuberance and honest error. But we must suspect the worst in light of the insolent assertion of NCPAC's director, Mr. Terry Dolan, that "a group like ours could lie through its teeth and the candidate it helps stays clean." No wonder the new chairman of the Republican Party, Mr. Richard Richards, was moved to say the other day that unaccountable political groups can "create all kinds of mischief."

In reality, NCPAC's record of deliberate distortion and its director's shocking rationalizing of lying are more than mere "mischief." Such immoral tactics are an assault upon the all-too fragile fabric of representative government. And despite Mr. Dolan's arrogant claim of immunity for his candidate from any sort of lie, the political history of this country cries out otherwise. Such contempt for the voters' intelligence and integrity cannot be concealed in the long run. Indeed, Sen. Eagleton's re-election last year, despite NCPAC's wicked stabs against him, ought to tell Mr. Dolan and everyone else that decency draws some limits, even in politics.

THE KANSAS CITY STAR
Kansas City, Mo., May 18, 1981

Political action committees (PACs) contributed millions of dollars to congressional campaigns last year. Why? To make candidates aware of their existence, to create a presence and to prepare an entrance if and when the organization needs to contact a member of the Senate or the House of Representatives. This was not, by any stretch of the imagination, philanthropy at work.

In fact, Common Cause has found that business-oriented PACs, corporate groups and those related to trade associations, dominated spending on races involving leaders and committee chairmen. "Almost two-thirds ($4.1 million) of the $6.5 million in PAC contributions received by these 54 key members of Congress during their last campaigns came from business PACs," the public interest lobby group points out. Common Cause expects, when all expenditures are computed, that business PACs will spend twice as much their labor counterparts—a marked reversal from 1976, when labor outspent business.

Sen. Robert Dole of Kansas is a good example. The Republican, who became chairman of the Senate Finance Committee after the GOP captured control of the Senate in the 1980 election, received $1,217,468 in contributions, according to the Common Cause study. Business PACs gave him $254,995 of the $328,055, or 77 percent, of all his PAC contributions. A similar pattern develops for Republicans and Democrats who chair the House Ways and Means, Senate and House Appropriations and Senate and House Budget committees.

Obviously, the PACs show no partisanship or philosophical tendencies when contributing to political campaigns. On the House side, Jim Jones of Oklahoma, a Democrat and chairman of the Budget Committee, received $114,951 in business contributions, a whopping 88 percent of all he was given by PACs.

Significantly, these leaders, both at the committee and chamber levels, are deeply involved in decisions that not only affect business, labor, trade organizations and other groups that form PACs, they affect us all. Question: How does the rank-and-file citizen make his and her presence felt in this decision-making process? We have the uneasy feeling that the large PACs will carry more weight in pushing their legislative objectives than the little man.

Don't be surprised if special interests score heavily in Washington.

THE SACRAMENTO BEE
Sacramento, Calif., May 9, 1981

There are encouraging signs for political reform in recent observations by Richard Richards, the new chairman of the Republican National Committee. Richards wants his party to begin changing the mechanics of presidential campaigns with an eye to shortening them and finding a way to restrain "independent expenditures" by groups other than candidates or parties.

Richards said the system which permitted organizations such as the National Conservative Political Action Committee (NCPAC) to spend millions of dollars to influence elections independently of any political party or any candidate is "fraught with mischief. Sure, we benefited more than the Democrats did. But if it's not a good system, then you can't justify it by who benefits."

As the national chairman sees it, campaigns by groups such as NCPAC against Democratic candidates on "single issues" such as abortion or gun control, could create a backlash of sympathy for some Democrats and could undermine the Republican strategy for winning conservative Democratic support for Reagan's economic program.

The real danger of having such groups as NCPAC collect and spend millions of dollars in political campaigns is that they are not responsible to any party and, in most cases, do not make it clear enough that they are not formally associated with the candidates. The "mischief" which Richards refers to comes when their spending to promote their "one-issue" politics skews the election and has the effect of denying candidates and parties the opportunity of running their own campaigns according to their own strategy.

Richards says when the Republican National Committee meets this summer he will appoint a panel to look into the activities of such independent expenditure groups and to suggest ways to restrain their activities.

On the question of the duration of the presidential campaign, Richards contends that the current system, under which presidential campaigns begin 26 months before election, sets a "killing pace for candidates and for everyone else." Richards says the GOP special committee should consider alternatives to the prolonged primary system such as regional primaries and the greater use of state party conventions to pick delegates for national presidential nominating conventions. And while there is no way to know what the committee will recommend, it will serve a useful purpose in considering the campaign problems and suggesting possible solutions.

We're heartened by Richards' remarks, first, because it's unusual for the leader of a winning party to acknowledge the defects of the system which his party mastered to achieve victory, and, second, because Richards' criticisms are both sensible and timely. Solutions to the problems Richards raises can be found if responsible and knowledgeable party members are committed to work on them.

The Dallas Morning News
Dallas, Texas, May 25, 1981

"You can't legislate morality," State Sen. Jack Ogg of Houston excused as he cast the only dissenting vote against the campaign reform bill in Senate committee.

Sorry, Jack, but that well-worn bromide just doesn't apply in this instance. While you can't force people to be honest, you certainly can make it more clear what's expected of them — such as defining how and when elected officials can accept and use political contributions.

The ethics package, a compromise between House Speaker Billy Clayton and Mesquite Rep. Ted Lyon, would tighten campaign finance regulations and make political action committees (PACs) disclose more about their memberships.

Among other things, the bill would limit cash donations to $100 and require reporting of all expenditures of campaign funds. It also would require PACs to report the occupation of anyone who contributed more than $50, and name the groups that control the committee.

Another needed provision would prohibit legislators and statewide elected officials from accepting contributions during or 30 days before and after a legislative session. That should help lessen the pay-as-you-vote pressure.

The reform package deserves to be passed and signed by the governor before the session rushes to an end. True, it can't guarantee morality, but it could allow voters to see who's supporting which official and where the money goes.

THE ATLANTA CONSTITUTION
Atlanta, Ga., May 12, 1981

Of all the dirty tricks in the world of politics, none is more reprehensible nor effective as The Big Lie. Deliberately misrepresenting a political rival's views is a quick way to end an opponent's political career.

So it is not surprising that Senate Minority Leader Robert C. Byrd, D-W.Va., is howling with indignation at the tactics of the National Conservative Political Action Committee which has targeted Byrd and other Democratic congressmen and senators for defeat.

Byrd says the committee is engaged in spreading "unmitigating lies" about him and other Democrats, and he has called on the media to reject such false and misleading political advertising. He specifically accused the committee of distoring his votes in support of the Panama Canal treaties and last year's budget resolution.

In the case of the Panama Canal, he said, the advertisement accused him of voting to give away the canal to a Communist country. He asserted that Panama was not a Communist country and that the canal was not given away.

The National Conservative Political Action Committee has taken credit for bringing election defeats of at least four liberal Democratic senators last November, and it already is working on defeating other liberal and middle-of-the-road Democrats next year.

If they can attain their goal by honestly reporting on the records of their opponents, then more power to the members of this political action group. But if they must resort to lies to win, they are engaging in a political practice that ought not be tolerated by the electorate for an instant. The media indeed should be careful not to become a party to any scheme to end a political figure's career by smearing him with lies and distortions.

SAN JOSE NEWS
San Jose, Calif., May 4, 1981

IN case you missed the last few elections, there has been something of a *coup d'etat* in American politics.

While voters still choose among Republicans, Democrats and assorted other candidates, the power and purse strings are increasingly controlled by a proliferation of independent — often right-wing — groups.

In the November election, for example, the National Conservative Political Action Committee poured $1.2 million into campaigns against six liberal Democratic senators. Four were defeated. Already, NCPAC has begun another million-dollar drive against four more Democratic congressmen for the 1982 election. And this is just one group.

We find this type of mean-spirited, narrow-minded politics distressing and, somewhat ironically, so does GOP National Chairman Richard Richards.

Although the Republicans have benefited greatly from such political zealotry, Richards notes correctly that this negative campaigning "hurts us more than it helps us." He points out that the growing number of political action committees "are not responsible to anyone," including the GOP or its leadership.

By putting candidates to an arbitrary litmus test on such questions as gun control, abortion and the death penalty, many ideological PACs are splintering the electorate over emotional, single issues. And by lavishing money and support on a candidate, they are subverting that politician's party loyalty. This, in turn, undercuts the political parties' ability to make policy, form a consensus and pass laws.

While parties are far from perfect instruments, they do serve to bring some order and responsibility to the political arena. Richards points to the case of Richard Nixon's 1972 campaign committee to show how circumventing the party's role can have disastrous consequences. The excesses of the president's money-raising organization, of course, led to Watergate.

Similarly, Jimmy Carter, by divorcing himself from the Democratic establishment, sowed the seeds of his own destruction. His inability to deal effectively with his fellow party members virtually assured the succession of defeats he suffered in Congress.

Of course, these examples can be dismissed as merely the tragic errors of two maverick personalities. But the implication of a growing collection of computerized and independently financed political interest groups threatens to cause broader problems for America's electoral system.

The nature of these groups' politics is negative: The strategy is to win by discrediting the opponent. Pandering to the narrow interests of voters overwhelmed by the complexity of modern life, these groups seek to advance political philosophies that are usually self-centered and dogmatic.

Parties, on the other hand, historically have tried to reach out to win wider acceptance with alternative programs. In some respects, the rise of special interest groups is a reflection of the major parties' failure to do this.

Further cause for alarm is the copycat response from a 33-year-old liberal political action committee, National Committee for an Effective Congress. For the first time, this organization has drawn up its own hit list — 66 members of the House and Senate that it is opposing with cash and services in 1982 because of their right-wing views.

Since money is still the mother's milk of politics, it appears that the financial war may continue to escalate in light of this challenge. To say the least, it is disturbing that these political groups, as Richards complains, "seem to be in the business of making money not to change the government."

The Chattanooga Times
Chattanooga, Tenn., May 20, 1981

In its effort to discredit congressmen who, in its view, have displayed hopelessly liberal political attitudes, the National Conservative Political Action Committee is relying on negative advertising campaigns that, on occasion, bend the truth. But that is no reason for the targeted congressmen to urge, in effect, that television and radio outlets censor or reject the material.

A case in point is Sen. Robert C. Byrd, D-W. Va., the former Majority Leader and an NCPAC target. Senator Byrd complained recently that NCPAC had distorted his vote for the Panama Canal treaties by releasing advertisements stating that he voted to "give away" the canal to a "Communist" country. Of course, both statements are false: Panama is not a Communist country and by no stretch of the imagination can the canal treaties be considered a "giveaway."

But NCPAC's assertions differ little from similar statements made by others, including many conservative politicians, during the debate over the treaties. The criticism by the committee, like the campaign-trail rhetoric during the 1976 and 1978 elections, is actually nothing more than hyperbole. If such talk were banned from the political scene, what would politicians talk about?

Besides, broadcasters subject to oversight by the Federal Communications Commission have enough trouble as it is trying to satisfy the provisions of the "equal time" rule. Obviously they try to prevent the airing of demonstrable falsehoods or personal attacks, but to require them to reject advertisements that merely exaggerate a charge would be an intolerable burden. Who wants the job of political censor?

A better response for the attacked politicians is to go on the offensive themselves, which is what a recently formed committee of well-known Democrats plans to do. Replying to NCPAC's hyperbolic negativism with facts, reasonably presented, will be much more effective than trying to stifle the opposition.

DAYTON DAILY NEWS
Dayton, Ohio, July 24, 1981

The Kansas City Times
Kansas City, Mo., June 12, 1981

An unpredictable, destabilizing and therefore dangerous force is working in American politics today. Where are the brave, decent elected men and women of Congress who love and live by politics who will stand up for the work they seek at the polls? This force was a shadowy fellow-traveler in last year's close senatorial race between Tom Eagleton and Gene McNary. The Senate race in Missouri was the only one of six in which its ends were not achieved.

It has surfaced in typical form in Maryland, well within radio and television broadcast range of the lawmakers on Capitol Hill and well ahead of the 1982 election. It has begun to poison the re-election of Sen. Paul Sarbanes, a Democrat from Baltimore who wears the latter-day hairshirt of liberal. Grown men and women who like to think of themselves as politicians of honor, intelligence, courage and vision are struck mute by the presence of this force. Unable to think of anything but their own re-election, they mumble and grumble among themselves, but say nothing publicly. They are afraid.

The force belongs to John T. (Terry) Dolan, director of the National Conservative Political Action Committee. Nick-Pack, as NCPAC is called in the trade of politics, is something of a new phenomenon in the business of getting people elected to public office and keeping them there, whether they deserve it or not. It is called an unaffiliated PAC, a political action committee without roots in a trade, labor or professional association that raises and spends money in campaigns as it wants.

Dolan and NCPAC aren't interested in keeping politicians in office. Dolan, a leader of the New Right, wants them voted out. He really doesn't care how he does that, or who is elected in place of the targeted politician. In Maryland, Sarbanes' defenders have rushed to the rescue with their own unaffiliated PAC, a twin of NCPAC in intent and style.

Tom Eagleton was smart and lucky. Next time NCPAC's target may be Jack Danforth, who comes up for his first re-election campaign. In 1984, it may be Nancy Kassebaum of Kansas.

The men and women charged with carrying out the will of the voters have a compelling duty to use their positions in politics to argue against the tactics of unaffiliated PACs as they are used today.

For a example of how our public life is being kinked by the New Right, look at the campaign announced by the National Conservative Political Action Committee against several members of Congress who favor an alternative to President Reagan's tax-cut plan.

"Nicpac," as it is generally called, says it will spend $500,000 to discredit these legislators via radio and TV commercials in their home districts. Their supposedly "liberal" crime is that, as Democrats, they prefer the Democratic tax cut plan developed in the U.S. House.

The partisan wrangling in Congress over the two approaches is heated. That's politics, and of a quite ordinary sort. But most of the differences between the plans would strike nonpartisans as ones reasonable persons could disagree about reasonably. Both approaches are basically conservative; neither is intensely ideological.

The Democratic plan would return more tax money than Mr. Reagan's to persons who earn under $50,000 a year and would give a good bit less to persons who earn more than $50,000.

Both plans provide substantial tax breaks for business, Mr. Reagan's by the simple device of faster depreciation on capital investments, the Democrats' with more tightly focused provisions.

Both plans raise the exemptions from inheritance taxation, the Democrats' a bit more than the GOP's.

Mr. Reagan's proposal would commit the nation to three years of tax cuts, the Democrats' to two years with a third-year cut conditional on certain improvements in the economy.

In its radio and TV spots, however, Nicpac will portray the Democrats who prefer their won party's plan as virtual traitors to the country, left-wing foes of American virtues.

Such distortions by the New Right put responsible members of Congress in the impossible position of trying to parry a meataxe attack with a lot of legislative fine points — and to do so before an audience of voters who do not have the time, means or inclination to study the details of complicated legislation.

The New Right's techniques in this and other campaigns give an edge to politicians who speak in red-white-and-blue slogans and put at a disadvantage whose who work with their sleeves rolled up, dealing with the real work of making law and policy.

The New Right misuses the once-healthy skepticism of Americans about politicians, converting it into a paranoid distrust that conditions voters to accept the worst face which any reactionary group is willing to put on the record of an official it opposes.

For now, the Republican Party is benefiting from this. But it might be wise for Republicans to begin wondering what their own fate will be after the New Right blows away the Democrats on its many hit lists and, as it must in order to keep the money rolling in from true believers, begins looking around for other targets.

THE COMMERCIAL APPEAL
Memphis, Tenn., August 26, 1981

THE FREE-SPENDING, free-wheeling folks at NCPAC — the National Conservative Political Action Committee — never were bothered about fairness before. In 1980 alone, the Arlington, Va.-based group spent $5 million to defeat candidates around the country with half-truths, innuendos and character assassination.

Now that television stations in five states have refused to run NCPAC advertisements against key congressional leaders, which the stations find to be in "poor taste" or deliberately misleading, the committee is crying foul.

NCPAC SPOKESMAN Stephen DeAngelo said the committee is being shut out of some broadcast markets because stations "do not understand the Fairness Doctrine," which requires them to provide time to respond to inaccuracies or personal attacks on political candidates.

"These were not personal attacks, they were political attacks," DeAngelo contends. With NCPAC, how do you tell?

Consider a commercial targeting Sen. Edward M. Kennedy (D-Mass.), which was turned down in his home state and neighboring Connecticut. Even though Kennedy isn't up for re-election until next year and even though nobody knows who — if anyone — will run against him, NCPAC hired an actor to impersonate him, complete with curly hair and Boston accent.

The 2½-minute ad features the actor making statements such as, "We have to pay Panama to take our Panama Canal," and "We must have more government spending, more bureaucracy, more taxes." One by one his audience walks out. And should the TV audience miss NCPAC's message, an announcer spells it out: "In Washington, they are not listening any more. He's been too liberal for too long."

Whatever one thinks of Kennedy, it is hard to think of NCPAC's advertising tactics as anything short of scurrilous. For that reason and others, its assaults on Sen. Paul Sarbanes (D-Md.) and Reps. Jim Wright (D-Texas) and Jim Jones (D-Okla.) have been refused by TV stations in Baltimore, Dallas-Fort Worth and Tulsa.

And while the group hasn't got around to Tennessee yet, it's likely to soon. Sen. Jim Sasser is on NCPAC's hit list, too, and it's earmarked $500,000 for his defeat.

WHEN NCPAC arrives, will it be concerned about what's fair not only to Sasser but to the people of this state? Or will it come in from Virginia to tell Tennessee what's best and who best represents it in Congress?

Whether Sasser is re-elected or retired isn't NCPAC's choice to make. Nor should the issues of that campaign be determined by NCPAC and its unnamed contributors — the only people to whom the group must answer.

Those decisions belong only to the voters of this state. Will NCPAC get their message?

ST. LOUIS POST-DISPATCH

St. Louis, Mo., June 7, 1981

From its earliest days, the American democracy has drawn much of its strength from the spirit of tolerance held by its citizens. As it had been with no other nation, the ideal of tolerance was firmly planted in the country's founding documents. The Declaration of Independence began with the observation of a "self-evident" truth, that *all* men were created equal and were equally entitled to pursue happiness. The Bill of Rights made freedom of religion, of speech and of the press the law of the land.

Throughout American history, tolerance has been far more than an abstract concept. America was made up of people who observed too many different religions, who came from too many national backgrounds and ethnic stocks and who were the products of too many social and economic classes to have survived without the give-and-take and sense of live-and-let-live that tolerance imposed upon its customs and political institutions. Practicing tolerance did not mean that Americans abandoned their beliefs in right and wrong or failed to act in accordance with them; it meant simply that they acknowledged the value of the espousal of different views.

To be sure, the spirit of intolerance has never been far below the surface of national life. Religious and racial persecutions are a part of America's history. Movements — some serving noble causes, others unworthy ones — have been based on intolerance. They have been directed against Catholics, Quakers, Jews, blacks, slaveholders, immigrants, Masons, drinkers and many other groups. Even so, propelled by the momentum of court decisions and legislation, the nation has moved steadily toward a greater level of tolerance, and that has helped enlarge individual liberties.

In recent years, a new and ugly strain of intolerance has become evident. Its appearance is most obvious in the nation's political life. Passionately tied to their causes, the new promoters of intolerance judge all politicians by their position toward a single issue, be it communism, abortion, gun registration or federal efforts on behalf of racial integration. No deviation is to be forgiven. The National Conservative Political Action Committee declares, for example, that Sen. Dennis DeConcini of Arizona supports abortion. Yet other anti-abortion groups note that the senator has voted "correctly" on 28 out of 29 abortion issues.

Through computer-generated mailing lists, such organizations have been able to amass huge treasuries to be used *against* offending candidates. "Hit lists," a phrase formerly associated with gangland murder, have become a political fact of life. Rep. Robert Young of St. Louis County recently resigned from the National Pro-life Action Committee when he found his name on the letterhead of a hit list calling for the defeat of nine fellow members of Congress. As yet, those senators and representatives have no opponents. The clear implication is that any politician, no matter how unqualified, is acceptable — as long as he is "right" on a single issue.

That remarkable philosophy was actually put into words last year by a NCPAC official, who denounced Sen. Thomas Eagleton on a few specific issues but conceded that the senator "did moderately well on his overall job rating." Traditionally, the "overall job rating" has been the criterion by which Americans judge their politicians.

Sen. John Danforth recently spoke out with courage against the new intolerance and its methods — the hit lists, negative advertising and deliberate spreading of misinformation. He described it quite accurately as "a meanness that doesn't accurately reflect the American spirit." Left unchallenged, that meanness ultimately will pervade the spirit; and America will become less tolerant and less free.

The Providence Journal

Providence, R.I., May 13, 1981

The Democratic and Republican national chairmen may not wish to admit it, but they seem close to agreement on one troubling issue: the growing power of independent political action committees, known in the political world as "PACs."

These are groups set up by corporations, unions and other interests to gather political donations and funnel them to selected candidates for Congress or the presidency, or to favorite causes. The PACs began proliferating after 1974, when revisions in the campaign finance law put a $1,000 limit on individual campaign contributions. In each election, primary and general, every PAC now is permitted to contribute up to $5,000 apiece to as many candidates as it wishes. And for PACs that are not tied to a particular candidate, there are no federal limits on spending at all.

The pace of PAC spending has been soaring: $12.5 million on the 1974 elections; $22.6 million on the 1976 elections; $35.1 million on the 1978 elections and (through last Oct. 15) $50.7 million for the 1980 elections. For both major parties, and for interest groups of every persuasion, this growth marks political action committees as a source of enormous leverage in elections to come. They have quickly mastered the fund-raiser's skills, and they know how to target their donations to the best advantage.

But the PACs' popularity has nettled both political parties. One Democratic beef is simple enough: corporation PACs, which largely support Republicans, have outdistanced the PACs run by labor unions that usually back Democratic candidates. Last year, for example, corporations were running 1,226 PACs while unions had only 318.

Other complaints, though, are heard from both parties. One is that the PACs' very independence undercuts the traditional roles of party and candidate as campaign organizer and distributor of funds. Richard Richards, the new Republican national chairman, said recently that the PAC system is "fraught with mischief." While he acknowledged that Republicans benefited far more than did Democrats in 1980, he added: "But if it's not a good system, then you can't justify it by who benefits." Candidates and parties, he added, should "be responsible for running their own campaigns." It's a good point. Political parties are in precarious health, as it is, and developments that weaken them further demand close scrutiny.

Mr. Richards' opposite number, Democratic National Chairman Charles T. Manatt, has raised a more pointed criticism, citing those PACs that deliberately target for defeat those candidates with whose stands they disagree. Among them: the National Conservative Political Action Committee, which spent more than $3 million last year and is believed to have contributed to the defeat of several liberal Democratic senators. The Democratic chairman says such groups have an "evil influence." The Republican chairman has come close to agreeing, saying they "create all kinds of mischief" and are "not responsible to anyone." Right again. Slanted, negative propagandizing against candidates of either party, often framed around a single narrow issue, is destructive both of good candidates and of the fairness of the political process. It ought not be encouraged by the fine print of a federal law.

Coming on an issue of such importance to the election process, this sign of bipartisan accord is important. The two parties may have separate reasons for being uneasy about the spread of PACs, and they might disagree on changes in the campaign laws they would recommend. But both parties have a stake in examining the PAC phenomenon closely, and they ought to cooperate in a joint study of how the PAC process really works. Neither the parties nor the voters can be sanguine about an independent money-raising system that is exercising a steadily growing influence on national elections.

Abortion Opponents Quit Lobby Group Over "Hit List"

The National Pro-Life Political Action Committee lost three leading congressional opponents of abortion June 3 when the committee issued a "hit list" of nine senators and representatives it wanted to defeat in the 1982 congressional race. All four congressmen asserted that they had not been asked to lend their names to the committee's effort, although their names appeared on NPLPAC letterheads. They were: Sen. Jake Garn (R, Utah) and Reps. Henry J. Hyde (R, Ill.), Marty Russo (D, Ill.) and Robert A. Young (D, Mo.). All four said they disapproved of the "hit list" tactic. NPLPAC Director Peter Gemma, Jr. defended the list, saying: "We're out to influence those congressmen, senators and candidates from both parties who are ambivalent or undecided on this matter of life versus death. If we can knock off some highly visible officeholders, it sends a signal to the 'mushy middle,' as I call them." The nine congressmen had been selected because they refused to support a constitutional amendment to ban all abortions.

The Washington Star

Washington, D.C., June 5, 1981

We venture to say that no one regards abortion as a positive good. Some think it a lesser evil when conception results from rape or incest, while others believe that it should be left, as recent Supreme Court decisions tend to leave it, to the individual conscience.

But if there is, on the permissive side, some ambivalence of feeling, there is an absolutist tenor to the opposition – so much so that in a recent Senate debate on the eligibility of rape and incest victims for publicly-funded abortion, Sen. Bob Packwood spoke of a "Cotton Mather mentality."

Those who find the Cotton Mather mentality inappropriate, as we confess we do, found it satisfying this week that the National Pro-Life Political Action Committee (NPLPAC) got a mild comeuppance. It had announced, with considerable fanfare, a "hit list" of senators and representatives who do not vote its views on abortion. The rather absolutist character of its criteria is suggested by the targeting of at least one representative who had voted "right" on four of five major abortion questions, and of Sen. Pat Moynihan, who favors the public subsidy of parochial education.

The mild comeuppance was the defection of several members of Congress who had been listed as NPLPAC sponsors, including Rep. Henry Hyde, who is not exactly soft on abortion. The defectors were probably inspired in part by a certain clubbiness. And we would not maintain that the camaraderie binding incumbents is more important than the abortion issue.

We prefer to believe, rather, that the defecting sponsors were inspired by deeper considerations, including the belief that single-issue zeal is an unfortunate preoccupation and that people of good will and sound mind may differ even about fundamental moral and ethical issues. Indeed, such differences spring less from infirmity of conviction about what is moral and ethical than from the conviction that when no one's religion may be established by law reasonable people

have a certain duty to forbear.

Beyond that consideration lies another: the need for variety and discussion when laws are framed. On a local radio talk show, the Rev. Charles Fiore, chairman of NPLPAC, asserted that the aims and activities of his group do not much differ from those of older political action committees, organized labor's for instance.

But that assertion is misleading. The politics of NPLPAC is not usual. Organized labor – and corresponding business lobbies – tend to take positions on a spectrum of public issues, not all (or even a majority) of which are of passionate concern to their members. They may favor one congressman or senator more than others, but seldom extend their favor on the basis of a one-issue test. The difference between their approach and NPLPAC's is the difference between politics and monomania.

Of course, many militant anti-abortionists regard *all* abortion, whatever the circumstance, as "murder." Morally and medically simplistic as such views may be, those who hold them cannot admit of degree or compromise;and their earnestness is not to be disparaged. But neither should they disparage the moral convictions of those who differ.

After this week's episode, Father Fiore was quoted as saying that he really doesn't care what members of Congress think about abortion in their "heart of hearts . . . We don't care if they see the light as long as they feel the heat."

Perhaps he was misunderstood or misquoted, for this is the deterrent theory of politics with a vengeance. Does Father Fiore mean to say that it is the aim of NPLPAC to prevail by intimidation entirely? Has motive nothing to do with the quality of a vote? If so, it is a startling example of single-issue single-mindedness in politics.

You might call it the Cotton Mather mentality in its pure state. That mentality would be appropriate in a theocracy. But this is not a theocracy.

The Salt Lake Tribune

Salt Lake City, Utah, June 6, 1981

An old, frequently misquoted phrase, "nothing became him so much as his leaving," springs instantly to mind in watching Utah Sen. Jake Garn resign from an advisory post with the ad hoc National Pro-Life Political Action Committee. The act was one of protest and timely for its implications.

As the senator explained, he has not dropped his opposition to abortion. Rather, he is dropping his official association with an anti-abortion group using seriously flawed tactics. In both a specific and general way, Sen. Garn makes an important distinction.

The ends do not always justify the means. Organizations such as the Pro-Life Political Action Committee need to understand that if the American political system is to survive and function as a guarantee of representative government in a large, pluralistic society.

Sen. Garn and the two U.S. House members who joined him in quitting the committee's advisory board pronounced themselves displeased with a "hit list" of House and Senate members the committee says it intends to help defeat because of "wrong" policies on abortion. They are properly distressed because they were not given an opportunity to consult on this form of political victimizing. Beyond that, they see the method as badly mistaken.

To a significant degree, the spite, vindictiveness and extortionate practices some single issue movements insinuate into United States politics constitute a definite threat to the more temperate, and often effective, give-and-take tolerance of different, various interests. Tyranny lurks in the assertion that every public official, regardless of position or party, who won't completely toe an inflexible, ideologic line, must be broken and defeated.

It must have been particularly awkward for Sen. Garn to find a group he is supposed to be advising had targeted for political ouster senators of his own party and those who he has worked with to limit federal financing for abortion. In fact, he and Reps. Henry Hyde, R-Ill., and Robert D. Young, D-Mo., when resigning from the advisory board, said members of Congress don't get cooperation from other members of Congress by endorsing "hit lists." Precisely.

Perhaps Sen. Garn will land on the Pro-Life Committee's "hit list" for his stand. It may compel him to repeat his personal and public position against abortion more times than would seem necessary. If so, it will be difficulty caused by courage, trouble more than compensated by a clear conscience.

CHICAGO Sun-Times
Chicago, Ill., June 7, 1981

You might liken it to a willful, malicious child turning against its parents: Last week one anti-abortion group so embarrassed three U.S. representatives and a senator who helped nurture it that the lawmakers have resigned from its advisory board.

The four—including the Chicago area's Henry J. Hyde (R) and Marty Russo (D)—objected to the National Pro-Life Political Action Committee's plan to target nine other members of Congress for defeat in the 1982 elections via a $650,000 spending spree.

To Hyde's and Russo's chagrin, the targets included a fellow Illinoisan, Democrat Paul B. Findley. That's not the way it's done among congressmen, the four said—and quit.

Was the zealot committee abashed at the decision? Hardly. Its executive director, Peter Gemma, said, "All we wanted was the use of the names of these congressmen to give credibility to a new organization. . . . We don't need them anymore. . . . I can get another 10 congressmen tomorrow. . . ."

Opportunism, arrogance, cynicism: Call it what you will, but it's typical of the dangers in single-issue political movements.

And we think negative, go-for-the-jugular campaigns, like those being mounted by the anti-abortion lobby and other well-financed pressure groups, will eventually turn off voters as well as former sponsors.

Hyde & Co. obviously want to put some distance between themselves and the creature they helped spawn. Yet they can't escape blame for encouraging such a narrow-minded, irresponsible group in the first place.

The State
Columbia, S.C., June 11, 1981

ONCE AGAIN single-issue zealots are showing how tough they can be in crusading for a cause. This time it is the National Pro-Life Political Action Committee.

The national anti-abortion group has named nine members of Congress to a hit list for the 1982 elections. They intend to beat the congressmen and senators because they don't vote "right" on the abortion issue.

"If we can knock off some highly visible officeholders," a spokesman said, "it sends a signal to the mushy middle . . . ."

Such tactics are well within the limits of the democratic system, of course. But the abortion issue itself calls for a conscientious decision which will rise from individual moral, religious, ethical or even political beliefs. Should that be punishable?

Should we elect members of Congress on this one issue only?

THE BISMARCK TRIBUNE
Bismarck, N.D., June 5, 1981

The National Pro-Life Political Action Committee the other day came out with its "hit list" on nine congressmen who are, in the words of the committee's executive director, "ambivalent or undecided on this matter of life versus death."

He added, "If we can knock off some highly visible officeholders, it sends a signal to the mushy middle, as I call them."

In reaction to the "hit list," three congressmen resigned from an advisory board of the political action committee. One of the congressmen, Rep. Robert A. Young, D-Mo., said, "I remain strongly committed to the pro-life movement ... but I also strongly believe that my name should not and will not be used in this sort of campaign tactics against other members of Congress."

Rep. Young is to be commended for his stand and for resigning from the board. And the National Pro-Life Political Action Committee and other organizations that compile "hit lists" based on a politician's stand on one issue deserve to be roundly criticized.

Such "hit lists" are the work of zealots who can not, or worse, will not, tolerate opposition to their positions. And those zealots are so egocentric that they believe their cause is the only cause that matters. Consequently, they believe, a politican's stand on "their issue" should determine whether that politican remains in office.

Never mind that a politician who disagrees with their stand may have an honest difference of opinion, something that should be tolerated and even welcomed in our society because it leads to intelligent debate. Never mind that a politician has positions on other issues that warrant his re-election.

No, the "hit list" mentality calls for replacing that politican with somebody who agrees with the authors of the "hit list" on their particular issue.

And that mentality gives rise to the single-issue candidate who may be an absolute dud when it comes to dealing in the realities of a complicated world with its numerous issues and numerous shades of gray ... a world that demands sophistication and wisdom.

Let us hope that more people affiliated with "hit list" groups recognize the wrongness of the tactic and disassociate themselves from such groups.

The tactic does not deserve a place in our political process or in our political psyche.

St. Petersburg Times
St. Petersburg, Fla., May 26, 1981

How does an officeholder who honestly disagrees with one of the New Right, single-issue hit groups survive in today's political climate? Five U.S. senators, including Florida's Lawton Chiles, have shown voters one particularly disturbing way. Unless voters organize to oppose the new pressure groups, there'll be more displays of political cowardice rather than fewer.

AMERICANS always have been divided on the issue of abortion. Before the U. S. Supreme Court in 1973 declared state laws prohibiting abortions as unconstitutional, a strong movement motivated by coat-hanger abuses worked against abortion laws. Since the court's decision, the anti-abortion movement has gained intensity steadily.

Even so, most Americans favor legalized abortion. In the latest Gallup Poll published in April, more than three-fourths of both Catholics and Protestants opposed a ban on all abortions. But those who favor a ban see the question as a moral issue on which they cannot compromise.

How does a public official deal with such an issue? There are several ways. Members of Congress for years have tried to avoid having to take a stand on the issue by keeping it from coming to a vote. After the right-to-life movement's political victories in 1978, some candidates avoided any confrontation by adopting its language and positions. One of those was Ronald Reagan.

Following the elections of 1980, the New Right collection of single-issue activists, including the anti-abortion movement, boasted of helping to defeat several opponents it had placed on its hit lists.

Last Jan. 8, Paul Brown, director of the Life Amendment Political Action Committee which plans to raise and spend $1-million in the 1982 elections, targeted 12 additional senators, including Chiles. He threatened: "The 12 senators named represent the 'death to the reborn child' mentality that claims millions of lives each and every year. We're sending another warning to the U.S. Senate. Either they vote our way and give us a pro-life amendment or we will vote them out of office." Brown falsely labeled Florida's senior senator as "totally anti-life."

Four of the targeted senators switched on a key vote last week. Chiles, Minority Leader Robert Byrd, Lloyd Bentsen of Texas and Howard Cannon of Nevada voted to deny federal funds for abortions to poor victims of rape and incest.

IF NATIONAL pressure groups can manipulate senators with such tactics, voters in the state lose their representation. One possible response would be for Floridians who oppose a ban on all abortions to promise to raise money to match the outside contributions, thereby hoping to neutralize them. The problem would be that moderates on the issue could not match the fervor or the computerized fund raising of the New Right.

Perhaps the voters' best protection against national zealots capturing their representatives is the understanding that no politician should rise or fall on one issue. Public affairs is a complicated business that requires intelligence, balance, judgment and integrity on many issues. Those who try to persuade voters otherwise should not be trusted.

Senate Opens Hearings on Legislation to Ban Abortion

The Senate opened hearings April 23 on a proposed statute that would define human life as beginning at conception, thus making abortion equivalent to murder under U.S. criminal law. The legislation, sponsored by Rep. Henry J. Hyde (R, Ill.) and Sen. Jesse Helms (R, N.C.) was the focus of intense controversy as the Senate Judiciary subcommittee on the Separation of Powers heard testimony on its first day from supporters of the Helms-Hyde law. The witnesses were five doctors, all of whom opposed abortion and believed that life began at conception. The two-hour session was interrupted twice by supporters of abortion, who were ejected from the chamber. In response to the charges that the hearings were biased, subcommittee chairman Sen. John R. East (R, N.C.) promised that "all points of view" would be considered. The hearings were adjourned until late May.

Lawyers, constitutional experts and one subcommittee member questioned whether the Congress would have the power to enact such a law. Sen. Orrin G. Hatch (R, Utah), himself an abortion foe, pointed out that the Supreme Court had legalized abortion in 1973. Constitutional experts, both pro- and anti-abortion, said that congressional efforts to outlaw abortion would violate the constitutional separation of powers between the legislative and judicial branches. The only way for a Supreme Court ruling to be overturned, they said, was by a constitutional amendment, not by an act of Congress.

Chicago Tribune
Chicago, Ill., April 23, 1981

In the near future, a subcommittee of the Senate Judiciary Committee will be holding hearings on one aspect of one approach to the perennially thorny issue of abortion. Sen. John P. East (R., N. C.) will be hearing medical testimony related to a pending "human life bill" which would define the term "person" in the 14th Amendment as including every fertilized human egg.

The many citizens unhappy with existing case law about abortion (because it legitimates abortion on demand in the first three months of pregnancy) have turned to agencies other than the Supreme Court. Some seek to outlaw abortion by means of either a "human life amendment" or a "human life statute." A bill sponsored by Senators Jesse A. Helms (R., N.C.), Alphonse D' Amato (R., N. Y.), and Rep. Henry J. Hyde (R., Ill.) would outlaw abortions performed or financed by government and would both empower the states to act against private abortions and immunize them from review of such action by federal courts.

Subtle and sophisticated arguments both for and against the "human life bill" are too complex to submit to brief summary. But it is readily clear that in the bill more is at stake than the abortion issue only, big though that is.

The efforts of anti-abortionists frustrated by the Supreme Court may result not only in giving the health of the fetus priority over the health of the mother, but in establishing sanctuaries from judicial review covering matters far beyond the single issue of abortion.

Impatience with disliked judicial decisions is sometimes justified, as the Supreme Court itself has recognized by openly reversing precedent at times. But such impatience is dangerous when it seeks to restrain the jurisdiction of the federal courts by declaring certain territories off limits to them. Their unwillingness to face constitutional challenge provides a sufficient reason for opposing sponsors of any bill, be it about abortion, prayers in public schools, or something else. If Congress can by simple majorities and with a compliant President protect a law from constitutional challenge in the federal courts, the Bill of Rights itself is diminished.

Not all countries with elected legislatures have judicially enforceable written constitutions. The parliaments of nations such as South Africa and the United Kingdom have almost unlimited powers. It is one of the glories of the United States that our Congress and President are not free to do whatever they please, but that statutes are vulnerable to court review of their constitutionality.

Citizens on both sides of the abortion issue should be able to join in resisting any and all bills that read, as the Helms-D' Amato-Hyde bill reads, "Notwithstanding any other provision of law, no inferior federal court ordained and established by Congress . . . shall have jurisidiction. . . ." Comprehensive judicial jurisdiction of constitutional claims is one of the essentials of the American system of government.

THE KANSAS CITY STAR
Kansas City, Mo., April 27, 1981

In its early stages, what's been billed the great debate is not so much a debate as a chorus delivered by selected experts with impeccable credentials most of whom could dot each other's "i's" and cross each other's "t's" without anyone noticing the difference. They affirm that life begins at conception.

The Senate, through Judiciary subcommittee hearings, has started work on a proposed human life bill that would ban all legal abortions and bypass the Supreme Court decision that a woman has a constitutional right to an abortion. The measure, introduced by Republicans Sen. Jesse Helms of North Carolina and Rep. Henry J. Hyde of Illinois, says: "For the purpose of enforcing the obligation of the states under the 14th Amendment not to deprive persons of life without due process of law, human life shall be deemed to exist from conception."

Emotions run exceedingly strong and convictions deep on both sides of the issue. Next to, and perhaps even surpassing, the matter of the national budget, the issue will engage the attention and energy of the whole Congress, making and breaking careers. If the bill survives the fray, not only will it touch the lives, directly or indirectly, of every citizen of the nation, it will mean that a relatively few politicians have done what mankind and the sages of its various disciplines including theology have been unable to do—define life.

Supporters of the bill, in and out of Congress, believe securing its passage by taking advantage of the new conservative mood of the Congress will be easier than getting a constitutional amendment prohibiting abortions.

It is both the significance and divisiveness of the issue that cry out for an open debate, inclusive of all shades of opinion and types of knowledge. A statement by the subcommittee chairman, John East, R-N.C., that later hearings will be expanded implies a more representative forum. That is imperative.

Whether or not the proposed law is constitutional—which even some supporters question—or if the clever idea holds the weight of moral imperative behind it—also questioned by some God-fearing persons—is not the point. The point is that unraveling one of mankind's greatest mysteries is not a task to be given over to a handful of politicians. We humbly admit some uncertainties. And a willingness to listen. The honorable legislators might be wise to do the same.

NEW HAMPSHIRE SUNDAY NEWS

Manchester, N.H., April 19, 1981

Some people are continually amazed at the low value placed on human life these days by others. Witness the recent tragedy in Lawrence, Mass., involving four juveniles — aged 13 to 15 — who beat to death an 82-year-old woman.

What set of values, what lack of morality is there in our societywhich fosters or permits such attitudes?

We think we have a part of the answer.

There was a debate at Dartmouth College last week on the subject of "elective" abortions. Arguing eloquently, as usual, against this baby-killing was Dr. Mildred Jefferson, president of the National Right to Life movement.

Arguing on the other side was one Charles Hartshorne, listed as professor emeritus of philosophy at the University of Texas. Just read what this gent had to say:

Not only unborn babies ("fetuses" in abortionists' parlance) but infants too are human beings but not "human persons," according to Hartshorne.

They are not persons because a person or individual must have rational thought. Children, he said, start to become persons and gain value in society as they learn to speak.

Not only abortion, but infanticide are legal rather than ethical issues. "Humans," said Hartshorne, "start as animals and become persons."

When a society has professors of supposed higher learning spouting such garbage, in effect saying that babies have no value, should one be surprised that other uneducated souls gain a warped impression of the worth of a single life?

THE PLAIN DEALER

Cleveland, Ohio, April 26, 1981

We oppose bills in Congress to overturn by legislative fiat the U.S. Supreme Court's controversial and divisive 1973 abortion decision. Enactment of these bills would constitute an illegitimate and, we believe, unconstitutional exercise of legislative power.

Lawmakers such as Sen. Jesse Helms, Republican of North Carolina, and Rep. Henry Hyde, Republican of Illinois, are pushing Congress to define precisely when human life begins. Their legislative proposals define life as beginning at the very moment of conception. Thus a fetus would be considered a person. The unborn would be entitled to 14th Amendment protection not to "deprive any person of life, liberty, or property, without due process of law."

Helms and Hyde propose to provide a political and legislative answer to a highly debatable and complex question on life which the Supreme Court tried to answer, but could not. The nation's highest court found that "the development of man's knowledge is not in a position to speculate as to the answer."

We agree with the concerns of Sen. Orrin G. Hatch, a conservative Republican of Utah. Hatch, a strong opponent of abortion, is extremely uncomfortable about the constitutionality of the Helms-Hyde bills.

"I'm second to no one in opposition to abortion, but I'm committed to sound constitutional principles," Hatch said.

And Rep. Louis Stokes, the liberal Democrat of Cleveland, accuses Congress of trying to play God. Stokes' view may be exaggerated, but he is correct in insisting that a determination of when life begins needs a precise scientific answer, not an arbitrary guess by Congress.

If enacted, these bills would substitute the political judgment of Congress for the constitutional judgment of the Supreme Court. Constitutional rights of citizens could be subjected to the whims of Congress. These whims can fluctuate, as legal scholars for the Congressional Research Service argue, with changes in "elective majorities." These are bad precedents.

These bills could also tamper with effective review by the judiciary. They are an intrusion into the Supreme Court's role of serving as interpreter of the intentions of the framers of the Constitution.

Regardless of how one feels about the highly passionate issue of abortion, the approach offered by these bills is constitutionally unacceptable.

SAN JOSE NEWS

San Jose, Calif., April 22, 1981

WHILE the rest of Congress wrestles with the nation's pressing economic problems, a group of conservative, anti-abortion senators is pushing ahead with a piece of legislation it calls the "human rights bill."

We think the proposal is badly timed and — despite its high-sounding and seemingly innocuous title — of dubious merit. Further, the political tactics behind it are suspect.

The measure takes the controversial position that a fertilized human egg is a "person" entitled to full protection of the 14th Amendment of the Constitution. This means that an embryo, at its earliest point, could not be legally aborted and that any physician or pregnant woman collaborating in an abortion could be prosecuted for first-degree murder or manslaughter.

Of course, all this is highly debatable, while running contrary to the law of the land: the U.S. Supreme Court's 1973 decision that abortion is legal. But there is more.

A literal reading of the bill, S. 158, indicates that certain contraceptives — such as intrauterine devices and some birth control pills that prevent the fertilized egg from attaching itself to the uterine wall — would be outlawed. This is certain to pose numerous legal problems.

Other questions arise over how authorities will monitor miscarriages to guard against "criminal abortions" and what "fetal personhood" will mean to American businesses, especially alcohol distillers and tobacco growers whose products are believed to damage fetuses.

Additionally, there is speculation that Sen. Orrin Hatch, R-Utah, will add to this bill his proposal to prohibit courts from issuing restraining orders or injunctions against federal, state or municipal anti-abortion laws.

Such legislation should concern those who value the judiciary's role in interpreting the Constitution. Since the anti-abortion forces admit they do not have the votes to pass a constitutional amendment outlawing abortion, they are pushing their "human rights bill" through Congress.

It is clear that the "pro-life" senators — led by Sen. John East, R-N.C., chairman of the Senate Subcommittee on the Separation of Powers — are trying to construct a legal-medical rationale to outlaw abortion while restricting the courts' authority.

This is a major social and constitutional question that demands a well-reasoned answer. The congressional hearings scheduled for Thursday and Friday have an important role in airing a wide range of concerns and issues.

But in an attempt to determine when life begins, Sen. East wants to limit discussion on this very complex matter. Thus far, he has insisted on hearing testimony only from sympathetic medical and scientific witnesses; eight doctors he and his staff have chosen to question are all known to support the view that a person exists from the moment of conception.

This arbitrarily narrow approach has understandably antagonized such pro-choice organizations as the American Civil Liberties Union and the Planned Parenthood Federation. These groups deserve an equal chance to express their views and to introduce other, dissenting medical testimony.

While we recognize the necessity of legislating certain social and constitutional rights, the East-Hatch attack on abortion is troubling.

Medically, there continues to be wide disagreement among scientific authorities, religious leaders and the American public about when life "begins." Politically, the debate for and against abortion has produced a complex array of thoughtful arguments.

The senators would be prudent to slow down and tone down their dogmatic anti-abortion campaign by opening their hearings to all viewpoints. Good law is rarely made in a political vacuum.

THE CHRISTIAN SCIENCE MONITOR
Boston, Mass., April 23, 1981

Americans have compelling reason to pay attention to the Senate subcommittee hearings on the Human Life Statute scheduled for today and tomorrow.

The intention of the statute is to negate the 1973 Supreme Court decision affirming a woman's right to choose to have an abortion. But it represents such a potential clash between the legislative and judicial branches of government that it has drawn opposition from legal scholars on both sides of the controversy over that decision. They question the constitutional authority of Congress to limit the jurisdiction of the courts as this statute sets out to do.

At the same time the Human Life Statute has divided those who want a constitutional amendment banning abortion: some see the statute as a diversion from the arduous drive for an amendment; some see it as a means of obtaining at least some results while the drive continues.

All in all, the need for the closest congressional and public scrutiny is clear.

This statute seeks to do what the Supreme Court did not consider it necessary to do in the 1973 *Roe v. Wade* decision: define when human life begins. Indeed, the court denied that the legislative adoption of "one theory of life" — in this case Texas's — may override a pregnant woman's rights. The Human Life Statute nevertheless seeks to adopt one theory by specifying that "human life shall be deemed to exist from conception, without regard to race, sex, age, health, defect, or condition of dependency; and for this purpose 'person' shall include all human life as defined herein."

The reference to "person" is meant to pin down what the term means in the 14th Amendment's provision against any state depriving "any person" of life, liberty, or property without due process of law. The reasoning is that states could then, for example, pass laws against abortion as murder, as depriving a "person" of life.

Roe v. Wade concluded that "the unborn have never been recognized in the law as persons in the whole sense." It anticipated the potential problems of a Human Life Statute by noting Texas's dilemma in urging that a fetus is entitled to 14th Amendment protection as a person. The court saw a problem arising here in any exception to a prohibition on abortion — such as permitting abortion on medical grounds to save the mother's life. It would appear to be out of line with the amendment's command not to deprive any person (now meaning the fetus) of life without due process of law.

Senator Helms, Representative Hyde, and other supporters of the statute offer a detailed argument on their side by Washington lawyer Stephen Galebach, a 1979 graduate of the Harvard Law School. He cites both the Fifth Amendment and the 14th Amendment as protecting the rights of "persons." He argues, in effect, that the statute would permit states to choose to protect the unborn "person" at any stage at the expense of the mother's currently protected rights — but would not compel them to do so.

The congressional discussion of the statute is an opportunity to shed light on whether the American public would like the grave questions raised by abortion to be left more to state-by-state judgment; whether it wants to test the authority of Congress to restrict the jurisdiction of the courts in this way; whether it prefers the usual method of constitutional amendment as a guide to the courts; whether it believes the need to stem the tide of abortion is such as to warrant using all legal means to this end.

The fresh focus on a poignant social issue also calls for renewed emphasis on the intelligent and ethical attitudes toward families and personal relationships that can prevent the situations in which the question of abortion arises. And the effort to define a "person" encourages individuals to consult their own highest concepts to define life beyond legal controversies as a touchstone for evaluating human existence.

Pittsburgh Post-Gazette
Pittsburgh, Pa., April 27, 1981

Abortion has so polarized the political process that every initiative in the area tends to be regarded as just one more skirmish in the same long battle.

In reality, however, the emotionalism surrounding the issue makes it all the more important that distinctions be drawn between "pro-life" proposals that vary greatly in their constitutional correctness, clarity of language and potential as precedents.

Fortunately, as a U.S. Senate subcommittee was holding (rather one-sided) hearings last week on a bill to try to circumvent the U.S. Supreme Court's abortion rulings, such important distinctions were indeed being drawn by "pro-life" as well as "pro-choice" advocates and by legal scholars of a wide variety of views.

The bill, which is sponsored by Sen. Jesse Helms and Rep. Henry Hyde and which has won favorable comment from President Reagan, aims to override the Supreme Court's abortion decisions not by constitutional amendment — which would require a two-thirds vote of the House and Senate and ratification by 38 states — but rather by a simple law requiring only a majority to pass. In addition to denying some lower federal courts the authority to negate anti-abortion laws, the bill would purport to enforce the Fourteenth Amendment by declaring that "human life shall be deemed to exist from conception," a formulation whose legal effects could extend far beyond prohibiting abortion.

The reason for the bill's focus on the Fourteenth Amendment is that in its landmark 1973 decision striking down state laws against abortion, the Supreme Court — needlessly, some scholars believe — addressed and rejected the notion that fetuses are "persons" under the amendment. The specific language about the beginning of life is a response to the high court's 1973 statement that it was "not in a position to speculate" as to when life begins. According to supporters of the Helms-Hyde bill, that statement was an invitation to Congress to take up that thorny task.

The constitutional rationale for the Helms-Hyde maneuver is that the Fourteenth Amendment gives Congress broad power to enforce its "due process" and "equal protection" protections by "appropriate legislation." The bill's advocates argue that the way for such legislation has been cleared by the Supreme Court itself, which in a landmark 1966 voting-rights case permitted Congress, pursuant to the Fourteenth Amendment, to outlaw literacy tests for voters of a kind that the court itself in the past had refused to declare unconstitutional.

It is a clever argument, but not a convincing one. And it has been ably anticipated by constitutional scholars such as Harvard's Archibald Cox, who has argued that Congress' authority to take a broader view of the amendment than the Supreme Court's is related to Congress' superior position as a "fact-finder."

For example, in the voting-rights case, Congress concluded that English literacy tests interfered with the exercise of the franchise by Spanish-speaking voters. The high court's acquiescence in the law restricting the use of such tests was not really a dramatic departure, Professor Cox has written: "The Court has long been committed both to the presumption that facts exist which sustain congressional legislation and also to deference to congressional judgment upon questions of degree and proportion."

Congress, containing as it does a good many politicians, knows a great many facts about how literacy tests affect the voting rights of various constituencies. On the other hand, the question of whether a fetus is a "person" under the Fourteenth Amendment is a more general constitutional question and one on which Congress cannot claim any more expertise than the Supreme Court possesses.

The difference is an important one, not only to pro-abortion forces but to legal experts of all persuasions who fear that the Helms-Hyde bill would threaten the independence of the Supreme Court by establishing a precedent for "backdoor" amendment of the Constitution. The list of law professors who have attacked the bill reads like a Who's Who of American constitutional scholarship. Many of the critics are prominent *conservative* legal scholars.

The point made by these critics, some of whom have criticized the Supreme Court's abortion decisions, is that congressmen who wish to override a major constititional decision must do so by the direct — and deliberately difficult — route of a constitutional amendment. That point is not an abstract nicety, or simply an argument seized on for tactical purposes by pro-abortion groups. It goes to the heart of the American system of separation of powers.

ST. LOUIS POST-DISPATCH

St. Louis, Mo., April 21, 1981

The Senate Subcommittee on the Separation of Powers is scheduled to begin hearings this week on legislation (S. 158) that would allow the states to pass laws outlawing abortion. S. 158 would declare that life begins at conception and would extend to the fertilized egg the protections of 14th Amendment. It also would prohibit federal district and appellate courts from hearing cases that challenged state laws and local ordinances pertaining to abortion. The legislation would do more than strip away constitutional freedoms now enjoyed by women of childbearing age. Through its assault on the federal judiciary, it poses a threat to the liberties of all Americans.

S. 158 and a companion bill in the House (HR 900) are efforts to achieve a national prohibition against abortion by statute instead of constitutional amendment. The latter course is considered to be fraught with too many political difficulties. A constitutional amendment requires two-thirds votes in each house of Congress in addition to the ratification by 38 state legislatures. To become law, a statute needs only majority votes in the House and Senate and the president's signature. Once it became law, S. 158 would invite state legislatures to approve the most stringent anti-abortion measures, notwithstanding the U.S. Supreme Court's landmark ruling in 1973 that declared states could not interfere with a woman's decision to have an abortion in the first trimester of her pregnancy.

In *Roe vs. Wade*, the court held that "the unborn have never been recognized in the law as persons in the whole sense." By investing the fertilized egg and fetus with the protections of the 14th Amendment, S. 158 is an attempt to redefine "persons" for constitutional purposes. Yet Article 3 of the Constitution clearly reserves for the Supreme Court, not Congress, the authority to interpret the Constitution. Hence, S. 158 and HR. 900 would appear to be drafted on the shakiest constitutional grounds.

The broader implications of S. 158 should give every citizen pause. If Congress can redefine the word persons to negate *Roe vs. Wade*, what is to stop it from redefining the word "rights" or "equality" or "religion" to get around other court decisions? What is to prevent Congress from using this technique to overturn any ruling that is unpopular with a majority of its members. A paramount function of the court is to safeguard the freedoms of Americans against momentary passions that sweep through the legislative or executive branch. If the framers of the Constitution had intended that document to be changed any time a majority could be mustered in Congress, they would scarcely have gone to the trouble of setting down the rigorous and time-consuming procedures that are required for amendments. Precisely because opponents of abortion realize that they probably cannot meet the test the Founding Fathers imposed, they now are turning to backdoor devices such as S. 158.

In attempting to exclude the federal courts from any consideration of abortion cases, S. 158 again would seem to fly in the face of the Constitution. The right to abortion, as *Roe vs. Wade* declares, is constitutionally protected. Yet under S. 158, federal courts would be prohibited from considering claims involving a constitutional right. If Congress can put the Constitution out of bounds for federal courts when abortion is concerned, it can do the same when the issue is racial discrimination or the right to speak freely. S. 158 is presented by its supporters as an attempt to extend the protections of the Constitution. In reality, by making them dependent on the whim of Congress, it would render them all but meaningless.

The Hartford Courant

Hartford, Conn., April 27, 1981

The U.S. Senate hearings last week on "when life begins" were an embarrassment even to many of the most ardent foes of legalized abortion.

Senators are elected to establish fiscal policy, and budget priorities, not to promote themselves as theologians. The question of when life begins is a worthy issue for doctors and clergy to discuss, but the answer will not come from a show of hands on Capitol Hill.

The hearings are a thinly disguised prelude to the introduction of an anti-abortion bill that would officially establish the "moment of conception" as the time when life begins. This backdoor attempt to avoid the U.S. Supreme Court's protection of the right to abortion will probably fail on constitutional grounds, if Congress has the bad judgment to allow such legislation to be approved.

Those who support the right of women to choose their own medical care do themselves no service, however, by dwelling on the fact that the Senate hearing is "stacked" with witnesses sympathetic to the anti-abortion forces, led by North Carolina Sen. Jesse Helms. Choosing friendly witnesses is hardly a new trick in Washington, and in this case, the issue is not whether the debate is fair, but whether it should be conducted at all.

Anti-abortion forces do not have the support of the nation's high court, the nation's medical establishment, a majority of the American people, or the support of enough state legislatures to ram through a constitutional amendment. To write a church document, masquerading as law, as a substitute for letting Americans decide whether abortion is a correct option, would be bad policy and hopelessly unconstitutional law.

The particular bill under discussion would have especially harsh consequences for users of certain birth control methods, other than abortion. Contraception that impedes the progress of a fertilized egg might well be considered murder, under a "life-begins-at-conception" doctrine. Any congressman who would vote for such damaged legislative goods should be required to serve on the first jury hearing such a murder case.

Under the best of interpretations, this particular anti-abortion proposal will provide good press for senators who generate large campaign contributions from anti-abortion forces, while not obligating other senators to take the measure too seriously. When law is distorted to make theologians out of politicians, and murderers out of mothers and doctors, the time has come to say, enough.

Los Angeles Times

Los Angeles, Calif., April 22, 1981

The 14th Amendment to the U.S. Constitution denies the deprivation of "life, liberty or property without due process of law." Some members of Congress would like to redefine when a person's life begins so that abortion would be illegal. They are seeking to throw out legislatively a Supreme Court decision that they lack the valid constitutional arguments to have overturned judicially or the political strength to change through the normal process of amending the Constitution.

On Thursday and Friday, a Senate subcommittee on the separation of powers will hold hearings on a bill sponsored by Sen. Jesse Helms (R-N.C.) and Rep. Henry J. Hyde (R-Ill.). It seeks to resolve a question left open in the Supreme Court's 1973 Roe v. Wade decision that legalized abortion. The question: When does life begin? The Helms-Hyde measure says life begins at conception. If passed, the bill would allow states to pass laws abolishing both abortion and some birth-control techniques that work after conception.

This attempt to redefine the Constitution is bad law and bad public policy, not to mention bad news to women in general. From the viewpoint of some anti-abortion forces, the bill is even bad politics. They disagree among themselves on what tactics would best achieve their ends—whether to reach for legislation that might well prove unconstitutional and would be unwieldly to implement, or for a constitutional amendment.

Doctors invited to testify this week must limit their comments to the immediate question of when life begins. There can be no discussion of the constitutional issues or of enforcement if such a simple-minded law were passed. Is this any way to write legislation?

If the Helms-Hyde bill passes, the damage to the Constitution and the tested methods of revising it could be irreparable. Those able to command a simple majority could then redefine anything, without having to submit fundamental changes to state legislatures as required now for constitutional changes.

And, if the Helms-Hyde bill passes, it will raise many more questions: Will an abortion after a rape be murder? Will there be a bureaucracy—a Federal Bureau of Pregnancy Investigation, perhaps—created to check on the termination of each pregnancy?

It is ironic that many of the same groups determined to get government off people's backs are trying to give government a new role in one of the most personal of all decisions—whether or not to bear a child.

THE MILWAUKEE JOURNAL

Milwaukee, Wisc., June 2, 1981

Whatever one's position on the troubling question of abortion, there is cause for concern in the present congressional effort to circumvent the US Supreme Court's 1973 abortion ruling. And the cautionary comments issued recently by six former US attorneys general are particularly worth pondering.

When the court ruled in 1973 that a woman's right to privacy permits her to abort a pregnancy in the first trimester, Justice Harry Blackmun wrote in the majority opinion that the court could not "resolve the difficult question of when life begins." Now, however, Sen. Jesse Helms (R-N.C.) and Rep. Henry Hyde (R-Ill.) have decided that Congress, in carrying out its obligation to enforce the 14th Amendment, may conclude that human life begins at the moment of conception.

Their notion is embodied in the Human Life Bill and their clear intent is to frustrate the Supreme Court ruling. The bill poses a threat to the balanced powers of the legislative and judicial branches of government. That is the point made by the former attorneys general, including both Democrats and Republicans, who admit to widely varying views about the Supreme Court's decision.

The former top lawyers were so concerned that they wrote a letter to the Senate subcommittee on the separation of powers. "Our views about the correctness of the Supreme Court's 1973 abortion decision vary widely," the signers wrote, "but all of us are agreed that Congress has no constitutional authority either to overturn that decision by enacting a statute redefining such terms as 'person' or 'human life,' or selectively to restrict the jurisdiction of federal courts so as to prevent them from enforcing that decision fully."

That's an opinion, true. It happens to be the opinion of Herbert Brownell, Nicholas Katzenbach, Ramsey Clark, Elliott Richardson, William Saxbe and Benjamin Civiletti.

DAYTON DAILY NEWS

Dayton, Ohio, June 9, 1981

The arguments over abortion itself aside, Congress is getting what is clearly good advice from most of the constitutional experts testifying on a anti-abortion bill that dodges constitutional procedures. The advice: Avoid the thing like the plague.

As even its sponsors admit, the bill tries to take a shortcut across the Constitution in order quickly to outlaw abortions once again. Chances are the law, if enacted, would fail; the Supreme Court is likely to find its methods themselves unconstitutional, making the whole exercise futile.

Worse, however, there is a risk the high court just might defer to the law. If so, the whole U.S. Constitution suddenly would be opened to dramatic changes, indeed to effective repeal, by mere legislative act.

The sober, reflective process that the Founding Fathers established for changing the Constitution would be replaced by knee-jerk legislative changes which could be enacted in the heat of a moment.

The Constitution, our fundamental governing compact, can be changed by amendments approved by two-thirds majorities in the House and Senate and ratified by three-fourths of the states.

This process has served Americans well, allowing for change to handle new circumstances but, with the exception of Prohibition, shielding basic constitutional principles from passing political fancies.

Rather than undertaking the serious process of amending the Constitution, some in Congress are pushing this tricky bill, which they figure would dump the Supreme Court's 1973 pro-abortion decision by expediently redefining constitutional terms. The court's ruling was based in part on a finding that fetuses under three months are not "persons" in the Constitution's meaning of the word.

If Congress can redefine words in the Constitution in order to get around applications of its principles that a hyperactive lobby dislikes, all the Constitution's basic provisions will be subject to impassioned, even whimsical changes.

Even the most committed abortion opponents, knowing they have an established process for constitutional change open to them, ought to recognize that the danger of wrecking the Constitution is too high a toll to pay for a joy ride on a shortcut.

The Cleveland Press

Cleveland, Ohio, March 24, 1981

As an archconservative, the powerful Sen. Jesse Helms of North Carolina sees himself as a defender of the Constitution. Yet he is trying an end run around the nation's basic law on the issue of abortion.

Helms and another leading foe of abortion, Rep. Henry Hyde, R-Ill., have introduced identical bills saying that "actual human life exists from conception." By treating fetuses as "persons" their measure would allow states to outlaw abortion as a crime.

The real target of the Helms-Hyde move is the 1973 Supreme Court decision that struck down most laws against abortion and upheld the right of a woman to terminate a pregnancy.

If one disagrees with the high court ruling, and we do not, there is a way to oppose it. This is to work for a constitutional amendment abolishing legal abortion.

However, it is difficult in a controversial matter to get the needed two-thirds vote in the House and Senate and the ratification of 38 states to amend the Constitution. So Helms and Hyde have chosen the easy, and illegal, way.

They are seeking to overturn a Supreme Court decision by simple legislation. If their bill passes (and unfortunately President Reagan has indicated he would sign it) it likely will be held unconstitutional by the high court.

But that is playing Russian Roulette with the Constitution. Suppose the Supreme Court ducked such a confrontation with Congress and allowed Helms-Hyde to stand. That would be a fundamental change, empowering Congress to rewrite the Constitution merely by passing laws.

The framers of the Constitution deliberately made it hard to amend. They did not want basic liberties and the structure of the Republic altered by transient majorities.

If the Helms end run succeeds and established Congress' supremacy over the Supreme Court, any one of the Bill of Rights could be revised or scrapped by legislative act, reducing the Constitution to whatever politicians want it to mean.

That is a terrible risk to run just for speeding things up for the anti-abortion lobby.

St. Louis Review

St. Louis, Mo., March 13, 1981

There is a scare campaign going on to distract peoples' attention from the violence done by an abortion. The scare campaign concentrates on the alleged bad consequences of enacting a Human Life Amendment.

Opponents of a Human Life Amendment charge that its passage would permit dependency tax deductions for unborn children and would prohibit a pregnant woman from horseback riding since that activity might endanger the unborn child.

The Committee for Free Choice is circulating pamphlets which ask questions like these:

Do you want a law that could require women who miscarry to prove that the miscarriage was in no way induced or the result of criminal negligence?

Do you want a law that could create legislative chaos within existing laws and systems relating to "persons" — including inheritance, tort, and tax laws as well as services based on population, apportionment of legislatures, census, etc.?

Then the pamphlet goes on to say: If your answer to any one of these questions is no, then you should not support a Human Life Amendment because that amendment would do all of this.

But, of course, amendments do not self-enforce. The principles laid down in constitutional amendments are applied and enforced by appropriate legislation and interpreted by the courts.

The Human Life Amendment would again permit the states to protect unborn human life. Presumably the legislation would be written by sensible men and women. No such ridiculous laws as suggested by the Committee for a Free Choice are to be expected.

The Committee is simply engaging in diversionary and delaying tactics — anything to stop a Human Life Amendment.

WORCESTER TELEGRAM.

Worcester, Mass., May 1, 1981

The Senate subcommittee hearings in Washington on the so-called Human Life bill have raised more questions that they ever will answer.

The testimony is supposed to determine when human life begins. Advocates of the new law claim that human life begins at conception and thus the fetus has all the rights granted to human beings. If that is written into law, they say, abortion automatically will be considered murder.

But no act of Congress can so easily decide a matter that has divided theologians, philosophers and doctors for thousands of years. Although there is no question that life begins at conception, the point at which that life takes on a human quality has been endlessly debated. Some say it is when the fetus develops its own functioning organs, including its heart. Others say it is when the fetus is fully formed and not an undifferentiated mass of cells. There is no consensus. Still others say the whole point is irrelevant to the real problem.

Aside from that, some constitutionalists see this proposed bill as an attempted end run around the Constitution. It would in effect amend the Constitution without going through the amendment procedure.

Still others regard it as another intrusion by the government in a realm where decisions should be made by individuals, not by lawmakers. It is plainly an attempt to outlaw abortions by overriding the U.S. Supreme Court decision of 1973.

Those who are pushing this new bill should reflect on American history. That history shows clearly that attempts to legislate morality succeed only when there is a wide agreement by the people on the goal to be achieved. Every poll taken in recent years shows that most people believe that abortion is a matter to be decided by individual choice, not by the government. There is no reason to believe that the majority favors any attempt by Congress to short-circuit the Supreme Court decision.

The issue is not when life begins, nor even when human life begins, but what is to be done in those tragic cases where a mother's welfare conflicts with her pregnancy. In some instances, her life may be at stake. In others, she may be the victim of rape, incest or disabling emotional trauma.

These are the difficult questions that the proposed Human Life Bill does not even deal with.

The Wichita
Eagle-Beacon

Wichita, Kans., November 11, 1981

The sanctity that should be afforded human life virtually dictates that abortion will remain a volatile national issue, regardless of congressional or judicial actions. But any efforts to alter the U.S. Constitution, either for or against the cause of abortion, would be a mistake. The resulting effect of limiting the jurisdiction of the courts would further politicize the controversy, as well as undermine the delicate system of checks and balances that has sustained the U.S. government for almost 200 years.

Recent congressional victories in banning the use of federal funds for abortions have spurred the introduction of legislation that either would ban all abortions in this country or give individual states the right to determine their respective abortion policies, as long as those policies are no less restrictive than any existing federal regulations. These measures are related closely to another pending bill that would define human life as beginning at conception.

There is a growing need for national reassessment for the manner in which abortion is used as a birth control device. Suggestions that legal abortions be confined to instances where rape, incest or the health of the mother is involved may have validity. But thwarting the constitutional intention for the courts to be the last resort for citizen redress would set a dangerous precedent. Leaving the fate of a matter as complex as abortion to the whim of partisan state legislatures, which are prone to shifting philosophical positions, in the long run would be more unsatisfactory than the present system.

It also is disturbing that the National Conference of Catholic Bishops has decided to endorse the bill for state determination of abortion regulations. The effect of a major religious organization pushing for the passage of legislation with such strong religious overtones borders closely on abridging the necessary separation of church and state. Rational arguments on the abortion issue could be diluted by the active intervention of established religious organizations in massive lobbying efforts.

There may be no answers to the abortion question that would satisfy all concerned parties. But the current system of deciding such issues on the basis of legal casework, rather than state or federal legislation, remains the best method of dealing with an admittedly difficult situation.

St. Petersburg Times

St. Petersburg, Fla., April 25, 1981

The 14th Amendment to the Constitution says that all persons "born or naturalized" in the United States are citizens entitled to equal protection and due process of law. The Supreme Court has held that this does not apply to fetuses. The words are plain enough.

Nonetheless, Rep. Henry J. Hyde, R-Ill, and Sens. Jesse Helms and John East, R-N.C., are trying to pass a law declaring that personhood exists from the moment of conception. This is intended to reverse the Supreme Court's historic abortion ruling of 1973 and require the states to prosecute women who have abortions and the physicians who perform them. It would outlaw some birth control pills and the intrauterine device. The bill makes no exceptions for rape, incest or pregnancies that threaten women's lives. So much for *their* equal protection.

WHAT HELMS, Hyde and East are trying to do demonstrates how impossible and unwise it is for political entities such as the Congress to attempt to decide when human life begins. The Supreme Court acknowledged itself unequal to that task, pointing out that neither doctors nor theologians have ever been able to agree on the question.

The bill is in profound conflict with society's established secular and religious practices. What happens when a woman miscarries for natural causes during the early stages of pregnancy? The law requires no autopsy, no inquest, no birth certificate, no death certificate, no burial. Religion affords no baptism, offers no funeral. Under the Helms philosophy, however, states would be neglecting the "rights" of the fetuses for failing to investigate each such spontaneous abortion.

IT IS A strange tactic for people who call themselves conservatives to be trying to change the Constitution by law instead of by amendment. Even the ranking legal adviser to the United States Catholic Conference, which supports an anti-abortion amendment, has said it is "utterly unrealistic" to expect the Supreme Court to uphold the legislation. And Sen. Orrin Hatch, R-Utah, whose conservative ideology is nearly that of Helms, has voiced his own doubts of the bill's constitutionality.

The most disconcerting aspect of all this is the arrogant misuse of power under which hearings began in East's judiciary subcommittee this week. East packed the witness list with people representing primarily one point of view. He refused to allow counsel for the Democratic minority to question them. He refused to schedule witnesses requested by the Democrats. That is the way dictatorships make laws, not democracies. Is that what America should expect from the New Right?

The Burlington Free Press

Burlington, Vt., July 19, 1981

Abortion is an issue that has been a subject of national debate for so long that the public probably has grown weary of the barrage of publicity that has been loosed for and against it.

Extremists on both sides tend to become shrill when they argue the merits and the drawbacks of abortion and often generate more heat than light in emotional exchanges on the issue. Rational discussion could provide some basis for reaching a compromise that might be acceptable to both sides. But proponents and opponents have adopted intransigent positions that seem to be frozen in stone.

Many persons,who oppose abortion on humane grounds, believe, and rightly so, that the decision on the procedure should be left in the hands of the family. Should a man and woman decide it is feasible to have an abortion, neither the government nor outside special interest groups should intrude on the couple's right to do so. Basically, it is a matter of free choice that is guaranteed by the Constitution to all citizens of the country.

That Congress is considering a "human life" amendment to the Constitution should be a matter of deep concern for all people who believe that the document was designed by the nation's founders to be an instrument for the protection of the individual's rights and not a license for the government to interfere in affairs that are outside its jurisdiction. As people have a right to choose when, where and how they will live, they must at the same time have a similar prerogative to make those decisions that will affect their lives for many years in the future.

What the "human life" amendment would do is to cancel the U.S. Supreme Court's 1973 decision that legalized abortion. Starting with the assumption that life begins at conception, the proposed amendment would outlaw all abortions, extending constitutional protection to the unborn. Such a step appears to be an unwarranted intrusion of government into family affairs that would usurp the power of free choice that now is exercised within the confines of the home. Choice would be abrogated by constitutional fiat.

Much of the energy that has been generated by those who defend the right to life has been spent on the protection of the fetus. The energy dissipates in many cases when the movement is asked to propose options. Many persons who oppose abortion are equally adamant in their stand against contraception. And they show little concern for the fate of the child who places an extra burden on the family after it is born. While they spend millions of dollars to protect the fetus, they spend nothing to assure that the children that are born as a result of their zealous defense of the right to life have a healthy and happy childhood.

Some proponents of abortion similarly squander their time and money on the single issue while neglecting to stress the fact that unwanted, or unneeded, pregnancies can be prevented by other methods that involve less trauma for women.

While medical techniques for abortion are highly sophisticated, they are not by any means as physically and psychologically painless as the treatment for the flu. Many women will attest to the fact that abortion leaves indelible scars on their memories that can last for years.

Even so, Congress should not propose a constitutional amendment that will take away a woman's right to have an abortion under conditions that are clinically safe and as comfortable as possible. Should such an amendment be approved, it is likely that the day of the back-room butchers will be revived and many women's lives will unnecessarily be placed in jeopardy.

Lawmakers should soundly defeat the proposal when and if it is brought to the floor on the grounds that it conflicts with other rights that are guaranteed to individuals under the Constitution and denies the right of free choice for the citizenry.

The Miami Herald

Miami, Fla., May 11, 1981

THERE is no single "right" answer to whether abortion should or should not be permitted. The rightness of the answer depends on the eye of the beholder.

That outlines clearly an area that generally is *not* the government's business. That is the basic reason there should be no Constitutional Amendment outlawing abortion. That is why Florida's House Judiciary-Civil Committee was wise to reject the call for a Constitutional Convention to consider such an amendment.

That action followed by a week the ill-advised approval of such a resolution by the state Senate. It makes it improbable that the full House will consider the resolution, which is just as well.

The key question is what role government should play in determining an individual woman's options when she becomes pregnant. People opposed to abortion generally believe sincerely that it is morally irresponsible to end pregnancy artificially.

Significantly, few of those people have stepped forward to pledge individual responsibility to the unwanted children — whatever race, religion, or potential — who would be born if they had their way. What they insist upon, rather, is imposing upon others their own moral and religious views.

The only fair compromise is what exists now: leaving as an individual and private decision what a woman does when she becomes pregnant. In a word, choice.

Moreover, this is not the time for a Constitutional Convention. The entire American system of government is not so hobbled that it should be put at the mercy of people so focused on a single issue. A convention could not be prevented from offering Constitutional Amendments on anything else that suited its fancy.

Supporters of a Constitutional Amendment outlawing abortion rejoin that two-thirds of the states must issue the call for a convention and that three-fourths of the states must ratify amendments to make them part of the Constitution. That argument sidesteps the obligation of the legislatures to keep government out of matters that aren't its business.

San Francisco Chronicle

San Francisco, Calif., May 5, 1981

CONGRESS SHOULD pay attention to the letter of warning from six former attorneys general who denounce as dangerous and unconstitutional the legislation being pushed by right-to-lifers that would overrule Supreme Court decisions on the right of women to abortions.

This legislation presents nothing less than a potential constitutional crisis, we believe, and must be judged in that light. For S. 158, the bill now being heard in the Senate Judiciary Committee, proposes to tell the Supreme Court "when life begins" and thereby to guide the hands of the justices in determining "the proper meaning of the word 'person' under the Fourteenth Amendment."

But the six former attorneys general say Congress can't constitutionally tell the Supreme Court how to interpret the Fourteenth Amendment.

"ALL OF US ARE AGREED," they say in their letter, "that Congress has no constitutional authority" to overturn the 1973 abortion ruling of the Supreme Court in *Roe v. Wade* "by enacting a statute redefining such terms as 'person' or 'human life'."

The point here is not that the six ex-attorneys general are of one mind on the abortion issue; they say, on the contrary, that "our views about the correctness of the Supreme Court's 1973 abortion decision vary widely." But the Court has declared the law, and it is not for Congress to "undeclare" it. *Roe v. Wade* held women to have the constitutional right, under the Fourteenth Amendment, to timely abort a fetus. The argument that a fetus is a "person" protected by the Fourteenth Amendment was rejected.

The anti-abortion bill, authored by Senator Jesse Helms, is thus "an attempt to exercise unconstitutional power," the former attorneys general said, and is "a dangerous circumvention of the avenues that the Constitution itself provides for reversing Supreme Court interpretations of the Constitution."

WHAT THE SUPREME COURT declares to be constitutional can be set aside through an amendment to the Constitution. It can't be done by a statute enacted by Congress, say the ex-attorneys general — Herbert Brownell Jr., Nicholas DeB. Katzenbach, Ramsey Clark, Elliot L. Richardson, William B. Saxbe and Benjamin R. Civiletti. Their legal judgment is impressively unanimous.

The Virginian-Pilot

Norfolk, Va., August 7, 1981

In his interview last week with The Washington Star, President Reagan was asked what he thought of the bills proposed in Congress that would limit the federal courts' jurisdiction over certain "social issues"—i.e., prayer in public schools, abortion, and school busing. Mr. Reagan replied: "Where we can accomplish something by legislation," he said, "I like that a lot better than by a judicial decision."

One is inclined to wonder: Did Mr. Reagan understand the question? Does he understand the issue involved in so curbing the federal judiciary? Other questions by Star editors offered Mr. Reagan the chance to clarify, but the president, alas, continued to reply as though the subject were as intelligible to him as calculus is to a fifth grader.

This is not the occasion to treat in full the variety of issues raised by the bills pending in Congress, of which there are now some 27. Suffice to say, however, that some constitutional lawyer in the Reagan administration—or outside it—ought to advise the president on this basic point: that while Congress is authorized under the Constitution (Article III) to regulate the appellate jurisdiction of the federal courts, including the Supreme Court, it is another question whether regulation of the type currently proposed in Congress is wise.

This is the chief issue raised by the 27 bills in question, not whether legislative decisions are better than judicial ones (which in most cases is true). And the problem with almost every one of the 27 bills is that, in stripping the Supreme Court of jurisdiction over the cases specified, whether abortion, busing, or school prayer, they would be establishing a precedent of dubious worth. For never before, despite the constitutional permission in Article III, has Congress under ordinary circumstances withdrawn jurisdiction over constitutional questions from the court. If it is done now, it could be done again, and done then, Mr. Reagan should note, for the sake of not conservative but maybe liberal ends.

Congress has every right, and duty, to engage the Supreme Court in the ongoing question of what is constitutional, and prudent legislation that would invite the court to change its mind has had that effect (as witness the congressional efforts earlier in this century to have the court reverse itself on child labor). But the current legislation is not prudent, it is not wise, for it seeks not so much to enter a discussion of constitutionality with the court as to deny the court of its reason for being—which is to exercise judicial review.

Supreme Court decisions of the past two decades have deformed the Constitution, but there is no point deforming the nature of our constitutional government in order to correct those deformations. Mr. Reagan may not be inclined to speak out against the deforming bills now pending in Congress, for the obviously constraining reason that they contemplate the conservative ends admired by the New Right. But it is not too much to ask that he at least demonstrate some awareness of the critical issue they raise.

The Chattanooga Times

Chattanooga, Tenn., May 2, 1981

To his credit, Sen. John East, R-N.C., has retreated from his clumsy effort last week to stack the testimony in favor of legislation that seeks to ban abortions. That issue is so controversial, and the legislation itself so controversial in its own right, that a one-sided hearing like the one he chaired mocks the idea that political debate necessarily requires the airing of opposing views.

More dangerous than Sen. East's high-handed tactics, however, is the legislation before the Senate Subcommittee on the Separation of Powers. The bill (S. 158, and a companion bill in the House, HR 900) would allow states to outlaw abortion by declaring that life begins at conception and thus the fertilized egg is a "person" eligible for the constitutional protections of the Fourteenth Amendment. Worse, it would prohibit federal courts from hearing challenges of state laws regarding abortion. At issue here is not whether abortion is right or wrong but a backdoor assault on the Constitution.

The legislation, sponsored by Sen. Jesse Helms, R-N.C., is an effort to get around the 1973 Supreme Court's *Roe vs. Wade* ruling which invalidated on constitutional grounds state laws prohibiting abortions. That decision held that a state may not inject itself into a woman's decision to have an abortion in the first trimester of a pregnancy. S. 158, therefore, is an effort to impose a national prohibition against abortion without going to the trouble of amending the Constitution. The latter process, of course, is more difficult. An amendment requires approval by two-thirds of both houses of Congress and ratification by at least 38 states. Legislation, on the other hand, needs only the president's signature once it has been approved by a simple majority of each house.

But in passing the law, Congress would have to decide by simple roll-call vote a question that has divided theologians and philosophers for nearly two millenia: when does life begin? Whether Messrs. Helms and East really believe such a bill will pass constitutional muster is questionable. The Supreme Court held in 1973 that "the unborn have never been recognized in the law as persons in the whole sense."

Again, the key issue is not abortion (or school prayer or busing, two other areas of judicial activity that are inspiring similar efforts), but whether Congress, riding the passions of isolated issues, will destroy vital constitutional protections handed down by the founding fathers. The danger is that if Congress voids *Roe* by redefining the word "person," the precedent would be set for another bill to negate other unpopular Supreme Court rulings by redefining other terms. The court, for example, has never precisely defined "due process" or "equal protection," for the simple reason that such terms are seen as concepts that change over the course of time. They mean different things in different contexts. But if Congress can decide what "person" means, why could it not make a similar decision on other words? S. 158 would in effect give Congress the authority to interpret the Constitution, thus conflicting with Article 3, which clearly assigns such responsibility to the Supreme Court. Small wonder, then, that the bill is creating concern among respected legal scholars.

Commenting on this issue recently in *The Los Angeles Times*, Judge Irving B. Kaufman of the 2nd Circuit Court of Appeals wrote:

"These proposed limitations on the power of federal courts to address constitutional problems do not bode well for the republic . . . Today, the controversial issues of school prayer, abortion and desegregation are in the forefront. Tomorrow, perhaps, there will be efforts to prevent the courts from hearing First Amendment free-speech and religion cases . . . Our scheme of government, in which Congress can only alter constitutional doctrines via the amendment process, will be subverted. Congress, in effect, will be able to nullify decisions of constitutional dimensions merely by passing laws removing jurisdiction from the federal courts. That is not how our founding fathers intended to safeguard our fundamental liberties."

The courts in this country were deliberately set up to protect fundamental freedoms from reckless actions flowing out of controversial, but transient, issues. But Sen. Helms' legislation, riding the passions spawned by the abortion issue, perverts that essential protection by avoiding the more difficult process of amending the Constitution. The nation's founders set up a complicated, time-consuming process for changing our Constitution. One purpose was to avoid frivolous alterations by any congressman able to persuade a majority of his colleagues to support a bill negating a Supreme Court decision dealing with constitutional issues. That point alone shows why Sen. Helms & Co., lacking the strength to amend the Constitution, have decided to deal with the issue through the back door.

S. 158 would ravage the Constitution in an effort to deal with an immensely complicated social, moral — and political — issue. The legislation deserves defeat.

TULSA WORLD

Tulsa, Okla.,
August 13, 1981

THE HOUSE of Delegates of the American Bar Association Tuesday voted overwhelmingly against efforts in Congress to restrict the jurisdiction of the Federal Courts. The delegates rightly denounced the move as "Constitutional tinkering."

Congress is once again toying with the idea of removing such controversial issues as school busing, school prayer and abortion from the purview of the Federal Courts. Congress cannot directly limit the jurisdiction of the U.S. Supreme Court. But it can limit the cases which lower Federal Courts can hear and which the High Court can then review.

Antlers attorney Joe Stamper best summed up the issue when he told the ABA delegates that it would be a "perilous precedent" for Congress to alter the subject matter jurisdiction of the Federal Courts simply out of dissatisfaction with those Courts' results.

Stamper and his fellow delegates are right. There is a Constitutionally prescribed manner for dealing with the volatile issues of busing and school prayer. Constitutional Amendment is the appropriate method for resolving at least the abortion and prayer questions.

But passing a Constitutional Amendment is not easy. So, Congress has tried to find a simpler way. Tampering with Federal Court jurisdiction is an ill-conceived idea. Congress should not try to stop the Courts from protecting recognized Constitutional rights.

Mormons & ERA: Feminist Ousted, Judge Scored

When a church demands that its members adopt a certain view on political issues, personal and professional conflicts may result. Such was the case in two instances involving the Equal Rights Amendment and the Mormon church in December 1979. Sonia Johnson of Sterling, Va., was formally excommunicated Dec. 5 for "spreading false doctrine" because of her public activity on behalf of ERA. The bishop who presided over her case ruled that she "was not in harmony with church doctrine concerning the nature of God in the manner in which He directs His church on Earth." The Mormon church considered ERA a threat to the family and to the legal protection of women on grounds that it would "stifle God-given instincts." Church officials said Johnson's excommunication was the result of her public activities, not her personal beliefs. Johnson rejected their explanation and called her trial "an issue of human rights, church and state, and how the church curtails it."

That same month, a Mormon federal court judge in Idaho was appointed to hear a suit by Idaho and Arizona against Congress' 1978 extension of the ERA ratification deadline. The two states also filed suit to allow their legislatures to rescind their approvals of ERA. The appointment of Judge Marion Callister was criticized by the National Organization for Women and other ERA supporters on the ground that Callister's religious beliefs were directly involved in the case and might affect his ability to rule objectively.

The Hartford Courant

Hartford, Conn., December 7, 1979

The Mormon Church's excommunication of Sonia Johnson for her political work on behalf of the Equal Rights Amendment goes far beyond the role distinctions in most religions.

The Mormon Church is not unique in the separate roles it grants men and women in its theology. As in many religions, and secular institutions, women in the Mormon Church do not perform the same work or have the same influence as men.

The Equal Rights Amendment, however, would not affect Mormon religious practice both because of other constitutional guarantees of religious freedom and the aim of the amendment itself: "Equality of rights under the law shall not be denied or abridged by the United States or by any state on account of sex." That applies to government-imposed or government-sanctioned distinctions, not religious belief.

Mrs. Johnson, a fifth generation Mormon, had the gall to lead some Mormon women in support of the ERA. The church leaders have been actively campaigning against the amendment. She and the other Mormon women were engaging in purely private political activity.

Yet, Bishop Jeffrey H. Willis, the judge at the trial which ended in her excommunication, wrote, "Your testimony and public speeches evidence in spirit that you are not in harmony with church doctrine concerning the nature of God and the manner in which He directs his church on earth."

It is ironic that a church, which at one time was politically persecuted, is itself unable to tolerate private, secular political work. Mrs. Johnson, who has refused to repent for her work as church leaders have demanded, remains committed to her religion.

"You don't abandon a good friend just because he does something unethical," she said. Church leaders should exhibit the same tolerance for what they consider to be her disharmony with their interpretation of church doctrine.

St. Petersburg Times

St. Petersburg, Fla., December 9, 1979

With the election of John F. Kennedy, most Americans thought they would never again hear a candidate asked whether he or she would follow, in a conflict, the dictates of conscience over those of church. That was almost 20 years ago.

Sadly, regrettably, Bishop Jeffrey Willis of the Mormon Church has exposed all of his coreligionists who would seek public office to precisely that question, as unfair and offensive as it may be.

In excommunicating Sonia Johnson, the Virginian who has campaigned for ratification of the Equal Rights Amendment (ERA), Willis raises what to many people are some unavoidable questions: Who's next? And for what reason? Could it happen to a public official, or a candidate, as easily as to a private person such as Mrs. Johnson? Considering the terrible consequences Mormons attach to excommunication — they believe it separates families and even spouses in the afterlife — it cannot be dismissed as mere harassment or as an idle threat.

A CAREFUL READING of what church officials have said implies that Mrs. Johnson was excommunicated not simply for supporting the ERA but for attacking the manner in which the men who run the church declared and executed their opposition to the ERA. It's a fine distinction and one that will be lost on most people. To imply that one can address only some aspects of a vital and political question is to be unfair. Mrs. Johnson, it should be noted, had argued in particular that what appeared to be grass-roots opposition to the ERA was in fact organized opposition. It is important to politicians, such as the state legislators who vote on ratification of the ERA, to know with which form they are dealing. By her activities, moreover, Mrs. Johnson demonstrated forcefully that by no means all Mormons oppose the ERA and that many support it.

In other words, was Mrs. Johnson punished not for supporting the ERA but for doing so too effectively? This question must be occurring to the many other Mormons who have worked for the ERA.

THIS IS A nation that separates church from state, so the conduct of the Mormon Church's own affairs, including discipline and admission or exclusion from membership, is in the last analysis a matter only for that church to decide. There is no appeal to the courts or to any legislature. Not even the Equal Rights Amendment, were it a part of the Constitution as it deserves to be, could bear on such a case.

But nothing prevents other Americans from expressing their profound admiration and sympathy for Sonia Johnson's courage and ordeal. Neither does anything prevent them from praying that in their review of her appeal, higher officials of the church will remember what it was that drove their ancestors to leave the East and make their historic trek to the Great Salt Lake.

It was nothing less than persecution . . . the denial of their equal rights under the Constitution of the United States.

Des Moines Tribune
Des Moines, Iowa, December 7, 1979

This is an editorial about two kinds of religious fervor: the kind that expresses itself in Christian love and the kind that expresses itself in ostracism.

On Monday, a Roman Catholic nun, Mother Teresa, will receive the Nobel Prize for Peace. Mother Teresa has spent most of her adult life working among the poorest of the poor in India. For her, religion is a loving force that unites the human race.

That is not the way Sonia Johnson has experienced religion in the last few months. Johnson is a fifth-generation Mormon, a wife and the mother of four. She also is head of a group of Mormons working for ratification of the Equal Rights Amendment, which is opposed by the church.

On Wednesday, she was expelled from the Mormon Church because of her work on behalf of the ERA. She said she was urged to repent, but could not, since "I haven't got anything to repent of. I wish I did, so I could repent."

The Mormons and other church groups have a right to discipline and expel members whose religious views are incompatible with church doctrine. But Johnson was espousing a belief that every human being should accept as a matter of course: that men and women are equal.

She put the matter with eloquence: "Equality was one of the principal messages of Christ." It was the kind of statement Mother Teresa might make about the poor of India. If it violates Mormon teaching to say that men and women are equal in the sight of God, and that they deserve equality under the law, then it's the church that needs to be changed, not Sonia Johnson.

Richmond Times-Dispatch
Richmond, Va., December 22, 1979

A myriad eyes have swelled tearful and red, and a multitude of vocal cords have been painfully stretched over the fate of Mrs. Sonia Johnson, the Fairfax County feminist expelled recently from the Church of Jesus Christ of Latter-Day Saints (Mormon). It is not a reckless guess to suppose that very few of the owners of those distressed eyes and voiceboxes considered Mrs. Johnson's trial and judgment according to their proper criteria, namely the discipline and doctrine of the Mormon Church. The weeping and wailing were not for Mrs. Johnson's soul. The religious controversy served as a foil for a major feminist political demonstration.

The well-publicized Johnson case is only the most recent of several instances in which radical feminists have made organized religious bodies tactical targets in their overall political strategy. In a lawsuit in New York, a plaintiff represented by the American Civil Liberties Union is contesting the "Hyde Amendment" against federal Medicaid spending for elective abortions. The plaintiff argues that, among other things, the legislation sets up an unconstitutional "establishment of religion" because its author, Republican Rep. Henry Hyde, is a practicing Roman Catholic whose views on the morality of abortion presumably have been formed by his religious training.

To uncover evidence of Mr. Hyde's alleged conspiracy against the Bill of Rights, the ACLU sent an agent to follow the congressman to Mass one Sunday. In an affidavit in the lawsuit, the civil libertarians' gumshoe solemnly described Mr. Hyde's participation in the ritual, including his queuing up for Communion. The ACLU also riffled through the correspondence in Mr. Hyde's congressional office and that of North Carolina Sen. Jesse Helms, an antiabortion Baptist (the two legislators had granted permission for this), in an effort to find letters from constituents who oppose abortion on religious grounds. The case is still pending.

This month the National Organization for Women petitioned to intervene in a lawsuit brought by the states of Idaho and Arizona challenging the constitutionality of the bill that extends ratification time for the proposed Equal Rights Amendment. The feminist group is seeking to have the judge in that case, Marion Callister of the Federal District Court in Boise, Idaho, disqualified because he is a regional representative in the hierarchy of the Mormon Church — and the Mormon Church's formal opposition to the ERA is well known. Judge Callister insists that he will rule impartially on the case according to its constitutional merits.

Both the plainly ludicrous campaign against Messrs. Hyde and Helms and the petition concerning Judge Callister are efforts to impinge dangerously on the religious and civil liberties of the men involved. The ACLU's assiduous search for evidence to prove that Messrs. Helms and Hyde are would-be theocrats — going to the point of trailing Mr. Hyde to his place of worship on Sunday — is a mocking contradiction of that organization's celebrated posture as a defender of the privacy of the individual conscience. Leo Pfeffer, a Long Island University constitutional law professor who often has sided with the ACLU and with secularists in religious freedom cases, has called NOW's challenge to Judge Callister "disturbing." Mr. Pfeffer has declared that to disqualify Judge Callister simply because of his religious affiliation would violate the Constitutions's dictum that "no religious test shall ever be required as a qualification to any office or public trust under the United States."

According to the arguments of the feminist lawsuits decribed above, Henry Hyde's fitness as a legislator and Marion Callister's fairness as a judge are presumptively diminished on account of their religious beliefs. That is an attitude that the author of the Bill of Rights, whether or not he would have favored the ERA, clearly would not have countenanced. Wouldn't it give more credibility to those who wish to write more "rights" into the Constitution if they would show that they agree with the protections of religious freedom already existing in the Bill of Rights?

Sentinel Star
Orlando, Fla., December 13, 1979

THE PROPOSED Equal Rights Amendment and the Mormon Church's opposition to it have sparked two related but very different questions. One is a matter for the church alone, but the other steps into the public domain because it embraces the matter of judicial integrity.

In the first case, Mrs. Sonia Johnson was excommunicated by the Mormon Church. The founder of "Mormons for the ERA," Mrs. Johnson said she was ousted from the church she was reared in because of her ERA activism.

For some, Mrs. Johnson's steadfast support and the resulting excommunication mark her as a martyr to the equal rights cause. But the church's wanting to sever her from the fellowship of the organization is its own business.

All churches have a right to make their own interpretations of divine will and to so define the conditions for membership. The Mormons are not denying Mrs. Johnson any of her constitutional rights. One is free to believe anything one wishes, but if one wishes to belong to an organization with a carefully defined set of beliefs as a requirement for membership, one must conform to the requirements.

But the issue is entirely different when those beliefs might reasonably interfere with the neutral setting of the courtroom. And that neutrality is what is being questioned in Boise, Idaho, where U.S. District Judge Marion J. Callister is scheduled to decide whether Congress could legally extend the ratification period for the ERA. Congress voted last year to give states until 1982 to ratify the amendment. It is now three states shy of the 38 necessary to make it part of the Constitution.

Judge Callister is a member of the church's Regional Representatives of the Twelve, which places him among the 100 highest-ranking Mormons. Mrs. Johnson, among others, has questioned whether the judge should remove himself from the case. The question goes right to the integrity of the courts and the public's perception of that integrity.

From the Johnson excommunication, it is apparent how strongly the Mormon hierarchy feels about the ERA. The church has condemned it as encouraging a unisex society, homosexuality and the deterioration of the family. For Judge Callister to rule on this important constitutional question when the church in which he is a leader so harshly criticizes the ERA is to cast dark shadows on the decision-making.

The model code of judicial conduct for the American Bar Association says that a judge should disqualify himself in a case "in which his impartiality might reasonably be questioned." This, certainly, is a case where a reasonable person would question the impartiality. The judge should step aside.

THE ARIZONA REPUBLIC
Phoenix, Ariz., December 20, 1979

THE CLASH between the rights of Sonia Johnson to support the Equal Rights Amendment and the rights of the Mormon Church to discipline her for pro-ERA activities is not, as some may be tempted to believe, a legal issue.

Yet, legal activists and pro-ERA groups are apt to leap into the fight on the side of the Virginia homemaker, hoping to have some court rule that her rights of free speech are being violated.

Such is not the case.

The Mormon Church, not unlike virtually every organized religion, has used the power of its individual doctrines to punish followers for violations of church codes.

As a Mormon, Mrs. Johnson has fully understood those codes and church laws. Her choice, like those of other church followers, is to adhere, to refuse and leave the church, or to disobey and face the consequences.

Mrs. Johnson, a mother of four whose husband supports her ERA activities, has been ordered to appear before a tribunal of the Church of Jesus Christ of Latter-Day Saints on Dec. 1. She faces charges that her ERA activities are harmful to church doctrine.

The worst punishment the church could mete out is excommunication and the least is probation.

The arguments center on whether the Equal Rights Amendment, if ratified, would alter the specific domestic roles of men and women as defined and supported by the Mormon Church, and whether Mrs. Johnson's support of ERA amounts to public repudiation of LDS doctrine.

Obviously such a question would tax the mind of a philosopher.

And just as obviously, the church's decision to force the issue with Mrs. Johnson is apt to create some dissidence within the church, just as the issues of women and homosexual priests and abortion have created schisms within other churches.

Although we oppose ERA on the grounds that it is superfluous and excess legal baggage, we are not prepared to condemn ERA on the grounds that it will absolutely destroy the American family.

Women who insist on being homemakers and mothers will be homemakers and mothers. And women who insist on being working women will be working women.

If the American family is destroyed it will not be because of ERA, but because of relaxed personal codes and social impulses that change the values of men and women, and weaken their obligations to one another.

The case for equality of *opportunity* for both sexes, however, is inarguable. There is not a profession or vocation today in which women are not needed and useful.

Had women, because of some 17th Century reasoning, been denied the right and opportunity to express their skills, the world would have been deprived of distinguished physicians, teachers, financiers, publishers, pilots, industrial executives, and scientists.

For more than 145 years, the Mormon church excluded blacks from priesthood. Now, church doctrine has been revised to admit them.

It's possible that if the case of the church vs. Sonia Johnson is argued and judged intelligently, the Mormon hierarchy may have a new awakening to a woman's harmless rights to work for what she believes are improved personal opportunities. □

The Idaho STATESMAN
Boise, Idaho, December 7, 1979

Had Sonia Johnson voiced her opposition to the Equal Rights Amendment through established anti-ERA organizations, she probably would not be in trouble with her church, the Church of Jesus Christ of Latter-day Saints.

But Johnson formed a group called Mormons for the ERA and took on her church in the political arena, which proved to be her undoing.

Despite the protests of church officials to the contrary, Johnson was excommunicated because of her political activities, and not because of differences with church authorities over religious beliefs or church practices.

That's wrong.

Johnson is — or was — a devout lifelong member of the LDS Church and a fifth-generation Mormon. To church officials, her devotion to her faith should be of more importance than her politics, no matter how she practices them.

Johnson's bishop, Jeff Willis, has maintained that she was not tried by church officials because of her advocacy of the ERA. Rather, her "testimony" and "public speeches" showed that Johnson was "not in harmony with the nature of God and the manner in which he directs his church on Earth," Willis said.

Johnson's "testimony" and "public speeches," however, were made in favor of the ERA. If she had not favored ratification of the ERA, it's doubtful she would have been excommunicated.

Other Mormons support the ERA and have not been before a church court.

But few have made as much noise about their opposition to the church's stand as Johnson has. Few have publicly questioned the church's opposition to the degree that she has. Johnson has traveled around the country carrying a pro-ERA message and arguing against the church's position. She testified at a Senate hearing and got into a debate with Utah Sen. Orrin Hatch, also a Mormon.

Johnson was exercising her right of free speech, a right that apparently isn't recognized by the Mormon Church, which, ostensibly at least, urges its members to take an active interest in civic affairs.

When it took up the cudgel against the ERA, the church entered the political arena, where it has no authority to set the rules.

Johnson's problems with the church stem less from her position in favor of the amendment than from her questioning of the church's opposition.

In the political arena, what's the difference?

The Johnson verdict would seem to indicate that church members can become politically active only as long as they espouse the official church line.

Johnson plans to appeal her excommunication to general church authorities. But it's too late for church officials to fully undo the damage that has been done.

Oregon Journal
Portland, Ore., December 12, 1979

Sonia Johnson may have lost her case before judges of the Church of Jesus Christ of Latter-Day-Saints, but it is equally obvious that the church won nothing in excommunicating her.

Sadly, she said, "I feel as Mormon as ever," as she announced the tribunal's decision, which reached her by letter. Her voice broke a little as she explained she had not had any time to cry. National interest in her disagreement with Virginia church officials over her support of the Equal Rights Amendment had demanded much of her time.

Most American women know their worth these days, whether they work for a paycheck or at home. In the West, particularly, women shared physical hardships side by side with the men — and this is not forgotten. When the Gold Rush lured most of the men in Oregon to California, wives and daughters ran the farms and ranches and held things together until the men returned.

It is not satisfactory to many American women to have personal worth recognized on sufferance. The demeaning attitude of some men toward women, and of some laws toward women, is offensive.

Laws concerned with Social Security are just one example. Passage of ERA is an important step in securing justice for women's financial and legal standing everywhere in America.

Mrs. Johnson's difficulty with the Mormon Church came about because its leaders (all men) are most active in lobbying against ratification of ERA. She objected to their political involvement. They object to hers. It is not a question of "Which came first, the chicken or the egg?"

Had the leadership of the church not moved into the political arena, Mrs. Johnson would have had nothing to criticize. As a sop, they contend that they have no quarrel with equal pay for equal work; they oppose the ERA "because it is vague," and would "strike at the family, the basic institution of society."

Her personal freedom was trammeled by the church over a political matter, not a religious one. Her excommunication is unjust and should be overturned by higher church authorities.

The Des Moines Register
Des Moines, Iowa, December 8, 1979

Sonia Johnson has learned, to her dismay, that she can't be both a feminist and a Mormon. Unwilling to "repent" of her belief in the full equality of men and women, she was excommunicated.

After she was cast out of the Church of Jesus Christ of Latter-Day Saints by a tribunal of men, she vowed to continue campaigning for the Equal Rights Amendment. She upset church leaders when she organized Mormons for ERA and then accused the all-male hierarchy of trying to arouse grassroots opposition to the amendment.

Johnson, a 43-year-old mother of four, said she was formally accused of knowingly advocating false doctrine, hurting the church's missionary effort, and undermining the authority of the church leadership. The presiding bishop at her closed trial in Virginia would only say that Mormon doctrine gives church leaders "a right to deal with their members for disorderly conduct."

This unusual drama furnishes a backdrop for the publication of what is sure to be a controversial book, "The Gnostic Gospels," by Elaine Pagels (see her article on the opposite page). The book draws on ancient documents, discovered in an Egyptian village, describing a community of early Christians who took a different course from that of fellow-believers who are remembered in history as the founders of the Christian church.

The Gnostic community (the name is derived from the Greek word *gnosis*, meaning knowledge) did not require a hierarchy of bishops and priests. The Gnostics thought that God was available to all persons, and that salvation was achieved through self-understanding that acknowledged a relationship with God.

The Gnostics believed in the equality of the sexes: God may have been mother as well as father of the created order; the soul is sexless. Christ, the Gnostics reminded other Christians, counted many women among his companions, of whom Mary Magdalene may have been his closest confidante.

The Gnostic texts show a deep hostility toward her among the apostles, and Pagels points out that her close relationship to Christ was all but erased by the bishops of the early church. The Gnostic community faded out of history, and, as Pagels notes, "It is the winners who write history — their way."

In recent years, ideas the Gnostics would have found compatible with their beliefs have been accommodated in some of the major denominations, but that is small comfort to Sonia Johnson, ex-Mormon. For many women (and male sympathizers), she will be a symbol of unfulfilled hopes for those who cling to the egalitarian context of the original Gospels.

BUFFALO EVENING NEWS
Buffalo, N.Y., December 8, 1979

If the punishment visited upon Sonia Johnson for her outspoken support of the Equal Rights Amendment were being decreed by any branch of government instead of by her own church, we would certainly have no hesitancy about springing to the defense of her right of free speech.

It is just because of the famous wall of separation between church and state, however, that a church's right to expel one of its own members from its flock is no more subject to proper scrutiny by outsiders than is the member's own right to defy the ecclesiastical authorities in any non-violent way she may wish. Both rights are deeply rooted in the same First Amendment.

For Mrs. Johnson, a fifth-generation Mormon, there is no doubt that the harsh penalty of excommunication is a bitter pill to swallow. Avowedly torn between her desire to stay in the church and her determination to speak out for the ERA and against her church's involvement in the campaign against it, she had hoped to have it both ways. And in fact she had made a strong case that her faith and acceptance of Mormon religious doctrine were as strong as ever, but that it was only against the church's delving into the political arena that she dissented.

But the church hierarchy obviously took a sterner view and excommunicated her — not, it insisted, for her stand on ERA, but for "knowingly" preaching false church doctrine, for hurting the church's missionary work, and for undermining church leaders by portraying them as woman-haters.

So Sonia Johnson has lost her battle to continue her pro-ERA campaign from within the Mormon Church. But whether in the end she will have won the war, by converting her excommunication into an effective mantle of martyrdom in the feminist cause, is another matter. Certainly this one highly-publicized incident, in which the Mormon hierarchy finds itself publicly on the defensive against one woman's cry of "misogyny" (woman-hating), has suddenly injected more life into the drive for ERA ratification than anything else that's happened to that seemingly moribund movement all year.

The Chattanooga Times
Chattanooga, Tenn., December 8, 1979

The decision of the Mormon Church to excommunicate Sonia Johnson, an enthusiastic and often outspoken supporter of the Equal Rights Amendment, strikes us as unduly harsh, especially in the light of the Church's seemingly contradictory explanations for the action. The decision has naturally dismayed Mrs. Johnson, a fifth-generation Mormon, who will appeal the ruling to a higher church court.

Granted, Mrs. Johnson didn't help her cause by stating at past pro-ERA rallies, according to the letter from the Mormon bishop who excommunicated her, that "our society, specifically including church leaders, has a 'savage misogyny' . . ." Her offer to repent for using "stronger rhetoric than necessary" was rejected by the church.

The Mormon hierarchy's opposition to the ERA is based on its judgment that "it is so broad that it would be left to the federal judiciary to decide what it means," as one church spokesman put it; of course, that is the judiciary's job for any aspect of the Constitution. But in the excommunication letter delivered to her, Bishop Jeffrey Willis wrote that she was "'not in harmony with church doctrine concerning the nature of God in the manner in which he directs His Church on earth."

The question, it seems to us, is whether the church considers the ERA to be a political or a doctrinal issue. In excommunicating Mrs. Jones, the bishop seems to have translated the church's opposition to the ERA (because of its allegedly harmful political side-effects) into a doctrinal matter by equating her approval of the amendment with absolute rejection of basic truths the church espouses.

Reasonable persons will not object if the latter is the case because a church can jeopardize its credibility and viability if its members consider its fundamental doctrines to be irrelevant. That doesn't seem to be the case with Mrs. Johnson, who apparently sees the ERA as merely a political way for women to achieve legal equality. Perhaps when her case is appealed, higher church courts will resolve this apparent anomaly.

The Detroit News
Detroit, Mich., December 19, 1979

The Mormon Church and the supporters of the Equal Rights Amendment are joined in bitter battle.

The remarks by well-known Mormon and former Michigan Gov. George Romney require little comment. In saying that the ERA movement is a haven for "moral perverts," Mr. Romney tells us more about himself than he probably wants us to know.

ERA advocates have meanwhile made a *cause celebre* out of the Mormon Church's excommunication of Sonia Johnson, who actively campaigned for the amendment and criticized the church's leaders and its political lobbying efforts against it.

But these incidents are only the periphery of the storm. At the center is a far more important issue: Can a federal judge who is a high-ranking official of the Mormon Church — given his church's strong anti-ERA bias — fairly decide a case involving the ERA?

The jurist is District Court Judge Marion Callister, and the case is a lawsuit brought by the states of Idaho and Arizona to challenge the constitutionality of extending the ERA deadline for ratification. The result, is vitally important to feminists because the extension was meant to win time for passage, and an anti-extension opinion from Judge Callister, even if successfully appealed, would use up crucial time.

Clearly, it would be a grievous error to assume that a judge's religious beliefs render him incapable of impartiality. Groups such as the American Jewish Congress rightly worry: "If a Mormon can't hear an ERA case, can a Catholic hear an abortion case, a Christian Scientist a medical case . . . ?" The U.S. Constitution stresses that no religious test is required of those holding public office.

Judge Callister, however, is not just a member of the Mormon Church. He is the equivalent of an archbishop of that church, one of 100 regional representatives who instruct local congregations in church doctrine.

It is natural to wonder, given the Mormon Church's outspoken anti-ERA position, whether Judge Callister will be torn between a duty to the law and a duty to the church in which he is a leader. The Justice Department is concerned enough about the possible conflict to ask the jurist to disqualify himself. Judge Callister has refused.

The issue has become embroiled in presidential politics. ERA supporters have been pushing President Carter to urge the Justice Department to appeal the judge's decision not to withdraw. Anger at Mr. Carter's refusal is one reason the National Organization for Women has withdrawn its support for his reelection.

While it is difficult to know what President Carter should do in this tangle of religion, justice, and politics, it is easy to see what wisdom and judiciousness demand of Judge Callister.

He should step aside.

THE PLAIN DEALER
Cleveland, Ohio, December 10, 1979

Sonia Johnson, a Mormon feminist, was excommunicated. She had been charged with preaching false doctrine. Mrs. Johnson said it was the church involvement in politics, not church doctrine, that was the cause. She said she had opposed the Mormon church's campaign against the Equal Rights Amendment.

The church appears to be within its right to conduct its affairs as it sees fit. Yet the description of her religious trial leaves a sense that it was less than fair, especially in comparison to modern secular trial safeguards, and that it is of public concern.

What has made the excommunication trial appear a public issue rather than solely a church issue was the church's involvement in opposing the Equal Rights Amendment and the public's perception of the element of politics, not religion, playing a key role.

Rep. Mary Rose Oakar, D-20, heightened this perception of religion and politics by raising this disturbing question: Can a federal judge who is a Mormon church officer rule fairly from the bench on the Equal Rights Amendment for women when the church has opposed the amendment?

She was questioning the impartiality of U.S. District Judge Marion Callister of Idaho after his refusal to drop out of a pending lawsuit which objects to the extension of time Congress allowed for ratifying the amendment.

We have no doubt that Callister has the capacity to be impartial and judge the issue on its legal merits. And we have no doubt that the appeals process has the capacity to correct whatever biasing error might creep into the case, no matter which judge presides over it.

Yet the underlying question Oakar raised is serious. It implies a challenge to the concept that the separation of church and state is workable. We believe separation is and should be possible, as required in the basic American social compact, the Constitution.

The Boston Globe
Boston, Mass., December 5, 1979

Sonia Johnson is a Mormon who supports the Equal Rights Amendment. The description is simple enough and yet it presents an elementary, if painfully clear, conflict of interest for the 43-year old Virginia woman and others like her.

On Saturday night Johnson stood trial before a three-man church tribunal on charges that that she had spread false doctrine by making pro-ERA speeches in Utah, Nevada, Arizona and Florida, states where Mormons have orchestrated successful anti-ERA lobbying efforts. Mormons say they aren't opposed to equal rights for women; they are simply opposed to the amendment that would guarantee them. Johnson doesn't buy this distinction and she may be excommunicated as a result.

Her dilemma dramatizes one that many men and women have lived in recent years as they've been pushed to weigh their own beliefs against the sometimes contradictory tenets of their religions. But, while the tribunal's verdict, expected any day now, is strictly church business, there's something at stake for all of us in a less private conflict of interest case that has surfaced in conjunction with the Sonia Johnson story.

Last August the Justice Department asked Marion Callister, a federal judge in the US District Court in Boise, Idaho, to disqualify himself from hearing a suit that challenges the constitutionality of Congress' extension of the deadline for ERA ratification. The case also involves the question of whether states that have already voted to ratify the amendment can vote again to rescind ratification. Callister, a member of the Mormon hierarchy, refused to disqualify himself in October despite the church's well delineated position on both questions. And the issue was dropped.

The Justice Department could have asked the circuit court of appeals to order that Judge Callister be removed from the proceedings. In fact it still can. That would certainly make more sense than having the National Organization for Women do the government's legal work. NOW announced on Monday that it will file an appeal with the 9th US Circuit Court of Appeals in San Francisco because the Administration has been lax in pursuing the question.

Even if Judge Callister were capable of separating his personal beliefs from the legal questions before him, his presence in the courtroom would certainly color, and possibly distort, the proceedings. And supposing Callister found in favor of the ERA? Would he then find himself in the same untenable position as Sonia Johnson? Would he face a reprimand or punishment from his church? For justice's sake and for his sake, the Justice Department should move quickly to see that Judge Callister is disqualified.

Pittsburgh Post-Gazette

Pittsburgh, Pa., December 21, 1979

Although the First Amendment's warning against the "establishment" of religion is explicitly directed only at Congress, it is settled law that the judicial branch of government should also steer clear of religious entanglements. But what constitutes such an unconstitutional entanglement? And at what point do efforts to keep court and church separate violate another provision of the First Amendment guaranteeing the "free exercise" of religion?

Those questions recently were plucked from abstraction by the National Organization of Women. NOW, with some support from the U.S. Justice Department, has been seeking to disqualify a Mormon federal judge from hearing a legal challenge to Congress' extension of the ratification deadline for the Equal Rights Amendment. Its argument, which has been echoed on this page by columnist Ellen Goodman, is that Judge Marion Callister's prominent role in a church that opposes the ERA constitutes at least an apparent conflict of interest. Arguing that the judge occupies a position equivalent to that of an archbishop, Ms. Goodman wondered: "Can the same man who has been part of one decision for the church have an open mind for the state?"

In the absence of proof that Judge Callister is disposed to mix Mormon theology with his legal interpretations, that question is mischievous — and so is the underlying assumption, that judges who lead active religious lives are incapable of objectivity in cases with religious overtones. Arguing for such a connection, Ms. Goodman cited the book "The Brethren," which, she says, shows that "judges are human, products of their own pasts and prejudices." But in the only incident from that book that is relevant to her argument, Justice William Brennan, a Catholic, is shown voting in favor of liberalized abortion despite the position of his church.

There is really no evidence that other judges, including Judge Callister, are incapable of a similar objectivity. And that is fortunate, for — as a respected civil liberties lawyer pointed out recently in a letter to The New York Times — the application of NOW's reasoning across the board could paralyze the judiciary. Catholic judges would be barred from hearing cases about aid to parochial schools, Jewish judges would be prohibited from deciding the constitutionality of Sunday-closing laws, conservative Protestant judges would be suspect where the issue was the teaching of evolution, and so on.

So far nothing about the Callister controversy justifies starting down that slippery slope.

Newsday

*Long Island, N.Y.,
December 8, 1979*

Can a prominent official in the Mormon Church be an impartial judge in a case that involves the Equal Rights Amendment? Here's why it matters:

A Mormon woman in Virginia has just been tried and excommunicated by the church for "spreading false doctrine" in connection with the ERA. The church vigorously opposes the amendment, and the excommunicated woman, Sonia Johnson, strongly believes the church is wrong.

Meanwhile, a suit to nullify the 30-month extension of the ratification period for the ERA is before U.S. District Judge Marion Callister, a regional representative of the Mormon Church in Idaho. Without the extension the ERA is dead, because it wasn't ratified by the necessary 38 state legislatures during the original seven-year period.

The Justice Department asked Judge Callister to disqualify himself. He refused, and this week the National Organization for Women filed an appeal seeking to disqualify him. On Thursday, eight House members urged the Justice Department to appeal, too.

According to Mormon beliefs, Sonia Johnson's excommunication will exclude her from heaven and eternal life. Surely it's not farfetched to believe that such a prospect might color the thinking of a high-ranking Mormon who also happens to be a federal judge. For his own sake and for the sake of fairness, Callister ought to remove himself from the ERA case.

The Kansas City Times

Kansas City, Mo., December 12, 1979

Mrs. Sonia Johnson, a Mormon and a committed feminist, was excommunicated last week from the church of her family for five generations. Sonia Johnson knew what she was doing when she opposed the leaders of the Mormon Church and was excommunicated by Bishop Jeffrey Willis, the same man who brought charges against her. She is convinced she did the right thing.

Mormon Church spokesmen say the decision against Mrs. Johnson needn't worry Mormons who support ratification of the Equal Rights Amendment; that she was expelled because she attacked the church hierarchy.

Now Judge Marion Callister of the federal district court in Boise, Idaho, also a dedicated Mormon and a lay leader for 12,000 persons, has refused to disqualify himself from hearing a case intended to kill the ERA drive in its tracks. The Johnson decision raises the question in the public's mind: Can Judge Callister weigh the case and rule impartially?

This is no everyday excommunication, and the case before Callister's court promises to be no ordinary case. Churches throughout American history have appealed to members to act politically at the ballot box and in petition and letter-writing campaigns. In the latest example, the Mormon Church comes forth as a persuasive and powerful force in a bloc of Western states where the battle over the ERA is under way. This is for historic reasons, but the ERA, like a handful of issues we know, has focused public attention on the influence a religion can have over political questions. Nothing improper in that. But the people should be aware of the origin of such opposition and the dogma behind it. In some states with high Mormon populations — Utah, Idaho, Montana, Arizona — the influence of the Mormon Church is considerable.

Perhaps Judge Callister can weigh the merits pro and con the ERA ratification extension to the satisfaction of all parties, but it seems highly unlikely. Regardless of his approach, it will be difficult for him to convey the appearance of justice in a decision for or against the ERA. That's because his church is deeply involved in opposing the issue before him and he is deeply involved in his church, as is his right. But he also should remove all possible doubt on this important case by taking it off his docket. In this case, unlike Mrs. Johnson's situation, Judge Callister does not sit in an ecclesiastical court. His decision would concern not just the doctrine of his church, but the entire nation, and in a political matter.

The Philadelphia Inquirer

Philadelphia, Pa., December 11, 1979

Should a judge who happens also to be a high official in an organization be allowed to rule on an issue in which that organization has taken an active political interest? When the organization is a church, the question assumes particular constitutional complexity, raising ticklish matters of religious freedom and judicial integrity.

A case of national importance now before a federal district court in Idaho poses the question. The case, brought against the federal government by the states of Idaho and Arizona, challenges the extension of time for consideration of the Equal Rights Amendment and seeks validation of a state's right to rescind prior approval of the ERA. The district court judge charged with ruling in the case, Marion J. Callister, is a high official of the Mormon Church, which opposes the ERA and the extension of time for its consideration voted by Congress last year. The church supports rescission.

Judge Callister ought to have removed himself from this case, given his high position in the Mormon Church and the church's opposition to the ERA. He did not. In fact he rejected a Justice Department motion that he disqualify himself. Following that rejection in early October, the Justice Department decided not to press further the matter of disqualification. That decision is misguided: The Justice Department should appeal to the Cir-

cuit Court of Appeals Judge Callister's decision not to disqualify himself.

If Judge Callister were simply a member of the Mormon Church, his position as judge in the ERA case would not be of such concern. The church has claimed that its members are free to support or oppose the ERA, though the excommunication last week of Sonia Johnson for her outspoken support of the amendment tends to call that assertion into question; but the church hierarchy has mustered its considerable political strength, especially in states in the West, to oppose the ERA.

Judge Callister is a member of that hierarchy, and whatever his personal views on the ERA, whatever his personal ability to judge the questions before him simply on the basis of law, his membership in that hierarchy at the very least creates a situation where his impartiality can legitimately be questioned.

To set a precedent whereby an individual judge's private religious beliefs could be used to disqualify him from a case would be a grievous mistake. However, the Mormon Church's active opposition to the ERA coupled with Judge Callister's position of leadership in that church make this a special case. The Justice Department should appeal the judge's decision that he should rule on the questions of the ERA extension and states' rescissions.

Minneapolis **Tribune**

Minneapolis, Minn., December 27, 1979

The National Organization for Women is right to seek to disqualify an Idaho federal judge in a case involving the Equal Rights Amendment — George F. Will to the contrary notwithstanding. The judge is a high-ranking official of the Mormon Church, and the case is over the legality of the time extension for ratifying the ERA. Will, in a column on this page Monday, contended that seeking to remove the judge from the case because he is a Mormon violates the constitutional guarantee that "no religious test shall ever be required as a qualification to any office of public trust under the United States."

Will missed the point. It would indeed be wrong to argue that the judge may not serve on the bench because he is a Mormon; that would violate the constitutional provision barring religious tests for public office. But no one is making such an argument. NOW's point is that the judge should be disqualified from deciding one particular case because the church he serves in a policy-making capacity has taken an official stand on the case's central issue.

That same argument was made by the U.S. Department of Justice, which initiated the effort to disqualify the judge. The judge's personal views might lead a reasonable person to question his ability to decide the case impartially, the department argued. In such circumstances, the appearance of impartiality is as important as the fact of impartiality.

Judges are often disqualified from hearing particular cases because of personal conflicts of interest. Many, perceiving the need to preserve the credibility of the courts, step aside voluntarily rather than risk even the appearance of judicial bias. Since the Idaho judge failed to do so, NOW and the Justice Department are right to try to force him off the case. Will is wrong to raise a false constitutional objection to a procedure that is not only common, but necessary to maintain the reputation of the judicial system.

The San Diego Union

San Diego, Calif., December 11, 1979

It is wrong, we think, that an important court test of the constitutional amendment process should become politicized over a judge's religious convictions. But that is precisely what is happening in Boise, where a federal judge is being asked to decide if the state of Idaho can revoke its ratification of the Equal Rights Amendment.

Federal District Judge Marion J. Callister, presiding, is a member of the Mormon Church. The church is officially opposed to the Equal Rights Amendment which it believes will undermine the foundations of the family, and the ERA proponents are charging that Judge Callister's religious convictions are in conflict with his judicial duties in this case.

Judge Callister says they are not. In the absence of some compelling evidence to the contrary, that should settle the matter. It is well understood that ethics of the legal profession require a judge either to set aside personal interests and personal philosophy or to step aside. Judge Callister has decided he can try the case without prejudice, and the solicitor general, who is defending the action of Congress, has taken him at his word.

However, the National Organization for Women has apparently been stampeded by the unrelated excommunication of Mormon feminist Sonia Johnson into petitioning the Ninth Circuit Court of Appeals to give it the status to seek removal of Judge Callister. Unfortunately, this ac-

tion adds weight to the political pressures being applied to the Justice Department by congressmen and other ERA proponents to act against a judge whose conduct, insofar as it has been demonstrated, has been irreproachable in this case and previously.

The unwisdom of such attempts to influence a judicial proceeding has been recognized by the American Jewish Congress, which also supports ERA. Its president, Nathan Dershowitz, said: "We reject as a matter of principle any assumption that a judge's membership, or even leadership in a particular religious group by itself, renders him incapable of deciding any case in accordance with the law and facts." We agree.

"New Right" Backlash Threatens ERA

The drive to ratify the Equal Rights Amendment slowed to a virtual halt in the late 1970s. By the time the amendment's backers had obtained an unprecedented three-year extension of the ratification deadline, it was not certain that even the extra time would help. Equal rights for women became as emotional an issue for the "New Right" as abortion. The ERA issue was a focus for women who resented the course of the feminist movement during the 1960s and 1970s. They objected to what they saw as the anti-housewife and anit-motherhood bias of the women's movement. Religious leaders who opposed the amendment were convinced that it would perpetuate the recent changes in American social patterns, such as the rising divorce rate and looser sexual standards. The ERA issue was made to stand for all that was labeled "immoral" about the women's movement. The drive to defeat the movement gathered momentum with surprising speed and intensity, indicating that its leaders had touched a raw public nerve. The amendment needed only three more states to reach the 38 required for ratification, but the months and years went by with no additions to the list. By the beginning of the 1980s, even some of ERA's most ardent supporters had begun to admit that the amendment was doomed.

The Hartford Courant

Hartford, Conn., May 18, 1980

You wouldn't think that a nation that for several centuries now has been committed to the principle of equality and justice for all would find it so difficult to pass a constitutional amendment securing the equality of more than half the population.

But the nation does find it difficult. The future of the Equal Rights Amendment, banning discrimination on the basis of sex, is now in the balance in Illinois. The General Assembly is about to vote on ratification of the amendment, and it's still too close to call.

If the amendment fails there, it may very well fail nationally. Three more states must pass the amendment by June 1982 if it is to become a part of the U.S. Constitution. Approval in Illinois could give the stalled ratification drive just the impetus it needs to get over the top. The campaign may not be able to survive another major defeat.

The ERA is depicted by its opponents as a symbol of social disintegration in America, harkening in an era of unisex bathrooms, homosexual marriages, abortions for all and the breakup of families.

In their predictions of impending chaos, opponents of the ERA closely resemble the advocates of divine-right monarchies before the revolutions in France and the United States. The world was carefully ordered, they thought, and if such radical ideas as democracy and equality were allowed to take hold, well, then, the entire social fabric would be ripped to shreds.

We see the proponents of divine-right monarchy as anachronisms now. We know that equality is not something to be feared. We know that it forms the basis of a free society, and that a free society is better than an oppressive one.

Don't we?

Richmond Times-Dispatch

Richmond, Va., September 19, 1980

Although the Equal Rights Amendment proposal will remain technically alive until June 30, 1982, Professor Andrew Hacker of Queens College, New York City, provides a post-mortem in the September issue of *Harper's* magazine.

His conclusion: Women, not men, killed ERA. And the main force of the opposition consisted of housewives.

True, most of the legislators are men in the 15 states that have not ratified the amendment and in the five which have voted to rescind earlier ratifications. But they acted, Professor Hacker declares, on the basis of their mail and other evidences of strong opposition to the proposal.

Professor Hacker's analysis of ERA's defeat runs this way:

Women saw ERA — at least as it was interpreted by its militant proponents — as threatening the family by downgrading the role of the housewife.

"This country still has many millions of women for whom caring for a home has been their lifetime calling. Moreover, most of them remember when the vocation of housewife was an honored estate. Some are old enough to recall when on radio or television a woman was asked her occupation, if she answered 'housewife' the rafters rang with applause.

"It does little good to tell these women that remaining at home is still a respectable option. They know the esteem is no longer there. Now, when asked what they do, they find themselves saying 'just a housewife' in apologetic tones. And from this grows an edge of anger over being made to feel outmoded."

Aspects of the women's "liberation" movement have tended to eliminate the moral and cultural pressures that kept marriages intact. "Men may have stayed married out of duty, but at least they stayed. It is in this sense that the ERA atmosphere threatens family life. Moral obligations that once bound partners cannot be replaced by provisos and demands."

Professor Hacker, it seems to us, has put his finger on a major cause of ERA's demise. True, the two dozen words of the amendment, isolated, seem relatively simple and hardly posing a threat to anyone. But their potential consequences, when applied in the everyday world in which most Americans live and want to continue to live, take on an ominous shading. The women's movement of recent years has brought needed reforms and has served to remove some of the injustices, particularly in the business world, that women suffered. But intentionally or not, the movement has tended to belittle the vitally important and traditionally respected role of the woman who is the homemaker. And the number of women — and men — who don't welcome this new attitude is large enough, when combined with persons who oppose ERA for other reasons, to keep the amendment from becoming a part of the U.S. Constitution.

The Detroit News

Detroit, Mich., April 7, 1980

Michigan Chief Justice Mary Coleman has called for a state constitutional amendment similar to the federal equal rights amendment (ERA) that still hasn't been adopted.

Michigan would seem to be a likely place for a state equal rights campaign: It ratified the federal ERA in 1972, and three efforts to rescind have since failed. But while a state ERA deserves support, it can only complement — not substitute — for a federal constitutional amendment. A state by state approach by itself would result in unfair variations; the status of women in Michigan would end up very different from that of women in a more conservative state like Utah. And state lines shouldn't be allowed to determine whether American citizens enjoy protection of basic rights.

Unfortunately, a Michigan equal rights campaign will probably revive the misguided criticisms that have stymied ERA proponents nationally. Now may be a good time — in the support of both a U.S. and state constitutional amendment — to answer some of the doubts aroused by ERA opponents. For example:

● Does the 14th Amendment provide legal equality for women? Are federal and state ERA's redundant?

The U.S. Supreme Court has rarely applied the 14th Amendment to sex discrimination cases. For example, women who claimed the right to vote under the 14th Amendment were rebuffed and did not gain suffrage until the passage of the 19th Amendment.

A constitutional amendment would not only address many sexually discriminatory laws now on the books — in such areas as insurance, credit, pensions, prison sentences, taxation, and Social Security — but also would prevent the future enactment of discriminatory laws.

● Will housewives lose their rights to support and Social Security?

Present laws do not require a husband to support his wife unless he wants to, at least as long as the couple stays married. In the case of divorce, an equal rights amendment's intent is not to abolish support of dependent wives and children, but rather to have laws base support obligations on the ability to pay instead of sex. ERA supporters can only assume that responsible state legislators will choose the ability-to-pay route.

Many changes in family relations have already been enacted in Michigan, without the dire consequences that ERA opponents predict. State divorce and alimony laws were changed in 1970 to eliminate sex discrimination: Either partner may be awarded alimony, and women do not have an automatic right to alimony, although they may request it. In addition, 1972 state child-custody and support laws make the interest of the child rather than the parent's sex the most important consideration in awarding custody (although single fathers may complain that tradition biases the court in the mother's favor). Non-custodial parents, regardless of sex, also may be asked to pay child support.

Further, a national ERA would not take away rights to a spouse's Social Security benefits, but would probably cause changes along the lines of recent court decisions giving husbands and widowers the same rights that female spouses enjoy.

● Will constitutional guarantees against sex discrimination put an end to single-sex schools and athletic teams?

State and national ERA's do intend to end the existence of publicly supported schools in which better facilities are available only to men. Private schools would not be affected.

● How about unisex toilets?

The U.S. Constitution protects the right of privacy. Equal rights amendments would have no effect on the privacy of personal functions, a fact established by various court cases.

● Does ratification of a federal ERA mean that women will be drafted?

President Carter recently requested that Congress pass legislation allowing the draft registration of women. He did not need the ERA to do it. Congress has always had the power to draft women and was in the process of enacting a bill to draft nurses when World War II ended. Women, like men, could be exempted for reasons of family responsibilities, and women draftees would not necessarily be in the front lines. Only 1 percent of military personnel ever sees combat.

● Will a state or national ERA legalize homosexual marriage and abortion?

The word "sex" in the ERA language refers to sexual discrimination based on gender not sexual acts or preferences. Abortion and homosexuality are single-sex issues, not matters involving sex discrimination.

These arguments have been repeated many times, but the amazing vigor of anti-ERA contentions derives from fear rather than fact.

The passage of a Michigan version of the ERA would be, as Justice Coleman says, of "symbolic" importance in proving the state's continued commitment to equal rights. But it should not detract from the real goal: guaranteeing equal rights for all American women.

Chicago Tribune

Chicago, Ill., June 21, 1980

If the Equal Rights Amendment fails, it will not be because there is any noticeable merit to the arguments against it. It will simply be because voters and legislators are getting sick of the spectacle which is put on by supporters and opponents of ERA alike whenever the issue comes up, and which makes a mockery of our legislative process.

This is nowhere better demonstrated than in the latest effort to get the measure through the Illinois House, which failed on Wednesday. There was the usual flurry of phone calls from the President, the governor, and the mayor of Chicago promising who-knows-what goodies in exchange for votes for ERA [the action was recently enlivened by several charges of actual bribery attempts]. There were confident assurances that the necessary 107 votes were in hand, and then there were last minute defections.

There were parades and demonstrations by chanting supporters of ERA [in green] and opponents [in red]. And there were impromptu press conferences at which the same old bromides were offered as arguments for or against the measure. [One 10-year-old boy carrying a "Stop-ERA" sign solemnly offered his opinion of ERA backers to anybody who was interested: "They kill babies."]

The truth of the matter is that there are no really solid arguments either for or against the amendment and that if adopted it is not likely to have much effect on life as it is lived. Most states, including Illinois, already have equal rights provisions on the books. If there are absurdities to be perpetrated in the name of equal rights, the opportunity already exists [see the next editorial].

The reasons we think ERA still deserves support are that it has come to be regarded a symbol of America's attitude toward women; that we demean ourselves in our own eyes and the eyes of the world by paying serious attention to the arguments against it; and that despite what opponents say, it has the support [if increasingly jaded] of most Americans—as well as most members of the Illinois House, which voted 102 to 71 in favor of it. Illinois requires a three-fifths majority, however, for passage.

The prospects for ERA are hardly auspicious. Thirty-five of the necessary 38 states have ratified it, but four have rescinded their approval. Not one state has acted since 1978, when Congress extended for three years the 1979 deadline for ratification. But Illinois is the only industrial state not to have ratified ERA and its approval is considered essential if others are to follow suit.

ERA will come up again in Springfield — though perhaps not until next year. When it does, we hope legislators will ask themselves whether they want Illinois to be blamed for the defeat of a measure which assures equal rights to women—even if its effect is mainly symbolic.

The Des Moines Register

Des Moines, Iowa, October 14, 1980

Some backers of the proposed Iowa Equal Rights Amendment are concerned about the stress being put on the charge by ERA critics that the amendment would pave the way for homosexual marriages. Not to worry. The charge is patently false and frivolous. If that's the chief argument against the ERA — and it seems to be — Iowa voters should have no difficulty seeing through it.

The amendment would prohibit unequal treatment on account of "gender." Opponents of the ERA have latched onto that word and have read a sinister pro-homosexual meaning into it. Never mind that there is not a shred of credible legislative history to lend support to the fear of legalized homosexual marriage. No court cases or experiences in other states support the contention that backing for the ERA equates with backing for same-sex marriage.

No one can issue an iron-clad guarantee about what courts will do. That's what makes the homosexual-marriage argument frustrating to combat. The ERA critics say that courts *might* interpret the amendment to favor homosexual marriage. A judge might declare that the Earth is flat, but the odds are overwhelmingly against it. In any case, if the far-fetched ever came to pass, the Legislature could revise the amendment if that's what voters wanted.

The addition of an Equal Rights Amendment to the Iowa Constitution would mark an important milestone for this state, which has a long tradition of respect for the rights of individuals. The amendment deserves thoughtful discussion. It deserves better than the baseless scare talk it has been getting about the specter of homosexual marriage.

SEX DISCRIMINATION:
Schlafly Denies Sex Harassment Problem for "Virtuous" Woman

Phyllis Schlafly, leader of the anti-Equal Rights Amendment group, Eagle Forum, told the Senate Labor Committee April 21 that "sexual harassment on the job is not a problem for the virtuous woman, except in the rarest of cases." "When a woman walks across the room," Schlafly continued, "she speaks with a universal body language that most men intuitively understand. Men hardly ever ask sexual favors of women from whom the certain answer is 'no'." Her statements were made in hearings on legislation to protect women from sexual harassment in the workplace. In support of the legislation, Eleanor Holmes Norton, former head of the Equal Employment Opportunity Commission, asserted that women were entitled to legal protection from demands for sex by supervisors or colleagues, from sexual remarks and from uninvited sexual contact. EEOC guidelines adopted in 1980 held an employer responsible if subordinate personnel were found guilty of sexual harassment. Women also were entitled to be reinstated with back pay if a court ruled that they had lost their jobs for refusing to grant sexual favors. An EEOC official added that the agency was studying 118 complaints of sexual harassment.

Rocky Mountain News
Denver, Colo., April 30, 1981

MEN seldom make passes at virtuous lasses.

This updating of Dorothy Parker's famous crack about girls who wear glasses came to mind as we read Phyllis Schlafly's remarks before a Senate committee looking into the problem of sexual harassment of women in the workplace.

Mrs. Schlafly, who someone has described as the nation's leading 19th-century spokeswoman, told the committee that "men hardly ever ask sexual favors of women from whom the certain answer is, 'No.'"

If what both Mrs. Schlafly and Dorothy Parker said were universally true, primness and pince-nez would be all the protection a working woman would need.

Unfortunately, countless innocent victims of sexual aggression from co-workers and bosses know it just ain't so.

THE PLAIN DEALER
Cleveland, Ohio, April 23, 1981

Even for Phyllis Schlafly, her remarks before the Senate Labor Committee recently were outrageous and we suspect that she knows they were. She went to extremes to express her hostility toward laws to protect women from sexual harassment in the workplace, and we can't believe she really meant what she said.

The virtuous woman, Schlafly said, rarely is harassed. By way of clarification, she offered: "When a woman walks across the room, she speaks with a universal body language that most men intuitively understand. Men hardly ever ask sexual favors of women from whom the certain answer is 'no.' "

Well, now, horsefeathers. It is not so much that men might hesitate to chance their luck with some women. But to suggest that a woman's defense is all that simple smacks of naivete or careless disregard of the truth.

Schlafly is, of course, a foe of feminism and even her opponents sometimes get loose with the facts. It is silly, even mischievous, to pretend that the proliferation of women, not to mention blacks and other minorities, in the workplace has not created tensions. In the case of women, sexuality must be considered a problem, not only for their male bosses if that is the situation, but for the women as well.

One expert in the expanding field of counseling business and industry in the art of handling race and sex relations says that there are three well-defined categories of problem for women and, by extension, men at work. They are sexism, expressed by men toward women; sexuality on the part of both; and harassment of women by men, often in the form of demands for sexual favors in exchange for job benefits. The male who is spurned can create an unlivable atmosphere for the woman.

The same expert attests that it is not easy for men to adjust to changing conditions at work. Often top management leaves such problems to subordinates who are ill prepared to handle them. That is why independent consultants are playing a bigger role helping companies train managerial staff to deal with such difficulties.

Schlafly falls back on mythology in her zeal to boot protective legislation out the window. She seems to contend that the woman, and the woman alone, invites her situation. Not so. Last year the Equal Employment Opportunity Commission, perhaps especially embarrassed by reports of sexual harassment within the federal bureaucracy itself, established guidelines to spare women such ordeals — or give them redress. We endorsed the guidelines then. We repeat our stand in the face of Schlafly's unthoughtful attack on them.

Detroit Free Press
Detroit, Mich., April 23, 1981

PHYLLIS Schlafly says "virtuous women" don't suffer sexual harassment at work, and no doubt she believes it. Almost by definition, Mrs. Schlafly's virtuous women are in the kitchen where they cannot be harassed by anyone except, she complains, "feminists and their federal government allies" pushing them to go out and get a job.

We don't make light of virtue — heaven knows the world needs all it can get — nor of women who find security and fulfillment within the home. But sexual harassment in the workplace has been amply documented. It might be reduced if "virtuous men" would keep their hands and their suggestions to themselves — but we haven't heard Mrs. Schlafly offering that as a solution. And if the Equal Rights Amendment, which Mrs. Schlafly so vigorously opposes, had been in effect years ago, working women would not be so heavily concentrated in subordinate ranks where — virtuous or otherwise — they are much more vulnerable to harassment of any kind.

But the worst aspect of Mrs. Schlafly's remarks is the injustice they do to women who have suffered real humiliation and injury. Over the years too many people — police agencies, juries, employers — have been too quick to conclude that if women get what they ask for, as Mrs. Schlafly suggests, then whatever they get, they must deserve — be it rape, harassment, ugly propositions or whatever. It's the same shoulder-shrugging logic every injured minority group has battled; it absolves us far too easily of the responsibility to correct real wrongs. Personal virtue is much to be desired, Mrs. Schiafly, but in an imperfect world it is no substitute for clearly enforced legal rights.

DAYTON DAILY NEWS
Dayton, Ohio, April 28, 1981

Phyllis Schlafly, president of Eagle Forum and most voluble foe of the Equal Rights Amendment, is doing her usual and often *non sequitur* thing at a Senate Labor subcommittee inquiry into on-the-job sexual harassment.

"The most cruel and damaging" sexual harassment, Mrs. Schlafly informs the senators, is that of "feminists and their federal government allies against the role of motherhood and the role of the dependent wife."

As for the woman who does get propositioned on the job, she probably asks for it, Mrs. Schlafly says — this by sending sexy signals "with a universal body language that most men intuititively understand. Men," she adds, "hardly ever ask sexual favors of women from whom the certain answer is 'no.'"

Society is indebted to Mrs. Schlafly for putting the working woman in her place: Back in the home. Baking brownies for her gainfully-employed husband and their 2.5 perfect children and raising prize-winning zinnias at the gate of their vine-covered cottage financed by a 30-year mortgage at — aren't they lucky? — a good old-fashioned 8 percent.

Meanwhile, back in the real world, 8.5 million families — 14.6 percent of all American households — are headed by women. Their incomes average about 50 percent of the median U.S. family income.

For many, then, it's a poverty-line struggle to keep the school age kids in school, a roof over their heads, clothes on their backs and food on the table, all without the help of that male provider Mrs. Schlafly idealizes.

Some do it with federal assistance. Plenty of them do it by holding down picayune dead-end jobs that often are the only kind available to those with outdated skills or little experience of the marketplace.

These women know that men don't ask sexual favors only of women they think will say "yes." They do it because they expect the answer to be "yes." After all, if it isn't, the woman loses a hinted-at raise — even the job. And tries to find new employment with a bad job reference.

Subjugation is not the essence of womanhood.

The Des Moines Register
Des Moines, Iowa, April 23, 1981

Stop putting us on, Phyllis Schlafly. Surely you must have been twitting those senators when you said that women who are sexually harassed bring it on themselves. The senators probably liked to hear that, but even they must know that the newspapers, courts and hospital emergency rooms are full of sad stories proving that virtuous behavior is no magic defense against lustful men.

We read that comment of yours, "When a woman walks across the room, she speaks with a universal body language that most men intuitively understand." You mean, of course, that the wiggling and jiggling must stop. Would you suggest giving up spiked-heel shoes, two-piece bathing suits, eye shadow and trips to the hairdresser?

Well, if you must, bring us righteousness in the dowdy look. Shield us from those brazen beauties who invite pinching, fondling and late-night hours at the office. And, thank you, Phyllis, for making life so simple, so clear, so unreal.

Pittsburgh Post-Gazette
Pittsburgh, Pa., April 24, 1981

By past attacks on the proposition that women can be happy elsewhere than in the home, Equal Rights Amendment nemesis Phyllis Schlafly has made herself the moral equivalent of long fingernails on the ERA's blackboard. Her performance before the Senate Labor Committee on Tuesday, however, raised her opposition to a new level of intellectual discordance.

In her testimony, Mrs. Schlafly did not accomplish what she set out to do: to raise doubts about Equal Employment Opportunity Commission guidelines for reporting sexual harassment on the job. Rather, she made it plain that her antifeminist campaign is driven by a view of human nature that ignores evidence of sex discrimination while accepting instead naive notions of self-fulfilling feminine virtue.

"Virtuous women are seldom accosted by unwelcome sexual propositions or familiarities, obscene talk, or profane language," Mrs. Schlafly told the Senate committee.

That she is plainly wrong could be determined from the results of an investigation among female federal employees that was presented to the same committee. Forty-two percent of the women surveyed said that they had been sexually harassed on the job. And of 130 cases referred to the EEOC, Acting Commissioner J. Clay Smith Jr. told the senators, specific evidence supported the charges in all but 12 cases. Well over half the cases involve demands for sexual favors. Almost half the cases were the result of unwanted sexual touching.

Presumably Mrs. Schlafly would argue that such sex-discrimination suits only reflect sour grapes. After all, 97 of the suits were brought by women who were either fired or quit their jobs, allegedly as a result of sexual harassment. But she did not offer any evidence of her own or even come close to refuting the findings of researchers whose independent investigations confirm the existence of a problem. Indeed, her view that virtuous women do not get harassed is really a hysterical corollary of the canard that nice girls do not get raped.

The Detroit News
Detroit, Mich., April 23, 1981

The acting commissioner of the U.S. Equal Employment Opportunity Commission told Congress this week: "Sexual harassment in the workplace is not a figment of the imagination."

Well, we never thought it was. But Phyllis Schlafly, who isn't always wrong, makes a fascinating distinction. Says she: "Virtuous women are seldom accosted by unwelcome sexual propositions or familiarities, obscene talk, or profane language."

In this instance, at least, Mrs. Schlafly doesn't know what she's talking about. The chief problem is not that men in shops and offices go about trying to seduce women (although some men do), but that many, many men conduct conversations about sex within earshot of women workers who don't want to hear them.

Such conversations are generally laced with snide references to female parts, and there's little a woman — virtuous or not — can do except lodge a formal complaint. If she protests to the offending men, she's likely to be assaulted by a wave of even greater and more personal crudities.

While women who elect to go out in the world should not be overly sensitive about occasional, risque chitchat, much of the time the chitchat is genuinely offensive to anybody — man or woman — who prefers some minimum level of propriety and civility in daily life.

However virtuous Mrs. Schlafly herself is, and we suspect her purity arouses the envy of the saints, she would be unlikely to tolerate workplace conversations that are deliberately designed to insult women.

Yes, there is pinching and patting in some offices, but there are laws against direct harassment. A far larger problem, we believe, is dirty, stupid talk.

Sentinel Star

Orlando, Fla., April 30, 1981

THE EQUAL Rights Amendment is a dead horse. But Phyllis Schlafly, the conservative heroine who single-handedly whipped it to death, is very much alive and kicking. What she's kicking now is sexual harassment in the workplace. Virtuous women, says this non-practicing lawyer, don't have problems with harassment.

When it comes to the various plights of women in the work force, though, Mrs. Schlafly is definitely an uninitiated outsider looking in.

But, heck, when you're convinced that women don't need ERA because they already have all the equality they need in today's equal opportunity market, it's easy to see that harassment couldn't exist without invitation. Isn't it?

ST. LOUIS POST-DISPATCH

St. Louis, Mo., April 26, 1981

When she testified before the Senate Labor Committee that "sexual harassment on the job is not a problem for the virtuous woman, except in the rarest of cases," Phyllis Schlafly did a great disservice to the women she claims to work for. Mrs. Schlafly calls herself a champion of the family. But in trying to keep the mother out of the workplace, she ignores the reality of the American family today.

More than half of American mothers with school-age children now work. Most married women find jobs so that their family income can keep pace with inflation. Many working women are the sole support of their children, and many of these families are barely above the poverty level. The days of housewives keeping beautiful homes and being available whenever husbands or children need them exist only in sitcom fantasy for many families. That may be regrettable, but those are the facts of today's economy.

Another fact that is more than merely regrettable is that many women are victims of sexual harassment. The *Wall Street Journal* recently reported examples in which male employees defended their advances on female coworkers as "something my wife likes or my girlfriend likes, and I was just teasing." In another reported case a man objected that his firing was too severe a penalty. His offense? He had refused to give a co-worker the cleaning materials she needed unless she consented to his sexual demands.

And the actual complaints are believed to be the tip of the iceberg, because women may say nothing in fear of losing their jobs or out of embarrassment. Mrs. Schlafly says that women who are sexually harassed have indicated through body language that they will comply. That inaccurate statement is an insensitive insult to working women, akin to the disproven, reprehensible idea that rape victims asked for it. Mrs. Schlafly is simply wrong. The only value of her testimony is to illustrate the continuing myths about working women.

The Washington Star

and Daily News

Washington, D.C., April 25, 1981

Eighteen million women sexually harassed on the job! Even the statistics on the street-corner purse-snatchers and parking lot rapists women confront when they leave the office can't touch that figure. Yet there it is. The Center for Women Policy Studies says the behavior of men working with women is that bad. J. Clay Smith, acting chairman of the Equal Employment Opportunity Commission, has been telling the Senate Labor Committee about the 118 sexual harassment cases under investigation at EEOC headquarters right now. Eleanor Holmes Norton, who used to be head of EEOC, has been telling the committee the same thing.

The volume of complaints lodged under the Civil Rights Act provisions covering sex discrimination is still small. However, there has been a survey of sexual harassment in the federal bureaucracy. The EEOC people get their outraged millions from extrapolations starting with that.

They admit that the totals have been going up as fast as they have partly because of more refined definitions of what constitutes harassment. Yesterday's bad joke is an actionable offense today. There's not yet a 1-to-10 scale for measuring leers, but even by Mr. Smith's count, slightly fewer than half the women complaining of sexual harassment were physically touched.

Phyllis Schlafly, who represents the other pole of a polarized situation, says that whatever happened to those women, they asked for it. Via body language, if nothing more audibly explicit.

To understand what's really going on in this morass of unlikely claims and counterclaims, it's useful to start with the big picture. This is but a skirmish in the war of the women's movement against a male-dominated society in general and the Reagan administration in particular.

Frustrated on the Equal Rights Amendment, threatened in the abortion area and hard-pressed on the welfare issues where their cause is up against the demand for spending cuts, some leaders of the women's movement are concentrating on the sex-discrimination aspects of the Civil Rights Act. To them, that means, along with affirmative action hiring and promoting policies, more policing of male supervisors who might be tempted to put down women as women or to advance the compliant bird of paradise before the merely efficient starling.

It doesn't take a Ph.D. in psychology to recognize that certain sparks do fly between males and females in any work force. They do occasionally affect managerial judgment.

There are men who use power to get sexual favors and sexual inuendo to exercise power. There are women who use sexual attractions, with or without the favors, to get power.

Phyllis Schlafly to the contrary notwithstanding, women no more provocative in dress and behavior than might be expected to catch the eyes of high-minded bachelors often do run into offensive remarks from the boss. It can be awkward to handle. It can be serious enough to warrent bringing unions or in-house grievance machinery into the picture. But most women don't find it necessary to make a federal case of it.

Certainly the woman employee subjected to passes, physical or verbal, accompanied by the suggestion that her response will have a lot to do with her future career, has a complaint that calls for remedy. But is making federal cases of such incidents by broadening EEOC powers to issue guidelines the way to do it? Will it do anything for either the productivity or the job-satisfaction of women in the work force to try to impose federal disciplines on men caught uttering condescending generalizations about what women are like?

We wonder. Just as we wonder about the 18 million.

The Evening Gazette

Worcester, Mass., April 24, 1981

Phyllis Schlafly may LACK tact, but she sure has guts.

She braved the hisses of a phalanx of feminists at a Senate Labor Committee hearing the other day to testify that "sexual harassment on the job is not a problem for the virtuous woman, except in the rarest of cases."

Thousands of virtuous women say she's all wet about that. For there to be no unsolicited sexual harassment on the job requires that the men as well as the women be virtuous.

But Mrs. Schlafly sincerely believes that "the most cruel and damaging sexual harassment taking place today is the harassment by feminists and their federal government allies against the role of motherhood and the role of the dependent wife."

As long as there is anything at all to be said along those lines, Phyllis Schlafly will be saying it, loud and clear. She is the nation's most prominent spokesperson for the traditional female role in society.

Mrs. Schlafly overstates her case. Like some of her feminist rivals, she has been too strident. But she has the courage of the embattled traditionalist. And she rather enjoys controversy. She speaks for more millions than her adversaries like to admit.

If there is a silent majority of traditional women out there, they have an effective and unsilent representative in Phyllis Schlafly.

SAN JOSE NEWS

San Jose, Calif., April 23, 1981

THE mind of Phyllis Schlafly is a national treasure. It should be ensconced in a dust-proof, climate-controlled glass cubicle in the Smithsonian Institution, where it could be preserved forever in its pristine, mid-19th-century condition, safe from the ravages of time and reality.

After all, what other contemporary American public figure still utters socio-politico-sexual theories that sound like they were lifted verbatim from a Jane Austen novel?

Viz. Mrs. Schlafly on sexual harassment in the workplace:

"When a woman walks across the room, she speaks with a universal body language that most men intuitively understand. Men hardly ever ask sexual favors of women from whom the certain answer is 'No.' "

Since feminine chastity is its own shield, Schlafly told the Senate Labor Committee, she sees no need for federal regulations against sexual harassment on the job.

Schlafly's interesting theory is open to question on a number of grounds. Even granting that "most men intuitively understand" women's "universal body language," what does one do about the minority of male klutzes who misread the signals? Worse, what does one do about those cads and bounders who deliberately disregard the signals and make their loathsome advances anyway?

Schlafly's quaint Victorian notions notwithstanding, sexual harassment *is* a problem in the American workplace, even for the most virtuous of women. If Schlafly truly doubts it, she should take her nose out of "The Mill on the Floss" long enough to talk to some of the thousands of working women who have been its victims.

the Charleston Gazette

Charleston, W.Va., April 23, 1981

IT IS POSSIBLE to conclude from the public assertions of Phyllis Schlafly, a charming and articulate defender of conservative positions, that the Far Right now views charges of sexual harassment on the job as liberal nonsense.

We assume that Mrs. Schlafly feels an obligation to pooh-pooh the issue because it is one pursued by feminists. Feminists, of course, are held out on the Right as the enemy of all that is decent and good. As for us, we've always assumed sexual harassment to be a bipartisan issue, if anything is. How could it be anything else?

In any event, we are disturbed by Mrs. Schlafly's unqualified testimony before a Senate subcommittee. To say flatly that women who are caressed and touched familiarly by men at the work site in fact invite these attentions by their own demeanor is not greatly different from the absurd assertions of some judges that rape victims invite assault with their dress and manner and that rapists in such cases should not be judged harshly.

In the first place, our own limited observations tell us that the most modest of women are subjected to sexual harassment. In the second place, we don't believe in open season on immodest women. If it is a woman's nature to be a coquette, surely she has a right to be selective in seeking the attention of men. She does not forfeit the protection of the ordinary rules of conduct.

A great number of recorded sexual harassment complaints, many from women who were fired because they refused to go along with propositions from male supervisors, make Mrs. Schlafly's observations sound just a bit silly.

St. Petersburg Times

St. Petersburg, Fla., April 26, 1981

Phyllis Schlafly, the prim wife of an affluent attorney, leads a sheltered life. Is it possible that she has no idea what goes on in the real world?

In Mrs. Schlafly's thinking, men only make passes at floozies.

In reality, a lot of women and men are subjected to sexual advances that they do not invite.

WHEN THAT happens on the job and affects a person's work performance, it's sexual harassment and it's illegal. But Mrs. Schlafly dismisses the problem with the ridiculous statement that in the workplace "virtuous women are seldom accosted by unwelcome sexual propositions or familiarities, obscene talk or profane language." How would she know anything about the workplace?

In testimony before a Senate Labor subcommittee, the anti-feminist also said, "When a woman walks across a room, she speaks with a universal language that most men intuitively understand. Men hardly ever ask sexual favors of women from whom the certain answer is 'no.' "

Mrs. Schlafly's view obviously is distorted. Sexual harassment on the job is a real problem.

J. Clay Smith Jr., head of the Equal Employment Opportunity Commission (EEOC), said Tuesday that sexual harassment in the workplace may be deeper and more widespread than his agency knows. "Sexual harassment is not a figment of the imagination," he said.

Backing up Smith, a study released last week by the Washington-based Center for Women Policy Studies estimated that at least *18-million* employed women experienced overt sexual harassment during 1979-80. And a study by the U.S. Merit Systems Protection Board found that 42 percent of a group of federally-employed women believed that they had been victims of sexual harassment.

Mrs. Schlafly grossly insulted all working women by implying that the 18-million or more victims of sexual harassment are people who deserve it.

Sexual harassment is not good-natured bantering between men and women who work together, a mutual attraction between two employees or an office romance.

SEXUAL HARASSMENT is a power play. Almost all complaints of that nature are made against supervisors by their subordinates. Of 118 charges which have been corroborated by the EEOC in the last year, 106 were perpetrated by supervisors or others in management and only 12 by co-workers. Some male bosses demand that women become sexually involved with them in return for a job, a promotion or a pay raise. Others subject women to unwelcome sexual contact, such as touching, hugging or kissing. Some women who refuse to engage in sexual acts are fired; others get so upset by such harassment that they quit.

Mrs. Schlafly owes working women an apology. The federal government owes them continued enforcement of the EEOC's reasonable guidelines on sexual harassment.

Lincoln Journal

Lincoln, Neb., April 24, 1981

Men seldom make passes, Dorothy Parker once concluded with erroneous whimsy, at girls who wear glasses.

Now, Phyllis "I'm-just-a-housewife" Schlafly has embroidered on that theme, with iron thread.

No whimsy or caprice this trip; just that streak of resurrected Cotton Mathering and judgmental superiority which so seems to animate Mrs. Schlafly and her political associates.

It is Mrs. Schlafly's view, confided to a Senate committee this week, that "virtuous women are seldom accosted by unwelcomed sexual propositions or familiarities, obscene talk or profane language... Men hardly ever ask sexual favors of women from whom the certain answer is no."

Men, Mrs. Schlafly says, can "intuitively" tell by a woman's body language which females are frosty and hostile to any sexual relationships and which are, well, not.

The fairly clear track down that particular line, of course, is that women who are sexually harassed — at home, at work, in public places or simply walking — fall into the class of being something other than virtuous.

That's just a nudge away from the really filthy, evil conclusion of too many pea-brains among us, that if a woman is raped or assaulted, somehow, just somehow, she got what she was asking for.

Other variations on the same idiotic wave length are that the rich are rich because they are deserving, and the poor are destitute because they are immoral. Or justice everlastingly prevails. Or that the wicked assuredly will be punished, that the stork brings babies.

Arrrgh!

Newsday

Long Island, N.Y., April 23, 1981

Did Phyllis Schlafly ever have a boss? Or did she make the transition from wife and homemaker to lawyer, writer, organizer and professional commentator without really having to cope with a typical office environment?

The questions arise from her almost contemptuous testimony on the subject of sexual harassment in the workplace before the Senate Labor and Human Resources Committee this week:

"Virtuous women are seldom accosted by unwelcome sexual propositions or familiarities, obscene talk or profane language," Schlafly told the senators. But sexual harassment can occur, she said, "when a nonvirtuous woman gives off body language which invites sexual advances, but she chooses to give her favors to Man A but not to Man B and he tries to get his share, too."

Instead of blaming sexual harassment on its victims, we hope the committee will pay serious attention to a very real problem. The head of the Equal Employment Opportunity Commission told the senators that 106 of the 118 charges it has corroborated involved supervisors or others in management. He called the 130 cases pending before the EEOC "the tip of the iceberg," and a study released this week by the Center for Women Policy Studies seems to bear him out: It estimates that at least 18 million employed women experienced overt sexual harassment in 1979 and 1980.

This is not the easiest problem for the federal bureaucracy or anyone else to deal with. But understanding its nature and breadth is a necessary first step. Speedy and firm action on complaints, by the EEOC and by the courts, should make employers more vigilant. More women in management should help, too. Unfortunately, insensitive comments like Schlafly's will not.

The Philadelphia Inquirer
Philadelphia, Pa., April 23, 1981

Phyllis Schlafly, voice of the anti-feminists, has some peculiar yardsticks to measure virtue in a woman. One is how she walks. The other is whether she's been subjected to sexual harassment. And one is closely tied to the other.

Mrs. Schlafly told the Senate Labor Committee Tuesday that "sexual harassment on the job is not a problem for the virtuous woman, except in the rarest of cases."

"When a woman walks across the room, she speaks with a universal body language that most men intuitively understand," Mrs. Schlafly said. "Men hardly ever ask sexual favors of a woman from whom the certain answer is 'no.'"

This undoubtedly comes as news to thousands of victims of sexual harassment. If virtue is as easily determined as Mrs. Schlafly would have everyone believe, a trip to the water fountain can become the equivalent of donning a red letter "A" and strolling through the town square.

Mrs. Schlafly's explanation of the whole problem of sexual harassment would be laughable if it didn't reflect a widespread misunderstanding of the serious problem that confronts women and men every day.

The purpose of the Senate hearing was to determine whether guidelines enacted last November by the Equal Employment Opportunity Commission are so restrictive they place too great a burden on employers, have the potential for infringing upon freedom of expression of others, and may create antagonism against women in the workplace.

J. Clay Smith Jr., acting chairman of the commission, asserted that the guidelines are necessary. "Sexual harassment in the work place is not a figment of the imagination. It is a real problem," Mr. Smith testified.

The guidelines hold an employer responsible for condoning sexual harassment and authorize the courts to order remedial action if called for. Since the guidelines were imposed, 130 cases have been forwarded to the EEOC for investigation. Most involve unwelcome physical contact of a sexual nature and, in 77 instances, demands were made to engage in sex, often in exchange for pay raises or promotions, according to Mr. Smith.

While Mrs. Schlafly is capable of linking the act of sexual harassment with virtue, and virtue (or the lack of it) with a person's gait, that sort of absurd logic won't prevail if the federal guidelines remain in place, as they obviously must.

The Chattanooga Times
Chattanooga, Tenn., April 28, 1981

Here's a message to all women who believe they've been sexually harassed on the job: It's your fault. We hasten to add that that's not our opinion but the view of Phyllis Schlafly, president of the Eagle Forum, a conservative organization opposed to most feminist goals. That includes, presumably, the goal of assuring women the right to work on a job unmolested.

Mrs. Schlafly told a congressional committee las' week that "sexual harassment on the job is not a problem for the virtuous woman, except in the rarest of cases. When a woman walks across a room, she speaks with a universal body language that most men intuitively understand. Men hardly ever ask sexual favors of women from whom the certain answer is 'No.'"

But Mrs. Schlafly's apparent belief that women victimized by sexual harassment brought it on themselves is merely another example of blaming the victim, which is what used to happen in most rape cases. Never mind the criminal motivation that leads a man to commit rape, this view holds; look instead to see whether the woman dressed or acted provocatively.

Mrs. Schlafly's testimony adopted the same reasoning, with the added filip of illogicality: She argued that those who raise the issue of sexual harassment on the job are a threat to the family. Why? Because "the feminist goal is to induce all wives and mothers out of the home and into the work force." Not only is such a charge a misrepresentation, consider its nonsense content. According to her reasoning, feminists are trying to persuade women who now stay at home to join the work force so they can be sexually harassed. Any takers?

CHARLESTON EVENING POST
Charleston, S.C., May 6, 1981

Phyllis Schlafly, a lady with a penchant for driving feminists up the wall, told the Senate Labor Committee not long ago that "sexual harassment on the job is not a problem for the virtuous woman, except in the rarest of cases." (That may or may not be reassuring to women who consider themselves virtuous.)

"When a woman walks across the room," Mrs. Schlafly continued, "she speaks with a universal body language that most men intuitively understand. Men hardly ever ask sexual favors of women from whom the certain answer is 'no.'"

Well, we don't know about that. Some men, having learned in puberty the sometimes astonishing value of the direct question, no doubt like to ask such questions from time to time just to keep their hand in, even when the odds seem formidable. Hope springs eternal, you know, and man's reach must exceed his grasp, etc., etc.

We don't want to make light of something so dastardly as sexual harassment on the job, but we think it important to keep such things in perspective. It should never, for example, be confused with innocent flirting which, we have observed, often leads to beautiful romance. It should never be allowed to provoke iniquitous countermeasures, such as outlawing slit skirts, slightly tight slacks and sweaters in season, perfumes and heels (except of the lecherous boss variety).

Working women's laughter must still be allowed to lilt; they must not be denied that certain smile. Feminine grace must not be buried under layers of baggy unisex clothing. The Chinese Communists tried it and the effect on productivity has been disastrous. (The effect on population growth in China remains an anomaly — there will soon be a billion Chinese.)

What a dismal place the world would be if all these things come to pass! Why it would hardly be worth any man's while to roll out of bed in the morning to go to work.

Come to think of it, maybe that explains those billion Chinese.

Post-Tribune
Gary, Ind., April 28, 1981

Phyllis Schlafly's standing in the Women's Liberation League was probably already so low that it may have been little affected by her recent testimony on sexual harassment before a U.S. Senate committee.

She said that most women who are subject to propositions or other unwelcome advances from men on the job are, in effect, asking for it.

We feel sure a number of women annoyed by office Lotharios will take exception to Mrs. Schlafly's assertions that "Men hardly ever ask sexual favors of women from whom the certain answer is "no'." and "Virtuous women are seldom accosted by unwelcome sexual propositions or familiarities . . . "

Perhaps she will be less directly challenged for saying that "When a woman walks across the room, she speaks with a universal body language that most men intuitively under-stand," but there will be different interpretations there, too.

The central point of debate appears to be over how much accosting may result from the natural attractiveness of a member of the feminine sex for a male, and how often that situation is aggravated by overt attempts to emphasize that attractiveness.

We don't agree with Mrs. Schlafly closely enough to decide that women need no protection from sexual harassment in the increasingly dual-gendered work force. But there is enough truth in what she says to alert legislators trying to draw too precise rules on the subject.

Women at work deserve protection within reason, but the Prohibition Amendment proved how difficult it is to legislate morality. Flirtation may be tougher to outlaw than the dry martini.

The Union Leader

Manchester, N.H., May 5, 1981

Columnist Phyllis Schlafly is such an effective spokesman for the views of what we perceive to be the majority of American women that it was unfortunate to see her stray so far off the "conservative reservation" during her recent testimony before the Senate Labor and Human Resources Committee on the Equal Employment Opportunity Commission's guidelines on sexual harassment.

Regrettably, her testimony rendered her vulnerable to the most effective of all retorts—ridicule.

If Mrs. Schlafly seriously believes some of the things she told the senators in public session, then she is not aware of life in the real world. Women who are victimized by sexual harassment on the job face a difficult enough problem without having to endure the kind of silly comments offered by the usually responsible profamily spokesman.

Tolerance toward sexual harassment most assuredly is contrary to the entire conservative philosophy. Yet, there sat Mrs. Schlafly offering the senators a veritable litany of inane comments:

"Virtuous women are seldom accosted by unwelcome sexual propositions or familiarities, obscene talk, or profane language. . . . "

"When a woman walks across the room, she speaks with a universal body language that most men intuitively understand. Men hardly ever ask sexual favors of women from whom the certain answer is 'no'. . . . "

"Sexual harassment can also oc-cur when a non-virtuous woman gives off body language which invites sexual advances, but she chooses to give her favors to man A but not to man B and he tries to get his share, too. . . . "

One need not be an expert on "body language" to know that Mrs. Schlafly has made light of a very serious problem by suggesting, as a general proposition, that most women invite sexual harassment. To be sure, some do —but that fact is irrelevant to the cause of the majority of those who do not, and particularly to the plight of those who find themselves victimized, in some instances being blackmailed with promises or threats related to their employment.

The statistic cited before the Senate committee by the Washington-based Center for Women Policy Studies — an estimated 18,000,000 employed women experiencing overt sexual harassment during 1979-1980 — hardly sounds credible, unless one includes in the category of sexual harassment vulgar or suggestive language, which in truth some women do invite by engaging in it themselves.

But the point is that one case of overt sexual harassment is one too many.

Mrs. Schlafly should reconsider her foolish comments before the Senate committee. They provide little comfort to those women who are courageous enough to fight back against sexual harassment on the job despite the embarrassment they must thereby endure and the difficulty of proving such charges.

BUFFALO EVENING NEWS

Buffalo, N.Y., May 1, 1981

We couldn't disagree more with the recent testimony of Mrs. Phyllis Schlafly before a Senate subcommittee on sexual harassment of women. "When a woman walks across a room, she speaks with a universal body language that most men intuitively understand," said Mrs. Schlafly, whose syndicated column appears regularly on this page. "Men hardly ever ask sexual favors from women from whom the certain answer is 'No.'"

In effect, she was saying that the male leer, the sexual invitation in the workplace, was almost invariably brought on by the woman herself.

No doubt that is sometimes true. But the Schlafly comments surely overstate the case and, in the process, insensitively seek to debunk the scope and seriousness of genuine instances of sexual harassment. The acting head of the U.S. Equal Employment Opportunity Commission, J. Clay Smith, said that among 130 sexual discrimination cases currently under review, 71 were brought by women who were fired and another 26 by women who quit their jobs "when the unwelcomed sexual activity became intolerable." It strains credulity to believe that all these women quit or were discharged over incidents they themselves invited.

To Mrs. Schlafly, "virtuous women are seldom accosted by unwelcome sexual propositions or familiarities, obscene talk, or profane language." It would be hard to imagine a more unfair or inaccurate statement.

THE LOUISVILLE TIMES

Louisville, Ky., April 27, 1981

Like other leaders on the political fringe when public opinion begins to swing their way, Phyllis Schlafly was faced with two options. She could draw toward the mainstream, thus attracting more supporters, or adopt ever more extreme positions in order to please the most radical of her followers.

Mrs. Schlafly showed last week that she has chosen the second option. The woman who became a household name by offering *A Choice, Not an Echo*, revealed herself as an echo, a self-parody of the writer-lecturer who has crisscrossed the country for almost two decades in a full-time crusade to confine women to *Küche, Kirche und Kinder*.

Her view, given to a Senate committee, that women who are sexually propositioned on the job are the ones at fault is so patently ridiculous, so plainly at odds with the truth that it renders her testimony worthless. Her use of the forum to speak out against the irrelevant issue of drafting women into the armed forces was, at best, gratuitous.

The issue before the Labor Committee was Equal Employment Opportunity Commission guidelines designed to curb sexual harassment in the workplace. The panel is seeking to determine if they are too inclusive and might be an unwarranted burden upon employers, who can be held responsible if supervisors or workers engage in sexual harassment.

Mrs. Schlafly did not enlighten the senators on that issue, except to argue that the laws and regulations weren't needed because, for the "virtuous woman," sexual harassment is not a problem "except in the rarest of cases." That implies that she would impose upon employers the obligation to hire only "virtuous" female employees. Think how many bureaucrats could devote how many bureaucratic hours to drafting an acceptable definition of "virtuous."

She was equally ridiculous in contending that affirmative action programs are unjust, especially to "the dependent wife and mother in the home whose breadwinner husband is denied a job, a raise or a promotion so that it can be given to a less qualified woman." That's bunk. Nothing in affirmative action programs requires employers to award jobs to the "less qualified woman" or member of a racial minority.

Mrs. Schlafly, it should be noted, entered law school at the age of 50. Somewhere in the country there is a young man who undoubtedly would have had a place in that class had she not been accepted. Was she not guilty of the very sin she attributes to the women who, unlike her in her full-time occupation, work full time because they are breadwinners: Displacing a male provider?

She complains that women in the workplace are "obsoleting the role of motherhood." Obsolete, in our dictionary, is an adjective. It describes Mrs. Schlafly.

POLITICS:
Goldwater, Noted Conservative, Takes "New Right" to Task

In a speech to Congress Sept. 15, Sen. Barry Goldwater (R, Ariz.) strongly condemned "special-issue religious groups" as "a divisive element that could tear apart the very spirit of our representative system, if they gain sufficient strength." Citing the Moral Majority organization, Goldwater, a long-standing conservative, pledged to fight such groups "every step of the way if they try to dictate their moral convictions to all Americans in the name of 'conservatism.'" "I don't like the New Right," he continued, "What they're talking about is not conservatism." He told Congress that "the religious issues of these groups have little or nothing to do with conservative or liberal politics" and they were "diverting us away from the vital issues that our government needs to address," such as "national security and economic survival." Goldwater charged that the energies of Congress were overly absorbed by special interest groups promoting their views on abortion, busing, school prayer, pornography and the Equal Rights Amendment. He said he was "frankly sick and tired of the political preachers . . . telling me as a citizen that if I want to be a moral person, I must believe in A, B, C, or D. Just who do they think they are?" The senator added that he was "even more angry as a legislator who must endure the threats of every religious group who thinks it has some God-granted right to control my vote on every roll call in the Senate." "We have succeeded for 205 years in keeping the affairs of state separate from the uncompromising idealism of religious groups," he declared, "and we mustn't stop now."

Democrat Chronicle
Rochester, N.Y., September 23, 1981

NO ONE has better conservative credentials than Sen. Barry Goldwater (R., Ariz.). But even he hasn't been able to abide what he described the other day as those single-issue "political preachers." They must, he said, "learn to make their views known without trying to make their views the only alternatives."

Mentioning the Moral Majority specifically, he added bluntly in a Senate speech: "The uncompromising position of these groups is a divisive element that could tear apart the very spirit of our representative system if they gain sufficient strenth." They cannot, he added, decree what the government must do or what people must think.

As if to make Goldwater's point for him, the Moral Majority's Rev. Jerry Falwell suggested that the senator had sealed his political doom by speaking so frankly. Well, more such frank speech is needed if the danger of the Moral Majority's doctrinaire rigidity is to be made plain to everybody.

ST. LOUIS POST-DISPATCH
St. Louis, Mo., September 17, 1981

"Mr. Conservative" has spoken: the New Right is not really conservative. In a both thoughtful and angry statement, Sen. Barry Goldwater of Arizona explains that groups such as the Moral Majority and Pro-Life have introduced divisive religious intolerance into American politics, undermining the constitutional principle of separation of church and state.

As a man of impeccable conservative credentials, Mr. Goldwater sees nothing conservative about this: a conservative would first of all conserve the Constitution and the representative system of government. Moreover, he says the single issues on which the New Right judges morality and politics have nothing to do with conservatism, or liberalism for that matter. Citizens on either side of the political center can and do disagree about such issues as abortion, school busing, prayer in schools, the ERA and so on.

The morality of such matters escapes the senator. In what Mr. Goldwater would no doubt disavow as "righteous" anger, he says he is sick and tired of being told that "to be a moral person, I must believe in 'A,' 'B,' 'C' and 'D.'" The moralistic presumption of these groups is astounding, and their concentration on single issues detracts from major issues of the economy and security.

Sen. Goldwater says, however, that the New Right will go on imposing its will on others unless people recognize that religious factionalism has no place in public policy. He adds that he will fight the self-appointed moralists every step of the way if they try to dictate their moral convictions to all Americans in the name of "conservatism." And that is a real consevative speaking.

THE ATLANTA CONSTITUTION
Atlanta, Ga., September 17, 1981

Sen. Barry Goldwater not only is known as the father of contemporary conservatism, but also for speaking his mind. He is on the money with his comments about the religion-dominated New Right — the mixing of conservative religion and politics threatens American democracy. It also threatens established religion.

The Republican from Arizona asked the question a lot of other people have been asking about the television preachers and others who presume to know what's best for all of us: ". . . from where do they presume to claim the right to dicate their moral beliefs to me?"

Goldwater, who ran for president as a conservative, said he is happy that the mood of the country has gone in that direction, but he said he objected to those groups who jumped on that pendulum and claimed they made it swing in the first place.

"One of the great strengths of our political system has always been our tendency to keep religious issues in the background. By maintaining the separation of church and state, the United States has avoided the intolerance which has so divided the rest of the world with religious wars," Goldwater told reporters.

The senator makes sense. Religion is a very personal thing. It varies from group to group and even person to person within those groups. History has shown when a political-religious organization gets to thinking it has all the answers and is best for all the people, there is trouble. One need only look at Iran and the killings, torture and imprisonment that are carried out in the name of religion. Look at the "un-Christian things" that were done to force people to convert to Christianity in the past.

Those pendulums usually swing both ways. The public is not easily fooled. When the public gets a bellyful of ultra-conservative TV preachers and their political ambitions — thinly veiled as old-time religion — there is likely to be a move against all organized religion, and that would be unfortunate.

Both religion and government are necessary for a civilized society. But whoever runs one should not be running the other.

The Times-Picayune
The States-Item
New Orleans, La., September 17, 1981

Few politicians can equal Arizona's brusque and august Sen. Barry Goldwater when it comes to venting righteous indignation. Of late, the 1964 Republican presidential nominee has trained his indignation on the Moral Majority and other elements of the "new right."

Last Tuesday, in remarks offered for the record on the Senate floor, the elder statesman of the Republican right accused them of endangering the basic American principle of separation of church and state by using the "muscle of religion toward political ends."

The "uncompromising position of these groups is a divisive element that could tear apart the very spirit of our representative system if they gain sufficient strength," warned Mr. Goldwater.

At the peak of his indignation, the senator said he was "sick and tired of the political preachers across the country telling me as a citizen that if I want to be a moral person, I must believe A, B, C and D. Just who do they think they are? And I am even more angry as a legislator who must endure the threats of every religious group who thinks it has been God-granted right to control my vote on every roll call in the Senate."

Congress could use more of the 72-year-old Mr. Goldwater's independence of spirit in responding to pressure groups that seek to impose their own moral convictions on both the public at large and the nation's political leaders. The "Mr. Conservative" of another era is performing a valuable public service by reminding Americans of the true definition of political conservatism, which he describes as adherence to the "proven values of the past" and a "deep abiding respect for the integrity of the Constitution."

True conservatism is dedicated to safeguarding the basic freedoms set forth in the Constitution — most pointedly, in this instance, freedom of religion, which means freedom from religious coercion.

While Sen. Goldwater, who appears personally afronted by the challenges of the "new right" to his concept of traditional conservatism, might be overstating the threat of the Moral Majority and its like, his outspokenness is reassuring. Less so is the relative silence of some of his younger colleagues who share his traditional conservative views.

THE COMMERCIAL APPEAL
Memphis, Tenn., September 17, 1981

WHEN SEN. Barry Goldwater accepted the Republican Party's presidential nomination in 1964 and told convention delegates that "extremism in defense of liberty is no vice," even some Republicans recoiled and criticized him as a radical.

But that was 17 years ago, and Barry Goldwater now expresses himself with greater clarity and finesse. At 74, he is no less a conservative than he was then, but by defining conservatism in terms of what has been happening to this nation in recent years he has won many friends for his concept of that philosophy, even among those who would prefer to be known as liberals. And justly so.

A fine example of his articulation of the conservative philosophy was offered in his breakfast talk with reporters earlier this week and in a Senate speech in which he dealt with the type of conservatism that the Moral Majority and other members of the New Right have been employing recently.

Members of such "special-issue religious groups" not only are uncompromising and unconcerned about upholding the integrity of the Constitution, he said, they are "diverting the Congress from vital economic and defense issues toward moral concerns such as abortion, busing, the equal rights amendment and pornography."

"That is no way to run the country," he said.

The religious issues of the New Right, he continued, have "little or nothing to do with liberal or conservative politics." He vowed to "fight them every step of the way if they try to dictate their moral convictions to all Americans in the name of conservatism."

In his breakfast remarks he specifically singled out Rev. Jerry Falwell and Sens. Jesse Helms and John P. East of North Carolina and Jeremiah Denton of Alabama — all fellow Republicans — as being among the targets of his criticisms.

It is not that Goldwater does not share some of the attitudes of the religious groups of which he spoke. He has said clearly that he, too, is opposed to abortion, for example. But what he does object to is the way those single-issue activists seek to impose their views on everyone else and to force the elected representatives of the people to bend to their will.

GOLDWATER HIT the mark when he said, "Freedom is what conservatism is all about" and the New Right religious groups are threatening freedom because they "make their views the only alternatives."

And he proved, too, that he is a realist in his conservatism. Asked what he thought of the so-called chastity law which is supposed to deal with adolescent pregnancy and parenthood and was enacted in July without discussion, Goldwater replied, "Oh, Lord, how in the hell are you going to regulate that? They've been trying to do that since the invention of the apple."

Wisconsin ⚑ State Journal
Madison, Wisc.,
September 22, 1981

As America's leading conservative spokesman for years, Sen. Barry Goldwater, R-Ariz., sees conservatism as a political philosophy built on free choice of the individual.

It does not, however, allow imposition of that choice upon others.

That is why Goldwater has taken angry exception to the Moral Majority's attempts to mix religion and politics and to prescribe "proper" behavior for American citizens and politicians.

"I will fight them every step of the way if they try to dictate their moral convictions to all Americans in the name of 'conservatism,' " said the senator in a statement for the Congressional Record.

For our emphasis on freedom and the individual's right to choice, there has been an ethic of conformity in America, an idea that, like machines, societies run best when their parts are mass-produced.

But societies are organisms, not machines. As uncomfortable as it may sometimes be, diversity, not conformity, is what gives strength to the organism.

In recent years, America has been stretched and pulled by new experiments in family, relationships, religion and ethics. Two reactions have developed — on the one hand, renewed appreciation of diversity as the seasoning of life; on the other, alarm and brittle intolerance.

The latter is voiced by the Moral Majority, whose hostile reaction to diversity has alienated those who recognize that intolerance is contrary to the American spirit.

Goldwater's remarks were echoed by A. Bartlett Giamatti, president of Yale University, in a speech to the institution's entering freshmen. Giamatti called the Moral Majority "peddlers of coercion" making a "radical assault" on pluralism.

In this time of experimentation, change and the shaking of long-held beliefs, people of deep religious convictions are concerned about immorality. But in a free society extremism, intolerance and insistence on strict conformity are among the greatest vices.

When the Moral Majority recognizes that, its members can become catalysts of discussion and introspection in America, rather than sources of anger and fear.

THE ANN ARBOR NEWS

Ann Arbor, Mich., September 18, 1981

TIME WAS when all you needed to know about Sen. Barry Goldwater could be learned by reading "The Conscience of a Conservative."

Since that thin book was published, the Arizonan has run for the presidency and stood for the Senate while earning a reputation for plain speaking.

He's getting on in years now and illness is taking its toll, but Goldwater **GOLDWATER** has not lost the style of discourse that never leaves doubt where he stands.

LIKE A few months ago, for instance, when he called Moral Majority preacher Jerry Falwell the east end of a horse going west.

Evidently Mr. Falwell and his right-wing colleagues are still getting under Goldwater's skin because he let the electronic evangelists have it with both barrels recently in a speech inserted into the Congressional Record. Goldwater said:

"I'm sick and tired of political preachers across the country telling me as a citizen that if I want to be a moral person, I must believe in 'A,' 'B,' 'C' and 'D.' Just who do they think they are? And from where do they presume to claim the right to dictate their moral beliefs to me?

"The religious factions that are growing in our land are not using their religious clout with wisdom. They are trying to force government leaders into following their positions 100 per cent.

"They are diverting us away from the vital issues that our government needs to address."

BOLDLY SAID, Sen. Goldwater.

Now it would be nice if other influential people in and out of government picked up on Mr. Goldwater's remarks. The type of authoritarian thinking the senator alludes to has also cropped up locally. The Washtenaw County Republican organization is having its set-tos with fundamentalists, although party stalwarts attached to the Milliken wing appear likely to repel any serious challenge from the religious right.

Of course, the mind-set of the religious/political right is not wholly a GOP problem.

Statewide, nationally and across party lines, the type of thinking Barry Goldwater assailed is attractive to those who frustrated with government and fed up with high taxes and inflation.

Still, most people prefer to make their own moral judgments. And because they do and because most people oppose church meddling in affairs of state, the New Right may be old stuff soon enough.

If more people follow Sen. Goldwater's lead, it'll be sooner.

The Wichita Eagle-Beacon

Wichita, Kans., September 20, 1981

Sen. Barry Goldwater, R-Ariz., in contributing an invaluable viewpoint to the ongoing controversy generated by the so-called "New Right" in a speech reprinted on today's Op Ed page, illuminates the disturbing element that lies at the core of the currently ascendant philosophy.

Almost uniquely qualified to analyze and comment on the subject, the unabashedly conservative Mr. Goldwater observes, "By maintaining the separation of church and state, the United States has avoided the intolerance which has so divided the rest of the world . . . The key word here is "intolerance," and it goes beyond matters of church and state.

Fails the Test

It is, unfortunately, the guiding, driving motivation that threatens to transform America's richly diverse cultural and intellectual landscape into a stark, barren two-dimensional environment where a person is judged either "right" or "wrong" on the basis of his views on a handful of simplistic single issues. Once so judged by those criteria, the individual then is perceived as either friend or foe, "for us or against us," and treated accordingly.

Ironically, much of the New Right claims to subscribe to the principles of Christian fundamentalism, but it is here that it fails the test, demonstrating not the kind of compassion and forgiveness the faith teaches, but the kind of intolerance that Sen. Goldwater cites.

The roll usually is taken on such issues as abortion, school prayer, busing and military spending. In the New Right's eyes, there are simple, definitive "right" and "wrong" answers to such questions.

Walking the Line

This, however, is not a simple world, and those certainly are not simple issues to resolve. How can anyone be absolutely certain of the rightness or the wrongness of any position on any of those complicated questions? Through dint of faith, members of the New Right proclaim they can be certain, and seek to impose their narrowly drawn views on those too reticent to articulate their own.

The world is an incredibly complex place today, and simply saying it isn't won't make it so, no matter how heavy an emotional investment one has in that premise. The fact that emotionalism plays so much a part in the New Right mentality accounts for why it is so difficult to argue to a rational consensus a point of difference with its adherents, There is no room for consensus — only for a strict ideological line that must be ascribed to if one is not to oppose it.

Understandably, Sen. Goldwater rankles at the thought that conservatism may be confused with "New Right-ism." The fact that the Sandra O'Connor Supreme Court nomination could not be undercut by New Right allegations of being out of step with conservative policy underscores the qualitative differences between the two philosophies. It also gives rise to hopes that distinction will be maintained, as it should be, rather than blurred.

Diversity to Be Desired

No one is saying the New Right is not entitled to express its viewpoints on matters of pressing concern to it — though the impression is that it would not afford others the same opportunity, if given the chance to rule on the matter.

The inclination to brook no diversity of opinion — no shadings of gray between the black and white of absolute right and wrong — is ultimately what must cause people to shrink back from the New Right's self-righteous, pious brand of political activisim. For it is that diversity of opinion — the challenge to think things through, instead of reacting to them only emotionally — that has made this nation great, and different from numerous others, where a powerful few are able to dictate an approved line of thought to the many.

The American tradition of freedom of thought, expression and religion can encompass such phenomena as the New Right, but it cannot be limited to them or by them.

The Idaho STATESMAN

Boise, Idaho, September 20, 1981

When it comes to commenting on the Moral Majority's condemnation of a "hellish" plan to condense the *Bible*, it's appropriate to quote Sen. Barry Goldwater.

Goldwater has decried the Moral Majority's efforts and demanded to know, "Just who do they think they are?" We have to ask the same question.

Religious issues are matters of individual conscience. Nobody — newspaper, government official or self-appointed Moral Majoritarian — has any business dictating how another individual or group should act on religious issues.

When the early books of the *Bible* were first written down by the ancient Israelites after the reign of King David, moral authorities probably cried "hellish." Without question, there were cries of "hellish" when the New Testament was added.

At whatever time in history, at whatever place on Earth, there's always been some know-it-all who claimed to have a direct line to heaven and the final word on the Word. The framers of the U.S. Constitution knew that. That's why they guaranteed religious freedom in the First Amendment.

It's all right with us if *Reader's Digest* puts out its condensed version of the *Bible*, but we don't understand one thing. More people might read the Scriptures if a new abbreviated version were available. Surely, the Moral Majority wouldn't oppose that.

The Seattle Times

Seattle, Wash., September 24, 1981

THE conservative credentials of Senator Barry Goldwater, the 72-year-old Arizona Republican, are impeccable. He carried his party's banner in the 1964 presidential election, and has since earned the title of "Mr. Conservative" in the Senate.

So when Goldwater says anything about American conservatism today, his words must be heeded.

That's why we were happy to hear his latest pronouncements on the "New Right" political-religious coalition that has tried to dictate its beliefs to the nation recently.

"Just who do they think they are?" Goldwater fumed. He said he was "frankly sick and tired of the political preachers across this country telling me as a citizen that if I want to be a moral person, I must believe in A, B, C and D. I am warning them today: I will fight them every step of the way if they try to dictate their moral convictions to all Americans in the name of conservatism."

Goldwater's anger at the New Right groups, which include the Moral Majority, Eagle Forum, and the Committee for the Survival of a Free Congress, was aroused last July when they opposed the nomination of Sandra D. O'Connor, an Arizonan, to the Supreme Court.

There are those who say Goldwater's recent statements prove he's getting old, crusty and irresponsible. They question his credibility. Some even hint that he's flipped.

If so, we'd say he's flipped in the right direction.

The Dispatch

Columbus, Ohio, September 20, 1981

IF THERE'S a wise old man in American politics today, it would have to be U.S. Sen. Barry Goldwater, R-Ariz. He has been in public service for decades, cares deeply about this nation and is respected by liberals and conservatives alike.

So it was with no little annoyance that we read this week that two political newcomers ignored and even ridiculed something the senator had to say. It seems that the Rev. Jerry Falwell, of the Moral Majority, and Nellie Gray, of the anti-abortion March for Life, have a lot to learn.

Goldwater warned that "single-issue religious groups...could tear apart the very spirit of our representative system."

"Can anyone look at the carnage in Iran, the bloodshed in Northern Ireland or the bombs bursting in Lebanon and yet question the dangers of injecting religious issues into the affairs of state?" Goldwater asked.

Gray immediately rejected what Goldwater had to say, and Falwell said that the senator could be "rebutted by almost any high school history student."

"It makes one wonder," Falwell added, "whether time has passed him by."

Well, to our way of thinking, wisdom, experience and perspective mature with age, and the views of people who have devoted their lives to serving this country are never out-of-date.

Indeed, the response to Goldwater's comments goes a long way toward proving their validity.

THE ARIZONA REPUBLIC

Phoenix, Ariz., September 22, 1981

BARRY GOLDWATER is bound to lose his fight with the self-styled Moral Majority and other religious groups that have injected themselves into politics.

This will not deter him. Goldwater has fought losing fights before.

The fact remains that religious groups have always taken part in politics in this country. They have as much a right to under the Constitution as anyone else.

Sometimes, they have served the nation well.

The Right-to-Life movement never wearies of comparing itself with the abolitionist movement. In the light of history, the abolition movement was a noble one.

The same can hardly be said of the campaign led by the Women's Christian Temperance Union. Prohibition gave birth to organized crime.

Religious groups that engage in politics are frequently offensive because they presume to have a pipeline to God.

The liberal National Council of Churches is just as sure as the conservative Moral Majority that it speaks for God.

As leader of the Moral Majority, the Rev. Jerry Falwell pretends to know even how God stands on the nomination of Sandra O'Connor to the Supreme Court.

Goldwater, who supports the nomination, is rightly outraged by this.

"Mr. Conservative" also is rightly outraged by Falwell's gall in lecturing him on how a conservative should vote in the Senate.

Many find the very name, the Moral Majority, offensive, since it clearly implies that anyone who disagrees with Falwell is a moral leper.

Actually, polls show that most Americans don't go all the way with Falwell on abortion. Thus, Falwell is saying that most Americans are moral lepers.

Goldwater rightly sees a danger in religious groups becoming political pressure groups.

Self-righteousness can lead to bigotry. It did during the 1928 presidential campaign, when many fundamentalist ministers urged congregations to vote against the Democratic candidate, Alfred E. Smith, because Smith was a Catholic.

It even can lead to bloodshed. It has in Northern Ireland, Iran and Lebanon.

Still, Goldwater might as well accept it. The Moral Majority and its allied religious organizations — armed with the sword of self-righteousness — will keep charging the political barricades.

They are well organized, they are zealous, and it takes great courage to fight them. Anyone who does opens himself to a charge that he's anti-God.

Goldwater has that kind of courage. And Goldwater doesn't have to fear such a charge.

San Francisco Chronicle

San Francisco, Calif.,
September 21, 1981

FEW POLITICIANS ON the national scene have as secure a claim to conservative credentials as Senator Barry Goldwater, the enduring Arizona Republican. His name alone brings a vision of the fellow in the helmet in the jet fighter, a fellow who totally symbolizes a sort of John Wayne patriotism.

Now he has performed a particularly valuable national service. Its value stems from the image he has created and from the constancy of his beliefs throughout his political career.

Senator Goldwater nas sharply reminded the New Right, the Moral Majority and others who want to see their fundamentalist religious beliefs enforced by law that this simply is not the American way. And, he stressed, the desire to see church and state wedded is not conservative in his view.

The country's founders, the senator said, were fully aware of the dangers inherent when church and state were indistinguishable.

* * *

"CAN ANYONE LOOK at the carnage in Iran, the bloodshed in North Ireland or the bombs bursting in Lebanon and yet question the dangers of injecting religious issues into the affairs of state?" he asked.

"Our political process involves give and take, a continuous series of trade offs. However, on religious issues, there can be little or no compromise. There is no position on which people are so immoveable as on their religious beliefs. There is no more powerful ally one can claim in a debate than Jesus Christ or God or Allah or whatever one calls his Supreme Being.

"But like any powerful weapon, the use of God's name on one's behalf should be used sparingly."

The senator deplored not only fundamentalists playing politics but all groups who look solely at one issue but pass judgment upon an entire career. "The uncompromising position of these groups is a divisive element that could tear apart the very spirit of our representative system if they gain sufficient strength," he said. And, as it is, he said, they are diverting the nation away from vital concerns over economic recovery and defense because they want total focus on such matters as birth control, the ERA, prayer in the schools and pornography.

AKRON BEACON JOURNAL

Akron, Ohio, September 17, 1981

THE AMERICAN public owes Sen. Barry Goldwater, R-Ariz., and the Rev. Jerry Falwell, leader of the Moral Majority, a debt of gratitude.

In almost simultaneous stinging attacks, these two political and religious opposites, who both travel under the banner of conservatism, have illuminated the emptiness and the pitfalls of simplistic political labels.

Sen. Goldwater, the acknowledged Conservative (with a capital C) of American politics since he ran for president 17 years ago, lashed out Tuesday against "the new right," and specifically the Moral Majority, whose uncompromising positions and attempts to force government leaders into following their positions threaten to "tear apart the very spirit of our representative system."

Sen. Goldwater vowed to fight "every step of the way" against efforts on their part to undermine or destroy the constitutional guarantee of separation of church and state. The senator said he treasures that independence and protection against the intolerance of any religious faction.

Invoking the same Constitution and its guarantee of freedom of speech, Mr. Falwell, in an article for Newsweek, accused "liberals" in churches and in government of politicizing what he called "basic moral values" of the country and of using the Constitution to restrict the church rather than to protect its freedom.

He left no doubt that the Moral Majority and the religious "conservatives" throughout the country will work politically for imposition of their version of morality and Americanism, and for the right of their churches to pursue political goals.

If Mr. Falwell's views do, indeed, represent "conservative" politics, then Sen. Goldwater must surrender his title. And conservatives and liberals alike should thank whatever gods they honor that it is he, not Mr. Falwell, who speaks for Americans in the halls of Congress.

The Philadelphia Inquirer

Philadelphia, Pa., September 17, 1981

"I'm frankly sick and tired of the political preachers across this country telling me as a citizen that, if I want to be a moral person, I must believe in A B, C or D. . . . I am even more angry as a legislator who must endure the threats of every religious group who thinks it has some God-granted right to control my vote on every roll call. . . ."

Some left-wing, godless cryptomarxist, right? Or at least one of the last of the liberal Democrats? No. Those words, and more, were spoken Tuesday by Sen. Barry Goldwater, the irrepressible grand old man of the American right. First at a breakfast meeting in Washington and then on the Senate floor, he attacked the Moral Majority, the so-called pro-life movement and their kindred self-assigned political-action hit-squads that are using religion, demagoguery and tens of millions of dollars of lobbying money, raised by mail-order campaigns, church collections and television appeals, to work their way into American laws, schools and bedrooms.

The Arizona Republican who ran against Lyndon B. Johnson has not abandoned the vision or principles that underlay his famous 1964 presidential campaign slogan: "In your heart you know he's right." Agree with him or not, and way back then Americans overwhelmingly voted that they did not, Sen. Goldwater is a conservative, and was so before a lot of the firebrands of the New Right were born.

And, in his judgment delivered on the Senate floor, "I don't like the New Right. What they're talking about is not conservatism."

Then what is it?

In the senator's words, they comprise "the religious factions that are growing throughout our land . . . a divisive element that could tear apart the very spirit of our representative system, if they gain sufficient strength." And to recognize their danger, he insisted, Americans should "look at the carnage in Iran, the bloodshed in Northern Ireland or the bombs bursting in Lebanon" — which he attributed to "injecting religious issues into the affairs of state."

At the height of his national political career, Sen. Goldwater fell, by many assessments, as a man of ideas whose time had passed. Times since have changed, of course, and much of his traditional conservatism is enjoying a new beginning. Today, there is a tendency to look upon the man as a voice from the past, to honor him affectionately as a noble article of nostalgia. There is nothing out of date, however, about his passionate affection for U.S. constitutional principles. There is nothing anachronistic about his faith in and defense of the deeply rooted strengths of American social values, especially that of abiding a variety of opinion, the enduring power of coexistent pluralism.

The expertly focused, lavishly funded, cynically manipulative forces of the so-called New Right are a serious and potentially growing threat to those fundamental American values and strengths — as any public figure who has come to be "targeted" for political destruction by them can attest. Vividly conscious of that, Sen. Goldwater vowed to his fellow senators that he would "fight them every step of the way if they try to dictate their moral conviction to all Americans in the name of conservatism" — and to that he could have added the names of moderation, of decency and of sanity as well.

The Star-Ledger

Newark, N.J., September 17, 1981

The New Right, a coalition of conservative religious groups, has been coming under increasing attack in recent months, mostly from liberal elements, its most prominent target.

But a surprising new element has been injected — Sen. Barry Goldwater, the feisty, blunt-spoken conservative who made a successful political career by tilting at liberal dogmas.

The Arizona Republican, in a speech on the Senate floor, said he was dismayed by the brand of conservatism preached by the Moral Majority and other New Right satellite groups — an ideology that, in his view, is not conservative in a traditional sense.

The intrusion of religion into politics and government, Sen. Goldwater charged, constitutes a threat to the "very spirit of our representative system."

Candor and courage have been constant characteristics of the senator's espousal of conservative doctrines, a disarming frankness that was admired by his liberal political colleagues on Capitol Hill, even though they sharply disagreed with his right-wing philosophy.

At 72, he remains unswervingly committed to the conservative cause that, ironically, has become far more widely accepted in the twilight of his political life than when he was the leader of the conservative wing of the Republican Party, and its presidential choice in 1964.

As evidenced by his blunt attack on the New Right, Sen. Goldwater has not been intimidated into silence by the influential presence on the political scene of the Moral Majority and similar religious-based groups.

This was one of the key themes in a recent address by the president of Yale University, A. Bartlett Giamatti, in welcoming the freshman class. In a wide-ranging attack on the Moral Majority and other conservative groups, he expressed concern that many of the nation's political and religious leaders appeared to have been intimidated into silence by the Moral Majority's appeals for a "closed society."

That could be the most damaging aspect of the current mood of conservatism generated by the New Right, a critical impingement on an open, pluralistic society that historically has been enlightened and enriched by the diversity of opinion, the basic freedom of its citizens to speak out, and to flail against social and economic injustice. A political silence spawned by intimidation diminishes and demeans our democratic heritage.

Chicago Tribune

Chicago, Ill., September 17, 1981

At first glance it may seem odd to find Sen. Barry Goldwater tilting against the Moral Majority. The so-called "new right," after all, had its roots in the 1964 Goldwater presidential campaign. But Sen. Goldwater's remarks against the Moral Majority are quite consistent with the conservative tradition of which he is a part, and they highlight both the practical legislative problem the Moral Majority creates and the ideological split within the American right.

Sen. Goldwater has accused the Moral Majority and other "new right" groups of trying to undermine the constitutional prohibition of an established state religion and guarantee of the free exercise of religion by using the "muscle of religion towards political ends." And he vowed to "fight them every step of the way if they try to dictate their moral convictions to all Americans in the name of conservatism."

This demonstrates the ideological split between conservatives who adopt the libertarian approach that government should stay out of the private affairs of individuals as much as possible and those who want government to promote a vision of American society that reflects a series of particular moral ideas including sexual restraint, religious worship, and temperance.

These approaches are fundamentally incompatible, the one emphasizing individual autonomy and social diversity and the other emphasizing the importance of shared—even enforced—moral values. Both have a basis in the conservative tradition. At the extremes, neither is acceptable.

A society without any set of widely shared moral values—even the value of the rule of law and respect for others' individual integrity—would soon tear itself apart. But a society with a rather precise set of government-enforced moral codes would be more stifling than Americans would accept.

The Moral Majority is a bit extreme. And in this case, extremism is indeed a vice, as Sen. Goldwater recognized. The country seems in little danger of extremism in defense of liberty just now. And it was quite appropriate for Sen. Goldwater to rise to state the libertarian objection to the moralists of the "new right."

But in addition to the theoretical objection, Sen. Goldwater noted a practical problem with the moralists' program. He argued that it was diverting Congress' attention from more significant and immediate economic and national security issues.

It would be easy to overstate the political impact the Moral Majority has had so far. The Reagan administration has hardly adopted its agenda. In fact, President Reagan has been accused of showing too little enthusiasm in this area. But the religious and secular interest groups that make up the moralistic "new right" have a prodigious publicity and fund-raising capacity that it would be folly to ignore.

Preserving the American tradition of freedom, tolerance, and diversity is a kind of conservatism that always needs to be alert and to renew itself.

ARKANSAS DEMOCRAT
Little Rock, Ark., September 19, 1981

Sen. Barry Goldwater's blast at "political preachers" is an uncommonly fierce one. What bugs the old Republican hero that he'd say he's sick and tired of the political moralists – the Moral Majority and the pro-lifers – telling him he's got to behave in a certain way to be a moral citizen?

Their positivistic manner, probably. The old man has been lobbied hard on these social issues, and appears to think they're personal rather than political. He seems to be saying that though he agrees in substance with a lot of what these people say, he won't have his soul and conscience examined or pass public tests of conformity.

But it isn't just the moralists and pro-lifers that rile Goldwater. He doesn't like single-issue groups in general, including ERA, and declares the whole social-moral issue bunch "divisive" and a menace to the republic.

That's too strong! These people may indeed exasperate lawmakers by trying to exact stands on issues some feel are more personal than political. But Congress and the courts have been taking action on these issues, so they are undoubtedly political – and many single-issuers argue rightly, moreover, that constitutional issues are involved. They say that if there's a menace to the republic, it's centered not in themselves but in Washington.

In any case, these people have a perfect right to bang senatorial ears on legislative and constitutional issues. For Goldwater or any other lawmaker to voice public warning against their "taking over" is demagoguery. They can't take over except by democratic means – and they can certainly point to what they consider past legislative and judicial "takeovers" by those of opposing social-moral opinion.

Anyhow, the bottom line is that any controverted public issue open to legislative or court action is political. And when laws and court opinions already enshrine what some think are wrong views, it's plain undemocratic for lawmakers to declare them out of political bounds when the opposition shows up.

THE KANSAS CITY STAR
Kansas City, Mo., September 18, 1981

When the patriarch of conservative politics in America speaks to other conservatives, more than reporters have good cause to stop what they are doing and listen. Carefully. When such a figure as Republican Sen. Barry Goldwater of Arizona takes the pains to chastise the doctrinaire followers of New Right politics, there comes a clear message: Stop this destructive single-issue nonsense or you'll wreck far more than you can ever salvage in this country. With admirable precision and characteristic bluntness, Mr. Goldwater struck at the heart of the religious New Right, its overriding and overbearing obsession with morality, particularly personal morality.

The primary issues, as Mr. Goldwater says, on the national agenda are the economy and the condition of national defense. The secondary issues are the others: abortion, busing, equal rights for women, school prayer and pornography. Depending upon the positions and arguments, we might disagree with Mr. Goldwater on how those issues should be ranked, but we do not part ways over their relative importance at this time.

Mr. Goldwater is Ronald Reagan's political godfather. It was at the 1964 Republican National Convention, when the conservative wing revolted and took over the party and nominated Mr. Goldwater to run against the incumbent creator of the Great Society, Lyndon Johnson, that Mr. Reagan issued his first edition of The Speech that he revised over the next 16 years until he reached the White House.

It says something about the condition of politics today that Mr. Goldwater, who scared the pants off the voter a decade and a half ago with his rock-hard positions, can be embraced as a man of rational, reachable moderation. His politics haven't changed that much—he remains a stalwart hawk on defense, for instance—but his place on the spectrum has been usurped and cantilevered into space by one-track religious leaders who wrap themselves in the garments of politicians. Mr. Goldwater has lost more fights than he has won during his Senate career, his position is more consistent than some of his colleagues', but his life as a politician continues because of an essential truth of this political system. It rewards give-and-take and compromise, a consensus wrought by coalitions and moderation.

Mr. Goldwater left no doubt to whom he was referring in his comments published this week in the *Congressional Record.* "In the past couple of years, I have seen many news items that referred to the Moral Majority, pro-life and other religious groups as 'the new right,' and the 'new conservatism.' Well, I have spent quite a number of years carrying the flag of the 'old conservatism.' And I can say with conviction that the religious issues of these groups have little or nothing to do with conservative or liberal politics.

"The uncompromising position of these groups is a divisive element that could tear apart the very spirit of our representative system, if they gain sufficient strength."

Considering the source, the New Right would be wise to listen. We are watching to see what Mr. Goldwater has done.

THE SUN
Baltimore, Md., September 20, 1981

Senator Barry Goldwater of Arizona has done the country, his party, conservatism and, perhaps, the Moral Majority a great favor by attacking the Moral Majority for its intrusion into politics. "I'm frankly sick and tired of the political preachers across this country telling me as a citizen that if I want to be a moral person, I must believe in 'A,' 'B,' 'C' and 'D.'... I am warning them today: I will fight them every step of the way if they try to dictate their moral convictions to all Americans in the name of conservatism," he said.

What can we say but, "Amen!"?

Criticizing the Moral Majority, the Rev. Jerry Falwell and the other political preachers is easy for liberals. So easy that the targets of the attack pay no heed. But when Senator Goldwater says it, then it is clearly time for them to listen. A "conservative" movement that offends the Arizona senator is obviously very narrowly based. A movement whose leader can say, "If you would like to know where I am politically, I am to the right of wherever you are. I thought Goldwater was too liberal!"—such a movement is not just saving the nation from liberalism. It needs to be reassessed. It needs to reassess itself.

We especially liked the fact that Mr. Goldwater criticized conservative politicians who respond to and even court the Moral Majority. He took to task the "New Right" in general—and Senators Jesse Helms, John P. East and Jeremiah Denton in particular.

While not quite in the same category, President Reagan also shares some of the blame for the aggressiveness with which the Moral Majority types have entered politics. Last year during the campaign he condemned use of the separation of church and state doctrine as a means of keeping religious values out of government. Now that Senator Goldwater has given the president an appropriate opportunity, Mr. Reagan ought to revise that statement and remind the nation there are other, better ways to inject religious values into government than single-issue, high pressure, moralistic political activity by organized sects.

BUFFALO EVENING NEWS
Buffalo, N.Y., September 24, 1981

Sen. Barry Goldwater, R.-Ariz., has now joined an increasing number of concerned Americans who have begun to speak out tellingly against the unyielding, single-issue tactics of the Moral Majority and similar groups.

But Sen. Goldwater's criticism takes on special importance, and should be listened to sympathetically by more moderate members of these groups, because they so often travel under the banner of conservatism — an ideology Sen. Goldwater has long championed and believes they have blemished.

Actually, he correctly stresses that what he questions here are attitudes and tactics that go beyond ideology — that is, the unusually strong commingling of religion and public issues, of church and state, and the implacable stands these groups take in trying, in the senator's words, "to force government leaders into following their positions 100 percent."

We do not believe that public discussion should be devoid of religious standards and ethics. Nor do the fundamentalists and the far right have a monopoly on uncompromising fervor in advancing their ideas. But Sen. Goldwater makes a valid point in asserting that such groups "must learn to make their views known without trying to make their views the only alternative."

What he fears is that the "uncompromising position of these groups is a divisive element that could tear apart the very spirit of our representative society, if they gain sufficient strength."

It could surely tear away at the tolerance that allows our dynamic society to preserve a reasonable distance between religion and government, so that neither dominates and controls the other, while encouraging freedom and a diversity of ideas.

St. Petersburg Times
St. Petersburg, Fla., September 17, 1981

Some people can't believe what they're hearing. Barry Goldwater, the moderate?

That's not the case at all.

Goldwater, the senior senator from Arizona, simply expressed the conscience of a conservative — a real conservative — in the *Congressional Record* this week. It was a remarkable, memorable document.

Excerpts follow.

"BEING A CONSERVATIVE in America traditionally has meant that one holds a deep, abiding respect for the Constitution. We conservatives believe sincerely in the integrity of the Constitution. We treasure the freedoms that document protects . . .

"One of the great strengths of our political system always has been our tendency to keep religious issues in the background. By maintaining the separation of church and state, the United States has avoided the intolerance which has so divided the rest of the world with religious wars . . .

"Can any of us refute the wisdom of Madison and the other framers? Can anyone look at the carnage in Iran, the bloodshed in Northern Ireland, or the bombs bursting in Lebanon and yet question the dangers of injecting religious issues into the affairs of state?

" . . . There is no more powerful ally one can claim in a debate than Jesus Christ, or God, or Allah, or whatever one calls his Supreme Being. But, like any powerful weapon, the use of God's name on one's behalf should be used sparingly. The religious factions that are growing in our land are not using their religious clout with wisdom. They are trying to force government leaders into following their positions 100 per cent.

" . . . THE RELIGIOUS ISSUES of these groups have little or nothing to do with conservative or liberal politics . . . I'm frankly sick and tired of the political preachers across this country telling me as a citizen that if I want to be a moral person, I must believe in 'A,' 'B,' 'C' and 'D.' Just who do they think they are? And from where do they presume to claim the right to dictate their moral beliefs to me?

"And I am even more angry as a legislator who must endure the threats of every religious group who thinks it has some God-granted right to control my vote on every roll call in the Senate . . .

"This unrelenting obsession with a particular goal destroys the perspective of many decent people. They have become easy prey to manipulation and misjudgment.

"A prime example was the recent nomination of Sandra O'Connor as a Supreme Court justice and the ensuing uproar over her stand on abortion. The abortion issue has nothing to do with being conservative or liberal. I happen to oppose abortion, but there are many fine conservatives who would go along with regulated abortions. In fact, my own wife believes that a woman should have the freedom of choice for herself whether she is capable of continuing the pregnancy and then raising the child. I disagree with her on that. Yet I respect her right to disagree . . .

"AND THE SAME goes for prospective Supreme Court justices. No single issue ever should decide the fitness of a Supreme Court justice. To think otherwise is to go against the integrity of the Constitution . . .

"The religious factions will go on imposing their will on others unless the decent people connected to them recognize that religion has no place in public policy. They must learn to make their views known without trying to make their views the only alternatives . . . We have succeeded for 205 years in keeping the affairs of state separate from the uncompromising idealism of religious groups and we mustn't stop now. To retreat from that separation would violate the principles of conservatism and the values upon which the framers built this democratic republic."

Goldwater did nothing but remind Americans this week what honest-to-goodness conservatism is all about. It's not the vituperation that passes for political debate these days. It's not the intolerant absolutism of people like Jerry Falwell, Jesse Helms and the other would-be moral monopolists.

THE TENNESSEAN
Nashville, Tenn., September 18, 1981

SEN. Barry Goldwater, R-Ariz., in more stinging comments aimed at "single-issue religious groups," has charged that they endanger America by "injecting religious issues into the affairs of state."

Senator Goldwater specifically mentioned the religiously fundamentalist and politically conservative organization Moral Majority and the anti-abortion group Pro-Life. "I am warning them today: I will fight them every step of the way if they try to dictate their moral convictions to all Americans in the name of 'conservatism,'" he said.

The senator added, "The uncompromising position of these groups is a divisive element that could tear apart the very spirit of our representative system if they gain sufficient strength."

Senator Goldwater's comments echoed in part an earlier and articulate address by the president of Yale University who saw the goals of a liberal education under attack by such groups.

Mr. A. Bartlett Giamatti said that "A self-proclaimed Moral Majority and its satellite or client groups, cunning in the use of a native blend of old intimidation and the new technology," threaten the goals of a liberal education.

"Angry at change, rigid in the application of chauvinistic slogans, absolutistic in morality, they threaten through political pressure or public denunciation whoever dares to disagree with their authoritarian positions. Using television, direct mail and economic boycott, they would sweep before them anyone who holds a different opinion," Mr. Giamatti said.

The Yale president went on to say, "I do not fear that these peddlers of coercion will eventually triumph. The American people are too decent, too generous, too practical about their principles to put up with the absolutism of these 'majorities' for very long."

Senator Goldwater and Mr. Giamatti are poles apart in some of their philosophical outlook, but both have sensed a disruptive effect of those groups parading under the banner of conservatism. Senator Goldwater sees the threat to representative government. Mr. Giamatti perceives it in the area of education, freedom and order.

The groups of which both spoke have shrugged them off as they would nitflies, but the fact that prominent people are beginning to speak out and warn that more is at stake than seems on the surface may be the first signs that reaction has set in against the absolutists.

CHARLESTON EVENING POST
Charleston, S.C., September 23, 1981

Sen. Barry Goldwater, incensed by the opposition of anti-abortion groups to the confirmation of fellow Arizonan Sandra Day O'Connor as an associate justice of the U.S. Supreme Court, lashed out the other day in the strongest possible terms against the Moral Majority, Pro-Life and others who would "dictate their moral convictions to all Americans."

"Just who do they think they are?" he asked. "... The uncompromising position of these groups is a divisive element that could tear apart the very spirit of our representative system, if they gain sufficient strength."

One does not have to march in the front ranks of those equally zealous for a woman's right to decide whether she will or will not carry her "fetus" to term, to know that Sen. Goldwater is correct. History is replete with examples of kingdoms and civilizations destroyed by the clash of competing religions and philosophies. One man's anathema is another man's meat. Thus it has been, and thus it shall always be.

The abortion issue *is* a terribly divisive one; it *is* splitting the conservative movement in this country, as Barry Goldwater's reaction shows so well.

Our view on abortion is that it is, except in a very narrow range of special circumstances, an abhorrent act, one that government has absolutely no business encouraging. At the same time, we believe the decision to have or not to have an abortion is a personal one that women must make after consulting their doctor, their conscience and, should they believe in one, their God. To insist, as many in this country now do, that the decision is somehow a collective one with society, more precisely a vocal *part* of society, exercising a veto, is more medieval than moral and, to be blunt, just as damaging to the human spirit as the act of abortion itself.

Newsday
Long Island, N.Y., September 18, 1981

It's not surprising for liberals, feminists, secular humanists or pro-choicers to attack the Moral Majority. But when someone with the impeccable conservative credentials of Sen. Barry Goldwater does so, his words deserve more than routine attention.

Goldwater is alarmed about the role of the Moral Majority and other so-called "new right" organizations in our society, for several reasons.

He thinks, for example, that they lack the true conservative's "abiding respect for the Constitution." He challenges their implication that God sides with them in every political debate. He is disturbed by their unalterable positions, which he warns could "tear apart the very spirit of our representative system." And he is perhaps most troubled by their failure to recognize the essentiality of the separation of church and state in American society.

"We have succeeded for 205 years in keeping the affairs of state separate from the uncompromising idealism of religious groups, and we mustn't stop now," the Arizona Republican said. "To retreat from that separation would violate the principles of conservatism and the values upon which the framers built this democratic republic."

Two things make Goldwater's denunciation of the Moral Majority important: His analysis of what's wrong with the arrogantly misnamed organization is sound, and he draws—perhaps for the first time—the clear distinction between mainstream American conservatism and the political-religious extremism of the Moral Majority.

"I am warning them today," Goldwater said. "I will fight them every step of the way if they try to dictate their moral convictions to all Americans in the name of conservatism."

The real majority, which is irrevocably committed (regardless of religious convictions) to the Constitution and the traditions of American political freedom and pluralism, can only say amen to that.

Roanoke Times & World-News
Roanoke, Va., September 26, 1981

In contrast to defections among the Democratic majority in the House of Representatives, the new Republican majority in the Senate has so far been remarkably unified. On the 101 recorded Senate votes this year on which most of the Republicans have lined up against most of the Democrats, Congressional Quarterly reports, the average Republican voted with his party 84 percent of the time. It's the highest party-unity score since CQ began compiling party unity scores in 1949.

The unity can be attributed mainly to the legislative skill of Senate Majority Leader Howard Baker and to the Reagan administration's decision to stress economic programs as its first priority. But now that more divisive social issues are coming to the fore, the GOP consensus may not endure. Issues like busing, school prayer and, above all, abortion threaten to divide not only moderates from conservatives. Such issues could also divide traditional conservatives from Republican senators close to the New Right.

Indeed, the fight between traditional conservatives and the New Right may have already begun, with Sen. Barry Goldwater's recent salvo against such groups as Moral Majority and Pro-Life, an anti-abortion organization also known as March for Life. Goldwater, the elder statesman of traditional conservatism, accused the New Right groups of trying "to dictate their moral beliefs to me." Among other things, Goldwater has not been happy about New Right criticism of Supreme Court Justice Sandra Day O'Connor, who is from Goldwater's home state of Arizona.

The response of to Goldwater's charges is revealing. Nellie Gray, head of March for Life, agreed she is trying to dictate her moral views: "Just as the abolitionists stood up against slavery, so the pro-life people shall stand up against the slaughter of innocents."

More than a century later, it is clear that the abolitionists were right to detest slavery; it is not so clear that today's pro-life (or, if you prefer, anti-choice) advocates are equally right to detest abortion in all its forms. In many other ways, however, the analogy is apt.

Like abolitionism, the anti-abortion movement tends to stress a single issue to the exclusion of all others, and it compensates for its minority status with a zeal derived from the belief that transcendent religious considerations are involved. Like abolition, the abortion issue does not follow the traditional lines of interest by which American politics have been traditionally organized. And like the abolitionists, the anti-abortion crusaders in their fervor sometimes adopt a shrill tone that is counterproductive because it simply turns off the unconvinced.

With its defiance of politics as usual and its goal of a radical change in the status quo, abolitionism can hardly be described as conservative. Neither, for the same reasons, can the anti-abortion movement. However right or wrong is the anti-abortion cause, Goldwater seems on solid ground in trying to distinguish it from the conservatism with which he has so long been identified.

Pittsburgh Post-Gazette

Pittsburgh, Pa., July 11, 1981

Unlike some nervous liberals, we don't think the shrill trumpets of the Moral Majority threaten imminently to bring down the constitutional wall between church and state. And we wonder if propagating that apocalyptic view doesn't actually help the radical religious right by exaggerating its influence.

Still, the self-righteousness of the Rev. Jerry Falwell and Co. *is* irritating, and so is their presumption to speak for all God-fearing Americans, whether the issue be national defense, television programming or a Supreme Court nomination.

For that reason, we found refreshing some comments Barry Goldwater offered this week on the subject of the MM and its leader. After Mr. Falwell's group pounced on Supreme Court nominee Sandra O'Connor, the 72-year-old Sen. Goldwater rushed to the defense of his fellow Arizonan and appended the salty suggestion that "every good Christian ought to kick Falwell right in the ass."

That the kicking the senator had in mind was political rather than physical was made clear by some further comments, in which he complained that the Moral Majority and anti-abortion extremists were arrogating to themselves the judgment as to whether a given judge or politician was really "conservative." Their obsession with social issues like abortion, Sen. Goldwater added, had distracted Congress' attention from truly conservative initiatives in economic and defense policy.

Sen. Goldwater's age and impeccable conservative credentials give him a freedom to speak out that few other members of Congress possess. His denunciation of the Moral Majority is thus unlikely to be echoed publicly by many of his colleagues, and certainly not in his (arguably too vivid) words. Still, in their hearts they know he's right.

The Virginian-Pilot

Norfolk, Va., September 19, 1981

Earlier this month Yale President Bartlett Giamatti attacked right-wing religious groups, conveniently, if inaccurately, referring to them all as the Moral Majority. September is apparently the month to moan the "Moral Majority blues," as we have called the tune, and in the past week the choir has been growing.

Senator Barry Goldwater became the first conservative Republican to blast the Moral Majority, when he did so Tuesday over breakfast in Washington. Here in Tidewater the attacks have been fast and furious, starting last week with educator Sol Gordon's criticism of the Moral Majority as "sanctimonious, authoritarian, and anti-Semitic." Wednesday was a big day for attacking the politically-minded, religious right, as both the Virginia head of the NAACP, Jack Gravely, and a University of Richmond humanities professor ripped into the Moral Majority.

What goes here? Why all these attacks? Some explanations—aside from the fact that the religious right is sometimes prone to rhetorical excess and thus invites criticism—seem obvious. Barry Goldwater doesn't like folks who call themselves conservative but who differ from him in their conservatism. Sol Gordon has bitterly debated Jerry Falwell and dislikes everything about him. The NAACP forecasts bad weather ahead, and the Moral Majority is a convenient place to lay the blame. The Richmond professor, like a number of academics, is easily persuaded that Jerry Falwell's real mission on this earth is to institute a theocracy in America.

Interestingly, none of these critics of the religious right is arguing against the right of Mr. Falwell and others to speak their mind. This is a sign of progress, inasmuch as when the religious right first appeared on the scene there were some—notably Anthony Lewis of the New York Times—who seemed ready to muzzle Mr. Falwell. Now, though—once you get behind some of the more emotional language of people like Mr. Gravely—you can detect a more subtle criticism of the religious right.

It is, simply, that while it is swell for people who hold religious opinions to speak out as they wish—this, after all, is a free country—actual legislation is quite another matter. And here the view seems to be that traditional religious beliefs should be excluded from any bearing at all upon public policy. Or, as Mr. Goldwater bluntly put it: "Religion has no place in public policy."

This seems to be a perspective common to all of those singing the Moral Majority blues. And it seems to be what drives many of them, in the final analysis, to attack the Moral Majority.

Yet surely this is an illiberal view—permitting people to be free to speak their views but unfree to have their views bear on public policy. And it is hypocritical because on many of the issues that concern the religious right—especially abortion—it can be said that everyone has a "religious" point of view of one kind or another.

As Paul Ramsey of Princeton University has pointed out, "any of the positions taken on controversial public questions having profound moral and human or value implications hold for us the functional sancity of religious belief." On the question of abortion, he writes, "each of the disputants has a religious faith in some kind of ethical creed"—whether it be secular individualism or "Ethical Culture" or Roman Catholicism or Baptist fundamentalism.

Public policy on matters like abortion inevitably requires an "imposition" of morality of one kind or another. And the Moral Majority, just like anyone else interested in such issues, should have every right not only to speak out but also to try to have their views influence legislation and policy. Perhaps the interesting question, in light of the recent attacks on the Moral Majority, is whether Messrs. Goldwater, Gravely, Gordon, *et al* will ever be tolerant enough to allow the religious right anything more than a quite limited freedom of speech.

Oregon Journal

Portland, Ore., September 26, 1981

When Barry Goldwater went down to a smashing defeat in 1964, it was assumed that the conservatism that he espoused was as much a contributor to Lyndon Johnson's landslide as were the latter's policies.

Some thought that right wing politics had been laid to rest, at least for a long time. They never would have foreseen the Ronald Reagan sweep 16 years later.

In fact, it is possible that Goldwater, even though crushed himself, may have provided the leadership that laid the groundwork for the comeback of the conservative philosophy in American politics.

But hardly anyone in 1964, looking toward 1981, would have predicted that one of the critics of the coming age of conservative leaders would be Barry Goldwater.

The Arizona senator, however, is emerging in that mold. He believes the cause for which he has labored and provided leadership for years has been subverted or compromised and used by single-issue and religious zealots.

Goldwater draws the line between a political philosophy to be applied to public issues and the closed-minded self-righteousness of some of the New Right.

He is particularly bothered by the likes of Jerry Falwell of the Moral Majority. The mingling of narrow religious views with public policy questions disturbs the senator.

He quite frankly labels some of the New Right organizations as posing a "serious threat to our liberty."

Furthermore, he believes the single-interest pressure groups — even the ones with which he agrees — distort the central issues of national security and economic stability.

This is not a liberal Democrat speaking. This is the Republican who has been the champion of the conservative cause for two decades and more. It just may be that the man who succeeded him in that role, now president of the United States, is listening, for Ronald Reagan seems to be trying to free himself from the embrace of the Falwells of the right wing movement without losing their affection in the process.

Yale University President Attacks Moral Majority

A. Bartlett Giamatti, president of Yale University, took the Moral Majority to task Aug. 31 in a speech to the incoming freshmen class. He singled out Falwell's group for special mention among the "peddlers of coercion." The "New Right," he declared, "threaten through political pressure or public denunciation whoever dares to disagree with their authoritarian positions." The Moral Majority claims a monopoly on truth, he continued, including "what God alone knows, which is when human life begins," a reference to the abortion controversy. A Moral Majority spokesman the next day denounced Giamatti's "unprovoked diatribe."

THE PLAIN DEALER
Cleveland, Ohio, September 3, 1981

The Rev. Jerry Falwell, television evangelist and founder of the misnamed Moral Majority, is burning. His so-called Christian fundamentalist political movement was rebuked thoroughly in a thoughtful and articulate manner by A. Bartlett Giamatti, the president of Yale University, who took the unusual step of disclosing his disdain in letters to Yale's incoming freshmen.

Three cheers for Giamatti for recognizing the hazards of a political organization so steeped in religious rigidity and absolutist views as to oppose constitutional principles, such as freedom of expression.

The trouble with Falwell and some of his followers is that they hold fast to a belief that they, and they alone, know the truth. Certainly, they have a right to their opinions. But their version leaves no room for diversity of opinion — for instance, anyone who believes in pluralism and has intellectual, cultural and secular beliefs is the archenemy of America and its free enterprise system. Thus, according to the gospel according to Falwell, thoughtful Americans who espouse diversity of opinion are immoral.

That kind of fundamentalism, as Giamatti so aptly pointed out, is fundamental nonsense.

The Union Leader
Manchester, N.H., September 2, 1981

While some of the Moral Majority folk come on a little too strongly at times, one wonders at the hysteria mixed with hypocrisy of those who seem to be fashioning a career out of attacking such groups while ignoring the beam in their own eye.

In May, for example, Yale University President A. Bartlett Giamatti used the unlikely occasion of Yale's commencement to attack the Moral Majority. Earlier this week he was back at the same stand. Hospitalized for surgery to remove a kidney stone, he sent prepared remarks to the in-coming freshmen in which he warned that the Moral Majority and other conservative groups are "shredding the fabric of our society," engaging in — shudder! — "public denunciation" of those who disagree with them, and pressing "uncompromising attitudes."

Interestingly, even as his remarks were delivered, a Catholic priest of liberal persuasion (and therefore acceptable to a Yale prexy), a gentleman who does everything Giamatti professes to deplore — i.e., he masks his ideological biases with professed concern over moral issues — was demonstrating what some might regard as an extremely "uncompromising attitude."

According to a statement issued Monday by Rev. Robert Drinan, clergyman, former Democratic congressman, president of the left-wing Americans for Democratic Action, he and his ilk will use more militancy in fighting the conservatism of the Reagan administration, whose victory at the polls, Drinan said, was strictly "a fluke."

Question for Giamatti: Does this "public denunciation," this belittling of the will of the majority of the people as reflected at the polls last November, this "uncompromising attitude," threaten to "shred the spiritual fabric of our society"?

Or is it the sort of exercise of free speech that members of the Moral Majority, and perhaps even a number of incoming Yale freshmen, feel is not the exclusive prerogative of liberals?

Chicago Tribune
Chicago, Ill., September 4, 1981

Yale University President A. Bartlett Giamatti lighted into the Moral Majority the other day in a statement to incoming freshmen. He charged that the Moral Majority has "licensed a new meanness of spirit in our land." And he characterized the religious movement this way: "Angry at change, rigid in application of chauvinistic slogans, absolutistic in morality, they threaten through political pressure or public denunciation of whoever dares to disagree with their authoritarian positions. Using television, direct mail, and economic boycott, they would sweep before them anyone who holds a different opinion."

This is strong stuff, but the Moral Majority had it coming. Mr. Giamatti stands for a tradition fundamentally threatened by Moral Majority-style politics. It is not a partisan tradition — liberal or conservative. Mr. Giamatti was as resolute against the know-nothing nihilism of the left in years past as he is today against the anti-intellectualism of the Moral Majority. He stands for a tradition that regards debate, free inquiry, and openness of mind as essential to the progress of civilization. It tolerates heresy, but subjects it to the same skepticism with which it views any other assertion. It trusts the informal devices of science and scholarship to the best way to grope toward truth. And if it distrusts authority, it does so only when authority imposes its beliefs through power rather than persuasion.

The Moral Majority does not welcome debate. Its truths are revealed, unchallengeable. It does not accommodate diversity, for this would represent an admission of uncertainty. It is illiberal, not because it is right-wing but rather because it is intolerant. It is not only — or even primarily — a religious movement. Rather it is a political pressure group designed to choke off a set of values (which it sneeringly calls "secular humanism") that it identifies with absolute evil.

Mr. Giamatti may have been intemperate when he accused the Moral Majority of creating the conditions for a resurgence of anti-Semitism and racism. But he was not out of line in suggesting that the politics of revealed truth creates a mood in which such malign forces thrive. He might have been more effective if his language were less venomous. He would probably not have become so exercised if the Moral Majority had not insisted on tampering with public education — through the demand for school prayer and the teaching of creationism and through silly objections to books that have become classics.

Understand, the issue here is not the authenticity of the Moral Majority's religious convictions. These are part of a strong American tradition, too, and no one should question anyone's right to a personal faith. But the Moral Majority has a decidedly secular side. It is playing into the realm of politics and authority. And what it wants there must be resisted.

Naturally enough, the Moral Majority has responded by accusing Mr. Giamatti of intolerance. The Rev. Dan C. Fore, its New York State chairman, tried to turn the Yale president's arguments against him. "We're not trying to coerce anyone," he said. "We're just trying to express a point of view. They're denying us every right to the pluralism they say we're trying to deny."

That, of course, is bunk. Mr. Giamatti has not called for government to ban Moral Majority ministers from television, or ordered fundamentalist literature out of the Yale library, or stricken the name of Jonathan Edwards from Yale's list of residential colleges. He is only opening the debate over whether the politics of revealed truth should prevail in a society that has prided itself on its openness and tolerance. And he understands, as the Moral Majority does not, that spirited debate is a tribute to our national character, not a menace.

THE COMMERCIAL APPEAL

Memphis, Tenn., September 4, 1981

IT IS PROBABLY instructive to note that the Moral Majority responded to the withering criticisms of A. Bartlett Giamatti, president of Yale University, not by praying for him but by forsaking him. The Moral Majority is much less given to Christian forgiveness than to political vengeance. That is why Giamatti's attack on the "polyester mysticism" of the Rev. Jerry Falwell and his flock was so welcome and so right.

Ronald Godwin, executive director of the Moral Majority, spoke nothing of love or salvation in reply to Giamatti. Instead, Godwin accused Giamatti of "liberal demagoguery" and suggested darkly that a "high White House official" was going to tell Giamatti a thing or two. So much for where the Moral Majority is coming from.

This exchange is significant in at least two respects.

First, it breaks the silence of the academic world on an issue of vital national concern and should give courage to other college and university presidents to speak out against what is potentially a major threat to academic freedom in this country. Business and religious leaders should also be prompted by Giamatti's example.

In fact, he called out to them. Pointing out that the members of the Moral Majority believe "they and they alone possess the truth," Giamatti said, "There is no debate, no discussion, no dissent. They know. There is only one set of overarching political and spiritual and social beliefs; whatever view does not conform . . . is negative, secular, immoral against the family, antifree enterprise, un-American.

"What a shame more of our captains of commerce have not seized the opportunity to speak up for free enterprise. What a shame such denials of our country's deepest traditions of freedom of thought, speech, creed and choices are not faced candidly in open debate by our political and religious leaders."

SECONDLY, THIS kind of assault is important because it forces the Moral Majority to defend itself, which is something it cannot do in any free contest of American ideas and ideals. Falwell and the Moral Majority have been trying to set the agenda for national debate, but Giamatti has gone a long way toward making them the central issue of that debate.

All sensible Americans should say, "Amen," and none too quietly.

THE BLADE

Toledo, Ohio, September 4, 1981

YALE President A. Bartlett Giamatti, fed up with the pretensions of the Moral Majority and other right-wing, would-be controllers of the thought waves, unleashed a blistering attack on such groups in his annual address to the freshman class.

"They have licensed a new meanness of spirit in our land, a resurgent bigotry that manifests itself in racist and discriminatory postures," the Yale president said. "We should be concerned that so much of our political and religious leadership acts intimidated for the moment and will not say with clarity that this most recent denial of the legitimacy of differentness is a radical assault on the very pluralism . . . our country was founded to welcome and foster."

Mr. Giamatti's attacks on what he called advocates of "polyester mysticism" — presumably a reference to the well-groomed television evangelists who use the medium as a mighty money-raiser — may at first glance be somewhat startling for a university president to use in a speech delivered to freshmen. They are, after all, on the brink of a new search for ideas among which, surely, will be those espoused by prominent members of the right-wing clergy. They represent part of the pluralism that is America, too.

But the acid test should be whether members of the Moral Majority are content to let their own ideas be tested freely in the marketplace of thought or whether they foreclose such tests.

One can smile when one learns that a school board member in a small Indiana town objected to two books, "Making it With Mademoiselle" and "Belly Button Defense," only to discover that the first dealt with dress patterns and the second was about basketball. But other books banned by stern-eyed inquisitors have included "The Diary of Anne Frank," for reasons one can never understand, and "1984," which ironically is about a state which exercises a ruthless form of thought control.

No doubt the critics of the Moral Majority are occasionally somewhat shrill, too. It would be well for all who attempt to prevent free and open discussion of ideas or access to differing points of view to remember an oft-quoted explanation of the rationale behind the First Amendment by the late Judge Learned Hand:

It presupposes that right conclusions are more likely to be gathered out of a multitude of tongues than through any kind of authoritative selection. To many this is, and always will be, folly; but we have staked upon it our all.

Some of our latter-day Cotton Mathers should tack that statement on the wall in front of their desks.

The Virginian-Pilot

Norfolk, Va., September 4, 1981

A. Bartlett Giamatti, the president of Yale University, has in recent years made speeches and led causes that have been right on the mark. He has defended high academic standards and argued for more challenging curricula. He has fought against government regulation of academic life. Now, this week, Mr. Giamatti has made another speech—this one to the freshmen at Yale—the burden of which was the Moral Majority.

The Moral Majority and its "satellite or client" groups are "peddlers of coercion" in "a radical assault" that threatens not only the life of the mind but also that of the nation, he said. "Angry at change, rigid in the application of chauvinistic slogans, absolutistic in morality, they threaten through political pressure or public denunciation whoever dares to disagree with their authoritarian positions."

The Moral Majority, said Mr. Giamatti, is intent on destroying "diversity of opinion" in the United States. Moral Majoritarians and their allies "presume to know what justice for all is. . .which books are fit to read, which television programs are fit to watch, which textbooks will serve for all the young . . . [and even] what God alone knows, which is when human life begins."

"They alone possess the truth," he said. "There is no debate, no discussion, no dissent. They know. There is only one set of overarching political and spiritual and social beliefs; whatever view does not conform to these views is by definition relativistic, negative, secular, immoral, against the family, anti-free enterprise, un-American."

Mr. Giamatti scored some points in this speech. Doubtless there are some members of the Moral Majority and other New Right groups who would squash opinion that conflicts with theirs, prescribe the books the rest of us should read, and contend that they alone know the truth and that whoever disagrees is Godless, and so on. Doubtless there are some folks in these groups we would not wish to invite to a keg party.

Yet Mr. Giamatti was at fault to lump the Moral Majority with other New Right groups, and to assume that the stands the organization takes are the same as those some of its members or allies, acting as individuals, have taken. His speech was obviously more polemical than careful. A phone call or two might have given Mr. Giamatti more accurate poop on the Moral Majority and the New Right. For example, when Mr. Giamatti linked the Moral Majority to the rise in anti-Semitism, he did so without knowing (one can only assume) that the Moral Majority is publicly committed (more strongly than most other groups) to the state of Israel, and that its president, Jerry Falwell, received an award from the National Conference of Christians and Jews last year.

More important than the details, however, is the big picture. Mr. Giamatti would seem to have no clue as to why the Moral Majority exists. Individualism is an American ideology, but so, too, is communitarianism, which is what the Moral Majority represents. American history happens to be the record of pendulum swings back and forth between the two, and during the past two decades the pendulum has swung in favor of individualism, in the form of the social and moral liberalism that has pervaded the nation and its institutions. In this context, it is no surprise the Moral Majority exists, and it will be no surprise if the nation does not experience a swinging of the pendulum in its direction.

What that may mean (if American history is any guide, any such swing will be small) would have been an interesting question for an academician of Mr. Giamatti's stature to have discussed. Apparently, Mr. Giamatti must think no good at all can come from the Moral Majority's efforts. Yet if that group's influence is such that more parents become more interested in their children's education, that television cleans itself up a bit, that some of America's porn shops go out of business, that the right of the fetus to life is given some weight in the balance that now only weighs the mother's right to abort that fetus—would all of these results be so bad?

The important point is that whatever happens does so after the sort of debate and discussion that Mr. Giamatti desires but says the Moral Majority is not interested in. If Mr. Giamatti's speech has utility, it will lie in testing that proposition, not in confirming the sort of fashionable intellectual prejudice that exists today against the Moral Majority.

Part II: Education

There is an old saying: "A little learning can be a dangerous thing." The clash between the "New Right" and the schools is an age-old conflict over the nature of education. The traditional purpose of education is to broaden a student's intellectual exposure. Human knowledge would not have progressed if it had not been for the exchange of ideas generated in schools and universities. However, this results in the well-known "generation gap." Parents find that their children come home from school with very different views from the ones they learned at home. The quest for knowledge leads away from the familiar, both in philosophical values and information.

American educators thought this problem was solved by the existence of private religious schools. Public education would be thoroughly secular, as befitted a pluralistic nation, while parents who desired to protect religious beliefs would send their children to special schools. In practice, however, religious education means extra expense, which many parents cannot afford. Since public schools are supported by tax money, parents conclude that they have the right to a say in how the schools will be run.

Part of the impetus for "New Right" activism has been the growing realization of serious deficiencies in public education. The impression that schools are failing to turn out literate students fuels pressure for a curriculum devoted to the "basics": reading, writing and arithmetic. Thus, the campaign to ban "subversive" books is at bottom a protest against poor educational training. Perhaps if Johnny could read well, there would be less concern over what Johnny was reading.

Biology & the Bible: "Creation Science" Gains Support

The famous "monkey trial" of 1925, in which Dayton, Tenn. teacher John Thomas Scopes was prosecuted for teaching Charles Darwin's theory of evolution, did not lay the evolution controversy to rest. On the contrary, Scopes lost the case, and Tennessee forbade the teaching of evolution until 1967, when the law was repealed after the Supreme Court ruled that it conflicted with freedom of religion. The evolution controversy continued to simmer afterward, never dying out entirely. As late as 1977, an Indiana Superior Court judge blocked the use of a ninth-grade textbook that said there was "no way to support the doctrine of evolution."

Anti-evolutionists quickly profited from the fundamentalist surge of the late 1970s. They were heartened in August 1980 by presidential candidate Ronald Reagan's remark that there were "great flaws" in evolutionary theory. He said he favored including the Biblical story of creation in addition to evolution in biology classes. The growing acceptance of "creation science" worried scientists, educators and religious leaders alike. Public opinion polls showed widespread sympathy for giving equal time to both Genesis and Darwin. The term "creation science" itself suggested that the "creationists" were not "anti-science" but were merely offering another interpretation of events that had no first-hand witness. Scientists were forced to become aware of just how out of touch with the public they were. The public took the word "theory" to mean "conjecture," whereas scientists used "theory" to mean an explanation of observed phenomena. The "creationists" had another powerful weapon in the scientific community's well publicized but imperfectly understood controversies. After all, the public reasoned, if scientists themselves could not agree on how life developed, why not consider "creationism" as just another possible explanation?

Sentinel Star
Orlando, Fla., March 12, 1980

THE Florida Legislature is considering a bill requiring that public schools teach the theory of creation according to Genesis as well as the scientific explanation for life on Earth.

If there is one scintilla of intelligence in Tallahassee, the bill, sponsored by Rep. Thomas R. Bush, R-Fort Lauderdale, will die a swift and permanent death.

The concept of injecting a formal religion into the classroom is both unconstitutional and a rank form of religious imperialism.

Mr. Bush ignores the fact that Florida has adherents of nearly the entire range of religions. Their children go to public schools. Their taxes support those schools.

Does Mr. Bush intend for the Legislature to also order children to learn the theory of evolution according to the Hindu faith, the Buddhist, the Taoist, the Moslem? And what about the Seminole Indians and their own view of how we came to be here? Surely, Mr. Bush's sense of basic fairness would dictate that their teachings also be recognized.

According to Mr. Bush, the biblical theory should be taught in public schools as part of a kind of "equal time" doctrine. But that, of course, ignores the existence of church schools where the children of parents with formal religious ties may send their children to learn the details of that religion of their choice. Those parents should not want public schools to take over that function.

The Florida Legislature should quickly do away with Mr. Bush's ill-conceived proposal and should do so by such an overwhelming margin that it will be clear such legislation will have no chance of passage anytime in the predictable future.

Chicago Tribune
Chicago, Ill., March 19, 1980

A number of earnest fundamentalists are mounting a national campaign to establish in the public schools, by statute, what they call "balanced treatment for scientific creationism and evolution." In Illinois, Sen. Robert Mitchler [R., Oswego] has introduced a bill to this end. The writers of several letters on this page join us in comment.

In the 19th century, some of our ancestors experienced a traumatic conflict between religion and science. Many found it hard to accept new insights in biology and geology, as evidence mounted that the processes of creation were slower than a literal reading of Genesis would suggest. With the passage of time, the conflict between religion and science receded, as people both with and without strong religious conviction found evolutionary thinking acceptable. William Herbert Carruth wrote a notable poem with the refrain, "some call it evolution, and others call it God." Or both.

But there are still those who find their theology at odds with generally received science. Members of the Creation Research Society contend that because the Bible "is inspired throughout, all of its assertions are historically and scientifically true." They want at least "equal time" in the public schools for their views.

The attempt to legislate the teaching of religious dogma in the public schools is contrary to our national laws and institutions, whatever the dogma might be. In the United States there is and should be no "established" religion. What children learn in the public schools should be secular knowledge, understanding, and skills. What the schools teach about the creation of the world should be undogmatic science, not the s a c r e d writings of Christian or Jew, Hindu or Buddhist.

Some contend that the public schools are not really religiously neutral, but are inculcating "secular humanism." Champions of "scientific creationism" represent themselves as raising a civil rights issue, as seeking "balance" and "equal time" rather than "establishment." But to put the force of law behind teaching one dogmatic theological position, "balanced" against the scientific consensus, would be establishing dogma, a single dogma.

The teaching of science in Illinois public schools should not be troubled by the enactment of Sen. Mitchler's bill. Dean Robert Paul Roth, of Luther-Northwestern Seminaries in St. Paul, was right when he said, "Equal time legislation will create bad science, bad theology, and bad pedagogy." Bad law, too.

The State

Columbia, S.C., March 12, 1980

PERSUASIVE testimony has been delivered to the S.C. Legislature against passage of a bill that would require public schools to give "balanced" educational treatment of origins of life. The General Assembly should take heed and keep the issue out of the lawbooks.

The bill under consideration is that of Rep. Robert Kohn of Charleston. His legislation would mandate "balanced treatment for scientific creationism and evolution" in classroom studies.

Legal decisions and opinions generally hold that it is unconstitutional to require a religion-based concept to be injected into public school teachings.

While Representative Kohn insists that his legislation makes no mention of "the Bible, religion or God," his bill is still deeply rooted in religious teachings. His semantics do not remove this.

The State said in an earlier editorial that there is no need, or shouldn't be, for legislation such as that proposed by Mr. Kohn. Be it science, history or other studies, lawmakers should not be dictating specific elements for educators to deal in.

Carl D. Evans, a University of South Carolina professor, stated this well, when he told the House Education Committee: "There is not a *bona fide* scientist anywhere who would be willing to allow state law to determine, much less define, the theories which he or she is permitted to advocate."

But as we also said earlier, there is room for acknowledgement in an educational setting of what the issue of origins of life is all about. The subject can, and should be, handled in an objective and historical perspective. It is impossible to ignore the role religious forces, including beliefs in divine creation, have played in shaping the history of mankind.

But to mandate the teaching of a specific theory in connection with a religion has no place in the public educational setting. Other institutions — families, churches, even private schools — exist to shape those beliefs based on faiths.

There is a residual danger in putting into law what Mr. Kohn proposes. It could open the door for other legislative proposals which would involve the state in religion-related fields, where the government does not belong. The Kohn bill should be put to rest.

The Evening Bulletin

Philadelphia, Pa., September 21, 1980

The sophisticates hooted when Ronald Reagan first proposed teaching the Biblical theory of creation in our public schools. Reagan is shooting from the hip again, they said.

On reflection, we think he has a point. This is not necessarily because we subscribe to this theory. We only think the nation's youngsters should be exposed to the widest range of human thought, including all theories of the development of life.

Except for those who cling to a literal interpretation of the story of Genesis, most established religions have come to live with English biologist Charles Darwin's theories of evolution and natural selection. Simply put, Darwin believed that life evolved from simple organisms. Survival depended on strength, speed, cunning. Species which adjusted, cell by cell and inch by inch, survived. Others were condemned to extinction.

Scientists today are saying they cannot reconcile Darwin's theories with current findings. Niles Eldredge of the American Museum of Natural History in New York told The Bulletin's Warren Froelich that prehistoric fossils show life evolved in quick bursts, from mutation or geographical isolation, not the gradual pace Darwin imagined.

For example, instead of the slow evolution of one form of prehistoric mollusk into another, Mr. Eldredge says fossils show the existence of one species, then suddenly another.

Defenders of Charles Darwin argue that Mr. Eldredge and his colleagues are playing into the hands of an increasingly vocal group of "creationists" who want the Old Testament version offered in school. Not so, says Mr. Eldredge. "If I come up with a challenge to cherished beliefs, that's too bad. The truth is the truth."

Niles Eldredge, naturally, is perfectly right.

Whether the Old Testament story of creation is literal truth or beautiful myth, there is no reason why it cannot be offered in our schools as one of several theories. It already is in New York, Florida, Virginia, Wisconsin and some Philadelphia suburbs.

The same sophisticates who would accuse the creationists of narrow-mindedness seem determined to cling to their own cherished beliefs, to deny young people the challenge of conflicting ideas.

Let the kids hear all the theories. They can decide for themselves which ones are right.

THE LOUISVILLE TIMES

Louisville, Ky., March 14, 1980

The Kentucky legislature, and especially the House Education Committee, deserve high marks for striving to acquaint our children with a broad range of ideas about the origins of earth and mankind.

A law already on the books allows teachers to tell students about the Biblical story of creation along with the theory of evolution.

The committee struck another blow for enlightenment this week when it approved a bill instructing the Textbook Commission to choose books on "scientific creationism" for use in biology classes.

What made the vote all the more admirable is that some members did not seem to know what "scientific creationism" means, and sponsor Claudia Riner of Louisville didn't have time to explain. Most agreed, however, that it's good for children.

But this must only be the beginning, so to speak, of the legislature's efforts to inform our youngsters of their ultimate origins.

Yet another bill must be written requiring schools to teach all the diverse and wonderful ideas about how people came to be on this swirling orb. To do less would be to deny young Kentuckians the freedom to choose.

For instance, kids ought to know the Aztec stories about Quetzalcoatl, the feathered serpent who created mankind.

Valuable lessons could be learned from a discussion of Oromazes, an old Iranian god of good. He, you may recall, made a deity who has few adherents in Frankfort, the god of good government. Then he plunked 24 gods in a cosmic egg, where they became forever entangled with 24 gods of evil. Does that sound a bit like the militants vs. the hostages? Or the governor and the legislature?

The youth of our river towns would be attracted by the Slavic myth in which god sends the devil to the bottom of the primordial waters for a handful of sand. From that material the world was made.

What Eastern Kentucky child would not be delighted by the Islamic teaching that god created two species, man and jinn, of which man is less inclined to evil? Are jinn perhaps politicians? Or strip miners?

Kentucky educators must obviously go beyond Darwin and scientific creationism if children are to be aware of all the possibilities. For Rep. Riner, a career spreading the word about the origins of our species is clearly evolving.

California Parent Loses Suit on Teaching "Creationism"

Kelly Seagraves, a San Diego religious teacher, lost his suit March 5 to force the California school system to include the Biblical story of creation in biology classes. Sacramento Superior Court Judge Irving Perluss ruled that the state educational system did not deprive Seagraves' three children of their First Amendment rights by teaching only the theory of evolution. However, Perluss ordered state officials to distribute a policy statement to local schools forbidding them to take a dogmatic approach to teaching the origins of life on Earth.

In his suit, Seagraves had charged that evolution was presented to students as the only explanation of the origin of life and was thus dogmatic and deprived fundamentalist students of their religious freedom. Seagraves, who headed the Creation Science Research Center in San Diego, sought to require public schools to include other theories about the origin of life, particularly the Biblical account. During the five-day nonjury trial, Dr. Thomas Jukes, researcher in biophysics and molecular evolution at the University of California at Berkeley and author of the state's guidelines on teaching biology, denied that the guidelines were dogmatic. He called the Biblical version of creation "a rigid concept frozen into the book of Genesis."

The Cleveland Press

Cleveland, Ohio, March 10, 1981

Just when everyone was expecting another Scopes "monkey trial," the plaintiffs in California's evolution trial switched signals.

In place of their demand that the biblical account of creation be taught in the public schools on an equal basis with the Darwinian theory of evolution, they were willing to settle for a finding that the teaching of the latter violated their religious liberties.

Judge Irving Perluss didn't oblige. He held that those liberties were already sufficiently protected — although he did order wider dissemination of a policy adopted by the California State Board of Education eight years ago.

The policy stipulates that evolution be presented in textbooks as a theory and not be taught as finished, dogmatic fact. This kind of conditional approach to truth is, of course, the essence of science.

It should also be noted that California students are already exposed to "creationism" along with other religious doctrines in social studies classes. This too is as it should be, and if they were wise, creationists would be content with that.

It is as undesirable for religion to try to compete with science as it is for science to become infused with religious fervor. The one exposes religious beliefs to ridicule (e.g., the Scopes trial); the other can have ghastly results (e.g., Nazi racial theories).

Creationists do not demand that biblical explanations of physical and mental disease as being caused by demons be accorded equal time in the nation's medical schools. Yet somehow many people are offended by the idea that they are closely akin to all of God's creatures, or that evolution could represent the working out of the Divine Plan.

But as Darwin himself urged in his "Descent of Man," the fact of man's having arisen from lowly origins "may give him hope for a still higher destiny in the distant future."

Not a bad thought for a sermon.

St. Louis Review

St. Louis, Mo., March 6, 1981

At Dayton, Ohio, in July, 1925, religious fundamentalists won a court case but lost a war of ideas. On July 10 of that year, John T. Scopes, a biology teacher in the Dayton schools, was brought to trial under a newly passed Ohio law prohibiting the teaching of "any theory which denies the story of the divine creation of man" and which teaches instead "that man is descended from a lower form of animals." Scopes was found guilty and fined $100, but the public ridicule occasioned by the trial effectively ended efforts to prohibit the teaching of the theory of evolution.

The Scopes trial had immense significance to fundamentalist Protestants, but had little impact on Catholics. Charles Darwin had first proposed the theory of evolution in his Origin of the Species published in 1859. As early as 1893, Pope Leo XIII, commenting on the theory, proclaimed that the Scriptures "did not intend to teach men those things in no way profitable unto salvation." The First Vatican Council in 1870 refused to condemn the theory of evolution and the Biblical Commission in 1909 stated that "free discussion of the six days of creation is permitted."

It is understandable then, that efforts to revive the controversy over evolution are not held as very important by most Catholics. Efforts are under way in California and elsewhere to require that in the public schools the doctrine of direct divine creation of each species on earth, including man, be taught.

Proponents of such legislation properly point out that the theory of evolution remains just that — a theory. No conclusive proof has ever been adduced. As a presidential candidate, Ronald Reagan was wiser than a number of his critics in noting that there is continuing questioning of the theory of evolution in scientific circles.

In addition, the philosophical consequences of the theory of evolution have been stretched beyond what is scientifically verifiable. Evolutionist philosophers use the theory to deny God and His creative power, extrapolating from the origin of man that evolution is a blind and random event, without an initiator, without a guide.

For the Catholic — scientist or layman — the possibility of the evolution of man's body from other forms of creation is no challenge to the beauty of God's creation, but makes His activity even more wondrous. Science should be free to prove or disprove the details of evolution as a part of the process of creation and children should be fully taught its current status. Even science, however, must realize its own limitations and give recognition to the ultimate Creator of all things, Almighty God.

Arkansas Gazette.

Little Rock, Ark., March 6, 1981

Religious fundamentalists at San Diego have brought civil suit in a California state court at Sacramento that is widely referred to in the Golden State as "Scopes II" although there are only superficial similarities in this trial and the criminal action against John T. Scopes at Dayton, Tennessee in 1925.

The plaintiffs in the California suit — their spiritual kin were often called Bible-thumpers in the rip-roaring days of H. L. Mencken — have asked that the California Board of Education be ordered to rewrite its science education guidelines to permit the Biblical version of creation to be taught alongside Charles Darwin's theory (or fact) of evolution in biology classes.

While the issue may seem simple, it actually is exceedingly complex, but some basic ideas about this controversy transcend even the legal process taking its own course in California. One of the plaintiffs is Kelly Segraves, director of the Creation Science Research Center, a non-profit foundation that lobbies in several states for the theory of supernatural creation of the earth and life. It also monitors textbooks and prepares teaching materials.

The essential distinction is clear enough to us: Belief in the literal Biblical version of creation presents not scientific theory but instead religious theory. Exposing students to a strictly religious interpretation of how it all began might be properly presented in a social studies curriculum that also includes other religious studies, but it has no proper place in a science curriculum.

Evidence in support of the general theory (or fact) of evolution is overwhelming among reputable scientists the world over. There may be minor disagreements on the details of how the evolutionary process took place, but the literal Biblical version of creation is not included among the points of legitimate scientific debate. Among the most thoughtful defenders of scientific evolu-

tionary theory are some pretty devoutly religious people who have not the slightest difficulty in finding their religious and scientific views congenial.

Curiously, attorneys for the plaintiffs in the California suit say their clients "seek protection for the right to believe in a cause." "The real issue," it is alleged, "is religious freedom under the First Amendment of the Constitution."

This is a revealing proposition, for the implication is that a religious "cause" and belief should be accepted as scientific theory for presentation in a science curriculum that already accepts, as does science everywhere, the validity of the theory (or fact) of evolution. Put another way, for a religious cause or belief to be presented to a biology class is to impose a particular religious view upon others who may not share that view, and infringes upon *their* religious freedom.

The plaintiffs have every right to believe in whatever cause they wish, and that right must be protected, but having that religious belief excluded from presentation to a biology class in no way abrogates the right. It can leave more class time, however, for a full presentation of legitimate scientific material.

This and related issues, we know, will never be put to rest, but they seem to crop up in some form or another in just about every state of the Union at one time or another. We are nibbling on the fringes of it again in Arkansas, but at least this time around, unlike 1925, the nation is dealing with civil law. John Scopes, the Tennessee teacher, was convicted of teaching evolution in violation of state law and fined $100, and the fervor of the time led Arkansas to adopt its own punitive law, which stayed on the books for four decades until the United States Supreme Court relieved us, finally, of the embarrassment. Let us not go through that disgraceful exercise again, whether it be in a criminal or a civil context.

ST. LOUIS POST-DISPATCH

St. Louis, Mo., March 10, 1981

Aware that the California evolution case was in danger of being turned into a boundless metaphysical debate, Judge Irving Perluss wisely kept the issue narrow and resolved it by declaring both sides winners. While holding that the state's guidelines on the teaching of evolution did not preclude belief in creation as presented in the Bible, Judge Perluss directed the state to do a better job of communicating to school districts its policy of tolerating the opposing belief.

Unlike the Scopes trial, in which a Tennessee school teacher was convicted of teaching evolution in violation of a statute prohibiting it, the California case raised the question of whether the schools were teaching that evolution was the sole credible explanation for the origins of mankind, thereby forcing students to repudiate their faith in the Bible. Evolution is certainly the only credible *scientific* explanation, the

biblical story offering no scientific evidence to support instant existence.

For this reason Genesis does not qualify for inclusion in a science curriculum, but is quite properly part of a social studies curriculum. That is exactly the way California handles the situation. Missouri, on the other hand, tells schools to include the biblical story of creation in biology courses.

No school district has the right to tell a student he must believe in evolution and that the creation story is wrong, which is what the California plaintiff contended was going on but which the judge found not to be the case — or at least not to be the policy. By the same token, if there is a conflict between a religious teaching and a scientific teaching, it is a distortion of the principle of neutrality in matters of religion for the state to reconcile the differing versions by saying they have equal scientific validity, which is what the creationists seem to want.

The Register

Santa Ana, Calif., March 5, 1981

"I am inclined to agree with Francis Galton in believing that education and environment produce only a small effect on the mind of anyone, and that most of our qualities are innate," naturalist Charles Darwin wrote in 1887 nearly 20 years after publishing his epochal theories on the evolution of man.

Darwin's words seemed especially ironic this week as evolutionists and creationists again squared off in a Sacramento courtroom over a renewed attempt to put the two theories side-by-side in California's science textbooks.

Darwin's theories alone are presented now. For the moment the case for divine creation can be found only in social science and philosophy texts.

Over the past 20 years, both sides have won and lost court and board-of-education battles over the issue. And no matter how the current case winds up, we suspect the fight will continue unless one theory or another is proven in a scientific sense.

The ongoing problem of evolutionists is that their theories while more than 120 years old, remain unprovable. Creationists are openly skeptical — and not without reason — of a theory proposing that man evolved from constantly positive mutations over tens of millions of years. To creationists it is far more logical to believe man, animal and plant life on planet Earth was divinely created.

It would seem elementary to include both theories in science textbooks. Science, after all, is the quest for truth and fact.

However, scientists are at the fore in keeping the creation theory off to the sidelines. They argue that the creation theory is religious or philosophical and thus "not within the realm of science."

Perhaps if the creationists were attempting to put Adam and Eve and the Book of *Genesis* in California's science textbooks, evolutionists would find wider support for their attempt to keep contrary ideas at bay. But after all these years, the evolutionists must know that whole texts produced by the creationists have managed to refrain from literal interpretations of the Bible. Zeroing in on scientific provability, the creationists have basically produced a theory they believe is far easier to accept scientifically than Darwin's theories.

In short, they believe fewer miracles are involved in accepting the creationist theory than the evolutionist theory.

If the school system wants to establish credibility, we fail to understand its current science guidelines restricting one theory while promoting another, when one is no more scientifically provable than the other.

RENO EVENING GAZETTE
Reno, Nev., March 12, 1981

California Superior Court Judge Irving Perluss acted both intelligently and compassionately last week in the latest lawsuit squaring religion off against Darwin's theory of evolution.

The judge ruled — as he had to — that the schools have a right to teach Darwin's prevailing scientific theory. But he also recognized — as he should have — the emotional and mental problems this teaching creates in children who believe literally in the biblical version of creation.

The Creation-Science Research Center of San Diego, which brought the suit, did not actually want Darwin banned from the schools. But it did want biblical creation taught as an alternate theory on an equal standing with evolution. And it claimed that creationist students' constitutional rights were being violated when biblical creation was not taught along with evolution. The judge would not buy that. No one's constitutional rights were violated, he said. But at the same time he ordered the state to distribute to local schools its official policy forbidding dogmatism in the treatment of the origins of life.

The judge's decision is a most practical one. It supports the schools, but also recognizes that the schools must do what they can to lessen the emotional stress facing fundamentalist children in science classes. This has pleased the creationists, who believe their children will be more sympathetically dealt with. They do not plan to appeal and thus the judge has prevented a lengthy constitutional battle which could drag on for many years without attending to the immediate problems of the children themselves.

Therefore the task immediately before the California public schools — and all public schools — is how to teach evolution so that its adverse effect on these children will be as small as possible. The main requirement is sensitivity: sensitivity of science teachers, but also of school administrations and publicly-elected school boards.

One solution is for the schools to excuse fundamentalist children from evolution classes. But this hardly solves the problem. Evolutionary theory is prevalent throughout society, and youngsters are bound to come into contact with it eventually. When they do, the same mental and emotional problems will occur. Also, exclusion from classes can make these children objects of speculation, if not insult, from fellow classmates who will be delighted to tell them all the information they are missing.

The better approach is to place more stress on the speculative nature of all scientific theory. Teachers could emphasize that even the most staunchly-held theories are overturned from time to time by later knowledge. One example is our conception of the universe, which is continually changing as new instruments reveal new facets of interstellar existence.

Whatever the schools decide, however, there is a broader question here — and that is the ultimate relation of religion to science. That relationship has by no means been fully settled, as the latest court controversy illustrates. But the best approach, surely, is to view religion and science in terms of synthesis rather than conflict.

Some notable efforts have been made in this area, particularly that of Pierre Teilhard de Chardin, a French paleontologist who just happened to be a Jesuit priest (or, if you prefer, a Jesuit priest who just happened to be a paleontologist).

Chardin accepted both evolution and Catholicism, and made a brilliant effort to synthesize them. He saw all existence as a continuing process of synthesis (or reaching toward Godhead, if you will): the first cells joined together to form a more progressive being, and eventually mankind created his own community, which was an improved type of synthesis.

De Chardin supports the religious belief that man is not just another animal by stating that man's brain was such an advance over the animal mind that it created an entire new sphere of existence. And he saw this process continuing, aided by modern communications, drawing men closer together until they attain an even higher level of synthesis and in effect a new level of existence. It

is not quite clear whether he intends this highest level to be akin to oneness with God, but in its structure it is clearly religious.

This is all very complicated, of course, and de Chardin's synthesis is neither totally successful nor totally clear. But the most important factor is not his ultimate success. It is the attempt itself — or, more specifically, the recognition that an attempt should be made.

We must remember that science, with all its powers, has not answered the ultimate question of creation. Whether we believe that the universe began when a "big bang" exploded a conglomeration of matter into stars and galaxies, or that the universe has always existed as it is, we are ultimately left with no answer as to where it came from. That answer still lies firmly in the province of religion.

Also, while scientific discovery might alter our religious concepts, it need not destroy them. The Biblical description of creation, moving from primordial nothingness to land and sea, then animals and finally man, fits the same general pattern as evolution. The Bible says that God created the world in six days — but surely "day" can be defined in many ways.

Religion can succeed best, one would think, not by denying knowledge, but by encompassing it.

The Des Moines Register
Des Moines, Iowa,
March 8, 1981

Did life on Earth evolve over millions of years following a gigantic celestial explosion eons ago, or were the world and its creatures created in six days a few thousand years ago?

The evolution vs. creation debate has gone to court again, this time in California, where fundamentalists contend that their children's rights are violated because the public schools don't give creationism equal time with evolution.

The creationists' theory is less bewildering than their insistence that its denial is somehow ungodly. If a religion needs miracles to confirm the existence of a supreme power, such miracles abound in nature's intricate methods of enabling delicate species to adapt to hostile environments.

What greater miracle could one ask than the evolution of humankind through the interaction of infinitesimally small carbon-based molecules into reasoning beings, capable of laying to rest the myths that misguided their ancestors? Given the magnitude of the miracle, what theological difference does it make whether it occurred over thousands or millions of years?

The Hartford Courant
Hartford, Conn., March 4, 1981

The state of California does not hinder fundamentalist Christians from teaching their children at home and in churches and private schools that God created the world and everything in it over a six-day period 6,000 to 10,000 years ago.

If the state did such a thing, it would be violating the constitutional right to the free exercise of religion. But California is violating no one's religious freedom by setting a guideline that effectively excludes the teaching of that fundamentalist religious belief as part of the science curriculum in public schools.

The fundamentalists are challenging that guideline set in 1978 by the State Board of Education, in a suit that is being tried before a California Superior Court this week. A group known as the Creation-Science Research Center is trying to clear the way for the teaching of "creationism" alongside Darwin's theory of evolution as a credible scientific explanation for the origin of life.

The creationists are more subtle than their fundamentalist forebears who brought teacher John T. Scopes to trial in 1925 for teaching evolution in a public school in Tennessee. They use slide presentations and other fancy sales techniques to advance their theory.

But they are still selling religion, not science. There is no credible scientific evidence to support the creationist contention. The theory of evolution is the cornerstone of all biological science, however much dissension there is among scientists over details of its application to explain specific relationships and phenomena. The evidence for its support is overwhelming.

If the creationists are successful in California, textbooks in that state might soon be forced to juxtapose evolution with religious belief disguised as science in a fatuous pretension to "equal time." Worse, the case could provide a precedent for similar efforts by fundamentalists in other states.

No state yet mandates the teaching of creation theory in public schools, although creationist legislation turned up in at least 11 states last year and may be introduced in even more states this year. The creationists have succeeded in intimidating some major textbook manufacturers to include a description of their beliefs in biology textbooks.

There is no more place for creationism in a science textbook than there is place for inserting an explanation of the theory of evolution in the Bible. We hope the court in California manages to uphold the distinction between science and religion, and thus the separation of church and state.

The News American
Baltimore, Md., March 13, 1981

The well-publicized trial in which fundamentalist Christians challenged the teaching of evolution in California classrooms ended with little of the drama predicted by observers and participants alike. Both sides greeted the ruling, which came last Friday, as a victory of sorts.

Creationists, fundamentalist Christians who see the creation stories in Genesis as a scientifically tenable explanation of the origin of human life, went to court because they were not satisfied that their views are given a hearing in the state's social studies curriculum.

Before the trial, there were hints the creationists might ask that their views also be presented in biology classes as a scientific alternative to evolution. Instead, they simply requested that biology teachers qualify lessons on evolution by describing the material as a theory, one of at least two possible explanations for the origin of human beings. They charged that presenting evolution as fact violates a young person's right to believe that the Genesis stories give a factual account of creation.

Judge Irving H. Perluss wasted little time deciding that the religious rights of fundamentalist Christians were not jeopardized by the state's curriculum. But, noting that the trial had taught both sides "more about understanding" each other, he cautioned educators to obey state guidelines stipulating that evolution be described as a scientific theory still open to debate.

The ruling will no doubt prod educators to treat the religious sensibilities of their students with proper respect. The fact remains, however, that most scientists familiar with the evidence — evidence that is abundant in virtually every area of scientific research — do consider evolution as fact, not theory.

Creationists should not be required to abandon their beliefs. But neither should religious beliefs become the yardstick for scientific proof.

To accept creationism as science would be to confuse the distinction between knowledge and faith, a distinction the Catholic Church disregarded to its lasting embarrassment when it branded as heresy Galileo's evidence that the earth revolves around the sun. Science and faith are different ways of knowing, and each must be understood on its own terms.

Science is not gospel, and gospel makes poor science.

AKRON BEACON JOURNAL
Akron, Ohio, March 6, 1981

COMING in an era when large numbers of the conveniences enjoyed by Americans are demonstrably the fruit of modern science, the California lawsuit seeking to force the state's public schools to teach the biblical account of the Creation as a "scientific theory" is disturbing.

The case is of special interest to Ohioans, because this is one of several states where efforts are reportedly being made this year to win passage of laws having the same effect.

Victory for the plaintiffs in California would severely hamper school efforts to help the young understand the scientific approach to problems, by blurring the distinction between questions of faith not accessible to science and questions of fact open to scientific investigation.

The suit and the legislative efforts are also puzzling. They seem to involve either a misunderstanding of the basic nature of science or a surprising willingness to subject a tenet of fundamental faith to the limitations inherent in all scientific theory.

The Genesis explanation — actually, its two differing explanations — of the Creation is already being taught to California public school children in their social science classes, as part of the study of religions and their role in society.

But the biblical version is not taught in physical science classes. In the state's educational guidelines for physical science courses, teachers are told that such matters as original creation and cause are beyond the reach of scientific investigation.

And along with other currently dominant scientific theories, the state favors trying to give students some understanding of the Darwinian theory of evolution. That is what troubles those now suing.

The Genesis accounts, they argue, should be taught as a scientific theory competing equally with Mr. Darwin's. This entails either misunderstanding or misrepresentation of the nature of science.

True science is an ever-continuing search for truth in questions open to approach through the examination of physical evidence. It involves recording and collating data and drawing reasoned conclusions that fit the data and explain relations among them.

Non-dogmatic, it is fettered only by the limitations of the human mind and technology at any given time.

The body of science is the best tool we have for understanding and coping with natural problems. And the habits of rigorous reasoning and of questioning assumptions that the scientific discipline requires are mankind's most powerful weapon against ignorance and the errors it causes.

Giving the young some understanding of the methods of science and encouraging their use are one of the most valuable contributions education can make to mankind.

Yet at any given stage science represents only the best that man has been able to do through intelligent examination and analysis of nature — not final and absolute truth. Its theories are subject to revision or abandonment when new data or more penetrating insights come along.

Thus if a sixth-grade teacher did in fact tell a youngster, as the boy testified in the California trial this week, that he "must believe" the Darwinian theory, the teacher was wrong. That is not science or the scientific approach.

The Darwinian theory enjoys respect by most — but not quite all — scientists working in related fields as the best available explanation for the evidence in geology and biology.

It is useful for people to understand it and how it was arrived at. This yields comprehension of how science attacks a puzzling problem by reasoning from available evidence, and helps people in coping with their own problems. But the theory remains a theory, not a dogma.

It seems strange that those suing California should be willing to characterize the Bible accounts — the events in which are by nature inaccessible to scientific examination — as subject to that same limitation. More commonly those of this persuasion hold that this is revealed, absolute truth, incapable of revision.

This is a question of faith, and people are entitled to believe what they will. But it is a distortion to clothe it in the garb of "science."

If they succeed, they will have thrown a roadblock in the path of efforts to equip the young with basic reasoning and analytical ability.

THE MILWAUKEE JOURNAL
Milwaukee, Wisc., March 6, 1981

The California "monkey trial" is fizzling as a mighty struggle between creationists and evolutionists. But if the trial ends "not with a bang, but a whimper," we still expect to hear more of the old controversy over the origin of human life.

Unlike its famed predecessor in Tennessee in 1925, the California trial does not involve a teacher accused of defying a state law by teaching evolution. Indeed, the plaintiffs have backed away from their earlier attempt to have the biblical version of creation taught in schools on a par with evolution. The creationists also have abandoned their contention that evolution was being taught in California schools as a "secular religion." At issue now is whether science-teaching guidelines will be rewritten to in some way accommodate the creationists.

Judge Irving Perluss, who is hearing the case, has said its central issue is how to assure "sensitivity, understanding and tolerance" for children whose religious views might conflict with what they are taught in the classroom. We agree — to a point. The Constitution's separation of church and state not only means that government must not sanction a religion; it means as well that the state must not manifest open hostility to religion.

Thus, there should be "sensitivity, understanding and tolerance" for the various religious or nonreligious views of students. Yet, the price of accommodating religious diversity must never be the placement in a curriculum of purely religious theories under the guise of respecting pluralism.

So, although some finely tuned editing of California's guidelines for teaching evolution may satisfy the plaintiffs in the present case, we doubt that this would quiet the clamor of some militant religionists who seem so bent on reopening the creation vs. evolution war. Those religionists, as they showed in November, can be politically effective. They have succeeded in having bills introduced in about 12 states that would require "equal time" for the teaching of divine creation along with evolution.

As the science vs. religion debate regrettably quickens, we can only wonder: Why is it not possible to advance the frontiers of science while understanding that, for many, there is an inner space filled by religion? And why is it not possible to hold a religious faith that, in St. Paul's words, is "the substance of things hoped for, the evidence of things not seen," while understanding that science may represent appropriate use of a divine gift of intellect?

THE DENVER POST

Denver, Colo., March 10, 1981

FIFTY SIX years after the famed Scopes "Monkey trial," the ongoing battle over teaching the theory of evolution in public schools has led to hardening of intellectual arteries on both sides.

While most Christians see no conflict between their religious beliefs and the scientific method, some fundamentalists still feel Darwin somehow undermines the Bible. Scientists, in turn, tend to stereotype the fundamentalists as narrow-minded clods such as those in the unforgettable movie "Inherit the Wind."

It is thus cause for rejoicing that Superior Court Judge Irving Perluss in Sacramento, Calif., managed to break fresh ground in a suit brought by the Creation-Science Research Center of San Diego challenging the way California teaches evolution in science classes.

The state's lawyers had mustered the usual phalanx of experts in support of evolution — and were stunned when the judge said he didn't care whether every scientist in the world supported Darwin or, for that matter, Genesis. Instead, he correctly ruled, the real issue is balancing both parts of the First Amendment mandate that there shall be no law "respecting an establishment of religion or prohibiting the free exercise thereof."

Manifestly, for the state to teach just Genesis is to "establish a religion." But it is also unconstitutional to give "equal time" for both Genesis and Darwin, as demanded in a bill introduced in the Colorado General Assembly by Sen. Sam Zakhem. It is not "balanced" to match a scientific theory against the views of only *one* of the hundreds of world religions.

That, of course, is old news. The refreshing new turn is Perluss's insistence the state show that teachers "have some understanding and sensitivity to the fundamentalist Christian child" and any other pupil whose religious beliefs might clash with their academic instruction.

That's a wise distinction. Genesis says: "So God created man in his own image." It doesn't specify the deity's *technique*, which could well have been the cosmic trial and error documented by Darwin. And Darwin, a stout Episcopalian, knew his theory did not exclude a possible *motive* for the process he catalogued.

The compatibility of science and religion shows even more clearly in astronomy. The Roman Catholic church once tried Galileo for heresy for suggesting the earth is not the center of the universe — a error it is now reversing. But, ironically, fundamentalist Christians today cite the triumph of astronomy's "big bang" theory as supporting the account of Genesis that the universe began when "God said, 'Let there be light,' and there was light."

Until the millenium foreseen by the theologians arrives, science and religion are simply different threads in the fabric of the human spirit. In the famous "five Ws" of journalism, it falls upon science to ask the "what, when," and "where." Religion is the province of the infinite "Who" and the ultimate "why."

Thus, if Sen. Zakhem does know of a few teachers who belittle the religious beliefs of students, then he should follow Judge Perluss' example and insist fundamentalists be treated with the same sensitivity due any other minority group.

But reacting to that problem by demanding the teaching of specific religious doctrine in public schools only shows Zakhem dwelled so long on Genesis he never read Proverbs 26:4:

Answer not a fool according to his folly, lest thou also be like unto him."

Sentinel Star

Orlando, Fla., March 14, 1981

IT WAS perhaps inevitable that the Orange County School Board would be faced with the issue of whether creationism should be taught in the public schools. Now that it has happened, it ought to be dealt with swiftly and decisively.

At "issue" is the debate over whether Judeo-Christian dogma on the origins of life on earth should be given equal time with instruction on the scientific theories of man's origins.

A recent California court case set what is probably the definitive answer in the argument, one fully accepted by both the preacher plaintiff and the California school board defendant.

The judge in that case refused to order the school system to give equal time to creationism but did order the schools to stress in their science and biology classes that Darwin's theory of evolution was just that, the prevailing theory perhaps, but not a fact. That would let science teachers touch on any number of theories, some incompatible with certain religions, others not.

Common sense would dictate such a course here as well.

The Chattanooga Times
Chattanooga, Tenn., March 7, 1981

Because the famous Scopes trial was conducted 56 years ago in nearby Dayton, Chattanoogans may have a more than passing interest in a similar legal battle now under way in Sacramento, Calif. And although the latest courtroom dispute differs in many respects from the legendary confrontation between William Jennings Bryan and Clarence Darrow, at least one principle remains at stake: free inquiry.

In the 1925 trial conducted in the old Rhea County courthouse, the issue was a state law prohibiting the teaching of Darwin's theory of evolution. Mr. Scopes, a local school teacher defended by Mr. Darrow, was ultimately convicted and fined $100, though the fine was never paid because the conviction was overturned on a technicality. The anti-evolution forces could legitimately claim a victory of sorts, however, since one effect of the Scopes trial was the virtual elimination of the teaching of evolution in science texts for more than 30 years.

The issue in the California case is whether the state should be required to rewrite its guidelines for teaching science to establish the biblical story of creation as one of two or more scientific "theories" for the origin of the universe, man included. Creationism, as it is called, is already taught in California schools, but in social studies, not science, classes. It is certain the outcome of the case will be watched closely by officials in other states where similar efforts to require the teaching of "creationism" are expected.

The creationists have marshalled a considerable body of "evidence" to support their position. But it seems to us they are trying to persuade a court to require the teaching as a scientific theory something that for centuries has been depended on a person's faith for its acceptance.

Obviously science is not without error, and it is not particularly well-suited to answer questions involving religion. But the conflict between the scientists and the creationists is interesting nevertheless, especially in the different approaches being taken on this issue. A scientist uses the evidence he discovers to propose a theory, with the latter changing as new evidence is found. The creationists start with a "theory" — the creation by a divine being of the universe and all it contains — and provide evidence that supports that view. Neither approach is wrong, obviously, but the latter, just as obviously, is grounded in a religious belief.

In the Scopes trial, the primary issue was the futile attempt to ban from the classroom an idea repugnant to fundamentalists who held to the idea of divine creation. In California today, scientists are seeking to ban from science classes a concept with which they disagree because it is "unscientific." If the doctrine of free inquiry has any validity whatsoever, it is logical to assume that if the two concepts are taught together, one or the other will be ultimately unpersuasive, at least in the minds of some students.

St. Louis Globe-Democrat
St. Louis, Mo., March 16, 1981

A California judge's verdict that schools should not teach Darwin's theory of evolution dogmatically did not really settle anything. It did raise an important question that isn't often discussed — have the courts and those opposed to prayers in schools succeeded in establishing secular humanism, which amounts to a state religion, in the public schools?

It appears that those who have used the courts so zealously to remove all religious influence from schools have paved the way for a secular humanist religion. This state-financed religion worships Humanist dogmas such as the belief that man himself is the sole judge of what is moral or immoral by such standards as whether something "feels good" or "doesn't hurt anyone else."

Some secular Humanists prefer to call their creed a "philosophy of life." But in the Humanist Manifesto I issued in 1933 the movement was called a "religion."

One of the problems that results from the state supporting secular humanism is cited by Dr. Daniel D. McGarry, retired professor of history at Saint Louis University, in his treatise, "Secularism in American Public Education:"

"The immorality that is spreading through our American society is largely due to a weakening of traditional religions and a substitution of reliance on considerations of secular humanism. It is partly a result of the exclusion of traditional religion from our schools, with a resultant monopoly of secularism in American public education."

The goal of Humanists, says Dr. McGarry, is to "substitute for traditional religions a 'religion of humanity,' in which man replaces God as the supreme entity."

In so doing, the Humanists have worked in public schools to exclude not only religious practices but the moral values that accompanied them. In their place, the Humanists have worked to establish their own "liberated" views concerning sex and human life.

In their Manifesto II (1973), McGarry says the Humanists declared that "We believe that...traditional dogmatic or authoritative religions...do a disservice to the human species."

The permissive Humanist influence in schools and our society in general may provide part of the answer on why there has been a disastrous drop in morality in the nation in the last 15 years and an equally marked rise in crime of all kinds. On this McGarry writes:

"An inevitable result of the sort of moral judgments allowed by secular humanism is to reduce morality to its least common denominator, i.e., to the minimum requirements that are agreed upon by all. In this case the lowest moral principles will prevail, and society will tend to become virtually amoral: that is almost without morals.

"The results of our growing abandonment of firm, religion-based morality are every day becoming more obvious. They include sexual promiscuity and sexual deviations of all kinds, premarital sex, extramarital sex, homosexuality between males and females, murder in the form of abortion of the yet unborn and euthanasia for the feeble aged, as well as suicide of the depressed, abandonment to unrestrained alcoholism, drug-addiction and widespread dishonesty and deception."

The inculcation of anti-religious values by Humanists in schools is not the intent of the First Amendment which says: "Congress shall make no law respecting an establishment of religion, or prohibiting the free exercise thereof..."

It is ironic that the interpretation of the First Amendment has produced almost exactly the opposite effect of what the amendment calls for. It has virutally established secular humanism as a national religion in public schools and is being used to discredit and injure traditional religions it purported to protect. If allowed to continue, this trend ultimately could result in a totally secularized society and the virtual elimination of traditional religion in the United States.

OKLAHOMA CITY TIMES
Oklahoma City, Okla., March 6, 1981

MUCH of the coverage of the so-called "evolution vs. creation" trial in California this week oversimplifies the real issue at stake. The case is more complex than a replay of the famous Scopes "monkey trial" of 56 years ago.

The lawsuit being heard in a Sacramento courtroom has interest in Oklahoma because of a recent effort to get legislation to require the teaching of creation along with evolution in the public schools. A bill called "Balanced Treatment for Creation-Science and Evolution-Science Act" was given a public hearing but failed to gain committee approval in the House.

Comparing the California case with the 1925 trial of a Tennessee biology teacher, John T. Scopes, charged with violating a state law against teaching Darwin's theory of evolution inevitably puts it in a framework of a battle between Bible "fundamentalists" and scientists. This approach overlooks important gains in knowledge compared to 1925.

The plaintiffs, three San Diego school students, are suing the state of California on grounds the state Board of Education is violating their constitutional rights by teaching the theory of evolution as the sole explanation of the origin of the species, a position that conflicts with their religion.

Regardless of whether one accepts the theory or not, it is intellectually dishonest not to acknowledge some rather substantial doubts have been raised about it, and not only among non-scientists.

As an example, one of the plaintiffs' witnesses in the trial is Dean Kenyon, biology professor at San Francisco State University. He says he was a "convinced Darwinist" but in the last four years has come to believe the theory fails to correlate data in astronomy, geology and biology. His doubts arose because of "gaps in the fossil record" that would demonstrate the kind of changes that evolutionists say had to occur.

Certainly, it would be hard to say his doubts are shared by a majority of scientists. Yet, as new information is developed, even proponents of Darwinism find it necessary to modify their views to a certain extent.

While the advisability of including "creation-science" in the public school curriculum may be open to question, those who advocate it appear to be on solid ground in objecting to the presentation of the theory of evolution as *fact* to impressionable children. A fact is defined as a truth that can be verified by any researcher at any time, repeatedly, so no doubt can exist about the statement.

One's approach to the discussion may be influenced by his religious views, or lack of same, but the issue is more than science versus religion. It is really whether the present body of knowledge supports a valid alternative to the evolutionist's theory of man's origin.

THE BLADE
Toledo, Ohio, March 10, 1981

MORE than a half century after the famed "monkey trial" in Tennessee over the question of whether public-school instructors could be prevented from teaching Darwin's theory of evolution, the issue has again arisen to plague the courts and the legislatures of several states.

There is one difference. Evolutionary theory itself was symbolically on trial in the hot, humid courtroom where Clarence Darrow and William Jennings Bryan fought their historic legal battle in 1925. The court case in San Diego, in which the judge affirmed that the teaching of evolution did not violate the rights of those who believe in the Genesis or creationist theory, was just the reverse of the earlier one. The California proceeding was designed to gain a legal foothold for teaching creationist theory in the science classroom.

The Scopes trial exposed an entire region of the country to ridicule as being incorrigibly backward, but it also had a chilling effect on publishers who, disliking controversy, shied away for many years thereafter from discussions of evolution in science textbooks.

The plaintiff in the California trial is a publisher of religious books, but his motives appeared to be as much ideological as commercial. Advocacy of the Genesis version of creation has become the talisman of resurgent religious fundamentalists' efforts to turn the country away from what they view as godless secularism in the schools.

It is not enough, apparently, that California guidelines apparently allow the creation story to be taught in social studies classes and that under the San Diego court's order the state must distribute to local schools a policy statement stating, in effect, that evolution must be labeled a theory rather than fact; the plaintiffs and other supporters of the creationist movement want the biblical account to be certified as scientific holy writ.

The recent efforts by creationists to promote their cause raises grave constitutional issues of separation of church and state, to say nothing of the problems that arise when religious groups attempt to prescribe what is orthodoxy for society. What the plaintiffs and those of like mind seek is for all children to be exposed, at taxpayers' expense, to a version of how earth was created that is essentially an eloquent statement of religious faith rather than scientific theory.

Any parent, of course, is free to affirm the centrality of mankind in a universe created and guided by a Supreme Being. Churches, private or parochial schools, and educational ventures abound to propagate this and other religious views. In a pluralistic society there is room in the public schools for discussion of the philosophical significance of the Genesis story of creation and, for that matter, other cultures' versions of how the earth and living creatures came to be. But this should not be done in a science class.

THE SACRAMENTO BEE
Sacramento, Calif., March 6, 1981

However one views the origin of the species and the evolution of Homo sapiens, as drama the Sacramento monkey trial, so-called, is a bust. Having begun with the promise of a bang, it is ending with a whimper. It is not a great clash of ideas and principles; it is not even the entertaining farce that was undoubtedly expected by the clutch of latter-day Menckens who came from far and near to view it. It is, finally, only an exercise in tinkering with the vapid rhetoric of a state curriculum guide and the disembodied words of a conventional textbook.

Consider what previous efforts, similarly motivated, have already foisted on the state's children (from the curriculum guide): "The process (of evolution) has been going on so long that it has produced all the groups and kinds of plants and animals now living, as well as others that have become extinct." Or again (from a California-approved textbook): "Besides the evolution theories, there are other theories that people use to explain the many different kinds of organism on the earth today. Some people believe that each kind of organism was created instead of being the result of gradual changes of living things over long periods of time . . . They believe that each species is an act of creation and that small differences will not change a species . . . " No wonder they're yawning in the courtroom. The same kind of stuff has long had them yawning in the classroom.

Who is speaking in that last passage? Is that the voice of a human being? Are the words designed to catch the interest of students, to arouse curiosity, to convey either vexing doubt or joyous certainty? No, this is the language of low profile — passive, without juice, without any redeeming social or pedagogical value except to protect the political flanks of those who circulate it. What sort of people are the "people" this refers to? What evidence do they adduce in support of what they believe, and why are they so passionate in their convictions? Is each set of beliefs as well-documented as every other set of beliefs? How does one choose between them, and does the choice make any difference? And what exactly is a student supposed to learn from such a passage? The hope appears to be that the student will learn nothing that can possibly offend anyone.

The real effect of the trial in Sacramento so far appears to be a lesson in the danger of writing textbooks in courtrooms or with courtrooms in mind — a lesson that can be variously interpreted but whose importance for education should not be ignored. There lurks in this case an important clash of rights and principles. Such issues, however, can't possibly be resolved by tinkering with the language of textbooks and curriculum guides, but only in the context of broader policy about who should be required to be exposed to what and under what circumstances.

If creationists don't want their children exposed to Darwin, maybe the state should find a way to excuse them from it. The attempt to write language to suit all sensibilities, on the other hand, results only in that disembodied, cautious voice that teaches kids that nothing in school makes a lot of difference, that no one cares, and that most intellectual activity is both tedious and inconsequential. So far, we haven't learned much about evolution, but we have learned a lot about why students are bored.

The Boston Globe
Boston, Mass., February 28, 1981

A California jury is probably no more likely to resolve the debate over the origin of the human species than those worthy Tennesseans who found schoolteacher John Scopes guilty of teaching evolution 56 years ago; but it will have to try.

Scopes was the defendant in the "monkey trial," so remembered as much for the courtroom goings-on as for the subject matter: the attempt to introduce into a high school biology class Darwin's theory that man was descended from the apes. Onstage in Sacramento is a suit filed by three San Diego students who charge that the Board of Education is violating their constitutional rights by teaching evolution as the sole explanation of the origin of mankind.

The case has serious political and scientific implications. The students and their supporters represent the "creationist" view that the gaps in the fossil record make it impossible to prove that amphibians evolved from fish, reptiles from amphibians, and so on — and certainly do not disprove the Biblical-based notion that each species represents an act of individual creation. Campaigning last fall, President Reagan said that if evolution is taught, creation should be also. Under pressure from creationists, textbook publishers are already beginning to hedge their evolutionist bets; a court victory could lead to rewriting of high school biology materials.

Just as the pontifical William Jennings Bryan and big city celebrities like Clarence Darrow and the young H.L. Mencken made the Scopes trial a national event, the California case will feature astro-glamorous Carl Sagan and a Beagle-full of biologists (on both sides of the issue). The saving grace this time around is that unlike the Scopes trial when, thanks to Darrow's Bible-baiting of Bryan, the humor was unintentional, this time it may be intentional. Says the coordinator of the Creation Science Research Center, "If we can keep ourselves from taking ourselves too seriously, we may have some fun."

San Francisco Chronicle

San Francisco, Calif., March 4, 1981

ALTHOUGH 56 YEARS have passed by and even the face of the globe has changed mightily in that time; there is now another Scopes' Monkey Trial underway in Sacramento. Time seems to have done little to quench some passions, at least when men get down to serious argument about the creation of the species. If you take the Book of Genesis literally, there is apparently little difference whether you were around in 1925 or are around in 1981. If you think that Charles Darwin was on the mark when he published "The Origin of the Species" in 1859, passage of time has probably not dimmed the tenacity of your belief.

But while there has been apparently little change in the dedication of adherents of either fundamentalist belief or of scientific theory, other things have indeed changed. In that storied Tennessee case, the state sought prosecution of teacher John Scopes for teaching evolution; in the current case, the state is being sued for teaching evolution but not also teaching "creationism," which amounts to governmental switch of sides. And the development of contemporary television and radio will bring this contemporary replay of the Scopes' trial live and almost instantly before us, altogether, we are inclined to think, poor substitutes for the earlier acerbity of H. L. Mencken in 1926.

AND THERE MIGHT BE another substantial difference; the original leading players in this legal drama were Clarence Darrow and William Jennings Bryan, two of the most outstanding barristers of the generation pitted in combat in a country courthouse. We hope that the arguments will reach the lucidity of Darrow and the dedication of Bryan but we will, however, not be disappointed if our hopes are not realized. That trial of more than five decades ago, we must remember, was "the trial of the century." And we are still in it.

Roanoke Times & World-News

Roanoke, Va., March 13, 1981

The outcome of the recent evolution trial in California apparently left both sides — public school educators and the creationist plaintiff — satisfied. Judge Irving Perluss upheld state policy for teaching evolution. But, he said, the schools should not be dogmatic about it.

There is no conflict. Good science, including the theory of evolution, should not be dogmatic. Dogma, including views of the university based on religious evidence, should not be considered good science.

In fact, the state policy upheld by Judge Perluss calls both for teaching evolution and for doing it undogmatically. The judge simply ordered that a 1973 statement by the California Board of Education, pertaining to the preparation of science textbooks, be circulated to local schools and to textbook publishers. That statement provides:

1. That dogmatism be changed to conditional statements where speculation is offered for origins.

2. That science emphasize "how" and not ultimate cause for origins.

Non-scientific pressures may have led to development of the statement, but it seems quite valid scientifically. By definition, the propositions of science are conditional, subject to continual testing and, as the evidence warrants, change.

For each question that is answered, new ones arise to be explored. Talking about "ultimate cause" — asserting where the questions end, or begin — is the task of religion, not science.

Important as it is to recognize the limitations of science, it is equally important to keep science uncorrupted by propositions not developed within these limits. There's a reason for the hold of evolution, despite its gaps, on the scientific community: It is, at the moment, the best theory to explain the known scientific evidence.

The creationists may be right. But until their views can be supported with the same rigorous examination of scientific evidence that supports the theory of evolution, creationism deserves little place in the science classroom. Interestingly, the California court challenge to evolution was based on alleged violations of students' *religious* rights.

During the trial, the issue was narrowed to whether the state was properly following its own policy. A showdown between science and biblical literalism was averted.

That's fortunate, because it allowed common sense to prevail. At the moment, evolution is science's best answer to describe how life developed on this planet. But let's not pretend that science has all the answers.

The Washington Star
and Daily News

Washington, D.C., March 13, 1981

Some of the correspondence on the recent California "evolution" trial reflect the usual displeasure with any suggestion that biological science (including evolutionary teaching) should be distinguished for educational purposes from "creationism."

But then it was the view of the California plaintiffs that they should not be distinguished that gave rise to the case, which ended on a mild note the other day. The judge agreed with the plaintiffs that biology should be taught with some regard to the sensibilities of fundamentalists. California is to revise its curricular guidelines accordingly.

That is a wholesome development, so long as it leaves the freedom to inquire and teach unimpaired. But it evades a basic difficulty. It is, by and large, the religionists, not the biology teachers, who insist on pitting evolution and "creationism" against one another in the same arena. But biologists are neither moralists nor theologians, and only bad biologists pretend to be. Their task is more modest and what they teach about the origins of the human species should be taught, like all science, in a spirit of inquiry, not of revelation.

But the present confusion about the implications of evolution — as about the relativity or quantum theories — exists mainly in the minds of those who confound two distinct logical realms, science with metaphysics — or, in the instance of the Biblical account of the origins of man, with poetic allegory.

Once the confusion starts, the ramifications are limitless. Some exception apparently is taken, for instance, to the description of *homo sapiens* as an animal species. But when biology classifies man as an "animal," it employs a convenience of taxonomy, proceeding from observable analogies with other forms of animal life. It is elementary confusion to make more of the terminological conveniences of biological classification than well-instructed biologists would themselves make of them.

Neither the classification of man as a "higher" primate, nor the consideration of fossil or analogical evidence about man's evolution from "lower" life-forms, need be theologically disturbing. These terms of art are disturbing only to those who believe them to contain, or imply, ultimate assertions about man's essence, worth or purpose — none of which science is qualified to pronounce upon with authority, either positively or negatively.

In a line from Shakespeare whose wisdom still resonates, Hamlet speaks of man as "this quintessence of dust." As almost every religious tradition affirms, most certainly that of the Book of Genesis, man is indeed "dust," at least chemically speaking. But those who believe that mankind, whatever its constituent material, is also a *creature* assert that there is more: a "quintessence," a fifth essence, beyond quantification or measurement, which is to say beyond the reach of scientific categories. Biology deals with the dust; belief, however elaborated or interpreted, is of the realm of the fifth essence.

In a properly ordered theory of learning, man-as-dust is the concern of science. It considers the observable and measurable — the minerals, proteins and chemicals and how they combine; life-forms and how they developed. It is unqualified to concern itself successfully with the fifth essence, call it soul or spirit or whatever, which is the proper realm of philosophy, theology and metaphysics.

That is why these pursuits belong in different classrooms, at least at the elementary level. Very different techniques of inquiry are appropriate to each of them, especially in the public schools of a nation that elects, for sound historical reason, to limit the state's interest (either of promotion or repression) in religion.

The "creationists" err, we believe, when they pursue a fruitless contention with biological science. It is, ironically, one sure way to make monkeys of men, though in the behavioral rather than the biological sense. Creationism, by claiming the trappings of science, makes too much in the wrong way of the limited powers of science, accepting the shallow convention of our time that the label "scientific" is the superior imprimatur of truth. It is, perhaps, the imprimatur of one mutable kind of truth, but not of religious truth, which of its nature is immutable and unbounded by the small wisdom of mankind. The rivalry is misguided, promoting confusion where light and sober learning are needed.

The Washington Post

Washington, D.C., March 3, 1981

OLD ISSUES never die. They just move to California. A San Diego publisher of religious books, Kelly Segraves, born 19 years after Clarence Darrow and William Jennings Bryan argued the 1925 Dayton, Tenn., trial of John T. Scopes, has sued California's State Board of Education, hoping to compel public schools to teach the Biblical story of creation as a valid scientific theory along with the theory of evolution.

In fact, the debate over inclusion of Biblical creation in the science curriculum has spread to 15 states, according to Philip J. Hilt's story yesterday, three of which—South Dakota, Wisconsin and Missouri—"now provide instruction on creation as part of public school biology." California schools "teach" creationist doctrine in social studies classrooms, not as gospel presumably (which would pose an obvious First Amendment problem), but as one set of arguments in a continuing political controversy that divides Christian fundamentalists not only from atheists and other non-Christians but from many of their modernist Christian brethren.

But by no means should the current California dispute be seen as a simple rerun of earlier Darwinist-fundamentalist battles such as the Scopes case. For one thing, Scopes was tried and convicted for violating a Tennessee statute that outlawed teaching evolution in state-supported schools at a time when creationist doctrines could not be challenged legally in the state's classrooms. In California, however, the *creationists* are suing to establish a beachhead in today's biology lecture halls. For almost a decade, moreover, the California State Board of Education has been a constant battleground on the issues. During the Reagan administration, a more pro-religious board tilted toward accepting the Biblical account of a six-day creation as scientifically respectable, but Jerry Brown's governorship brought a resurgence of support on the board for the evolutionary account of creation as a process that has taken thousands of years. Even under Mr. Reagan, the board conceded that "most scientists agree that the theory of organic evolution is the best scientific description we have to account for the complex forms of life in the past and present."

Teaching the Biblical doctrines of creation as *scientific* truth violates the First Amendment rights of non-believers today just as much as in the past. As matters stand, the creationists in California get a thorough—though not uncritical—hearing in social studies classrooms. Their beliefs deserve no more display in *biology* classrooms than do the dogmas of scientists in the realms of politics and ethics.

Even the creationists' historic enemy, H. L. Mencken, found it necessary to concede that modernists like himself confronted an underlying dilemma on the issue. For Mencken, "the Tennessee anti-evolution law, whatever its wisdom, was at least constitutional . . . the yahoos of the State had a clear right to have their progeny taught whatever they chose, and kept secure from whatever knowledge violated their superstitions." Change "constitutional" to "understandable," "yahoos" to "people" and "superstitions" to "religion," and less sardonic observers might defend the right of California creationists to teach their doctrine in the schools—though not as science, a cumulative and self-corrective process of analysis, but as one of any contending moral philosophies that deserve scrutiny in a pluralist republic.

THE COMMERCIAL APPEAL

Memphis, Tenn., March 8, 1981

THE COURTROOM was in Sacramento, not Dayton, Tenn., but the cause argued half a country away and half a century removed from the Scopes "monkey trial" could affect us all the same.

"Creationist" Kelly Segraves brought suit against California but not because he wanted Genesis to be taught in its public schools. The state already allows it in social studies courses.

Segraves wanted the biblical story of creation to be part of California's *science* curriculum. And, because California has the biggest school system in the nation, its course content and textbook orders influence what is taught throughout the United States, including Tennessee.

"WE ARE NOT trying to ban evolution," Segraves' lawyer said. "We seek protection for the right to believe in a cause. The real issue is religious freedom under the First Amendment of the Constitution."

So it is — and that is where Segraves went wrong. He not only confused church and state by seeking to require the schools to teach religion; he also confused science and religion. Both seek to explain the miracle of life, but they are separate disciplines which approach the subject in different ways.

Religion tries to make sense of the world through faith in the power of a divine being, whose handiwork is what we see. The world was created in six days, and on the seventh day God rested, according to the Jewish, Christian and Islamic texts. Every civilization on Earth, from the most primitive to the most developed, has its own story of creation, however.

Would Segraves be willing to give other versions equal time with the Bible in the science classroom? Would Segraves even entertain what most Western theologians believe: that God's day does not have to be clocked in 24 hours?

Scientists take a different tack in trying to explain the universe. They observe the world, sift the evidence they find, and try putting it together in rational ways to understand nature and to improve our control of it.

This was the approach Charles Darwin took in traveling the world and chronicling what he saw. His theory of evolution, which first appeared in his "Origin of Species" in 1859 and got Tennessee schoolteacher John Scopes in trouble some 66 years later, grew out of his efforts to relate the animals he found on islands to the animals he observed on nearby continents.

Scientists today approach life much the same way, only the matters they deal with are often as small as an atom or as large as the cosmos:

• Only last week the Congress for Recombinant DNA Research met to discuss how gene-splicing laboratories are studying the building blocks of life in hopes of conquering hereditary diseases and producing new, more effective vaccines.

• Only last week astronomers identified a galaxy estimated to be 10 billion light years away, some 2 billion light years farther than the most distant galaxy previously found. In other words, the light from that galaxy, traveling at 186,000 miles a second, took 10 billion years to reach their observatory. Their finding may lend further credence to the "Big Bang" theory of how the universe was formed. What that theory doesn't answer is: Who or what caused the Big Bang in the first place?

THUS, THE WORLD comes full circle. The youngster who is taught evolution in the classroom must reconcile any differences with what he is taught at home. Asking questions to arrive at answers for yourself is what education is about. It is the same whether the subject at hand is science or literature or the world's great religions. It is the same whether the student is a child or an adult.

If man evolved from the apes, where did the apes come from? If the apes came from reptiles and amphibians, where did they come from? What about amoebas and other single-celled creatures? If life came from hydrogen, oxygen, carbon and nitrogen, where did these elements come from?

In the beginning and at the end, both science and religion depend on faith in their search for truth. But that doesn't mean they are the same thing, or should be taught as such.

Arkansas Passes Law Requiring "Creationism" in Biology Classes

A bill requiring Arkansas public schools to give equal treatment to the Biblical account of creation and the theory of evolution was signed into law March 19 by Gov. Frank White. The bill had been passed by the State Senate, 22–2, and by the State Assembly, 69–18. It stated that requiring the "creationist" teaching along with Charles Darwin's theory was intended to "prevent the establishment of theologically liberal, humanist, non-atheist or atheist religions." In 1928, Arkansas had enacted a law prohibiting the teaching of Darwin's theory in public schools, but the U.S. Supreme Court had declared that law unconstitutional in 1968.

The Oregonian

Portland, Ore., March 22, 1981

The Arkansas Legislature, in passing a bill requiring that so-called scientific creation be given equal time in the state's classrooms if evolutionary topics are taught, has mandated the public teaching of a narrow religious theory. The action is bad science, bad for religion and a disgrace in a nation that prides itself on its scientific understanding and religious tolerance.

Science is not a body of belief, a dogma or an article of faith. It is an open-ended process of information gathering, usually through observation, experimentation and identification. If it works toward a predetermined or unassailable conclusion, it is not science at all.

In contrast, scientific creationism, a rank contradiction in terms, is a narrow religious doctrine that knows the answer before it starts searching for any proof. Facts are warped to support conclusions that hinge either on faith or on sectarian interpretations of holy writ.

Arkansas' legislators, fearful of voter disapprovals (some said) in their Bible-belt districts, voted the way they did in the hope the courts will take them off the hook by declaring their action unconstitutional. That excuse is yet to be used by the misguided sponsors of similar legislation in Salem, where a public hearing was held this week.

Passing the buck to the courts does not erase the promotion the legislative act gives textbook publishers who stand to reap profits from national efforts to promote scientific creationism as a classroom subject. Further, the legislators have cowardly dumped the issue on the public schools. Teachers, if evolution is mentioned, will have to give "balanced references," whatever that means in a rural Arkansas community, to the purveyors of a special doctrine that not even all Christian believers accept.

It is also disgraceful that a legislative body even pretends that all the major scientific journals of the world are to be doubted, that the achievements of biology, astronomy, geology, paleontology and anthropolgy, resting as they do on the framework of evolutionary discoveries, are to be weighed against a special religious doctrine.

Worse, the burden of finding such an unchartable course beween science and creationistic beliefs is to be loaded on the backs of harassed elementary classroom teachers. Surely, legislators in Oregon would not want to do that.

THE SUN

Baltimore, Md., March 19, 1981

Twelve years ago the U.S. Supreme Court threw out Arkansas's old anti-evolution law. Now, just when you thought it was safe to go into Arkansas again, the legislature has passed and the governor is expected to sign a new anti-evolution law.

Though it is labeled otherwise, make no mistake that is what the Arkansas law would be. It is a brazen effort to demean science's attempt to explain the development of life in natural terms, by equating that with theology's attempt to describe it in supernatural terms. The latter has been given the name "creation science," but it is not science in any way, shape or form. All scientists working in related fields accept evolution at least as an unassailable scientific generalization, and most accept it in an even more specific sense. The scientific community's respect and support for evolution has never been greater. No scientists (and not many theologians) accept creation science as a scientific explanation for anything.

Even if there were an argument for some scientific approach other than evolution to the study of origins and classifications, the so-called creation scientists have not presented it, in Arkansas or anywhere else. This is disguised religion, and not very disguised. Here is one "finding of fact" that led the legislature to pass this ignorant bill: "Public school presentation of evolution-science without any alternative model of origins abridges the U.S Constitutional protection of freedom of belief and speech of students and parents, because it undermines their religious convictions and moral and philosophical values...." That's not the language of a science. It is the language of a cult.

We said this law attacks and demeans science. It also attacks and demeans other religions which do not share the creationists' narrow view of the origin of man. It would create a preferred status in Arkansas schools for a particular religious view. That, of course, the Constitution strictly forbids, in order to protect "freedom of belief." When this law is tested in court, it will fail, as will all others like it.

The Miami Herald

Miami, Fla., March 22, 1981

SCIENTISTS seeking evidence of man's ability to make a monkey of himself need look no farther than Little Rock. There, legislators have made Arkansas the first state to require the teaching of "creationism" in the public schools.

Arkansas probably won't be the last state to do so, however. The Education Commission of the States reports that virtually identical bills have been introduced in several other states.

Those bills apparently are modeled after "An Act to Require Balanced Treatment of Scientific Creationism and Evolution in the Public Schools." Copies have been circulated nationwide by a South Carolina group.

The issue here is not the validity of Charles Darwin's theories. Nor is it the assertion of some creationists that the Biblical account of creation must be taken literally.

Rather, the issue is academic freedom. Although many school policies quite properly are determined by elected officials, the academic content of particular courses is not. That is best left to the expertise of teachers and professors, rather than to politicians and popular sentiment.

If the Arkansas Legislature's approach had prevailed throughout the history of Western civilization, the whole era of scientific progress would have been impossible. The populace would still be taught that the Earth is flat and at the center of the universe, or that disease is caused by demons.

The consequences of the intrusion of politics into science are nowhere more evident than in the Soviet Union. For more than three decades there, research in genetics was hamstrung by the Communist Party's doctrinaire insistence that the students be taught the ridiculous theories of Trofim Lysenko. The Soviets still lag in this area.

In the United States, the effort to require the teaching of "creationism" seems to be motivated by the demonstrably unfounded fear that the teachings of science will destroy young people's religious beliefs.

Such legislation was introduced in the Florida Legislature last year by Rep. Tom Bush of Fort Lauderdale. If a similar bill reaches the floor of either house this year, it should meet the same fate — defeat. Academic freedom demands no less.

ARKANSAS DEMOCRAT
Little Rock, Ark., March 21, 1981

It has Governor White's signature – the Arkansas legislature's bill calling for the teaching of "scientific creationism" alongside evolution in state schools. Whatever the scientific evidence for the creative event itself, the law wouldn't stand a constitutional chance without that "scientific" tag – and may not survive in spite of it.

The U.S. Constitution bans any direct government involvement in religion. So without its scientific tag, Sen. Jim Holsted's law would be a clear example of a state's adopting an "establishment of religion" and directing that it be taught in public schools.

Even with its scientific shield, the law will surely be taken to court, where some judgment should be made on the Creationist belief – one not given in a recent California case – that there's scientific evidence of a Supreme Being's suddenly creating the earth and its creatures whole – just as they are today.

There is, of course, no scientific evidence of any such instantaneous event – unless it's the Big Bang (exploding universe) theory of creation. Within limits, the BB theory suits creationist arguments almost as well as it does those of the evolutionists. However, the scientific evidence for Big Bang is not at all conclusive. Big Bang is just theory – for the good reason that its scientific backers are only reasoning from what they think (but can't prove) is after-the-fact evidence of such a beginning. That is to say, they are looking through their scopes at an "exploding universe" and reasoning backward to an explosion.

Creationists have equal trouble with Big Bang. It doesn't jibe with biblical accounts of the creation – of which, of course, there's no scientific proof at all. Moreover, Creationist science, as such, amounts mostly to archaeological evidence of biblical truths. For example, the equating of a historical flood of several thousand years ago with the biblical flood. As many a scientist would be happy to point out, correlations don't amount to proof of relatedness – science's supreme test of truth.

But the main trouble with proofs of biblical events is that they don't address the original event – Creation itself. But, then, neither does evolution, necessarily – and, worse for evolution, it itself can't parade as fact.

Science has strong presumptive evidence for evolution – which is why it is taught in the schools – but science simply cannot prove that the earth's plentiful fossils – including those of "early man" – conclusively demonstrate an ascent of life forms from earlier types. In positing a connected chain of mutations dating back billions of years and ending in what we call Man, science must – like Creationists arriving at faith – make its own "leap in the dark."

It's unfortunate that a great deal of "science" is indeed taught as fact instead of hypothesis or theory – but that's the result of the mistaken modern belief that the scientific method infallibly adduces truth

In fact, science mostly adduces evidence of varying reliability pointing to possible truths.

That applies to the theory of evolution, which – alone among claims of scientific fact – strikes sparks of anger from those who find its postulates at odds with received religious doctrines. Many of the faithful of all faiths look on evolution as an enemy of religion. Except in cases where scientists actively seek to discredit religion, that isn't true. Evolution is neutral on the subject of religion. It doesn't deny creation; it simply tries to explain it in terms of evidence pointing to progressive mutations.

Nevertheless, the theory of evolution is too often perverted by scientific scoffers who cite it as proof that all religions are wrong and that there's no basis for the spiritual side of man.

There is, because even the scientists are brought up at last against the Great Unanswerable – how it all happened and why. At this point, Creationist and Evolutionary theory need not collide. The scientists go on guessing and the religious go on believing.

Instead of trying to meet science on its own grounds with unprovable assertions of Instantaneous Creation, Creationists should – like the man in the California case – be content with an agreement on the part of educators that evolution will not be taught either as fact or as an alternate materialist "faith" – one antagonistic to the spiritual side of man and hostile to belief in a Creator.

That kind of junk isn't evolution; it's atheism, parading as science.

Predictably, it's the Arkansas Civil Liberties Union that has been first to challenge the new law – and, realistically, ACLU has a chance of winning its suit on the argument that the legislature has created an establishment of religion under guise of calling for the teaching of a scientific theory competitive with the theory of evolution. But let's see whether ACLU sticks to the constitutional approach – or whether it interlards its arguments with attacks on religion itself. ACLU's well known know-nothing attitude toward the free exercise of religion suggests it may do just that.

Arkansas Gazette.
Little Rock, Ark., March 19, 1981

The Arkansas House, like the Senate last week, succumbed to its worst instincts Tuesday and rushed through to easy passage a measure (SB 482) that requires the public schools to teach "creation-science" alongside evolution, giving "balanced treatment" to each. Equally distressing is the announcement by Governor Frank White's office that he will sign the bill.

Arkansas thus has become the only state in the Union to impose its police powers upon the classroom teacher on behalf of, shall we say, a religious view of how all matter, including life, originated. The convoluted language of the legislation seeks to paint "creation-science" as a purely scientific offering, without reference to religion. But then it makes the incredible assertion that teaching evolution alone abridges the First Amendment rights of those who accept only the religious view of creation.

The language of the bill could be argued all day, but the fact is that the legislature has now isolated this state as a bastion of know-nothingism in the teaching of science.

It behooves those who care about intrusions upon the classrooms and the actual rights of all students and teachers alike to bring a lawsuit in federal courts as soon as possible. Perhaps the Arkansas Education Association, or the American Civil Liberties Union, will be alert to the need. Provisions of SB 482 will not take effect until the fall of 1982, in any event, leaving time for the courts to act.

The House, like the Senate, does have a few enlightened members, such as Representative Mike Wilson of Jacksonville, who led the fight against SB 482, and Representative Lloyd George of Danville, a former teacher of biology and physics, who called the measure ridiculous, adding: "It's the state meddling where it shouldn't. Teachers are not qualified to give equal time to teaching the theory according to Genesis."

Arkansas's legislature, in short, has once again made our state the laughing stock of the nation, although enforcing such a spurious statute will be difficult in any case. The Senate sponsor acknowledges that he got the model bill not from a scientist but instead from a minister. But whatever the genesis of the legislation, a state legislature has no business writing school curricula in any subject area. Yes, once again it will be up to the federal courts to save us from ourselves.

The Charlotte Observer

Charlotte, N.C., March 19, 1981

The Arkansas legislature has approved a bill requiring the state's public schools to give "balanced treatment" of "creation science" and "evolution science." The bill would, in fact, write the Protestant fundamentalist view of creation into the school curriculum without calling it that — a subterfuge that deceives no one, least of all the Protestant fundamentalist backers of the bill. (It would, for example, require teaching of "separate ancestry for man and apes.")

This isn't the first time that people convinced that they possess Divine Truth have wanted the government to adopt their version of it. A similar effort hit the South in the 1920s.

The anti-evolution crusade in North Carolina peaked when William Jennings Bryan appeared in Raleigh to urge passage of a law to ban the teaching of evolution in public schools. The attempt, in 1925, drew opposition from, among others, a 28-year-old legislator named Sam Ervin.

"I know nothing about evolution," Mr. Ervin told his fellow legislators. "Neither do I care anything about it. . . . I don't see but one good feature in this thing, and that is that it will gratify the monkeys to know they are absolved from all responsibility for the conduct of the human race."

"The passage of this legislation," he said, "would be an insult to the people of North Carolina. I don't believe the Christian religion's endurance depends upon the passage of some weak-kneed resolution of the General Assembly of North Carolina. It is too big, too strong for that."

Mr. Ervin believes the Constitution requires government to be neutral regarding religion, neither promoting nor discouraging it, nor favoring one religion over another. "A religion that needs the government's help to do its teaching is a mighty poor religion," he said recently.

The question is not whether the Genesis version of creation is true; that's a matter of personal belief. The question is whether government has any business favoring the Genesis version over, for instance, the Crow Indian version, which holds that the earth and its creatures were made from mud gathered by Coyote from a duck's foot. It doesn't, as Arkansas legislators will probably find out when the law is challenged in court.

The Evening Bulletin

Philadelphia, Pa., March 19, 1981

The evolutionists and the creationists are still at war over what our children can be taught in school. The kids have every right to be confused by what's going on.

Kelly Segraves, a Christian fundamentalist, recently brought suit against the California public schools, arguing that evolution should not be taught as the only theory of mankind's origins. The Biblical story of Genesis should be included in the science curriculum.

Superior Court Judge Irving Perluss ruled that the school system wasn't guilty of religious persecution. However, he directed that Darwinism should not be presented to students as "the ultimate cause of origin."

This is hardly a decisive ruling, which is sorely needed. Now, Arkansas has carried the confusion one step further by passing legislation requiring public schools to teach the "theory" that God created man. On the surface this sounds alarmingly unconstitutional. In 14 other states, similar laws have been dispatched on such grounds.

However, Arkansas' bill does not require that all students be given lectures on both creation and evolution. Classes dealing with the history of man, however, would have to present "a balanced treatment to creation-science and evolution-science."

This law raises more questions than it answers.

Evolution is a theory. Although it isn't conclusive, there are scientific findings to support many of its assumptions.

The story of creation, however, is based not on science but on belief. There is no evidence to support it, nor can it be verified. Its acceptance depends on faith.

As part of man's history, culture and evolving religious thought, there's no reason we can see why the story of creation should not be taught in history, philosophy, or social studies classes.

The Arkansas law appears irresponsible in limiting instruction in both theories to "scientific evidence." Classes "must not include any religious instruction or reference to religious writings," it reads. This ignores the basis for creationist belief.

Creationism is based on religious writings — the Old Testament. It is intellectually dishonest to teach it without revealing its source and historic context.

The law places an incredible burden on the Arkansas schools. As written, its intent can't be carried out.

Creationism is not a science. It should not be taught in science classes. Faith and science must not be confused.

The Cleveland Press

Cleveland, Ohio, March 26, 1981

Fifty years ago, foes of evolution were pushing laws to keep the subject out of the schools. Today, they're supplicating state legislatures to require the schools to give creationism equal time.

They have apparently won their first victory in Arkansas. Gov. Frank White has signed a bill mandating the state's public schools to provide "balanced treatment to creation-science and evolution-science."

The bill also specifies that classes and books "must not include any religious instruction or references to religious writings." So that leaves out the Christian version of creation, as well as that of any other religious body.

Even so, the bill, which will become law in 90 days and is supposed to go into effect in the fall of 1982, strikes us as patently unconstitutional. It is a bald attempt to establish a religious teaching in the public schools — essentially a Judeo-Christian teaching, since not all religions posit the all-at-once creation of man separately from other living organisms.

We wonder how creationists would react if a state passed a law requiring Sunday schools to present a "balanced treatment" of scientific humanism in every church that enjoys tax-exempt status.

It is time for scientists, that vast majority of whom know that evolution is a fact as firmly established as any other scientific fact, to mount a unified resistance to attempts to diminish what is one of the most revolutionary and productive discoveries of the human mind.

Pittsburgh Post-Gazette

Pittsburgh, Pa., March 25, 1981

A few weeks after a California judge dealt a defeat to the forces of "creationism" — the pseudo-scientific movement to smuggle Genesis back into biology classrooms — the anti-evolution movement has won one. Arkansas, which has the dubious distinction of being the state whose law prohibiting the teaching of evolution was struck down by the U.S. Supreme Court 13 years ago, has just enacted a law that would require biology teachers to give equal time to "creationist" theories.

Whether this law will survive judicial scrutiny is doubtful, as one exasperated legislator told his colleagues. "As a lawyer, I will tell you the courts will hold this bill unconstitutional as quickly as it gets to court," Rep. Mike Wilson pleaded in vain.

There is a good reason for the courts to consign the Arkansas "equal time" law to the same constitutional graveyard as its predecessor. Notwithstanding coy arguments that creationism is simply one scientific theory among others, the fact is that its proponents are motivated not by scientific induction but by devout (and, in their sphere, constitutionally protected) religious beliefs.

For whatever the origins of man might be, the origins of the theory of creationism are clear: They can be located in the teachings of a highly specific religious tradition, fundamentalist Protestantism. That this religious tradition is widely adhered to in Arkansas no more justifies a creationist approach to biology instruction than the presence of Indian immigrants in a certain school district would justify that district's use of Hindu creation stories as scientific texts. There is a place in public schools for the sensitive exploration of various religious traditions, but it is not the science classroom.

No one can pretend that the teaching of science can be totally harmonized with solicitude for each and every religious belief. There would be no way for a physics teacher, for example, not to offend a student who believed as a matter of faith that there is no such thing as the law of gravity. Evolution is admittedly less of a clear-cut case: Scientists vociferously argue among themselves about the speed and the direction of evolution, and about a host of subsidiary issues. But no expert in the field doubts the *fact* of human evolution.

The campaign for "creationism" in the classroom springs from entirely different objections, *religious* objections. For that reason, legislators who enact "equal time" laws are flouting their oaths to uphold the Constitution, which includes a prohibition of governmental establishment of religion.

Louisiana Follows Arkansas With "Creation Science" Bill

Louisiana became the second state to enact a law requiring the teaching of "creation science" in public schools, when Gov. David C. Treen signed the bill July 21. The wording of the bill avoided mention of the Bible or God, in consideration of the First Amendment prohibition against mixing church and state. State Sen. Bill Keith, sponsor of the legislation, said: "The teaching of scientific creationism is totally separate and apart from the Genesis account. . . . The Genesis account explains what happened. Scientific creationism, through scientific data, explains how it happened." The bill required that the "scientific evidence" of creation by a divine power be discussed in biology classrooms along with the theory of evolution. The law was slated to go into effect in September 1982. Besides Arkansas and Louisiana, 18 states had similar laws in various stages of preparation.

THE ARIZONA REPUBLIC

Phoenix, Ariz., May 11, 1981

HUMAN evolution — the center of a stormy debate in the nation's schools — is far less certain than Darwin and his followers would have the world believe.

The Chinese, for one, are not convinced humans derived from apes.

They report finding the first complete skull of a Ramapithecus, a forerunner of man believed to have lived 8 million to 14 million years ago.

Studies of the reconstructed skull indicate Ramapithecus walked on two legs. The Chinese say this makes him a likely predecessor of man rather than the ape.

If the Chinese finding is verified, it would change the hypothesis of paleoanthropologists for the past 20 years — that man evolved primarily in eastern and southern Africa, and that Ramapithecus was clearly more apelike than man.

Not only is the latest finding closer to early man than had been presumed, the Chinese report, but it also differs signficantly from fossils found in Ethiopia.

The Chinese discovery raises, perhaps, as many questions as it answers.

That is the precise position of those who challenge Darwin's theory of evolution. It's a theory — nothing more nor less.

The Washington Star
and Daily News

Washington, D.C., March 5, 1981

There is a startling sense of *deja vu* in the news that Adam and Eve are once more challenging Darwin for the hearts and minds of the young. Surely the Scopes trial settled all that! After sharp Clarence Darrow got through with corny William Jennings Bryan nobody would suggest that a Bible story could be taken seriously if it contradicted the pronouncements of certified scientists.

There it is, though. From New York to California, schools and legislatures are under pressure from so-called creationists to give biology classroom time to what Genesis has to say about how the world began. It is a switch on the Scopes trial, which, more than half a century ago, weighed the Darwinian theory of evolution against the complex of law and community mores that kept it from being taught in a Tennessee public school.

This time around, it's yesterday's dogma trying to get back in where another world view now exercises the authority it once had. Creationism's resilience after so many setbacks would not have surprised H.L. Mencken. The Baltimore iconoclast who covered the Scopes trial for his newspaper and cosmopolitans everywhere came away from Tennessee stronger than ever in his conviction that the boobs, as he called unsophisticated people, never learn.

Recently, to be sure, the fundamentalist view has had some encouragement. It did not cost Ronald Reagan the election to disclose doubts on the Darwinian theory. And while,

as president, he has conspicuously not brought creationists into his administration, having him in charge seems to some of them to add respectability to their beliefs.

Their years in the wilderness have also forced creationists to try to defend their side with the enemy's weapons at least as they understand those weapons. More and more, anti-Darwinians are turning to evidence and systematic argument to vindicate revelation. They have yet to convince the faculties of most universities, or indeed any segment of scientific opinion, but the fact is that there are now people questioning evolutionary theory in ways that give comfort to the creationists.

The controversy is a reminder that scientific hypotheses are never beyond modification through fresh insights, reasoning and experiment. It is a further reminder that scientific thought is never too detached to respond to changes in the cultural climate.

Still, there are those who see the rise of creationism as the beginning of a night of unreason. Unreason is powerful all right, and insisting that poetic truth can or must be the same thing as what laboratories establish does not reflect the highest qualities of either the mind or the imagination.

But moving closer to the intellectual mainstream should influence the creationists to bring their faith to terms with the best of science. They might even come to see where one leaves off and the other begins.

Arkansas Gazette.

Little Rock, Ark., January 9, 1981

A group of scientists got together under the aegis of the American Association for the Advancement of Science the other day to answer directly the "know nothing" campaign remark of President-elect Ronald Reagan that evolution "is only a theory."

Mr. Reagan's remarks were uttered to an appreciative audience of evangelists at Dallas in August, when he said: "I have a great many questions about it. I think that recent discoveries down through the years have pointed up great flaws. It is not believed in the scientific community to be as infallible as it once was believed." At another point in his talk, Mr. Reagan said that if evolution is going to be taught "then the Biblical story of creation, which is not a theory, should also be taught."

The group of AAAS scientists, meeting at Toronto, called Reagan's remarks "tremendously unfortunate," but they also serve notice that the scientific community will not remain silent if religious fundamentalists, taking a cue from the president-elect's comments, try in the next four years to dismiss the obvious facts about evolution.

One of the experts on hand at Toronto was Porter M. Kier, senior scientist at the Smithsonian Institution, whose views seem to reflect, at least generally, those of his colleagues who also were present.

Scientists, said Dr. Kier, may argue about the details of evolution — presumably, we would add, about the various theories of how the process occurs — "but they agree that evolution is a fact. The evidence for evolution has been accumulating for several hundred years," he added. "New age-dating methods have proven that rocks at least 3½ billion years old contain evidence of life. Over the eons, we know beyond doubt, life has changed dramatically, changing from simple, unicellular organisms into animals as complex as man. This knowledge is based on unassailable evidence, the fossil remains of thousands and thousands of species of plants and animals which no longer exist."

Unfortunately, Kier reminds us, those who do not accept the evidence are vocal in their attacks and are promoting their creationist views in many forums. Therefore, he added, "Those of us who know the overwhelming, incontrovertible evidence and the conclusions to which it leads must be equally outspoken if we are to provide the public with what it needs to know on this important subject."

Dr. Kier and his associates surely know what they are letting themselves in for. Evolution has been bitterly debated in political, social and religious contexts in the United States for many years. It has been only 10 years or so since the last state law — Arkansas's — prohibiting the teaching of evolution in public institutions was tossed out as nonsense by the United States Supreme Court. Diehards persist, here and elsewhere, and remarks such as those by Mr. Reagan will only encourage their resurgence. Responsible members of the scientific community, such as those at Toronto, will have to be speaking out with increasing forcefulness and clarity as new skirmishes break out across the land.

Portland Press Herald

Portland, Maine, July 20, 1981

The Bible doesn't need equal time in public school science classes. And it doesn't belong there. No matter how many signatures dot a petition circulating in Caribou to inject the biblical account of creation into science classrooms there.

Truth is not the issue. And it never has been. The real issue is separation of church and state, a constitutional precept that's been repeatedly affirmed by the courts.

Fundamentalists intent on taking Genesis to referendum in Caribou will probably encounter that precept if they persevere.

Beyond the constitutional issue, however, Caribou should carefully evaluate the concept on which the petition is based—an assumption that science is somehow anathema to religious thought.

No less a scientist than Albert Einstein once observed that "science without religion is lame, religion without science is blind." In saying that, Einstein recognized that both knowledge and faith have their place.

The petition to put the Bible into public school science classes make no more sense than substituting Charles Darwin's "Origin of the Species" for Genesis in theological schools.

TULSA WORLD

Tulsa, Okla., July 27, 1981

THE PEOPLE who brought America the so-called Scopes Laws of the 1920s are back again.

The Scopes Laws, in different versions, prohibited the teaching of "Darwinism" or scientific theories of evolution in public schools. These statutes were adopted in several States, including Oklahoma. They were laughed into oblivion soon after the celebrated trial of a Tennessee high school teacher named Scopes. He was convicted of lecturing on the teachings of the English botanist, Charles Darwin.

The early laws were promoted on religious grounds. They were based frankly on the idea that Darwin's theories and similar teachings were an affront to the Christian religion.

The Courts have long since ruled that religious censorship of this kind has no place in public education. So the new Scopes Law advocates have taken an indirect approach. They say their belief in the instant — rather than evolutionary — creation of man is not religious, but "scientific."

They do not propose to censor Darwin and other scientists out of the classroom. But they want to require the teaching of their own ideas of "scientific creationism" in addition to the accepted scientific facts and theories.

The old Scopes Laws, absurd as they were, made a lot more sense than the modern version. At least, they were supported with honest motives. There was no "scientific" subterfuge.

The point is, of course, that science and religion are not interchangeable and not in conflict. Religious beliefs are based on faith. They need not, indeed should not be required to pass any scientific test. Christians believe in everlasting life, for example, but no one seriously suggests that this belief can be proved in a laboratory.

But the new "Scientific Creationism" is neither science nor religion. As science, it is a joke. And the very people who advocate it deny (perhaps with their fingers crossed) that it is a religious teaching.

It's hard to believe this kind of unscientific science or non-spiritual religion — whichever you prefer — could be taken seriously. But don't laugh.

Arkansas and Louisiana have adopted the new Scopes Laws. Oklahoma could be the next target.

The News American

Baltimore, Md., October 20, 1981

One of the bills awaiting legislators in Annapolis merits notice as a particularly bad idea. Delegate Patrick Scannello of Glen Burnie is proposing that public schools in Maryland be allowed to teach creationism along with scientific theories of the origin of life.

Creationism is the belief held by some fundamentalist Christians that the creation stories in Genesis provide a scientifically tenable explanation of the origin of human life. But creationism rests on theological assumptions; the Genesis stories do not pretend to present scientific fact. Confusing theology with science is an injustice both to religious faith and to scientific knowledge.

Creationism has no place in a science classroom, and we were glad to see that the Maryland State Teachers Association was quick to make that point in a resolution passed at its convention here last week. We hope legislators will be equally sensible.

The Times-Picayune
The States-Item

New Orleans, La., July 12, 1981

If Louisiana is not to have religious doctrine imposed on its public school teachers and children, Gov. David C. Treen will have to veto the Legislature's approval of a bill mandating the teaching of "scientific creationism" in public schools where evolutionary science is taught.

The Legislature, with its support of "scientific creationism," has once again passed the burden of leadership on to the governor. The governor should veto this ill-advised legislative act. The state has no business mandating the teaching of religious beliefs in our public schools, where some teachers and students might hold beliefs contrary to those being imposed upon them.

There is nothing scientific about "scientific creationism," which is a contradiction in terms. A religious theory based on the biblical story of creation found in the Book of Genesis, it is not subject to scientific verification utilizing universally accepted scientific methods.

By avoiding any reference to the Bible or religion, the term "scientific creationism" represents a clear effort by its proponents to circumvent the federal prohibition against the teaching of religion in public schools. It is appalling that the Legislature should capitulate to this subterfuge.

Scientific creationism is more than a narrow-based assault on the study of evolution; it necessarily challenges, in addition, the validity of the sciences of geology and paleontology, on which the study of evolution depends, and, by extension, the whole scientific process.

Although it evidently is not understood by a majority of our legislators, the effort to force the teaching of scientific creationism in the public schools is widely perceived by many church leaders to be a threat to religious freedom. In Arkansas, a coalition of educational and religious leaders, including representatives of many of the established churches, have joined in a suit challenging a new state law mandating the teaching of scientific creationism in the public schools.

Freedom of religion and scientific progress are integral and essential parts of our heritage and our democracy. Many scientists are, in fact, deeply religious, and many devoutly religious individuals have no problem conceding to science that which belongs to science. Only a misguided minority and occasionally befuddled legislators cannot let well enough alone.

New Orleans, La., July 22, 1981

It comes as no great surprise that Gov. David Treen has signed the "creationism bill." In doing so he expressed grave doubts about the wisdom of the legislative action, but reconciled these doubts in the light of the "mandate" of the Legislature.

We consider his action to be ill advised, even though he suggests that the bill merely grants authority to school boards and others to exercise their own judgment.

The governor provided a list of 10 points about the bill as passed. What he seems to have intended to demonstrate is that the bill is not that bad because it is so vague that local boards and teachers can implement it any way they want to. But vagueness is a common ground for declaring laws unconstitutional.

Mr. Treen glides by a central problem of the bill with his contention that "it does not provide for the teaching of religious belief." "Scientific" creationism is in fact an article of faith, not a body of knowledge built up through scientific inquiry, and the faith is that of the Old Testament, accepted as scripture by Christians. Thus, giving creationism whatever form of serious equal time in science classes is not only teaching religious belief but teaching one religion's belief to the exclusion of others — Greek, Nordic, Hindu, Egyptian, et al — that are not accepted as revealed scripture.

On the other central issue, the governor argues that even if the bill requires rather than simply permits — another vagueness yet to be analyzed — teaching creationism, the educational process will not be damaged. "Academic freedom," he said, "cannot be harmed by inclusion. It can be harmed by exclusion." But there can be no academic freedom when the content of a course is prescribed by law for reasons having nothing to do with educational judgment. Evolution, should new evidence or new interpretations of current data prove it false, would forthwith no longer be taught by reputable science educators. But creationism, regardless of any evidence, would be on the books and in the classrooms until the Legislature repealed the law.

Politics clearly played more of a part in all this than education. The Legislature, looking at the powerful and sophisticated resurgence of fundamentalism and all the votes it represents, passed the bill perhaps hoping Gov. Treen would take them off the hook with a veto (and get hung on it himself). Gov. Treen perhaps saw all those votes too, and hopes the Legislature next time (the act does not go into effect until 1982) will take him off or that the courts, where the issue will surely go before then, will do it.

Any way you figure it, it has been a sad performance all 'round. We could have expected better from people whose task is not only to represent and reflect constituents' views and interests, but also to lead where required.

The Des Moines Register
Des Moines, Iowa, December 26, 1981

Believers in creation are religious; believers in evolution are atheists, the line goes. It is voiced with increasing frequency in the debate over teaching "creation science" in public schools, and in the Arkansas trial where a law requiring that schools provide equal time for the Old Testament story is under challenge.

Evolution holds that Earth's creatures evolved through a complex series of mutations over millions of years; creationists contend that the world began around 4004 B.C., with its life forms coming into being within a short time span, fully formed, through the manifestation of a divine will. Many creationists further contend that belief in divinity and belief in evolution are mutually exclusive, that divinity is real only to those who accept Genesis literally. They have thus theologically exiled most members of many major religions.

A fundamentalist religious tract making a case for creationism masterfully describes the complexity and delicate beauty of a variety of life systems, argues that they could not have developed by accident, then charges that to believe in evolution is to deny God and any meaning to life.

That leap of logic denies any possibility of divine direction in the evolutionary process. To be religious, by this definition, means that one must believe not only in a divine creation but in a particular method by which the handiwork was accomplished.

Ever since humans have been able to reason, they have plugged the gaps in their understanding of life with belief in everything from magic to miracle. Science has stripped away the magic but reinforced the miracle of life by pointing out the intricate interactions through which it evolved.

To demand that theists accept only one theory as to the genesis of the miracle is to erect needless and divisive barriers to understanding. "Creationism" or "evolution" — either one would be a miracle.

Legal Challenge Begins Against "Creation Science" Law

The American Civil Liberties Union filed suit in May against the Arkansas "creation science" law. Joined by 22 other plaintiffs, the ACLU called the law a violation of the First Amendment separation of church and state. It was a familiar battle for the ACLU, which had chosen Clarence Darrow as defense counsel in the 1925 Scopes trial and had led the successful suit in 1967 against Tennessee's 1929 anti-evolution law. That law had forbidden the teaching of any "doctrine that mankind ascended or descended from a lower order of animals." Fourteen years later, the ACLU and the state of Arkansas were adversaries over evolution. This time, the law did not seek to prohibit teaching of any particular theory. Instead, it sought to add "creation science" to evolution. Carefully avoiding the mention of God or the Bible, the law defined "creation science" as "scientific evidences . . . that indicate: sudden creation of the universe, energy and life from nothing; the insufficiency of mutation and natural selection" to explain the development of life on earth, "separate ancestry for man and apes; explanation of earth's geology by catastrophism, including the occurrence of a worldwide flood," and "a relatively recent inception of the earth and living kinds" no more than 6,000–10,000 years ago. Arkansas Gov. Frank D. White summed up what many saw as the basic significance of "creation science." When asked why he signed the bill without having read it, he replied: "I'm a Christian, and I believe in the Bible."

The Cincinnati Post

Cincinnati, Ohio, August 22, 1981

It is a good time for creationists, those who now claim that the biblical story of creation is a science and must be taught on equal terms with the theory of evolution in public schools.

Arkansas and Louisiana have passed laws ordering the teaching of so-called "creation-science." Even without state laws it is widely taught in Texas, Minnesota, South Dakota and parts of Florida and West Virginia.

Since fundamentalist Christians have political power in many other states and legislators fear the accusation of "voting against God," the teaching of creationism is sure to spread. That is unfortunate on constitutional and intellectual grounds.

Of course parents in the home and clergymen in churches have a perfect right to instruct that man was placed on Earth in his current form by a divine creator about 6000 years ago. There's nothing wrong, in fact, with noting that's what some people believe when investigating theories of creation in a classroom. But teaching religious dogma under the guise of science cannot be done in public schools without violating the principle of separation of church and state. That is a crucial difference.

In the 125 years since Darwin proposed the theory of evolution, creationism has steadily lost out among scientists through the free competition of ideas. The fact that Darwin's theories themselves are now being subjected to some withering criticism in scholarly circles is evidence that truth is indeed a hard deer to hunt.

But today's creationists do not merely seek "equal time" with evolution in the classroom. They are well aware of their influence with school boards and after "creation-science" is in the schools, they will try to downgrade or eliminate the teaching of evolution.

If they succeed, we will not only abridge the rights of those who do not believe that the Bible is the literal word of God. We will also be training a generation of scientifically incompetent students.

In Arkansas, parents, teachers, scientists and leaders of the Roman Catholic, Presbyterian, United Methodist, African Methodist and Episcopal churches and the Jewish faith have filed suit to overturn the creationism law.

In the interests of religious tolerance, the First Amendment stricture on the establishment of religion and openness of scientific thought, they deserve to win.

ST. LOUIS POST-DISPATCH

St. Louis, Mo., July 14, 1981

Fifty-six years after high school biology teacher John Thomas Scopes was convicted in a Tennessee court of violating the state's law against the teaching of biological evolution, the Arkansas Legislature has revived the issue by enacting a statute requiring that public school teachers in that state who teach evolution also teach the religious belief that a Divine Being suddenly and at once created all forms of animal and plant life. Although Scopes was found guilty, his conviction was reversed on a technicality by the Tennessee Supreme Court; and the idea of teaching divine creation in the public schools was discredited as an unacceptable intrusion of religion into public education.

A 1928 Arkansas statute, similar to that of Tennessee, was struck down by the U.S. Suprme Court in 1968 as a violation of religious freedom as guaranteed by the First Amendment. But apparently Arkansas has not learned a lesson from its own ill-fated law or from the original so-called Scopes "monkey trial." Its new law has now been challenged in court by the American Civil Liberties Union in behalf of plaintiffs who include officers in Presbyterian, Episcopal, Methodist, Baptist, African Methodist Episcopal, Roman Catholic, Jewish and educational organizations in Arkansas. The principal basis for the legal challenge is that the law violates the constitutional requirement of separation of church and state. The First Amendment to the U.S. Constitution — and, by extension, the 14th Amendment as applied to the states — forbids laws respecting "an establishment of religion." Arkansas, by mandating the teaching of religious doctrine, is clearly violating this prohibition.

Many religious bodies, such as those who are parties to the Arkansas suit, realize that their interpretations of doctrines differ. Therefore, understandably, they prefer to confine religious teaching to religious educational institutions, churches and synagogues and to keep it out of the public schools, where the state controls what is taught. Their view is consistent with the traditional American political concept under which the state is — and should be — neutral on religious matters. But religious fundamentalists — who backed the Arkansas statute and who have been promoting similar laws in a dozen states, including Missouri — seem to think that they have a monopoly on truth and that the teaching of their version of doctrine should be compulsory.

Such an attitude not only reflects intolerance for diversity in religious thinking but also intolerance for accepted methods of education, in which theories such as evolution must be buttressed by scientific evidence. One of the basic objectives of education is to foster skepticism and free inquiry. That objective is undermined by mandated dogma. So is the long proven concept that religious freedom can flourish only when the state keeps it hands off religion.

THE CHRISTIAN SCIENCE MONITOR

Boston, Mass., August 12, 1981

Louisiana's new law that requires public schools to give equal treatment to so-called "creation-science" whenever the theory of evolution is taught raises disturbing questions concerning the separation of church and state.

It is true that neither this law nor the similar statute enacted last year by Arkansas explicitly mandates religious teaching as such. Nevertheless, the "creation-science" which the statutes do mandate is a version of the literal interpretation of Genesis which Christian fundamentalists espouse.

This is especially clear in the Arkansas law, which, unlike the Louisiana statute, includes a definition of "creation-science." This "science," it says, includes the sudden creation from nothing of the universe, energy, and organic life substantially in their present forms. It explains Earth's history in terms of catastrophes, especially a global (Noah's) flood. It maintains that Earth and the universe were formed at a specific time and recently, within the past 10,000 years or so.

Many Americans are concerned that such views, if introduced in the schools by law, will not only do great damage to the quality of science teaching, jeopardizing the training of the nation's future scientists, but lead to the overt introduction of sectarian instruction in them. That is why a number of religious organizations and religious leaders, as well as scientific organizations and individuals, have joined with the American Civil Liberties Union in a court test of the Arkansas law. The ACLU says it will challenge the Louisiana law, too.

Certainly creationists have a right to interpret the Bible as they wish. However, for a state to force that view on public school teaching amounts to establishment of one brand of religion by governmental authority, which is forbidden by the First Amendment to the United States Constitution.

The public schools now teach human evolutionary theory as it has developed within the broad scientific community. This does not mean, however, that persons teaching such theory would or should claim that it repre-

sents the final truth about man and the universe. Given the many revolutionary changes in scientific thought in the 20th century, scientists themselves would be the first to admit they are far from understanding the laws underlying reality or even what reality is. Reasonable explanations of physical phenomena today become myths tomorrow. Good teachers of science will strive to cultivate open and inquiring minds in their students, reminding them that there do exist other approaches, including religious ones. But tax-supported schools should not start down the course of teaching the views of a particular religion.

There obviously is a deep longing among many segments of the American public for a greater affirmation and application of religious faith in everyday life, especially in a society grown so secularized. Perhaps what is needed is a recognition that the quest of scientific thinking is not necessarily in conflict with religious values and the concept of ultimate spiritual reality.

ARKANSAS DEMOCRAT

Little Rock, Ark., June 7, 1981

Atty. Gen. Steve Clark says he'll stand alone in defending the state's Creationism Act. We don't begrudge him his big chance to gain the notoriety and political preferment victory might bring — and we think he's dead right to reject all offers by religious groups to intervene in the state's interest.

That would likely be fatal to his planned presentation of the act as a straightforward right-to-know measure, aimed at illuminating rival non-religious theories of world origins.

Clark doesn't have to make any case for "creation science" — only for the lay nature of both the act and the theory it subserves. The law does that for him — and he can leave the evolution to the Arkansas Civil Liberties Union. ACLU has the double burden of establishing evolution as explaining the world in its entirety — and of proving that the act, despite its many disclaimers and caveats, is hidden religion.

As for any attacks it might make on the act as violating academic freedom — making teachers teach creationism against their will — it would be a great opportunity for the court to point out that academic freedom doesn't run to refusing to teach state-prescribed course materials. Anyhow, academic freedom sounds pretty hollow when put up against Clark's argument that kids aren't hurt by having their minds broadened — so long as they aren't being preached to.

Indeed, the chief result of the trial may be to broaden all our minds — and ACLU certainly won't like that. ACLU wants to ban all school discussion of "original" ideas, evolution excepted, as religious per se. It doesn't scruple to get there any old way. It presents the Legislature as an enemy of the Constitution — the devious promoter of a code version of the Old Testament's account of world origins. Reading the ACLU suit after reading the act, you have to marvel as much at the venom of the attack on the act as at the weakness of the evidence offered against it.

Little Rock, Ark., November 24, 1981

An AP-NBC poll shows 76 per cent of Americans favoring the teaching of both evolution and biblical creation in public schools. What does the ACLU's Sandra Kurjiaka, deadly foe of the creationism act, think about that?

She says that 76 per cent is speaking out of ignorance — probably with the thought that such teaching would do no harm. But what people fail to realize, Kurjiaka says, is that such teaching would set the country up for a "state-sponsored religion."

First Amendment-wise, that would mean a "Church of the United States," to which we'd all have to conform. Of all bugaboo-threats ever raised against our liberties, that's the feeblest. We could easily take Kurjiaka to task for playing high priestess of civil liberties to the dum-dums — misleading us deliberately. But we know she isn't really talking about a national church when she warns of a "state sanctioned religion."

What she means is that by tolerating or sanctioning the teaching of "biblical creation" — government would be acknowledging that christianity is America's overwhelming religion. All anti-religionists hate and fear that admission. So do many non-Christians. The fears of the latter are groundless. Since the First Amendment bans any official interference with the free exercise of religion, all other faiths and the free exercise of them are safe.

You might think that professed libertarians, like the ACLU, would at least point that out. Since ACLU doesn't, you have to ask whether what really underlines its hostility to de facto acknowledgment of christianity as our prevailing religion isn't opposition to religion, especially, christianity itself. We're inclined to think that this virus does indeed underlie much of the frenetic opposition to "mixing church and state" and the attack on the creationism law as well.

That law, of course, studiously avoids the teaching of "biblical creation" and speaks of creationist science. But ACLU's court attack is based overwhelmingly on the argument that the law is sneaking christian fundamentalism.

There's no mistaking the shrillness. It expresses an almost paranoid fear that somebody — somewhere — in authority might one day acknowedge that America is fundamentally a religious - even christian — country and that courts might then cease to hamper christianity's free exercise. That wouldn't endanger the free practice of other religions — but ACLU doesn't mind exploiting that fear in its frantic warnings of a "state sponsored religion."

The Hartford Courant

Hartford, Conn., July 30, 1981

Pity the poor public school student in Arkansas or Louisiana.

The legislatures of those two states have deemed that each student must — repeat, must — be taught "creationism," right alongside the theory of evolution, whenever the origins of matter and life are discussed in the classroom.

What next? Will they order that children also be taught the theory that the world is flat, or that females get fevers from intellectual activity?

It is a dangerous precedent for government to approve specific doctrines and to mandate that those doctrines be taught in public schools.

The theory of evolution is taught in public schools because most science educators agree that it offers a testable explanation for life, not because some politicians ordered it to be taught.

Creationism would be included in textbooks, without government fiat, if the theory were able to compete with evolution with hard evidence, in studies using scientific methods, and reported in reputable scientific journals.

But it cannot, and has to rely on Bible-thumping legislators to force it into school curricula.

The laws in Arkansas and Louisiana are being challenged by the American Civil Liberties Union on the grounds that the government is violating the First Amendment to the Constitution by forcing religious instruction in public schools.

The theory of creationism, even under the rubric of "creation-science," is founded upon the literal interpretation of the Bible. That interpretation is a matter of faith, which defies scientific inquiry. It is religion in the guise of science.

For the sake of the students in Louisiana and Arkansas, who might never learn the difference, we hope the courts declare laws forcing the instruction of creationism unconstitutional.

Arkansas ⚜ Gazette.

Little Rock, Ark., June 1, 1981

Few thoughtful persons who are familiar with the bitterly divisive issues that often become all wrapped up in an adversary discussion of "creation-science" and/or evolution will relish the idea that Arkansas must now endure a federal court challenge to Act 590 of 1981. This is the unspeakable law requiring the public schools to teach "creation-science" if evolution also is taught.

Just because we and others do not relish the idea does not mean that the lawsuit filed last week by the American Civil Liberties Union on behalf of 23 plaintiffs, most of them religious leaders or religious organizations, is not welcome. To the contrary, the ACLU should be applauded for seeking relief in the federal courts, and if one result will be an embarrassing trial it certainly cannot be as embarrassing as the fact that our legislature and governor have imposed the law upon Arkansans.

Enactment of Act 590 clearly was the result of an effort to inject into the classroom one particular fundamentalist religious view. Many proponents will deny this assertion, but it is plain enough to anyone who has closely observed the social and political attitudes of this state. Certainly it has not been missed by those other figures of religion that do not share the particular view held by Act 590's sponsors and who now may be counted among the plaintiffs. "Creation-science," say the plaintiffs, amounts to religion, masquerading in the clothing of science.

Even Arkansas's attorney general, Steve Clark, is unenthusiastic about fulfilling his duty to defend the constitutionality of Act 590 in the federal courts. The state will make a "good faith effort," he says, but he has "personal qualms" about whether the law is "good for the state and whether it's a legitimate state interest." Clark favors changing the law, adding: "Setting the curriculum ought to be left to the Department of Education and local school boards."

Some legislative leaders acknowledge that the General Assembly committed grievous error in approving the measure so hastily and want to repeal Act 590 at the first opportunity. Their efforts should be encouraged, although they apparently can count on little help from Governor Frank White, who signed the measure without reading all of it.

The trial would be rendered moot by early legislative repeal, but if it is held as scheduled in the court of Federal Judge William Overton, there will be extraordinary opportunity to develop the issues fully. The ACLU already has lined up an impressive list of expert witnesses to assist the plaintiffs and their testimony can be an uncommon educational experience itself. The list includes Dr. Carl Sagan, the famous astrophysicist from Cornell perhaps best known for his book and television series *Cosmos*; Dr. Niles Eldredge, a curator at the American Museum of Natural History and a professor of geology at Columbia University; Dr. Thomas Jukes, professor of biophysics at the University of California at Berkeley; Dr. Richard Dickerson, professor of chemistry at the California Institute of Technology; Dr. William McLaughlin, professor of history at Brown University; and William V. Mayer, professor of biology at the University of Colorado and director of the Biological Sciences Curriculum Study Center at Boulder.

It is apparent that the ACLU is prepared to attack Act 590 with an extraordinary array of intellectual and legal talent, just as it entered the battle against a Tennessee law banning the teaching of evolution in 1925. Arkansas may become the site of "Monkey Trial II" but we have no one to blame except ourselves — i.e. the legislature and the governor.

Little Rock, Ark., October 29, 1981

Arkansas's attorney general filed last week in federal court at Little Rock the state's brief defending the constitutionality of Act 590 of 1981, the act that requires the public schools, starting the fall of 1982, to give "balanced treatment" to "creation-science" and evolution in the classroom.

Many contrasts, some sharp and others subtle, are drawn with the brief filed earlier by attorneys for the American Civil Liberties Union, which represents 23 plaintiffs, including 16 religious leaders. The stage is well set, in any event, for the trial scheduled to begin on December 7 before Federal Judge William R. Overton.

In one particular, for example, the state contends that "creation-science" is a theory "well-supported by competent scientific evidence" and its list of expert witnesses indicates that some scientists will testify to this point. The ACLU, on the other hand, insists that "creation-science" is actually religion in the guise of science, and its list of witnesses supporting this point includes perhaps the best-known scientist, Carl (*Cosmos*) Sagan, in the nation.

Certainly the trial has promise of becoming an intriguing intellectual exercise serving a worthy educational purpose in defining the perimeters of science and religion. To be sure, it is an important constitutional question that brings the "creation-science" law into federal court, but the general issues that the suit raises will not likely be settled whatever decision the courts reach. Science and philosophy have argued these issues for centuries and, if the world does not destroy itself in the meantime, the debate will rage for centuries into the future.

THE MILWAUKEE JOURNAL

Milwaukee, Wisc., June 5, 1981

One of the most fundamental, cherished freedoms in America is the right to individual religious belief, unimpeded by official action of the government. Thus, every true believer in religious freedom should applaud the legal challenge filed against the State of Arkansas and, by implication, against the so-called creationists who want to impose their beliefs on everyone.

The federal lawsuit challenges a new Arkansas law requiring that any teaching of the scientific theory of evolution in public schools be balanced with the teaching of the view that life was created suddenly by a Divine Being. The suit was filed by the American Civil Liberties Union and leaders of such major faiths as the Presbyterian, Southern Baptist, Roman Catholic, Jewish, Episcopal and Methodist.

The creationists seek to portray the theory of evolution as a religious view, so that — presto! — they can demand equal attention to their own viewpoint in the classroom. Arkansas lawmakers apparently swallowed such fallacious thinking.

Although there are some scientific questions about evolutionary theory, it certainly is not a religious belief. (Even if it were, the creationist viewpoint would be only one of several different beliefs about the origin of life that could demand equal attention.)

The Arkansas law, which the creationists are urging other states to enact, does not merely mandate the teaching of religion in public schools. It requires the teaching of a *particular* religious belief.

It should be clear to people of every faith, as well as to those with no religious belief, that a state requirement of this kind is fundamentally at odds with the concept of religious freedom. If the creationists can impose their beliefs on the public schools today in Arkansas, what other particular religious view will be required somewhere else tomorrow? The answer presumably would depend on just which religious group could muster sufficient political power to win enactment of its own view as official state policy.

Clearly, the survival of full religious freedom in America is at stake in this important lawsuit.

Arkansas "Creationism" Law Goes on Trial

Hearings opened Dec. 7 in Little Rock on Arkansas' controversial law requiring the teaching of "creation science" in public schools alongside Charles Darwin's theory of evolution. The American Civil Liberties Union had filed suit against the law on grounds it violated the constitutional separation of church and state. The ACLU sought to prove that "creation science" was a religious teaching and should be barred from public education. Defenders of the teaching intended to prove that it was a scientific theory no less valid than evolution. In his opening statement, Arkansas Attorney General Steve Clark said: "The state will prove that neither 'creation-science' nor 'evolution-science' is science under the strict definition. . . . 'Creation-science' is at least as scientific as 'evolution-science.' " Robert Cearley of the Arkansas ACLU replied that the law "is an unprecedented attempt by the legislature to use its power and authority to define what science is," and that it represented "a clear and dangerous breach in the wall of separation between church and state." The Arkansas law defined "creation science" as "Sudden creation of the universe, energy and life from nothing; . . . separate ancestry for man and apes; explanation of earth's geology by catastrophism, including the occurrence of a worldwide flood; and a relatively recent inception of the earth and living kinds."

THE CHRISTIAN SCIENCE MONITOR
Boston, Mass., December 9, 1981

Both Protestant and Roman Catholic clergymen have testified that Arkansas's now challenged "creation-science" law bears a direct if unstated relationship to the Book of Genesis. They were among the first witnesses in a suit brought by the American Civil Liberties Union and others attacking the law as contrary to the First Amendment guarantee of separation of church and state. The law requires that Arkansas teachers who teach the theory of evolution give "balanced treatment" to creation-science. The outcome of the case could affect not only Arkansas but other states that have or contemplate similar laws.

We discussed this subject at greater length when Louisiana passed such a law last summer. The constitutional separation of church and state must be maintained for the protection of all. At the same time the yearning for religious insight on the most fundamental questions of human life must be respected. The advocates of creation-science argue that it can be taught without violating the Constitution. Some also argue that evolutionism itself is a form of religious belief.

It is well that the issue has been brought before the judgment of the courts. It needs full clarification and adjudication.

Newsday
Long Island, N.Y., December 10, 1981

"Creation science" is the name recently bestowed on the antiquarian view that the earth and living things came into existence all at once about 6,000 years ago. Modern physics, astronomy, geology and biology point to a body of evidence that the process took billions of years; evolution is their explanation for life's variegated forms.

A federal court suit brought in Little Rock by the American Civil Liberties Union would strike down Arkansas' new requirement that "creation science" be taught whenever and wherever evolution is part of the state's public-school curriculum. The ACLU holds that "creation science" is no science, but a set of fundamentalist religious propositions cloaked in scientific jargon.

Members of the clergy and others representing Catholic, Protestant and Jewish organizations have joined the ACLU suit as co-plaintiffs. Perhaps more eloquently than most, they support the Constitution's strict separation of church and state.

These people espouse religious education in their own particular ways and by their own particular lights, but they oppose the imposition of any faith's tenets, however elaborately disguised, by a state legislature. They also know that the Bible is not a scientific textbook, and that evolutionary theory is no substitute for religion.

THE SAGINAW NEWS
Saginaw, Mich., December 13, 1981

The trouble with laws is that they are, well, legal. That's where Arkansas made its mistake in the creation vs. evolution debate on the origin of mankind. Michigan should avoid making the same mistake.

The debate has become a federal case in Arkansas. The American Civil Liberties Union says a state law mandating "balanced treatment" in public schools of the conflicting theories violates the separation of church and state.

We agree. Although Arkansas cloaked its law in academic trappings by calling the theory "creation science," it's plainly rooted in the biblical account of Genesis.

But we also see nothing wrong with telling students in public schools that evolution, generally accepted as a science — that is, subject to testing, challenge, revision — isn't the only theory of how we all got to be here. In fact, there are numerous theories, depending on which faith you follow or which anthropologist you ask.

Noting the beliefs of religion doesn't "teach" religion any more than mentioning the word "Christmas" in the classroom. A teacher should be able to do both — but not be *forced* to do either.

Both the Arkansas law and the ACLU, as we understand its argument, miss that point. The law mandates the teaching of a religious doctrine — one out of many held by American citizens — as a "science." The ACLU would prohibit any mention of the simple truth that there is such a thing as belief in creation.

Off and on during the past year, there have been movements in Michigan to put the same kind of law on the books.

The Legislature should not be led into the temptation to insist that schools promote any particular set of beliefs. That will only invite a challenge that may impose a different sort of absolutism.

Either case would violate the principle that our faith should not be a province of government or law, but a personal, private matter.

Richmond Times-Dispatch

Richmond, Va., December 11, 1981

If there is anything certain on this Earth it is that the origin of the Earth is uncertain. All of the wisdom and knowledge that mankind has acquired through the ages has failed to produce a universally acceptable, demonstrably true account of how it all began.

Among the most prominent theories, the New Columbia Encyclopedia reports, "are gravitational condensation hypotheses, which suggest that the entire solar system was formed at one time in a single series of processes resulting in the accumulation of diffuse interstellar gases and dust into a solar system of discrete bodies." Life emerged from all this, evolutionists say, and gradually developed into forms that exist today. Assuming that such hypotheses are soundly based, a baffling question remains: Who, or what, made all of those gases and all of that dust? Which is to suggest that even after science has taken us as far back as it can, we find ourselves face to face, still, with a mystery.

Creationists ascribe the origin of the universe to the act of a supernatural power — God. In their view, the Earth and all living things came into being within a fairly short period of time no more than 10,000 years ago. But like the "gravitational condensation hypotheses," this is an unproved theory that has failed to gain universal acceptance.

How the Earth began is now being debated, in a sense, in an Arkansas courtroom. The issue is there because of a state law that requires the creationist theory to be taught in any school that teaches the theory of evolution. Supporters of this theory, who call it "creation science," argue that they have as much right as the traditional physical scientists to present their case in an academic setting. But those who are challenging the law — a coalition of traditional scientists, religious leaders and civil liberties organizations — insist that creation science is really a religion and that teaching it would violate the constitutional requirement for separation of church and state. The Arkansas law, it is important to note, expressly forbids the use of religious writings in teaching the creationist theory and forbids the use of such courses for religious instruction.

Our sympathies are against the law — and against the basic argument of the people who are challenging it. We are inclined to think that it is unwise for the state to compel the teaching of any particular hypothesis, whether in the field of physical science or in philosophy, by statute. But the presentation of the creationist theory in the classroom, as long as it is not accompanied by evangelical efforts to persuade the students to become a member of any particular religious organization, does not appear to be the horrifying threat to the doctrine of separation of church and state that its critics allege it to be. Whether scientific purists like it or not, creationism is a view held by many in our society, and prohibiting any discussion of that view in classrooms would clash with the principle that education in a democratic society should guarantee access to ideas and freedom of inquiry.

How a particular subject is to be taught in public schools is a matter we would prefer to leave to the people responsible for running the schools — the education specialists who plan courses and choose textbooks, the teachers who teach and the laymen who serve on school boards and committees. This is not to say that legislative bodies are never to get involved. But statutory dogmatism either for or against a particular theory in any field of study is wrong.

Sentinel Star

Orlando, Fla., December 11, 1981

THE Arkansas court battle involving the creationist theory of man's beginnings and the Darwinian theory of evolution, symbolic of a widespread national controversy, is as predictable as it is unfortunate.

It was spawned primarily because people who should know better lost sight of the line separating scientific theory and dogma.

What happened in Arkansas is really not all that different from what has happened in too many public schools across the country: High school science instructors teach Charles Darwin's theory of gradual evolution as fact rather than emphasizing that it is merely the prevailing theory.

They do this for a number of reasons, not the least of which is convenience. It is easier to concentrate on the dominant theory than to clutter up lesson plans with alternative lines of thought. It is also uncommon for high school teachers to have a deep, well-developed store of knowledge about the subject.

The tone of the instruction is what angers religious folk as much as the content: Darwin is taught as fact with the clear, albeit implicit, conclusion that all else is fantasy.

In fact, there is a significant and growing element of the academic and scientific community that is questioning Darwinian theory on purely academic and scientific grounds, aside from any religious factors.

But all of this does not validate what the Arkansas Legislature did when it ordered balanced treatment for instruction of creationist views on how we all came to be here. The Arkansas lawmakers erred because creationism is also not presented by its backers as theoretical. To them it is fact, not theory.

It further is not supported by such commonly accepted scientific means as radioactive carbon dating and accepted laws of thermodynamics. The only legitimate point the creationists make in the Arkansas case is one that Americans everywhere, particularly those involved in public education, should acknowledge: Too many schools fail to foster the spirit of open-mindedness and inquiry and are instead shutting young minds to alternatives.

That is the real issue. Darwin's theory should be taught as such: the dominant theory in the scientific effort to explain the origins of life on Earth. It should not be taught at the expense of other respected theories on life's beginnings.

Once you've taught the Darwinian theory, there's room to recognize other theories and, indeed, even question their validity. But dogma should never be allowed to enter public classrooms under the guise of science.

The Charlotte Observer

Charlotte, N.C., December 15, 1981

A court in Little Rock is hearing arguments about an Arkansas law requiring the teaching of "scientific creationism" alongside the theory of evolution in the public schools, and efforts are underway that could lead to a similar law in North Carolina.

North Carolina shouldn't revive that misconceived debate. The desire of fundamentalist religious groups to convert others to their views is understandable, but the public school classroom isn't the place for such evangelism. "Creation science" is simply a new name for the old belief in the biblical story of creation. It isn't science, it's religion, and teaching one group's religious views isn't the business of public schools.

Science is a self-correcting enterprise. As new discoveries are made, scientists revise or even reject theories that once represented the best in scientific thought. That isn't true of "scientific creationists." They believe what they believe, every word, now and forever. On this question, at least, they lack the quality essential to scientific inquiry: an open mind.

This does not mean that science is more "true" than religion, and certainly not that science is more important than religion. Science is, however, *different* from religion. A law requiring public schools to teach a religious belief as if it were a scientific theory would be a disservice to both religion and science.

Science is mankind's effort to understand and control nature. Explanations such as "The devil did it" or "It was God's will" are not scientific explanations. The interest of science is, the natural, not the supernatural.

The most important questions of life, however, are not scientific but moral. What values should human beings live by? How should we treat each other? Why do the evil prosper and the good suffer? Are our lives just random flickers in the darkness of time, or does each life have a purpose?

The Bible has not endured for 2,000 years because of its comments on biology and geology. It has endured because of its wisdom about our relationships with each other and with God. The Bible should be cherished for what it is, not twisted into something it isn't; and one of the things it isn't is a high school science textbook.

ARKANSAS DEMOCRAT
Little Rock, Ark., December 8, 1981

What's on trial in the ACLU's suit against the state's creationist law, Act 590?

You can hear a lot of answers, but we'd agree with Atty. General Steve Clark that it isn't the Bible, let alone the superiority of any one scientific theory of origins over another that's on trial – it's the free flow of ideas in the classroom. Who'd quarrel with that?

Why, the American Civil Liberties Union. ACLU sees curricular freedom as curricular indoctrination and Act 590 as a fundamentalist effort to smuggle the Old Testament into the schools under guise of science – thereby violating the constitutional ban on an "establishment of religion."

How does ACLU propose to prove that?

In two ways. Its lawyers will labor obvious parallels between creationism's supposed scientific evidence and biblical events like the flood and its scientific witnesses will try to demolish creationism as a science. More important, the lawyers will argue that the law violates "academic freedom" in requiring teachers either to teach both creationism and evolution – or teach neither.

How will the state respond? It won't couple science and religion in any way except negatively. Clark's argument is that the law requires nothing more than the teaching, solely as a matter of education, two rival scientific theories of origins – the evolutionist and the creationist – and doesn't require teachers to be neutral in their teaching.

The state, too, will have its witnesses arguing for the validity of creationism as a science – and the clash between experts will be educational in itself. But since neither side can offer any butt-shut, dovetailed scientific case for its origins theory, the creationists shouldn't have to do more than show that their evidence meets the tests of scientific methodology.

And if this isn't a trial between two scientific theories, neither is it, as Clark says, a case of judging either theory by chance relations to religion. The word creationism, he says, doesn't denote a personal creator. And if the evidence for "creationist science" happens to recall certain biblical events, that doesn't make creationism a religion in its essentials: Not any more than does the incorporation of evolutionist elements in many religious beliefs make evolution one.

No amount of scientific theorizing on origins, however, is going to be conclusive. The decision could turn on something else – the widely different definitions of "academic freedom" that the ACLU and Clark offer against and for the teaching of creationist science. Clarks's, we think, is the most reasonable.

He says that academic freedom calls for as broad a lay curriculum in origins as possible – that teachers should support him in thinking that no idea or theory of origins should be excluded on the alarmist ground that teaching it is preaching it. Clark says academic freedom has no constitutional standing as a separate right conferring on teachers freedoms denied the rest of us.

ACLU's view is, to say the least, a revisionist one for those who think of academic freedom as a teacher's right to teach without officialldom telling him what to say or what not to say. Academic freedom, most libertarians think, is free speech and nothing more. But ACLU says it is a constitutional right confined to teachers – that under it any teacher who finds creationism personally offensive can choose not to teach origins at all, thereby losing his or her academic freedom. More likely his or her job, we'd say. But if academic freedom is a matter of conscience-over-curriculum, how about the teacher who doesn't want to teach evolution? Would ACLU limit cases of academic conscience to teachers who oppose creationism? Would others have the choice of confessing error or being harried out of the the schools as yahoos?

And while we're on the subject of rights, how about student rights? Clark's brief cites cases in which the courts have held that forcing anyone to participate in an activity that offends his religious *or non-religious beliefs* contravenes his First Amendment rights. That's a stunner, isn't it? It covers the First Amendment's guarantee of both free speech and the free exercise of religion.

Wouldn't it be great to see the decision turn on these libertarian axes without even the mention of religion? Why not a ruling saying that a pluralistic origins curriculum offends less that a single one? Such a ruling should please all who respect one another's rights. If there's any libertarianism stilll stirring in ACLU's crabbed view of those rights, how could it quarrel with that? There's not a word of religion in it.

We have hopes yet that ACLU will one day quit chasing the phantom of official religion through schools and city halls and over courthouse lawns? Why not now? It's Christmas, if ACLU will pardon mention of it.

Little Rock, Ark., December 14, 1981

Creationist-trial judge William R. Overton apears dissatisfied with the state's contention that the word "creation" isn't necessarily religious – doesn't necessarily denote a personal creator. It's a key ACLU argument, of course, that it does. A few comments.

Webster's Unabridged assigns to the word "create" both religious and non-religious meanings – defining it in the latter context as "to cause or occasion; to form – said of natural physical causes."

That, we'd think, should give the word scientific standing in a statutory context. The state's witnesses must still of course establish a scientific case for "creationism." But if they do produce evidence that is even arguably a product of scientific methodology – then any parallels between that evidence and such biblical "creationist" events as ACLU reads into Act 590 ought to be irrelevant.

Lay observers, meanwhile, must have been surprised to hear ACLU's prime biologist-witness, Dr. Harold Morowitz of Yale's department of biophysics and biochemistry, testify that evolution doesn't offer a theory of the beginning of life. The study of life's beginnings, Morowitz says, is the concern of biologists; their studies are separate from the study of the fossil evidence upon which geologists base their theory of changing life forms.

Morowitz goes on to offer the non-expert opinion (he's no lawyer) that the creationist language of Act 590 "assumes a creator and implies a supernatural explanation of natural phenomena." Armed with Webster, Atty. Gen. Steve Clark can readily answer, no; creationist science assumes no creator – only creation by scientific causation, meaning natural, not supernatural, agency. He might also ask generally why – if evolution posits no life-origins theory of its own – the ACLU's biologist-witnesses (including high school teachers) defend evolution as the definitive scientific explanation of origins.

Arkansas Gazette.

Little Rock, Ark.,
December 10, 1981

Federal Judge William R. Overton has wisely rejected attempts to limit expert testimony during the early stages of the trial testing the constitutionality of Arkansas's "creation-science" law, Act 590 of 1981. It has been clear from the time of the bill's introduction in the state legislature that it was simply an attempt to impose religious fundamentalism upon science instruction in the public school classrooms, as if oil and water do mix after all.

Nothing that has been said either in testimony or outside the courtroom alters this observation. Events instead have served to enhance the obvious nature of Act 590's challenge to the First Amendment's prohibition against an establishment of religion.

State Senator Jim Holsted of North Little Rock, who sponsored Act 590, told reporters during a break in the proceedings on Monday that God had spoken to him and told him to sponsor the bill.

Holsted acknowledged, in testimony the next day, that he got a model law from creationists and sponsored it partly because of his deep religious convictions. He testified as well that he believes in a literal interpretation of the Bible.

Attorneys for the American Civil Liberties Union, representing the 23 plaintiffs seeking to have the law declared unconstitutional, have outlined in their "findings of fact" a kind of capsule history of Arkansas's experience this year with the "creation-science" movement. In this "scenario," the chairman of Citizens for Fairness in Education, which is identified as part of the evangelical fundamentalist movement, drafted, in consultation with others of like view, a model statute calling for "balanced treatment" of "creation-science" and "evolution-science" in public schools. A copy was sent to a person in Arkansas, who gave it to Holsted.

As the ACLU points out, the bill had an all-too-brief journey into state law. The Senate didn't even hold a hearing on or debate the bill before passing it. The House held a hearing of only 15 minutes and opponents were not allowed to testify. Neither house consulted the state Education Department, which surely would not have supported it, and as voted into law, the bill's language was almost precisely the same as the model bill. Especially revealing is that the "findings of fact" section of Act 590 contains language identical to "findings of fact" section in the model act. Indeed, it would take almost as much time to read the 12 paragraphs on "findings of fact" in Act 590 as it did to debate it and to vote upon it. If the legislature could truly make so many "findings of fact" in so short a period of time, there must have been some Divine Intervention!

Certainly the outcome would be consistent with the Creator's instruction to Senator Holsted that set the legislative wheels into motion. Is "creation-science" religion? Of course it is.

Little Rock, Ark., December 12, 1981

And on the sixth and seventh days they rested, to resume the federal court trial Monday on the constitutionality of Arkansas's "creation-science" law, Act 590 of 1981. The brunt of the testimony so far seems to be directed at defining science and religion. Out of this thicket will emerge a ruling on whether Act 590 runs contrary to constitutional principles, especially the prohibition against an establishment of religion found in the First Amendment.

Some of the front-line troops — three teachers and a science co-ordinator from the public schools — took the stand in the closing stages of direct presentation by the plaintiffs, represented by the American Civil Liberties Union, to explain some of the impossibilities that would be imposed upon them in discharging their classroom duties if and when Act 590 takes effect next fall.

What, indeed, is a teacher to do, when he or she seems to be directed by law to teach what he or she knows is professional nonsense? Act 590, it should be recalled, insists in its direct language that "creation-science" is indeed science, but read in other context it is saying that teaching "creation-science" is necessary to protect students' religious beliefs. If the point seems to get a little foggy in this observation, then imagine how the language of the act might be read and interpreted by the teacher charged to teach within its non-scientific strictures.

Certainly the overwhelming body of scientific thought in the United States considers "creation-science" as simply religion, and rejects evolutionary theory as religion. The public school teachers testifying seem to support this view, saying they believe that "creation-science" cannot be divorced from religion and that biology cannot be taught properly without references to evolution.

Consider, briefly, a couple of other points raised in testimony of two high school teachers in the Pulaski County School District, one a biology and psychology instructor and the other a teacher of social science and world history.

The biology-psychology teacher notes that giving "balanced treatment" could destroy his credibility with students because he would have to use religious references in answering questions about "creation-science" material. He said he knew of no scientific basis for the law's requirement to deal with such subjects as the sudden creation of the earth and the worldwide flood, which Act 590 specifies, concluding: "Without scientific evidence, I don't know how I can implement Act 590. By nature, I'm very much inclined not to comply with Act 590."

The social science-world history teacher says his history classes would be affected because he believes the law would require him to discuss creationism if he discussed prehistoric man. Some students, he says, are inclined to monitor teachers for compliance, saying he could "see how students might become sort of vigilante groups."

"Creation-science," in short, may be religion but it is not science. Under Act 590, teachers would be forced either to teach this religion as science, or not teach evolutionary theory at all, unless they chose to defy the law. Modern science cannot be taught without reference to evolution. Therefore, Act 590 would effectively erase acceptable science instruction from the public school curriculum. It would a terrible penalty for Arkansas children to pay.

"...SPEAKING OF EQUAL TIME IN THE CLASSROOM..."

Arkansas "Creation Science" Ruled Religious, Not Scientific

A federal district judge in Little Rock, Ark. Jan. 5 declared unconstitutional the state's law that required the teaching of "creation science" along with the theory of evolution in public school biology classes. In his 38-page decision, Judge William Ray Overton flatly rejected the "creation science" supporters' contention that their Bible-based theory had equal scientific merit with Charles Darwin's theory of the origin of the species. The believers in "creation science," he ruled, "cannot properly describe the methodology used as scientific, if they start with a conclusion and refuse to change it regardless of the evidence developed during the course of the investigation." Supporters of "creation science" asserted that the universe, the Earth and all living creatures came into being instantaneously less than 20,000 years ago and that living creatures had not undergone any substantial physical changes since then. Overton said the "creation science" law "simply makes a bald assertion" about the origin of life and was "purely an effort to introduce the biblical version of creation into the public school curricula." The creationists, he said, "take the literal wording of the Book of Genesis and attempt to find scientific support for it." He criticized the creationists for asserting that "one must either accept the literal interpretation of Genesis or else believe in the godless system of evolution." Evolution, he observed, "does not presuppose the absence of a creator or God." Overton concluded that the state law failed the constitutional requirement of separating church and state. Creationism, he ruled, had "no scientific merit or educational value," its "only real effect" was "the advancement of religion," and its application to public schools would "require state officials to make delicate religious judgments."

ARKANSAS DEMOCRAT
Little Rock, Ark., January 21, 1982

In an interesting piece on this page Tuesday, a Los Angeles Times writer opined that Judge William Overton's ruling in the creationist trial added nothing to the jurisprudence of the First Amendment's religion clause.

We agree. But only to the extent that the writer means that Overton ruled according to the First Amendment ban on an "establishment" of religion — saying nothing about the "free exercise" of religion.

Free exercise, of course, holds equal space with the establishment ban in the First Amendment. But, as the writer says, the reason the judge didn't address it was that the state never raised it — didn't, in fact, want to. Steve Clark's job was to defend the "creation science" that the act would have introduced into the state's schools. So any argument for the free exercise of religion would have been irrelevant — and meat for the ACLU.

Of course, as things turned out, the judge — in a shoddy show of scientific and religious expertise — turned science into religion anyway. However presumptuous he was in his reasoning — or hostile he may be at bottom to religion — Overton did add to the voluminous jurisprudence of the establishment ban by declaring that religion can't masquerade as science in public schools.

The Times reporter's point is that the free exercise of religion doesn't need any such cover to win its place in schools or elsewhere. Federal courts, he says, are now bursting with explicit free-exercise cases and they reflect a new "tension" between the two parts of the religion clause that arises from a resurgence of fundamentalism.

He quotes a California professor of constitutional law as saying that the Arkansas case was unusual for the number of constitutional arguments on both sides and that he has sympathy for those who complain that government's limitation of origins curricula to a single theory is a denial of free exercise — not an upholding of the establishment ban.

Because of the nature of Act 590, Clark didn't and couldn't make that argument. He called the exclusion of creationism from schools a denial of academic freedom, and that was the Democrat's view throughout — academic freedom in our view being an aspect of free speech. That argument, however, isn't a religious one, and the California professor's view is that the creationist case for pluralistic origins curricula may yet prevail via the free-exercise-of-religion approach. That was the line that critics of Arkansas' handling of its creationist defense favor, and which Louisiana hints it may take in defense of its own creationist law.

The free exercise argument isn't complex; it's just that the establishment ban has preempted it. In essence, its argument is that in excluding creationism from origins curricula states are not obeying the establishment ban — they're limiting the free exercise of religion. Why? Because our constitutionally guaranteed free exercise of religion covers both the religious and non-religious — those who believe in a creator and those who don't. The non-creationist camp rules the public school curricula simply because judges as Overton did) are almost sure to exclude the teaching of creationism as amounting to an official establishment — a state-sponsored religion.

That tendency is buttressed by the irrelevant assumption — which Overton fell for — that scientific origins theory (evolution) represents the only real explanation of origins and that creationism represents (as the Gazette so quaintly puts it) 'the forces of darkness.''

But that description better fits the constitutional know-nothings who see the establishment ban as preempting the whole religion clause of the Constitution. Courts, too, in too many rulings, appear to take that view — with results that are positively anti-religious. It is time that the more important side of the religion clause, its very heart — free exercise — had its day in court.

THE CHRISTIAN SCIENCE MONITOR
Boston, Mass., January 8, 1982

Americans can be thankful that a federal district judge has overturned the Arkansas law requiring the teaching of "creation science" in schools along with the theories of evolution. The ruling is bound to have impact in many other states having or considering similar legislation. It certainly helps preserve the constitutional line of separation of church and state, thus benefiting all citizens whatever their religion.

Defenders of the Arkansas law argued that "creationism" is a science deserving equal treatment in the classroom. But Judge William Ray Overton rightly concluded that "it was simply and purely an effort to introduce the biblical version of creation into the public school curricula" and therefore was aimed at advancing religion.

Advancing a particular denominational viewpoint, we might add. The fact is, there is more than one account of creation in the Bible and there are many differing interpretations of biblical history. Fundamentalist church groups which advocate the teaching of "creationism," for instance, take the first 11 chapters of Genesis literally and even pinpoint the date of creation. But a large majority of Christians would not go along with that interpretation. Many denominations treat the Bible accounts in a metaphorical or symbolic sense. Some Christians make a clear distinc-

tion between the evolution of a physical universe and the transcendant reality of a spiritual universe created and sustained by God, a distinction they believe is evident in the two different accounts of creation in Genesis.

Given the wide divergence of views, communities and schools would open themselves to unimaginable dissension by legislating the teaching of religious theory. Surely the proponents of "creationism" are themselves in the long run protected by Judge Overton's ruling. For if they succeed in injecting their beliefs into public education contrary to the First Amendment, one day they may be subjected unwillingly to the views of others.

This is not to slight the importance of religious training. It is also not to impugn the motives of those concerned about bringing up their children with spiritual values, a concern we share. But surely the natural scientists can go on researching and teaching human theories of evolution without conflicting with the religious beliefs of parents or children, without claiming that their theories represent the final truth, and without denying that other approaches exist.

The judicial ruling in Arkansas may be appealed. But this first judicial test of a state "creationism" law is reassuring. It is a victory not of state over church but of all churches over imposition by any one.

Arkansas ⚜ Gazette.

Little Rock, Ark., January 7, 1982

Federal Judge William R. Overton has found unconstitutional the 1981 Arkansas statute requiring the public schools to give "balanced treatment" to "creation-science" and evolution. "Creation-science," Judge Overton ruled Tuesday, is not science at all but instead religion and thus Act 590 constitutes an establishment of religion in violation of the First Amendment.

Certainly no one who had followed the history of Act 590 of 1981 closely, through the state legislature and then through the voluminous testimony of the challenge brought against it in federal court, could have expected any other outcome. As Judge Overton expressed the point, "the evidence is overwhelming that both the purpose and effect of Act 590 is the advancement of religion in the public schools."

In reaching his conclusion about Act 590, Judge Overton went into great detail to explain the conclusion. The opinion is a record of some note, and by choosing to treat with the evidence and arguments in such a comprehensive way, the judge may well discourage attempts elsewhere to force creationist views upon the schools. Act 590, with only minor exception, followed the language of a model "creation-science" statute drafted by a South Carolina respiratory therapist and distributed to believers in creationism throughout the nation. Interestingly enough, a footnote in Judge Overton's opinion says that the original model act had been introduced in the South Carolina legislature, but had died without action after the South Carolina attorney general had opined that the act was unconstitutional. Louisiana has passed its own version, which is being tested in federal court there, and the Mississippi Senate has just opened the 1982 session by approving its own version. Proposals are said to be pending in perhaps 15 additional states.

Whether the defendants, represented by Arkansas Attorney General Steve Clark, will appeal Judge Overton's ruling to the Eighth United States Circuit Court of Appeals will be determined later. The bill's legislative sponsor, state Senator James L. Holsted, and the state leader of the Moral Majority, Rev. Roy McLaughlin, seem to think that the higher courts will reverse the district court. Governor Frank White, a "creation-science" supporter who had signed Act 590 into law without having read all of it, says he will leave an appeal decision up to Clark, which is easy enough because it is the kind of decision that an attorney general must make anyway. Governor White adds, curiously and certainly gratuitously, that "I will forever support the power of the legislature to pass legislation." Even if, Arkansans are left to believe, the legislation is clearly in violation of the United States Constitution, as amended.

Indeed, the suggestion is sometimes heard that if Act 590 should be struck down, a second attempt would be made to write a bill that would satisfy the federal courts. It is difficult to imagine, in even one reading of Judge Overton's 38-page opinion, how language could be devised to skirt the inescapable point that "creation-science" is religion and therefore may not be taught in the public schools as science. The best advice the Arkansas legislature can have — and the same goes for the governor — is to forget any effort to mandate the teaching of religion as science, even if the legislature, down to the last member, favored such a course, especially in light of this paragraph from Judge Overton's opinion:

"The application and content of First Amendment principles are not determined by public opinion polls or by a majority vote. Whether the proponents of Act 590 constitute the majority or the minority is quite irrelevant under a constitutional system of government. No group, no matter how large or small, may use the organs of government, of which the public schools are the most conspicuous and influential, to foist its religious beliefs on others."

The ruling, in one of many interpretations, is a reaffirmation of the constitutional principle that the "wall of separation" between church and state must be maintained.

As a result of this important decision, Arkansas school children this fall will not have to be taught creationism as the scientific equivalent of evolutionary theory. This should come as a great relief to many parents and most teachers, for children taught such nonsense as acceptable science would face disabilities upon entering college, whether in this state or elsewhere.

Finally, a word of gratitude is in order for the 23 plaintiffs who challenged Act 590 in the federal court and to the American Civil Liberties Union, whose lawyers presented such a powerful case. There comes a time in which to stand up to the forces of darkness in all walks of public life. The place in 1981 was Arkansas and the issue was Act 590.

The Salt Lake Tribune

Salt Lake City, Utah, January 8, 1982

A federal district judge correctly assessed the Arkansas "Creative Science" law as a vehicle for teaching a particular religion in the public schools. His decision should not, however, inhibit efforts to make accounts of the biblical creation story available a part of education's broad focus.

The disputed "creation science" includes the creation of all things by some supernatural force: the belief in separate origins for human beings and animals and the relatively recent origin of the world, a beginning that included the earth-consuming flood. Evolution science, normally taught in public schools, holds that humans evolved from lower forms of life over millions of years.

Whereas the former relies on faith, the latter is based on widely accepted, but still incomplete, scientific data. Evolution is universally taught in public schools. The Arkansas law was an attempt to get equal billing for the version of creation contained in the first chapters of Genesis.

The law's backers were not altogether wrong. The biblical version of creation should be made known to students in public schools because it is a part of the Western religious and cultural heritage. An educated person should know it just as that person should know something of the world's other religions.

Whether the biblical creation account can be taught under the cover of "science" was the issue before the federal court in Little Rock. The judge said no. That decision should not discourage public schools from presenting the biblical creation account in more realistic ways.

CHICAGO Sun-Times

Chicago, Ill., January 8, 1982

In striking down the Arkansas "creation-science" law, a federal judge struck a blow for education—and for religion.

The law, which required public schools to give equal time to creation science and evolution, had no "legitimate educational purpose," said District Judge William R. Overton.

Actually, it was the antithesis of education, which is supposed to teach people to draw conclusions from facts and to change the conclusions if new facts are found.

Creation science, as Overton noted, starts with a conclusion (the creation as described in the Book of Genesis), adorns it with facts that seem to support it and refuses to change the conclusion "regardless of the evidence developed during the course of the investigation."

A person who learns that method of "scientific inquiry" is getting religious indoctrination, not education.

Religious training has its place, but its place is the church or the home, not the public schools. Unfortunately, some religious groups can't understand that the way to keep religion strong is to keep it out of the grubby hands of politicians—as Overton has done.

When religion is written into the statute books, through government-mandated creationism or school prayer, it becomes subject to the pushes and pulls of the political process, like any other law.

Once the churches have turned over their authority to legislators, they'll have trouble getting it back. They'll be simply another special interest group lobbying every year to prevent the legislature from altering the government's version of religion.

Fortunately, the nation has a Constitution that prevents that—and judges like Overton to enforce it.

Pittsburgh Post-Gazette

Pittsburgh, Pa., January 7, 1982

The Book of Genesis can bring a greater appreciation of the mysterious wonder of creation, the still uncomprehended vastness of the universe and the puzzle of human existence. Yet even many religious creeds have conceded that the Genesis account doesn't rest upon factual authenticity. So, fortunately, U.S. District Judge William Overton decided Tuesday with resonant firmness that such religious poetry should not be elevated in the curriculum of Arkansas public schools to the status of science.

Judge Overton's landmark ruling against the Arkansas law requiring public schools to teach "creationism" as a theory in competition with the scientific doctrine of evolution was unequivocally based upon the U.S. Constitution's separation of church and state. Arkansas sought to establish a fundamentally religious point of view as a scientific theory. The judge wisely recognized that that expansion of the public school curriculum would have represented the fossilization of knowledge, not a credible refutation of the evidence found in fossils.

The trial in Little Rock showed that in some cases proof for the theory of creationism is eccentric not only in its relation to established scientific views but also even in relation to traditional interpretations of Genesis. One creationist defendant, for instance, told Judge Overton of his belief that life came to earth in the tail of a comet.

Creationists are necessarily caught in a paradox. While claiming that the Genesis account should compete in public schools with the scientific view of evolution, fundamentalist Christians tend to overlook the fact that other religions embody myths of creation that compete with Genesis. So for consistency in teaching creationism, should they not also seek equal time for, say, Hindu explanations of the origins of life? Those legalistic nuances to the dispute thankfully will be avoided because of Judge Overton's assertion of the separation of church and state education.

Just as in Genesis God said "Let there be light," so the public ought to recognize that there was constitutional brilliance shed on the controversy over creationism this week in an Arkansas courtroom.

THE SAGINAW NEWS

Saginaw, Mich., January 7, 1982

The federal judge who struck down an Arrkansas law requiring that the creation theory get equal time with evolution in science classes made the right judgment call.

But we hope the decision won't remove all judgment from what happens in our public schools.

Testimony during this latter-day "monkey trial" left little doubt the Arkansas law forced the teaching of biblical theory. Depending on individual convictions, Genesis may be a valid belief — but it remains a religious one, not a science subject to testing, revision or independent challenge. We should respect each other's faiths (or lack of them) enough to not force them on each other's children.

Two Michigan legislators say the ruling won't keep them from proposing a state law along the same line — but, they say, not crossing it. Rep. Alan Cropsey, R-DeWitt, said his bill will assert that teachers can teach both theories.

As we said here earlier, we see nothing wrong with noting that some persons don't subscribe to the evolution theory. That is a fact. Schools should not ignore facts. Unless the Arkansas ruling says they should, we don't see the need for any special law on the subject.

The line that should be followed is the one between forcing and allowing specific classroom discussions. There's a world of difference — no matter how it came to be.

San Francisco Chronicle

San Francisco, Calif., January 7, 1982

WE HAVE GREAT RESPECT for the clear-headed reasoning of the Arkansas federal judge who has ruled that "creation science is not science" but rather a smokescreen for the advancement of religion in the public schools, contrary to the Constitution. Unlike so many pious and hypocritical Bible-thumping politicians who seek to pick up votes and money from the Moral Majority and other fundamentalists, Judge William Overton has the courage to blow the whistle on the scientific travesty that this so-called "creation science" is.

In throwing out the Arkansas law requiring "creation science" to be taught alongside evolutionary theory, Judge Overton says its proponents were motivated solely by their religious beliefs. "They take the literal wording of the Book of Genesis and attempt to find scientific support for it." But by its own terms their "creationism" is dogmatic, absolutist and not subject to revision. Thus it is not a scientific theory, and the effort to slip it into the classrooms of Arkansas for "balanced" treatment with the theory of evolution "was simply and purely an effort to introduce the biblical version of creation into the public school curricula." This, the judge ruled, would violate the Constitution's guarantee of separation of church and state.

THE TEACHING OF the Bible version of creation is the privilege of fundamentalists, working on their own time, but to force it to be studied as serious science can only be considered intellectually preposterous.

The Dallas Morning News

Dallas, Texas, January 10, 1982

The way the modern federal judiciary construes the First Amendment, no surprise whatever is possible concerning the downfall of Arkansas' creation-science statute.

The merest whiff of religion has become impermissible in the public schools, though formerly the First Amendment was understood to enjoin government neutrality as between denominations, not as between religion and non-religion.

This judicial sea-change doomed the Arkansas law, which in effect if not in outward profession would have accorded the religious theory of creation equal time with more "scientific" theories.

Whether another great blow has been struck for secularism remains unclear. America's public schools, being creatures of the state, carry heavy, state-imposed burdens, such as putting up with indiscipline, shuffling children around to achieve racial balance and teaching junk unworthy of inclusion in any serious curriculum.

This has precipitated a headlong flight from the public to the private schools: which flight the federal courts, by banning even tangential religious references in public-school classrooms, probably do no more than hasten. Parents wanting a certain kind of education for their children, and not finding that kind available from the state, will go out and purchase it.

Sometimes, if you're a federal judge, you can't win for losing.

BUFFALO EVENING NEWS

Buffalo, N.Y., January 8, 1982

There were highly emotional issues involved in the trial concerning the "creation science" law in Arkansas. They were some of the same issues that dominated the famous "Monkey Trial" of biology teacher John T. Scopes in Tennessee in 1925, but fortunately the court avoided a needless clash between religion and science.

Federal District Judge William Ray Overton refused to get into the kind of debate that aroused the nation in 1925, when famed criminal lawyer Clarence Darrow and devout William Jennings Bryan debated the theory of evolution. Judge Overton wisely decided the case on one narrow question — whether creation science is essentially religion or science.

He decided it was the former, and that therefore, on the basis of the First Amendment separation of church and state, creation science had no place in a public school science curriculum. Act 590 (the Arkansas law in question), he ruled, "was simply and purely an effort to introduce the biblical version of creation into the public school curricula."

He found the Arkansas law flawed not only consitutionally but scientifically. The essential characteristics of science, he noted, are that it is based on natural laws, testable against the empirical world and subject to change when new evidence is discovered. None of this could apply to the assertions in Act 590. Thus he lightly concluded that "state entanglement with religion is inevitable under Act 590."

A noteworthy difference from the Scopes trial is that the creationists sought only "balanced treatment" for their beliefs along with the theory of evolution. The Tennessee law that was upheld in the Scopes trial prohibited the teaching of anything but the biblical account of creation. While the Arkansas case was limited to the constitutional issue, the old religious-scientific debate was not far below the surface. The state law noted that creation science proclaimed a "separate ancestry for man and apes" — recalling the famous remark of British statesman Benjamin Disraeli: "Is man an ape or an angel? . . . I am on the side of the angels."

Fortunately, in this free and diverse land, there is room for many religious beliefs and many scientific theories. The proper place for the teaching of religion, however, is in the church and the home, not in the public schools.

While the ruling was a blow to the conservative religious groups that had favored the Arkansas law, Judge Overton avoided any implication that the decision was anti-religious. The theory of evolution, he correctly noted, "does not presuppose the absence of a creator or God." And, indeed, Catholic and Protestant church leaders in Arkansas were numbered among those opposed to Act 590 as a violation of the constitutional separation of church and state.

The Seattle Times

Seattle, Wash., January 8, 1982

GIVEN the Constitution's ban on mixing affairs of church and state, a federal judge scarcely could have ruled any other way in this week's decision against an Arkansas law requiring public schools to give equal time to rival theories about the origins of man.

United States District Judge William Overton declared the Arkansas statute (enacted only last March) to be "simply and purely an effort to introduce the Biblical version of creation into the public-school curricula."

Christian conservatives lobbied for the Arkansas law (and a nearly identical one in Louisiana) by asserting a need for "balanced" teachings on the enduring argument over Charles Darwin's theory of evolution vs. the "creationist" view that man was created by a Supreme Being.

The equal-time approach sought to avoid the fate of the Tennessee law ridiculed in the celebrated "Monkey Trial" of 1925. That measure had attempted a flat ban on public-school teaching of "any theory that denies the story of the divine creation of man as taught in the Bible."

Contemporary debate over classroom teachings on man's beginnings includes the conservatives' assertion that instruction on the theory of a "godless evolution" in itself amounts to state sponsorship of a religion, one they call "secular humanism."

In this state, Judge Overton's decision caused the Clover Park School District in Pierce County to suspend its 10-year-old policy stating that if either evolution or creationism is to be taught, instruction must be given in both.

The equal-time approach is flawed not only on constitutional grounds but because of a practical problem. Christian teaching on creationism is only one of several religious explanations of man's origins.

Efforts to introduce religious teachings on creation into the public schools of today are remarkable if only because they are an outgrowth of the controversy unleashed by Darwin in 1859. Instead of subsiding through the years, the issue seems to have intensified.

This week's court ruling is not likely to quiet the storm, because there are no absolute truths about the beginnings of man. As anthropologist Ashley Montagu noted recently, the difference between science and creation-science is that "science has proofs without any certainty. Creationists have certainty without any proof."

St. Louis Review

St. Louis, Mo., January 15, 1982

The well-publicized judicial ruling of Federal Judge William Overton striking down Arkansas' "creation science" law has done little to clarify the fundamental issues involved.

Arkansas and Mississippi have recently enacted legislation requiring that creation science be taught in schools where evolution is taught. It may well be that the Arkansas legislation was incautiously drawn since Father Bruce Vawter, CM, testified that its description of "creation science" could only have come from the Book of Genesis.

The ruling in this case should not be taken as conclusive evidence that it is not possible to have legislation calling for a presentation of creation which would be constitutional.

Judge Overton declared that the teaching that the world is created "out of nothing" is to promulgate a religious idea, since "in traditional Western religious thought, the conception of the creator of the world is a conception of God."

Cosmology which deals with the origin, processes and structure of the universe is a study which antedates the Christian era. There is ample leeway in the study of cosmology to examine religious, philosophical and scientific explanations of the origin of the universe. In this context the religious and cultural reflections on the origin of the world which posit some form of creation can be studied side by side with latter-day scientific hypotheses.

The Catholic Church has long held that there is no contradiction between science and religion. What is disturbing is the viewpoint of some scientists that there is a basic incompatibility.

Whatever its merits, the evolutionists' theory of the origin and development of the world is merely a working hypothesis incapable of ultimate proof. Yet, its adherents propose it with religious zeal.

An editorial in the Wall Street Journal of Jan. 7, 1982, set forth the reason for fundamentalists' attempts to insist on the teaching of creation in our schools. It stated in part: "We suspect that efforts to break down societal mores and standards of conduct that have a religious base are more than a little bit responsible for the fundamentalist backlash . . . We are not sure the courts have considered what it might be like if they insist on divorcing government entirely from spiritual thought . . . We hope the forces who have won this narrow battle in court won't labor too long with the notion that they have scored some major victory against religious belief."

And so say we.

THE PLAIN DEALER

Cleveland, Ohio, January 7, 1982

"Scientific creationism," the assertion that the world and its inhabitants were cut from whole cloth with divine scissors a few thousand years ago and did not evolve, over millenia, from cosmic dust and lower forms of life, was judged and found wanting this week.

Hallelujah. The federal district judge, after a heated and much-publicized trial, found that there was precious little science but much religion in the beliefs of scientific creationists. That, he found, was more than sufficient reason to invoke the constitutional injunction concerning separation of church and state. An Arkansas law, due to go into effect this fall, would have forced educators to teach creationism as equal to the theory of evolution in scientific weight and credibility, which is quite simply not the case. Evolution is true scientific theory — the observations, investigations, findings and extrapolations of trained minds, continually open to revision and refinement, always responding to new evidence or new interpretations of old evidence. Creationism is dogmatic. It begins with a flat premise: The world was created in the way described in the first few chapters of Genesis. Any stray facts or anomalies that coincidently match that belief or appear to contradict evolution are vacuumed up and glued tightly onto the whole "theory."

Most of those behind the creation science movement are honest, sincere, God-fearing souls whose primary concern is that their children might be confused or misled by science into questioning their religious beliefs. The answer is not to muddy science, but strengthen religion — in the home, and in the church. Science is science and faith is faith. Hybridizing the two will help neither.

And sincerity, per se, is no measure of right or wrong. There are those who sincerely believe Earth is hollow, and that other beings live inside. They offer many pseudo-scientific calculations and hundreds of testimonials to support their case, but would anyone else want to see this "theory" taught as "science" to children?

The essentials in this creationism maelstrom are politics and power. If a tiny, vocal special interest group — the fundamentalists — can successfully wangle a place for "scientific creationism" on the slates of America's public schools (and other states besides Arkansas are fighting the same fight), then the next tiny, vocal special interest group begins pushing its beliefs, and the next, and the next. The end result is education by political whim, by coercion. And that is wrong.

Each person has the right to believe what he or she will, and teach his or her children to believe the same. But everyone also operates under societal laws and the Constitution, which are specifically designed to ensure that the dogma of a few isn't force-fed to the many. Science, the scientific method and objective information belong in public schools; belief and faith must come from the home.

Lincoln Journal

Lincoln, Neb., January 6, 1982

The attorney for the American Civil Liberties Union in Little Rock was carried away by the moment's delight Tuesday.

U.S. District Judge William Overton's ruling, finding gross constitutional fault with Arkansas' creation-science law, almost certainly has not dealt a "fatal blow" to the effort engineered essentially by the Christian fundamentalist movement. The ACLU lawyer temporarily confused hope with reality.

If only that hope could become a reality!

Abandonment of the joyless, authoritarian crusade to install a particular religious orientation in the public schools would spare all parties of needless turmoil, friction and hard feelings between peoples who should be cooperative.

How quickly Nebraska religious fundamentalists were reassured was the assertion of Grand Island Sen. Howard Peterson immediately after he learned of the Arkansas judicial holding.

The creation-science bill Peterson said he was considering sponsoring in the 1982 Legislature would be "much more specific that creation-science is a science."

Yes, and the world is flat, too.

You can substitute a word here, add a clause there, but the driving force behind the creation-science campaign will be the same eternally.

It is, as Judge Overton wrote, suffused with "an inescapable religiosity."

From which follows the American constitutional judgment: "No group, no matter how large or small, may use the organs of the government, of which the public schools are the most conspicuous and influential, to foist its religious beliefs on others."

Houses of worship and contemplation, and our homes, should be the indestructible founts of religious belief, guiding lives and daily conduct.

The particular notions of a religious community — for example that the planet's age is from 6,000 to 20,000 years — may be proper subjects for student examination in classes on comparative world religions.

But they do not fit the tests of science, as Judge Overton carefully detailed, and they certainly should not be armored with the power of the state, to be forced down the minds and throats of public school pupils.

Chicago Tribune

Chicago, Ill., January 9, 1982

Federal Judge William Ray Overton made all the right distinctions between science and religion in overturning an Arkansas state law that would have required creationism to be taught along with evolution in public school science classes.

Science, the judge wrote, proceeds by hypotheses that are tentative, that are tested against empirical data, and that admit of the possibility that some data might disprove them. Creationism derives from a sacred text. It is invulnerable to disproof because disproof of the word of God is inconceivable to the faithful. The veneer of science that creationists have laid over the doctrine in recent years is a thin one. Its arguments are lawyers' arguments, mustered on behalf of a predetermined cause. While it is true that some scientists sometimes behave like lawyers in defending their theories, science as a whole gropes ahead, casting off failed ideas, continually testing and retesting. And its most glorious achievements occur when a new proposition or a new set of data overturns the existing conceptual order.

But Judge Overton's decision, powerfully reasoned as it is, will not end the effort to establish creationism as an equivalent to evolution in public school science teaching. As Fred M. Hechinger pointed out the other day on the Perspective page, science textbook publishers already are hedging their bets by including discussions of creationism in their new books. The publishers are averse to risk, and they do not want to be left out of big markets in states where the evolution issue is still politically potent despite the federal judicial decision.

The creationists will undoubtedly continue their efforts with renewed vigor. Their belief is as strong as their religious faith. And though it is hard to imagine Judge Overton's ruling being reversed on appeal, there are bound to be other tests of the distinction between science and religion in the matter of the origin of life.

Opponents of creationism in public school curricula (who may be deeply religious themselves, for evolution theory is not an anti-religious concept) will have to continue to resist. And though the faith that drives them cannot be called religious, it is still quite profound. It is a faith that nature may be induced to yield up her secrets to man and that the tentative, groping, ever-incomplete methodology of science is the best avenue to empirical truth.

The Boston Globe
Boston, Mass., January 8, 1982

"Creation science" was dealt a powerful blow this week when a federal judge in Little Rock struck down Arkansas Act 590, which required "balanced" classroom treatment of the opposed theories of evolution and creationism.

The decision was important because it was the first judicial test of a type of law that has been introduced in some 20 states. Although Arkansas may appeal Judge William Ray Overton's ruling, his rejection of the Balanced Treatment Act slows the political advance of the fundamentalist religious wing of the so-called New Right. The law had been seen as a stalking horse, through which fundamentalists aimed to reintroduce their religious beliefs into public school curricula.

Evolutionary theory dates the beginning of the world at several billion years ago, and explains the gradual development of life forms through mutation and natural selection. Creationism explains the origin of the world in terms derived from the biblical Book of Genesis, dating creation of the universe "from nothing" a few thousand years ago.

The 38-page opinion is powerful because it moves from careful definitions of "creation-science" and "evolution-science" to a detailed analysis of the contrasting methodologies. It concludes bluntly that the doctrine of creationism is not science, but rather a means of advancing religion. The ruling upholds the American Civil Liberties Union argument that the Balanced Treatment Act violated the First Amendment requirement for separation of church and state.

Before and during the trial there was much fretting in the scientific community and among political liberals about the creationist threat. This was warranted because the Arkansas law would have required equal classroom time (and, presumably equal textbook coverage) for science and pseudo-science. Academic freedom would have been violated because science teachers would have been required to teach what they know not to be true. An extended examination of creationist doctrine might be valid in a course on comparative religion, but not in the study of the natural world.

Still, "creation-science" should not be cast aside, even by science teachers. It should be voluntarily preserved for use in the science classroom because it provides a useful handle for grasping an important and slippery question that has troubled generations of students (and not a few teachers): What is science, anyway?

Scientific knowledge is usually presented to students as an accumulation of data, "facts" and "laws" that are uncomfortably similar in appearance to "received" religious dogma. As a result, many laymen regard science as a rigid, deterministic, faintly alienating form of knowledge.

Science is more interesting and humane than that. It is a creative process, filled with mystery, in which all facts and laws are tentative intellectual models. The moment of revelation in science, when a Copernicus or an Einstein grasps a new vision of reality, is hard to distinguish from art.

Yet scientists accept the burden of validating their insights. Theories are tested by experiment, treated as truth only so long as data support them, and then modified, elaborated or scrapped. Science is always an unfinished business, fundamentally different from static dogma.

Creationism should be of value to science teachers because it is an alternative model that can shed light on science by demonstrating what it is not. Judge Overton's opinion deserves close attention in the classroom, and so does creationism, as long as no law requires "equal time" or presents science and religious belief as "two sides" of comparable merit.

Stiff-arming the creationists was necessary because of their political incursion. Now that that's been done, alert teachers of science will accept their contribution with thanks.

THE  SUN
Baltimore, Md., January 7, 1982

Federal Judge William R. Overton was correct to throw out as unconstitutional the Arkansas "creation science" law. That is beyond dispute. If it is ever safe to predict what appeals courts might do, it is safe to predict they will uphold Judge Overton. He was right on the facts and right on the Constitution.

The Arkansas law would have required the teaching of religious beliefs and values that are not any sort of science. Established constitutional doctrine says flatly that government may not pass a law in this sensitive area unless it "has a secular purpose" that "neither advances nor inhibits religion . . . [and does] not foster an excessive government entanglement with religion." *All three* prongs of that test must be met. But consider this:

According to trial evidence from leaders of the national movement to enact similar laws in every state, the Arkansas creation science law is meant to further the cause of those who believe the teaching of evolution undermines the precepts of fundamentalist Christianity. Trial evidence showed clearly that the theory ordained by the law is based on the Book of Genesis and related literature, not scientific inquiry. It became equally clear that in order to implement the law, state officials would become involved in the details of overseeing every textbook and lecture to ensure that the favored religious ideas were included.

So the law failed the three-prong test on all three prongs: religious purpose, religious effect, state entanglement. Since failure on a single prong makes a law unconstitutional, Judge Overton had no choice but to invalidate it.

The judge's ruling was a great victory for those secular organizations such as the American Civil Liberties Union that are ever on the alert for the first toeholds of established religion. It was a victory for educators who don't want politicians legislating curriculum. It was a victory for those religious organizations that don't want the government favoring one religion over another. A point worth remembering is that among those who went to court to have the Arkansas law overturned were the resident bishops of the United Methodist, Episcopal, Roman Catholic and African Methodist Episcopal churches, the principal official of the Presbyterian Church in Arkansas, Southern Baptist clergy, the Union of American Hebrew Congregations and others.

Such plaintiffs cannot be accused of being antireligious or of being disrespectful toward the Book of Genesis. We trust no one will consider us antireligious or disrespectful when we say that the study of Genesis and related works—in Arkansas, in Maryland and in every state—belongs in classrooms where comparative religions are being studied, or not in classrooms at all.

TULSA WORLD
Tulsa, Okla., January 7, 1982

LITTLE has changed in 56 years.

In 1925, the Tennessee Legislature enacted a law which forbade the teaching of evolution in a publicly-supported school.

In 1981, the Arkansas Legislature passed a law requiring the teaching of "creation-science" in public schools where evolution was taught. (Creation-science was defined as the theory that everything was created suddenly from nothing.) Tuesday, U.S. District Judge William Overton rightly struck down this attempt to turn public schools into pulpits.

Proponents of the Arkansas law adopted a new tack, labeling as "creation-science" what has always been viewed as a tenet of religious faith. But calling a religious belief "science" does not transform it. The Arkansas effort was an attempt to introduce a particular religious view into the classroom disguised as science.

The law would not have required the teaching of creationism in the public schools *unless* evolution was taught. It was unclear, therefore, whether the objective was to get pubic schools to teach creationism or to stop teaching evolution.

The evolution-creationism debate is nothing new in this country. Arkansas has heard it all before. In 1928 the state adopted a law prohibiting teaching evolution in public schools and universities. Forty years later, the U.S. Supreme Court declared the statute an unconstitutional violation of the First Amendment's establishment clause.

In the most recent round, Arkansas argued that public schools should teach what the public wants. While there is a germ of truth in that contention, school curriculum should not be a matter for majority vote. That is especially true when school classes touch on religious belief. The Constitution stands as a bulwark against the tyranny of majority rule.

Few people would object if the public schools noted during discussion of evolution that many people believe, as a matter of faith, that God created the universe. But creationists argued that creation-science is not premised on religious faith at all.

Were we talking about the "big bang" theory of the universe, that would be true. But Judge Overton was absolutely correct in stating that "creation of the world 'out of nothing' is the ultimate religious statement because God is the only actor."

Creationists are entitled to their religious beliefs about the universe, but they should not attempt to have the public schools preach those beliefs under the guise of teaching science.

THE MILWAUKEE JOURNAL
Milwaukee, Wisc., January 7, 1982

The biblical account of creation in Genesis is an awe-inspiring story. However, it is religion, not science; it has no place in a public-school science classroom. The misguided attempt of the State of Arkansas to teach this religious story in its science classrooms has been rebuffed by a federal court.

Admittedly, the law did not refer explicitly to the Genesis story, and it forbade the use of religious texts. However, as Federal Judge William Overton found, the law's definitions of "creation-science" and of evolution clearly were based upon the ideas of religious fundamentalists, for whom the Genesis account *is* the explanation of the Earth's beginning.

Thus, the judge ruled — after hearing nine days of testimony — that the Arkansas law, which purported to balance the teaching of creation-science and the teaching of evolution, "was simply and purely an effort to introduce the biblical version of creation into the public school curricula." The US Constitution, which separates religion and the state, forbade such action by Arkansas.

Moreover, even the law's supposed prohibition of religious references or religious discussion was constitutionally defective. Overton ruled that the law would have required administrators to screen texts for prohibited religious references. It would have required teachers to monitor classroom discussion to uphold the ban on religious instruction. Necessarily, Arkansas' teachers and school administrators would have been required "to make delicate religious judgments." Thus, there would have been an inevitable "state entanglement" with religion.

Overton clearly and forcefully pointed out the unscientific and essentially religious nature of "creation-science." His ruling makes it difficult to see how legislators anywhere could assume that a constitutionally proper "creation-science" law could be written. Yet the effort goes on. Indeed, on the day of Overton's decision, the Mississippi Senate overwhelmingly passed a creation-science bill.

Such efforts are woefully misguided. The success of the creation-science movement would require the teaching of a particular theological view, and it would expose students to alleged "science" that meets none of the tests of scientific inquiry.

Religious instruction is most appropriately given in the home and in the houses of worship to which the faithful repair. Perhaps that thought was what motivated a number of religious groups and religious leaders in Arkansas to join the legal challenge to the state's unwise injection of religion into the classroom.

Portland Press Herald
Portland, Maine, January 7, 1982

The decision this week by a federal judge overturning an Arkansas law requiring "balanced" teaching of creationism should put an end to this effort to introduce religious beliefs into the classroom.

It should, but it probably won't. On the very day U.S. District Judge William Ray Overton ruled the Arkansas law unconstitutional, the Mississippi Senate approved similar legislation. Other state legislatures are also weighing such proposals.

The movement to pit the "science" of creationism against the "theory" of evolution under the guise of academic freedom is, as Overton said, "simply and purely an effort to introduce the biblical version of creation into the public school curricula."

Further, it is an assault on academic freedom in that it seeks to compel by law the teaching of biblical dogma. And plainly it violates First Amendment guarantees of church-state separation.

But regardless of the Arkansas decision, the creationist debate has already spawned some unfortunate results. It has underscored the vulnerability of public schools and teachers to political pressures. And some textbook publishers reportedly have begun to tone down chapters on evolution and include references to creationism, apparently as a safeguard against sales losses.

Unhappily, the court ruling which strikes down the Arkansas law cannot undo the more subtle damage to academic freedom which may have resulted from this continuing public controversy.

The Wichita
Eagle-Beacon
Wichita, Kans., January 7, 1982

While the results of the nine-day creation science trial in Arkansas undoubtedly dismayed some religious fundamentalists, the court's decision was a proper one. The separation of church and state has been an essential factor in the growth, development and survival of U.S. democracy. The removal of such a necessary safeguard could have ramifications more far-reaching than those envisioned by creationist supporters.

Tuesday, U.S. District Judge William Overton ruled that an Arkansas law requiring the teaching of creation science in Arkansas public schools that teach evolution is unconstitutional. He called the law "...an effort to introduce the biblical version of creation into public school curricula." Judge Overton's decision went against fundamentalist arguments that creationism is a science rather than religious teaching.

Since the basis of creation science is the first book of the Bible, and educators are unable to develop lesson plans without religious references, the court had little option other than to rule the law violated constitutional provisions against the intermeshing of church and state.

While the ruling may be appealed, and a similar case is pending in Louisiana, any resulting court decisions should come to the same conclusions. The framers of the Constitution realized the potential for abuse when they decided that government should be run by laws and that religious beliefs should remain a personal matter. That should not be seen as a repudiation of any individual's religious beliefs, but as a protection of the individual and his or her right to practice those beliefs independent of government intervention or persuasion.

Richmond Times-Dispatch
Richmond, Va., January 7, 1982

The 18th-century sages who framed the Bill of Rights of the U.S. Constitution could not have been attempting to referee the precise religion-vs-science dispute over creation that has swept the Southland like a seven-year plague of locust.

Not until the 19th century and Charles Darwin's theory of evolution was the biblical version of creation seriously challenged in the Western nations. From the earliest times, man explained his presence on Earth as the result of some supernatural force; primitive tribes used various gods to explain this great mystery.

But the Founding Fathers, in writing the First Amendment, did wish to prevent the state from forcing religious doctrines on individuals. Believing devoutly in liberty, they exalted the right of Americans to be free to practice (or not practice) religion, and to be free *from* any state-established religion.

The U.S. Supreme Court, most notably in its 1962 *Engel v. Vitale* decision, has interpreted this constitutional separation of church and state to mean that government may not propagate a particular religious faith or practice in a public school classroom. In voiding a prayer officially prescribed for public schoolchildren by the New York State Board of Regents, the high court said the authors of the Constitution thought religion "too personal, too sacred, too holy"(in the words of the late Justice Hugo Black) for any civil authority to sanction.

Thus in reviewing an Arkansas law that required public schools to teach "creation science" whenever evolution was taught, federal District Court Judge William Overton had the basic task of ascertaining if "creation science" is, in fact, a science or if it is a religion. Mustering impressive fact and logic, the judge ruled that it is a religion — the end result, in fact, of a religious crusade — and, therefore, the state cannot consti-

tutionally require that it be taught in public schools.

The judge found that creation science fails several tests of a science. Its basic tenets are right out of the first 11 chapters of the Book of Genesis. Its assertions of a sudden creation "from nothing" and of a catastrophic worldwide flood (as in the Old Testament story of Noah and the Ark) depend on the intervention of a supernatural force rather than the workings of natural law. Scientific theory is tentative and always subject to revision or deletion on the basis of new evidence, but creationism is "by its own terms dogmatic, absolutist and never subject to revision" and therefore cannot qualify as a science, the judge wrote.

The decision does not disparage religious belief in the existence of God the Creator or the merit of the Bible. Evolution is a theory, not an atheistic creed; it leaves wide open the possibility that God set in motion the evolutionary processes that may have begun millions of years ago. Despite the battle lines being drawn between science and religion by some religious crusaders, many Christians, including many scientists, believe the truths of the Bible and the theory of evolution are perfectly compatible.

Judge Overton ruled on a narrow point of law: May a legislature legally require a tenet of religious faith to be taught in public schools? Relying on ample precedent, he ruled that it may not. The power of a legislature or a state board to shape the secular curriculum was not at issue.

The Arkansas ruling may not be the Final Word on the subject of state-mandated teaching of the biblical account of creation. A similar law in Louisiana is facing a court challenge, and other state legislatures are considering such measures. Ultimately, the Supreme Court may be asked to decide. But the Overton ruling seems to be in line with previous interpretations by the nation's highest court.

THE BLADE
Toledo, Ohio, January 11, 1982

A FEDERAL court decision in Arkansas striking down a state law mandating the teaching of creationism alongside evolutionary theory is encouraging, but one should not suppose the matter will end there.

A similar court test is planned in Louisiana which has a law patterned after the one in Arkansas. That such topics are a hot potato in a state with a strong flavor of religious fundamentalism is evidenced by the fact that the Arkansas act was whooped through the legislature and quickly signed into law by Gov. Frank White even though he did not read all of it.

U.S. District Judge William Overton wrote that the Arkansas law "was simply and purely an effort to introduce the biblical version of creation into the public school curricula." As such it simply could not be taught in a secular manner, he ruled.

It goes without saying that the decision does not prevent the creation story found in the book of Genesis from being taught as part of regular religious instruction in the proper setting — a church, synagogue, or parochial school. But in no way should it be presented in public schools as a full-blown course of instruction on a par with other courses in the sciences.

Judge Overton's decision, of course, makes sense, but his arguments will fall on deaf ears insofar as the creationist lobby is concerned. The issue is simply a wedge used by right-wing political groups who seek to reverse what they regard as overemphasis on secular values in public school education.

The real harm is not in the danger that creationism actually will be given much credence in the classrooms as a scientific approach to questions about the origin of the universe. What is more disturbing is the likelihood — in fact, it is already happening — that scientific textbook publishers, anxious to avoid controversy, will downgrade mention of evolutionary theory and of the contributions to it by Charles Darwin and scientists who followed him. Teaching of science in the public schools is on a shaky enough foundation as it is, and the nation simply cannot afford this kind of subtle censorship.

It is well that a federal judge in Arkansas has struck down an absurd law. It would have been better, though, if the legislature had not passed it and the governor had not signed it. That they did so is tribute to the perceived power of politically inclined religious fundamentalists, whose zeal is not likely to be diminished by the adverse court decision.

ST. LOUIS POST-DISPATCH
St. Louis, Mo., January 6, 1982

A U.S. district judge in Little Rock predictably has voided an Arkansas law that would have mandated what in effect would be the teaching of religious doctrine in the public schools. Enacted early in 1981 at the behest of Christian fundamentalists, the law required public schools that teach the theory of evolution to give balanced treatment to the so-called theory of creation science — that is, that the world (as related in the Genesis story) was created suddenly by a supreme being over a short period of time.

The Arkansas statute was challenged in federal court by the American Civil Liberties Union in behalf of educators, scientists and religious leaders of many faiths. The ACLU argued that the law violated the constitutional separation of church and state. Although the law states that its purpose is not to advance religion, Judge William Overton ruled that the only inference that could be drawn from the circumstances under which the act was drafted and passed was that its purpose was religious.

At the nine-day trial in December, scientists ridiculed the notion that any credible scientific evidence supports the law's creationist theory. And religious leaders, who favor religious education but not in the public schools, testified that the doctrine required to be taught came from a religious text. In invalidating the law, Judge Overton accepted their arguments and held that the act violates the First Amendment's prohibition against laws that advance religion. This should end the nationwide efforts of one religious group to impose its views on others through the instrument of the public schools. But their zeal is not likely to be curbed until there is a final ruling against mandated creationist teaching by the U.S. Supreme Court.

The Morning News
Wilmington, Del., January 17, 1982

THE DILEMMA OF THE creationists is their need to deny in the name of "science" that their discipline springs from an article of religious faith. They would have the public schools teach "creation" without a "Creator," in the faint hope of satisfying the constitutional requirement of the separation of church and state.

They propose for the sake of "balanced treatment" to include in public school science courses the view of the origins of life, the Earth and the Universe set forth in Genesis. And they would legislate this leap from faith to "science" by forbidding in such courses "any religious instruction or *references to religious writing.*"

In short, it has been their hope to institute such teachings in the public schools as "science" with a simple legislative statement that all this has nothing to do with religion. They failed miserably in Arkansas, where U.S. District Judge William Overton ruled this month that the state's new law requiring the teaching of creation science was unconstitutional. He did so, he said, because the new law "was simply and purely an effort to introduce the biblical version of creation into the public school curricula."

A similar proposal in Delaware's General Assembly, House Bill 358, has been put "on the back burner" by its sponsor, Rep. Terry Spence, R-Stratford, pending appeal of the Arkansas ruling. Included in the "Declaration of Purpose" of this "non-religious" bill are these revealing intentions: "Insuring freedom of religious exercise for students and their parents," and "preventing establishment of theologically liberal, humanist, nontheist or atheist religions."

Implicit in that declaration are both the unreasonable fear of those uncertain of religious tolerance and the zeal of those whose evangelistic convictions constitute a form of religious intolerance. It springs from the same paranoia that considers religious freedom incomplete until prayer is imposed by law on the public schools.

RELIGION AND SCIENCE have been at odds since the beginning of scientific inquiry, each time evidence of things previously unknown challenged the accepted dogmas of "revealed truth." And the fear and suspicion of science are greatest among those whose rigid religious faith considers knowledge not freedom but sacrilege.

The creationists are demanding that the public school system, in the name of "balanced treatment," secularize their religious beliefs to make them constitutionally palatable. The implications of their demands on genuine science are staggering. They would turn science — from anthropology to zoology — on its head. They would have us dismiss the mountains of evidence on extinct forms of life, natural selection, geological transformation and the venerable age of the Earth itself as the instant and very recent act of a cosmic prankster.

To the true scientist, doubt is an article of faith. Even when he is reasonably sure of his conclusions, it is still necessary to look for error. To the creationist, doubt is a repudiation of faith. He must seek always the evidence to support what he already believes to be true. His most difficult task is to substantiate for the unanointed his designation of creationism as science.

Rocky Mountain News
Denver, Colo., January 10, 1982

THE ruling by a federal judge striking down the Arkansas law favoring the teaching of the biblical story of creation as "science" in public schools is a victory for the Constitution and common sense.

U.S. District Judge William Overton clearly saw that the law was an effort to require the teaching of religion in public schools and that creationism is "simply not science."

The law's goal was to force equal time for so-called "creation-science" in the vast majority of schools which teach the theory of evolution. It was whooped through the Arkansas Legislature by members afraid of being accused of "voting against God" and was signed by the governor before he read it.

In a lengthy trial before Judge Overton, leading scientists and theologians testified that no scientific evidence exists to support creation-science. Witnesses supporting the law advanced no credible evidence for creationism, and most said they were motivated by the belief that the Book of Genesis is "literally true."

It is important to note that Overton's decision does not abridge anyone's religious rights. Fundamentalist parents who wish their children to learn that God created the universe and all creatures in it in six days can teach it at home or send their children to churches and Sunday schools where it is taught.

The ruling does, however, prevent fundamentalists from pressing their beliefs on other people's children in public schools, handicapping pupils by feeding them pseudo-science, and breaching the wall between church and state.

Any hope, however, that Overton's decision will settle the issue is in vain. About 20 other states face bills promoting the teaching of creationism in public schools, and the issue will have to be litigated in each one.

Unfortunately, even as their unconstitutional proselytizing lost in one federal court, the creationists were making progress. Textbook publishers, fearful of losing sales and profits, are cutting references to evolution in science books.

That shows what happens when a vocal, zealous minority goes to work on businessmen who worship the bottom line. The right of students to know gets trampled. Public education suffers.

The Courier-Journal

Louisville, Ky., January 7, 1982

THERE WAS little surprise in the ruling that Arkansas can't force its schools to teach fundamentalist religious doctrine as an alternative to scientific theories about the origin and development of life and the universe. The nation's courts have preserved through two centuries the principle that the power of the state may not be used to impose *any* kind of religious indoctrination.

The surprise, if any, was that the nine-day trial illuminated the issues so effectively. Tennessee's 1925 Scopes trial, in which a teacher was prosecuted for informing students about the concept of evolution, was mostly a circus. The Arkansas trial dealt with issues, not personalities, and thus stripped away much of the confusion.

The issue in Arkansas was new in only one respect — the disguise in which this particular form of religion was attempting to enter the classroom. The aim was essentially the same as that of the now-void Tennessee law that prohibited teaching any scientific theory that conflicted with "the story of the Divine Creation as taught in the Bible." It was no different from later state laws, which fared no better in the courts, that attempted to bar evolution from the classroom without mentioning religion.

As the trial clearly showed, the new and somewhat more confusing tactic amounts to claiming that the Bible is itself a scientific text, intended to provide guidance on physical facts as well as spiritual matters. An elaborate doctrine called "scientific creationism" has been constructed to couch the biblical language in scientific terms.

The claim that this doctrine should be taught as a rival to generally accepted scientific findings in biology, geology, astronomy and several other sciences appeals at first glance to a sense of fair play. If there are two sides to a story, why not tell both?

That view is valid only if "scientific creationism" is science. The trial found otherwise. As Judge William Overton observed in his ruling, nothing that starts with a conclusion and rejects evidence that may stand in the way can be called scientific.

The Creation Research Society, a principal developer of the creationist ploy, requires members to believe that the Book of Genesis is "historically and scientifically true in all of the original autographs.". So it follows, in this reasoning, that the earth and all its living species were created at the same time, 6,000 to 20,000 years ago, and that living creatures haven't changed since.

Acceptance of this view as the route to scientific knowledge leads to pernicious consequences. If the Arkansas law were accepted, students would be asked, in effect, to choose between a religious creed and science as accepted by scientists. The creationist doctrine implies that evolutionary theory presupposes the absence of a creator or God — which is distinctly untrue. Scientists may be religious or non-religious. But as scientists, they study the natural, not the supernatural.

The choice between science and religion implied by the Arkansas law surely was one of the reasons that led a coalition of leaders from major religious denominations — Catholic, Episcopal, Methodist, Presbyterian and Southern Baptist — to join in the suit against it. Some of these leaders may have had varied views on the proper height of the fence between church and state. But none could relish a law that offered the state's young people the implication that one must choose between science and religion.

The logic and facts in the court decision surely won't stop the creationist movement. Even as the judge issued his ruling, Mississippi's Senate was voting for a similarly unconstitutional law in that state. In fact, cynical politicians will feel all the more safe in voting for such laws, confident that the courts will overturn them.

But the Arkansas trial has at least removed the excuse of ignorance among legislators who vote for "scientific creationism" laws to appease comparatively small but highly vocal groups of supporters. It may even have awakened voters who don't normally put pressure on legislators to the pernicious choice the creationists are trying to impose on the schools.

The Oregonian

Portland, Ore., January 6, 1982

The creationists have a problem with truth in packaging. They failed to convince a federal court during nine days of extensive testimony that the sole purpose of a law rammed through the Arkansas Legislature last March without public hearings was not to advance religion in the public schools.

In ruling that the law violated the U.S. Constitution's First Amendment prohibition against advancing or inhibiting religion, U.S. District Judge William Overton has found the creationists' teachings come directly from the Book of Genesis. "The definition of creation science conveys an inescapable religiosity," his opinion said.

In citing creationist views that the world was created out of nothing, the judge found, "This is the ultimate religious statement because God is the only actor."

In attempting to impose their narrow, fundamentalist views of the Bible on all the school children of Arkansas through a public law requiring classroom teaching of their biblical version of the creation of the Earth and its inhabitants, the creationists threaten the beliefs of other religions. Leaders of other churches testified that the law did more to threaten religion than to enhance it. They raised fears that biblical literalism would become an established part of public education, defying other viewpoints, including those of Christians.

The damage the law has done to the economic community in Arkansas was recognized by those who wanted to repeal it last summer. The Chamber of Commerce has received poor signals from businesses that would rather take their technology to states where science is better understood and appreciated.

The judge recognized the misleading effort by those who believed they could teach about a spiritual creator's works without being religious, arguing as one creationist witness did, "It is possible to believe that God exists without necessarily believing in God."

The court understood the essence of the issue when it noted that creationist methods do not take opposing scientific data and attempt to reach a conclusion. Darwinism, unlike creationism, is subject to alteration, change and even abolition if the facts warrant, because it is subject to scientific tests and methods.

The victory in the Arkansas court for the American Civil Liberties Union will not end the debate because the organized forces of creationism are busy writing legislation they hope will prove more difficult to attack in future trials. Not only science, but also all religions have a stake in seeing that a narrow construction of the Bible is not enacted into state laws under the cloak of science.

The Hartford Courant

Hartford, Conn., January 7, 1982

The same day this week that U.S. District Judge William Overton delivered his opinion overturning the Arkansas "creationism" law, the American Association for the Advancement of Science was holding its annual meeting in Washington, D.C.

It was a fortuitous coincidence, since the discussion at the AAAS meeting was an implied affirmation of Judge Overton's decision.

He ruled that the law, which required that creationism be given equal weight in public school whenever evolution is also taught, was an unconstitutional violation of the separation of church and state and could not be executed.

Not surprisingly, Mr. Overton found that that there was no scientific merit or educational value to teaching so-called creation science in public schools.

The law, he said, "was simply and purely an effort to introduce the biblical version of creation into the public school curriculum."

Christian fundamentalists, in Arkansas and elsewhere, have been promoting their belief that the world and everything in it were created in the interim of one week fewer than 10,000 years ago.

Scientists at the AAAS meeting, however, were more concerned about the cause of the extinction of dinosaurs, who apparently passed away from existence on earth without benefit of the Book of Genesis: 65 million years ago.

The Columbus Dispatch

Columbus, Ohio, January 11, 1982

FEDERAL DISTRICT Court Judge William Overton reached the only decision he could when he ruled last week that an Arkansas law requiring the teaching of the creationism origins of the world was unconstitutional.

The law maintained that creationism, a theory derived from the Book of Genesis, was a science and should be given equal treatment with the evolution theory of the world.

The judge ruled, correctly, that creationism is not a science in the commonly accepted sense of the word and concluded that the law's purpose was the advancement of religion in public schools in defiance of the constitutional separation of church and state. It is silly, however, to say that creationism has no place in the education of children in public schools.

The idea that the world was created within a relatively short time by God is a facet of religious belief. Religion has been one of the most powerful forces in the history of the world. Whether one believes in a supreme being or not, the world he or she lives in has been shaped to a great degree by the actions of people carrying out religious dictates or expressing spiritual convictions.

Some of the world's greatest art, some of its most beautiful music, some of its most humanitarian societies have emerged from religious thought. Religious convictions have also precipitated warfare and persecution, conquests and suffering.

To say that the U.S. Constitution, a document that guarantees the free exchange of ideas, precludes the treatment of any religious topics would be to deprive children of vast amounts of information needed to construct the historical context of which they are the beneficiaries.

Consideration of the creationism theory of the origins of the world has its place in education, and it should be guaranteed its place in the common sense way that the Columbus Board of Education has approached the issue. Addressing the matter for the first time a full decade ago, the board has this policy to guide its staff:

"Teachers in all fields are encouraged, when considering or teaching the origin of life or the universe, to present all major theories, including those of creation and evolution. These should be stressed as theories, rather than established fact, and accorded proper treatment in time, emphasis and attitude to protect the rights of all students. An adequate amount of reference material shall be provided by the Columbus Public School Libraries to lend support to each theory. Teachers should supplement Board of Education adopted texts with materials which attempt to provide unbiased information about the various theories of the origin of life and the universe."

That statement, in its simplicity and calmness, stands in stark contrast to the forces that collided to create the folly recently played out in Arkansas.

If people would approach education in a well-meaning manner that respects the views of others, there would be no politics played with children's lives.

Des Moines Tribune

Des Moines, Iowa, January 12, 1982

A federal district judge has declared unconstitutional an Arkansas law requiring public schools to present "balanced" treatments of both "creation science" and "evolution science." The ruling is based on the judge's finding that "creation science" is derived wholly from the story of creation and worldwide flood in the book of Genesis and "the ideas are not merely similar to the literal interpretation of Genesis: They are identical and parallel to no other story of creation."

Even without the obvious parallelism, creation science amounts to religion rather than science, Judge William Overton wrote, since "creation of the world 'out of nothing' is the ultimate religious statement because God is the only actor." Thus, Overton said, the law, in effect, required religious instruction in public schools in violation of the U.S. Constitution.

Overton noted that the law — which defined six principles of creation science and six principles of evolution science — was taken almost verbatim from Institute for Creation Research writings and presented "a contrived dualism which has no scientific factual basis or legitimate educational purpose." The institute — and, by adoption, the Arkansas Legislature — present as the only alternative to the Genesis story a version of evolution that misstates the theory.

Creation science makes no use of scientific method in propounding theories, testing and revising on the basis of evidence. It garners what its advocates consider evidence in support of a dogmatic position derived from the fundamentalist interpretation of Genesis, rejecting carbon-dating, basic principles of geology and major bodies of accumulated scientific knowledge and theory.

Judge Overton's harsh words are directed at creation science, the pastiche that its advocates insist is a science worthy of equal public-school attention, although no recognized scientific journal has ever published an article espousing it. His words were not directed at sincerely held religious convictions. Those who hold them are free to preach in churches and church-school classrooms.

It is a basic distinction, but it seems to have escaped the legislators in Arkansas — and those in Louisiana, where another creation-science law will soon be in the courts.

The Times-Picayune / The States-Item

New Orleans, La., January 7, 1982

The ruling by U.S. District Judge William R. Overton of Little Rock that the Arkansas "scientific creationism" law is unconstitutional does not legally affect the similar Louisiana law now heading for the courts. But it would be a blessing if the federal court in Baton Rouge being asked for a similar ruling by the Louisiana Department of Education would so rule with dispatch. That would save the people of Louisiana a lot of money — in court time, teacher time and textbooks.

"The evidence is overwhelming," Judge Overton wrote, "that both the purpose and the effect of (the law) is the advancement of religion in the public schools.... No group, no matter how large or small, may use the organs of government, of which the public schools are the most conspicuous and influential, to force its religious beliefs on others."

Louisiana Attorney General William J. Guste Jr., who will defend the Louisiana law should it get to trial, says there are "substantial differences" between the Louisiana and Arkansas laws, specifically that the Arkansas law "mixes science and religious teachings; Louisiana's law does not." But Judge Overton's ruling is based on his finding that scientific creationism is itself a religious belief, and David A. Hamilton, the Louisiana Department of Education counsel who asked for a ruling in Baton Rouge, says, "Whether it's in Arkansas, Louisiana or Mississippi, it (scientific creationism) is the same animal."

If the unconstitutional entanglement of church and state was the central unwisdom of the scientific creationism law, another bit of unwisdom was the legislative interference in curricula on other than valid educational grounds. To require that science classes, which must teach the theory of evolution because it is the backbone of numerous sciences, also teach the views of the life sciences' equivalent of the Flat Earth Society is totally unacceptable. The people elect school boards and pay school administrators to run schools professionally.

This issue has been granted far more importance than it is worth, and the argument has gone on long enough. If the Arkansas ruling is not signal enough that creationist laws cannot stand in principle, a paired Louisiana ruling may be signal enough that court challenges will see to it that they will not stand in practice.

THE COMMERCIAL APPEAL

Memphis, Tenn., January 7, 1982

FREEDOM of religion is stronger in Arkansas today.

In overturning the Arkansas law that required "balanced" classroom treatment of evolution and "creation science," U.S. Dist. Judge William Ray Overton found:

• "Creation science" is not science.

• The only effect of the law was to advance religion.

• The law violated constitutional guarantees for separation of church and state.

But the case didn't pit science against religion. Representatives of six religious denominations entered the case in opposition to the law. As The Commercial Appeal's religion editor, Michael Clark, pointed out in yesterday's editions, there's an "essential alienation" among U.S. churches on the issue of whether creationism should be taught in the public schools.

There's also a vast difference between religion, as such, and attempts to use a public institution to further the cause of a particular religious crusade. Such attempts threaten the right of individuals to hold and pursue their own religious beliefs free of government influence.

THE CASE documented that Christian fundamentalists pushed the Arkansas law to enactment to make their view of creation a required part of the school curriculum. Their argument that the law prohibited any religious teachings, including reference to a supreme being, was simply part of a legislative strategy designed to counter constitutional objections. Some of them even said they couldn't separate their religious beliefs from their support of the law.

The crusade, however, continues. The Arkansas law was modeled after one that was drafted in South Carolina. Similar laws have been introduced in 18 other states. Louisiana has passed one, which also faces a court test. The Mississippi Senate approved a nearly identical bill Tuesday, just hours after the Arkansas ruling was announced.

Supporters of "creation science" seem to have seized upon this model law as a missionary tool with which to stake out new territory for conversion. Judge Overton apparently thought so. He called the introduction of "creation science" into the schools "part of their ministry."

But such a ministry, if successful, would clearly entangle the state with religion. And it would do so at the expense of other beliefs contrary to those of the fundamentalist creationists.

THE ZEAL WITH which "creation science" laws have been promoted underscores the need for strong, objective courts to protect freedom of religion and the separation of church and state from infringements dominated by emotion. In Mississippi, one of the prime movers of the approved bill urged his fellow senators to "take the offensive" against those who "desire certain things not be taught." The senators, fully aware of how unpopular negative votes might be among religiously conservative constituents, fell into line, 48-4.

Fundamentalists have powerful political leverage on their side. They can turn legislative votes against their causes into single-issue election campaigns against those who opposed them. In Tennessee a few years ago, the same kind of political contest developed over passage of antipornography legislation that was patently unconstitutional and that was later overturned in court. After the fact, some Tennessee legislators said they voted for that legislation without giving it serious enough thought.

Similarly in Arkansas, some legislators publicly regretted their votes for the creation science law. They apologized for the embarrassment the law had caused the state and promised to try to rescind it if the court didn't find it unconstitutional.

And yet, in Mississippi, a comparable measure whips through without committee discussion and with hardly any floor debate. When fundamentalist flames have been fanned, legislators proceed warily lest they be burned. Perhaps they think that the courts will douse the fire eventually.

BUT STATE legislatures shouldn't depend on the judicial system to resolve difficult legislative issues. They shouldn't abandon their responsibilities for the sake of political convenience, or saddle the taxpayers with the cost of expensive suits to avoid having to defend what may be momentarily unpopular votes.

Religious crusades have no place in the public schools or any other public institution. Constitutional restrictions against government involvement with particular religious points of view are the most important guarantee Americans have for everyone's religious freedom.

The Idaho STATESMAN

Boise, Idaho, January 8, 1982

A federal judge upheld one of the fundamental American principles of liberty — the separation of church and state — when he ruled Tuesday that creationism cannot be taught in Arkansas' public schools.

If U.S. District Judge William Overton had reached the opposite conclusion, a rivulet of rights violations would have begun trickling through the Arkansas school system, eating away at our country's base of religious freedom.

As the legislatures of other states acted on bills similar to the statute Overton threw out, the rivulet could have become a stream, washing away a right that Americans hold dear.

The danger is not overstated. Louisiana already has a law that's similar to Arkansas'. Like the Arkansas statute, the Louisiana law was based on a model drafted and promoted by creationists. On Tuesday — the day Overton's ruling was announced — the Mississippi Senate passed a bill based on the same model statute.

The basis of Overton's decision has an importance of its own. It might, of course, be the subject of an appeal ruling, but in addition to that, Overton's decision gains importance because it met the issue head on.

The Arkansas law required that creationism be taught whenever evolutionary theory is taught. It was challenged by the American Civil Liberties Union on three points, but Overton dealt only with one of them in concluding that the statute abridged the First Amendment's guarantee of religious freedom.

The Arkansas law "was simply and purely an effort to introduce the biblical version of creation into the public school curricula," Overton said. There isn't much doubt that he's right.

One of the creationists' key arguments was that creationism is a scientific theory, like the theory of evolution. Overton rejected the argument, saying the only evidence for the story of creation is religious belief. Obviously, the argument was tailormade to achieve the creationists' goal — not to advance the study of science.

Overton also rejected a second key argument of the creationists — that the public schools should teach what the public wants. "The application and content of First Amendment principles are not determined by public opinion polls or by a majority vote," Overton said. "No group, no matter how large or small, may use the organs of government, of which the public schools are the most conspicuous and influential, to foist its religious beliefs on others."

In that statement, the judge identified the danger and gave the solution. Many God-fearing, upstanding citizens believe that a little religion in the schools is good for kids. These people don't want to abridge others' freedoms, but they fail to appreciate how fragile rights can be. Overton recognized the fragility of our freedoms and protected against breakage.

School Prayers Persist Despite Supreme Court Ruling

In June 1963, the Supreme Court ruled that requiring prayers or Bible readings in public schools violated the First Amendment. The 8-1 decision was handed down in two cases involving a state law and a city school board. In the first case, Mr. and Mrs. Edward Louis Schempp filed suit against the state of Pennsylvania because it required schools to schedule a reading of "at least 10 verses from the Holy Bible, without comment, at the opening of each public school day." The Schempps, who were Unitarians, said this violated the constitutional rights of their two children. The second case was filed by Mrs. Madalyn Murray O'Hair, a prominent atheist activist, and her son, William, against a Baltimore school board's requirement of daily Bible readings and the Lord's Prayer. The Supreme Court majority declared that "in the relationship between man and religion the state is committed to a position of neutrality." The court added that teaching the Bible or religion in connection with Western history was acceptable. (Seventeen years later, William Murray publicly apologized for his role in the case. In May 1980, he wrote to a local Texas newspaper that he regretted "the 33 years of life I wasted without faith and without God. . . .")

Pressure for prayer continued, nevertheless. The Wall Street Journal reported that September that Bible readings and prayers were still required in public schools in at least nine states. Compared with the other problems facing the public school system, enforcing the prayer ruling received little attention. Some states left the choice of prayer and Bible readings to individual teachers; others set aside a period for "optional" prayer.

the Charleston Gazette

Charleston, W.Va., January 7, 1976

The Chicago area is experiencing a resurgence of the "Put prayer back in the schools" movement. It is a movement based upon a misunderstanding so widespread that a *Chicago Tribune* columnist, James Robison, was moved to attempt an explanation. The *Chicago Tribune* doesn't employ or publish the work of fuzzy-headed, left-leaning columnists, you may be sure.

Robison points out, as we have done in this space so many times, that a 1963 court decision prohibits only compulsory or organized religious exercises from the public schools. It does so in recognition of the First Amendment and the fact that the public schools are supported by taxpayers of all religious persuasions and taxpayers of no religious convictions at all.

The decision wasn't rendered by Madalyn Murray O'Hair, as commonly contended in our own Readers' Forum, but by the United States Supreme Court. Nor did Mrs. O'Hair influence the ruling of a federal district court in West Virginia which held that prayer sessions, organized and led by a clergyman on school grounds at recess time, did injury to the First Amendment and the tradition of separation of church and state.

If no court has ruled in the case of an individual voluntarily praying during school time, it is because such a practice obviously doesn't conflict with the customary interpretation of the First Amendment. We can think of no constitutional prohibition, no statute, no custom, which would prevent a student from murmuring a voluntary prayer as he approaches a difficult algebra test. Those who believe prayers must be uttered in unison and directed by a leader in order to be effective have, it seems to us, an insecure grasp on faith.

If the courts don't outlaw voluntary prayer, neither do they outlaw teaching "about" religion in the public schools. In this connection, the courts are concerned only that no particular religion is advanced as more desirable than others.

In his opinion concurring with the 1963 decision, Justice William Brennan, a Roman Catholic, said:

"The holding of the court today plainly doesn't foreclose teaching about the Holy Scriptures or about the differences between religious sects in literature or history."

Justice Arthur Goldberg, a Jew:

"It seems clear to me from opinions in the present and past cases that the court would recognize the propriety of teaching 'about' religion as distinguished from the teaching 'of' religion in the public schools."

Justice Tom Clark, a Protestant:

"One's education isn't complete without a study of comparative religion . . . and its relationship to the advancement of civilization."

We find ourselves agreeing with Robison that the "Put prayer back" people would be well advised to abandon their shaky constitutional position in favor of a movement to inaugurate comparative religion courses in public schools.

We doubt, however, that such a movement will take form. Zeal for school prayers is based largely upon the desire to indoctrinate a captive audience. It is difficult to envision this kind of zeal giving way to dispassionate and objective discussion.

In any event, we urge our readers to understand that their children may pray in public schools. To date, court decisions say that they may not be *required* to pray and that schools must not lend themselves to the organization of religious exercises.

The Birmingham News

Birmingham, Ala., November 16, 1976

Since the 1963 U. S. Supreme Court ruling against holding prayer in school the short "quiet time" at the beginning of the day has all but disappeared from the classroom.

And in many cases pandemonium has prevailed. Starting off a day of study and concentration takes a certain amount of organization—and it's just easier to begin quietly with a formal welcome to the day.

Public school officials in Philadelphia are turning back to the time when the Pledge of Allegiance to the U. S. flag was recited and students bowed their heads for a moment of silent meditation.

The silent minute is not an attempt to circumvent the court prayer ban, a school board member explained, but "if a student wants to begin his day by getting in touch with God, or simply putting his day in order in his own mind, that's his personal choice."

Starting the school day in an orderly and quiet fashion sets the emotional and intellectual mood for learning. It can be of immense benefit to the teacher who must deal with a classroom filled with rambunctious youngsters.

As for Philadelphia and its school board's courageous example—a silent moment of thanks. To all the other schools in the country—go thou and do likewise.

Rocky Mountain News

Denver, Colo., April 10, 1976

Surely, you would think, the issue of prayer in the schools is kaput, gone the way of debate over slavery, say, or other once-searing questions that have been satisfactorily resolved.

But no, some U.S. senators, including Colorado's William Armstrong, have voted for an education bill amendment to restore the "right of voluntary prayer" in public schools. The move is viewed as an effort to take jurisdiction over the prayer issue from the Supreme Court, which ruled in 1963 that prayers in the schools violate the Constitution's intended separation of church and state.

It really shouldn't be necessary to go over all the old arguments again, but maybe it should be pointed out to the senators that, even today, a student can bow his head and pray silently if he chooses — no one can or would try to stop that. In that sense, "voluntary" prayer in schools exists today.

And no one, the senators might keep in mind, has outlawed prayer in churches or homes. Schools are public institutions attended by persons of a variety of faiths and no faith at all, and the government shouldn't be in the business of imposing or promoting any religious view.

The Courier-Journal & TIMES
Louisville, Ky., January 11, 1976

THE INDIANA legislature opened its 1976 session with introduction of a resolution on one of those tried and true issues designed to wow the folks back home.

The issue is prayer in the schools. It is still a controversial topic — and one that is little understood — more than 13 years after key Supreme Court rulings on the subject.

Some politicians who should know better, and some who, indeed, do know better, scream that the Supreme Court "threw God out of the classroom."

Actually, the Supreme Court simply upheld the First Amendment to the Constitution, which forbids the government from making laws establishing religion or limiting religious freedom. Our nation-founding forebears were all too familiar with the experience in other nations, where the only religion tolerated was the one officially sanctioned by the state.

In landmark rulings in 1962 and 1963, the Supreme Court simply said that public schools must be absolutely neutral when it comes to religion. Whether prayers be "voluntary" or not, public-school teachers cannot lead religious services.

". . . In this country," said the Supreme Court, "it is no part of the business of government to compose official prayers for any group of the American people to recite as part of a religious program carried on by government."

The ruling did NOT outlaw courses in religious history, the reading and discussing of the Bible as literature, or mention of the deity in national ceremonies and patriotic oaths.

Many church groups and ministers have subsequently applauded the decision as an important safeguard for our constitutional principle of separation of church and state. Unfortunately, a few, including some opportunistic politicians, like to seize on the issue and distort it. Several states, including Pennsylvania and New Hampshire, have passed laws permitting "voluntary" prayer at the option of local school districts.

In the Indiana legislature, Representative Clifford Arnold of Michigan City introduced a resolution directing Congress to explore means to reverse the Supreme Court prohibition against organized prayer recitations in school.

The resolution quickly drew co-sponsors from a majority of the 100-member House. Undoubtedly some legislators fear they would be branded as being antiprayer if they failed to support the resolution.

"I'll support this resolution," commented one Hoosier legislator, "but I think it's a waste of time."

It's just a shame that the resolution isn't directed to the parents, instead of to Congress. As the Supreme Court has noted, religion in our society has properly been advanced "through a long reliance on the home, the church and the inviolable citadel of the individual heart and mind."

Many ministers, priests and rabbis say that prayer and religion need buttressing at home, not in public assemblies. Recent sociological studies show that the average family spends many hours a week glued to television, but seldom, if ever, spending any time discussing religion.

If the Hoosier legislators are serious about making prayer more a part of a child's life, they would address their resolutions to the parents. For starters, why not a resolution urging that families believing in religion forgo watching TV one night a week in order to teach their children about their religious heritage?

Pittsburgh Post-Gazette
Pittsburgh, Pa., May 24, 1976

As the surprising success of a recent "silent prayer" amendment in the U.S.. Senate demonstrated, opposition to the Supreme Court's prohibition of prayer in public schools persists. For that reason, there is likely to be considerable sympathy for Lloyd Fink, a Warren County elementary-school teacher who was fired for refusing to stop saying prayers and reading the Bible in his classroom.

That sympathy would be misplaced. Mr. Fink, whose dismissal was upheld by the state Education Department this week, was found to have disobeyed a direct order from his superiors to refrain from religious readings. That sort of insubordination would be objectionable in any case, but is especially galling in the sensitive area of religion.

In prohibiting official school prayer in 1963, the Supreme Court acted on the self-evident constitutional principle that schools operated by the government for all children should not serve the proselytizing or devotional purposes of any one religious tradition, no matter how "established" it might seem. Those who would regard Mr. Fink and like-minded teachers as martyrs for traditional values should ask themselves how they would react if *their* children were subjected to — or, just as objectionable, forced to seek exemption from — the religious exercises of a "foreign" faith.

Mr. Fink, who has filed suit against his school board, argues unconvincingly that the landmark Supreme Court decision on school prayer has been misread by Pennsylvania officials, and that his right of academic freedom should allow him to do what the school administration cannot — mix public education and religion. Such arguments, like Mr. Fink's misguided behavior, shouldn't have a prayer of receiving public support.

The Union Leader
Manchester, N.H., January 5, 1978

It would appear that the leadership of the National Education Association is as much concerned about political ideology as it is about enhancing the prestige and financial security of the nation's teachers.

Recently the NEA announced that it would assist in the court case of a North Carolina high school teacher who claims he lost his job because he questioned the legality of school prayer. The NEA contends that the teacher was employed during the 1976-1977 school year in Albermarle with the prospect of eventual promotion to an administrative position when the high school began broadcasting prayers to classrooms over the public address system.

The teacher is supposed to have questioned the school principal, a defendant in his $1,000,000 suit in federal court, about the legality of school prayers, contending that they were unconstitutional.

When daily prayers were replaced with a silent prayer while religious devotions were conducted in the school auditorium before school classes began, the teacher again protested and questioned the legality of allowing tax-supported school facilities to to be used for such purposes.

It is alleged that school officials told him last February that his promotion to an administrative capacity no longer was possible because of community opposition to his activities against religious excercises in the schools.

Whatever the facts of the case — and these will be determined in court — and whatever the outcome of the trial, the NEA cannot avoid the appearance that it is "reaching" for a cause to support, that it opposes school prayer even before the start of classes, and that it is willing to go beyond what the Supreme Court proscribed in its prayer rulings and to seek to ban the use of school property for any purpose that is religious.

Lest it be contended that the NEA is more concerned with other considerations, such as protecting what it views as the rights of a member, it should be emphasized that the teacher in question is NOT a member of the NEA.

School Prayer Issue Revived By Sen. Helms

An amendment designed to restore voluntary prayer in public schools, sponsored by North Carolina Sen. Jesse Helms,' was the topic of Senate debate April 5-9. The measure was eliminated (53-40) from a bill establishing a separate federal Department of Education and was attached instead to a Supreme Court jurisdiction bill giving the high court almost total control in determining which cases it would hear. The prayer provision was approved by a 51-40 vote, and the amended jurisdiction bill, sponsored by Arizona Sen. Dennis DeConcini, was sent to the House by a 61-30 vote.

The prayer amendment would bar the Supreme Court from reviewing any state law that related to "voluntary prayers in public schools," and would prevent federal district courts from hearing such cases. Accordingly, two previous Supreme Court rulings (made in 1962 and 1963) which held that state-sponsored prayers in public schools violated the Constitution's ban on the establishment of religion by government, would be invalidated.

The Carter Administration, which strongly supported the creation of a separate, Cabinet-level Education Department, was concerned that the Helms amendment jeopardized its passage. "I personally don't think that the Congress ought to pass any legislation requiring or permitting prayer being required or encouraged in school," Carter told reporters at a news conference April 10.

The Chattanooga Times

Chattanooga, Tenn., April 17, 1979

We commended the Senate yesterday for removing from a bill to create a new department of education the amendment by Sen. Jesse Helms, R-N.C., to prohibit the federal courts from exercising jurisdiction over state laws authorizing "voluntary prayer" in public schools. When Congress returns from its Easter recess, it should lose no time in rejecting the education department bill.

The White House, aided in no small measure by lobbyists for education, attaches great importance to the bill, which provides that federal education programs would be removed from the Department of Health, Education and Welfare for administration by a new Cabinet-level secretary. A news story several weeks ago quoted Vice President Mondale making the point that the United States is the only major democracy in the world without a department or ministry of education. And he added that education is hindered "because its highest official is not at the Cabinet table speaking directly to the president."

But merely because the U.S. doesn't have a department of education, does that necessarily mean education is suffering? Well, it is and it isn't. Take the latter point first.

Fully three - fourths of today's young people graduate from high school nowadays and more than half of secondary school graduates go on to college; that figure may be higher if you count the ones who enroll in college after working a few years or serving in the military.

But would an education department really alleviate education's central problem, that of an alarming number of ill-educated students? We think not. If anything, such a department would add another layer of deadening bureaucracy to the present effort of trying to administer proliferating federal education programs.

Obviously the federal government is heavily involved in education, which is still primarily a state and local responsibility. Helpful as some of the federal programs are, however, we think it would be a profound mistake to concentrate them into a Cabinet - level department that would, by virtue of its greater "clout," enlarge the federal government's role in education.

Besides, we simply don't buy the proponents' argument that the new department would respect state and local education priorities and merely coordinate federal funds and programs — all in a more efficient manner. Anyone who believes that will be the case ought to be sentenced to reading federal education manuals written in "education-ese."

We don't foresee the federal government ever easing itself out of the education business. But it ought to be satisfied with using and improving the means now available to achieve its purposes. There is absolutely no need to crank up a new department that eventually will evolve into nothing less than a mouthpiece for the National Education Association.

AKRON BEACON JOURNAL

Akron, Ohio, April 14, 1979

SEN. JESSE HELMS to the contrary notwithstanding, the still-hot issue of prayer in the public schools cannot be settled by a congressional effort to limit the Supreme Court's power to interpret the Constitution.

The North Carolina Republican, usually pictured as an ultra-conservative, may or may not see how radical his pro-prayer effort is, and may or may not be serious. In politics it is often hard to distinguish between honest purpose and phony posturing.

But it is obvious that not all the other 50 senators who voted for Mr. Helms' curious measure this week could be serious about it.

By attaching it as an amendment to another Supreme Court measure, they made a package regarded even by Mr. Helms as having zero chance of survival in the House. Thus they could indulge in a little ritual sham — a bid for future votes from pro-prayer folks back home without any possibility of real consequences.

Sen. Helms' amendment, like several similar measures fruitlessly tried in the Congress since the 1963 ruling against compulsory prayer in public schools, undertakes to nullify the court's action. The method this time is of a kind in which no Congress has succeeded since John Marshall's time: It would by statute deny the Supreme Court jurisdiction over certain state laws, regardless of appeals based on the U. S. Constitution — in this case, any state law relating to "voluntary prayer" in schools.

In the early years of the republic there was dispute among the three branches of the federal government as to who should be the final interpreter of what the Constitution requires. Chief Justice Marshall settled the question with such force and logic that his view has never been successfully challenged: Questions of constitutionality are essentially judicial, and thus it must be up to the Supreme Court to answer them. No alternative protecting the Constitution's "supreme law" force has since been found.

Thus the Congress, if foolish enough to beat its head against such a wall, faces certain failure. Any congressional attempt to tie the Supreme Court's hands in this fundamental role would surely be thrown out as unconstitutional the first time it was tested.

If the proponents of school prayer hope for real victory, their path to it must itself be constitutional, not congressional. They must sell the nation a constitutional amendment either nullifying the First Amendment or erasing from it the part forbidding governmental "establishment of religion" — which, in turn, would open the way for government to dictate religious practices and beliefs.

The Washington Post

Times Herald

Washington, D.C., April 14, 1979

IN EVERY ONE of the last 17 years, an effort of one kind or another has been made on Capitol Hill to put prayer back into the public schools. This year, an especially strong push has been made by Sen. Jesse Helms (R-N.C.), who has persuaded the Senate to pass a proposal that purports to strip the Supreme Court of the power to hear cases involving "voluntary" prayer. Its passage appears to have been an election-oriented gimmick; several senators who know better voted for it in the belief that the proposal will be quietly buried in the House. It should be, partly because it is of doubtful constitutionality and its enactment would create a horrendous precedent, but mostly because its purpose is fundamentally wrong.

The Supreme Court was right in 1962 when it ruled that daily recitation of a "nondenominational" prayer in the public schools violates the First Amendment. It was right the following year when it said that daily Bible reading and devotional exercises have no place in the public schools of a nation that has barred the establishment of religion and guaranteed to all the right to worship, or not worship, as they see fit. Now Sen. Helms says, show me a child "who has ever been harmed by voluntary prayer in the public schools." But what kind of a standard is that? It is an irrelevant test. Harm (or help) to a child who has prayed is not the issue. The issue is one of keeping faith with the Constitution.

The strangest aspect of this (and every) year's drive to restore "voluntary" prayer to the schools is that truly voluntary prayers have never been expelled. No student and no teacher is forbidden, under the court's rulings, to say a private prayer any time he or she wants to. What is forbidden is that scene in which the teacher tells the students to "voluntarily" bow their heads and pray together.

Schools, like any other place, are appropriate for personal, private prayer. They are inappropriate for group exercises that have the sole purpose of imparting to students beliefs that the Constitution, and the basic principles of the nation, say should be imparted at home or in a house of worship.

The Boston Globe

Boston, Mass., April 11, 1979

It is some consolation that, through parliamentary maneuverings, the school prayer amendment approved by the Senate Monday was attached to a minor piece of legislation whose defeat will shake neither the Republic nor any of its special interests. Thus, the forecast is that this specific proposal will die. But the re-emergence of the school prayer controversy, the troubling form in which this measure won Senate approval and the political posturing that surrounded its passage are all regrettable.

The merits of the issue itself have been thoroughly discussed in the past. The First Amendment requirement of church-state separation makes public school prayers unacceptable in the oft-stated view of the Supreme Court. Various approaches to get around the court's rulings have been attempted, without success.

The difficulty inherent in all of them was articulated the other day by President Carter, certainly the most religious occupant of the White House in recent years. "If everybody else in a classroom is engaged in public prayer and doing it voluntarily, for a young seven- or eight-year-old to demand the right to leave is a difficult question to answer." The President's approach was right on the mark: "I think the government ought to stay out of the prayer business...."

Of course, those on the other side of the question have not and do not now find such arguments compelling. But even they should be offended by the legislative language approved by the Senate. It does not seek simply to authorize school prayer; instead, it seeks to bar the Supreme Court from reviewing any state law or rule governing school prayer. In other words, its intended result is to have Congress, for the first time in history, limit by statute the Supreme Court's jurisdiction. At best, such an approach is unconstitutional. At worst, it could open the way to barring Supreme Court review of virtually any class of state statutes.

One might have thought the approach would have been chased off the Senate floor. But already sights are set on the 1980 senatorial and presidential elections and mere constitutional problems apparently are not to be allowed to obscure the view. Instead, what was clouded was the view of the electorate. Some senators managed both to vote for the school prayer amendment and then to go along with the parliamentary moves that made it unlikely ever to win final approval.

The goal of the school prayer amendment is unwise. The specific approach taken to reach that goal is at best unconstitutional, at worst a dangerous tinkering with the balance of powers. And the Senate's duplicitous resolution—to give the amendment its approval with one hand while seeking to bury it with the other—does no credit to the institution.

The Evening Bulletin

Philadelphia, Pa.,
April 10, 1979

School prayer seems to be one of those highly charged issues where it is difficult to find members of Congress willing to vote against it in public — even when they may be worried about it as a practical matter.

Thus the Senate voted 47 to 37 last week to restore the right of voluntary prayer in public schools. Then last night the Senate voted 53 to 40 to attach the measure to a minor judicial system bill almost certain to be defeated.

The original school-prayer vote had been on an amendment to a bill that would establish a new Cabinet-level department of education. It was attached by Senator Jesse A. Helms (R-NC). Mr. Helms accused the U.S. Supreme Court of having a "myopic and narrow view of the history of the Constitution" in its decisons against school prayer, beginning in 1963.

His amendment would deny the high court jurisdiction over any state laws relating to voluntary prayer in schools.

We can't find precedent for excluding the Supreme Court from any Constitutional questions, and we wonder about Senator Helms' motives in bringing the question to the Senate floor at this time.

In any case we think the idea of a separate, Cabinet-level governmental structure to handle education should stand or fall on its own merits and not be clouded by the emotion attached to prayer in the classroom. Likewise, school prayer is a subject for discussion at another time and place.

Support for the proposed federal education department — coming principally from the National Education Association, the largest teacher's labor organization — is built on lofty terms rather than practical improvements in the quality of learning. We agree that education is as important to our nation and society as energy and transportation — concerns which have their own departments. But we are not convinced that an expanded bureauracy will produce better administration of education programs.

The Adminstration-backed education department bill reportedly was in trouble in Congress even before the prayer amendment. A broader version of the bill was adopted last summer by the Senate but was not considered by the full House.

Regardless of the fate of the education department proposal — and we think it should be rejected — mixing in religion was a bad idea.

Register-Republic

Rockford, Ill., April 10, 1979

Will voluntary prayer return to public schools?

A proposal to that effect is bouncing around the United States Senate — although it may not be considered on its merits since it is an amendment to a very controversial bill creating a new U.S. Department of Education, which President Carter wants.

Frankly, we hope the prayer measure survives — and passes muster in the House as well.

Praying could be handled in the same way that the teaching of evolution now occurs in Rockford grade schools. Those parents who object to the Darwinian theory and think it does harm to biblical teachings are notified in writing in advance.

If they disapprove, their youngster is transferred to other productive assignments. If they agree, the child studies the theory of evolution along with other members of the class.

This solution may not be considered perfect by everyone involved, but it does work. And it does force anyone to take part in any activity which is in opposition to their specific religious beliefs.

This issue has not generated any furor about "separation of church and state" — although it could easily generate far more substantive concerns than a head bowed in prayer within a classroom.

Banning voluntary prayer has always equated itself, from our point of view, with the singing of Christmas carols in school — or taking a school vacation at Easter.

What's the big objection?

The Hartford Courant

Hartford, Conn., April 11, 1979

The U.S. Senate vote to once again permit government-sponsored prayer in public schools is a mistake that the House of Representatives will have to correct.

To avoid the obvious unconstitutional flaws in the school prayer amendment, the Senate seeks to forbid Supreme Court jurisdiction over state laws on school prayer. Such an assault on the First Amendment deserves retribution at the polling places, as well as rejection by the House.

As a practical matter, the Senate legislation is doomed. It has been attached to a relatively unimportant bill that the House will be inclined to reject. As a final impediment, President Carter, true to his Southern Baptist tradition of church-state separation, has threatened to veto legislation with the prayer amendment.

But the temporary victory will not be reassuring. America is faced with the unsettling fact that its most powerful legislative body is still capable of sabotoge against the First Amendment.

In whatever legal arguments such activity is draped, it cannot be condoned. Religious activity encouraged or endorsed by government, does not belong in public schools.

To limit jurisdiction of the highest court in the land, based on a show of hands, is dangerous business. Congress has not dared to mount such an assault on the Constitution since the 1860s.

There is no justification for a calculated weakening of First Amendment protections for so indefensible a principle as government endorsement of religious observations. And if Congress does find a worthy issue on which to battle the high court, let that battle be fought through a constitutional amendment, not a five-minute exercise of ayes and nays.

THE BLADE

Toledo, Ohio, April 13, 1979

FOR a case of the pot calling the kettle black, consider Sen. Jesse Helms. The North Carolina Republican strongly suggested that his colleagues were playing a demagogic game when they reversed themselves and transferred his school-prayer amendment from the bill to create an education department to another measure predestined for oblivion. And he was probably right.

But it is difficult to believe that Senator Helms is not himself engaged in a similar exercise with the adoption of this issue for his latest legislative crusade. He vows that he will bring up again and again his amendment purporting to restore prayer to public schools. That is as sure a sign as any that he perceives an irresistible opportunity to ride this political mount for a long time. And it would be surprising indeed if Mr. Helms had given no thought to the almost endless string of headlines he can expect along the way.

Granted, Senator Helms may feel that his roots in the so-called Bible belt of the Southeast make him particularly qualified to espouse the school-prayer cause. Yet President Carter, whose credentials in that regard are well known, was unequivocal in declaring his opposition to the Helms proposal on grounds that "the Government ought to stay out of the prayer business." As a Baptist, Mr. Carter said, he agrees with the Supreme Court that a pupil should feel no constraint to pray while in public school.

What most arouses suspicion about the senator's campaign, however, is his tactic. One would suppose, in light of his proud claim to righteous archconservatism, that Mr. Helms is a stout defender of strict constitutional principle. Yet here he is, trying to use a statutory provision to upset a Supreme Court decision based on the First Amendment in the Bill of Rights. What is that if not a spurious attempt to make an end run around the Constitution itself? Were it possible for Congress to so easily circumvent the basic charter of our national existence by merely passing laws, the Constitution would have been worthless from the beginning and long ago ravaged by the assaults of a parade of Jesse Helmses who have marched across Capitol Hill.

Removal of the school-prayer rider should have no bearing on the fate of the education-department bill; that proposal ought to die on its own merits. So also should the Helms amendment, however many times it is brought up.

The News and Courier

Charleston, S.C., April 12, 1979

The words, from the First Amendment to the U.S. Constitution, seem clear enough. But what a torrent of judicial and legislative argument they have caused to be rained on the American people over the years!

Last week, Sen. Jesse Helms, R-N.C., opened a new chapter in the controversy. He succeeded in attaching a pro-prayer amendment to the Carter administration's bill to establish a separate department of education. The Helms amendment would deny the U.S. Supreme Court review authority over any state law or regulation dealing with voluntary prayer in the public schools. It would also touch off a first-class constitutional crisis by directly challenging a 1963 ruling by the court which held that prayer and Bible reading in the schools violated the First Amendment language quoted above.

Sen. Helm's victory in the Senate was short-lived, however. Monday, Senate Democrats stripped the Helms amendment from the education department bill and attached it instead to another bill certain to wind up in the congressional graveyard. Sen. Edward Kennedy, D-Mass., spoke out strongly against the Helms amendment, terming it "the greatest assault on the jurisdiction of the Supreme Court ... in the 200 years of its existence," while warning that it would "establish a precedent for all types of mischief."

Well, we doubt that voluntary prayer in the public schools is as threatening to the security of the Republic as Sen. Kennedy and others make it out to be. And we feel that the Supreme Court in 1963 indeed ventured into waters it would have been well to steer clear of.

In any event, the issue is not likely to go away. Sen. Helms has promised to attach his amendment to "every available bill" and to continue his fight for its passage. We look forward with interest to the outcome, believing that it does no harm to pull the Supreme Court's chain from time to time, and that this is as good a vehicle to accomplish that as any.

Pittsburgh Post-Gazette
Pittsburgh, Pa., April 9, 1979

In an unexpected action that probably dismayed some of its nominal supporters, the U.S. Senate voted last week to restore the right of "voluntary prayer" in the public schools. Not only would this mischievous measure satisfy the lobby to "put prayer back in the schools"; it would do so in an audacious and dangerous way, by attempting to deny the U.S. Supreme Court jurisdiction to act on any state law involving school prayer.

The staying power of the school-prayer movement is puzzling. This newspaper and others often receive letters expressing the view that allowing schoolchildren to begin their class day with a prayer — any prayer, no matter how diluted or nondenominational — would somehow bring about dramatic changes in the nation's moral climate.

But even more puzzling than this view is the support for school prayer from political conservatives, who ordinarily emphasize the importance of insulating the family — and family values like religion — from state interference. What greater violation of individual and family rights can there be than an official moment of prayer or even "meditation" at a state-run school which is attended by children of all — and no — religious beliefs?

Far more disturbing than the content of the Senate's school-prayer amendment is its legal reasoning. The question of Congress' role in determining the jurisdiction of the courts is a complex one. But whatever legitimate role Congress might have in that area, it cannot be perverted to overrule Supreme Court *holdings* — like the ban on school prayer — that some or even a majority of congressmen don't like. If Congress did have such authority, the Constitution and the independence of the judiciary would mean nothing.

When the Senate takes up the school-prayer amendment again this week, it is expected to behave more responsibly than it did last week. And perhaps that near-miss will teach some senators not to cater to demands from their constituents that offend the Constitution.

The Miami Herald
Miami, Fla., April 9, 1979

THE UNITED STATES has been spared much of the sectarian strife that afflicts far too many lands. By wisely separating church and state, the framers of the Constitution made possible a society in which a rich diversity of religious thought could thrive without rending the fabric of society.

This cherished principle led the U.S. Supreme Court in 1963 to rule against mandatory prayer and Bible reading in the public schools. Such

Helms

practices, the court said, amount to an establishment of religion and thus are prohibited by the First Amendment.

The ruling was misinterpreted — sometimes deliberately — by critics such as Richard Nixon and Everett Dirksen. Senator Dirksen even proposed a Constitutional amendment to reverse it.

The amendment has stalled — and for good reason. The American people generally don't want school boards and principals telling their children how to pray. That's a private matter for the family, the church, and the individual to decide.

During the past week, however, the U.S. Senate — which can't seem to discipline its own errant members or abide by its own ethics code's income limits — suddenly "got religion."

To a bill creating a Cabinet-level Department of Education, the senators attached a preposterous amendment devised by Jesse Helms, the right-wing extremist whose 1978 re-election campaign set a record for special-interest contributions.

Senator Helms seeks by statute, not by Constitutional amendment, to deny the U.S. Supreme Court jurisdiction in the area of prayer in schools. The proposal thus flies in the face of the separation-of-powers doctrine as well as the First Amendment's prohibition against establishment of religion.

The wonder is that a majority of the senators present — including Florida's pair — voted for a proposition that should not have had a prayer of succeeding in a group that likes to think of itself as the world's greatest deliberative body.

Senators ought to reconsider — after solemn meditation, of course. And if they don't, the House ought to kill the amendment. But if both chambers persist, President Carter ought to veto the bill without hesitation. This nation does not need the strife that would surely come eventually if the wall separating church and state is breached.

The Philadelphia Inquirer
Philadelphia, Pa., April 9, 1979

Sen. Jesse A. Helms of North Carolina may have performed a public service with his amendment, adopted 47-37, to the Carter Administration's bill to create a separate Department of Education. The amendment, one of the rightwing Republican's favorite crusades, purports to restore the "right of voluntary prayer" in the public schools. It would do this by stripping the U.S. Supreme Court as well as the federal courts of jurisdiction over state laws permitting "voluntary prayers in the public schools."

It is, of course, almost certainly unconstitutional. There is nothing in the Constitution which prevents anyone from praying wherever and whenever they want, but the Supreme Court has prohibited any government entity from requiring religious exercises in the public schools, including "voluntary" prayers which in reality are not voluntary.

Whether one agrees with the Supreme Court's decisions or not, Congress cannot reverse constitutional rulings by legislation. So if the Helms amendment remains in the bill, it is quite possible, as one of the bill's cosponsors, Sen. Spark Matsunaga (D.,-Hawaii), declared, that "the bill itself may die."

There will be little cause for mourning if it does. The administration asserts, as budget director James T. McIntyre Jr. has testified, that "the question before the Congress is simply this: 'How do we most effectively manage more than 150 federal education programs?'," and answers the question by proposing to set up a separate Department of Education.

But the proposal itself rather begs the question. If the answer is to establish a separate Department of Education, why has the administration excluded so many educational functions from it, from veterans to Head Start to Indian education and more? The answer is that their special constituencies persuaded the administration to sacrifice much of the principle of coordination in order to reduce the political opposition.

The administration has not made a persuasive case that the new department would result in better management. Indeed, a case can be made that unhooking education from related functions of health and welfare would make it more rather than less difficult to coordinate.

There is, though, a more important question. That is, as Rep. Shirley Chisholm (D., N. Y.) put it, whether the new department "would significantly upgrade the quality of instruction and acceess to educational opportunities available to the nation's children." Rep. Chisholm says she remains "unconvinced," and so do we. The Senate may (and should) reverse itself today on the Helms amendment, but even without it the bill should be killed.

THE CHRISTIAN SCIENCE MONITOR
Boston, Mass., April 10, 1979

The nice thing about praying – in school or anywhere else – is that Congress or any other legislative body does not have to give anyone the "right" to do it. It's an inherent right and privilege, granted by an authority much higher than any human legislative or judicial body. And therefore restrictions on mandatory audible prayer in public schools in no way diminish the opportunity available to all to pray at any time and in any place.

The question, then, which the Senate must weigh in considering Senator Jesse Helms's proposed amendment to restore the "right of voluntary prayer" in public schools is not the right to pray voluntarily. The question is whether public schools in America's free and changing society are the proper place to impose religious worship.

There was a time when religious standards were commonly held in a community; prayer in the schools was not then an issue. Today, however, society grows increasingly diverse. In such conditions, prayer mandated by school authorities, even though with broad community support, could impinge on the sensitivities and rights of pupils who would wish not to join in prayer. A minority could claim discrimination under such a breach of separation of church and state.

We tend to agree with President Carter, who remarked, ". . . the government ought to stay out of the prayer business and let it be between a person and God, and not let it be part of a school program under any tangible constraints, either a direct order to a child to pray or an embarrassing situation where the child would feel constrained to pray."

The Helms amendment, moreover, raises serious constitutional questions. It would deny the Supreme Court jurisdiction to act on any state law or ordinance relating to prayers in public schools. On the surface, it seems highly unlikely that Congress can constitutionally restrict the court by specifically denying it the right to upset any state law or ruling.

In the home and places of worship is where children should be taught how to pray. Thank goodness, there can be no restrictions on where and how they can do so privately and individually – in the school corridors, walking along the street, or in a classroom. The opportunities are infinite. Freedom of prayerful thought is inviolate.

St. Petersburg Times
St. Petersburg, Fla., April 11, 1979

Sure, it's tough for a member of Congress or any elected official to take a stand "against prayer," whether in the public schools or elsewhere. Some have done so and subsequently gone down to defeat.

But that's no excuse for the U.S. Senate. On the other hand it says a lot for the honesty and courage of President Carter.

Twice in five days a Senate majority has voted to overturn the Supreme Court's ban on organized praying in school. The second time, it did so in the face of a warning by Carter that prayer is a private matter, in which officialdom ought not to meddle.

THE SENATORS voting to exempt so-called voluntary school prayers from the high court's ruling did so in the knowledge that nothing could come of their action. Also, most of those thus proclaiming themselves in favor of piety, virtue, morality, godliness and clean living probably recognize that the Supreme Court's decision was right. Certainly Florida's two — yes, they voted "for" prayer — are that smart.

The court acted under the First Amendment, which bars government action "respecting an establishment of religion, or prohibiting the free exercise thereof." The court said organized prayers or prescribed Bible readings in public schools fall afoul of that constitutional ban.

It said this was so even in the case of a so-called nondenominational prayer — whatever that is — and even where children not wishing to participate were permitted to be excused from the room.

Since the court first ruled on this issue, in 1962, members of Congress have mounted numerous efforts to amend the First Amendment, as they said, to "put prayer back in the schools." Despite sincere help they got from theologians and lawyers, the efforts all failed.

FIRST THEY tried to write a nondenominational prayer and discovered it couldn't be done. ("To whom it may concern" was the way one suggested model began.) They fiddled with language specifically to legalize "voluntary" praying in school and concluded that on an individual basis this already is as legal in school as anywhere else. On any other basis, it's not voluntary.

So much for the latest senatorial posturing, which came not on a proposed constitutional amendment but on a lame legislative attempt to limit the high court's jurisdiction. Aside from its dubious legality, the bill has no chance of final enactment.

ITS EFFECT is to revive a dead issue. Its effect is to encourage belief that the Supreme Court, in thus trying to protect children from being either proselytized or embarrassed, is merely being narrow and picky. Carter, talking to a group of visiting editors, conceded that the question before the Senate was tough, but he made no effort to duck it.

"In general, I think the government ought to stay out of the prayer business," Carter said, "and let it be tween a person and God and not let it be part of a school program under any tangible constraints, either a direct order to a child to pray or an embarrassing situation where the child would be constrained to pray."

Maybe that wasn't the most polished statement ever delivered by Carter. But it was one of the most perceptive. As a born-again Christian, Carter on this issue is in better position than most to make an intelligent judgment. And fortunately he has the guts to say what he thinks.

The Oregonian
Portland, Ore., April 11, 1979

The U.S. Senate's approval of an amendment that would permit voluntary prayers in the public schools leaves to the House or the courts the task of stifling the proposal. The legislation is unwise, unneeded and unconstitutional.

Anyone can pray anywhere now. Also, places for community worship abound: churches, temples, even homes.

What the amendment would do is endorse group prayer in a government institution where individuals must be present, where possibly they would be influenced against their will or that of their families.

The Senate proposal would clash with the principle of separation of church and state, violating Article I of the Constitution — "Congress shall make no law respecting an establishment of religion, or prohibiting the free exercise thereof. . . ."

It also would sorely test the separation of powers, in that the measure would deny the Supreme Court the power to address the issue.

Similar moves to permit school prayers have been tried, without success, since the Supreme Court ruled in 1962 and 1963 that prayers and Bible readings in the public schools violated the First Amendment.

Since then, civil disobedience has abounded in every degree, from open classroom praying to the singing of Christmas hymns, which many consider to be prayers. The Pledge of Allegiance phrase, "one nation, under God," recognizes what the Supreme Court said in a 1952 decision (Zorach vs. Clauson), "We are a religious people whose institutions presuppose a Supreme Being."

Nevertheless, the First Amendment was drawn to protect citizens of this country from mandated religion. Endorsing any form of worship in government institutions is a step in that direction.

Persons who wish their children to practice their religion can better guide that practice when they are present. Congress has no business mandating otherwise.

The prayer of a free people might best be that government not intrude on their ways of worship.

The Providence Journal

Providence, R.I., April 16, 1979

It is quite natural, one supposes, that the controversy over prayer in the public schools periodically resurfaces, despite the U.S. Supreme Court's prohibition 16 years ago. Over the years, Congress has considered various proposals to amend the Constitution but none has received enough votes for consideration by the states.

Sen. Jesse Helms of North Carolina has taken a new tack, this one hardly more promising than the rest. He would exempt any and all state laws and regulations dealing with voluntary school prayers from review by the high court. In other words, he would carve out this area of the court's jurisdiction and declare it off limits to the nine justices.

This approach itself raises serious constitutional questions. Does Congress, the legislative branch of government, have power to restrict the judiciary in this manner or is this right reserved to the highest tribunal? Any such legislative abridgement of judicial authority is apparently unprecedented. Moreover, it is inconceivable that under a system of three co-equal branches one branch might assume such pre-eminence without creating constitutional mayhem.

President Carter told a group of editors at the White House last week that he opposes the Helms amendment, which was first attached to the proposal for a separate Department of Education and then transferred to a bill of somewhat lesser significance. "In general," he said, "I think the government ought to stay out of the prayer business and let it be between a person and God, and not let it be part of a school program under any tangible constraints, either a direct order to pray or an embarrassing situation where the child would feel constrained to pray."

The latter point is one that proponents of voluntary prayer in the public schools often lose sight of. Minors are not free to exercise individual will during school hours. They are subject to the authority of their teachers and principal and are constantly exposed to the influences of their peers. The choice of participating in "voluntary" prayer or not would in fact be illusory. Fear of incurring displeasure, either that of a teacher or of classmates, in many instances would make that optional moment set aside for prayer more obligatory than an occasion for individual choice.

It was the First Amendment's ban on government establishment of religion that the Supreme Court invoked in 1962 and 1963 in striking down mandatory school prayers. It has not ruled on state laws that permit certain types of voluntary prayer, but many believe it would also frown on quasi-voluntarism for the reasons cited above. Thus Senator Helms' attempt to proscribe high court review of this emotional issue.

If in fact Congress upsets this misguided attempt to stage an end run around the court, it will strengthen the constitutional fabric without in any way denigrating the quality of prayer. And in terms of church-state separation, that is precisely the stand that government ought to take.

The Wichita Eagle

Wichita, Kans., April 13, 1979

An amendment proposed by Sen. Jesse Helms, R-N.C., that would revive prayers in public schools poses a double-barreled threat to some of the basic rights that serve as a foundation for this country.

Most obviously, the school prayer amendment would blur the line between church and state that finally has been established after so many years of debate and court decisions. President Carter had the right idea last weekend when he said, "I think the government ought to stay out of the prayer business."

Mr. Carter, a person with deep religious convictions himself, realizes that, although the Helms amendment would not provide for mandatory prayers in schools, the measure would bring very real pressures on school children who would prefer not to participate in any formal religious activity.

Real freedom of religion encompasses not only the right to worship according to the faith of one's choosing, but the right not to worship, nor to feel compelled by the state to worship.

The second, and no less worrisome, aspect of Mr. Helms' proposal has to do with the procedure for guaranteeing that no law reinstituting school prayers could be struck down as unconstitutional. To achieve that end, the law would make it illegal for the U.S. Supreme Court to consider cases growing out of conflicts over such school prayer legislation passed by any state.

The chilling effects of such a move on constitutional government should be clear. If Congress can dictate which laws the Supreme Court can rule on and which ones it must ignore, there is no need for a judicial system. The legislative branch would, in effect, not only be writing the laws, but applying them and ruling on them as well.

Theoretically, the Congress could go on from banning religious cases before the Supreme Court to stripping the court of its right to review murder cases, civil rights suits, or any type of litigation that the Congress felt wouldn't stand up under glaring exposure to the U.S. Constitution.

The frightening thing is that Sen. Helms' amendment was approved by a 47-37 margin in the Senate on a preliminary vote. Apparently some senators feel they can safely vote for such radical legislation, knowing it stands little chance of passage, and then tell their constituents that, "Yes, by golly, I voted for prayers in schools and apple pie and Mom and the flag and all those other American things we hold near and dear."

Unfortunately, if enough senators succumb to that line of thinking, the Helms amendment, which will probably bounce from one bill to another, in search of passage, could make it through the Senate.

The Supreme Court ruled reasonably in 1965 when it banned formalized prayers in public schools. The religion-in-school question has been properly resolved, and to undercut the working relationship that has grown up since that decision now would be a mistake of the first magnitude.

And, trying to end-run the Supreme Court on its constitutional responsibilities by passing limits on the types of cases it can hear would be just as irresponsible. It was no overstatement on the part of Sen. Edward Kennedy, D-Mass., when he said the Helms amendment, if enacted, would represent the most serious assault on the U.S. judicial system in 200 years.

The Morning News

Wilmington, Del., April 12, 1979

No agency of government — no state legislature, no municipal council, no state or local school board — can tell your child when, or where, or how to pray.

That is the essence of the 1963 ruling of the United States Supreme Court which, despite all the misinterpretations and sinister motives attributed to it, was one of the great blows struck for freedom of religion. Emphasis is on the word "freedom," because in no other way can religion be practiced in this country.

This week, a slim majority of the United States Senate tried taking another end run around that ruling. First, the Senate attached to the bill creating a federal Department of Education an amendment which denies the Supreme Court jurisdiction over any state law relating to voluntary prayer in the public schools. When that made the sponsors of the education department bill nervous (their bill has enough problems of its own), the amendment was shifted to another bill on court procedures.

Under whichever umbrella, the amendment has only a very slim chance of clearing the House of Representatives. The senators know that. And that divides those who voted for the amendment into two groups: those who sincerely believe that the government can and should prescribe a form of prayer — they are merely wrong — and those who get a free ride on legislation they know will be knocked down by another house or a court.

Sen. Jesse Helms, who sponsored this legislation, managed in fact to get athwart the Constitution twice in this instance. Not only is he trying to carve out a portion of the First Amendment which would be immune from interpretation by the federal courts ("Congress shall make no law respecting the establishment of religion, or prohibiting the free exercise thereof . . ."), but he has run into the Fourteenth Amendment as well. A section of that amendment reads: " No state shall make or enforce any law which shall abridge the privileges or immunities of citizens of the United States. . . ."

One of those privileges is the right to sue in the federal courts for protection of an individual's constitutional rights; one of those immunities is from the pressures of state-established religion.

The authors of our Constitution, who had a lot of experience in the matter, were determined that religion and government in this country were to be kept separate to the extent that neither could exert undue influence on the other. They were not necessarily irreligious men, nor were they so unrealistic as to believe that Americans, then and now, are an irreligious people. But they knew that both religion and government are healthier if they co-exist, and the people are free to worship God if no agency of government tells them where and when and how to do it.

Jimmy Carter, who is one of the more ostensibly religious presidents we have had in a long while, put the whole issue much more simply when he said last week that he believes that government "ought to stay out of the prayer business."

THE MILWAUKEE JOURNAL

Milwaukee, Wisc., April 12, 1979

If politicians were sure that the public understood the true meaning of religious freedom, they probably would not be afraid to oppose such foolish measures as Sen. Jesse Helms' "prayer amendment." But many lawmakers seem to believe that a vote against the measure would be misinterpreted as a "vote against God."

So they indulge in a charade, voting for the provision but allowing their leaders to sidetrack it with legislative maneuver. That has just happened in the US Senate, but the issue will be raised again and again. How much better it would be if the lawmakers overcame their timidity and started explaining to the public exactly what is involved.

Helms' proposal, like others before it, attempts to sidestep the Supreme Court's proper decision that public schools have no right to prescribe prayers for their students. The court did not say there was anything undesirable about praying, in school or elsewhere. It just defended the constitutional right of each individual to practice religion in his or her own way, without assistance, guidance or interference from any arm of government.

It's important to guard that right jealously. If one school principal is allowed to make pupils recite a relatively bland, "nonsectarian" prayer, what is to keep another educator from imposing his own particular religious beliefs on the student body? The only sure way of protecting each person's religious liberty is to maintain strict separation between the activities of government and those of religion, a fact that the Supreme Court appreciated when it said prayer could not be a required part of public schooling.

Helms' proposed legislation doesn't attack the Supreme Court ruling head on; that is, it doesn't say the right to make school prayers mandatory should be established. Rather, it speaks of allowing voluntary prayers in schools and other public buildings.

Well, there's no way to stop really voluntary prayers, and nobody is trying to stop them. Certainly no act of Congress is needed to protect voluntary praying.

The trouble with Helms' proposal is that it goes far beyond saying the right of voluntary prayer exists. It says the Supreme Court would not even have the power to review any case arising out of a state law that allows voluntary praying in schools or public buildings. In other words, if voluntary school prayers were converted into prescribed prayers, the Supreme Court could do nothing to make that abuse of power yield to the First Amendment's guarantee of religious freedom.

Although President Carter places a high value on prayer, he has been willing to point out the folly of Helms' proposal. Unfortunately, too few members of Congress have been willing to take an equally responsible position.

THE KANSAS CITY STAR

Kansas City, Mo., April 17, 1979

There is nothing wrong with praying in the classroom, and we would guess that many pupils do it frequently in the face of final examinations. But the nonsense now perpetrated by the U.S. Senate — an attempt to tell the Supreme Court it cannot involve itself in state laws concerning prayer in the public schools — is something else. It hits at the First Amendment guaranteeing freedom of religion. It is a futile exercise in political grandstanding that can only stir anguish and most unChristian emotions.

Prayer is not an act that requires unison recitation, communal silence or any set-aside time or place. Whenever any of those factors enters the picture, then coercive elements are inevitable. The authority figure of the teacher cannot order a roomful of children to observe silence for "meditation" or bow their heads in quiet or deliver thanks without infringing on the right of Americans to pray in a certain manner or not to pray at all. In the same manner, certainly, thought control cannot be imposed against a silent prayer in the mind at any time.

Such has always been the unconquerable method of the truly devout.

We would assume that people who demand a demonstration of prayer in the public schools would very carefully guide the religious lives of their own children with frequent church attendance, regular family prayer and religious training for those children in a church school if they so desire. That is all commendable. When they insist on regimented prayer in a public classroom, aren't they really thinking of the children of others? Their own, surely, are well-nurtured in the beliefs of the parents. It is not their place to force a mode of relationship with God on anyone else. In fact, the basic law of the United States forbids it.

To oppose prayer in schools supported by taxes is not to promote atheism or harm the beliefs of anyone. It is to say that no American can be forced into a structure of worship, and that religious beliefs cannot be imposed upon anyone. That is not antichurch. It is the sort of atmosphere in which religions are free to flourish.

BUFFALO EVENING NEWS

Buffalo, N.Y., April 14, 1979

"Sometimes a student might object even to so-called voluntary prayer when it's public and coordinated. It might be very embarrassing to a young person to say 'I want to be excused from the room because I don't want to pray.' So I don't know all of the Constitutional aspects of this very difficult and sensitive question but I think that it ought to be an individual matter between a person and God."
—President Carter in this week's news conference

The day between Good Friday and Easter Sunday is probably as good as any other to consider the implications of a Senate-passed bill to forbid the Supreme Court from interfering with any state-authorized voluntary prayers in public schools.

The bill, sponsored by Sen. Jesse Helms (R., N.C.), has passed the Senate twice now as a kind of rider on other legislation. It is not offered as a constitutional amendment, as numerous similar prayer measures have been in the past, nor does it even attempt to alter any of the previous Supreme Court decisions holding prescribed prayers and Bible readings as part of religious exercises in public schools to be unconstitutional.

What the Helms bill would do, very simply, is deny the Supreme Court jurisdiction to act on any *state* law or regulation relating to *voluntary* prayers in public schools. It would in effect give each state's highest court the final say on that question.

During brief Senate debate, Sen. Edward F. Kennedy (D., Mass.) called the Helms bill "clearly unconstitutional." But we (and evidently the 51 senators who voted for it) aren't so sure. Sen. Kennedy may well be right in saying that no Congress has ever "voted to exclude from federal courts" any matter of "individual rights and liberties enshrined in the Constitution." But the Constitution itself says very plainly (in Art. III, Sec. 2) that, in all cases "arising under this Constitution," where the Supreme Court is not given explicit original jurisdiction, it "shall have appellate jurisdiction, both as to law and fact, *with such exceptions, and under such regulations as the Congress shall make.*"

That power of Congress to restrict Supreme Court jurisdiction, moreover, has generally been interpreted very liberally in Congress' favor. In fact, the very bill to which the Helms rider is now attached is, ironically, a "routine" Supreme Court bill, backed by all nine present justices, to remove from their jurisdiction many types of minor, time-consuming cases that do not involve principles of wide public concern.

So maybe the right question to ask is not whether Congress constitutionally *could*, but whether it *should*, strip the federal courts in general, and the Supreme Court in particular, of appellate jurisdiction over any state laws on voluntary prayer. In our view, it should *not*.

We say this not because we have any more objection in principle to voluntary prayers in public schools than we do to the opening invocations still used in the House and the Senate and, indeed, in the Supreme Court itself. We say it rather because we do not believe that any part of the U.S. Constitution — least of all, any of the fundamental provisions of the Bill of Rights — should be put beyond the reach of Supreme Court review.

There are twin dangers, as we see it, in the Helms bill's effort to do this, even on so-called "voluntary" prayers. One is that if Congress once starts chipping away the Supreme Court's jurisdiction in one area involving individual constitutional rights, there may be no stopping it from extending the same device to other areas. Today, voluntary prayers; tomorrow, school busing, abortion, obscenity, or almost any other hot-potato issue one could name.

The other danger is that, if the Supreme Court can't touch any state law relating to voluntary prayers, then it would be doubtful whether it could touch one which only purported to be voluntary but in fact raised very profound First Amendment issues "respecting an establishment of religion or prohibiting the free exercise thereof."

We agree with President Carter, in short, that on "this very difficult and sensitive question," Congress ought not to be tampering with the Supreme Court's constitutional jurisdiction.

Minneapolis Tribune

Minneapolis, Minn., April 12, 1979

Children are unharmed by prayer, says Sen. Jesse Helms, as if that were the issue. The real issue is whether prayer and Bible readings in public schools violate the constitutional separation of church and state. They do. A ban on such practices was upheld by a 1963 U.S. Supreme Court decision. To get around it, Helms and a majority of his colleagues support an amendment to remove school prayers from the jurisdiction of federal courts. Doing so would be a mistake.

Aside from its disturbing constitutional questions, the Helms amendment is an affront to good sense. To oppose the amendment is not to oppose religion; indeed, one encouraging aspect of public life today is the readiness of many political leaders to acknowledge the importance of their private beliefs and to gather for prayer with like-minded colleagues. It is a commendable practice in Congress, as in the Minnesota Legislature.

But making private beliefs a part of public education would be a contradiction. Nothing now prevents the exercise of religious ethics in schools or elsewhere. Moreover, condoning prayer in public schools suggests that religion is inadequately nourished in church and family, and that government should therefore intervene.

The frequently undesirable, sometimes calamitous effects of mixing religion and politics have been depressingly evident in strife of recent years: between Catholics and Protestants in Northern Ireland, Moslems and Jews in the Middle East, Hindus and Moslems in South Asia. A grim irony of Iran is that vendettas in the name of religion have made "ayatollah" synonymous with "repressor."

Framers of the U.S. Constitution recognized such dangers. James Madison wrote of the "zeal for different opinions concerning religion," which he said was among the reasons competing factions were "more disposed to vex and oppress each other than to cooperate for their common good." That is why the First Amendment so bluntly proscribes laws that would establish or regulate religion.

The Senate voted twice the past week to dilute the First Amendment by permitting school prayers. We regret that Minnesota's David Durenberger voted yes both times. Rudy Boschwitz voted no. The Easter recess would be an appropriate time for Durenberger and allies to reflect on the separate roles of church and state, to return with a change of mind and to join Boschwitz on the side of the angels.

Democrat Chronicle
Rochester, N.Y., May 9, 1979

THE HOUSE Judiciary Committee, headed by Rep. Peter Rodino (D-N.J.), has before it a minor judicial reform bill that, if passed, could have major constitutional consequences.

It's called the Judicial Jurisdiction Bill and was passed by a 61-30 vote in the Senate last month. It would give the Supreme Court almost complete say over which cases it will hear.

The bill itself seems reasonable enough. It has been endorsed by a cross-section of lawyers as well as by all nine Justices.

The danger lies in a school prayer amendment sponsored by Sen. Jesse Helms (R-N.C.) which, ironically, would nullify some of the bill of which it is a part.

It seeks to bar the High Court and other federal courts from reviewing any state law concerning "voluntary prayer in public schools or public buildings."

If passed by the House, the school prayer amendment would enable states to sponsor prayer in public schools. This violates the Constitution's First Amendment which prohibits government from establishing religion anywhere.

But there's also another danger: The amendment would prevent citizens against public school prayer from challenging it in the High Court.

OPPONENTS OF the school prayer amendment point out 1962 and 1963 cases (Engel v. Vitale and Abington School District v. Schempp) in which the Supreme Court forbade state- and church-written prayer.

They also accurately say that the Helms amendment could set a precedent for Congress to establish unconstitutional laws abridging public freedoms while killing the process of judicial review.

"If the Congress . . . is prepared to exclude jurisdiction of the Supreme Court in one particular area . . . " said Sen. Edward Kennedy (D-Mass.), "why cannot the Congress . . . virtually establish a religion . . . and provide for the Supreme Court exclusion from ruling on the appropriateness of that enactment?"

Indeed, Congress can control the High Court's range of cases. Section 2 of Article III of the Constitution gives Congress authority to determine Supreme Court appellate jurisdiction except on questions "affecting ambassadors, other public ministers and consuls, and those in which a State shall be party."

This may be true, but this power must be weighed against the public's right to freedom of religion.

Sen. Charles McC. Mathias (R-Md.), said he fears Congressional power to flout the Constitution would spill over into other categories.

"There is no subject that cannot be reached by a simple act of Congress altering the jurisdiction of the courts to control the outcome of cases," Mathias said.

Other problems include determining what kinds of prayers would be permitted and how the Congress could pass a law that, in effect, would tamper with the outcome of a potential legal case.

THOSE IN FAVOR of school prayer base their arguments on shaky premises.

For example, Sen. Strom Thurmond (R-S.C.) said, "Our nation was founded upon religion. Today it is acknowledged in the government and we ought to remember it." He was referring to the fact that each Senate session opens with a prayer.

Thurmond also said, "If we . . . who make the laws, approve of prayers . . . then what is wrong with letting little children in school pray if they want to?"

First, our nation was founded upon the principles of democracy and freedom by many "God-fearing" men, not on religion. In America, all religions would be protected, but so would the rights of people who did not believe in religion.

Second, people — whether children or adult — already have the right to pray anywhere and any time they please. This is the basis of the First Amendment's section on freedom of religion.

What is to prevent a child from praying during study hall, lunch, or during an exam? What is to prevent an adult — in this case a teacher — from praying during chemistry lab or during a free period?

And, most important, what is to prevent either child or adult from suing the school that tells them to stop?

Prayer advocates such as Sen. Ted Stevens (R-Alaska) say the Helms amendment may be unconstitutional, but that it should be passed so its constitutionality can be tested in the Supreme Court.

This can be done only in the High Court. And if that court has no authority to hear such a case, then how can the amendment's constitutionality be tested?

President Carter — a God-fearing Baptist himself — summed it up when he said, "I think the government ought to stay out of the prayer business and let it be between a person and God." Amen.

St. Louis Review
St. Louis, Mo., April 20, 1979

Since the U.S. Supreme Court rulings of 1962 and 1963 which outlawed mandatory prayer in public schools, a succession of distinguished senators have led a valiant but unsuccessful fight to permit voluntary prayer in public schools. The baton taken up by the late Senator Everett Dirksen has, in recent years, been taken up by Senator Jesse Helms (R-N.C.).

Senator Helms has proposed a legislative rider which would strip the federal courts and the U.S. Supreme Court of all jurisdiction over state laws permitting voluntary prayers in the public schools and other public buildings.

Senator Helms has been able to win a slim majority for the amendment, but the Senate has studiously avoided attaching the rider to any viable piece of legislation. In this way, Senators can go on record as being in favor of prayer in public schools, while avoiding any meaningful action which would secure implementation.

The Helms device is one which was suggested in a St. Louis Review editorial some time ago. Though rarely invoked, the U.S. Constitution does provide the legislative branch of government the power to limit the power of the judiciary. If the Congress successfully limited the jurisdiction of the courts over prayer in public schools, there would certainly be a widespread demand that state laws regulating abortion also be removed from the jurisdiction of federal courts and the U.S. Supreme Court.

Quick to sense the implications of this initiative, Senator Edward M. Kennedy, Chairman of the Senate Judiciary Committee, stood in opposition to the rider, declaring that it would mark the first time in 100 years "that the Congress has voted to exclude from jurisdiction of federal courts subjects involving individual rights and liberties enshrined in the Constitution." Senator Kennedy's championing of human rights has never included the right to life of the unborn.

The continuing encroachment of the federal judiciary into the field of legislation demands some such drastic action as that proposed by Senator Helms. If judicial legislation continues at its present pace, the legislative branch of government will become an expensive anachronism.

Chicago Tribune

Chicago, Ill., April 20, 1979

For a few days, the Carter administration's bill to create a separate Department of Education was burdened by a controversial amendment denying the Supreme Court power to review any state law permitting voluntary prayer in public schools. To the surprise of many observers, the Senate voted 47 to 37 to accept the amendment to that effect sponsored by Sen. Jesse Helms [R., N.C.].

Sen. Helms is a persistent campaigner on the subject of prayer in schools. Last year he tried to attach his amendment to a bill sponsored by Sen. Dennis DeConcini [D., Ariz.] and backed unanimously by all members of the Supreme Court. That bill was to enlarge the power of the court to refuse review without explanation. This year, Senate Majority Leader Robert Byrd [D., W. Va.] suggested that the Helms amendment can most suitably be considered with a pending bill about the operation and jurisdiction of the Supreme Court. The Senate took his advice, and that bill, with the Helms amendment, has gone to the House.

Backers of a separate Department of Education are no doubt glad to be rid of the Helms amendment, which was considered a handicap to passage. Tacking on irrelevant amendments to reduce a bill's chances is a standard legislative device, and Sen. Helms need not be blamed much for resorting to it. But the separate Department of Education bill should be judged on its own merits, which are so meager as to compel any sensible legislator to oppose it.

As for the Helms amendment itself, it is not universally considered genuinely pro-prayer. The Baptist Joint Committee on Public Affairs has called it "an abridgement of the First Amendment and in no way an aid to religion or the religious exercise of prayer." Most church spokesmen that have commented on the Helms amendment have been against it. Most thoughtful people believe there is no way to make classroom prayers either theologically neutral or genuinely voluntary.

Probably the most significant dimension of the Helms amendment is that discussed by Patrick Buchanan in a recent Perspective column — the power of Congress to limit the appellate jurisdiction of the Supreme Court. Sen. Helms is more confident than many others that the Constitution gives Congress the right to limit the Supreme Court's jurisdiction anywhere it wishes. Yet the Supreme Court, rather than Congress, is the now universally accepted arbiter in questions of constitutionality.

Early in the history of this country President Andrew Jackson defied the authority of the Supreme Court in a case involving the rights of the Cherokee Indian tribe. Noting that the judicial branch lacks means to enforce its rulings, President Jackson simply disregarded the Supreme Court's directive. Among the events that this country does not need is a conflict between two branches of government that poses a constitutional question in the absence of an accepted umpire.

ST. LOUIS POST-DISPATCH

St. Louis, Mo., April 14, 1979

The House of Representatives ought not to go along with the Senate's approval of a Jesse Helms proposal to bar the U.S. Supreme Court from reviewing state laws on the use of prayers in the public schools. Efforts to return formal group prayer to classrooms have been made repeatedly since 1962 when the Supreme Court held that "each separate government in this country should stay out of the business of writing or sanctioning official prayers and leave that purely religious function to the people themselves and to those the people choose to look to for religious guidance."

Proponents of measures like the one Mr. Helms has just sponsored consistently ignore that every child has the right to pray in his or her own way at any time. What is constitutionally unacceptable is a public body promoting a prayer, a type of religion or any religion at all. Making participation in a formal group prayer "voluntary" does not get around the undesirability of institutionalized approval of religious expression. As children are extremely vulnerable to peer pressure, many may feel compelled to participate in the prayer against their beliefs or inclinations. And the children who choose not to participate are likely to be harassed or ostracized.

Religion and prayer are very personal matters and ought to be left to the choice of each individual as he or she sees fit. They should not be debased into a daily recitation of a generalized prayer to a generalized God. Should the prayer in a public school go beyond generalization, a religious choice must be made. And that choice would be a clear and unacceptable violation of the constitutional prohibition against governmental establishment of religion. Mr. Helms expects the current offering to die in the House, and it deserves to. Congress would better serve the public if it continued the status quo where every child can offer individual prayers, but no one is coerced into praying through "voluntary" group sessions.

The Evening Gazette

Worcester, Mass., April 16, 1979

Back in 1962, when the U.S. Supreme Court ruled the daily recitation of a nondenominational prayer in the New York State public schools to be unconstitutional, members of both houses of Congress denounced the decision and introduced bills to amend the Constitution to permit reading of prayers in public schools. The feeling was just as intense a year later, when the Supreme Court ruled against recitation of the Lord's Prayer and Bible verses in public schools.

Today the pendulum seems to have swung at least partly the other way. The school prayer amendment proposed by Sen. Jesse Helms to override the First Amendment seems like an anachronism. A whole generation of students has passed through the public school system without prayer or Bible verse recitations.

To many parents, prayer isn't much of an issue any more. They are more concerned about the education their children are receiving. Other parents are worried that their children might be attracted to religious cults. They prefer keeping religious instruction in the home and community of faith. The explosive growth of religious beliefs in recent years — from born-again Christian to Hare Krishna to charismatic Catholic — makes any meaningful common prayer problematical.

Whatever the reason, the Helms rider to the bill to create a separate Department of Education seems misguided in these changed times. President Carter, a staunch Baptist, opposes Congress' passing legislation "requiring or permitting prayer being required or encouraged in school." Carter calls prayer an individual matter between a person and God and says that it might be "very embarrassing" to a young person to have to ask to be excused from so-called voluntary prayer at school. Many Americans agree with that point of view.

Changing perceptions about mandated prayer in public schools — even among the deeply religious — should give people pause. The Constitution should be timeless; popular issues are peripheral.

The Seattle Times

Seattle, Wash., April 16, 1979

THANKS to a slick parliamentry maneuver, the push to get prayers back into the public schools is where it should be — buried under the dead weight of some unpopular legislation.

The prayer amendment had been attached as a rider to the administration-supported Department of Education bill, even though the President is opposed to returning prayers to the schools.

Senator Robert Byrd, West Virginia Democrat, resorted to a parliamentary procedure that got the rider off the education bill and onto a Supreme Court jurisdiction bill, which is unlikely to pass.

Supporters of prayers in the classroom believe that somehow the nation can turn the clock back to 20 years ago, when schools were attended by homogeneous groups of children sharing the same socio-economic status and often the same religion.

In years gone by, many families chose their neighborhoods according to the church in the area, the school, affordability, and race.

While affordability is still a major factor in choosing a neighborhood, so are open-housing laws. Desegregation plans are obscuring the neighborhood-school concept, and the location of one's preferred house of worship is not a factor because of high mobility.

Neighborhoods today are extremely diverse in terms of religion, a fact that underscores the inappropriateness of prayers in schools.

Ethnicity and choice of religion, or lack of it, are sources of pride. The United States is not a nation under one God, but under God, Allah, Jehovah, Buddha and no God, depending on one's preference.

And even if there were some universal prayer that could apply to all, it would not change the inalienable right of children to worship or not as they and their families choose in private, or at a time and place of their own choosing.

THE SACRAMENTO BEE
Sacramento, Calif., July 2, 1979

The best thing that can be expected of the bill creating a separate federal Department of Education is that it will sink under the weight of the amendments that have been loaded on to it. Among those amendments — both passed by the House recently — is one that would encourage "a daily opportunity for prayer or meditation" on a voluntary basis and another which would prohibit the use of racial or sexual quotas or busing for integration in local public schools.

The bill and the amendments deserve each other. Neither has much relevance to good education; the bill is sponsored and backed by the Carter administration to pay off a political debt to the National Education Association, the country's largest teacher organization which has been pushing for a separate Department of Education for years and which may well be the dominant influence in the new department should the legislation pass. The amendments, at best, are gestures on highly emotional issues which cater to certain political groups without providing anything of legislative substance.

Yet in one respect the bill and the prayer amendment are different. While the bill is merely foolish and unnecessary — certainly not something that will create the efficiency promised or effectively reduce the enormous bureaucracy now housed within the combined Department of Health, Education and Welfare — the amendment once again caters to the idea that "voluntary" prayers can be conducted without violating either the Constitution or the religious beliefs of millions of children and their parents.

The fact is that there can be no such thing as a genuinely voluntary prayer in a setting in which attendance is required by law. Nor is there such a thing as freedom of religion — either for believers or nonbelievers — where the state writes, sponsors and leads the prayers.

While neither the future of the Republic nor the education of American children will be much affected by the fate of the Department of Education proposal, free religion, free expression, and the separation of church and state are jeopardized each time some house of Congress casually flirts with "voluntary prayers." The Department of Education proposal can be allowed to die a quiet death. Hopefully the prayer amendment, which must yet be approved by a Senate-House conference committee, will not die without some loud "amens."

Lincoln Journal
Lincoln, Neb., April 16, 1979

There remains in this country a hard core of opposition to the U.S. Supreme Court's laudable 1962 decision saying that denominational Bible readings in public school classes are unconstitutional.

The strength of opposition to the court's religiously-neutral holding was demonstrated again recently. The Senate voted, not once but twice, to forbid the Supreme Court from prohibiting denominational prayers in public schools. State courts would be able to do so, but not the federal bench.

The first time senators voted, they attached the court restriction on the bill creating a federal Department of Education, thereby making a bad proposition even worse. Subsequently, Senate leaders were able to slide the denominational praying-in-school rider off the education measure and on to a minor bill relating to the jurisdictional authority of the Supreme Court itself. At least it's germane there.

It is with no joy, but no real surprise, either, that one notes both Nebraska senators favor the return of organized religion in tax-chartered and tax-supported classrooms.

Maybe Sens. Zorinsky and Exon aren't even aware that the Nebraska Supreme Court outlawed denominational Bible reading in Nebraska public schools way back in 1902. And the holding was written by a chief justice named John J. Sullivan, no less.

Regardless of what the U.S. Supreme Court has said or ever may say, there is no possible way any government can prevent a student from silent prayer. That voluntary act is a demonstration of the divinely free mind, and commendable humility. We suspect many students, on their own, pray in schools today. So why all the fuss?

No, what the leaders of the Senate effort really want is restoration of some bleached, inoffensive forms of group denominational worship. Beside being coercively objectionable, that would be poor and pallid religion, a kind of prayer carefully and inoffensively addressed: To whom it may concern...

What more public schools could constructively do — and with the Supreme Court's approval, too — is teach **about** religion, and the driving force religion has played in shaping the history of humankind. That kind of classroom emphasis is badly lacking.

THE COMMERCIAL APPEAL
Memphis, Tenn., April 24, 1979

SOME TENNESSEE legislators always seem determined to prove they know more about the U.S. Constitution than does the U.S. Supreme Court.

There have been the moves to pass legislation to allow prayer in schools, to prohibit the teaching of the theory of evolution and to pass laws regarding obscenity.

Now a handful of Tennessee senators claims to know more than the court about the constitutionality of automatically exempting women from service on juries.

The Supreme Court decided that issue early in 1975 when it ruled on a Louisiana law similar to one which has been on the Tennessee books.

The court said such laws were unconstitutional because they deprived a criminal defendant of a trial by jury that is representative of the community.

But when Sen. James White (D-Memphis) sought to get a House-passed measure to wipe that law from the Tennessee statutes, he was able to muster only 8 of the needed 9 votes in the Senate Judiciary Committee on two tries, and on the third try got only 7 votes.

DON'T THOSE senators who opposed removal of this law read the newspapers to learn what the Supreme Court has said on the issue?

The state law already is being ignored in a number of counties, including Shelby, because of the overriding Supreme Court decision.

But the fact that the state law still is observed in the remaining counties opens the way for appeals of decisions in those counties that will unnecessarily burden the courts, to say nothing of the costs to the state and the defendants.

There is no evidence that submission to the Supreme Court decision has worked undue hardships on women in the counties where it has been accepted.

The Supreme Court after the Louisiana decision refused to accept a challenge of a Florida law which grants exemption from jury duty to pregnant women and mothers of children under 18, if they claim it, which surely takes care of whatever serious objections the Tennessee senators may have to calling women for jury duty.

THE OBLIGATION to serve on state juries can be reduced even more if counties will move into the progressive juror utilization and management programs which are beginning to catch on around the nation.

That system, which began in Houston in 1971, has been adopted in at least 18 states.

The new program, which provides for computerization of jury selection lists, reduces the number of citizens called for the jury panels at one time and drastically shortens the time a juror must serve on such panels. The system has been endorsed by the Law Enforcement Assistance Administration of the Justice Department, which is offering $1 million in grants to help establish it where it has not yet been adopted.

The system depends in part on wiping out almost all the existing exemptions from jury duty.

It's time Tennessee joined that movement, and wiping out the already overruled automatic exemption for women for jury duty would be a good place for the legislature to start.

TULSA WORLD

Tulsa, Okla., April 14, 1979

THE U. S. Senate resolution purporting to restore prayer in schools is probably harmless enough. Since Congress cannot repeal any part of the U. S. Constitution, it can be safely assumed that any such presumption by lawmakers will be thrown out quickly by the courts.

But it is troubling, nevertheless, that people who take their religion the most seriously cannot see the danger of turning public school classrooms into places of religious worship even in the most benign "non-denominational" way.

The truth is that religion taken seriously is not always "non-denominational."

There are many denominations and they all have different ideas about prayer.

No one argues that the nation could not be improved with some more attention to religious and spiritual matters. But religious evangelism, even in the form of "non-denominational" prayers, has no place in the public school systems.

Most religious people, while holding respect for the views of others, are not "non-denominational." Roman Catholics do not teach their children to pray in the same way as Baptists.

To suggest that these differences are unimportant and that everyone should agree on a "non-denominational" way of praying is another way of saying that religion itself is not very important.

Arkansas Gazette.

Little Rock, Ark., April 12, 1979

Some constitutional issues are long since settled, and clearly so, even with a changing Supreme Court. One of these has to be the old question of holding prayer in the public schools, a practice held unconstitutional in a decision that will stand undisturbed, surely, even if it should reach the court that has four justices "cloned in the image of Richard Nixon" (the line belongs to Robert Sherrill writing in the April issue of *Playboy*).

Not even the present Supreme Court, we dare say, would want to reopen the prayer case or the Bible-reading case and try to redefine the rule against imposing religious exercises on public education. The Court has all it can handle, Lord knows, since it tried to rewrite the rules governing what is obscene.

In the circumstances it is doubly unfortunate that the United States Senate has now dragged out the prayer issue, again, in an amendment purporting to restrict the jurisdiction of the federal courts over state laws sanctioning classroom prayers. The Senate has hooked the amendment on to a routine bill regarding court jurisdiction, while declining to put it on a bill to establish a federal Department of Education. The vote on the amendment was 51-40; in an earlier test vote, it was 47 to 37.

It is unfortunate that the Senate is wasting so much time on a spurious provision purporting to tell the United States Supreme Court where it can define a constitutional right, in this case the constitutional right to freedom from an "establishment of religion." Holding religious exercises in the tax-supported public schools is a purely classic illustration of the practices in an establishment of religion.

The amendment is an exercise in demagoguery sponsored, inevitably, by Senator Jesse Helms, the North Carolina Republican who has become probably the best known among the Senate's contemporary cave dwellers. Helms asserts that his amendment will "restore the right of voluntary prayer in public schools." The claim is false because the right of voluntary prayer has never been taken away; the courts have made it clear that the individual pupil may pray any time he chooses anywhere in school that he chooses. What the school, the teacher, the class majority, may *not* do is hold an organized prayer that might infringe upon the religious views of an individual in the class. President Carter framed the issue one day last week when he remarked that "prayer should be a private matter between a person and God," adding:

"There are constraints that are placed on students other than ordering a child to pray. If everyone else in the classroom is engaged in public prayer and doing it voluntarily, for a young seven or eight-year-old child to demand the right to leave the room is a difficult question to answer. But in general, I think the government ought to stay out of the prayer business...."

It was an eloquent statement from a man who, incidentally, is perhaps the most devout president the country has had in this century.

At best, the Helms amendment is meaningless and hypocritical; at worst, it is another effort to subvert the First Amendment to the Bill of Rights. It may never clear the House of Representatives; if it does, it may be riding a bill that the President can veto; and if it should become an act of Congress it would be without standing in the courts. It is unlikely that the Supreme Court would even receive the question on appeal. The amendment is vintage demagoguery.

There is one more point, which is distasteful to mention, but necessary. In the roll call, Senator David Pryor of Arkansas voted with Helms, while Senator Dale Bumpers, of course, voted against the amendment. You can count on Bumpers in matters of this kind, almost every time, but David Pryor is still throwing kisses to the peanut gallery after the pattern he set in last year's Democratic primaries. With his next election six years away, Pryor votes even now as if he were frightened of his shadow. It is a bad augury for Pryor's term, a sad business all around.

The Idaho STATESMAN

Boise, Idaho, April 12, 1979

Sen. Jesse Helms, R-N.C., must simply be spoiling for a good fight. Why else, with all the important issues facing this country, would the senator seek to take up Congress' time debating such a cockamamie, archaic, ill-advised, emotional scheme as getting prayer allowed in the public schools?

Helms' proposal is archaic and ill-advised because we are no longer a nation of homogeneous living groups. Perhaps at some point in our distant history, when almost every person in a community held to a common belief, prayer in the schools was an acceptable practice. Now, however, that condition of homogeneity no longer prevails. Almost every American community is a diverse collection of religious beliefs, including agnosticism and atheism, to which it would be impossible to speak in a common prayer. As a result, prayers acceptable to the majority would be imposed. But religion is not politics; individual choice rather than majority rule is the guiding principle. Each person must have the right to choose from or reject all religious persuasions.

Supporters of Helms' proposal argue that the prayer would be entirely voluntary. Right, voluntary, like Nurse Ratched's therapy was voluntary in *One Flew Over the Cuckoo's Nest.* "Now Johnny, you can either pray like any normal little boys or be a stupid, idiotic little twit, and we'll all laugh at you, right class? Now which will it be, Johnny?"

President Carter, himself no slouch when it comes to prayer, personally opposes the legislation on grounds that it would be difficult for a child to seek relief from prayer without being subjected to painful ostracism. Carter says, and we agree, that prayer is a personal matter, between oneself and his diety. To expect that prayer in the schools will either save the schools, as Helms suggests, or incite new interest in religion, is preposterous.

As Carter's remarks indicate, there is no need to worry about the Helms bill. In the unlikely event Congress should pass it, Carter will most certainly veto it. However, it remains unnerving and irritating that a member of Congress can demonstrate such dumbness as Helms has demonstrated with this proposal.

Moreover, although it seems to be accepted by Congress that Helms' legislation is legitimate, we fail to understand how Congress can, under our Constitution, take away the Supreme Court's jurisdiction over a constitutional question simply because the court's decisions in that area are not equally appreciated by all quarters. If Congress has this power, it would seem there is a sizable chink in our vaulted separation of powers doctrine, to which we hold with so much vigor as our best defense against the abuse of public power.

The late Sen. Everett Dirksen of Illinois similarly championed a constitutional amendment to allow prayer in the schools. In Dirksen's case, the crusade was the quaint, charming idiosyncrasy of an old man, much the same as Dirksen's perennial battle to have the Marigold named our national flower. Helms is not old, and his crusade is neither quaint nor charming; it's ridiculous, and the sooner it's laid to rest, the better.

"Voluntary" Prayers
Introduced in Schools

The Supreme Court struck down mandatory school prayers in 1963; as a result, supporters of prayer responded with legislation to require "voluntary" prayer sessions. The laws avoided direct conflict with the Supreme Court's ruling by specifying that students who did not wish to participate could leave the classrooms. In addition, no particular prayers were mentioned, in order to avoid the charge that the public schools were promoting a particular religion. The requirement of separate time for "voluntary" prayer existed in nine states as of 1980: Connecticut, Florida, Maryland, Massachusetts, Mississippi, Nevada, New Hampshire, New Jersey and Texas.

The Boston Globe
Boston, Mass., February 7, 1980

The first back-to-prayers days have come and gone and there has been no pandemonium in the corridors nor, apparently, much in the way of moral uplift, either. There had been some concern, before the new law took effect, that students who had dismissed themselves from their first period classrooms rather than participate in a voluntary prayer led by a classmate would be roaming the corridors unsupervised, getting into all the expected kinds of trouble.

We could have saved our concern, as apparently there have been few volunteer prayer leaders, at least at the high school and junior high school (for which read: "mischief-prone") level. It may be that no one knows any prayers anymore, that they have all been unlearned since the US Supreme Court ruled that mandatory prayer in the public schools was unconstitutional 10 years ago. But, as the new law reads, if there is no volunteer, there is no prayer, and thus everyone stays in his seat and skims through his homework, gets the day's gossip started, or does whatever else one does in homeroom these days.

The expected constitutional challenge to the new voluntary prayer law has been filed and there will be some fun days ahead for the lawyers. But so far, the best evaluation of the matter has come from a Barnstable High School student who said he felt that "if someone wants to pray, they should pray at home or go to church before they come to school. School is for learning, not prayer."

THE MILWAUKEE JOURNAL
Milwaukee, Wisc., March 17, 1980

The US Supreme Court, invoking the constitutional ban on official sanction of religion, struck down prayers in public schools years ago. But some politicians, often more concerned with posturing than with piety, keep trying to slip prayer back into the classroom.

"Not here," the Massachusetts Supreme Court has properly told state officials. The court has barred enforcement of a new state law that required teachers to ask if any student wished to lead a prayer. Students who did not wish to participate could be excused from the room.

Although state officials argued to the contrary, the Massachusetts high court found that the law was an example of state involvement in religion because it required the prayer as part of the daily opening exercises in schools, because the religious activity was conducted on public property during school hours, and because it was supervised by teachers, who are public employes.

If government is to respect freedom of conscience, as both the Constitution and the American ideal of liberty require, it cannot logically mandate religious ceremonies in school.

Moreover, a strong case can be made that compulsory religious exercise of the kind represented by mandatory prayers in schools is not even a valid expression of religion. It is doubtful that any depth of religious conviction is to be found in the rote exercise. Almost any prayer that would be offered would be meaningless to some students and offensive to others.

For the believer, religious expression — prayer, ritual or ceremony — is a manifestation of personal faith. The late US Supreme Court Justice Robert Jackson put it well when he wrote "It is possible to hold a faith with enough confidence to believe that what should be rendered to God does not need to be decided and collected by Caesar."

Thus, Massachusetts did religion no favor when it sought to impose a religious faith — even the faith of a single student in a public school classroom — on everyone. And the state breached the wall of separation between church and state. Such an infringement is unworthy of a state whose founders sought freedom to practice religion according to the dictates of conscience.

the Charleston Gazette

Charleston, W.Va., March 15, 1980

YET ANOTHER attempt to put a religious exercise in the public schools has been struck down by the courts. It is but a matter of time, of course, until yet another state legislature adopts yet another unconstitutional device for thrusting religion upon students and yet another court will strike it down.

The latest failure was in Massachusetts where, Thursday, the state Supreme Court ruled that a new state law reintroducing prayer in public schools violates First Amendment guarantees of a separate church and state.

The rejected statute called for teachers to ask if any student wished to lead a prayer and for the student then to lead the prayer. Provision was made for students not wishing to participate to leave the room.

It would be impossible for both sides of the school prayer issue to agree on a definition of "voluntary." Apparently the Massachusetts Supreme Court does not accept the state Legislature's definition in the case of a prayer solicited by a teacher on school time.

School prayer advocates know that students are perfectly free to pray individually and silently at their desks. The zealots insist upon some kind of organized prayer program not because the opportunity for individual prayer is limited but because of a desire to make religion a fixed part of public school instruction. Who has not heard "the Godless schools" disparaged? Who isn't familiar with the plea for instruction in religious — usually meaning Christian — morality in the schools?

We do not believe a school in which there are no religious exercises is a "Godless school" any more than we believe a food market in which there is no daily prayer is a "Godless store." Some day, perhaps, school prayer advocates will understand that separation of church and state does not mean an official stand against religion. On the contrary, separation strengthens the defenses of religion against state control.

Since state support is very likely to lead to state control, we are puzzled by a readiness to enforce religious belief with the power of the state. Such a readiness cheapens religion, suggesting that it cannot stand on its own. Compulsion is hardly the way to sustain faith.

The Idaho STATESMAN

Boise, Idaho, April 11, 1980

With all the stories that a teacher can read to her class, why has an Arkansas teacher persisted in reading *Bible* stories when it has been apparent for years that public schools and religion don't mix?

The parents of a 7-year-old Mountain View, Ark., boy have taken the local school district to court after school officials ignored their request that stories based on the *Bible* no longer be read in class. The school district's superintendent — who is the husband of the teacher who has been doing the readings — said the parents' request was an "intrusion" into the responsibilities of school officials.

But are school officials being responsible when they turn their backs on the explicit wording of the Bill of Rights and U.S. Supreme Court decisions that ban religious activities in the schools?

No one is arguing that young people may benefit from hearing the *Bible* stories. But, as the boy's mother and an attorney from the American Civil Liberties Union point out, such teachings are better handled by parents or church leaders, not teachers.

The federal judge hearing a lawsuit brought over the *Bible* readings has asked the lawyers in the case to file legal briefs within 10 days. The judge also has said she would read the book containing the *Bible* stories.

Reading the briefs and the book is fine, but all the judge really has to read is the First Amendent to the Constitution. The parents are obviously in the right.

Arkansas Gazette.

Little Rock, Ark., April 18, 1980

In 1963 the U. S. Supreme Court handed down its famous decision against Bible reading in the public schools. This decision, along with the one forbidding official prayers in the schools, established a proper delineation of the constitutional mandate for separation of church and state. If the point of constitutional law was settled 17 years ago, there are still school systems that disregard or try to circumvent the law, usually in the expectation that no one will challenge the school policy.

Now at Mountain View, Ark., a school policy allowing teachers to read Bible stories has been challenged forthrightly by the parents of a pupil in the Mountain View Elementary School. The issue has been taken into U. S. District Court at Little Rock and presented to U. S. Judge Elsijane Trimble Roy. The plaintiff's suit was filed by the American Civil Liberties Union, in its familiar role as guardian of constitutional right. It is not entirely clear whether the religious exercises at Mountain View now include the actual reading from the Bible as a religious exercise but the record does show that at least one teacher — the wife of the school superintendent — reads to her class twice a day from a "Children's Story Bible," which, of course, is derived directly from one or another version of the Bible itself. The preface to the book states that it is faithful to the Bible as the "inspired and infallible word of God."

It is also established that two lay evangelists of the North Arkansas Gospel Association visit the Mountain View School once a month and tell Bible stories in all five grades, the stories exemplifying the Christian way of life.

The full detail of religious exercises conducted in the Mountain View School may not have been developed in the one-day hearing in federal court, but we doubt that any further evidence is needed. It is clear that the School District is engaged in the most transparent attempt to get around the Supreme Court's decision. The plaintiffs happen to be Roman Catholics, and one would imagine that their own precepts of Christianity have been abraded by the interpretations advanced in the Children's book or in the appearances of the speakers for the gospel group, but the plaintiffs stipulate that what they oppose is the teaching of religion in the classroom.

Plainly, the Mountain View School District has been permitting, and encouraging, religious exercises in the school. The use of a children's Bible book instead of the Bible is the slenderest kind of screen for the practice. In the circumstances, we are somewhat puzzled by a remark of Judge Roy's in the courtroom that "restrictions on religious activities should be kept to a minimum." The question is not one of restricting religious activities in church, or any of the other places where they belong; the question is in restricting religious activities in the public schools in accordance with the order of the U. S. Supreme Court, which, in turn, is acting under the First Amendment's prohibition of an establishment of religion.

Judge Roy asked for briefs in 10 days and advised the Mountain View superintendent to draw up some guidelines on the use of religious materials. We should think that 10 days would be plenty of time to decide this one, and would not envy the district court that tried to support, at the appellate level, any decision except the obvious one.

THE ATLANTA CONSTITUTION
Atlanta, Ga., December 18, 1980

An eighth-grader at an Atlanta public school has complained that she and fellow pupils are forced each day to hold prayer sessions as part of their homeroom activities. The girl's parents and others in the community are demanding that it be halted -- and rightly so.

The 13-year-old says that the sessions take up about half the 20-minute homeroom period and consist of reciting Scripture, the Lord's Prayer and silent praying. The teacher then allegedly tells the pupils to turn to the next person and say, "Jesus loves you."

The girl's parents complain the school has done nothing about it and the American Civil Liberties Union has intervened, advising school officials of the constitutional provision of separation of church and state. The ACLU says, in its opinion, the practice is clearly unconstitutional.

Now, there will be those who will commend the teacher in question for taking matters into her own hands and teaching the youngsters scripture and prayer. These people will be those who consider themselves of the Christian faith. They should put themselves in the place of someone who doesn't share that faith.

How would they feel if forced to take part in activities related to someone else's religion?

How would they feel if forced to take part in activities related to someone else's religion?

The Founding Fathers were wise in establishing the doctrine of separation of church and state. They knew — sometimes from personal experience — of the kind of insensitive actions that grow out of trying to practice one's religion in a place not meant for such things, especially a place where one is required by law to be, such as a public school.

We certainly are proud of our heritage of freedom of religion, but we know that it means freedom to practice whatever religion we want to follow — or even no religion at all if that's our desire. Freedom of religion also means, therefore, freedom from religion.

There are numerous places of worship for one to go where religion can be practiced by those who share similar ideas and ideals. That and the home are the proper places for it.

The teen-ager who complained said the teacher badgered her if she didn't take part and recently told her she could leave the room during the service, thus singling her out in front of her peers. That's exactly why our nation has the separation doctrine. The girl's mother said she is a Christian but the activity is against the law and by violating the law, the teacher is not teaching children to respect it.

Religion in public schools is permitted when taught as history, and we think such courses taught by qualified instructors would go a long way toward helping us understand each other. But other religious activities are prohibited for very good reasons and the law should be upheld.

AKRON BEACON JOURNAL
Akron, Ohio, October 31, 1980

TIRESOME as most campaign rhetoric has become, the need of most representatives to go home and fight for re-election may have served the voters well in at least one respect.

It interrupted an attempt in the House to force to a floor vote still another in an 18-year-long list of school prayer proposals. And a bill that would have undermined the U. S. Supreme Court's 1962 ruling on school prayer is now not expected to be revived in this session of the Congress.

The bill in question, passed by the Senate last April, dealt with Supreme Court discretion over what cases it would hear. It became a very controversial issue after Sen. Jesse Helms, R-N. C., succeeded in adding an amendment that would bar the Supreme Court from reviewing any state law that related to voluntary prayer in public schools.

In effect, that would allow local communities or state boards of education or legislatures to draw up guidelines for prayer in public schools, perhaps even recommending the specific prayer to be used. And, as long as the proposals were upheld in state courts, they could not be challenged in federal courts, even though the Supreme Court in 1962 and 1963 specifically struck down state laws in New York and Pennsylvania regarding school prayer.

The word "voluntary" in the Helms amendment is a ploy that fools no one — not those who want formal prayer as a part of school day activities, and certainly not those who believe in separation of church and state.

Voluntary prayer has never been banned anywhere, and the Supreme Court couldn't ban it in schools even if it wanted to.

As the Rev. R. G. Puckett, executive director of Americans United for Separation of Church and State, testified, the court "never prohibited any child from praying at any time he or she chooses."

Mr. Puckett, a Southern Baptist, was joined by leaders of most major faiths and denominations, as well as a National Congress of Parents and Teachers' spokesman, in opposing the bill.

The fact that the school prayer amendment would violate the constitutional First Amendment right of freedom of religion is not the only argument against it, though that is reason enough to continue to fight back repeated challenges to religious freedom guarantees.

Perhaps an even stronger argument against Sen. Helms' maneuver to restore supervised prayer to the classroom is his effort to accomplish that by limiting the power of the Supreme Court to deal with a specific issue. If he were successful this time, it is frightening to contemplate what other civil right might be removed from court protection by legislative action.

Yet, the narrow-minded senator — who did not bother to attend hearings in a House subcommittee or testify on his own proposal despite an invitation to do so — vows that he will continue to submit similar proposals until one is passed. Apparently he is untroubled by the threat to individual freedom that is inherent in his "voluntary" proposal — a threat so well described by Richard Cohen of the Washington Post:

"The real problem with the bill is that word 'voluntary.' The notion is that a child can either pray or not pray. When the time comes for the prayer, that child, in his maturity and wisdom, is supposed to tell the teacher that even though the school wants him to pray (why else would everyone be doing it?) and all his classmates are praying, he will not.

"That kind of volunteerism makes for a 99 percent voter turnout in Russia."

Chicago Defender
Chicago, Ill., December 2, 1980

In 1962, the Supreme Court banned prayer and religious ceremonies in the public schools. The opinion rested on the ground that any such exercise in contravention of that view was clearly violative of a specific constitutional provision.

Pressures by a number of parents and religious zealots reached such a crescendo of emotional feelings that Congress felt obliged to submit the issue to legislative consideration and finality. That was the purpose of the constitutional amendment on school prayers which was defeated in the House.

The amendment backers pushed to allow school prayers reads: "Nothing contained in this constitution shall abridge the right of persons lawfully assembled in any public building which is supported in whole or in part through the expenditure of public funds to participate in non-denominational prayer."

Had the amendment passed, it would not only have been in contravention to a long-established constitutional principle, but also a dangerous repudiation of a judicial mandate, the end result of which would be a lessening of the influence and power of the U. S. Supreme Court. Such a precedent would threaten the whole fabric of our judicial system.

St. Petersburg Times

St. Petersburg, Fla., May 7, 1980

Something sad and shabby is happening in the Florida Legislature.

Shallow politicians are flailing the school-prayer issue again.

The combination is both unholy and unconstitutional.

But too few legislators seem to be decent or dutiful enough to put down this mischief and bigotry. The duty they shirk is the oath they all took to uphold the state and federal constitutions, which prohibit any law "respecting an establishment of religion."

THE SUPREME Court ruled almost two decades ago that this forbids forced prayer and Bible-reading in the public schools, no matter how "voluntary" or "nondenominational" such exercises purport to be.

Those were wise decisions. There is no possible official religious exercise that does not conflict with someone's right to hold different beliefs or no beliefs at all.

Allowing children to be excused is no remedy, because it forces them to display their differences and expose themselves to prejudice and harassment.

HISTORY overflows with cruel proof of the necessity to separate church and state. Ayatollah Khomei-

ni's tyranny over Iran is one vivid example.

The Inquisition burned Jews and heretics at the stake as an *auto-da-fe* — literally, "act of faith." Protestants and Catholics stained Europe with each other's blood.

Even in colonial America, religious freedom came late. Puritan Massachusetts hanged four Quakers. In Virginia, the penalty for breaking the sabbath three times was death. In the 1940s, mobs brutalized Jehovah's Witnesses for refusing, on religious principle, to salute the flag.

"A UNION of government and religion tends to destroy government and to degrade religion," said Justice Hugo Black, a devout churchman, in the 1962 school prayer case. He recalled James Madison's warning that " . . . It is proper to take alarm at the first experiment on our liberties."

Opportunistic politicians continue to exploit that decision for votes. Hearing them, one would think the court had also forbidden prayer in the home and in the family and in the church. What makes prayer in schools of such consuming importance? Is it the 20th century's *auto-da-fe?*

In Tallahassee this week, a House education committee voted 7 to 6 for a

bill requiring public schools to hold prayer sessions each morning. Student volunteers would lead the prayers — in whatever fashion they wish. No nonsectarianism complicates this bill.

ON MARCH 26, according to the committee staff, the Massachusetts Supreme Court declared a very similar law to be unconstitutional.

Rep. George F. Hieber II, R-St. Petersburg, voted for the Florida bill despite its equally glaring unconstitutionality.

The sponsor, Rep. Wayne Hollingsworth, D-Lake City, displayed his disdain for the minorities whom the prayers might offend. "If they don't want to be excused," he said, "they can stick their fingers in their ears."

Hollingsworth's mind is as narrow as his mouth is big. Decent people can only hope that enough other legislators will eventually remember their duty to kill his very bad bill.

Hollingsworth has another bill, an alternative, that would permit school boards to schedule up to two minutes of silent meditation at the outset of each day. This is inoffensive but also unnecessary. Many schools do this now. Why is it that the politicians don't tell you that?

The Dallas Morning News

Dallas, Texas, July 10, 1980

IN MANY ways, democracy is a dizzying high wire act. We've been tiptoeing along for 204 years now, balancing the public good with the private right. It's never easy.

In a case that has come up at Highland Park High School, the difficult question is: Should a small group of students be able to banish daily prayers at a school if most of the students wish to keep them?

On one side there are six students who argue that they are a "captive audience" for the daily devotionals read over the public address system. Although the prayers are not state-mandated, the protesting students argue that the prayers violate the separation of church and state. In effect, they argue their right not to have prayer in school is greater than the right of other students to have such devotionals.

The majority of the student body, on the other hand, has voted in favor of the devotionals, and the student council has endorsed the practice 86-6.

After hearing arguments from both sides, the Highland Park school board voted this week to continue the daily

prayers. The vote came after the school attorney reported he could find no U.S. Supreme Court rulings to indicate the program is unconstitutional, because the prayers are not state-mandated and participation is not required.

The dissenting students have indicated they are considering going to court against the school system. The irony is that the dissenters rejected a compromise whereby they would be allowed to leave the classrooms during the readings. They argue they do not wish to be "singled out" — and yet they themselves have earnestly sought to have their rights singled out and given priority above those of the majority of their classmates who want the prayers.

In recent years, we have increasingly seen organizations, groups — even the electorate itself — frustrated at every turn by something called "the minority veto." While it becomes easier and easier for one small faction or another to prevent the majority from doing anything, it becomes harder and harder to see evidence that the principle of majority rule still applies. And if majority rule does not work, democracy

does not work.

Checks and balances originally built into our system to prevent a majority from heedlessly steamrollering the rights of a minority have been turned around. Now almost any minority, no matter how small, can throw up one obstacle after another to block the majority from moving in any direction toward the goals on which it agrees.

Built-in protections meant to ensure due consideration for minority rights have too often been misused to produce the virtual paralysis of the majority. By constant threats and uses of the minority veto, various small interest groups have managed to impose in many constituencies what can accurately be called the tyranny of the minority.

And that, we should all keep in mind, is what the American Republic was supposedly designed to prevent.

Perhaps at Highland Park and elsewhere a gentle reminder is in order: The right to dissent is not the only democratic tradition. There's also the practice of compromise, which often protects the fine balance between public good and private right.

More States Join Drive to Enact "Voluntary" Prayer

Since the 1963 Supreme Court's ruling was decided on the basis of cases involving mandatory prayer, the move for "voluntary" prayer spread to many states. Legislation called for "meditation" periods, "voluntary prayer" periods or "a moment of silence," but it all had the same purpose: to reintroduce some kind of prayer into the school day without directly mentioning religion. Usually, the federal and appeals courts that heard objections ruled that there was a direct connection between the "voluntary" sessions and prayer.

Portland Press Herald

Portland, Maine, November 4, 1981

Those who would return prayers to the public schools never seem to tire in their efforts to elbow past the constitutional prohibition against such a policy.

Once again, legislation has been introduced in Augusta to establish a period of silence in the schools to be devoted to prayer or meditation by the students. The sponsor of the bill, Republican Sen. Thomas R. Perkins of Blue Hill, explains, "We're trying to get the religious concerns back in our lives at least in a reflective way."

But what the Perkins bill attempts to do is to raise those religious concerns in a legislative way, and that's where the proposal collides with constitutional guarantees of religious freedom.

There's nothing wrong with local school systems providing a period of silence for their students, so long as it is not specifically earmarked for prayer. In fact, several schools established just such a period a few years ago—Sanford is one example—following an opinion by then-Attorney General Joseph E. Brennan that it was legal.

Said Brennan: "In my opinion such a period of silence, not intended and not identified in any way as a religious exercise, would not offend the Establishment Clause of the federal Constitution."

But the Perkins bill would go considerably beyond that. It would make the period mandatory for all Maine schools, thus taking away the option of school boards to decide for themselves on the basis of local needs and desires. And it specificies that the period is to be devoted to "meditation or prayer," thus needlessly reopening the old church-state-separation controversy.

This bill is both undesirable and unnecessary. It deserves a quick, merciful death.

ALBUQUERQUE JOURNAL

Albuquerque, N.M., October 15, 1981

Let us all observe a moment of silent despair for all the public money, time and animosity about to be wasted in the Las Cruces Public School's attempt to back-door permissive prayer into public schools.

The Supreme Court of the United States has said unequivocally that such uses of public school and time violate the separation of church and state doctrine of the U.S. Constitution.

However, Rep. Randall Sabine, R-Dona Ana, a lawmaker but no lawyer, assured school officials "it was completely legal and wouldn't get us in trouble," according to a school spokesman.

It was Sabine who introduced a bill passed by the last Legislature that allows school districts to set aside up to one minute per day for " "contemplation, meditation or prayer."

The American Civil Liberties Union, which salivates like Pavlov's dog in a chime factory at the merest hint of church and state cohabitation, has risen to the bait. State ACLU officials say the Las Cruces school action will be challenged in court.

The utter absurdity of the whole affair is best brought into focus by considering what the "silent minute" will accomplish. Children of devout households will probably say a silent prayer during the minute. They probably used to say a prayer during math lecture anyway, if they felt the need.

Other children will use the minute to ridicule their companions obviously praying, shoot spitballs or rubber bands, compose an excuse for why their homework isn't completed, or flirt with the girl (boy) at the next desk.

It begs the question of the "silent minute's" constitutionality, but if school officials and community religious zealots were sincere, they could add the "silent minute" at the end of each school day, with children being given the option of remaining to celebrate it, or leaving.

But they won't, because central to the proponents of prayer in the schools is this idea that somehow they must impose their views on others.

The Constitution prohibits it. And after the spending of much time and money, both public and private, the fanning of much animosity, and the stirring of much disruption in the Las Cruces School System, the courts will so rule.

Men of true piety and conscience must bow their heads in despair of the pending strife in Las Cruces, launched in the name of prayer.

THE ANN ARBOR NEWS
Ann Arbor, Mich., July 15, 1981

WELL, not really. Prayer is back in the schools only in the sense that some people want to put it there.

Moral Majority types, mainly. And Rep. Ethel Terrell, a Highland Park Democrat who has introduced a bill in the Legislature to require public schools to provide time for prayer.

If Rep. Terrell is trying to create a more wholesome atmosphere and a better moral climate, fine. Worthy goals.

But she should know the law of the land bans mandatory prayers in public schools.

And the Constitution is simplicity itself: "Congress shall make no law respecting an establishment of religion, or prohibiting the free exercise thereof."

THE SUPREME COURT decision in 1962 is one that is persistently misunderstood.

The Court did not decide against prayers. The Court did say that the appearance of sponsoring prayer in state-run schools violated the separation of church and state.

Set-aside time in public schools for silent religious meditation is a questionable enough practice; Rep. Terrell's bill goes significantly farther.

Her bill requires schools to provide non-instructional time for voluntary prayer or silent meditation.

Don't be taken in by that word voluntary. The language of the bill taken in entirety is flat-out state sanction of religion. How can it be read any other way?

As such, the prayer bill is clearly unconstitutional. The courts would throw it out.

But will legislators pass the law (and the buck) anyway and let the courts do the dirty work?

No one wants to appear to be against prayer, let alone children at prayer. That may be too powerful an issue for legislators, however, especially those fearful of making Moral Majority hit lists.

AS PRIVATE and personal as prayer is, any attempt to institutionalize it in the schools by government should be resisted.

Religious tolerance and the separation of church and state have taken this country a long way.

The appropriate place for prayer is outside the area of state influence. If certain groups still want to incorporate prayer into the likes of public classrooms, they can seek to amend the Constitution.

Roanoke Times & World-News
Roanoke, Va., June 8, 1981

Giles County children will be allowed to receive religious instruction, the School Board there has agreed, but not on school property. The move is a good one. School officials had rightly been concerned about the constitutionality of a previous program conducted in the classrooms. Under the new setup, expected to pass constitutional muster, those who wish will again be able to learn more about a subject indisputably important in American life.

To hear some people tell it, you'd think almost every problem in the country is attributable to a couple of Supreme Court decisions in the early '60s. In one, *Engel v. Vitale,* the court ruled that the New York State Board of Regents had no business composing an official prayer for recommended daily use in the public schools. A little later, in *Murray v. Curlett* and *Abington School District v. Schemp,* the court ruled that Maryland and Pennsylvania had no business requiring public school students to begin the day with classroom Bible-reading or recitation of the Lord's Prayer.

The decisions did not prohibit instruction about religion in the public schools. In one opinion, the court noted pointedly that the study of Bible or religion, "when presented objectively as part of a secular program of education," was not being declared unconstitutional. The option to offer such a program was available to Giles officials; instead, they elected to go with a more sectarian program that must be offered away from the schools.

Since the landmark cases of the '60s, some members of Congress have sought, so far unsuccessfully, to undercut the rulings. For a while, proposals to amend the Constitution were in vogue. More recently, Sen. Jesse Helms of North Carolina has pushed for legislation to bar the federal courts from hearing challenges to state laws that provide for "voluntary prayers" in public schools.

The issue remains alive partly because the questions involved can be rather close. Exactly where, for instance, is the line between government establishment of religion and government interference with its free exercise, both of which are prohibited by the First Amendment? At exactly what point does objective religious or moral instruction shade off into the propagation of religion?

Wisely, the courts have tended to take a common-sense, empirical approach in their answers. A state-sponsored moment of meditation carries coercive overtones for a 6-year-old child that it doesn't for an adult. The Ten Commandments cannot be posted on Kentucky school walls because the first four, after all, promulgate specific religious doctrines rather than general ethical principles. Public schools can allow students to attend voluntary programs of sectarian religious instruction away from the school grounds, as Giles County has chosen to do, but cannot rent out school property for that purpose.

Drawing such fine lines is sometimes criticized on the ground that it trivializes religion or, in the words of an editorial several months ago in *The Wall Street Journal,* "reduc(es) it to the level of historical artifact." But the greater risk of trivialization lies in not drawing the lines. What is blander, and thus more offensive to many believers, than a state-composed prayer designed so as to offend nobody?

Reasonable men may differ as to where the line of constitutionally permissible practices should be drawn. But it *has* been drawn, by courts charged with the difficult task of interpreting and upholding the Constitution. The apparent ability of Giles County to adhere to the law without giving up religious instructions suggests that the line is not impossible to find. It also raises questions about the real motives of politicians like Helms in keeping the issue alive.

AKRON BEACON JOURNAL
Akron, Ohio, May 21, 1981

THE AKRON school board faces a difficult issue in trying to decide whether the public schools should be used as places of worship and religious training. They are intended, by law and public policy, to be schools, not churches. They should remain schools, not churches.

In addressing this question, the school board will best serve the entire community and all its students of varying religious faiths and denominations if it proceeds with great caution. The board and its administrative staff have done so thus far.

The board has heard, at its public hearing Monday night, from sincere people on both sides of this question. Witness, for example, the fact that the leading spokesmen on each side were both well-known and well-respected ministers in this community.

The Rev. Charles Billington, pastor of the Akron Baptist Temple, urged the school board to allow students to conduct voluntary prayer and religious sessions during non-class hours in public school buildings.

Dr. Gordon McKeeman, pastor of the Unitarian-Universalist Church, urged board members not to permit such use of the schools, pointing out that "the use of public property for religion is financial assistance for religion."

Not at issue in these discussions was whether the schools should impose sanctioned religion and prayer on students during regular classes. The U. S. Supreme Court addressed that issue in 1962 when it ruled that state-prescribed prayers in the public schools violate the principles of the U. S. Constitution that give Americans the freedom to worship but protect them from any state-ordered religion.

The current debate in the Akron school system is an offshoot of that proper and often misunderstood court ruling.

The court said that any school student was free to worship, especially to utter a silent prayer in school. It said the schools should not and cannot lawfully be used for specific religious purposes.

Since then, the court has ruled on a variety of proposals and policies, all intended in one form or another to circumvent its original ruling.

Many religious leaders have consistently supported the court's rulings. The General Board of the American Baptists has reaffirmed "our historic Baptist belief that religion should not be mandated and that religious practices should not be established or prescribed by law or by public policy or officials."

The Southern Baptist Convention has recorded its "opposition to attempts, either by law or other means, to circumvent the Supreme Court's decisions forbidding government-authorized or sponsored religious exercises in public schools."

The Union of American Hebrew Congregations has said, "The public school does not provide the proper atmosphere for religious devotion. True understanding and acceptance of prayer cannot occur in this secularized environment." And the General Assembly of the United Presbyterian Church in the U. S. A. has urged that "religious observances never be held in a public school (because) Bible-reading and prayers as devotional acts tend toward indoctrination or meaningless ritual and should be omitted for both reasons."

The proposal before the school board to permit voluntary religious meetings in the schools would open the door to the dangers cited by these and many other religious groups. Under such a program, at what point does a school cease being a school and become a church, supported directly by tax dollars, and promoted for a particular religious faith and its spokesmen? What if all religious faiths in an area sought to use the schools — public property — under such a policy? Which would be permitted and which would be denied on the basis of cost, the religious beliefs of school board members, or the fervor and clout of those seeking to use the schools?

The proposal raised before the school board is fraught with such questions and potential dangers. in addition, the board has the strong advice of its own lawyers that such use of the schools would not be legally proper.

Finally, it was significant that the placards carried by well-meaning supporters of such use of the schools said, "LET US READ OUR BIBLE!" and "LET US PRAY!" Significant because no one is suggesting or should suggest that anyone be denied such rights. Churches and individual personal places of worship abound in American society and in this community. To assure religious liberty for all and for all time, those are the best and most legally appropriate places for Bible-reading and prayer — not the public schools, which must remain free from any vestige of a state-ordered or state-sanctioned semblance of religion.

Minneapolis Tribune
Minneapolis, Minn., June 19, 1981

In 1977, the Minnesota State Board of Education adopted a policy on religion in the public schools. The First Amendment requires schools to avoid either promoting or disparaging any religion, the policy declared. Public-school education and religious programs and practices "shall be kept separate." Few have quarreled with the spirit behind that policy, but schools have had occasional trouble putting it into practice. Where should the line of separation be drawn? What is permitted, and what is not?

The result has been controversy: over prayers at official school events, for instance; over Christmas programs; over participation by school organizations in religious ceremonies. Last week, for the first time, the board provided some clear answers, which should help end such controversies — and make the 1977 policy statement a reality throughout Minnesota. The answers came from a task force appointed in February to develop guidelines for teaching about religiously sensitive issues in all curriculum areas and for resolving conflicts over school-wide customs and practices. It was a broad-based group, whose membership included First Amendment purists like Matthew Stark of the Minnesota Civil Liberties Union and religious educators like the Rt. Rev. James Habiger of the Minnesota Catholic Conference.

The group's agreement on guidelines is significant because it tells school districts throughout the state specific things they should do — and not do — to protect the right of all students, parents and teachers to be free from an imposed religion, and to be free to hold diverse beliefs. The guidelines do not ban religion from the schools. On the contrary, they recognize the need for teaching about religion.

Religions have been an important part of human culture throughout history, the task force noted, and no one's education can be complete without an understanding of these beliefs. Moreover, such teaching can foster understanding and respect for all forms of belief.

But the guidelines draw a sharp, and necessary, distinction between teaching *about* religion and teaching religion. Teaching about religion involves no proselytizing; such an approach, the task force said, "does not give preferential or derogatory treatment to religions in general or to any single religion, and . . . does not constitute a religious practice." Thus a school may "expose students to all religious views, but may not impose any particular view"; it should "study what all people believe, but should not teach a pupil what he should believe."

What constitutes the improper promotion of religion? The guidelines list specific practices to avoid. For example, schools must avoid indoctrination in any religion, whether that religion is Christianity or Judaism — or agnosticism, humanism, yoga or transcendental meditation. They may not incorporate religious worship into school-sponsored programs — like including prayers in graduation ceremonies. They may not permit official school musical groups to take part in religious services under the school's auspices.

Such guidelines, zealously observed by all school districts, should help assure that all Minnesota students learn to recognize the important contributions religious faith has made, and continues to make, to human culture. Equally important, they should assure that no student's right to belief — or nonbelief — is violated by a public school.

Senate Passes Amendment Endorsing School Prayer

In a highly emotional debate, the Senate Nov. 16 passed a resolution prohibiting the Justice Department from blocking voluntary prayers in public schools. The resolution was in the form of an amendment to the appropriations bill funding the Justice, State and Commerce departments for the 1982 fiscal year. It had been passed by the House as well, but its effect was unclear, since the Justice Department was not currently involved in any lawsuits concerning school prayer. However, Sen. Lowell Weicker (R, Conn.), who led the fight against it, warned that its passage would "send a signal" that voluntary prayer was permitted. He denounced the amendment as an "outrageous, unconstitutional action" and threatened to lead a filibuster against it. (The issue was defused after President Ronald Reagan vetoed the entire appropriations bill seven days later.)

At one point during the debate, Sen. Ernest Hollings (D, S.C.), a supporter of the amendment, referred to an opponent, Sen. Howard Metzenbaum (D, Ohio), as "the senator from B'nai B'rith," a Jewish social service organization. In the uproar that followed, Metzenbaum, who was Jewish, replied "in sadness and embarrassment" that Hollings' comment was "in bad taste." Hollings immediately apologized, saying he had "said it in a moment of levity. . . . I had no intention to make fun of his religion." Metzenbaum accepted Hollings' apology and called the matter "closed." Weicker remarked that the incident "makes us all understand why religion should not be debated on this floor."

ARKANSAS DEMOCRAT
Little Rock, Ark., November 20, 1981

Sens. Dale Bumpers and David Pryor both voted earlier this week against a bill providing for voluntary prayer in public schools. Unconstitutional, they said. But the bill passed the Senate overwhelmingly – as it had the House. Now, Sen. Lowell Weicker of Connecticut says he'll filibuster to keep it from going to President Reagan. Will our senators join him?

Not if they rethink the meaning of the First Amendment's guarantee of the "free exercise" of religion. Yes, the Supreme Court outlawed school prayer in 1962 – but only when it is specified by state law or conducted by a teacher on his or her own. The ruling was proper. But voluntary prayer doesn't "mix church and state" – even if schools set a time for it.

We need a broader understanding that the Constitution's first guarantee is of the "free exercise" of religion. Not only does the Constitution order government not to interfere with religion – it also tells it not to try to set up an official religion and make people adhere to it.

Somehow, the courts have extended that ban on official religion (aimed only at broadening religious freedom) to impose a whole array of piddling no-nos on any contact between government and religion – such as forbidding the building of creches on the grounds of public buildings and even disallowing prayer on the campus of a state university.

It all comes to constitutional know-nothingism and denial of free exercise of religion. But since it's federal court doctrine, it's no wonder that many people believe that religion and government mustn't touch at any point – though they obviously do.

However, it's a mistake to assume that voluntary school prayer is automatically to be lumped in with the ban on official prayers as just more unconstitutionality. Why deal another mistaken blow to the free exercise of religion? Let the prayer bill pass into law – and give the Supreme Court an opportunity to show whether, this time at least, it can read the heart of the First Amendment's religion clause the way the Framers meant it to be read.

St. Louis Globe-Democrat
St. Louis, Mo., November 18, 1981

Sen. Ernest F. Hollings, D-S.C., an advocate of prayer in public schools, displayed something less than Christian courtesy in referring to Sen. Howard M. Metzenbaum, D-Ohio, an opponent, as "the senator from B'Nai B'rith."

Hollings apologized later, saying his remark was meant "only in fun" during the heat of debate.

Hollings may be the best judge of what motivated his original remark, but an apology sincerely offered ought to be accepted.

Equally regrettable is the effort by the pro-prayer group to attach their pet project to an appropriations bill.

Controversial issues ought to be decided on their own merits, and not through the subterfuge of attaching them to money bills.

Prayer in public schools is an issue on which citizens in good conscience are divided. The nation is ill-served when parliamentary devices are used to gain an advantage in a matter such as this.

The effort to tie prayer to appropriations is just as much out of place as was Senator Hollings' tasteless remark.

THE MILWAUKEE JOURNAL
Milwaukee, Wisc., November 16, 1981

Freedom of religion is one of the most treasured of American liberties, yet some devout people have trouble understanding that it is a two-way street. While they are glad that the government does not interfere with their own private beliefs, they do not mind if the government helps impose their beliefs on others.

Throughout much of the nation's history, public school classrooms were used for the promulgation of religion — through prayer and Bible reading. Granted, it was usually a sort of homogenized Protestantism, not a narrow denominational variety, but it was religion nonetheless. And it was an infringement on the freedom of persons who held other beliefs or were nonbelievers.

Against that background, the US Supreme Court wisely ruled in 1962 that state officials could not require that any official prayer be recited in public schools. Since then, politicians have made repeated efforts to reverse, weaken or somehow circumvent the court decision. They are at it again.

The House and the Senate, in their present session, seem determined to pass a measure that would forbid the Justice Department to "prevent the implementation of voluntary prayer and meditation in the public schools."

On the surface, the measure may seem meaningless. Truly voluntary prayer or meditation obviously cannot be "implemented" by anyone except the worshiper and certainly cannot be prevented by the Justice Department. In fact, the department has had virtually no role in the challenging of prescribed prayer. Still, the legislation would encourage those state officials and school personnel who would like to restore prescribed school prayer in the guise of volunteerism.

Sen. Lowell Weicker (R-Conn.) is threatening a filibuster to block final passage of the measure. Although we deplore the filibuster as a means of thwarting majority rule, we hope the lawmakers will abandon the unwise proposal.

THE TENNESSEAN
Nashville, Tenn., November 23, 1981

THE Senate of the United States has pride in being called the greatest deliberative body and its unwritten rule is that of having great courtesy to one another no matter how heated the "deliberations" become. There are exceptions.

The fight over one of the New Right's pet issues — school prayer — provoked an uproar last Monday when Sen. Ernest Hollings, D-S.C., an advocate of school prayer, referred to opponent Sen. Howard Metzenbaum, D-Ohio, as "the senator from B'nai B'rith." B'nai B'rith is a U.S.-based Jewish social service organization.

Senator Metzenbaum, who is Jewish, said he was filled with "sadness and embarrassment" at the "bad taste" remark. Senator Hollins apologized, saying he was speaking "only in fun" and in the heat of debate. It was tasteless, even "in fun."

It makes one wonder how some of the "distinguished gentlemen" can argue so vociferously over the issue of prayer, an act of humility and supplication, and so easily forget for what and why it is done.

the Charleston Gazette
Charleston, W. Va., November 26, 1981

FREEDOM of religion is a cherished fruit of American democracy, yet, paradoxically, its greatest threat comes from the devout. These well-meaning people assume that their faith will flourish in partnership with government. History teaches us that religion flourishes on its own merits.

Even benevolent government is constrained to discipline whatever comes under its control. In ages past, religions which sought the support of the state invariably became the handmaidens of the state. This should give pause to those who believe, for instance, that prayer in public school would always be the prayer *they* prefer.

No matter how you slice it, to demand prayer in the public schools is to demand government support of religion — prohibited by a First Amendment intended as a rule for avoiding the bloody strife of centuries past. In spite of the warnings of history, however, another effort has been mounted to fuzz the distinction between religion and government.

A prayer-in-school measure recently passed by the Senate seems innocuous. Like all the other prayer bills, it conspicuously contains the word "voluntary." But its sponsors obviously do not mean voluntary prayer in the sense that we understand it and which already is permissible in the classroom — that is, prayers murmured spontaneously by individuals.

When classroom prayer advocates say "voluntary" they mean formal religious exercises attended on a voluntary basis. The Supreme Court has struck down several state laws aimed at this objective, and it should be clear that such an approach violates the constitutional prohibition. Still, congressmen, with the hot breath of constituents on their necks, contrive to resurrect just such exercises.

Some congressmen can be counted on to pander to the more popular prejudice when a fierce, emotional issue presents itself. That is why we commend Sen. Robert C. Byrd and Sen. Jennings Randolph for their votes to table the school prayer measure. Their votes were not anti-religion, but votes against a threat to religion.

The Kansas City Times
Kansas City, Mo., November 18, 1981

The matter of religion in the classroom has come to a crossroads of decision with the action in the U.S. Senate. Tagging along with the House, the Senate took the wrong road, formally endorsing voluntary prayer in public schools. Dismay at congressional direction is not opposition to prayer, but protest at government intrusion into an area traditionally and purposefully private, by law and practice. Properly so.

Without going into the Senate's coercive strategem of wedding the policy to Justice Department funding, the endorsement in an amendment is bad as a symbol, bad as a loophole that thwarts Supreme Court decisions prohibiting organized worship in public schools and alarming in its potential for destroying constitutional guarantees of religious freedom. That privilege, some seem to forget, includes both the right to choose among religions and expressions of such affiliation and the right to choose none. In specifically barring government from establishment of religions, the Constitution's framers wisely reserved all related decisions to the individual. Congress now seeks to usurp that power.

Parents are quite fit to mold the spiritual lives of their children including whether to pray, how to pray, when and where. It is not the business of politicians to supplant them, by adding the job to the duties of teachers whose beliefs or lack of them may contradict the faith and customs of the family. At the very least, it will encourage some teachers to flout the law. It is going on now, even with strict regulations to prevent it. No imagination is needed to envision what can happen if Congress gives its tacit approval.

Denying such intervention by pointing to its purported "voluntary" nature is pure hypocrisy. Adults play with such distinctions as "voluntary." Most children cannot.

The hope that this start down a dangerous path can be stopped short lies in the integrity and courageous stand of leaders like Missouri Sen. John Danforth who voted against the amendment, Sen. Thomas F. Eagleton who in the past has been opposed to similar proposals, and Sen. Lowell P. Weicker Jr. of Connecticut who vowed to lead a filibuster against the bill. The day it passes is a day Americans will look back on in shame.

THE CHRISTIAN SCIENCE MONITOR
Boston, Mass., November 18, 1981

Children's prayers are too important to become a political football. Not that legislators cannot legitimately challenge the federal and state court rulings against prayer programs in the public schools through the constitutional amendment process. Yet there are continuing congressional efforts to weaken the separation of church and state by means short of that process.

In the latest development the Senate has now joined the House of Representatives in tacking a school prayer amendment onto an appropriations bill. It is a largely symbolic step. It prohibits the Justice Department's use of federal funds to prevent the implementation of programs of voluntary prayer — which the department has not been doing anyway. But the amendment could encourage states to try more of the "voluntary" prayer programs that so far have been found unconstitutional in line with the Supreme Court's 1962 ruling against government-sponsored devotions in the schools. Senator Weicker promises a filibuster against the measure, and its demise would be welcome.

The senator's own defeated alternative amendment would have been an improvement. It would have banned Justice Department action only against "constitutional programs," in effect reaffirming the status quo.

But no new law is necessary to protect the right to genuine voluntary prayer — the prayer between an individual and God. This individual voluntary prayer has been ruled constitutional. Even if it had not, no government could invade the realm of thought in which prayer can be invoked to meet every human need, whether learning math or solving any other problem.

Here is where it is so essential to honor the diversity of America, ensuring each child's freedom from official pressures against the individual practice and belief fostered by home and religion. Such pressures could be heightened by school prayer programs, however "voluntary." These also risk the promotion of some generalized and diluted sort of civil religion, chipping away once again at that wall between church and state which is so necessary to America's precious religious liberty. Thus each stand for this constitutional principle must be applauded, whether by a senator now, or the Massachusetts court that held the line last year, or voices in the future contending with what appears to be a growing tendency in the other direction.

The Evening Bulletin

Philadelphia, Pa., November 19, 1981

You may have thought that issue of prayers in public schools was settled in 1962. The Supreme Court ruled then that prayers in schools violated the Constitution's First Amendment separation of church and state. But the U.S. Senate is now trying an end run around that ruling.

That's the first thing wrong with its action — bad method. It was an amendment, barring the Justice Department from using federal funds to halt programs of voluntary prayer in the public schools, tacked onto an appropriations bill.

Supreme Court interpretations of the Constitution should not be changed by majority votes of Congress. If Sen. Jesse Helms and his allies are serious, let them go for a constitutional amendment. They ought to have the guts to let their proposal be tested in that tough forum, not this quicky vote.

But that's only the start of what is wrong with this amendment:

□ If it became law, it could force Justice Department officials to violate their oath of office to uphold the Constitution. They would be asked to ignore violations of Supreme Court rulings.

□ The amendment has a secret agenda. Individuals, not the government, now bring almost all school-prayer suits. So the amendment would have little immediate impact. Its backers hope passage would deliver a message that would encourage organized worship in public schools.

□ With the country skidding into a deep recession, Congress ought to have better things to do than trying to set itself up as a second Supreme Court.

□ Debates of this kind can degenerate into the kind of tawdry slur Sen. Ernest Hollings got off the other day in calling Sen. Howard Metzenbaum "the senator from B'nai B'rith." Hollings's apology does not mask his mindset.

Sen. Lowell Weicker has pledged a filibuster to block the bill. We're not a filibuster fan, but we wish him strong voice.

The Cleveland Press

Cleveland, Ohio, November 29, 1981

It has been 18 years since the Supreme Court ruled that state-mandated prayers and other religious exercises in the public schools violated the Constitution's prohibition against an "establishment of religion."

The decision has long since been accepted, and supported, by such prestigious bodies as the National Council of Churches and by numerous religious groups of all faiths.

Yet Congress, almost every session, entertains measures designed to circumvent the ruling, usually by a constitutional amendment or by limiting the court's jurisdiction.

Just the other day, though, with much more pressing matters to attend to, the Senate found time to stage a heated and silly debate over a proposed amendment to an appropriations bill that would bar the Justice Department from interfering with "programs of voluntary prayer and meditation in the public school."

The amendment, or a similar measure passed by the House, would have little practical effect, since the Justice Department has had almost nothing to do with enforcing the 1963 decision. Most cases have been brought by private individuals.

But the school-prayer issue is bitterly divisive and wholly unnecessary. It would be unfortunate if Congress were to encourage those groups, chiefly fundamentalist, who continue to make it an issue.

There is nothing "voluntary" about formal, scheduled prayers in the classroom under any guise we have seen tried in the past 18 years, no matter how neutralized and generalized the prayer formula. Even when nonparticipating students are excused, they are marked out and set apart from their fellow students.

Truly voluntary prayer is and always has been constitutionally protected, in houses of worship, in other places and gatherings not supported by public funds, in the private heart — and in the home, where faith and morality are best taught and learned.

Maine Sunday Telegram

Portland, Maine, November 22, 1981

□ When, in 1830, the news reached Andrew Jackson that the Supreme Court had struck down as unconstitutional a state law which the president supported, Jackson is reputed to have said: "John Marshall has made his decision, now let him enforce it."

Today, Congress seems intent on taking Jackson's dictum one step further. Unwilling to accept a Supreme Court decision forbidding official prayers in public schools and unable to amend the Constitution, some members of Congress want to prevent the Justice Department from enforcing the law of the land.

The Senate last week approved an amendment (opposed by both Sens. William S. Cohen and George J. Mitchell) prohibiting the Justice Department from using federal money to "prevent the implementation of programs of voluntary prayer and meditation in the public schools."

It is doubtful that the proviso could stand a constitutional test. It is unlikely any court would hold the legislative branch could legally deny the right of the executive department to uphold the First Amendment.

Apologists for the measure defend it by saying the Justice Department has played virtually no role in the area of school prayer, since most cases have been brought by individuals.

That sort of pernicious reasoning worse than none at all. If Congress believes it has the power to forbid the Justice Department from defending the First Amendment, what is to prevent it from forbidding the enforcement of, say, the 14th Amendment in civil rights cases? Plainly, nothing at all.

The 1962 Supreme Court decision, which struck down an "official" prayer used in New York state schools by students on a voluntary basis, remains as right as it is controversial. Such prayers, wrote the late Justice Hugo L. Black constitute a religious activity barred by the constitutional clause forbidding the establishment of religion by the government.

That First Amendment clause, Black wrote, expresses the principle that "religion is too personal, too sacred, too holy, to permit its 'unhallowed' perversion' by a civil magistrate."

The state, under the Constitution, has absolutely no role to play in the establishment of a religion, particularly prayers composed by agents of the state as part of a governmental program to further religious beliefs.

Opponents of the court's sensible decision have never understood that the decision was not hostile to religion but rather designed to assure governmental neutrality towards all religions. In attempting to bar the Justice Department from upholding the law, the Congress indicates it understands neither the decision nor the Constitution.

FORT WORTH STAR-TELEGRAM

Fort Worth, Texas, November 20, 1981

Sen. Jesse Helms, R-N.C., said in the U.S. Senate the other day that the courts in ruling on cases involving prayer in schools were "meddling in something that was never their business in the first place."

Amen, Sen. Helms. And the Congress, too, is meddling in something that was never its business — prayer. Helms had been addressing his colleagues in regard to an amendment attached to an appropriation bill for the departments of State, Justice and Commerce. The amendment prevents the Justice Department from using funds to prevent the implementation of programs of voluntary prayer and meditation in public schools.

Religion cannot and should not be legislated. The courts must become involved in school prayer issues simply because there are some who cannot understand that religious freedom means not only that individuals are free not only to worship as they please but to not worship, or pray, at all if they so choose.

Religious freedom does not give a person or group the right to impose prayer or meditation upon those who do not wish to participate. Prayer is a private matter between the person who prays and the god to whom he prays.

The public schools are for learning and they are supported by taxpayers of all faiths and those of no faith. If a student chooses to pray in school, he or she can do so without involving the remainder of the student body. A prayer, of any sort, should not be part of the public school program.

Schools are for education and they would do a better job of that if congressmen and others would cease involving them in matters of non-education.

"Sex education belongs in the HOME--a little RELIGION, however...."

Newsday

Long Island, N.Y., November 20, 1981

Constitutional issues aside, one of the worst features of the school prayer debate is the nastiness it brings out in people.

It seems unnecessarily snide, for example, for one member of the Senate to call another "the senator from B'nai B'rith" for defending the 1962 Supreme Court ruling that organized prayer in the public schools is unconstitutional. Of course, people have been called worse: B'nai B'rith is a respected Jewish service organization, the parent body of the Anti-Defamation League.

The name-caller was Sen. Ernest Hollings (D-S.C.), who was on the winning side of a largely symbolic Senate vote amending an appropriations bill to prohibit Justice Department lawyers from opposing reinstatement of voluntary prayer in public schools.

The amendment had been adopted previously by the House. Its practical effect is slight because almost all challenges to prayer in public schools come from private organizations and individuals rather than the federal government.

But as both supporters and opponents of the measure know, its enactment into law would send a message—the wrong one, in our view—that local school districts have little to fear if they go ahead with prayer programs.

The attempt to bring back school prayer doubtless will go on; there's no denying widespread sentiment for overturning the Supreme Court's prohibition. Whether authentic religious concerns would thereby be satisfied is doubtful, for there are such easy remedies available to those who want their children to pray: The nation's houses of worship—and its homes—provide far more appropriate opportunity for religious activity.

The Burlington Free Press

Burlington, Vt., November 18, 1981

Senate approval of voluntary prayer in the public schools not only represents a victory for a coalition of fundamentalist ministers and congressional conservatives but also an attempt to undermine the Constitution by blocking the Justice Department from challenging programs of voluntary prayer or meditation in the schools.

The legislation would effectively take the Supreme Court out of the issue by creating immunity for schools that permit it. Thus Congress has crossed the fine line that separates the legislative and judicial branches of government and cast a cloud over the court's function as the arbiter of constitutional issues. Lawmakers have in effect reversed the court's 1962 decision that outlawed prayer in the public schools on the grounds that it violates the constitutional provisions on separation of church and state.

Supported by Sen. Jesse Helms, R-N.C., the powerful leader of the coalition, the provision was included in an $8.6 billion appropriations bill for the State, Justice and Commerce departments. Opponents have vowed to block the passage of the bill by the Senate until new language is incorporated in the measure that would hold to the 1962 court decision. Their chances of staving off passage seem to be slim indeed on the basis of Senate votes on the issue.

What is most alarming about the Senate action is that it sets a dangerous precedent for overturning court decisions on other controversial issues such as abortion and school busing. Congress thus becomes the interpreter of constitutional law by fiat. And the courts no longer function as the repositories of the law and the shapers of its meaning. Congressional interference with the Constitution can mean that the courts are rendered impotent.

While many people in the nation may support the idea of prayer in the public schools, the constitutional strictures against the mingling of the interests of church and state must be observed as interpreted by the Supreme Court.

The Constitution cannot be dismantled simply because it does not suit the purposes of one or another special interest group.

Detroit Free Press
Detroit, Mich.,
November 19, 1981

THE SCHOOL prayer bill, which is introduced regularly in Lansing to save us all from moral decline, might be dismissed as hopelessly irrelevant to Michigan's real problems were it not for the intrusion it threatens on privacy and religious freedom. After all, the rationale behind the bill — that prayer in the public schools will elevate our moral tone, rescue the American family and save the nation from Darwin and communism — falls somewhere between wishful thinking and pious fraud, as most lawmakers would admit if they knew the Moral Majority wasn't listening.

But prayer is too personal and religion too important for the Legislature and local school boards to intrude on. The relationship between human beings and whatever deity or ethical system they place their trust in is as central and deeply personal as any that life provides. It grows from family, faith, experience. And it comes in far too many varieties to be fairly encompassed in a single form of prayer.

And if it has not taken root outside the public schools, it will not be acquired in the minutes between the taking of attendance and the opening of the math book. What prayer in the public schools will do is embarrass the non-participating children, tempt teachers and administrators to push their own expressions of belief and breach the wall between church and state. Although the bill directs school boards to set aside time for voluntary prayer or meditation, the voluntary character of the ritual will not be apparent to young children. The outcome will be especially wounding to those whose religion places them in a minority in their classrooms, or whose families request that they not participate.

The courts have repeatedly made it clear that the right to worship as one pleases is so private and so sensitive that government must maintain absolute neutrality, must in fact absent itself from the entire process. The school prayer bill tramples around heavily on ground that should be left to parents, church and conscience.

Despite the noise from the religious right, most Americans understand that. It is a smokescreen to talk about "the right of little children to pray," as the Moral Majority does, when what you mean is the power to compel religious conformity. On this issue, the Legislature should recognize that the path of righteousness leads straight back to the Constitution — to the sanctity of private worship and the integrity of the public schools.

The Hartford Courant
Hartford, Conn., November 18, 1981

Trying to prevent the passage of reactionary measures could become a full-time job for Connecticut's Republican senator, Lowell P. Weicker. He spent months earlier this year in a holding action against an amendment that would have limited the power of federal courts to order the busing of students for racial integration.

Sen. Weicker now promises to lead a filibuster against an amendment, passed Monday, that would bar the Justice Department from trying to "prevent the implementation of programs of voluntary prayer and meditation in the public schools."

He succeeded Tuesday in having his own amendment — this one guaranteeing freedom of religion for children, a right they already have under the Constitution — approved by the Senate to partially countermand the impact of the original amendment. More parliamentary maneuvering on the issue is expected today.

If the original school prayer amendment were allowed to stand, it would tell public schools around the country that they would not have to worry about possible federal interference if they decide to set aside school time for "voluntary" prayer. The Supreme Court has repeatedly declared such organized school prayer unconstitutional.

Although the amendment would have little practical effect on the Justice Department, which is not now involved in school prayer cases, it would signal Americans that they have congressional approval to ignore the Supreme Court on this issue.

Interestingly, the same people who are most vociferous about the encroachment of government on the family are also most insistent that the public educational system encourage prayer, a personal activity from which government involvement is constitutionally barred.

The separation of church and state is guaranteed by the First Amendment, which prohibits Congress from making any law "respecting an establishment of religion."

The school prayer amendment could also be blocked if Sen. Weicker succeeds in his filibuster of the appropriations bill to which it is attached.

Any time Sen. Weicker spends on filibustering or disarming this and other antibusing and anti-abortion bills, now percolating to the surface in the Senate, is time well spent.

It may be the only way to prevent the moralists of the right from marching through Congress with legislation that poses a threat to the civil liberties of all Americans.

The Chattanooga Times
Chattanooga, Tenn., November 19, 1981

The fact that the Senate vote on Tuesday to endorse "programs of voluntary school prayer" was purely symbolic does not obscure the fact that it represents a triumph of politics over common sense. To that extent, the vote cheapens the very thing it presumes to enhance.

Ever since the Supreme Court banned compulsory prayer in public schools, the decision has been used by many, in Congress and out, to justify the argument it is Congress' responsibility to "return God to the classroom." We have even seen it argued seriously that many of the social problems that plague the nation have increased in intensity since the decision, the apparent point being that compulsory prayer in public schools would have prevented many of those troubles. And while they have been careful to disavow any intention to reimpose compulsory devotional periods, they have focused on the word "voluntary" as one way to get around the court's ruling.

Of course, there is nothing "voluntary" as far as students are concerned when a school system sets aside a formal meditation period which, presumably, would be led by the teachers. Besides, the legislation in question is nothing more than a dangerous tinkering with the Constitution's First Amendment guarantee of church-state separation. That amendment not only forbids Congress from establishing a state religion but passage of any law that prohibits the free exercise of religion.

Many who disagree with the Supreme Court's decisions on school prayer argue, incorrectly, that those rulings prohibit the free exercise of religion. The fact is that anyone who wishes can pray in school any time he or she wishes. That should be sufficient to dissuade the Senate in engaging in the legislative absurdity of barring the Justice Department from using federal funds to "prevent the implementation of programs of voluntary prayer and meditation in the public schools," especially when you consider that most cases challenging such programs have been brought by individuals. The Justice Department has had virtually no role in such litigation.

The Senate's vote, then, can be accurately described as nothing more than grandstanding on a emotional subject. It seems not to bother some senators that their action trivializes a vital activity — the issue is sometimes framed by its advocates as a vote for or against God. Worse, it foists upon the gullible the notion that Congress can indirectly mandate a "voluntary" school prayer program without violating constitutional principles that are designed to protect all Americans, whatever their religious beliefs.

St. Petersburg Times

St. Petersburg, Fla., November 22, 1981

Like some pernicious social disease, anti-Semitism continues to infect even the nicest people. Witness last week's appalling incident in the U.S. Senate where, during a debate over school prayer, Sen. Ernest Hollings, D-S.C., referred to a Jewish colleague as "the senator from B'nai B'rith." (B'nai B'rith is a Jewish service organization whose affiliate, the Anti-Defamation League, opposes prayer in the public schools.) Hollings' public record is not that of a bigot, yet at that moment he sounded like one. His lapse, in the heat of debate, is a timely reminder of the staying power of religious intolerance.

It is also a vivid example of the reasons why prayer, however "voluntary," should not be introduced into the public schools. If even a respected U.S. senator can succumb to the temptation to mock the religion of a colleague, what is to stop children from persecuting other children when religious differences intrude into the classroom? The surest way to inject those differences is to begin to conduct religious observances, as in the guise of "voluntary" prayer.

"VOLUNTARY" prayer can no more remain voluntary than "separate but equal" schools ever became equal. Inevitably, students who do not want to participate — or whose parents instruct them not to — are exposed to harassment from their peers. And for what? Does anyone believe that pro forma devotions really make children more devout?

The world's religions teach their followers to pray in so many different ways that it is hard to construct any prayer that is both meaningful and nonsectarian (and impossible to write one that respects the rights of nonbelievers.) That is one reason why many religious organizations oppose school prayer, and why senators of at least 12 different denominations voted against it. (But Florida's Paula Hawkins and Lawton Chiles were among the 51 voting to encourage religious intolerance.)

The school prayer issue is largely a manufactured controversy which some politicians exploit deliberately, heedless of the prejudices they arouse or to the great harm that can come out of it. There is nothing to prevent any student from praying silently at any time — whether before a meal, a test or the day's first class. Indeed, many schools set aside a moment of silent meditation each day, offending no one. People who insist that the schools make a ritual out of public prayer are trying, whether they realize it or not, to misuse the power of the state to force their religion on other people's children.

THE CONGRESS now wants to forbid the Justice Department to use any federal funds to "prevent the implementation of programs of voluntary prayer and meditation in the public schools." In practical terms, this does nothing — every lawsuit dealing with school prayer has been brought by private parties. In a symbolic sense, however, it is terrible. It signifies the Congress' willingness to throw the Constitution to the winds of passion and prejudice. It declares that, in the nation Thomas Jefferson helped to found, religious minorities are now political scapegoats. As Lowell Weicker, R-Conn., warned the Senate, "all we'd be doing is inviting the states and local government to produce all sorts of unconstitutional prayer programs."

This episode is yet another of Sen. Jesse Helm's schemes to use appropriations bills to remake America in his image of intolerance and bigotry. His contempt for the Constitution would destroy that which has made it possible for America's multitudinous ethnic and religious groups to live together in comparative peace and tolerance. No one's religion, no one's liberties, would be safe.

Pittsburgh Post-Gazette

Pittsburgh, Pa., November 24, 1981

In a rather striking contradiction, conservatives who like to insist that education in "values" is the job of parents, not the public schools, are bent on opening those same public schools to an even more personal activity: religion.

Last week, by a disgraceful 51-34 vote, the U.S. Senate approved a fatuous amendment to an appropriations bill that would prevent the federal government from spending any tax monies "to prevent implementation of programs of voluntary school prayer and meditation in the public schools."

Never mind that no such federal activity has taken place in the real world; that inconvenient fact could not stand in the way of congressmen desperate to put themselves on record in favor of "voluntary" school prayer and against a sensible Supreme Court ruling abolishing compulsory prayer and Bible reading in public schools.

The word "voluntary" in the bill must be set inside very large quotation marks.

In the realm of theory, a child might be free to opt out of school-sponsored prayers or religious exercises. Realistically, however, how many children would have the self-confidence to mark themselves as different by affirmatively withdrawing from a classroom exercise?

Congressmen who support a return to prayer in the schools — either through symbolic legislation like last week's rider or in more mischievous bills aimed at preventing the courts from interfering with school prayer — insult both the Constitution and religion.

For, as many perceptive clergymen have observed, the fixation on prayer in the schools demeans not only religion in general — by equating it with a few mumbled prayers at the beginning of a class — but also the distinctive beliefs and practices of individual traditions.

Even religious Americans should pray that Congress comes to its senses on this issue.

THE LOUISVILLE TIMES

Louisville, Ky., November 20, 1981

Some unholy motives underlying the effort to introduce organized prayer into public schools showed up on the floor of the U. S. Senate Monday.

During debate on an appropriations bill amendment that would prevent the Justice Department from prosecuting classroom-prayer cases, one senator angrily attacked another with an anti-Semitic slur. Then, by a 51-34 vote, the Senate refused to go on record in favor of the Constitution. It did so by rejecting a move by Sen. Lowell Weicker that would have barred the Justice Department from · moving against school-prayer programs that the courts had ruled to be "constitutional."

That unsuccessful effort to put the Senate and the Justice Department on the same team as the Supreme Court and the Constitution indicates that school-prayer advocates are willing, if necessary, to flout the law.

The religious slur was uttered during a tense moment in the debate when a supporter of classroom prayers, Sen. Ernest Hollings of South Carolina, slammed Ohio Sen. Howard Metzenbaum, an opponent, as "the senator from B'nai B'rith." (B'nai B'rith is a Jewish religious and service organization.) The attack may have been instructive, as Sen. Weicker suggested: "It makes us all understand why religion should not be debated on this floor."

Nor, according to the Supreme Court, should it be a standard element of classroom life. When the court struck down daily classroom prayers in 1962, the late Justice Hugo Black observed that Americans' respect for individual religious beliefs has always been a primary lure for those who were persecuted in other lands. From 1620, when the Pilgrims set foot on Plymouth Rock, until today, insistence upon religious tolerance has been a hallmark of democracy.

Daily classroom worship undermines tolerance because, when it is allowed, the government embraces a particular creed. The danger in that is clear: A philosophy that is in favor one day can be the target for persecution the next. Justice Black justifiably concluded that a "... union of government and religion tends to destroy government and to degrade religion."

The Supreme Court's conclusion about classroom prayer made sense 19 years ago, and it still does today. The failure of 51 senators to recognize that brings no credit to that body.

The News and Courier

Charleston, S.C., December 12, 1981

It was during a heated floor debate recently, that Sen. Fritz Hollings slipped verbally and referred to Sen. Howard Metzenbaum as "the senator from B'nai B'rith." He quickly apologized, the apology was accepted and the exchange stricken from the Congressional Record.

The only reason to even recount the incident is the significance of the subject that evoked such heated passions — voluntary prayer in schools. Eventually, as a sop to the Moral Majority and the New Right, the Senate, by a 51-to-34 vote, put a rider on an appropriations bill denying the Justice Department any money to block voluntary prayer or meditation in public schools.

The Supreme Court has ruled in a series of decisions starting in 1962, that prayer in public schools, voluntary or any way, is a violation of the constitutional separation of church and state.

The pro-prayer forces would reverse those findings through a constitutional amendment, if necessary. This is a time consuming, laborious process and we're against tampering with the Constitution on such issues in the first place.

There is a middle ground worth pursuing. In its landmark decisions, the Supreme Court ruled that a prescribed prayer cannot be read in the nation's public school classrooms. But the decisions did not answer the question of how prayer can be banned without, in the same breath, endorsing atheism.

The courts therefore, have one further decision to make — if prescribed prayer is banned what *is* permissible? When our forefathers separated church and state they didn't mean to abolish religious practice.

The Des Moines Register

Des Moines, Iowa, December 2, 1981

As part of the effort to bring prayer back into public schools, both houses of Congress have approved a proposal to bar the Justice Department from upholding a portion of the Constitution. Only the threat of a filibuster by Senator Lowell Weicker (Rep., Conn.) stands in the way of the measure's being adopted.

The proposal, tacked onto a fiscal-1982 appropriations bill, would prohibit the Justice Department from using its money to "prevent the implementation of programs of voluntary prayer and meditation in the public schools."

The U.S. Supreme Court has ruled that most such "voluntary" prayers in public schools are unconstitutional. People who don't agree with the Supreme Court's rulings are free to work for a constitutional amendment to bring prayer into the classroom. School-prayer supporters realize that it would be difficult to get such an amendment adopted. They have thus chosen an easier route: trying to restrict the ability of the government to uphold the Constitution.

Their first effort is the proposal to bar the Justice Department from getting involved in school-prayer cases. Next in line is a proposal to bar the Supreme Court from hearing cases on "voluntary" prayer in public schools.

Representative Neal Smith (Dem., Ia.) noted that the Justice Department has not been actively involved in school-prayer cases. Challenges to public-school-prayer programs have been brought by individuals. But it is wrong in principle to bar the Justice Department from upholding the Constitution.

We regret that all eight members of Iowa's congressional delegation voted for this unwise amendment.

The Virginian-Pilot

Norfolk, Va., November 19, 1981

The Senate voted Monday to bar the Justice Department from using federal funds to "prevent the implementation of programs of voluntary prayer and meditation in the public schools." Note the language: The Justice Department would be *barred* from *preventing* the implementation of *voluntary* prayers in the public schools.

The first problem with this is that *voluntary* prayers in the public schools are permissible. There is nothing amiss if someone says a prayer in private or even in public, so long, of course, as the school itself — the agent of the state — has not in any way been involved with drafting the prayer in question.

The second problem is that the Justice Department does not stand athwart the public school door as some Madalyn Murray O'Hair, poised to keep out all those who would lead America's children in classroom prayer — whether of the voluntary or state-sponsored variety.

So the Senate has voted to stop the Justice Department from doing something that it isn't doing, and to stop it, moreover, from moving against something (voluntary school prayer) that isn't controversial anyway.

The purpose of the vote, as it happens, is something else. By supporting voluntary school prayers, the Senate — or at least some of its membership — is trying to send a signal — albeit a feeble one — that it supports state-sponsored school prayer and meditations of the sort that were outlawed by the Supreme Court decisions of 18 and 19 years ago. And of course this is the real issue whenever the words "school prayer" are uttered: whether the Supreme Court was wrong when it said that prayers composed by and said in the public schools constitute an "establishment of religion."

We don't agree with many of the decisions involving the First Amendment's "establishment clause," but in the school prayer cases it seems to us that the court drew the right conclusion. Yet even if one disagrees with the school prayer decisions, it is another question whether returning such prayer to the public schools will accomplish everything its proponents say it will.

We doubt that the social problems of the age — crime, racial conflict, drug abuse, sexual promiscuity and so forth — would be significantly affected by the recitation of a state-endorsed prayer. Much more than school prayers — which in many places were theologically bland — is needed to shape the character of the young in a more virtuous way than some of our public schools currently do. The proponents of school prayers surely must recognize that the problem of character education goes far beyond some one-minute prayer. Yet here they are, expending their energies in behalf of school prayer instead of using them to, say, push for more private schools that could address the issue of character in an explicitly religious fashion.

And they are expending their energies in a way that may not be the best means for securing the end they desire. The Senate vote came in the form of an amendment — a "rider" — to one of the many money bills now moving through Congress. Legislation by this method is a questionable business, not least because often the riders are conspicuously irrelevant to the appropriations at issue. Conservatives aren't the only ones who've resorted to this technique; liberals have played the game, and we recognize, alas, that it is unlikely ever to stop.

Even so, it is worth noting in this instance that the Senate Republican leadership had asked those concerned with school prayer not to use the rider technique but to wait until the end of the year, or the first of next, when their issue would be considered singly, and thus could be decided on its own merits. But they rejected this request, thus losing, perhaps, the chance of having a better shot at influencing public debate, as might happen when the issue could be discussed by itself and as it should be—with attention centered on state-sponsored school prayer.

And it is worth asking, too, whether any kind of legislation on school prayer is the best way to rub out the court's prayer decisions. After all, there are other alternatives for those who disagree with the Supreme Court. Proponents of school prayer are free to try to persuade the court through litigation that it was wrong; and they are free to propose a constitutional amendment that would permit school prayer. We don't endorse their ultimate goal, but proponents of returning prayer to the public schools should know that what they did Monday was to win a big headline, but little more.

The Boston Herald American
Boston, Mass., December 1, 1981

The Senate voted recently to put one of those brief but politically potent riders on an appropriations bill. It is the will of a majority of senators that the Justice Department may not use any of its money to try to block voluntary prayer or meditation in the public schools.

Inasmuch as the Justice Department has shown no inclination to wade into the sensitive area of school prayer, the vote can be regarded as symbolic rather than a mandate from the Senate for a new federal policy. But what does it symbolize?

By one interpretation, the 51-to-34 vote sustaining the rider reflects the strength in Congress of the "New Right" — the conservative bloc that is unhappy with Supreme Court decisions on school prayer, abortion, busing, and several other issues.

A better test of the strength of the pro-prayer forces, we think, would come with a vote on measures that attack the issue more directly. Would the same senators vote for a bill that would take jurisdiction in school prayer cases away from the federal courts? Or for a constitutional amendment that would legalize school prayer?

Congress may be unable to avoid a full-blown debate on the issue, as bitter and divisive as it would certainly be. The intemperate words exchanged in the Senate recently are an indication of what to expect.

The country, not to mention Congress, would be better served if this issue could be resolved by the public conscience and the courts. Significantly, public opinion polls show consistently that the majority of Americans are not offended by the idea of giving children an opportunity for prayer in the schools. But how?

The landmark Supreme Court decisions of 1962 and 1963 have established that, under the First Amendment, prayers and Bible-reading cannot be a prescribed activity in a public school. But neither those decisions nor any coming later have answered the question of how prayer can be banned in a school without implanting a "religion of secularism" in its place.

Having banned any coercive aspect of religion in the schools, the courts have yet to define clearly what is permissible. This remains to be done. For, in separating church and state, the Constitution does not empower governmental abolition of religious practice.

THE COMMERCIAL APPEAL
Memphis, Tenn., November 18, 1981

THE ANGRY outbursts that broke the usual decorum of the Senate during a debate on school prayer were witness to the wisdom of the First Amendment.

The debate centered on an appropriations bill rider, which would ban the use of federal funds "to prevent the implementation of programs of voluntary prayer and meditation in the public schools."

At one point, Sen. Ernest Hollings (D-S.C.), who supported the rider, referred to Sen. Howard Metzenbaum (D-Ohio), an opponent, as "the senator from B'nai B'rith." Metzenbaum is Jewish, and B'nai B'rith is a Jewish organization.

Hollings apologized, but he couldn't undo the ill will that had flared up. Sen. Lowell Weicker Jr. (R-Conn.) commented, "If it (the prayer issue) does this to us, imagine what it's going to do to the people out there...It makes us all understand why religion should not be debated on this floor."

Both sides say that the rider would have little practical effect, because most cases challenging prayer in the schools are brought by individuals. The Justice Department is seldom involved. But the rider would be a symbol of congressional opposition to the federal courts.

Hollings said, for instance, that he thought the Supreme Court had misinterpreted the Constitution when it banned organized worship in schools. And Sen. Jesse Helms (R-N.C.), a leader of the movement to overturn that ban, argued that failure of the rider would tell the courts "to keep on... meddling in something that was never their business in the first place."

But the Constitution clearly separates church and state. The Supreme Court has a right and an obligation to interpret the Constitution's meaning. If legislative acts to "correct" constitutional decisions became common practice, there would be no end to congressional "meddling" in the judicial branch of government. The American system of checks and balances could be upended.

HELMS APPEARS to be trying to require that the prayer issue be settled by his rules, or rules that would favor the pro-prayer groups that could bring critical pressure to bear on local school boards. Other groups lacking the same leverage would be left without any legal recourse, if Helms were successful in going even beyond the rider and removing the prayer issue from federal court jurisdiction.

What would that, to repeat Weicker's concern, "do to the people out there"? School prayer should not become the focus for political battles, pitting schools and parents against one another and feeding the demagoguery of single-issue candidates. Religious divisiveness should not spill into everyday affairs or make more difficult the civility of government, even as it did, if briefly, in the Senate.

The Miami Herald
Miami, Fla., June 2, 1981

THE United States, a pluralistic nation if ever there was one, has enough social tensions already without adding religious strife to the list.

Yet sectarian disputes almost certainly would arise if religious zealots persist in their efforts to convert this secular nation into a latter-day theocracy.

The zealots not only are hard at work to impose their view of morality on the rest of the population. They're also pushing religion itself.

According to spokesmen for a new coalition called "Project Prayer," a majority of the Senate Judiciary Committee now favors or leans toward a school-prayer bill sponsored by Sen. Jesse Helms and Rep. Phil Crane.

The Helms-Crane legislation is in sharp contrast with traditional conservatism. It proposes a radical step: forbidding the Federal courts from ruling in school-prayer matters.

If the bill were to become law, the U.S. Supreme Court purportedly would have to ignore wholesale assaults on the First Amendment's guarantees of freedom of religion as commonly understood during most of this century.

Instead, citizens would be left to the tender mercies of their state legislators, who would be empowered to enact laws concerning school prayer.

Thus the simmering national debate that followed the U.S. Supreme Court's widely misunderstood decision barring state-prescribed prayers in public schools could be transformed into a raging controversy in state capitals.

In many states, Roman Catholics might be pitted against Protestants, Christians against Jews, believers against dissenters, the majority against the minorities.

Who needs the trouble? One might have thought the ruins of Belfast and Beirut — in lands being destroyed in part by sectarian strife — would have offered persuasive testimony as to the perils of entangling church and state. Adherents of different religions who begin by shouting at each other, end up too often by shooting at each other.

Or one might have thought that conservatives would be appalled, as James Kilpatrick was, by the violence this proposal does to the traditional Constitutional functions of Congress and the Supreme Court.

But the true believers of the far right, flush with their newfound wealth and sense of power, apparently want to keep their momentum going regardless of the consequences. Unless Americans who support religious liberty resist, this tightly knit minority of zealots will prevail by default.

ST. LOUIS POST-DISPATCH

St. Louis, Mo., November 18, 1981

Both houses of Congress have now, in effect, told the Justice Department not to intervene on the side of the Constitution as interpreted by the Supreme Court. That is the clear meaning of an amendment to an appropiation bill in which the Senate, following the example of the House, forbade the department to use federal funds to "prevent the implementation of programs of voluntary prayer and meditation in the public schools." In 1962 the Supreme Court ruled that a program of so-called "voluntary prayer" in New York state schools was an unconstitutional "establishment of religion."

What the congressional proponents of school prayer have in mind is no more voluntary than the invalidated New York prayer. Students already have the right to pray voluntarily if they choose. The prayer proponents want officially sponsored school prayers that would in effect be enforced in scheduled time by the pressure of peer and teacher example. The coercive nature of such programs cannot be camouflaged by the terms "voluntary" and "nondenominational." Such programs unavoidably line up the state on the side of an establishment of religion and against those students who do not want to engage in any religious worship or do not like the form of worship provided.

In the heat of debate, Sen. Hollings of South Carolina, a prayer proponent, provided an unfortunate example of just how divisive the issue can be. He referred to Sen. Metzenbaum, a prayer opponent and a Jew, as "the senator from B'nai B'rith." Although Mr. Hollings promptly apologized, the slur is indicative of the kind of hurtful friction between students that would be engendered by prescribed prayer programs. Since the Justice Department has had almost no role in prayer litigation, Congress is really sending a message to the courts to ignore the freedom of religion guarantee in the First Amendment of the Constitution.

The Philadelphia Inquirer

Philadelphia, Pa., November 23, 1981

Sen. Ernest F. Hollings (D., S.C.) undoubtedly meant no harm when, during floor debate over "voluntary prayer" in public schools, he referred to Sen. Howard M. Metzenbaum (D., Ohio), as "the senator from B'nai B'rith." Sen. Hollings quickly apologized for a remark intended, he said, "only in fun." Sen. Metzenbaum accepted, and the exchange was stricken from the Congressional Record.

The episode, though, may have served a useful purpose in reminding everyone of the reason that the Founding Fathers, in their wisdom, erected what Thomas Jefferson called the "wall of separation" between church and state.

The men who signed the Constitution were well aware of the passions that religion can evoke and they were determined that in the nation they were founding the religious quarrels of the Old World would be, if not avoided, at least abated.

Those passions showed up on the Senate floor the other day. At issue was a proposal to bar the Justice Department from intervening to "prevent the implementation of voluntary prayer and meditation in the public schools." Sen. Lowell P. Weicker Jr. (R., Conn.) offered an amendment to neutralize the proposal and maintain the status quo.

Sen. Jesse Helms (R., N.C.) thereupon declared that if the Weicker amendment were passed, the federal courts would get the message "to keep on doing what they are doing — meddling in something that was never their business in the first place."

Not for the first time, Sen. Helms has things exactly backward. The Supreme Court has ruled, in a series of cases, that prayer in the public schools, "voluntary" or otherwise, is a violation of the constitutional "establishment of religion" clause. It is the courts' business to interpret the Constitution. It is *not* Congress' business to substitute its whim. Nor is it Congress' business to instruct the Executive Branch not to enforce the Constitution.

The principle is clear enough beyond the issue of school prayer: If the executive is "instructed" to forgo doing its job in one area, what will be the next: Enforcement of laws against stealing from the public till? What if the Congress instructed the Justice Department not to prosecute legislators for corruption?

The Senate nevertheless did so instruct the Justice Department on the matter of prayer. It was wrong.

"In the relationship between man and religion," the late Justice Tom C. Clark wrote for the Supreme Court majority which in 1963 struck down Pennsylvania's and Maryland's school prayer laws, "the state is firmly committed to a position of neutrality."

Nothing in the Constitution prevents anyone from praying anywhere, anytime. Nothing in the Constitution prevents the public schools from instilling moral principles in their pupils. Yet one of those principles is surely obedience to the law of the land. The Senate, like the House earlier, flouted that principle in amending the appropriations bill for the departments of Justice, State and Commerce.

Thanks to Sen. Weicker's determination to lead a filibuster against this "outrageous, unconstitutional action," Sen. Helms has decided not to press for a final vote on his amendment, but he promises that "we'll go at it again next year." Is it too much to hope that next time around a majority of senators will decide to abide by their oath to preserve, protect and defend the Constitution of the United States?

THE SACRAMENTO BEE

Sacramento, Calif., December 2, 1981

The other day the Senate tacked to an appropriation bill for the State, Commerce and Justice departments a largely symbolic amendment concerning school prayers. Earlier the House tacked the same amendment to its version of the bill. "No funds," says the rider, "may be used to prevent the implementation of programs of voluntary prayer and meditation in the public schools." Since in fact no funds are being used in such a manner, the rider is more or less academic. It will certainly have no direct bearing on the existing constitutional prohibition against prayers in the public schools.

Still, if the rider has enough symbolic importance for someone to vote for it — as did the majorities in both houses — it has enough importance to oppose it, as did a dozen members of the California delegation and some 40 other members of the House. At best, an affirmative vote among those members of Congress professing to respect the line between church and state is therefore a small piece of political hypocrisy. Worse, it encourages those who want to reinstitute their form of religious exercise in the public schools to increase their efforts.

The school prayer issue has always been a matter of principle — the principle of separation based on the certainty that no matter how worded or presented, any prayer or any other religious exercise is likely to be offensive to the religious sensibilities of some group in the community. The introduction of such exercises is thus almost always divisive and very often conducive to religious animosities.

To the extent there is any establishment of religion with state support, there is also an infringement of someone else's liberty. Congress should affirm that principle, not approve gestures against it, no matter how hollow they may be.

Supreme Court Allows Prayer on Public University Campus

The Supreme Court ruled, 8-1, Dec. 8 that state universities did not have the right to bar private student prayer groups from meeting on campus. In its ruling, the court drew a distinction between public institutions of higher learning and elementary or secondary schools. The case involved the University of Missouri at Kansas City, which was sued by Cornerstone, a Christian evangelical organization that was prohibited from holding weekly services on campus. Writing for the majority, Justice Lewis F. Powell Jr. agreed with Cornerstone that the university policy violated the First Amendment's freedom of speech clause. Cornerstone's activities did not conflict with the First Amendment's separation of church and state, he wrote, because "having created a forum generally open to student groups, the university seeks to enforce a content-based exclusion of religious speech. Its exclusionary policy violates the fundamental principle that state regulation of speech should be content-neutral. . . ." The university must allow private religious groups to meet, Powell added, since it allowed other private student groups to use the campus. Powell asserted that there was no church-state issue involved in the decision. "An open forum in a public university does not confer any imprimatur of state approval on religious sects or practices." Justice Byron White, the lone dissenter, wrote that if "no line may ever be drawn" between spoken religious worship and other kinds of speech, then "the majority would have to uphold the university's right to offer a class entitled 'Sunday Mass.'" In the majority's opinion, universities were "public forums" for the study of different views, including religion. This definition was not extended to elementary and secondary schools, which was why the court refused to review a decision barring voluntary school prayer in a New York State high school. A group of students in Guilderland had been prohibited from holding voluntary prayer meetings on school property before school hours. An appeals court had ruled that the meetings were a violation of the separation of church and state, and the Supreme Court's refusal to hear the case left the appeals court decision intact.

The Chattanooga Times

Chattanooga, Tenn., December 14, 1981

The Supreme Court's decision on Tuesday that public colleges and universities may not prevent campus organizations from conducting religious services and other activities on campus reaffirms in a valuable way the First Amendment's guarantee of free speech without, in our view, doing harm to the doctrine of church-state separation.

The case concerned the University of Missouri's ban on organized prayer and Bible reading at its Kansas City campus. The university officially recognizes more than 100 student organizations and provides facilities for their use. One of those organizations was Cornerstone, a Christian campus group that had used a facility from 1971 to 1977. In 1977, however, the university said Cornerstone could no longer use the facilities, primarily because its meetings included prayer and Bible reading. To do otherwise, it said, would violate the First Amendment "establishment of religion" clause. Student members of Cornerstone argued that the ban not only denied them their constitutional right to a free exercise of religion but infringed upon their free speech rights as well.

Justice Lewis Powell's majority opinion is worth quoting at length, for it clearly distinguished between the two rights at issue in the Missouri case. The university, Mr. Powell wrote, "has discriminated against student groups and speakers based on their desire to use a generally open forum to engage in religious worship and discussion. These are forms of speech and association protected by the First Amendment." Speech may not be regulated or banned because somebody doesn't like its content, he wrote, adding: " . . . Having created a forum generally open to students groups, the university seeks to enforce a content-based exclusion of religious speech," an exclusion that "violates the fundamental principle that a state regulation of speech should be content-neutral . . ."

Justice Powell also disposed of the UM argument that allowing Cornerstone's activities would amount to state sponsorship of religion. He wrote that "an open forum in a public university does not confer any imprimatur of state approval on religious sects or practices" any more than allowing the Young Socialist Alliance to meet on campus gives state approval to socialism.

The lone dissenter, Justice Byron White, wrote that if the majority were right that "no distinction may be drawn between verbal acts of worship and other verbal acts," then all of the cases concerning religious worship in public institutions would have to be reconsidered.

But most of those cases have concerned public elementary and secondary schools whose students are obviously more impressionable than college students. Further, the former can be considered a "captive audience," whereas the latter are not, especially since most religious campus groups are extra-curricular. If universities are scrupulously neutral in their dealings with campus organizations, they need not fear violating the Constitution.

TULSA WORLD

Tulsa, Okla., December 10, 1981

THE U. S. Supreme Court has held that a university can't bar religious groups from using public buildings for meetings.

In doing so, the court reversed by an 8-1 vote the ruling of a lower court which upheld University of Missouri officials who argued such meetings violated the Constitutional separation of Church and State.

The high court decided such a ban would infringe on freedom of religious expression.

Legalities aside, however, there are practical reasons in favor of the court's decision.

First, universities are not grade schools. Students there are young adults, under no obligation to attend religious gatherings on the campus. (The issue is entirely different from that of so-called "voluntary" prayer in common schools. In the school prayer cases, the question was whether children — a captive audience in the classroom — should be exposed to officially-recognized religious exercises which may violate their own or their parents' spiritual beliefs.)

Secondly, it would be very difficult for a university to separate religion from philosophy, for example. Would it ban a philosopher whose beliefs happened to include traditional religious ideas?

Or would it ban a minister whose basic ideas of social justice led him to speak out on secular matters but with a religious point of view?

Or how about the out-and-out atheist, who in discussing his viewpoint must of necessity discuss religious thought, even if only to debunk it?

Had the court decided otherwise, universities would have been required to continually examine and pass judgment on the views of a large majority of people who routinely speak on U. S. campuses.

It is a sound decision.

The Des Moines Register

Des Moines, Iowa, December 25, 1981

Religious speech must be accorded the same First Amendment freedom from government censorship as non-religious speech. That is the principle enunciated by the U.S. Supreme Court earlier this month in holding unconstitutional a rule of the University of Missouri at Kansas City that barred a student religious group from using meeting rooms generally available to other student organizations.

The university had imposed the ban in the belief that it was required by the First Amendment prohibition of "an establishment of religion." The court's 8-1 decision was consistent with its precedents on establishment of religion as well as freedom of speech.

On the freedom-of-speech issue, the court has held that governments issuing parade or meeting permits or granting use of buildings must be neutral toward the content and subject of those parades or meetings. That means, said the court, that if the university allows meetings of philosophical groups expounding atheism (or anything else), it must allow the religious group called Cornerstone to meet for Bible-study and hymn-singing.

Such permission meets with ease the three rules the court has used to test for violation of the Establishment Clause:

• Does the action have a secular legislative purpose? Providing meeting rooms for 100 or so varied organizations does that.

• Is its primary effect to advance or inhibit religion? The religious group derives some incidental benefit — in the same way that a church, although tax-exempt, derives benefit from tax-supported fire and police protection.

• Does the action foster "excessive governmental entanglement"? There is no entanglement so long as university authorities are not monitoring groups to see if they discuss religion.

That kind of entanglement seems to be what Justice Byron White proposed in his solitary dissent when he suggested that the university could distinguish between religious discussions and religious study that might be classed as worship.

It is proper for a university to promote a forum for the exchange of ideas and opinions. If that exchange is unfettered, some of the ideas and opinions are bound to be of a religious character. The court is right. This is a case in which preservation of free speech must inevitably grant freedom to speech that is religious in nature.

EVENING EXPRESS

Portland, Maine, December 10, 1981

Sometimes, less is more. And it was that way this week in the U.S. Supreme Court.

In an 8-1 decision, deliberative and carefully drawn, the court affirmed the right of state university students to meet together to discuss religion as freely as they meet to do anything else. No more. No less. But equal.

The case before the court turned on a regulation adopted by the University of Missouri, prohibiting the use of university property "for purposes of religious worship or religious teaching."

The regulation was challenged by Cornerstone, an evangelical Christian student group at the university, one of more than 100 student organizations recognized by the school.

Defending its regulation, the university argued that to allow Cornerstone to pray and discuss religion on campus would, in effect, give Missouri's "symbolic approval" to the worship and breach the Constitution's clear mandate for separation of church and state.

But the supreme court has ruled that free speech, not religion, is the issue.

"The university has opened its facilities for use by student groups, and the question is whether it can now exclude groups because of the content of their speech," wrote Associate Justice Lewis F. Powell Jr. in the majority opinion. The answer, he said, must be "No."

A state, Powell wrote, can discriminate against constitutionally protected free speech only if it can show that it is necessary to protect "a compelling state interest." And that interest must be narrowly defined.

A state-owned university that allows student groups to meet to talk politics, medieval poetry or music cannot deny equal access to a group that wants to discuss religion and pray.

Basing its opinion carefully on free speech and not on free exercise of religion, the court wisely steered clear of the issue of teaching religion in schools.

It is one thing to use a public school classroom to teach religious beliefs to students required by law to attend and quite another to protect the right of university groups to discuss whatever they please.

Certainly, no one would suggest that free speech must stop where religion begins.

Richmond Times-Dispatch

Richmond, Va., December 14, 1981

Homosexual and Marxist groups had the right to hold meetings on the campus of the University of Missouri, but a group of Christian students was forbidden to meet there for religious services. University authorities said there was nothing in the U.S. Constitution to prevent homosexuals and Marxists from using state property for meetings, but there was something — the First Amendment's establishment-of-religion clause — that denied the religious group use of the public facilities.

It is beyond the wildest speculation that the Founding Fathers intended that any such topsy-turvy situation should exist on public property in this nation. Fortunately, the U.S. Supreme Court last week put the matter in perspective when it overturned the university's ban.

The court, in an opinion written by Justice Lewis F. Powell Jr., based its decision on the First Amendment, but on the freedom-of-speech clause, not on either the establishment or the freedom-of-worship clause.

If a university opens its facilities to the free speech of student organizations in general, it cannot deny use of those facilities to one group because of the content of the speech of that particular group, wrote Justice Powell for himself and six of his colleagues.

"Religious worship and discussion," he said, "are forms of speech and association protected by the First Amendment." Government may discriminate against a particular type of speech only if it can "show that its regulation is necessary to serve a compelling state interest...." There was no evidence, declared Justice Powell, that any compelling state interest was served by the ban on the Christian group's meetings.

The university — which said that the ban was in accord with previous court rulings on religion in the public schools — argued that allowing the religious group to meet and hold services would amount to state sponsorhip of religion.

Not so, said Justice Powell. An open forum in a public university does not confer state approval on religious sects or practices any more than allowing a meeting of the Young Socialist Alliance would constitute state approval of socialism.

One intriguing question arises: What relation, if any, does this decision have to the court's ban on prayers and Bible reading in the public schools?

The court majority said in a footnote to its opinion that unlike grade school children, "university students are, of course, young adults. They are less impressionable than younger students and should be able to appreciate that the university's policy is one of neutrality toward religion."

Well and good. But Justice Byron White, in a dissenting opinion, argued that the proposition that religious worship is no different from other forms of expression is "plainly wrong." If the proposition were right, he said, all of the earlier cases concerning religious worship in public institutions would have to be reconsidered. On that latter statement — concerning the reconsideration of earlier cases — we're not sure that Justice White doesn't have a valid point.

In any event, last week's decision is significant in giving free-speech protection to religious worship on state property. Could this be the beginning of a trend toward opening a crack in the wall the court has erected in some of its decisions against religion in the public schools and on other government property?

OKLAHOMA CITY TIMES

Oklahoma City, Okla., December 10, 1981

ANY COURT ruling that deals with the constitutional issue of freedom of religion is bound to raise more questions than it answers.

So it is with the U.S. Supreme Court's decision this week that the University of Missouri at Kansas City violated students' constitutional right of free speech by banning the use of a student center for religious purposes. The university claimed allowing meetings by a student religious organization would violate the Constitution's "establishment" clause that bars states from advancing religion.

The court's opinion said the religious worship and discussion for which students used the center are forms of speech and association protected by the First Amendment.

That raises an interesting question in Oklahoma, where several school districts have been sued for allowing student groups to use classrooms for voluntary before-school Bible study. The court has treated grade and high schools differently from colleges in such cases but if they are all tax-supported institutions, that line is hard to follow.

Pittsburgh Post-Gazette
Pittsburgh, Pa., December 11, 1981

Two groups will be disappointed by the U.S. Supreme Court's sensible ruling this week that the First Amendment does not prohibit — and in fact requires — the use of state-university facilities for voluntary religious meetings.

The first group comprises Moral Majoritarians who like to argue that the Supreme Court is populated by aggressive secular humanists who won't give religion the constitutional time of day. The second group, which is not completely a figment of the Moral Majority's imagination, is made up of civil-liberties fundamentalists who see the First Amendment as a bar only to governmental activities that make life easier for religion.

What both groups tend to overlook is that the First Amendent contains what legal scholars call a "fork" on the issue of religion. One of its clauses guarantees the free exercise of religion; another forbids Congress (and by later extension the states) from using its power to encourage particular or general forms of religious belief.

There is some tension in the two guarantees. Especially in the 20th century, when government is intimately involved in sponsoring a wide variety of enterprises, officials must sometimes walk a middle ground between policies that can be interpreted as partial to religion and others that unfairly penalize religious freedom.

In the case that produced this week's 8-1 ruling, the University of Missouri at Kansas City had prohibited a student religious group from making use of facilities that were available to other voluntary student associations. Its fear was that such permission might constitute "establishment" of religion. In fact, the exclusion had the effect of penalizing groups whose common interest was religion rather than poetry or civil rights or the Democratic Party.

Justice Lewis F. Powell Jr.'s majority opinion in the Kansas City case focused on that unfair treatment, and made two other important points. One was that a university does not lend its imprimatur to a religious group simply because it allows it to meet on university property. The other is that the ruling "in no way undermines the capacity of the university to establish reasonable time, place and manner regulations" for such meetings.

Some instant analysis of this week's ruling asked if it might give aid and comfort to congressmen and others who want to roll back the high court's decisions against official prayer in public schools.

That is a far-fetched scenario. The "voluntary" prayer that conservative congressmen wish to see reinstated in the public schools would be voluntary in name only. Under such proposals, the state, in the form of the public school, would clearly be taking the initiative, with the burden to opt out of religious exercises falling on the individual child. By contrast, what was at stake in this week's ruling was the right of students of mature years — not young children — to form associations of a religious character and receive the same treatment accorded other voluntary student groups.

The Cincinnati Post
Cincinnati, Ohio, December 14, 1981

The Supreme Court was right the other day to strike down a University of Missouri ban against student groups using campus facilities for religious-oriented meetings.

University officials stretched the U.S. Constitution's separation of church and state requirement to a ridiculous extreme to justify denial of the use of a room to Cornerstone, an evangelical Christian student group, for Saturday night meetings.

Cornerstone was one of more than 100 recognized student organizations at the university's Kansas City campus. Justice Lewis Powell, writing for the court majority, said a ban on such voluntary organized prayer and Bible reading is a ban on free speech.

"An open forum in a public university does not confer any imprimatur of state approval on religious sects or practices," Powell said, any more than allowing Young Socialist Alliance meetings gives state approval to socialism.

The Supreme Court ruling should not be seen, however, as an opening to attack previous court rulings against prayer in public elementary and high schools.

Voluntary gatherings of religious-oriented groups on university campuses are far different from prayers or other religious activities imposed on youngsters in elementary and secondary classrooms.

The Virginian-Pilot
Norfolk, Va., December 16, 1981

Legal scholars have noted that Supreme Court decisions regarding the First Amendment's religion clauses lack coherence. Two actions by the court in the past week only promise to add to the confusion.

The first raised the question of whether the University of Missouri was right to prohibit an evangelical Christian group named Cornerstone from meeting in campus buildings. The university reasoned that allowing the organization to meet in taxpayer-financed facilities constituted sponsorship of such meetings, and thus an "establishment of religion."

To this argument, all the court had to say was that there is a distinction between merely permitting a meeting to take place and actually sponsoring it, and that the latter is an establishment of religion, in accordance with the court's prayer decisions of almost 20 years ago, but the former is not. Strangely, though, the court failed to make this simple rebuttal.

Instead, it agreed with Cornerstone's argument that religious worship is a form of free speech entitled to protection under the First Amendment's free speech clause, and concluded that a university cannot ban a particular speech because of its "content" (in this case religious).

Where this unprecedented interpretation of religious worship and free speech will lead us is uncertain. Justice White, the lone dissenter, rightly wondered what can now be distinctive about the religion clauses of the First Amendment, since this case could be reduced to one about freedom of speech. And if religious worship — if, more particularly, prayer — is a form of speech, the court would seem to be inviting litigation defending prayer in public school.

It is hardly clear, however, that the court is ready to change its mind on prayer in the public schools. This week the court let stand a circuit court ruling that barred high school students from holding prayer meetings in a vacant classroom before school. It is a risky business to infer from silence by the court, but it is puzzling that the same court that one week lets a voluntary religious group meet on a public university campus decides the next week not to take action that would let a voluntary religious group meet on a public school campus.

Questions arise in the wake of these two actions, chief among them whether religious worship is a form of speech for college students, but not for high schoolers. Furthermore, does the establishment clause only apply to public education at the primary and secondary levels, but not at the college and university level? Do voluntary religious meetings on a high school campus really constitute an "establishment of religion," as the circuit court's decision held but as the Supreme Court has yet to rule? And, finally, how does the free exercise clause figure in any of this? Suffice to say, the court has unfinished business, and with its explicit identification of religious worship as a form of free speech, it may have opened up new possibilities for First Amendment incoherence.

ARKANSAS DEMOCRAT
Little Rock, Ark., December 13, 1981

Here's one for the American Civil Liberties Union and other people who can't seem to understand that there are two sections to the First Amendment's religion clause – the negative "establishment" clause and the positive "free exercise of religion" clause.

By an 8-1 vote, the Supreme Court has awarded the protection of free speech to student groups conducting religious exercises on campuses of tax-supported universities. Religion, the justices say in overthrowing the University of Missouri's ban on such meetings, is a protected form of free speech – in the context of campus discussions-groups.

How about that? Religious free speech! The court said that if the university lets 100 other student groups meet and talk, it can't bar the one simply because its purpose is religious.

The court could easily have affirmed the tax-supported university's argument that its deliberate assent to campus religious exercises would violates the constitutional ban on an "establishment of religion." That was the obvious route. But the court didn't take it – and neither did it rule – as it might have ruled, and as the religious students asked it to rule – that the university was violating their First Amendment guarantee of "the free exercise of religion."

"Free exercise" would have been the logical and better ruling. But the justices haven't got that far yet in liberalizing it in public contexts. They chose free speech because constitutionalizing the free exercise of religion – as such – on a state-supported campus might have looked like blessing an "entanglement"

between church and state. "Entanglement" is one of the court's tests for determining violations of the "establishment" ban.

But even in invoking free speech to justify the free exercise of religion, the justices curtail the scope of the "establishment" ban. And that's all to the good, even if they weasel-worded their free speech ruling. In the majority opinion, Justice Lewis F. Powell wrote: "...We are unpersuaded that the primary effect of the public forum, (the religious meeting) open to all forms of discourse, would be to advance religion."

But of course the meetings do advance religion – what else would they do? The justices simply chose a defensible way of saying that any rote upholding of the university's sterile establishment ban would have limited the free exercise of religion. In other words, it's silly to push the establishment ban so far as to see church-state entanglement in campus praying – simply because a school is tax-supported.

Unhappily, the logic of any Supreme Court decision is limited to its context – to the issue at hand. So the prayer ruling doesn't automatically extend free-speech protection to all religious exercises on public property – especially since the Supreme Court has so far treated public schools differently from universities. Though carol singing in public schools is now blessed as basically traditional, ACLU can go on trying (as it is doing now and does at every Christmas season) to push creches off court house lawns. It can also go on fighting voluntary prayer or the circulation of religious materials in public schools.

But the "free speech" thrust of the new campus ruling is a big step toward sane interpretation of the "free exercise of religion" clause. In time, the baneful establishment ban will be relegated to the minor constitutional role intended for it.

Meanwhile, there's no reason why the logic of the new "free speech" approach shouldn't also apply to pluralistic teaching of origins in public schools – without the judges stumbling over the establishment ban. In the creationist trial, the ACLU has done its best to mask the free-speech issue by inviting the court to read Act 590 as a proxy Genesis. Maybe worse, it is trying to use free speech (academic freedom) against itself in the name of establishmentarian science.

The creationist law's requirement that both evolution and creationism – or neither – be taught would violate a teacher's academic freedom, ACLU says. How? Well, if a teacher found creationism intellectually distasteful and chose not to teach origins at all rather than teach it, she (or he) would lose the right to teach as one chose.

But if that's so, why hasn't ACLU through the years ever raised a cry against Arkansas teachers' being required to teach evolution alone? Surely, some teachers are intellectually opposed to teaching evolutionary theory as cold petrified scientific truth – to the exclusion of any other theory. Has their academic freedom been denied all these years? Ask ACLU – which has manufactured this phony one-sided view of "academic freedom" for the creationist trial and caught a lot of boobs by cynically peddling it as a constitutional right.

One last word. If the high court can call outright campus religious meetings free speech, why shouldn't it see the free speech issue in an academic case whose only connection with religion is ACLU's frantic use of supposed parallels to read religious fundamentalism into a law that rejects all religion on its face?

Lincoln Journal
Lincoln, Neb., December 14, 1981

Reaction seems fairly muted to the U.S. Supreme Court's 8-to-1 decision of a week ago, permitting a variety of religious and denominational activities to be conducted on the property of a publicly-owned university

The test case centered on a conflict at the Kansas City campus of the University of Missouri.

Those who won were, naturally, elated. But the country has not necessarily been rocked with hosannahs, thanking the Deity that a godless Supreme Court majority finally has glimpsed the guiding light.

The Journal would be among those in the camp of the restrained.

We also venture that this decision may be anything but favorably appreciated in the future by some of the same religious personalities, especially Christian fundamentalists, who think highly of it today.

The issues are succinctly stated and wrapped up by Newhouse News Service reporter Jack Landau elsewhere on this day's opinion page.

Understood, too, is the court's cautionary statement that the holding in the case is narrow. That's to suggest one should be wary about projecting ramifications.

From a public campus perspective,

however, it's probably now wide open for any sort of group which classifies itself as religious — mystical, spiritual, etc. — to be accorded taxpayer-financed meeting space.

A complete reversal has been enfranchised.

Heretofore, by saying no to space or subsidy requests from each and every student-related religious organization — established as well as aborning — university and college executives spared themselves the torture of drawing lines, of trying to determine who was genuine.

Now, they almost dare not reject any such request, even a deliberately kook outfit, for fear of being accused of showing religious bias.

One can quite understand and follow the logic by which the Supreme Court reached its constitutional judgment and still have reservations about that judgment.

We are, of course, passionately supportive of free speech. That's what the Missouri appeal turned on.

But equating vigorous free speech and particularlized religious practices as equally eligible for public accommodation may end up inviting trouble — religious trouble.

THE SUN

Baltimore, Md., December 17, 1981

The Supreme Court ruled this month that state universities which provide facilities for other discussion groups may not deny religious groups the same treatment. This is the first time the court has so ruled. However, the ruling is not an invitation to public educators generally to get back in the religion business.

What the court said, in a decision by Justice Lewis Powell, is prayer, hymns and Biblical discussions are just a form of speech under certain circumstances. The First and Fourteenth Amendments to the Constitution, which forbid laws "respecting the establishment of religion" by the federal or state governments, also forbid national or state suppression of free speech.

The case involved the University of Missouri at Kansas City and a group of evangelical Christian students known as Cornerstone. The university's stated policy was to allow student groups to hold meetings in university buildings. All students paid activity fees to help support such meetings. Some 100 groups took advantage of the policy. But UMKC denied a request from Cornerstone on the grounds that state support would be involved, and that would violate the Establishment Clause of the First Amendment, which the Fourteenth Amendment imposes on the states. The students sued and now have won.

Justice Powell emphasized that the decision was meant to be a narrow one: when colleges assist student groups to exercise their right to free speech, they may not deny other groups the same right just because the speech involved is religious in nature. College age "young adults," says the opinion, are not likely to interpret such an evenhanded treatment as state "approval" of the particular group's views, much less as state "establishment" of a preferred religion.

Letting the Young Socialists use the same meeting hall does not imply that the university believes in socialism. Letting students pray does not mean the university believes prayers are answered—or even heard. As long as the university policy is one of equity and neutrality for all groups concerned, the right of free speech of religious groups deserves protection under the U.S. Constitution.

It goes without saying that the same reasoning does *not* apply to public schools below the college level, where children might mistake neutrality for approval and even coercion. A few days after the UMKC decision, a related appeal came before the Supreme Court. A lower court had upheld a school board's right to forbid voluntary prayer meetings on high school property. The Supreme Court refused to hear the students' appeal, thus sending a message, we trust, to those who have been fighting "to put God back in the classroom," that the UMKC decision is not the beginning of a retreat under public pressure by the Supreme Court.

ST. LOUIS POST-DISPATCH

St. Louis, Mo., December 16, 1981

In two cases only a week apart, the U.S. Supreme Court has in effect made a signicant distinction between the use of public college property and of public high school property for religious worship. In the first case the high court held that, under the free speech and free exercise of religion guarantees of the First Amendment, the University of Missouri at Kansas City had improperly barred a student religious group from using a university building for its meetings. The court held that as long as the public forum of the university was open to all forms of discourse, the student religious group had a free speech right to use the facility — although the university could still regulate the time, place and manner of such meetings.

The second case was not ruled on directly by the Supreme Court. But it let stand without comment a decision by the 2nd Circuit U.S. Court of Appeals in which that tribunal held that a high school in upstate New York had improperly allowed a student group to hold prayer meetings in a classroom before the start of school each morning. That practice, the appellate court said, involved the state in "an excessive entanglement with religion" in violation of the First Amendment ban on state support for an establishment of religion.

In its ruling in the New York case, the appellate court made several points that show the distinction between use of high school and university facilities for worship: The high school prayer meetings were conducted before class but still "during official school hours." Supervision would be needed to "guarantee that participation in the prayer meetings would always remain voluntary." To impressionable high school students, school involvement might indicate that the state had approved "a particular religious creed." All of these things, the court suggested, meant that the school was advancing religion rather than remaining neutral. In the Missouri case, the university could more easily remain neutral.

The San Diego Union

San Diego, Calif., December 14, 1981

In an eminently sensible decision handed down last week, the U.S. Supreme Court defined the correct constitutional distance between religion and the state, which has become indistinct through previous rulings.

By an eight-to-one vote, the court said state universities that permit student groups to use campus facilities for meetings must also let these same groups hold worship and study sessions in those facilities.

The case arose from the prohibiting by the University of Missouri, Kansas City, of use of university property for religious purposes. A student religious group sued, asserting its First Amendment rights of free speech and free exercise of religion had been violated.

A lower court held the university was correct in banning religious use of its facilities because of the constitutional ban on state "establishment of religion." But, the students prevailed when an appeals court overturned the lower court, ruling that the issue was not promulgation of religion by the state university but denial of a category of speech, namely religious speech.

In upholding the appeals court, Justice Lewis Powell, writing for the majority, said university openness to religious groups was not a state advancement of religion. But Justice Byron White in his lone dissent asked this troublesome question: If all religious worship comes under the protection of free speech, what additional purpose is served by the constitutional guarantee of free exercise of religion? He said, if the majority opinion is correct, the court should review its ban on school prayers and the mandatory posting of the Ten Commandments in Kentucky's public schools.

The difficulty is that the court, in guarding against state religious entanglement under the Establishment Clause, has sometimes prohibited religion altogether.

The resulting confusion has led institutions and the judiciary such as the University of Missouri and a lower court to think that no religious group could meet in a university facility, which was otherwise available to homosexuals, Communists, Democrats, and even Republicans.

Who can seriously believe the founding fathers entertained such an intention when they wrote the Constitution? It is heartening to see now that the Supreme Court does not think so.

St. Petersburg Times
St. Petersburg, Fla., December 11, 1981

A U.S. Supreme Court decision this week cast some light on two other controversial issues, prayer in the schools and the Florida Legislature's attempt to cut off the funds of any public university that allows some groups to meet on campus.

THE CASE arose in Missouri when the University of Missouri at Kansas City refused to permit an evangelical Christian group named Cornerstone to use a meeting room. The court said the refusal violated the students' right to free speech. It said that as long as the university permitted secular groups to meet in campus buildings, it must allow student religious groups the same privilege. The court said that state regulations on free speech issues "should be content-neutral."

Associate Justice Lewis F. Powell wrote in the majority opinion: "The university has opened its facilities for use by student groups and the question is whether it can now exclude groups because of the content of their speech. Religious worship and discussion are forms of speech and association protected by the First Amendment."

The court emphasized that the case was decided on narrow grounds and was not directly related to its opposition to officially sponsored prayer in public schools. But the ruling still should help the public understand the difference between the state's neutral position in providing university meeting space and the non-neutral position of imposing a "voluntary" prayer on impressionable children forced by the state to attend public school.

THE DECISION also sends a message to the Florida Supreme Court, which has before it an attempt by the Legislature to cut off funds to any public university allowing groups to meet on campus that might advocate sex between unmarried persons. The measure was aimed at homosexuals. The Florida law clearly is unconstitutional because it excludes groups "because of the content of their speech." Most Floridians can make distinction between their disapproval of some sexual practices and petty laws that violate basic American freedoms.

The Birmingham News
Birmingham, Ala., December 17, 1981

The United States Supreme Court handed down curiously contradictory rulings about providing space in publicly supported colleges and secondary schools for religious meetings this week. But, though they do conflict, they also make good sense.

In the case of colleges, the high court struck down a silly ban on such religious gatherings at the University of Missouri. There, university officials prohibited the use of school facilities by an evangelical Christian student group known as the Cornerstone, though it allowed some 99 other recognized student organizations access to them.

The court said, in effect, that if other student groups — such as, say, the Young Socialist Alliance — are allowed space for extracurricular sessions, then religious organizations should be offered the same privilege, otherwise the college is, in effect, censoring the free speech of those who desire to meet voluntarily for religious reasons.

On the surface, that ruling seems in striking contradiction to the justices' decision in a similar case concerning high schools. In a case where students of Guilderland High School, near Albany, N.Y., wanted to hold prayer meetings in a classroom before school, the justices said no.

The court unfortunately did not comment on its reasoning, but the ruling continued a long tradition by the court of treating colleges and high schools differently in such matters. And that probably is a necessary distinction.

Few people would object to allowing an unused high school room to be used for religious meetings, but many more would object to the same being provided for the myriad of political groups such as inhabit a college campus. To have ruled otherwise would have opened a Pandora's box for high school administrators.

The Providence Journal
Providence, R.I., December 14, 1981

It would be wrong to read too much into the U.S. Supreme Court's recent ruling that public universities must permit student groups to meet on campus for religious discussion and worship. The 8-to-1 decision is narrowly drawn with no reference to prayer in the public schools, Nativity scenes erected on public property or any other church-state issue.

An evangelical Christian group at the University of Missouri had been denied permission to hold meetings on campus under a policy that prohibited the use of university property "for purposes of religious worship or religious teaching." The students argued that if other groups could meet for secular purposes, prohibiting religious activities would deny the rights of free speech and association.

The U.S. Court of Appeals for the Eighth Circuit agreed with the students, and fortunately the high court last Tuesday upheld that decision. College campuses ought to be open forums for the unlimited exchange of ideas. To bar religious study and worship would be to proscribe an area of learning and belief that for many is central to the academic process.

There may be merit, to avoid confusion, in noting what the court did not do in this case:

● It did not consider the right to freely exercise religion. Associate Justice Lewis F. Powell Jr., writing for the majority, said it was not necessary to do so because the free-speech finding prevailed. "The university has opened its facilities for use by student groups," he wrote, "and the question is whether it can now exclude groups because of the content of their speech."

● It did not rule on separation of church and state, which the university cited as the rationale for its exclusionary policy. "The university policy," Justice Powell wrote, "misconceives the nature of this case" by focusing almost exclusively on the establishment clause.

● It did not alter its ban on officially sponsored prayer in public schools. It was emphasized that "the basis for our decision is narrow," applying only to voluntary religious activities at state-supported universities.

● It did not decide whether the right of free speech for college students who wish to meet for religious purposes also applies to secondary school students. The U.S. Court of Appeals for the Second Circuit upheld the refusal of the board of education in Guilderland, N.Y., to permit students to hold religious meetings on school grounds. The high court has not yet said whether it will consider the case.

The subtleties of church-state questions impose a heavy burden on the American public. Constitutional restrictions sometimes seem contradictory. For some it may be hard to understand why a government-sponsored Nativity scene is disallowed while a government-sponsored university is required to host religious meetings and services. But there is a difference based on constitutional rights that come into play and sometimes must compete for preeminence.

In the University of Missouri case the court is clearly on solid ground.

Christmas, the Public & the Public Schools

People frequently complain that the true meaning of Christmas has been degraded by department stores, television and commercialism. However, when the complaints turn into action to remove Christmas from the public arena, intense controversy results. The same people who admit that Christmas preparations are tasteless and unnecessary take offense at suggestions to ban decorations from public places and give the holiday less attention in the public schools. The American Civil Liberties Union has been at the forefront of the drive against state involvement in Christmas, and even some religious leaders agree. In Sioux Falls, S.D., the ACLU took up a case on behalf of Roger Florey, who objected to his son's participation in a school Christmas pageant. A federal court ruled in favor of the pageant in 1979, and an appeals court upheld the decision. The Supreme Court refused to hear the case in 1980, thus letting the decision stand. The appeals court had ruled that the Sioux Falls school pageants were "not unquestionably religious in nature." The court added that Christmas carols had "achieved a cultural significance that justifies their being sung in the public schools." Also in 1979, ACLU filed suit to remove a Nativity scene from city property in Denver, Col., but the suit was refused by a federal judge in December 1981. (The case is under appeal.) Admittedly, it is hard to make a distinction between religious and popular when the majority of people celebrate a particular religious holiday. The state, too, blurs the distinction by making Christmas an official day off, closing libraries, schools, post offices and other government bodies. More than any other religious holiday, Christmas is closely entwined with public observance.

The Cincinnati Post

Cincinnati, Ohio, December 20, 1979

How sad that in this season of goodwill to men, people are once again quarreling with each other about where and to what extent the return of Christmas may be acknowledged in public.

Saddest of all is that the arguments take place in front of the children.

In the most extreme incident we've heard about, a teacher's aide in an elementary school in Rockville, Md., took a Christmas tree out of the school office and tossed it in the parking lot. She had "strong feelings about the separation of church and state," she said.

The American Civil Liberties Union, of course, has long championed the same "separation," as it perceives it. And while we may not always agree with the ACLU, we have to acknowledge its consistency.

The ACLU has just won a suit in U.S. District Court in Denver in which municipal authorities have been ordered to remove a manger scene from the city hall. Meanwhile, in St. Louis, the ACLU is appealing another U.S. District Court ruling upholding the singing of Christmas carols in the public schools.

We are tempted to cry "Bah, humbug!" on all those who drag the spirit of Christmas through the courts. Yet we realize that serious Constitutional questions can be involved (the Denver case would seem to qualify). And we know that the commercialization and secularization of Christmas is a real and valid concern to churchmen.

It's just that we keep thinking of the children, to whom Christmas is supposed to belong. How bewildered and confused they must be, and how funny they must think grownups sometimes act.

Chicago Tribune

Chicago, Ill., October 8, 1979

Not all is calm in Sioux Falls, S.D. Not all is bright. The city is in an uproar over a suit by the American Civil Liberties Union asking for a federal court injunction against the singing of "Silent Night" and other religion-oriented Christmas carols in the public schools.

An ACLU attorney, acting on behalf of the father of a kindergarten pupil, argued before the 8th U.S. District Court of Appeals that the Supreme Court's ruling against prayer in public schools applies equally to caroling.

Silly, isn't it? With drugs, indiscipline, and racial strife tearing the nation's public schools apart, do we need a snarling Scrooge of an ACLU lawyer silencing the tiny voices of a kindergarten Christmas choir?

Unfortunately, we do. The ACLU's case is unpopular, and it probably could be pursued in a more productive manner, but it is valid. The principle of separation of church and state is enshrined in the Constitution and supported by a large body of Supreme Court rulings. The widespread acceptance of Christmas caroling as innocent, beautiful, and uplifting does not invalidate that principle. The introduction of religious observances into public schools amounts to support for a particular religion, Christianity in this case. The fact that a single parent objected is sufficient evidence that the acceptance, though widespread, is not universal.

Christian parents who are annoyed by the ACLU case should imagine the situation in reverse, with them living in a neighborhood that is predominantly, say, Moslem, and with a local school that holds prayers and Koran readings, and closes the cafeteria during the Ramadan fast. The Christian parents would protest, and the school board would need no court order to ban the prayer, halt the readings, and reopen the cafeteria. The general Christian population outside the Moslem neighborhood would not be likely to sympathize with any objections by the Moslem parents.

Still, it seems silly to make a federal case of the Sioux Falls "Silent Night." It is like using an elephant gun to kill a mosquito—the offending bug will be blasted, but so will lots of other things. If the courts rule in favor of the ACLU, will judges next decide which carols are acceptable and which are not?

It would be more productive to persuade school boards, administrators, and parents that they must be sensitive to religious views that differ from those of the majority. One person's harmless Christmas carol may be a religious intrusion to another. To invite a judicial and categorical definition of which Christmas carols and customs are religious and which aren't would be asking for trouble; one might even question whether Christmas itself should be a legal holiday. The place to draw these fine lines should be in local communities, not in the courts.

If "Silent Night" can be sung in a particular school without offending minority religious sensitivities, splendid; let the voices ring. If not, "Silent Night" will not be silenced. It will thrive in Sunday schools, church choirs, homes, and, needless to say, department stores.

THE ANN ARBOR NEWS
Ann Arbor, Mich., December 19, 1979

THE AMERICAN Civil Liberties Union is again observing its dreary tradition of threatening court action against communities where Christmas displays appear on public property.

Detroit's corporation counsel, George Matish, himself an ACLU member, rightly says the ACLU "has more important fights to fight".

Responding to the ACLU's demand for removal of a nativity scene from in front of the City-County Building in downtown Detroit, Matish says "My recommendation to the mayor will be that if we allow other religious groups, like the Hari Krishnas, to solicit members and money in front of other public buildings, it cannot therefore be wrong to allow another religious group to memorialize one of their most holy days."

If the ACLU is seriously intent on providing income for lawyers by initiating court suits against government-sanctioned observances of Christmas, it should not merely attack symbols. Instead, it should be going to court demanding that government agencies — including courts — remain open for normal business on December 25.

The same logic would call for an ACLU suit demanding that President Carter withdraw his executive order granting most federal employees an additional holiday on December 24, a Monday, and another ACLU suit demanding that Carter remove the national Christmas tree and the 50 small trees representing U.S. prisoners in Tehran from the public park near the White House.

The essential point ACLU leaders are missing is made by Matish, when he points out that no one's religious or non-religious beliefs are infringed by government so long as competing religious groups are free to use public property if they wish to do so.

* * *

IN MENTIONING Hari Krishna solicitations on public property, Matish reminds us of this relevant fact:

During recent summers, visitors to the Great Smoky Mountains and some other national parks have been accosted on park property by Hari Krishna members asking for money while wearing wigs and imitation park ranger uniforms, and often refusing to identify themselves. Some claim to be collecting money for "Indian schools" or "nature study". A court test as to whether this deceptive activity is entitled to First Amendment protection would be one good example of the "more important fights" the ACLU should be fighting.

THE ATLANTA CONSTITUTION
Atlanta, Ga., September 13, 1979

Silence "Silent Night"? Really now, ACLU, that's a little much.

The American Civil Liberties Union has fought some good fights in its time, and it had has been on some good sides, but on this one, the union is on the wrong silly side. It has taken up the fight for a South Dakota father who doesn't want his son to take part in Christmas assemblies. ACLU wants to ban Christmas carols from public schools on the grounds that carols go against the U.S. Supreme Court's decision banning prayer in public schools.

Hogwash.

If the ACLU can make a case that singing "Silent Night" is praying, then it should be busy as the proverbial bee making cases against some of the real injustices in this society, because if it can make the carol case stick it's an incredibly persuasive organization.

Frankly, we don't think ACLU is that persuasive. At least we hope it isn't. After all, if this case is decided for ACLU's position, where would it all end? Who's to prevent some nut from making a case that Christmas decorations in schools should be banned because they are religious in nature and go against the Supreme Court decision?

And how about banning Santa Claus?

Come on, ACLU. With all the battles that need fighting on the civil liberties front, surely you realize that this is one on which you're wasting valuable ammunition.

But even if ACLU doesn't realize how silly is this suit, surely the 8th U.S. Circuit Court of Appeals will.

Des Moines Tribune
Des Moines, Iowa, December 25, 1979

We can't recall a year when the season of peace on Earth has produced so much angry confrontation. The subject of the hassle is Christmas in the schools.

Christmas is a religious holiday that, because of its innate appeal (love, kindness and gift-giving) and commercial potential, has become the fulcrum for the American business year as well as the focus for much American family life.

It is little wonder that hosts of parents and not a few newspaper columnists have gotten wrought up about schools that have attempted to bar all signs and symbols of Christmas — even trees and Rudolph, the Red-Nosed Reindeer — from classrooms and halls in the name of maintaining the constitutional separation of church and state.

Schools that try to weed out the religious — "Silent Night," stars and manger scenes — and keep the secular have little better luck. In a Metro Poll of Des Moines-area residents, 89 percent said they had no objection to religious themes in school Christmas programs.

The American Civil Liberties Union wants a new Sioux Falls, S.D., school board policy declared unconstitutional. The policy allows carol singing as long as it is clearly not a religious observance. Nativity pageants are banned, and religious symbols must be presented in a context of teaching about religion and not as part of a religious observance. These rules have been approved by a federal judge.

The suit, ironically, was inspired by a 1977 kindergarten program that has few if any defenders. In it, the tots sang "Away in a Manger" and participated in a "Beginners' Christmas Quiz" that amounted to a Sunday School catechism. A parent complained to the school board, which adopted a new policy to guide 1978 Christmas pageants. The parent and the Civil Liberties Union found the new policy also unacceptable, hence the suit.

The Sioux Falls rules under challenge appear to be based on the landmark Supreme Court decision on Bible-reading in the schools, Abingdon Township School District v. Schempp: "Nothing we have said here indicates that such study of the Bible or of religion, when presented objectively as part of a secular program of education, may not be effected consistently with the First Amendment."

Christmas, alas, is one human institution that persistently refuses to be separated into neat secular and religious compartments. Church authorities, over the years, have attempted to purge such pagan trappings as decorated trees and Yule logs — with about the same success as pastors today enjoy when they inveigh against the myth of Santa Claus (or against the commercialization of Christmas).

Civil authorities and civil-liberties organizations who have fought for constitutional principle by trying to purge the trappings of the holiday from public property have done little but earn themselves a niche alongside Scrooge and the Grinch.

Although it is grounded in tenets of a particular faith, Christmas expresses ideals common to all religions — and the moral principles of those who reject religion.

School observances, to be true to these ideals, must steer clear of proselytyzing or preaching. But to deny such a major element of American culture by attempting to purge all references to it is shortsighted educationally and verges on the "religion of secularism" against which the Supreme Court also warned in 1963.

Rocky Mountain News

Denver, Colo., December 19, 1979

IT'S KIND OF like becoming a god, the way some judges see it. You just put on your judicial robe, take your place at the bench and suddenly you're the fount of all wisdom.

Subscribing to that dubious theory, apparently, is U.S. District Judge Richard P. Matsch, who found it impossible the other day to confine his remarks to the legalities of the case before him.

Instead, in ruling that Denver should take down a Nativity scene erected on City Hall steps, he gratuitously slammed Mayor William McNichols on matters far removed from any legal considerations. Matsch talked about "abdication of responsibility for decision making" and explained himself thusly:

"It should be recognized that all who hold public office have an equal obligation to adhere to the United States Constitution. The courts should not be used merely for the convenience of those who wish to avoid the unpleasant consequences of a required resistance to the majoritarian view on a clamorous issue."

In other words, Matsch was saying that McNichols knew good and well that putting up the Nativity scene was unconstitutional and allowed it to happen because that was the popular thing.

Well, is it really that overwhelmingly clear that the Nativity scene is a violation of constitutional guarantees of separation of church and state? All kinds of tax-supported institutions recognize Christmas one way or the other, have done so for decades and have never been told by the courts to cut it out. Even Matsch will probably get the day off on this religious holiday. Mayors prior to McNichols had Nativity scenes put up at City Hall without anyone worrying overly much about it. And Matsch says it's OK for the Christmas lighting display to stay on the building, although it would be hard to argue convincingly that those lights have no religious connotations. Where, precisely, should the line be drawn? Seems to us, a fairly muddy issue — something reasonable people could debate.

And another point: It wasn't McNichols who wanted this matter taken to court. It was the American Civil Liberties Union. As this paper has previously maintained, the suit was really kind of silly because nothing much was at stake. Can anyone except a fanatic absolutist really believe that the principle of keeping religious propagation out of government hinged on this case? The whole thing was on the order of taking someone's driver's license because he went 55½ miles an hour in a 55-mile-an-hour speed zone. There are all kinds of reasons to keep religion (as opposed to religiously inspired moral beliefs) out of government, but things like City Hall Nativity scenes, White House Christmas trees, placing "In God We Trust" on coins, permitting prayers in Congress and playing religious music on public radio are minor exceptions that do no real harm to anyone. They certainly don't presage an American theocracy.

So why did Matsch feel compelled to deliver his little lecture? Our only answer is that the longer some judges sit on the bench, the more all-knowing they come to consider themselves.

THE DENVER POST

Denver, Colo., December 23, 1979

THERE'S A DIFFERENCE this year in the crowds at the annual Christmas display at Denver's city hall. In the past, most adults and children alike focused on the bright lights or Santa's workshop and Rudolph. Now, they pause at the creche for long periods of contemplation.

The reason is obvious. Last Monday, U.S. District Judge Richard Matsch ordered the Nativity scene torn down. Tuesday, the 10th U.S. Circuit Court of Appeals stayed that order, allowing the display to remain at least for this holiday season while arguments continue.

That was followed by an astonishing display of zealotry by the American Civil Liberties Union, which vowed to take the case to the U.S. Supreme Court in a desperate effort to banish the Nativity scene from the view of Civic Center's Christmas throng. To date, the nation's highest court has shown no signs of interrupting the nation's serious legal business to wrestle with the matter of a Christmas display — but the crowds continue to flock to the creche before it's too late.

It is always thus. We are prone not to value what we have until someone tries to take it away. And any attempted censorship, whether directed at subjects sacred or profane, whets our appetite for the message our "protectors" would forbid us from seeing.

The holiday season is inherently religious in nature, though by no means exclusively Christian. But we often lose sight of its message amid its hubbub and commercialism. The nugatory and grinchine assault on the holiday display, ironically, has done more to turn our thoughts to the real holiday values than the creche, left unmolested, could have done. That deepened comprehension may indeed be the "gift of the Grinch."

Turning specifically to the legal issues in the case, Judge Matsch's opinion is flawed. But it does point to a way to resolve this trivial tempest in a fashion that would expand freedom of expression, not constrict it.

The First Amendment to the U.S. Constitution forbids the government equally from establishing a particular state religion and barring the free exercise of religion.

The necessary government neutrality can be achieved in two ways: banning all official recognition of religion or recognizing all faiths equally. Our disagreement with the plaintiffs in this case is based on their insistence that only the restrictive approach is permissible. The proper remedy is not to censor the Nativity scene but to elevate other viewpoints to an equal status. Judge Matsch's opinion at least alludes to that possibility.

The current controversy has an interesting relevance to the issues raised by the U.S. Supreme Court in a case involving prayers in public schools. Generally, schools properly take the view that religion is too important a part of American life to be ignored. Instead of promoting a specific creed, however, they discuss all even-handedly. Such an educational exercise, a celebration of our cultural heritage, is clearly appropriate for the city.

The city could readily sell the creche to private groups and give them the responsibility for erecting it. That reduces the question to whether such private displays may be made on public property. We believe they could be if other religious viewpoints were allowed equal access on such dates as are appropriate to their own faiths. This is the approach which allowed Pope John Paul II to conduct religious services on public property during his recent U.S. visit: no "establishment" of religion was involved since all groups had reasonable access to the same privilege.

By ultimate ACLU logic, we should ban the Christmas lights as well as the creche and stop letting public employees of any religious faith off work on their sacred holidays. But Matsch rightly noted the lights are not at issue in this case — and while they have religious significance to many, their meaning is not exclusively Christian.

The creche and comparable exhibits from other religions may be offensive to some. But the First Amendment does not confer the right to silence beliefs with which one may disagree — only to equally express one's own views.

Such a response to this controversy would increase understanding of all elements in our pluralistic society about the values and tenets of each other's beliefs. If that is the outcome, we may indeed rejoice for the gift of the Grinch.

Post-Tribune
Guarding Your Interests Daily

Gary, Ind., December 20, 1979

So far as we know, our area schools have made it through another season without anyone going to court charging that the singing of "Silent Night" violated the Constitution.

But hold your applause. Next year it might be different. The issue of religious carols in schools hit the high courts in South Dakota and probably will end up in the laps of the U.S. Supreme Court.

Despite a fondness for the First Amendment and its essential safeguards against governmental meddling, this persistent challenge to carol singing is a bit much. It's out of harmony with the melodies that sing in our hearts this time of year.

It's a darned, irritating nuisance. But it has to be dealt with. There is a constitutional prohibition against establishing religion by law. Nobody can challenge that with much rationality. The South Dakota case involves some parental complaints about the religious content of a 1977 Christmas program put on by two Sioux Falls kindergarten classes. One federal court says the program is OK. An appeals court is pondering the case now. Next, the highest court of all — human court, that is.

It is foolish to predict that the outcome will be, but it is probably safe to suggest that we have not heard the last of this issue, no matter what the ruling in the South Dakota case.

What we all should do is to take a good look at the issue. Is there an argument against the use of religious carols in school programs? Most of us find it hard to see one. Anyone who has sat misty-eyed through a Christmas program presented by kids of any age in school is not thinking about the Constitution. The thoughts are about how warm the music makes us feel.

Those who challenge such programs may be doing us all a good turn. Attempts to force religious thoughts on children would be intolerable — that is not the function of public schools.

We have seen no threat to the First Amendment in any area school program, nor do we believe there is any. If that is based on a prejudice in favor of old habits and traditions — well, so be it.

But courts do not, and should not, allow sentimentality to influence decisions. Devotional use of the Lord's Prayer and daily Bible readings in public schools have been ruled unconstitutional. Those seem to be more obvious threats to freedoms than the singing of carols, but don't count on a court feeling that way.

We have no profound thought to end this discussion with. One thing sure, nobody should blindly react to these challenges as some kind of anti-God, kooky deeds. We will gain more by poring over the Constitution and sorting out our thoughts.

Having been forced to do that, some of us may receive a Yule gift we had not expected: A better understanding of the document that guarantees equal rights to everybody. Not bad, right?

The Miami Herald
Miami, Fla., September 14, 1979

THE *Silent Night* will be silent, indeed, if an American Civil Liberties Union suit from South Dakota succeeds in banishing Christmas carols from public-school assemblies. That would be a shame and, worse, a perversion of the Constitutional principle of the separation of church and state.

Americans may not be told by any government that they must pray, or how to pray. Nor may any government deny an individual the right to worship in his own way. For that reason the U.S. Supreme Court was correct when it ruled in 1963 that schools may not require the recitation of prayers or Bible verses.

The ACLU, which ordinarily has a fine sense of subtle distinctions, now unwisely seeks to extend the prayer ruling to include songs with religious themes — specifically, Christmas carols in schools' holiday assemblies. The argument misses the distinction between the practice of religious worship and the mere appearance of religious trappings in the popular culture.

Silent Night is a song, not a prayer. It has a religious theme, of course, as do *Swing Low, Sweet Chariot, Battle Hymn of the Republic, Amazing Grace,* and the fourth verses of *The Star Spangled Banner* and *America.*

But it's nonsense to assert that every performance of these songs is intrinsically an act of worship. Too many choruses of *When the Saints Go Marchin' In* have echoed under too many barroom rafters to sustain that argument. One can sing *Adeste Fideles* without professing the divinity of Jesus as readily as one can sing *Santa Claus Is Comin' to Town* without believing in Santa.

Art, literature, drama, and music are filled with religious themes that students ought to know. Religious content must be matched with a worshipful context before the rightful separation of church and state is breached. Only if the school assembly is, in fact, a worship service, rather than a mere holiday festival, is the Constitutional principle violated.

If a school system maintains a proselytizing attitude toward "encouraging" Sunday School attendance, emphasizing the doctrinal aspects of Christmas and Easter holidays, and ignoring non-Christian or nontraditional views, history, and practices, then it probably shouldn't be allowed the temptation of a Christmas program at all, whether carols are sung or not.

But if a school generally is respectful of religious diversity — including the students' right to freedom *from* religion — and throughout the year is sensitive to a variety of religious holy-day observances, it should not be prohibited from including *Silent Night* in its Christmas assembly.

The First Amendment's intent is to protect individual religious freedom. That goal is well-served by keeping group worship out of the schools. There is no need to substitute the opposite evil of turning the public school into an anti-religion censor that snips every reference to religious themes from the expressions of popular culture or art.

Court Bars Ten Commandments, OKs Christmas in Schools

During November, the Supreme Court was asked to decide on two cases of religious observance in the nation's public schools. In a case that received much attention, the court Nov. 17 ruled, 5-4, that a Kentucky law requiring public schools to post copies of the Ten Commandments in every classroom violated the constitutional separation of church and state. The Kentucky law had been enacted in 1978 and specified that the funds for supplying the copies of the Ten Commandments should come from voluntary contributions, not taxes. The legislature thus hoped to avoid the constitutionality question. The law was challenged by a number of Kentucky religious leaders. The Supreme Court ruled that the law was "plainly religious" even though no public money was used. The justices said the Ten Commandments could be included "in an appropriate study of history, civilization, ethics, comparative religion or the like."

In an earlier case, the court Nov. 10 refused to review, thus letting stand, a South Dakota practice of staging Christmas plays in public schools. A parents' group in Sioux Falls had objected to hymns and religious pageants in schools during the Christmas season. The court agreed with an appeals court ruling that the productions were "not unquestionably religious in nature" and that Christmas carols had "achieved a cultural significance that justified their being sung in the public schools."

Roanoke Times & World-News
Roanoke, Va., November 20, 1980

The drive, or coincidental movement, to scrub from public property all traces of the country's Judeo-Christian religious heritage continues willy-nilly. Now the U.S. Supreme Court has ruled, 5 to 4, that it was unconstitutional for Kentucky to pass a law permitting the posting, at private expense, of the Ten Commandments in public school classrooms. It would be similarly unconstitutional, under the same reasoning, for the Supreme Court to paste on its walls, just above and behind the justices, the admonition: Thou Shalt Not Bear False Witness. Stated in a secular fashion, that would be all right. But no, *never*, should an American public building show a trace of its religious heritage.

This, recall, is the same Supreme Court which convenes to the bailiff's cry, "and God save this Honorable Court." The chief justice of this same court, come Jan. 20, will administer an oath to an incoming president whose hand will be on a Bible and who will swear to protect and defend the Constitution of the United States, "so help me God."

Considered in a certain way, the law and the decision are trifling matters. Most states do not have such a law and presumably the children in them are educated as well as those in Kentucky. Content is more important than form; what is in the heart is more important than what is on the wall; religious nuts can be as pestiferous as the patriotic nuts. Considered in such a way, the law and the decision don't make a dime's worth of difference. But take a look at a dime:

● The dime could be unconstitutional itself! On it is inscribed *In God We Trust*. Here we have the government of the United States exercising one of the most exclusive of sovereign powers: coining money, and it inscribes a religious statement on the money!

Well, it was bad enough when they took the silver out of the silver dime and made it not worth an old-fashioned copper penny. The coming event has cast its shadow. The deity, whether viewed as a person or a concept, should not be associated with something as meager as the dime has now become. Libertarians, to arms! Man the ramparts, sound general quarters! Summon the American Civil Liberties Union! The Supreme Court should next be asked to scrub an offending statement from the state-authorized memento.

THE INDIANAPOLIS NEWS
Indianapolis, Ind., November 22, 1980

What the Supreme Court needs to do now is to rethink its recent rulings on the principle of separation of church and state.

The recent ruling on the posting of the Ten Commandments in Kentucky public schools illustrates the weakness of applying this principle well beyond what the Founding Fathers had in mind.

The court, by a 5-4 vote, declared that the state law requiring the Ten Commandments in every classroom was unconstitutional. "The pre-eminent purpose for posting the Ten Commandments on schoolroom walls is plainly religious in nature," the court ruling declared. "The Ten Commandments is undeniably a sacred text in the Jewish and Christian faiths, and no legislative recitation of a supposed secular purpose can blind us to that fact."

Obviously the origin of the Ten Commandments is "religious." But does the religious origin of a statement or assertion intrinsically make the assertion a violation of the First Amendment? All the First Amendment states is: "Congress shall make no law respecting an establishment of religion, or prohibiting the free exercise thereof."

Did the Founding Fathers intend with this clause to forbid the posting of the Ten Commandments in public school classrooms?

Elton Trueblood, a retired Earlham College philosophy teacher and eminent writer, thinks they had something else in mind.

Earlier this year he wrote some thoughts pertinent to this recent ruling: "The Founders knew very well, by first hand experience, what establishment meant, and this is all that they forbade. Establishment means putting one denomination in a favored position with public financial support.

"The authors of our Constitution were familiar with the establishment of what we call the Church of England, and this was what they were determined to avoid," he continued. "Valuable as establishment is in Great Britain, with the manifest power of the bishops and with reverent coronations in Westminster Abbey, our ancestors did not wish to perpetuate the practice in North America. But, at the same time, they did not wish to eliminate religious experience from the life of the new nation. If they had wished to do so, there never would have been the practice of opening the session of Congress with prayer or the use of the Bible in the inauguration of presidents and other officers of government."

Perhaps the Founding Fathers were mistaken. Perhaps they should have said something to this effect: "Religious assertions shall not be advanced in the public sphere." But that is not what they said. Those who wish they had said it perhaps should advance this concept in the form of a constitutional amendment. Meantime, the court needs a wholesale review of its recent rulings on the establishment clause.

The Miami Herald
Miami, Fla., November 19, 1980

A RARE and welcome display of sensitivity issued Monday from the U.S. Supreme Court. The Court last week had let stand a lower-court ruling to permit some forms of Christmas observances in public schools. It followed that controversial, though sensible, decision with another that clearly signals the Court's commitment to barring religious trappings from public schools.

Without even waiting to hear arguments in the case, the Justices voted 5-4 to preclude the schools of Kentucky from posting the Ten Commandments in every classroom. The closeness of the vote was misleading; some of the dissenters merely wanted to hear the arguments before ruling.

Thus the Court rejected the Kentucky law's subterfuge that the Ten Commandments have "secular application" as "the fundamental legal code of Western Civilization and the Common Law of the United States." The Justices correctly countered that, while commandments such as "Thou shalt not kill" have application in secular law, others referring to sabbath observations, worshipping only God, and taking the Lord's name in vain are indisputably religious.

In a study of history or religion, the commandments, parts of the Koran, the writings of Martin Luther, and many other religious texts might be appropriate. The difference is that they would be studied, not endorsed by school authorities. By posting the Ten Commandments in every classroom, even at private expense, the state clearly was taking the side of a particular set of religious beliefs. Such an activity is expressly prohibited by the First Amendment ban on "an establishment of religion."

By issuing this ruling soon after the Christmas-observance decision, the Court indicated that the earlier ruling was not intended to reopen the door to religious indoctrination in public schools.

The Justices sensibly acknowledged in the South Dakota case that Christmas is a secular holiday as well as a religious one. In the Kentucky ruling they properly underscored the principle that no religious document, not even one so generally recognized and accepted as the Ten Commandments, may be allowed to take on the aura of a public policy.

The Court has carefully sought to distinguish between popular culture and religion. Its efforts should be applauded — and heeded — by school administrators throughout the nation.

THE KANSAS CITY STAR
Kansas City, Mo., November 19, 1980

The point is not that the powerful moral imperatives of the Ten Commandments would hurt or fail to benefit children and teachers if posted in the public schools of Kentucky. The point is, as the Supreme Court majority has said, that "it is undeniably a sacred text in the Jewish and Christian faiths . . . " and that while adherence to the Ten Commandments might be "desirable," it is "not a permissible state objective under the establishment clause" of the Constitution.

The decision that the Kentucky law was an "establishment" of religion by the state will be argued on both sides by sincere people of good will and by a few who truly would like to force their own beliefs on all humankind by any means available, including the power of the state.

But does not one person's freedom of religion end with the promotion of another religion in institutions of the state? The Supreme Court is not, of course, "outlawing" the Ten Commandments or denying their power and majesty. It is simply saying they are scripture and, as such, cannot be promoted by the taxes of those who might follow other beliefs. Are there no longer homes, churches and religious schools?

Suppose a public school district should come to encompass a majority of Moslems or Buddhists. Would that majority then have the right to post quotations from the Koran or Sutra in the schools for the benefit of all, including the Christian and Jewish minority?

The Constitution must apply to all and with equal weight, not just when it is convenient or only a tiny minority might be relieved of rights. Over two centuries the United States has found benefit in the wall between church and state advocated by Thomas Jefferson.

THE LOUISVILLE TIMES
Louisville, Ky., November 19, 1980

The message the U.S. Supreme Court sent Monday was clear: A 1978 Kentucky law requiring the posting of the Ten Commandments in public schoolrooms is unconstitutional. Therefore, the displays must come down.

The law's unconstitutionality was so obvious to five justices that they refused even to seek briefs or to hear oral arguments. Two of the other four parted with the majority because they wanted the court to grant a hearing.

So an end should be written to Kentucky legislators' attempt to thwart both the intent of the Founding Fathers and the First Amendment's prohibition on laws giving any religion the state's endorsement.

The law tried to evade the Constitution by placing what amounted to a disclaimer on the Ten Commandments. It required that each classroom display contain a phrase stating that the commandments are "the fundamental legal code of Western Civilization and the Common Law of the United States."

That ruse was never convincing. When the Kentucky Supreme Court upheld the law last April, Justice Robert Lukowsky wrote: "It is inescapable that the Ten Commandments are a religious creed." His words failed to carry the day in Kentucky, but they were in step with the nation's highest court which, in its unsigned opinion, expanded the idea:

"The Ten Commandments is undeniably a sacred text in the Jewish and Christian faith and no recitation of a secular purpose can blind us to that fact."

The court also demolished the fiction that the state wasn't offering support to a particular religious viewpoint because private contributions paid for printing, framing and posting the commandments. No matter how financed, "the mere posting of the copies under the law of the legislature provides the 'official' support of the state ... government' that the establishment clause prohibits," the opinion stated.

No doubt the fundamentalists who rammed the bill through the legislature will portray the court's ruling, as they have its decision banning mandatory prayer in the schools, as a sign that the high court wants to eradicate religion from the national experience.

This is disproved by the refusal, just a week ago, to hear a challenge to a Sioux Falls, Iowa, rule that allows public schools to observe holidays "which have a religious and secular basis ... (and) have achieved a cultural significance."

Such observances are a legitimate part of education when they are offered in a way that enriches youngsters culturally without imposing any faith or creed. Nothing in the rule the high court upheld made the observances mandatory.

The decision striking down Kentucky's law was consistent. The justices said that it is entirely acceptable to integrate the substance of the commandments into the school curriculum, since "the Bible may constitutionally be used in an appropriate study of history, civilization, ethics, comparative religion or the like."

The decision was a proper acknowledgment of the nation's pluralistic religious heritage. State officials, in that same spirit, should acknowledge it and remove the commandments from their classroom walls.

FORT WORTH STAR-TELEGRAM
Fort Worth, Texas, November 21, 1980

Religion is not a commodity to be sold like soap and it is not something that can be force fed to people as though they were geese to be fattened.

But there is a segment of our society that insists that religion will cure all our worldly ills. And that segment may be right. The question we ask then is: which religion?

The framers of our Constitution were religious men, but they deliberately wrote that document to include a separation of the church and the state. That division is clear. Disputes have arisen, however, over what constitutes separation or abridgement of separation.

Most prominent has been the argument over prayer in public schools. The use of the Bible in public schools also has been an issue. In 1962, the United States Supreme Court ruled in Engle vs. Vitale that school prayer was unconstitutional. There have been attempts since that ruling to pass in Congress a constitutional amendment to permit prayer in public schools. The recent conservative shift in Congress, particularly in the Senate, has given new fervor to that desire to install prayer in public schools.

And the president of the Fort Worth school board said recently that he would like to see prayer returned to the classroom.

In the face of the new rise of the prayer advocates, the Supreme Court this week ruled that a Kentucky law requiring the posting of the Ten Commandments in public school classrooms was unconstitutional. The ruling was 5 to 4.

Earlier this year, the Massachusetts Supreme Court ruled that a new state law that required teachers in public schools to grant time for prayer was unconstitutional.

And the battle goes on.

If the advocates of religion in public school persist and win, in the Congress and in the courts, as they may, which religion are they going to use? And which prayers, which bibles and which gods will be attended to in such public religion breaks in our school curriculums?

There are about 50 million Roman Catholics in this nation and about 2 million Muslims and there are countless denominations of Protestants and a few million Jews. And there are many who have no religion.

Religion is a matter of personal choice. It is a function of the churches and the home and not a function of government, whether it be in the legislature or in the public schools.

DAYTON DAILY NEWS
Dayton, Ohio, November 20, 1980

Religion did not suffer from the Supreme Court's decision to strike down a Kentucky law requiring that a copy of the Ten Commandments be posted in every public school classroom.

It's hard to see how a first grader would find relevance in a daily reminder not to "covet thy neighbor's wife" or "thy neighbor's ass"; or why a math teacher should be held criminally liable for neglecting to have the scripture tacked to the classroom-wall.

Education should teach values, but that task requires more than merely posting them. In any case, youngsters are moved more by example than by poster preachments.

Teachers who do think moral philosophy has its place in the school will find no constitutional strictures against displaying the best thought of all great religions in appropriate classes. Surprising how universal and similar they are; and how much youthful sensibilities may be broadened by discoving that the general guidelines for living in harmony with one's fellow human beings are much the same the world around.

TULSA WORLD
Tulsa, Okla., November 19, 1980

THE U.S. Supreme Court has struck down a Kentucky law which required public schools to post copies of the Ten Commandments. Five of nine Justices said the mandatory display of a religious document violated the "establishment of religion" clause in the Constitution.

This is a bad decision — not because it is entirely wrong, but because it is Pecksniffing and trivial. The Kentucky fuss could have easily been ignored by the nation's highest Court with no great harm to religious freedom.

In the narrowest technical sense, the majority may have been right. The Constitution has consistently been interpreted to prohibit the State from forcing purely religious instruction or activity on citizens. The Constitution wisely sets religion aside as a private rather than an official activity in this country. American law and custom clearly reserve religious choices to individuals and prohibit interference in these choices by the State. Well and good.

But if there is an offense against the principle in this instance, it is so minor and so murky that the principle itself seems to be trivialized. As an affront to religious freedom, for example, the Kentucky law cannot compare to the odious practice of forcing prayer services on public school children against their parents' wishes.

The Court held that the Ten Commandments are religious in nature and "the pre-eminent purpose for posting (the Commandments) is plainly religious in nature."

But despite their religious roots, the Ten Commandments also have a broad ethical and moral importance in Western Civilization not tied to any exclusive spiritual belief. They may be read as purely Judeo-Christian religious doctrine — or they may reasonably be seen in the same light as the Magna Carta or the Declaration of Independence as part of a wider legal and philosophical heritage that applies to the civilization as a whole.

It can be contended both ways. The Court's big mistake was to allow itself to be dragged into this hairsplitting argument in the first place.

We agree with Oklahoma Education Association director Weldon Davis.

"It seems frivolous," Davis said, "when there are so many other problems confronting schools."

It's the kind of decision that gives religious freedom a bad name.

The Des Moines Register
Des Moines, Iowa, November 22, 1980

The Supreme Court's 5-to-4 decision striking down a Kentucky law that required the posting of the Ten Commandments in every public school classroom was welcome but hardly surprising. It was in line with the court's 1962 and 1963 rulings against Bible readings and the reading of an "official" prayer in public schools.

In those cases, the court held that such officially sanctioned religious activities violate the First Amendment injunction that "Congress shall make no law respecting an establishment of religion, or prohibiting the free exercise thereof."

The Kentucky Legislature thought it could get around the Supreme Court rulings by having the copies of the Ten Commandments bought with contributions and by posting the following notice with each copy: "The secular application of the Ten Commandments is clearly seen in its adoption as the fundamental legal code of Western Civilization and the Common Law of the United States."

The Supreme Court saw these efforts for the ruse they were. The majority said: "The Ten Commandments is undeniably a sacred text in the Jewish and Christian faiths, and no legislative recitation of a supposed secular purpose can blind us to that fact." It pointed out that several of the commandments (for example, "Thou shalt have no other gods before thee") are clearly religious.

Unfortunately, the court's ruling is unlikely to end efforts to bring religion into public classrooms. There have been repeated efforts in Congress to get around the Supreme Court's rulings on school prayer. Last year, the Senate approved a measure that would bar federal courts from reviewing state laws relating to "voluntary prayer in public schools."

The recent elections have brought more supporters of school prayer into Congress and have elevated one of the strongest advocates, Senator Strom Thurmond (Rep., S.C.), to the chairmanship of the Senate Judiciary Committee.

It would be unfortunate if the school-prayer advocates were to succeed. Imposing on public school students any Bible readings, the Ten Commandments or prayers derived from the Judeo-Christian heritage would trample on the beliefs of children from other religious traditions.

There is a place for religious instruction and indoctrination. That place is not the public school classroom.

THE MILWAUKEE JOURNAL
Milwaukee, Wisc., November 21, 1980

Some church people may think the US Supreme Court went out of its way to strike a blow against religion when it ruled that Kentucky must not require the posting of the Ten Commandments in public school classrooms. Actually, the decision was just a logical application of the Constitution's required separation of church and state.

Granted, the commandments in one sense are part of the secular moral code, and several of them have been incorporated into civil law. First and foremost, however, the commandments are a central element of the Jewish and Christian religions. And, under the American political system, it is not the proper business of the state to impose religious doctrine on schoolchildren.

Those who object to the court's ruling might ask themselves if they would be willing to have the tenets of an alien faith exclusively promoted on the walls of their children's classrooms. If the answer is no, then perhaps they can begin to see what's wrong with giving *any* religion favored treatment in the public schools.

SYRACUSE HERALD-JOURNAL
Syracuse, N.Y., November 20, 1980

The Supreme Court hasn't detoured around its landmark decisions over the last two decades, but continues refining what's meant by religious freedom in the First Amendment of the Constitution.

Students for Voluntary Prayer sued the Guilderland High School (near Albany) to obtain a classroom for their prayer meeting. The court said, "No way!"

This would breach the wall that separates church and state, the court said, but added, "We can't be critical of their objectives."

Neither can we.

* * *

Nor, we think, would their parents or pastors.

Thus we suggest with the court, that the students meet at members' homes and churches. That's not so inconvenient, is it?

In another opinion, the Supreme Court shot down a Kentucky law ordering public school administrators to post a copy of the Ten Commandments in every classroom of the state.

Said the court after a 5-to-4 vote: "The preeminent purpose for posting the Ten Commandments on schoolroom walls is plainly religious in nature. The Ten Commandments is undeniably a sacred text in the Jewish and Christian faiths, and no legislative recitation of a supposed secular purpose can blind us to that fact."

* * *

Youngsters aren't isolated from such teachings as "You shall not kill," or "You shall not commit adultery," or steal, or lie about a neighbor or covet another's wife and property.

Children's parents and grandparents, their teachers in private and public schools let them know what's required of everyone as law-abiding citizens who honor their parents.

Nine years ago, the court created a three-part test for determining whether state law violates the First Amendment's the "establishment" of religion. Chief Justice Burger wrote:

● "First, the statute must have a secular legislative purpose;

● "Second, its principal or primary effect must be one that neither advances nor inhibits religion;

● "And finally, the statute must not foster an excessive government entanglement with religion."

* * *

Forcing school districts to solicit funds for the posters isn't secular enough, the text is obviously sacred and promotes two religious groups, and, finally, state government shouldn't be in the business of promoting either.

Those three measurements aren't a bad test.

What can be done and should be done at home, doesn't have to be done in school.

THE ELEVENTH COMMANDMENT: DISREGARD THE FIRST TEN
— THE U.S. SUPREME COURT

St. Petersburg Times

St. Petersburg, Fla., November 22, 1980

Almost two decades have gone by since the Supreme Court drew the line between public school and Sunday school, yet the decisions remain profoundly misunderstood.

In prohibiting prayer and Bible-reading exercises, the court said that the Constitution does not allow government to promote religious practice among its schoolchildren, who are a captive audience. At the same time, the court virtually invited public schools to present the Bible, and other aspects of religion, in their educational context. To teach, yes; to preach, no. Courses in religious history, in the Bible as literature, in comparative religion — if honestly and fairly taught — these all would fall within the legitimate purview of the public schools. So said the court.

THE DIFFERENCE ought not to be hard to see, but few educators and even fewer politicians have been able to open their eyes. Comparative religion is taught rarely. The Bible, though it contains some of humanity's most exquisite poetry, is still neglected in the literary sense. About all that happened is that irresponsible politicians found in the decisions another opportunity for irresponsibility. The tried to evade the decisions and failed. Now they are trying again.

It was one of these exercises of pretentious orthodoxy and deep-seated hypocrisy that led the Kentucky legislature, two years ago, to require that the Ten Commandments be posted in every public school classroom. It was an insincere, pointless act. Does anyone imagine the schoolchildren of Kentucky lining up to ponder the ethical and historical implications of that writing on the wall? What it was, and nothing more, was the Kentucky legislature thumbing its nose at the Supreme Court and at the Constitution of the United States.

Predictably, the Supreme Court struck down that law this week. Five justices didn't even see it close enough for oral argument. The court was right. And once again, it invited the nation's public schools to teach religion in its proper, constitutional perspective. This is what the court said:

"The pre-eminent purpose for posting the Ten Commandments on schoolroom walls is plainly religious in nature . . .

"**THIS IS NOT** a case in which the Ten Commandments are integrated into the school curriculum, where the Bible may constitutionally be used in an appropriate study of history, civilization, ethics, comparative religion or the like. Posting religious texts on the wall serves no such educational function."

Once again, the court has drawn a distinction *and* a difference. Teach yes, preach no. But is anyone listening?

The Cincinnati Post

Cincinnati, Ohio, November 22, 1980

We would like to think that the Supreme Court's refusal to review a lower court decision in South Dakota permitting limited religious holiday observances in the public schools will soften some of the controversy surrounding this perennial issue.

It's probably a fond hope, however. The court's action, or nonaction, does not set a binding precedent on lower courts. Many people will continue to have inflexible opinions, on both sides.

In the present case, all the Supreme Court did was let stand an appeals court approval of a set of guidelines established by the Sioux Falls school board.

Teachers may explain to students "the historical and contemporary values and the origin of religious holidays." But they are prohibited from trying to indoctrinate students in any way.

In a parallel case, the Supreme Court knocked down a Kentucky law requiring the display of the Ten Commandments in all public schools. While we basically agree with the ruling, we think an additional point needs to be made: Learning about the Ten Commandments is not an exercise in religion. That ancient code is such an integral part of our Judeo-Christian tradition that it forms a basic building block in the heritage of Western man.

As such, no person—a believer or not—can be considered adequately educated if he or she does not possess an understanding of the commandments and the historic role they have played in forming our civilization and its values.

The Sioux Falls guidelines, nonetheless, seem to be a sensible compromise between the need to keep the schools religiously neutral and the need of children to learn about and, if they wish, to celebrate certain things that are part of their common cultural heritage.

ARKANSAS DEMOCRAT

Little Rock, Ark., November 15, 1980

The Supreme Court has blessed the singing of hymns and carols and the staging of religious plays in public schools on religious holidays. Hallelujah!

The court has finally begun to realize that "the free exercise of religion" is what the First Amendment is all about — and that official sanction of religious activity on public property doesn't "mix church and state," to use the ignorant unconstitutional term that misstates the relationship.

How about school prayer, distribution of bibles in schools and the erecting of religious displays (like Christmas creches) on public property?

No, the ruling applies only to religious holiday observances in public schools. Yet, the court has affirmed the momentous principle that public bodies can associate themselves with religious observances without 'mixing church and state" – without, that is, foisting an official "establishment of religion" on the people. It will be hard to hold that principle in check.

The objection raised against prayer or distribution of bibles in schools is the same as that that was heard against school hymns – that a public body cannot associate itself with any religious observances, however passively, without being guilty of trying to set up an official "establishment of religion, meaning a government church.

But now that the court has brushed the "establishment" objection aside in the case of school hymns, how will it be able to see an establishment of religion in other passive associations of government with religion on other days of the year.

The court's decision seems to be based on Christmas. Christmas is our greatest public event, and the justices, no doubt, realized the silliness of trying to keep its observance out of schools. But religious holidays are part and parcel of religions in general, and it would be even sillier – once the permissibility of state-church association is established – to limit the association to "religious holidays only."

After all, the test of an establishment of religion is one of official intent – whether the public body associating itself with a religious activity is "pushing" religious observances of its own. In all the religious activities mentioned, the question, "Who wants this religious observance – the public body or the people?" yields the answer, 'The people, obviously." So if government says no to the people, it isn't refraining from pushing its own religion on them – far from it. It is interfering with their "free exercise of religion."

It is this free exercise that the First Amendment guarantees and aims at maximizing when it tells government (1) not to interfere with the innumerable private exercises of religion and (2) not to reduce those many religious exercises into any "state religion" and make everybody conform to it.

If the court and the country can grasp the fact that only government can mix church and state and that government is guilty of doing so only when it "pushes" religious observances of its own with a view to a takeover, old fears of religious exercises on public property will drop away – and the free exercise of religion that the founders did their best to guarantee will finally come into its own.

THE SAGINAW NEWS
Saginaw, Mich., November 17, 1980

The Supreme Court last week freed public schools to include religious music and materials in programs marking holidays such as Christmas.

Our reaction is a muted, cultural, secular "hallelujah."

Some South Dakota parents asked the court to review whether religious content of any kind should be allowed in public schools. The court refused, and let stand a set of local guidelines that allow singing of Christmas carols, for instance.

We wish the court had issued the same decision after hearing the case. A full opinion could have made two things clear. First, the role of religion and religion-based holidays in American culture and history is a proper topic in the classroom. Second, the court is sanctioning neither formal religious exercises, such as prayer periods, nor teaching of religious doctrine.

As it is, local districts will have to take care to protect the rights of all students. Our diverse society includes many who either do not believe in religious observances, or believe that public schools aren't the place for them. On this emotional issue, the potential for abuse is great.

But the court majority clearly felt that it would be pointless, even hypocritical, to order schools to pretend that religion does not exist in American life. Taken to its logical conclusion, such an absolutist legal approach would lead to banning Christmas as a paid holiday for public employees.

The South Dakota guidelines restricted use of religious symbols, music or literature to teaching about the cultural heritage of the holiday. That makes sense. We hope Saginaw-area educators use them — and don't exceed them.

The Knickerbocker News
Albany, N.Y., November 13, 1980

The Supreme Court just upheld the right of schools to hold Christmas pageants using religious hymns and dialogue about the birth of Jesus.

We have long advocated keeping church and state separate, so we were tempted to say "Hooray for the Supreme Court!" — but it's not that simple.

The entire topic creates a no-win situation. The attempt to sanitize our public institutions free of every jot and tittle of religious contamination is being carried to silly extremes. This instance and the attempt several years ago to ban Christmas carols from a Midwestern school are two cases in point.

On the one hand, the widespread use of Christmas carols, for example, by Christians, non-Christians and persons uninvolved in religion, has secularized them to a great extent. By, in effect, recognizing this in its latest decision, the Supreme Court is offending those who object to having a symbol of their religion secularized by judicial fiat.

On the other hand, those who think that despite this secularization the court is breaking down the church/state separation are offended.

The situation is further muddled when one considers the case of the Guilderland students who have been unsuccessful in getting court approval to use a vacant classroom for a before-school prayer group. That certainly is not a secular activity, and the courts so far have banned it.

We don't have the definitive answer, but there appears to be a subtle shading of thought that marks the almost-uncharted border. The Supreme Court let stand an appeals court ruling that said: "The First Amendment does not forbid all mention of religion in public schools; it is the advancement of or inhibition of religion that is prohibited."

A prayer group is obviously "advancement." But a pageant — the presentation of religiously oriented material (for what purpose — education? entertainment? Certainly not worship) — is on the other side of a faded, thin line.

There are some things that are, quite simply, so integral a part of Americans' cultural and psychological heritage they can never be obliterated. The Pilgrims, for instance, were religious refugees; their very dress was dictated by religion.

The Christmas tradition is very strong in much of the country. Even many of those whose religious faith doesn't include the birth of Christ still observe a holiday season of good cheer, gift-giving and reverence for tradition with their Christian neighbors. And even those who don't can hardly evade the festivities (and the commercial hoopla) around them. Even those who don't have much of a religion at all "believe" in Christmas.

We are a nation committed to God, though we have many different ways of defining and identifying Him. Toleration of religious differences has always been America's watchword.

Our public institutions should never promote any religion. But neither can we expect our schools or city halls to be washed clean of any hint of our religious heritage. It can't be done. Even if it could, we shouldn't allow it.

The Hartford Courant
Hartford, Conn., November 16, 1980

The U.S. Supreme Court apparently doesn't feel up to the task of formulating a definitive policy on the usage of hymns, carols and plays with religious themes in the nation's public schools.

The court refused to review a lower court ruling approving school board guidelines that permit music, art, literature and drama with religious themes to be used in holiday programs in Sioux Falls, S.D. The decision of the U.S. Circuit Court of Appeals is now law in seven states.

Many Americans will no doubt find themselves perched precariously and uncomfortably on the fence on this issue, somewhere between the Moral Majority and the absolutist civil libertarians.

Of course, it is proper that groups like the American Civil Liberties Union and the American Jewish Congress continue to test with vigor this country's adherence to the constitutional principle of separation of church and state.

Their efforts are particularly important now, when national sentiment for prayer in school and a general recognition of the United States as a Christian nation seems to be ascendant.

Further, there were some practices endorsed by the school board in Sioux Falls that seem particularly dubious.

But is is unrealistic, at best, to try to hermetically seal public schools off from the rest of American society, which is unmistakably preoccupied after Thanksgiving by the Christmas holiday.

Christmas has become an intrinsic part of our culture and history. In fact, so secularized and commercialized has Christmas become that the most common complaint about it is that it has lost its religious significance altogether.

Public schools cannot, and perhaps should not, proceed oblivious to the fact that Christmas existed and that it is, at root, a religious observance of a majority of people in this country.

Christmas should be acknowledged in public schools, like Rosh Hashana or Ramadan, as part of the diverse cultural heritage of this nation.

Public schools must surely abstain from promoting any religion, but they are not educating children by trying to artificially insulate them from the significance of religious holidays or their manifestations in music, art, literature or drama.

To delete any reference to religion in our public schools amounts to censorship, a precarious and uncomfortable position for civil libertarians.

The Register

Santa Ana., Calif., November 27, 1980

Two court decisions of some significance were rendered last week on the matter of religion in the public schools. As is often the case when the interests of church and state become entangled, shades of gray are everywhere and the clear line of demarcation we would like to believe exists between God and government is, in fact, very hard to locate. But, on the basis of distinctions we find helpful to draw, we suggest that the jurists were right in one instance and wrong in another.

Our dividing lines are these: First, whether the activity in question was prescribed by school administrators or initiated by students, and beyond that, whether religious themes are sounded in the course of classroom work to lend them official sanction or merely to recognize their undeniable role in historical and contemporary thought.

By these standards, the U.S. Supreme Court's ruling against the state of Kentucky ordering placement of the Ten Commandments on perpetual display in all classrooms is appropriate. The banning of before-school prayers by a federal appeals court in New York is more suspect.

When considering the Kentucky decision, we ought to be clear right off about what the Supreme Court did *not* do, lest we allow this decision to be broadly interpreted the way an earlier court's 1962 decision on mandatory school prayers has been. In the pursuit of this clarity, the lead paragraph in our news service account the following morning is regrettable: "The Supreme Court Monday barred the Ten Commandments from the walls of public school classrooms." Only if one stretched the literal meaning of that sentence would it be correct. Its essence is wrong: the language used by the court in 1980 no more forbids religious text from occupying its respective place in instructional displays than the 1962 ruling prohibited children from saying prayers on their own.

What the court said was that the state couldn't order specially prepared copies of the commandments to occupy space in the way that symbols of the government of which the schools are a part — like the flag, or the Constitution — often do. Kentucky officials tried to sidestep the church-state separation by funding the project privately and printing a disclaimer on each copy, but the thrust of the required display remained obvious. Some argue that the Ten Commandments are deserving of special status because of their contribution to Western civilization, or because the Founding Fathers of this nation made reference to God's inspiration in their earliest works of state. The answers to these contentions are, first, that other artifacts of our culture's development are not accorded similar treatment in Kentucky or elsewhere, and second, though respect for the divine may be part and parcel of our law, the specifics of *Exodus 20* are not. Kentucky, for example, no longer has laws against adultery and Sunday work, and neither do California and many other states.

Where the highest court confined itself to matters of state action in Kentucky, the New York appellate panel drifted into what are largely affairs of the individual in its refusal to allow prayer meetings at a high school near Albany.

The court could argue, and did, that the provision of a tax-paid facility to the Students for Voluntary Prayer organization constitutes "an improper appearance of official support" for religion. But to do so is to ignore the substance of what was occurring, in the same way that the state of Kentucky attempted to deny the religious nature of its wall display. In New York, the students met together like any other school club, on their own time and at the school building for purposes of convenience. Allowing them to do so connotes no more state approval for their agenda than it would for the hobbies or interests of countless other recognized organizations. The essential point is that the state must be neutral to religion, not single it out for special treatment propitious or adverse.

(In the New York case, it should be noted that the prayer sessions were held immediately prior to the commencement of classes, lending them the unfortunate appearance of routinization. According to the *New York Times* report, the justices made reference to this temporal proximity to the start of classes, but didn't say that their ruling revolved around it.)

The search for some proper balance of church and state in the schools will continue, and probably as long as government-run institutions maintain their dominant role in the teaching of the young. The ideal solution would be to allow for a real choice in schooling by relieving private-school parents of the burden of taxes for facilities they don't utilize. In the meantime, though, the state schools remain the cutting edge in a debate over the place of religion in a secular world, and we can only hope for clearer and more consistent opinions from the courts in that regard.

The Evening Gazette

Worcester, Mass., November 20, 1980

Within a week, the U.S. Supreme Court made two decisions that seem to contradict each other: It ruled unconstitutional a Kentucky law requiring posting of the Ten Commandments in classrooms, but refused to hear an appeal of a South Dakota ruling that religious symbols, music and literature may be used in school holiday celebrations.

In the Ten Commandments ruling, the 5-4 majority found that posting the commandments, even though not at state cost, violated the First Amendment prohibition of establishment of religion. Even though there may be secular reasons for teaching the Ten Commandments (because they are important to the cultural and legal traditions of our country), the court determined that the commandments are "undeniably a sacred tradition in the Jewish and Christian faiths."

Their posting, framed on schoolroom walls, not discussed in the pages of history books, clearly intends them to be a model for students — certainly a religious model. The commandments may be superb ethics, but they are religious, too.

As for holiday celebrations, the Supreme Court let stand a South Dakota appeals court ruling that celebrations of some religious holidays could be allowed because the days have acquired "a significance which is no longer confined to the religious sphere of life. It has become integrated into our national culture and heritage."

In these matters, firm lines are hard to draw. Some feel that Christmas and Santa Claus have become so secularized as to be harmless. Perhaps the Easter bunny can be squeezed in under that reasoning. But it plainly would go against the spirit of the First Amendment to permit purely religious celebrations to be held on school property and on school time, even if those celebrations are based on beliefs shared by the majority.

It is precisely this crucial distinction — between learning about religion and observing it — that was cited by the American Civil Liberties Union in appealing the South Dakota ruling. In the Ten Commandments case, the Supreme court saw that distinction; in the South Dakota case, it did not.

Our nation's currency, engravings on official buildings, mottoes and pledge of allegiance reflect a traditional recognition of a Judeo-Christian God. It is an uphill task to maintain the separation of church and state required by the Constitution. The Ten Commandments outlawed in Kentucky schools paradoxically are emblazoned on the walls of the Supreme Court building. If the line is to be clearly drawn anywhere, however, it is in the schools, where children meet and absorb the lessons on which our society is based.

The Chattanooga Times

Chattanooga, Tenn., November 21, 1980

In striking down a Kentucky law that required the posting of a copy of the Ten Commandments in each public school classroom in the state, the Supreme Court in effect wrote a new one: "Thou shalt not trivialize the Ten Commandments." The court's 5-4 decision was a wise one.

The court held that the law amounted to an unconstitutional "establishment" of religion, a point that gains strength in light of the state's efforts to depict the Commandments as something other than religious in nature. The Kentucky legislature had written into the law a requirement that each copy of the Ten Commandments include a small-print notice that the Commandments serve as "the fundamental legal code of Western Civilization and the Common Law of the United States." Another diversionary effort was the legislature's decision to underwrite the project with voluntary contributions collected by a foundation, not tax dollars.

It is true that the Ten Commandments serve as one basis for the legal codes of the United States and other nations. It is also true that the imperatives contained therein constitute a valuable guideline by which to live. But more important, the Commandments are first of all a part of the Jewish and Christian religions' sacred texts. And that is the point which undermined the constitutionality of the Kentucky law.

It's hard to question the legislators' good intentions; apparently they believed that posting the Ten Commandments in the classrooms would encourage more young people to learn right from wrong. But that responsibility is two-fold. The state, through the schools, can encourage young people to be law abiding citizens by teaching them, for instance, that it is wrong to steal. Most of the Ten Commandments, however, are purely religious in nature. Teaching compliance with those requirements is hardly the state's role. Posting the Commandments as Kentucky did trivializes their importance.

CHARLESTON EVENING POST

Charleston, S.C., November 17, 1980

They're going to have Christmas in Sioux Falls, S.D., after all.

Last week, the U.S. Supreme Court upheld a ruling by a Circuit Court of Appeals saying that public schools can conduct Christmas pageants that include the singing of traditional carols and dialogue about the birth of Jesus.

A suit had been brought by individuals in Sioux Falls who argued that the pageants "inhibit members of the minority faiths by relegating them to the status of outsiders."

The First Amendment to the U.S. Constitution says that "Congress shall make no law respecting an establishment of religion, or prohibiting the free exercise thereof...", and it is on this that those bringing the suit based their case. They contended that Christmas pageants, conducted in the public schools, violated the doctrine requiring separation of church and state. The courts did not agree. Neither do we.

America is a country of great ethnic and religious diversity, and it should remain so. The idea of a perfect "melting pot" is, we believe, repugnant to many who believe that they and their country are enriched by the freedom not to conform. For all that, ours is also a country steeped in tradition, proud of a distinctly American heritage. To contend that Christmas is not part of that heritage, and that it is something the young must be protected from, is to argue nonsense.

Those who seem intent to get Christmas out of the schools should try instead to get dicussion of their religious or moral beliefs into them. The youth of America today need all the help in this area they can get.

Charleston, S.C., November 19, 1980

Just when we begin to think the U.S. Supreme Court has acquired a bit of common sense (see our last Monday editorial, "Church And State"), a new nonsensical decision is handed down.

This week the nine wise men held, in a 5-4 ruling, that it is unconstitutional to post the Ten Commandments in public schools. "The pre-eminent purpose for posting the Ten Commandments on schoolroom walls is plainly religious in nature," the court said. "The Ten Commandments is undeniably a sacred text in the Jewish and Christian faiths, and no legislative recitation of a supposed secular purpose can blind us to that fact."

Beautiful. Just beautiful. Which of the commandments, do you suppose, did the justices find most objectionable? Which do they believe would prove most dangerous to young and impressionable minds?

Honor thy father and mother?

Thou shalt not kill?

Neither shalt thou commit adultery?

Neither shalt thou steal?

How could anyone in command of his faculties say that these things serve a *"supposed* secular purpose"?

We don't know either.

The Boston Herald American

Boston, Mass., November 23, 1980

The Supreme Court has realistically acknowledged the impossibility of hermetically sealing the public schools against religion. Its decision to allow the singing of Christmas carols and the observance of other religious holidays in the schools of Sioux Falls, S.D., is a reasoned response to an effort by the American Civil Liberties Union to banish religious influences in the schools.

Now Sioux Falls children can have Christmas programs, even sing "Silent Night" along with "Winter Wonderland" in their classrooms. But it remains clear that the purely religious aspects of church holidays must be reserved for the home and church. In upholding a ruling that the schools may celebrate holidays with "a religious and secular basis," the court has invited a strongly secular dilution of observances by students. Christmas, Hanukah, Easter and Passover will be treated as cultural, rather than spiritual experiences.

This, perhaps, is inevitable if religious holidays are to be observed at all in the cosmopolitan racial, cultural and religious mix of American public schools. But to emphasize Santa Claus, for example, at the expense of spiritual values is a diminution of Christmas which must be rectified outside the schools.

By allowing the most religion that can be tolerated by the Court in secular public school systems, the Court has properly assumed that home, church and synagogue will continue to take responsibility for the spiritual education of young people.

Chicago Tribune
Chicago, Ill., November 25, 1980

The Supreme Court has summarily struck down a Kentucky law requiring that the Ten Commandments be posted in every public schoolroom in the state. It is the kind of decision that will make the Moral Majority groups seethe.

As a matter of constitutional law the decision is so unremarkable and correct that it is at first difficult to imagine why four justices voted against it. The Ten Commandments, while embodying some universally held ethical tenets such as the prohibition of murder, is also a distinctly Judeo-Christian religious code. It speaks of idolatry, the Sabbath, and the worship of a single God.

For a government to insist upon the posting of such a sacred religious text in public schools is a clear violation of the First Amendment of the Constitution that prohibits the state establishment of a religion. It is in the interest of religious tolerance, in which religion can thrive, that the secular Constitution includes this commandment. No majority — moral or amoral — should be allowed to use the power of government to advance a particular creed.

Two of the four dissenters in the case voted only to hold a full scale oral argument in the case before disposing of it. Only two suggested that on the merits they saw something persuasive in the state's defense of its misconceived law. Perhaps it would have been more politic for the court to have afforded the advocates of the law more of a chance to present their case. The Supreme Court has been acting recently more and more like a potentate issuing edicts than like a court of law.

But this should not distract attention from the central issue of principle. The Constitution does not keep government out of affairs of the spirit in order to stifle the spirit but rather to allow the individual human heart room to choose and worship freely. When the state remains secular and tolerant, the faithful have nothing to fear from the state.

The Hartford Courant
Hartford, Conn., November 18, 1980

The U.S. Supreme Court did not rule against God on Monday. The justices did not ban the Bible from classrooms. The high court did not endorse "secular humanism," nor did it forbid teaching about religion.

The court did remove the Ten Commandments from the walls of every public school in the state of Kentucky. Despite all the bombast that is sure to follow, the decision was constitutionally sound, has common sense on its side, and was consistent with other Supreme Court decisions for some time.

What the justices, in their 5-4 decision, essentialy told public school educators and state legislatures was not to be lazy about things religious. The majority opinion emphasized what has been said by the court in other cases involving prayer or Bible reading in public schools: School systems are free to teach about religion, but they are forbidden from directing religious practices, or placing a government stamp of approval on certain religious practices or texts.

An ethics class of any public high school legally still can be awash with copies of the Ten Commandments, just as a literature class reading of Archibald MacLeish's "J.B." could refer to the Book of Job in the Old Testament. A public school curriculum need not pretend that religion is any less important in the history of man than economics, science or politics.

What the Supreme Court demands is a realization that public schools are not chapels, not places of worship. The Kentucky case merely removes the Ten Commandments from the corridor walls; it does not exclude religion from the schools.

Now that the heavy-handed Ten Commandments state law is declared unconstitutional, perhaps Kentucky legislators can be convinced to purge the statute books of another shaky law that permits local school systems to require the reading of the Lord's Prayer every morning. A course on church-state relations might be more beneficial to the children of Kentucky than the arbitrary state insistence on religious observance.

Rockford Register Star
Rockford, Ill., December 1, 1980

While pressures grow that would blur the separation of church and state in this country, two recent court rulings clarify that the "wall of separation" between church and state remains sturdy and functioning.

The United States Supreme Court led off with its ruling negating a Kentucky law requiring the posting of the Ten Commandments in every public school classroom in the state.

The high court said the Kentucky law was unconstitutional because it involved "establishment" of religion by the state.

Kentucky legislators had tried to avoid such a ruling by the U.S. Supreme Court by requiring that each copy of the Ten Commandments bear a message in small print pointing out that these commandments serve as "the fundamental legal code of Western civilization and the common law of the United States."

The high court responded: "The Ten Commandments is undeniably a sacred text in the Jewish and Christian faiths, and no legislative recitation of a supposed secular purpose can blind us to that fact." The Supreme Court allowed as how it might be "desirable" for everyone to adopt these commandments as a personal ethical code, but "it is not a permissible state objective" under terms of the Constitution.

Next came a New York case in which Students for Voluntary Prayer at the Guilderland High School near Albany sued their local board of education for denying them classroom space to pray prior to the start of classes each morning.

Judge Irving R. Kaufman, writing on behalf of a unanimous federal Appeals Court of three judges, cautioned against "an improper appearance of official support" for religion. The court issued an order barring the prayer sessions from classrooms.

"We must be careful that our public schools, where fundamental values are imparted to our children, are not perceived as institutions that encourage the adoption of any sect or religious ideology."

Judge Kaufman said he did not challenge the students' claim that prayer was necessary to their religious beliefs. But he said students are free to hold such prayer sessions before or after school and on weekends "in a church or any other suitable place." A public classroom would not be such a suitable place, he added.

He explained why. "To an impressionable student, even the mere appearance of secular involvement in religious activities might indicate that the state has placed its imprimatur on a particular religious creed. This symbolic inference is too dangerous to permit."

He continued, "Religious activity under the aegis of the government is strongly discouraged and in some circumstances — for example, the classroom — is barred."

Having said that, Judge Kaufman directed his comments to the students who practice voluntary prayer, specifying that "we cannot be critical of their objectives. Introspective activity that seeks to strengthen the moral fiber of our nation's young adults deserves our support, but only in our role as private citizens."

"We hope," he continued, "that the Students for Voluntary Prayer can conduct their prayer meetings and religious discussions at another place and at different times. To permit these activities to occur in the classrooms of a public high school prior to the commencement of the school day, however, would contribute to the erosion of principles articulated by our colonial fathers and embraced by religious dissenters for several hundred years."

It is a carefully worded statement — one that should buttress religious beliefs without the entanglement of the state.

The Courier-Journal
Louisville, Ky., November 19, 1980

THE SPEED with which the U. S. Supreme Court acted on Kentucky's "Ten Commandments" law seems to have left unclear the question of removing the 16-by-20-inch plaques from public-school classrooms. But that's a minor flaw in a constitutional holding that should be welcomed by both religiously minded citizens and those with no beliefs.

There are three reasons to prize Monday's majority opinion of the court: It is politically well-timed. It pierces a legislative pretense that the 1978 law's purpose was purely secular. And it ultimately will add to the religious freedom guaranteed by the Constitution.

The timing was apt. Members of Cong ed to the timidity of Kentucky judges who let the law survive so long. In addition, the decision puts lawmakers on notice that, if they would change the legal status of church and state, they must take the onerous constitutional amendment route. The court appears determined to close off statutory avenues.

Yet, just as in last week's decision on Christmas pageants — an educational exercise that exposes children to the practices of other faiths — the court showed flexibility. It said in the Kentucky opinion what it has said before, that the Bible may legitimately be used in history, civilization, ethics and comparative gress are searching for new constitutional vulgarities to commit; one example is discussed in the editorial above. The incoming adminstration supports a "school prayer" amendment to the Constitution, to overturn the 1963 ruling against state-imposed prayers in the classroom. And many office-holders are bowing and scraping before "morality" politics.

In this atmosphere, the Supreme Court was able, through the Commandments decision, to reinforce the guidelines on church-state cases. The majority acted expeditiously, without formal briefs or arguments, forgoing what might conceivably have been a 7-2 ruling.

This forthright action may be contrast-

religion courses.

The violence done by Kentucky's law to the First Amendment was due to its "plainly religious" purpose. The court dismissed the legislature's pretense that its purpose was only secular; likewise it rejected the notion that the private donations for the placards mitigated state involvement. Ordering the posting of the Commandments fostered a particular faith or faiths. Such an "establishment of religion" was wisely opposed in the lawsuit supported by the Kentucky Civil Liberties Union.

Ultimately, such laws threaten the integrity and independence of the Christian, Jewish and all other faiths. Some day, had this law been upheld, controversy about the correct Decalogue text could have forced a state agency to choose one enumeration and wording of the Commandments. But once the civil government became so deeply involved in judging belief, would any religious observance be safe?

The State
Columbia, S.C., December 2, 1980

A LOT of sincerely religious people were appalled by the U.S. Supreme Court decision striking down a Kentucky law that required the Ten Commandments — the ancient Law of Moses — to be displayed in public school classrooms.

Other equally religious persons, those who revere the Constitution's church-state separation doctrine, were cheered by this reaffirmation of the First Amendment's prohibition of the establishment of religion by the state.

This decision, by a 5-4 margin, was predictable in that it is entirely consistent with rulings banning prayers and Bible reading in the public schools. Those were issued almost two decades ago.

The Kentucky Legislature was aware of those precedents when it passed a law in 1978 that required the permanent posting of copies of the Ten Commandments in every public elementary and high school classroom. The lawmakers tried to get around the prohibition by requiring that the copies be paid for by private contributions. The law also stressed the non-religious aspects of the Commandments: "The secular application of the Ten Commandments is

clearly seen in its adoption as the fundamental legal code of Western civilization and the common law of the United States."

The high court did not buy either of these efforts at circumvention, nor should it have. By ordering the hanging of even privately financed posters, the Legislature gave official state sanction to the practice.

The court admitted that certain of the Commandments were "arguably secular" in nature, such as honoring one's parents and abstention from killing, stealing, adultery, bearing false witness and covetousness. But it correctly pointed out that the Law of Moses is not confined to these matters, but defines the religious duties of believers: avoiding idolatry, worshipping the Lord God alone, not using the Lord's name in vain and observing the Sabbath day.

The court's majority ruled on the secular-religious nature of the Commandments without hearing full arguments. Chief Justice Warren Burger and Justice Harry A. Blackman joined the dissent because they felt a full hearing was important. We agree that a fuller discussion would have been useful, but we are not persuaded the result would have been different.

The Commandments are inarguably a part of the foundations of the Jewish and Christian religions. If some of the principles found their way into the law of nations, that does not change their fundamental character.

Therefore, the state-ordered posting of them served more of a religious than secular purpose and was, therefore, offensive to the Constitution.

In agreeing with the court, we in no way denigrate the Ten Commandments as a moral code and as a vital part of church and family life. Children need to be exposed to them, and to learn to appreciate them through those institutions.

Nor do we suggest that religious values do not have a place in government or in school life. The Supreme Court pointed again to their proper function in education when it said:

"This is not a case in which the Ten Commandments are integrated into the school curriculum, where the Bible may constitutionally be used in an appropriate study of history, civilization, ethics, comparative religion, or the like."

Indeed, a study of religion is essential to becoming a fully educated person.

The Union Leader

Manchester, N.H., December 6, 1980

One of the greatest mistakes the Supreme Court of the United States has made is the barring of prayer in schools. Their entire concept of separation of Church and State is completely mistaken.

The founding fathers were conscious of the state churches of both the Protestants and the Catholics in Europe and they wanted to avoid the existence of any state church in America.

They certainly, however, did not want to separate the people from religion. This is what the Supreme Court has been doing.

For instance, the state of Kentucky had a state law requiring the posting of a copy of the Ten Commandments in every public school classroom in the state. By a vote of 5-4, however, the Supreme Court recently ruled this unconstitutional.

What a tragedy! The children are now to be deprived of this early knowledge of the Ten Commandments as a guide for their basic behavior.

Certainly the Ten Commandments could not be declared as denominational. They are universal. They are not only a part of the Protestant and Catholic teachings, but after all, Moses, who brought down the Ten Commandments from Mt. Sinai, was a Jew. So, the Ten Commandments are accepted equally in the Jewish religion.

Just as Chief Justice Warren E. Burger and Associate Justice Harry A. Blackmun said in dissenting, the courts should hear the arguments in the case rather than decide on the basis of legal briefs as they did.

Something must be done to reverse this attack on religion by the Supreme Court. Somehow or another, the court never seems to pay much attention to the First Amendment or the Bill of Rights, which says, "Congress shall make no law respecting an establishment of religion or prohibiting the free exercise thereof; or abridging the freedom of speech . . . ."

The difference between the question of an established religion and just religion per se should be so obvious that no judge of the Supreme Court would have any difficulty understanding it. But such, unfortunately, has not been the case.

THE INDIANAPOLIS STAR

Indianapolis, Ind., November 20, 1980

Three striking figures are centered on the carved marble pediment of the rear pavilion of the Supreme Court Building in the nation's capital.

To the left stands Confucius, the Chinese philosopher and teacher. On the right is Solon, the master codifier of Greek law. The dominant center figure is Moses, bearing the stone tablets on which were inscribed the Ten Commandments.

In the courtroom itself, the justices sit beneath magnificient carved friezes honoring a galaxy of history's brightest legal lights. Again the great bearded Moses, with his tablets, is present.

Yet this week the Supreme Court ruled that it is unconstitutional for Kentucky to post copies of the Ten Commandments in public school classrooms, even though the copies are paid for by private funds and carry the following factual notation:

"The secular application of the Ten Commandments is clearly seen in its adoption as the fundamental legal code of Western Civilization and the Common Law of the United States."

What do we do now? Insist that the court's curators cover the offending tablets with fig leaves?

THE ATLANTA CONSTITUTION

Atlanta, Ga., November 19, 1980

Despite a too-narrow 5-to-4 vote, the U.S. Supreme Court's decision to "ban" the Ten Commandments from public classrooms is wholly consistent with the First Amendment, with the Protestant tradition and with its own history.

The court has banned Bible reading, school prayers and now the Decalogue from schoolrooms for the good and sufficient reason that how a man, or a child, worships is nobody else's business — least of all the state's.

And it has done so in the face of clear indications that the American public feels very differently about it all.

Though written in stone and in the bedrock of Judeo-Christian tradition, the commandments are no longer to be hung on classroom walls (as till Monday they were in Kentucky, where the constitutional challenge arose) unless they meet the test of "secularity" devised by the court in a notable 1971 ruling.

Under that standard a biblical text of any sort is acceptable for class study only when it fulfills a "secular legislative purpose," when it "neither advances nor prohibits religion" and when it clearly does not "foster an excessive entanglement religion."

When the makers of the Protestant reformation spoke of religious liberty they had in mind not the Ten Commandments but an 11th, one which the Supreme Court has embodied in numerous decisions of recent years: The state shall not interfere in matters of individual conscience.

Is it wrong for a child to recite the Ten Commandments or utter a prayer in the required presence of those who happen not to share his religious views? It is indeed a small tyranny that he exercises. But it is well for us to remember that it is nevertheless a tyranny.

Textbooks & Libraries Made Targets of Censorship

The new evangelical wave swept over school textbooks and library books, giving fresh strength to a simmering controversy. For years, parents had sought to keep out of schools certain books containing ideas that conflicted with religious and moral standards at home. Kanawha County, W. Va., was the site of a particularly violent confrontation in 1974 between conservative parents and the school board over books that were labeled "vulgar, profane, violent, critical of parents, depressing, seditious, revolutionary, anti-Christian and immoral." Almost every other state had had its brush with local objections to certain books and reading assignments. Chief among the objections was the charge of pornography and the use of obscene language. Other books were ordered removed from the curriculum and library shelves because the authors had a permissive attitude toward sex or opposed U.S. government policies. Such authors included major American writers as Kurt Vonnegut, Bernard Malamud, Richard Wright and John Steinbeck. The fundamentalist movement gave new impetus to the book-banners by adding the weight of a nationwide movement with growing political respectability. The controversy was more than a simple desire to protect children from exposure to inappropriate materials. It raised the question of whether the state had an obligation to reinforce parental values in public education or whether it should expose children to a wide range of ideas.

THE SACRAMENTO BEE

Sacramento, Calif., November 30, 1978

The National Council of Teachers of English reports that censorship of books in classrooms and school libraries is on the increase. Some 30 percent of 2,000 schools surveyed by the council ban certain books from library shelves, among them *The Diary of Anne Frank, To Kill a Mockingbird, The Grapes of Wrath, A Separate Peace, The Scarlet Letter* and, in some places, certain dictionaries containing what school boards regard as objectionable words.

Whether the titles listed by the council are indeed representative of the books banned from schools, and whether there is, in fact, a real increase in censorship as reported by the council are both matters subject to question. It may simply be that more incidents are reported — that what used to take place quietly, or through consensus among teachers and school administrators — is now becoming a matter of controversy. But there is no question that school censorship of distinguished literature, including some classic American novels, continues to plague many schools.

Maybe it's only coincidence that reported incidents of censorship are rising while scholastic competence and literacy, as measured by standarized tests, are on the decline. Although there is no evidence that teen-agers would be better or more passionate readers if every book in the En-

glish language were readily available in every school, both phenomena seem to reflect the same disrespect for literature and the same lack of interest in good reading and good writing.

In many places, teachers themselves seem to share the disrespect and to disdain everything but the most narrow professional reading, but that hardly mitigates the message conveyed by official censors no more interested in good literature than the students whose academic skills are subject to so much criticism.

Virtually any book worth reading contains some ideas, some language, some scenes which can be regarded as objectionable by some people. It's those very elements which give good literature its tension, its moral conflict, its interest and its power. Trying to find works which are free of all objectionable elements therefore tends to select out almost everything but the dull and banal. Moreover, the effort itself indicates — to students and teachers — just how much the authorities, in this case administration and school board members, really care about how well their students read and think. Any school board genuinely concerned about the academic skills of its students should be fighting to get the best and most compelling literature into the hands of its students, not trying to keep it away from them.

The Providence Journal

Providence, R.I., August 8, 1976

Book-banning by school or public libraries is, and always should be, frightening and abhorrent.

Although there are probably no instances in which book censorship has been permanently victorious, the occasional attempts at it represent a continuing assault on the right of free inquiry. That is no less a right than freedom of speech.

One of the latest examples of such demagoguery was the recent decision of a school board in Levittown, N.Y., to continue its ban on nine books that had been removed from junior and senior high school libraries and from the school curriculum. Among the banned books are *Slaughterhouse Five* by Kurt Vonnegut Jr., *The Fixer* by Bernard Malamud, *The Naked Ape* by the anthropologist Desmond Morris and *Soul on Ice* by Eldridge Cleaver.

These and the other books initially were purged from school libraries in Levittown last April on the grounds that they contained material "offensive to Christians, Jews, blacks and Americans in general."

But nothing in these books could be more offensive than the school board's determined effort to impose literary censorship on an entire community's teenage school population. What makes it even more stupid is that most of the books on the banned list were best sellers that can be bought freely at almost any paperback book store or borrowed from any public library.

Some Rhode Island communities have had bouts with potential book-banners. Last year, for example, the Scituate School Committee rejected the demands of the Rev. Ennio Cugini, Fundamentalist pastor of the Clayville Community Church, who wanted it to bar from use in town schools three books he found unpalatable. They were *Catcher in the Rye* by J.D. Salinger, *1984* by George Orwell and *Death of a Salesman* by Arthur Miller, three modern classics.

Scituate residents were luckier than those in Levittown, whose unenlightened school board was guilty of a grave injustice.

It is unimaginable that any valid case can be made for public agencies to "protect" young minds by denying them exposure to certain forms of literature. Even if they contain volumes that some elements of the community might find repugnant, school libraries are designed to broaden students' intellectual horizons, not limit them. Standards of taste are individual matters, and should not arbitrarily be set by public officials.

The Burlington Free Press

Burlington, Vt., April 12, 1978

CITIZENS OF totalitarian states meekly accept the fact that their books and newspapers are published under the restraints of strict censorship.

Under the Nazi regime, offending books were burned to protect the people from their subversive ideas.

But there are still those in free countries who would censor the reading material of their neighbors. They demand that school boards, library officials and selectmen take a hand in the book selection process.

They do not wear brown shirts and swastika armbands; they wear business suits and righteousness as their emblems. But they are just as dangerous, for all the innocence of their appearance. What is not to their liking they would deny to all. As self-appointed censors, they would either destroy or lock away those books that do not meet with their approval. They would set the standards of reading for their fellow citizens.

The latest incident in Vermont has occurred in Springfield where an irate citizen has demanded that the selectmen do something about the presence of pornographic books in the community's public library. If the board does not act, he has vowed to seek a 25 percent cut in the library's budget next year. Because he objects to the offering of a pornographic book by the library, he has asked that such books be placed in red jackets and placed in the front of the library.

When the town took over the library three years ago after it had been a private institution for several years, the selectmen made it clear they would have nothing to do with the selection of books. That chore would be left to the library staff.

As a result of the complaint, however, the selectmen have decided they want library officials to explain how the books are selected.

If the selectmen follow through with their demand, they will be politicizing the library for once and for all and they will be guaranteeing that the staff will be more than cautious in making future book selections.

The new censors will have won another round in their battle to dictate the reading habits of their fellow citizens and will have denied them the right to read what they wish.

The people of Springfield should not surrender that freedom lightly, for it could be the beginning of more serious trouble for them.

The Seattle Times

Seattle, Wash., August 20, 1978

A COUPLE of years back, it was "Catch 22" that was under fire in the Bothell School District.

Now it's "Catcher in the Rye," in Issaquah.

Elsewhere and in other years, it has been "One Flew Over the Cuckoo's Nest," even "Life With Father," or anything by James Baldwin, Ogden Nash or Joan Baez.

Whether because of the language they employ or the ideas they present, books and the way they are used in public schools increasingly are targets for efforts at censorship.

Edward Jenkinson, an English professor at Indiana University, in a report last year to the National Council of Teachers of English, attributed the increase in such crusades to social unrest in general and the relative accessibility of schools in comparison with other levels of government.

The concerns of those crusaders who fear for the erosion of values that have been important to this society for generations are valid.

But in their zeal to protect such values, they jeopardize others, primarily those associated with the equally cherished principles of the free flow of ideas and interpretation.

No matter the degree of censorship or the limitations of its application, it is still censorship, and censorship is incompatible with freedom of expression.

The Washington Star

Washington, D.C., January 7, 1978

We're all for free speech and the First Amendment, aren't we? Of course nobody should be stopped from expressing ideas just because they're unpopular ideas! Or even repulsive ideas. Voltaire summed it up for all time in "I disagree wholly with what you have to say and I will defend to the death your right to say it." At least he is said to have said that.

But when you get down to cases, somebody is always deciding that what somebody else wants to say is out of bounds after all. Human inconsistency will play out its comedies. If you don't think so, ask the American Library Association.

The librarians often encounter at least the outer ripples of free speech issues in their work. Choosing to have one book on the shelves and not another looks like censorship to some people. If a book isn't readily available, it's the same as if it was banned, isn't it? On the other hand, for a library to stock material that offends a particular school of thought can be denounced as racism, sexism, obscenity or communism.

In fact, such problems come up so often for librarians that the ALA decided to stimulate some discussion that might improve public understanding of what they are up against. The ALA commissioned a film dramatizing a standard free speech dilemma: the familiar scenario of a club inviting a controversial speaker and being pressured into withdrawing the invitation.

A great idea, except that — you guessed it — the film turned out to be too controversial for half the librarians.

"The speaker" in the film was modeled on Dr. William Shockley, the Nobel prize physicist who was prevented by force from airing his theory of black inferiority at Harvard. Even as a springboard for discussion of how far down the road it would be wise to follow Voltaire there was too much dynamite in that one for many of the librarians. As of now, however, efforts to ban or limit distribution of the film under ALA sponsorship have been unsuccessful.

Whatever happens next — and an all-out battle is expected in the organization's executive board before the film's future is settled — it may have justified its existence in a real life dramatization of how and why free speech can be a fighting issue, even among people who think they believe in it unreservedly.

There is no principle of government or private morality without its troubled edges, where the exceptional cases make their claims against the clean simplicity of absolute rules. Good is always colliding with good and one set of rights is always contradicting another. There are always dangers to be weighed against each other.

For our kind of government, there cannot help being an uncertain boundary where free speech begins and ends, short of that false fire report in the crowded theater. How far can a society committed to free speech go in protecting itself against those who want to abolish free speech? Is it ever justifiable to defend widely held concepts of public decency by restricting free speech?

The uproar among the librarians over "the speaker" shows how much alive these issues are. It also shows how much confusion there can be about them. There are those who seem to think a controversial speaker is denied First Amendment rights simply by not being invited to speak. There are others who see no First Amendment wrongs in hounding a controversial speaker off a legitimately occupied platform if the views being expressed are considered outrageous.

A sound doctrine of free speech, of course, must reject both positions. We hope the librarians make widespread use of their censorship film. Showing its power to stir indignation, it has shown how much it is needed.

Local Pressure to Ban Books Spreads Across the Country

Along with the influence of the "New Right" movement, the movement to ban certain books from schools spread across the country with surprising speed in the late 1970s. Parents' groups were inspired by the successes of other groups in other states. In many areas, the school boards themselves were solidly in favor of the censorship of school materials. The public had lost confidence in the public school system over the past decade, and the book-banning was a symptom of this disillusionment. Parents were upset at news stories of children who could not read or manage the simplest tasks in arithmetic. The "back to basics" move in education was in part the result of parental pressure on the schools to improve their preparation of students. Book-banners believed that many reading assignments were not necessary to their children's education or, indeed, prevented them from learning. The traumas of the 1960s and early 1970s were blamed on the "wrong" books as well as on lax educational standards. Once again, the schools were held at fault for the ills of society.

St. Petersburg Times

St. Petersburg, Fla., December 16, 1979

From our nation's founding, the free expression of thoughts and ideas has troubled some citizens. Angered or frightened by mere words on a printed page, they have set out to protect society from the words and ideas they considered offensive or threatening.

Well-intentioned or not, censorship does not work and must not be endured. When one suppressor prevails, another is inspired. When one book is banned, another awaits attack. Each time the censor succeeds, American freedom is undermined.

The public schools are particularly vulnerable to such self-appointed censors. Some, rankled by the rapid changes in social mores in the last two decades, have tried to turn the world back to more innocent times by organizing emotional protests to the instructional materials selected by professional educators.

NEWSWEEK reports that a recent survey by the National Council of Teachers of English found that the number of teachers who "felt subject to censorship pressures" from parents or school boards has risen 50 percent since 1966. The American Library Association reports about 300 book-banning incidents in schools during the 1977-78 academic year.

The Pinellas County School Board withstood such censorship pressures a few years ago. This year, the Lee County School Board in Fort Myers is preparing to confront a small, vocal group of ministers and parents who want to ban six library books — including *Catcher in the Rye* by J. D. Salinger and *Catch 22* by Joseph Heller.

No student is forced to read any of the books. They are assigned reading, but teachers substitute other volumes if students or parents complain.

That approach is reasonable and fair, offering freedom of choice while preserving freedom of information, and the Lee County board should firmly resist the book-banners. The First Amendment demands — and the proper functioning of the educational process requires — that the removal of books from a school library or classroom curriculum must be based on educational considerations — not on political, ideological, moral or religious views.

BUT THE CONCERNS of the irate parents cannot be ignored, and the Lee County board should provide an open forum for their dissent. Communication will advance understanding and build public confidence in the selection of teaching materials by professional educators.

Then, perhaps, a constructive balance can be struck between the freedom of teachers to teach and the right of thoughtful parents to influence the educational process for their children.

Certainly, some reading material may be considered inappropriate for certain adolescents. That judgment is for individual parents. It must not be imposed on everyone.

The Washington Post

Washington, D.C., May 10, 1979

ACCORDING TO THE American Library Association (ALA) and a new report of the National Council of Teachers of English (NCTE), the censorship of school books is on an alarming rise. The NCTE report cites places, such as Cedar Lake, Indiana, where the school board ordered the American Heritage Dictionary removed from the high schools because among its nine definitions for "bed" it included "a place for lovemaking." An education commissioner in Texas found four other dictionaries unfit for young eyes because of such words as "horny" and "queer." Beyond individual words, current objections are said to include: "Overconcern with minority racial and ethnic groups"; "anything that might show disrespect (or questioning) of authority"; and "any anti- or un-American stance." All of which would seem to suggest that as goes the country, so go the books.

That's one way of looking at it and, from a historical base, an understandable way, since there have always been plenty of vigilantes around—to the left as well as to the right—eager to purge the shelves of anything that seems to bisect their angle of looking at the world. Whenever that happens—when a "liberal-minded one bans Richard Wright's "Black Boy" —clearly, you may call that censorship. On the other hand, when a parent sees that a reading list for a high school English class consists solely of "Soul on Ice" and the collected works of Kurt Vonnegut, and raises holy hell to the point of persuading a school board or librarian to replace that book, it sounds more like the exercise of thoughtful discrimination on the part of a directly concerned adult as to what his or her child grows up to regard as literature.

The point is that the issue of censorship may be both less interesting and unimportant than the process that goes on in every school every year—one that determines what a teen-ager learns of heroism, tragedy, irony, beauty, honor, wit and any other of the high moments of life that a great book gives. A teacher who chooses Kurt Vonnegut to provide such things is kidding himself and his students. He is taking what is current (or was current), and merely current, and trying to force-feed it with all the standards of a "Hamlet," thus creating the goose, without the pâté. To object to this is not only reasonable, it is right; and it is certainly not censorship. There may be nothing wrong in reading Kurt Vonnegut for the fun of it, but the development of taste takes more than that.

Of course, the trouble occurs when some kook or group of kooks in or outside a school system rants against a particular book or author on political grounds, or on any grounds extraneous to the heart of an education. When that occurs, organizations such as the ALA and NCTE rightly sound the alarm— just as they ought to, in fact, whenever a teacher chooses a book for political reasons as well. But the alarm should never be so shrill as to drown out the thoughtful public who have a right and an obligation to look hard at what their children read—knowing all the while that this is no area for perfect judgment, and that books will change and opinions differ. As several great works prove, the people are never quite so dangerous as they're made out to be.

The Hartford Courant

Hartford, Conn., April 24, 1979

A generation ago, school children, if they were lucky, learned the names of the capitals of the world powers and perhaps were exposed to the cultures of a few European countries.

Africa, Asia and Latin America were vast continental unknowns. America consisted of the Pilgrims and Puritans and their progeny, perhaps the black slaves and the immigrants who melted into the mainstream in the nineteenth century.

A curriculum in Enfield (and other schools around the country) teaches fourth graders about the peoples and customs of places like Nigeria and Brazil and India. Stories in the anthropology and sociology book recount the experiences of black and Indian migrants to American cities and of the coal-mining residents of Appalachia.

Some parents are trying to have the textbook, published by Holt, Rinehart and Winston, banned because they think it shows too much poverty, desperation and oppression. The Board of Education wisely ignored their objections, but now a parent-teacher group has voted against its use and the superintendent of schools must decide

what to do. He should keep the book in the classroom.

Opponents object to stories about African tribes whose men use drugs and whose women are sometimes beaten; about a social club in Brazil which bars the majority of the town's residents, the poor; about black immigrants to Harlem who found rural life was better and about Irish immigrants to the United States who experience discrimination.

Little, if any, of the book could be pointed to as untrue or unrealistic. Its purpose is to show Enfield youngsters — and youngsters across the country — how people in various countries live. Its purpose is not to promote an American, Horatio Alger approach to the world; the youngsters will receive that in other classes.

Taking the books out of the classroom will not serve the education of Enfield youngsters. Putting the book in perspective and explaining to children how their way of life compares to that of other lands will help them become more educated and aware citizens of the world. That, not censorship, should be the goal of parents and teachers.

ARGUS-LEADER

Sioux Falls., S.D., December 20, 1979

We don't question the right of parents to complain about "Blues for Mr. Charlie," by James Baldwin, or any other book or play which they may feel is offensive and shouldn't be used in course work at Washington Senior High School.

We think their complaints should be heard. A joint commission of parents and educators has done that and cleared the book for use in the modern literature curriculum at the high school.

The book has strong language and a characterization of sex and violence that were offensive to some parents. Defenders of the book said Baldwin depicted racism in the South as it appeared from the blacks' point of view. He is regarded as one of the foremost spokesmen for American blacks.

Why not let Sioux Falls public high school students read his ideas?

Mrs. Deloris Huether says she will appeal the decision of the committee to the Sioux Falls Board of Education. Her complaint should be carefully considered by the board members.

While parents have every right to exhaust all means at their disposal to challenge books with which they disagree, we don't share their views that such works should be kept out of sight and out of mind.

We think the students are better served by the availability of contemporary and classic literature and the insight it may give them to the real world.

We also think the commission which cleared "Blues for Mr. Charlie" was on sound ground in recommending "that no special interest group, including this committee, seek to impose on others their own moral, religious or aesthetic view as the standard for directing what specific instructional materials should or should not be taught within the public schools."

A friend tells us about the librarian in a small high school who snipped articles from Time magazine so students wouldn't see references to sex, morals, "bad books" and other topics in the news that the librarian considered offensive in the early 1970s.

That is an extreme example of misguided intentions. This is what the commission sought to avoid in recommending that no group impose its views on the students.

Both parents and students were well served by the careful work of the commission, of which Robert Caselli, Washington principal, and Jan Nicolay, a Washington teacher, were co-chairpersons and the Rev. Tom Tucker was spokesman.

The Times-Picayune
The States-Item

New Orleans, La., December 27, 1979

A small-minded organization calling itself "Decency in Education" has succeeded in persuading school authorities in various parts of the country to ban a number of literary works, and some citizens have demonstrated their devotion to the civilized virtues by burning books in public.

The sinister implications of such barbarities presumably escape the perpetrators, and it is unsurprising, though depressing, to find so many prim and self-righteous cranks ready to play censor and suppress what they are apparently unable to comprehend. Indeed, it must be strongly suspected that many books have been proscribed unread; the banning of Charles Dickens in Anaheim, Calif., for instance, is one of the greatest mysteries in the annals of philistinism.

The parental obligation to provide guidance for the development of a child's reading habits might, from time to time, necessitate the decision that certain works are unsuitable for juvenile consumption, although youngsters have a way of escaping the shackles well-meaning adults attempt to place on their curiosity.

But when writers like Salinger and Heller are removed from library shelves, we repudiate the qualities of wit and imagination embodied in major accomplishments of American culture and risk stunting the intellectual growth of our children.

Indeed, men capable of producing great books, almost by definition, will say many things calculated to outrage the less enlightened denizens of American suburbia. But we cannot allow the intolerance of self-appointed censors to condemn adolescents to a diet of bromides and dehumanized role models.

"Decency in Literature" supporters are, no doubt, more deserving of pity than abuse, but the authorities who have bent to their demands merit unmitigated rebuke. They have cravenly yielded to pressure for the sake of their own political futures; they have shamefully neglected their obligation to nurture the minds and sensibilities of their charges, to ensure that they do not grow up with the warped and repressive attitudes that afflict some of their parents.

We constantly prate about the personal liberties enjoyed in America, yet we seem forever under pressure to conform — often to some prudish and unintelligent notions like those espoused by "Decency in Literature."

Shakespeare, of course, appears on some banned lists, perhaps because of the frequently-heard but idiotic argument that *Othello* is racist and *The Merchant of Venice* anti-semitic.

It is difficult to know what to make of people who would deprive students of the ennobling effects of the world's greatest poetic dramas. But it is abundantly clear that their attempts to interfere must henceforth be met with sterner resistance from the forces of reason.

The Honolulu Advertiser

Honolulu, Ha., May 28, 1979

One sign of the current conservatism in social matters is the surprisingly large incidence of textbook censorship in schools across the nation, something many people may have though vanished long ago.

Depending mostly on the Newsletter on Intellectual Freedom of the American Library Association, a researcher found that from the start of the Bicentennial year to late last year there had been at least 66 censorship cases involving 205 books and five magazines in 32 states. (Hawaii was not one).

BOOKS REMOVED from classrooms and libraries are as diverse as the reasons given for the banning or the places the banning occurred. In Brighton, Michigan, the school board banned all 29 textbooks on drugs and sex education. Levittown, L.I., outside New York, led with not only the most books but the most prestigious, award-winning writers banned.

J.D. Salinger is a favorite of book banners, as he has been since "Catcher in the Rye" was published. Other well-known authors on lists nationwide are John Steinbeck, Ernest Hemingway, Richard Wright, Alexander Solzhenitsyn, Bertrand Russell, Leon Uris, Kurt Vonnegut and Ken Kesey.

Some of the most often banned books are anonymously or collectively written: "Go Ask Alice," a horrifying tale of a teen-ager hooked on drugs; "Our Bodies, Our Selves," by the Boston Women's Health Book Collective and the American Heritage Dictionary, banned apparently for "offensive" sexual definitions.

Dictionaries seem an unlikely target for book banners but Webster's New World Dictionary of the American Language was knocked off Texas purchasing lists because of criticism by a non-profit "book analysis" organization there that mails reviews of books it finds objectionable to parents across the country.

THE RESEARCHER FOUND the pressure for banning books is shifting; instead of coming from organized citizens groups as in the past it increasingly comes from seemingly unorganized action by individual parents despite the increasing complexity of textbooks which makes it hard for parents to keep track.

Not all the protesting groups are right-wingers or social conservatives, either. Feminist groups have protested sex stereotyping in textbooks; Indians objected to their depiction in a Vermont history and black parents in New Trier, Illinois, had Mark Twain's "Huckleberry Finn" removed from a reading class over ACLU protests because of the word "nigger."

There are some positive signs in the right-to-read battle, however, including pro-textbook court decisions that follow strong presentations by the library association, the National Education Association and others. In Boston a U.S. District Court ruled that a school board may buy or not buy a book but once on display the book cannot be removed without violating First Amendment rights.

PARENTS DO HAVE a legitimate interest in how their children will be educated, so a number of school boards have moved to make textbook selection a more cooperative, consultative process. This is better than dismissing protests out of hand as bigotry or repression.

In some cases school boards allow for reconsideration of material that has been legitimately questioned by concerned parents and some have set up procedures for handling protests with less pain and vituperation than before.

"In the future," concluded the researcher, "while there may be more protests and hence more parental influence on textbooks and other school materials, it is anticipated that there will actually be less removal and destruction of them."

THE SACRAMENTO BEE

Sacramento, Calif., April 15, 1979

There has been no end of complaints about the alleged illiteracy and general ignorance of the current generation of high school students. Their miseducation — some would call it lack of education — has been attributed to everything from food additives to permissiveness. At the same time, the prescribed solutions have covered a spectrum that's even broader and, for the most part, just as lacking in the sort of evidence on which educational policy can be based.

In recent weeks, however, new indications have accumulated that among the causes of that miseducation is a perverse desire among many adults to maintain the ignorance about which others complain. Among the more obvious examples of that desire is a resurgent censorship of school library and textbooks instigated by parents and community groups; a growing belief that, as the president of the Anaheim high school board said recently, "if they teach grammar properly, they will have no need of further books;" and a return to the kind of "fundamental" education which not only regards all art, music, literature and history as frills but which in many instances appears to define "basic education" as a sort of punitive exercise designed to drive all curiosity out of the classroom.

In the '60s, the reformers, pursuing "relevance," accepted all manner of silliness as proper curricular fare. Now, in their attempt to compensate, a growing number of counterreformers are confusing boredom, meaningless rote exercises and virtually anything labeled fundamentals with the essence of good education. Thus they substitute one sort of ideology for another, but the remedies they propose have little more chance of generating any love of learning or, indeed, any more respect for academic discipline.

The belief that it's possible to implement a mechanical production system that automatically makes children learn and the belief that through censorship it's possible to keep them from learning the wrong things are, obviously, part of the same illusion. Yet the fact is that real learning and real teaching — which is to say real education — are risky enterprises, risky not only because they sometimes fail, but also because it's impossible to predict with certainty where they'll lead. As soon as such certainty is expected, there is bound to be disappointment; as soon as attempts are made to impose it through censorship or coercion, the only assured result is failure. Like everything else, fundamentals will be learned only because they are either fascinating or useful. They can be taught only by people who respect them sufficiently to believe in them. If they are used instead as instruments of torture — as punishment — they will be treated accordingly by the hapless students on whom they're imposed.

The Courier-Journal

Louisville, Ky., December 30, 1979

THE EFFORT to suppress ideas by banning books has a long and dishonorable history. Some lands and some ages have been especially susceptible to the censorial impulse, but no time and place — including America in the final days of the 1970s — is entirely immune.

School officials in a number of communities across the country are under mounting pressure to protect youngsters from such allegedly corrupting literature as *Catcher in the Rye, Soul on Ice,* and (in Anaheim, California) most of the works of Shakespeare, Dickens and Mark Twain. The pressure, according to an *Associated Press* story, is coming from parents and "decency" committees who claim the offending literature teaches "secular humanism" or contains profanities.

The likelihood that most of the protesting parents are sincere and well-intentioned makes their intimidation of educators and librarians no less objectionable. Presumably the Kremlin censors who excluded a number of American and Israeli publications from the recent Moscow Book Fair also were quite sincere. They truly believe that decent Communists shouldn't be exposed to literature that didn't jibe with official Soviet views.

And when it comes to fighting "isms," the opponents of secular humanism aren't the only ones who claim the welfare of children as their pure and sole motive.

Others are battling to purge textbooks of sexism, racism, capitalism, socialism and even deism. In a society as diverse as ours, and as prone to dissent, there's a constant clamor for public education to accomplish any number of goals, some of them mutually exclusive.

Faced with these demands, the conscientious educator can only steel himself for a barrage of criticism and select books he hopes will give students some notion of the wealth of ideas that have shaped civilization. With luck, the choices will inspire more inquisitive youngsters to read further, or at least show that literature can delight, as well as instruct.

That doesn't mean parents have no legitimate role in this aspect of their children's education. Most teachers doubtless would be happy to meet with individual parents to discuss reading assignments and to offer alternative titles when particular books are unacceptable.

But parents have obligations, as well as rights. One is the duty to have a clear idea — beyond the rumors generated by "decency" committees — what supposedly offensive books actually contain. That, of course, would require a little reading. And if this led to livelier and more frequent family discussions, the result could be more educational than any number of hours Johnny spends alone with an assigned book.

The Miami Herald

Miami, Fla., August 9, 1979

UNPOPULAR ideas are like mushrooms. Bury them in a dark cellar to suppress them, and instead of shriveling they'll flourish. But plant them in a windowbox, alongside competing ideas, and they'll prosper only as they can withstand the light of inquiry.

That's what the Island Trees School Board in Long Island, N.Y., tried to ignore when it banned 11 books — including two winners of the Pulitzer Prize — in 1976. That's what a Federal judge acknowledged this week when he upheld the board's Constitutional authority to ban the books while criticizing the "misguided educational philosophy" behind the banning.

The titles of the books don't matter. What matters is the principle. And no matter what arguments are offered in favor of such censorship, all are muted by this inescapable fact: The potential harm from suppressing unpopular ideas inevitably is greater than the potential harm from allowing them to clash with other ideas.

U.S. District Judge George Pratt implied this when he said the Island Trees board's decision was unwise but legal. The American Civil Liberties Union, which sued the board on behalf of five students, says it will appeal. It should. This case raises such profound questions for every school board that it should be decided by the U.S. Supreme Court, which never has ruled on the question.

The legal arguments are much narrower than the principle that contains them. Judge Pratt may be quite right in ruling that a school board, its members elected to set educational policy, has the authority to declare certain books unsuitable for high-school students. There may be some merit to the argument that the schools are acting *in loco parentis,* in place of the parents, while a child is in class. Under that logic, the schools would be empowered to deny a child access to ideas — whether in books, films, photographs, or other media — that some parents might not want their children to see.

But that argument wilts under the heat of inquiry. None of the books involved has been declared pornographic. As a group, the books advocate no -ism likely to corrupt fundamental values or to seduce innocents. The books are purely and simply perspectives of writers whose experiences reflect not the mainstream of American life, but the eddies and whirlpools in which many Americans work and live.

So the question is not whether a school board *can* ban books from school libraries. The question is, *should* it?

The answer must be no. No because no person, young or old, can assay his own ideas if contradictory ideas are removed from the scale. No because education should stretch young minds, not partition them off. And, finally, no because suppression has never yet killed any unpopular idea. It has, instead, only filled history's cellar with mushrooms.

Book-Banning: The Criteria Varies

Literary merit was one of the last considerations in objecting to a book. Conservative parents opposed both American classics like John Steinbeck's *Grapes of Wrath* and faddish teen novels like Judy Blume's *Blubber*. In one county, a book might be on the "banned" list; elsewhere, it might be tolerated. There was no predictable standard. The "New Right" was not always alone in objecting to certain works. Shakespeare's *The Merchant of Venice* and Mark Twain's *Huckleberry Finn* drew protests from minority groups. However, it was the "New Right" that mounted a sustained campaign to withdraw books permanently from school libraries. Other groups objected merely to individual reading assignments or requested that additional material be given to the students to provide "balanced" treatment.

The last opinions to be solicited were those of the students themselves. They were rarely asked which books they found morally objectionable. Very often, the books that were the targets of censorship were not the most popular ones—but controversy was sure to change that. In the case of popular authors like Judy Blume, students were emphatic in their determination to read her words, in spite of (or perhaps because of) parental objections. At times, it seemed as if the book-banning movement intensified the very problems the book-banners hoped to solve.

THE CHRISTIAN SCIENCE MONITOR

Boston, Mass., October 24, 1980

Book-banning, it seems, is on the rise in public and school libraries across the United States. Anyone doubting this should ask Mary Poppins, the genial high-flying nanny in the popular children's book of the same name, who has recently been grounded by San Francisco's public library.

The book-banning trend seems to reflect heightened public concern about outdated and demeaning racial stereotypes, obscenity, and vulgar language in literature accessible to children. And that is understandable. But any action that threatens to infringe on authors' and publishers' First Amendment rights and the free dissemination of ideas is dangerous and should be undertaken with the greatest of care. The problem with even high-minded censorship is how to reign in overzealousness.

Mary Poppins ran afoul of the censor in tolerant San Francisco because of what a library committee considered the book's derogatory treatment of minorities. It was said to depict them "in the old English view of the 'white man's burden'. . . That is naturally offensive to minorities and others as well." Even a re-edited version from which some offensive passages had been deleted by the author failed to assuage the censors. Other children's books, such as "Huckleberry Finn" and some early Nancy Drew mysteries, have drawn similar criticism in other places.

More often than not, however, censorship has been practiced in the name of decency — to keep foul language and obscenity out of the classroom or library. And in a society that many consider too permissive, there is a need to be alert to such mental pollution. But it is also true that today's youngsters, at an earlier age than was true of previous generations, are forced to face up to a confusing array of moral and social questions once looked upon as "adult," and these further complicate the work of parents and educators in selecting suitable books. One librarian's reasonable elimination of a book frequently is another's example of excessive censorship.

One suggestion that might make censorship a bit easier to swallow would be for educators to make a distinction between books assigned to youngsters as required reading and those simply made available in the public or school library. A parent who objects to a teacher assigning a book he or she does not consider appropriate would have less reason to complain where the choice of whether or not to read it is the student's. Moreover, how a teacher presents a book to a classroom is important. Outdated racial stereotypes properly treated as such need not be offensive but, to the contrary, can be an effective tool for bolstering students' understanding of past racial attitudes and the abuses spawned by them.

Such efforts will not likely satisfy extremist groups that would bar any book they deem antigovernment, anti-Christian, or antiparent. But as Judith Krug, director of the American Library Association's Office of Intellectual Freedom, cautioned in regard to the ban on "Mary Poppins," "Everyone wants to protect the children. The problem is, they're going to be so protected they won't be able to function in the year 2000."

Des Moines Tribune

Des Moines, Iowa, February 29, 1980

The subject of censorship, which apparently holds few terrors for the Kanawha school board, got more attentive treatment when two dozen literary people met recently in New York for two days of discussions. The participants, most of them writers, exchanged horror stories of the pressures they have felt from governments, community groups and publishers.

Susan Sontag recalled that her high school library in North Hollywood banned an anthology of Tom Paine because of how the revolutionary pamphleteer was depicted in a novel ("Citizen Tom Paine") by Howard Fast. "Paine was being banned 200 years later because Howard Fast had written about him," Sontag said in dismay.

When Toni Morrison learned that her novel "Song of Solomon" was not displayed in Atlanta bookstores and libraries, she asked a friend there to find out why. She was informed that a leader in Atlanta's civil rights movement objected to the book because "black people aren't that way."

Morrison said it is "scary" when a citizen who acquires community prestige or political clout can intimidate booksellers and librarians to hide or remove books that do not satisfy some private standard. This is a sinister form of censorship because it is usually unknown to the public and, therefore, shut off from public questioning.

Russian poet Joseph Brodsky observed that official censorship forces artists to devise new symbols and ironies to try sidestepping the censor. But the result of such deceptions is that an author then is usually understood only by an elite intellectual group that can decipher the vague symbolism.

When the Kanawha school board members decided that "The Grapes of Wrath" was not fit for high school students to read, they joined a long, and probably unending, line of censors. Maybe they don't think of themselves that way, but that is what they are. They represent a repressive force not only against those who want the freedom to read but against those who yearn for the creative vigor to help find answers to life's puzzles.

The Hartford Courant

Hartford, Conn., November 7, 1980

While some educators shield students from intellectually challenging material, others shield them from early awareness of cultural and social diversity.

In Ledyard, a curriculum revision committee decided that certain pages in two books about Eskimos had to be ripped out before being used again this year for a Grade 6 social studies course.

Although there have been no complaints about the books from anyone in the 12 years they have been in use in Ledyard, the committee has now decided the children aren't ready to face harsh truths about Eskimo life as it once was during some bitter winters.

Particularly objectionable, in the committee's eyes, was material that described the abandonment of old people, the fatal neglect of newborn girls and the sharing of wives.

Any teacher or administrator who believes that an 11-year-old child reading such stuff in the textbook would be shocked or disoriented, obviously doesn't own a television set.

But more to the point, a child immersed in the distinctive culture of Ledyard, Conn., is not likely to adopt the discordant values of an old, alien culture just by reading about them.

We wonder whether the committee is more interested in protecting children from "unsuitable" information or protecting the school system from potential controversy.

OKLAHOMA CITY TIMES

Oklahoma City, Okla., November 13, 1980

THE "new wave" of censorship feared by librarians across the land should be recognized for what it is, the venting of a long-smoldering resentment against what many Americans perceive as a degrading of traditional values.

The American Library Association reports an increase, almost coinciding with the Nov. 4 election, in attempts to censor books on library shelves and in school reading programs. The director of the ALA's office for intellectual freedom sees the trend as the beginning of a "major assault" on the ability of libraries and schools to maintain free access to materials representing diverse political, social and economic viewpoints.

The timing is not accidental. If the election results marked a basic shift to the right in this country's political philosophy, as most observers agree, they also brought to a boiling point the frustration of people not willing to accept the thesis that the so-called "new morality" is inevitable and irrevocable.

Yet the growing tendency to vent that frustration by attempted censoring of the material people read is a disturbing one. It cannot help but be destructive and counter-productive in the end.

The selection of books for school and public libraries ought to be a function of local community decision-making based on what the majority of citizens believe is wise and proper. It should not reflect the wishes of a narrow but vocal interest group.

Extremist actions from either side — from the book burners on the one hand to the literary libertines on the other — are certain to lead to equally extreme counter actions. Then the community suffers.

Libraries ought to exercise good, common sense in their selections, especially where the institutions are tax-supported and the patrons include children. The problem, as always, is where to draw the line. There is no easy answer to this, and the line could vary from community to community. Surely, though, librarians would not want to stoop to the kind of material found in adult book stores.

Restraint must be used in condemning book selections. Unbridled censorship is unacceptable in a democracy; it invites deliberate reaction and all-out licentiousness. Diversity of taste and opinion must be recognized.

The ideal alternative is to elevate the level of individual moral standards through religious training and enhancing a child's appreciation for good literature by challenging his intellect.

Granted, this is a long, slow process. But it is immeasurably preferable to an extremist approach that compromises on our ideals of individual freedom and responsibility.

The Des Moines Register

Des Moines, Iowa, February 17, 1980

The Kanawha Board of Education is more to be pitied than reviled for its vote removing "The Grapes of Wrath" from sophomore English class reading lists. The board members who voted against this American literary classic showed once more how the human mind can be numbed when prejudice is combined with misused authority. It is sad to see.

Someday, we are confident, at least a few of the young Kanawha scholars who will be deprived of John Steinbeck's work now will take time to read it. They will follow a family of poverty-stricken Oklahoma farmers from the abandoned Dust Bowl to what is supposed to be the land of promise in California. The story may help these young readers to better understand the human tribulations that were the common lot of thousands of Americans in the Great Depression.

The parent of one student, after reading parts of the book, called it "profane, vulgar and obscene." A lot of other people, including an Oklahoma congressman and a nationally syndicated columnist, had similar reactions after the book was published in 1939. Such indictments were short-lived compared to the book's lasting importance to American literature.

The fictional members of the Joad family, around whom Steinbeck builds his story, are crude, ignorant and thoughtless at times. Yet there is something ennobling about their devotion to one another in desperate struggles against natural catastrophes and the oppression of the rich and powerful.

The parent complained that the book "takes the Lord's name in vain dozens of times." A lot of Kanawha farmers probably would, too, if they were about to lose their land to a banking syndicate. Which is the greater sin — the poor man's profanity or the rich man's oppression?

A reader who has time only to jump around in the book will miss the biblical allegories Steinbeck weaves into his story: the exodus from a land of famine plagued by whirling dust storms; the wilderness experience where the migrants improvise a new social order with its own rules of conduct; a promised land where the newcomers are despised and virtually reduced to slavery.

It is really an old story placed in a new-world setting in a traumatic period of American history. It is also a commentary on the phony pieties, political and economic as well as religious, that blind so many Americans.

Four decades after it was published, "The Grapes of Wrath" continues to prick American consciences. Is that what the Kanawha school board doesn't like about it?

Des Moines, Iowa, August 31, 1980

The Kanawha school board caused far more of a flap than it could have imagined when it voted last winter to remove "The Grapes of Wrath" from sophomore English class reading lists. This contemptuous treatment of an American literary classic didn't go unnoticed in the Soviet Union.

The incident helped feed Russian suspicions of U.S. government policies that were interpreted as attempts to disrupt cultural exchanges between the two nations. According to an article in a Soviet publication, reprinted in the current World Press Review, these suspicions range from federal restrictions on the dissemination of Russian books and magazines in this country to the censorial practices of local governing bodies on American reading materials.

The article, written by Iona Andronov for the weekly publication of the Soviet Writers Union, contains this paragraph: "There are 200 regional censorship organizations in the U.S. that engage in ideological 'weeding' of libraries in thousands of municipalities, schools and colleges. All the seditious works of history, novels, poems, short stories — particularly those written by American authors who enjoy wide popularity in the Soviet Union — are pitilessly removed. The most recent example was the ban in Iowa against John Steinbeck's novel 'The Grapes of Wrath'."

The reference to the Kanawha incident is blown out of proportion. It may be a deliberate misstatement to reinforce an impression that Americans don't practice the freedom they preach, or the Russians may just have missed something in the translation.

Whatever the reason, the incident is an embarrassment to American interests. That doesn't mean that U.S. leaders must glance over their shoulders to find out how their actions are perceived by the Russians. They ought to firmly uphold democratic practices and ideals.

But book censorship, even in the limited dose prescribed at Kanawha, is a retreat to authoritarian methods — about which the Russians know a great deal — rather than an expression of the democratic faith.

The Providence Journal

Providence, R.I., December 16, 1980

Banning books by applying some supposedly universal standard is one of those practices that the average American deplores in principle. The outrages of Nazi Germany sent the world a powerful message on that point nearly a half century ago. All the more distressing are signs that many Americans are altering that message to suit their own purposes.

Censorship, in short, is on the rise.

The old put-down for would-be censors, that the best way to get a book on the best-seller list was to have it banned in Boston, isn't that funny any more. Disparaging the cult of "book-burning" doesn't seem to have the same effect it once did. Influential groups and individuals are attempting (and in some cases successfully) to create a new air of respectability for the kind of thought-control that would have appalled most Americans a few generations ago.

Listen to the Rev. Jerry Falwell, leader of the newly ascendant Moral Majority: "Textbooks are Soviet propaganda. Textbooks are destroying our children. (We must) rise up in arms to throw out every textbook not reflecting (our) social values."

The sad fact is that many are not only listening to this kind of evangelism but believing it. Judith Krug, director of the American Library Association's Office of Intellectual Freedom, explains. "It seems that many people feel that the time is ripe (for censorship)...and so many of them ...are identifying themselves as aligned with the Moral Majority or fundamentalist churches."

Lest anyone assume the political right alone is guilty, Jewish groups have excoriated books that include alleged anti-Semitism and black groups have lashed out at books containing racial stereotypes. Moral, ethical, religious, racial, ethnic, political and sexist reasons are among those cited by the purists for whom the fear of exposing children to alien ideas has risen to a level of paramount importance. Ironically, the antidote they choose to ward off this evil is their own indoctrination agenda purged of any alien hints or connotations.

To give some idea of the lengths to which the book banners will go, Prof. Edward Jenkinson of the University of Indiana cites the example of a banned book called "Making It with Mademoiselle" which turns out to be a collection of dress patterns for teenagers.

Most examples contain little humor. There is nothing funny, for instance, about classics being banned by school boards and library selection committees because a parent offended by a given word or phrase has pressed his or case for its removal. Incredible as it seems, even dictionaries and popular weekly news magazines have been swept away for fear that impressionable students would be compromised.

"If the students are learning one set of values at home and another set at school," says a prominent Texas censor, "that causes psychological harm — like teenage suicides, crime, violence, VD, unwanted pregnancy and vandalism. What the textbooks are teaching are causing all of them," this self-appointed judge of what is right and proper thus contends.

That intellectual freedom is the loser in all of this seems less and less a problem in this society. For those who stand four square for the U.S. Constitution except when the freedom to speak and write and publish are rubbed against their cherished preconceptions, it seems no problem at all. "They don't want the children to be taught how to think," says Dorothy Massie of the National Education Association. "They want them to be taught what to think."

Democracy cannot survive and flourish in a climate of narrowness, hostility and thought control. It will happen only if imagination, curiosity, and healthy skepticism are allowed room to subject ideas to interplay and testing. The censors may not realize it, but open and closed societies are only that far apart.

The Idaho STATESMAN

Boise, Idaho, December 26, 1980

Though depressing, it comes as no surprise that the Moral Majority chapter in North Carolina is trying to rid the public schools of books it considers improper. What is ironic is that the religious zealots are trying to stifle works that any reasonable person would have to conclude are morally uplifting and even profess traditional Judeo-Christian values.

Take one book on the censors' hit list, Aldous Huxley's *Brave New World*.

Apparently, the Moral Majority's problem with *Brave New World* is that the book describes a future world-state in which sexual promiscuity is not only accepted, but encouraged. What those of the Moral Majority don't seem to understand is that Huxley was not advocating promiscuity. He was trying to warn about where current social trends might lead the world — toward a totalitarian state in which sexual gratification is seen as a tool to pacify the masses, rather than as an element of loving, human relationships.

"There are already certain American cities," Huxley wrote in the foreword to a 1950's edition of *Brave New World*, "in which the number of divorces is equal to the number of marriages. In a few years, no doubt, marriage licenses will be sold like dog licenses, good for a period of 12 months, with no law against changing dogs or keeping more than one animal at a time. As political and economic freedom diminishes, sexual freedom tends compensatingly to increase. And the dictator will do well to encourage that freedom. In conjunction with the freedom to daydream under the influence of dope and movies and the radio, it will help to reconcile his subjects to the servitude which is their fate."

These are not the words of a pornographer from whom we should protect our youth. They are instead the words of a man who — like those of the Moral Majority — was profoundly concerned about where society was headed.

Recently on this page columnist James J. Kilpatrick stated that "barbarians," like all other citizens, should have a say in how public dollars are spent for such public amenities as school books and libraries. It's true, they should.

But the rest of the public — the moral and sensible majority made up of all kinds of people with all kinds of social and ethical ideas — must beware of allowing the narrow-minded to impose their views on everyone else.

The Seattle Times

Seattle, Wash., March 4, 1980

WHO would have ever thought that some day there might be a market for fake ID for a minor to get into a section of a public library?

R-rated bookshelves? It conjures up a vision of a mustachioed man in a trench coach lurking in the south wing of the library, whispering: "Psst, kid, feelthee books?"

It's still up to the Library Board in Roseburg, Ore., but the county commissioners gave their support last week to setting up a restricted area for books found to contain sexually explicit material. The commissioners acted after a minister denounced some of the library's books as "glorified smut," unfit for young minds. The county librarian said he had never heard of a restricted shelf in any public library.

There always will be arguments over what is acceptable literature for a public library. But the solution isn't to create a "dirty books" section — for adults only.

The Washington Star
and Daily News
Washington, D.C., February 28, 1980

The news that Judy Blume's novel *Blubber* has been taken off the Montgomery County public school library shelves reopens some touchy questions. Should children's reading be censored at all? And if it should, on what grounds?

We'll say an unequivocal "Yes" to the first one. As for the second, the chief — and perhaps the only — test would be whether or not a book's impact would uphold or subvert civilized values in people too young to have their own standards either sorted out or securely internalized.

New York's Roaring '20s mayor, jazzy Jimmy Walker, used to say that no girl was ever seduced by reading a book. It made a good one-liner, but it doesn't hold up next to the evidence that people of all ages *are* influenced, for better or for worse, by what they see in print. The irony is that nobody believes this more strongly than defenders of the Judy Blume kind of reading; who else has been demanding a cleanup of schoolbooks that show girls baking cookies and boys playing baseball?

Judy Blume's novels, beamed at children from the second grade up through the high school years, are the most popular of a new genre of juvenile fiction that claims to be morally neutral realism. Underneath the authenticity of the settings and dialogue, though, these stories turn out to be more like tracts peddling the values of anything-goes hedonism.

They show children encountering problems over sex, honesty, group loyalties, family conflicts and relations to authority. *Blubber*, the one that has caused the excitement in Montgomery County, is about a class of 10-year-olds tormenting a fat child because she is fat. It worries traditional parents because, unlike yesteryear's tales of children ganging up on the person who is different, it does not build to a repudiation of the persecutors. Also, its permissiveness covers a child calling the teacher a bitch.

All this is a far cry from the 19th-century readers that laced their introductions to the alphabet with threats of hell for the child who lied or stole or disobeyed a grownup. It's also a far cry from certain great works of art that, with great boldness and verisimilitude, show the underside of human behavior as children experience it.

Huckleberry Finn, after all, is about unfit parents, child abuse and truancy, not to mention boyish fantasies of the outlaw life. But, because all of these appear in a framework of civilized values, Mark Twain offers no challenge to morality that could be considered corrupting to children.

Perhaps the most ominous part of the Judy Blume uproar is the author's own defense. "If libraries want kids to read," she says, " . . . then how dare they put down the books that the kids want to read. That's saying kids have no taste, that kids don't know what's good for them, that kids don't know how to decide."

Behind such thinking is the myth of the noble savage and such related myths as the one that says children, given a choice, will eat carrots and prunes rather than potato chips and chocolate bars. The people who advertise sugar smacks on Saturday morning TV cartoon shows know better.

So should parents and so should librarians. Children like Judy Blume's books because, implicitly or explicitly, they legitimize feelings and behavior patterns that have been traditionally tabooed. And children are pathetically in need of guidance on such matters. Without it, they do *not* have taste, they do *not* know what's good for them and they do *not* know how to decide.

A statement of that sort invariably calls forth allusions to Nazi book-burnings and the way the Soviet Union prevents people from reading any but approved writings, There's a difference, though, and it's at least as great as the difference between grownups and children, maturity and immaturity.

The Boston Globe
Boston, Mass., March 10, 1980

Some grown-ups are afraid of books their children love. In a few communities, they're so scared by what their kids are reading that they've burned the offending volumes as trash. In many more, they've simply removed them from the library shelves or crossed them off the reading lists in public schools. For years, parents, school boards and librarians have wrestled over J.D. Salinger's "Catcher in the Rye" and William Golding's "Lord of the Flies." More recently, some grown-ups have sounded the alarm about the less literary but extremely popular work of Judy Blume.

Blume has written adult books, such as "Forever" and "Wifey" that are not intended for the juvenile shelves in the library. But her main body of work deals with the pain of growing up, with real life as it is faced by children. She writes about divorce, menstruation, masturbation, shoplifting and the primitive nature of kids' relationships with one another. In books like "I was a Fourth Grade Nothing," her characters talk like kids talk, act like kids act and think like kids think.

Apparently, this shocked the grown-ups in Montgomery County, Md., a wealthy Washington suburb where schools are "good" and parents are said to care. Last month, they cared enough to push "Blubber," Blume's story of a fat girl tormented by her classmates, out of open circulation in the schools. They were disturbed because the book doesn't make judgments. As one parent explained: "There's no adult or another child at the end who says, 'This is wrong. This cruelty to others shouldn't be.'"

Some grown-ups work up steam when truth is faced, when books show kids for what they are, when books help them understand themselves and the complex things they feel. Some grown-ups think TV is safer. They almost never turn it off because the stories always have a moral despite the sex and violence. The truth will out, crime never pays, love conquers all.

On television, kids are cherubs — cute, clean, basically decent, obedient and kind. Of course, their halos slip sometimes. They make mischief, get into scrapes, cross acceptable lines of behavior. Their problems are blown up for easy resolution between commercials. Because the networks frown on dirty words and favor happy endings, the scripts are played for hollow laughs and empty tears, a formula which never threatens.

But kids are so much smarter than they're given credit for. They know that some books have a life that TV doesn't. They're not afraid despite their parents' fears. Too bad some grown-ups just don't understand.

The Charlotte Observer
Charlotte, N.C., December 21, 1980

When there's conflict at the schoolhouse, it's often between parents' duty and right to guide their children's lives and the school's duty to educate their children. That initially was the nature of the conflict this fall at North Iredell High School. The issue was whether a 10th-grade English student ought to be required to read Aldous Huxley's satirical novel, "Brave New World."

We don't think any public school student should be required to read "Brave New World" or any other particular work of fiction if the parent objects to the ideas or language it contains.

We also don't think any parent, or any group of parents not assigned by school officials to screen reading material, should have the ultimate authority to remove a book, even temporarily, from compulsory or optional reading lists, or from school or public libraries.

School administrators and teachers can head off many such conflicts by making sure parents see reading lists and inviting parents who object to a particular book to discuss their concerns.

Teachers should explain why they believe the book is worthwhile and suitable for student reading; and they should make clear that if, for religious or other reasons, a parent does not want a child exposed to a particular book, the student can be assigned alternative reading or study. Those are sensible guidelines, supported by the National Council of Teachers of English.

North Iredell's principal, Kenneth Wilson, says such an option was offered to Charles Campbell after Mr. Campbell told school officials Oct. 30 that he found "Brave New World" to be "anti-family and anti-Christian" and objected to its being required reading for his daughter, Lisa. Other good books could help Lisa Campbell understand the concept of satire.

But Mr. Campbell, reported to be a Moral Majority member, is pursuing the matter in an attempt to have the book taken off the required reading list for *all* students, not just his daughter. That's the issue the Iredell County school board must decide when it meets Jan. 5.

So the situation at North Iredell High now involves more than parental rights; at issue now is censorship. It has gotten to this point, however, not just because of Mr. Campbell's insistence, but also because of a policy of the Iredell County school board.

The board requires that when a school gets a complaint from a parent about a particular book, the book must be removed from all classes while the dispute between the school and the parent is being resolved. So, during what can be a lengthy appeals process, the reading of all students is, in effect, controlled not by educators, but by a single parent or group of parents.

We believe that's a bad policy. Whatever process a school board sets for dealing with complaints regarding books, the books at issue should be removed, if at all, only at the end of that process, not at the beginning.

As Book-Banners Organize, So Do Their Opponents

The campaign to withdraw books from classrooms and libraries became an organized, nationwide effort as local groups discovered that their pressure brought results. The U.S. textbook industry, with $940-million worth of business a year at stake, was sensitive to local complaints. In more than half the states in the U.S., textbooks were chosen by a central authority, and pressure from local groups could make the difference between healthy sales and uncomfortable losses. Chief among the "New Right" textbook reviewers were Mel and Norma Gabler of Longview, Texas. Their Educational Research Analysts rapidly grew into a national network reviewing history, literature and biology textbooks and lobbying for changes. They criticized modern textbooks for lack of patriotism, a negative attitude towards capitalism and disregard of religious and moral values.

Opponents have begun slowly to organize against groups like Educational Research Analysts. The American Library Association's Office for Intellectual Freedom and the National Coalition Against Censorship have advised local groups on mounting challenges to the banning of books from school libraries. In a test case, an appeals court judge ruled in March that students in Island Trees, N.Y. could bring suit against the school board's 1976 order banning nine books. Judge Jon O. Newman said the issue posed a "sufficient threat to the free expression of ideas within the school community to establish a First Amendment violation." He ordered the case, *Pico v. Board of Education, Island Trees,* to be heard by a U.S. District Court, despite the school board's objection. The books included works by Bernard Malamud, Kurt Vonnegut, Eldridge Cleaver, Desmond Morris and Piri Thomas.

The Seattle Times

Seattle, Wash., August 9, 1981

IT IS bad enough that library and school officials across the nation are reporting an increase in attempts to censor books and films in classrooms and school libraries.

What is worse is that the crusade against books and publications deemed objectionable by self-appointed censors seems to be working.

The dismaying trend is reported in a survey sponsored by the Association of American Publishers, the American Library Association, and the Association for Supervision and Curriculum Development.

Analyzing information obtained from questionnaires sent to nearly 1,900 elementary-and-secondary-school superintendents, principals, librarians, and library supervisors in 50 states and the District of Columbia, the report said at least half the respondents said "some degree of restriction or censorship was ultimately imposed on the challenged material."

Challenges were based most frequently on writings and films containing references to sexuality and obscenity and objectionable language, the report said.

Earlier this year, library officials had reported a substantial increase in the number of complaints about library materials, probably because of the publicity given censorship pressures advocated by zealots attached to such organizations as the Moral Majority.

The Rev. George Zarris, chairman of Moral Majority in Illinois, had said last December that "some stuff is so far out, you have to (ban) it . . . I would think that moral-minded people might object to books that are philosophically alien to what they believe. If they have the books and feel like burning them, fine."

Encouraging that line of thought inevitably produces ludicrous results. Among the works under recent challenge, according to the new report, were novels by Ernest Hemingway, J.D. Salinger and Nathaniel Hawthorne, and classics such as Shakespeare's "Merchant of Venice" and Mark Twain's "Huckleberry Finn."

Maintaining strong citizen interest in libraries and what youngsters are reading is one thing. But urging censorship and even book burning is an intolerable attack on one of the most cherished traditions of a free society.

Rockford Register Star

Rockford, Ill., August 19, 1981

That image of irate parents seeking to purge public school libraries isn't too far off target. It's gotten so the mere thought of such a confrontation impels more principals and teachers to censor books, just to avoid trouble.

"Censorship pressures on books and other learning materials in the public schools are real, nationwide and growing," a new study shows. It was conducted by the Association of American Publishers, the American Library Association and the Association for Supervision and Curriculum Develpment.

These are some of the volumes that figured in 1980 censorship battles: The American Heritage Dictionary, Shakespeare's "The Merchant of Venice," Wilt Chamberlain's autobiography, E.B. White's children's book, "Stuart Little," Mark Twain's "Huckleberry Finn," J. D. Salinger's old chestnut, "Catcher in the Rye," and George Orwell's "1984," as well as Solzhenitsyn's "One Day in the Life of Ivan Denisovich."

Chicago writer Studs Terkel, whose interviews of working people produced the book, "Working," saw his own work banned. Terkel said the censorship contains sadness because ideas scare people. "Their own fear takes over and they put it in their kids."

We totally agree with Terkel's advice to principals: "The very experience of having been exposed to works of human and artistic merit will enable (children) to throw out the schlock. Good stuff would put the bad stuff out of existence."

Post-Tribune

Gary, Ind., February 7, 1981

There was this minister, setting fire to books, album covers, comics. It was a sick act of violence. And there were dozens of children watching. Some show.

The Rev. Lars Wessberg of Omaha said the material, including a National Geographic and some Batman stuff, "hindered Christian lives." He asked kids in the church school to bring in the awful stuff for the bonfire.

Now, Wessberg has a right to be wrong. But why should he teach kids to be wrong, too?

It was quite a media event. A crowd of kids gathered around, while he officiated at the purification rites, or whatever it was. We did not find out, in the news story about this fire, what the minister found offensive in a Daffy Duck comic. But it was among the targets.

Book burning is therapy for some. It is easier than reading. It's a kind of cosmetic exorcism that brings a temporary, deluding satisfaction. But the practice of book burning is progressive.

So what will go into the flames next, wherever they burn? Why, more "bad" books, of course.

Portland Press Herald
Portland, Maine, May 8, 1981

The Baileyville School Committee is getting into the book-banning business. The committee says "365 Days," a book of vivid Vietnam war sketches, is unfit for the eyes and minds of high school students in the Washington County community.

There's nothing new about school board censorship. Every so often a school board will succumb to the temptation to impose its collective judgment as to what ought to be permitted on school library shelves.

Elected school officials ought to be wary of accepting that kind of responsibility. By and large, they constitute some of the worst book reviewers in the country. School boards in Maine in recent years have banned books by Alexander Solzhenitsyn and J. D. Salinger. Others have banned such authors as Kurt Vonnegut, Richard Wright, and Bernard Malamud.

The Baileyville book, by Ronald Glasser, was enthusiastically reviewed when it was published a decade ago and was nominated for a National Book Award. In the 10 years it has been on the shelves at the Woodland High School library about 30 students have borrowed the book.

The literary quality of Glasser's book, however, is less important than the ominous question of censorship which is raised whenever a school board bans a book from a school library. In the Baileyville case, like most of those which have preceded it, the school board acted after the parents of a student complained.

Two points need to be made here. First, Glasser's book was not required classroom reading. Second, parents and school board members have little business imposing their own moral values upon the voluntary reading pursuits of others.

The action of the Baileyville School Committee, however well intended, amounts to nothing less than governmental censorship. It ought to be resisted.

St. Petersburg Times
St. Petersburg, Fla., August 1, 1981

From the standpoint of many Pinellas County teachers and residents, former School Supt. Gus Sakkis' eloquent defense of academic freedom in 1975 was his finest hour. At least 350 parents bristling with righteous indignation had attended a school board meeting to demand that "dirty books" be stripped from high-school library shelves. Sakkis made a lot more sense than the censors.

"Students have to have the right to read and professionals have to have the right to handle controversial subjects," Sakkis said. "If you're going to educate citizens who have the ability to think for themselves, then you can't begin to restrict what they can discuss and what they can read."

CAUGHT IN the middle of common sense and emotionalism, the School Board voted unanimously to back Sakkis, leaving the review of library books to the educators. The board made the right decision.

Considering a new and alarming study on censorship, this is an appropriate time to recall Sakkis' firm stand against censorship of schoolbooks.

"Censorship pressures on books and other learning materials in the public schools are real, nationwide and growing," says the study, based on a survey of 1,891 librarians, principals and superintendents. One public school in five comes under pressure each year to purge from its shelves books that someone finds offensive. The number of censorship attempts is growing and half the time the effort succeeds — the book is either removed from school or access to it is restricted.

All parents have a right, of course, to voice their opinions about the education of their children. Their views about textbooks and school library books ought to be considered. But professional educators should have the final say.

WHAT'S NEEDED is a balance between the freedom of teachers to teach and the right of parents to express their views about how they want their children educated. The removal of books from a school library or classroom curriculum ought to be based on educational considerations — not on parents' political, ideological, moral or religious views.

But in most cases, people who demand that books be banned from public schools do so for those very reasons. Two hundred books were subjected to censorship pressures last year, the study says. Nearly half of the challenges were based on the charge that the book was obscene, used objectionable language or dealt with sexuality. In all, 30 reasons were given, including the way books portrayed the U.S. role in history, the way they dealt with evolution or what they said about traditional family values.

One of the most disturbing findings of the survey is that efforts to censor schoolbooks often are initiated by teachers or prinicipals to avoid trouble. Censorship, unfortunately, is common in schools that have experienced book-banning controversies. Having gone through one battle, principals try to omit books that might cause protest.

THERE IS a remedy. The study said that schools with formal written policies and procedures for considering challenged books were less vulnerable to censorship pressures. Parents retain their right to object to books used in public schools, but a committee of professional educators has the final say.

During the 1975 dirty-book controversy in Pinellas County, the School Board set up formal procedures for book selection and reviews that have worked well.

Although parents ought to decide what their children read at home, their views should not be imposed on every student in public schools.

St. Louis Review
St. Louis, Mo., September 11, 1981

Book censorship is re-emerging as a controversial issue in American society fueled somewhat by the political clout of rightist organizations like the Moral Majority. The main focus of the new disputes involves the use of controversial books in public schools.

This issue gets very complicated because it involves parental rights on the one hand and freedom of speech on the other. In many cases it is not easy to disentangle the issues.

Protestant theologian Harvey Cox, who is no right-winger, recently said: "One of the major problems in this country is that people don't give a damn what is being taught to their children. If I were to discover my children were being taught things that went

completely against my beliefs, I would complain too."

There are certain rights that parents have regarding the type of education their children receive. The public is not entirely at the mercy of schools and libraries regarding available reading matter. In this as in all matters of public life there is a tension between individual rights and group rights.

But on the other hand we must recognize that fundamental to any free people is the right of access to printed matter without prior censorship. The First Amendment was added to our Constitution in part to protect words and ideas which the majority might find objectionable. The rights of the minority are important too. A great deal of balance and common sense

need to be applied to the application of these principles.

The history of book banning has certainly not always manifested common sense and balance. A display on book banning that was presented at West Virginia State College in the seventies listed among periodicals once banned Today's Health, National Geographic and Ebony. Books listed included Milton's Paradise Lost, Mark Twain's Huckelberry Finn and Tom Sawyer. Even the Bible was included.

We do have a serious problem with books and parents should be interested in what their children read, but we must try to handle the issue dispassionately.

THE COMMERCIAL APPEAL
Memphis, Tenn., March 29, 1981

THOSE AMERICANS too young to remember for themselves can read how books were burned in Hitler's Germany and recognize it for what it was: the symbolic destruction of words and thoughts that offended the Nazis' sense of "morality." The burning was all the more heinous to American sensibilities because it also destroyed the essence of democracy. People were denied knowledge and information and the right to choose from competing ideas.

HOW COULD an action which seemed so foreign then find a home now in the United States?

• A Longview, Texas, couple, Mel and Norma Gabler, run Educational Research Analysts, Inc., a mom-and-pop operation which does nothing but rate books for their "acceptability." The firm, considered the 16th member of the 15-member Texas school textbook committee, convinced the state to recommend against purchasing the American Heritage Dictionary and four other standard dictionaries because of "vulgar language" and "unreasonable definitions."

• Three national news magazines — Time, Newsweek and U.S. News & World Report — are among the latest targets of censorship in the schools, according to the National Council of Teachers of English.

• The Kanawha, Iowa, school board removed John Steinbeck's "The Grapes of Wrath" from the sophomore reading list after several parents complained that this classic tale of migrant farm workers in the Great Depression contained language that was "profane, vulgar and obscene" and "takes the Lord's name in vain dozens of times."

• An Abingdon, Va., preacher has pressured the public library to remove best sellers by Sidney Sheldon, Harold Robbins and Philip Roth after readers requested their purchase. Failing that, Rev. Tom Williams asked to see the circulation records. The library maintained the list was confidential and held its ground for itself and its patrons. The issue promises to remain hot until next fall's election. Some officeseekers plan to run on the promise to cut off all library funds.

• "Our Bodies, Ourselves" hasn't been banned in the hometown of its authors, the Boston Women's Health Collective, but it's been taken off the shelves in the State College, Pa., high school library and is under attack in Alpine, Calif. This book on female physiology was written to help women understand and participate in the medical decisions affecting them. It presents the facts of life and leaves moral conclusions to its readers.

• When a Montello, Wis., book review committee decided "The Magician," by Sol Stein, could be included in a high school novels course, nine "concerned citizens" checked 33 other books out of the school library. The citizens are challenging 10 of the books, including two by Judy Blume, and say they may challenge the rest, among them, "The Great Gatsby" by F. Scott Fitzgerald, "Catcher in the Rye" by J. D. Salinger and "Diary of a Young Girl" by Anne Frank, the first-person account of a Jewish adolescent and her family hiding from the Nazis.

ARE THESE CENSORSHIP efforts isolated brushfires and the result of spontaneous combustion, or is there an organized effort? Both. Individuals do object for isolated reasons, but more and more networks have sprung up to inflame the grassroots. The Gablers of Texas send mailings to like-minded people around the country. The Moral Majority in North Carolina is developing an "official list" of the "right" books for students in grades 1-12.

To judge by the nature of the complaints, however, the printed word isn't under attack only from the far right. Some books have been condemned for dwelling on violence or hinting at racism, sexism, bias against the handicapped, ethnic prejudice and the like. Mark Twain and the Brothers Grimm are only three of the writers who've been attacked on this score.

New Right critics focus elsewhere: on publications which are sexually explicit, from best sellers and Playboy in Braille to medical information written in laywomen's terms, and on books which espouse beliefs that differ from their own or that are morally neutral. They gladly pass out copies of selected passages they find offensive, never stopping to consider that if the Bible were dissected and disseminated verse by verse, it also would contain many "wrong" elements.

This willingness to destroy all but the "right" books and thoughts is a dangerous business. We will all be the poorer if it isn't stopped. So will future generations, who will never know what America was like, much less Nazi Germany, because the "wrong" books won't be around for them to read.

The Hartford Courant
Hartford, Conn., September 9, 1981

Schools, in a democratic society, should be places where children are encouraged to explore and question their world, where they are given the skills to think for themselves. Schools should not be just another institution reinforcing old orthodoxies.

This is the simple yet basic view the state Board of Education will consider today in a proposed policy statement on academic freedom. If the nine-member board approves this enlightened policy, it will make Connecticut the first state in the country to officially support the students' right to be free from unreasonable censorship.

The policy would not be binding on local school boards. It would, however, give them a clear reference point for deciding for themselves how to respond to the growing demands to withhold certain books, facts, or ideas from inquiring young minds.

There have been 17 instances in the last six years where state officials believe students' academic freedom has been threatened. In one celebrated case, a South Windsor anthropology class was attacked because a textbook told students about an Alaskan Eskimo tribe that practiced polygamy.

Too often, these reasons bear the bitter fragrance of fanaticism. Too often, parents are not just objecting to having their children exposed to the material they find offensive; they can usually remove their children from these classes or make other arrangements. The problems arise when a few parents do not want the books or subjects taught at all.

The proposed policy statement offers a useful approach for dealing with these cases, asking local school officials to "demonstrate substantial or legitimate public interest in order to justify censorship or other proposed restrictions upon teaching and learning."

There is a difference, the statement notes, between teaching and indoctrination. "Schools should teach students how to think, not what to think," it adds. "To study an idea is not necessarily to endorse an idea."

Local school boards properly will remain the arbiters of what this means in practice, although their decisions are always subject to review in court when conflicting legal rights come into question.

Hartford, Conn., September 11, 1981

It is just one more sorry sign of these socially confused times that as mild and unbinding a policy statement as the one the state Board of Education just approved on academic freedom should encounter such fevered opposition.

The statement offers local school boards an enlightened perspective to help them deal with the growing number of complaints against the diversity of ideas introduced in classrooms. Local boards are free to adopt it or ignore it.

When faced with a request to remove a course or book or idea from the curriculum, the statement recommends that school officials "demonstrate substantial or legitimate public interest in order to justify censorship or other proposed restrictions upon teaching and learning."

But even this flexible standard is too confining for the state board's critics. At a hearing this week, there were complaints that the policy would sap parental authority in town schools and promote teaching of objectionable topics. This is nonsense.

The statement simply outlines a responsible role for schools to play in democracy. "Public schools represent a public trust," it notes. "They exist to prepare our children to become partners in a society of self-governing citizens. Therefore, access to ideas and opportunities to consider the broad range of questions and experiences which constitute the proper preparation for a life of responsible citizenship must not be defined by the interests of any single viewpoint."

The statement further encourages public participation in the process but acknowledges that people should "respect the constitutional and intellectual rights guaranteed school personnel and students by American law and tradition."

Parents who are concerned about what their children are being taught should and usually do have opportunities to insulate them from objectionable subjects. But just because someone feels some idea is inappropriate for one child does not justify censoring it from everyone else.

The Idaho STATESMAN
Boise Idaho, August 6, 1981

It didn't come as much of a surprise last week to read about a study outlining a surge in censorship of U.S. school books. That's what makes the situation doubly sad. Everywhere you you look these days, ignorance and nonsense seem to be winning battles.

Down in Los Angeles, for example, there's an anti-Semitic group that spends $100,000 a year telling people that the Holocaust never happened. "The Holocaust is about as real as the emperor's new clothes," says Lewis Brandon, publisher of the high-sounding *Journal of Historical Review,* which lists 11 people with doctorate degrees on its editorial advisory board.

It's a bizarre notion, right? Denying history, denying the tragedy of the 6 million Jews who died at the hands of the Germans, denying the ovens and gas chambers and the political nightmare that brought them about.

The temptation is to label Brandon and his supporters as kooks to whom nobody in his right mind would listen. We would all like to believe that Americans are wise enough to see through such lies. But *are* people that wise? And, if so, will they continue to be so wise another 20 years down the road when there are no more Auschwitz survivors to tell the story and show the tatooed numbers on their arms?

We wonder, particularly when we see irrationality winning the day in other arenas — like the public schools.

That study of censorship by a coalition of educators, librarians and publishers found that more than 200 books were subjected to censorship pressure in 1980. As usual, the list included classics like *Huckleberry Finn, 1984,* and *The Merchant of Venice.* Just as Brandon the anti-Semite tells people that the Holocaust never happened, somebody somewhere is telling people that Huck Finn, George Orwell and Shakespeare are dangerous. Those who believe put pressure on schools and then — in too many cases — the schools defy common sense by restricting the readership of literary treasures.

Perhaps most alarming is the study's finding that in many cases where books were challenged, "the challenged material was altered, restricted or removed prior to a formal review." In other words, the schools chose to cave in and avoid trouble rather than defy their ignorant tormenters.

That worries us. Teachers — and everyone else with good sense — should stand up and scream bloody murder when they find ignorance, foolishness and just plain lies being foisted on the public.

the Charleston Gazette
Charleston, W. Va., December 1, 1981

FOR YEARS those who identify themselves as being among the righteous have suffered mild discomfort when asked if they have read any of the books they condemn as un-Christian and un-American.

Now they have an answer to this embarrassing question. It is this: The books they condemn are too dangerous to read. One of the three major groups endeavoring to seize control of young American minds by regulating what young Americans read is Mel and Norma Gabler's Educational Research Analysts. This outfit warns parents in its national mailings that textbook content "appears so natural, reasonable and convincing" that they should not risk reading it.

What should parents do then? The Gablers have the answer to that, too. They are prepared to supply parents with thousands of book reviews which tell just how wicked the innocent-appearing textbooks actually are. That takes the job of judging out of the hands of parents where moralists once said it belonged. Now, parents, themselves, are not trusted to select their children's reading material.

Anyone who believes there is no possibility of resumption of the textbook strife of the last decade in Kanawha County is optimistic, indeed. The radical religious right has not lessened but has increased its efforts to capture the minds of students. The campaign is coordinated by Jerry Falwell's Moral Majority, the Gablers' Educational Research Analysts, and Phyllis Schlafly's Stop Textbook Censorship Committee.

Mrs. Schlafly reasons that dread "secular humanists" now censor all textbooks. Falwell has said that most textbooks are nothing more than "Soviet propaganda," and the Gablers, as we have observed, believe that parents cannot recognize what is bad for their children. They call for a purge of reading material that is inconsistent with Moral Majority orthodoxy. Their efforts to save America from wickedness recall John Birch techniques. Here, taken from a report prepared by People for the American Way, an anti-Moral Majority group, are some samples of Gablerism.

▲ Discussions of the civil rights movement and the slogan "Freedom" should be prohibited in schools because all persons in this country have always been free unless they were in jail.

▲ Discussions of whether computers are capable of creative thinking should be prohibited. The objection: "Infers (sic) that there can be more than one answer."

▲ Descriptions of America as a nation of immigrants from other countries should be prohibited because they present a derogatory view of America that does not foster patriotism.

▲ Discussions of women's contribution to history should be prohibited because they undermine women's traditional role.

Sound familiar? These observations are very much like those made by the vocal minority that frightened thoughtful Kanawha Countians into silence in the mid-'70s. It could happen again. If it does, many of us must decide whether we shall speak out against intolerance or stand apart from the fray, as before, and watch democracy suffer.

The Miami Herald
Miami, Fla., August 12, 1981

CONSIDERING the test performance of America's high-school seniors, you'd think the chief worry of parents and school officials would be that too many pupils are graduating who can't read — or don't.

In an increasing number of school districts, however, the chief worry appears to be that the pupils will read books deemed naughty by the self-appointed censors from the fringes of American politics.

A new report, *Limiting What Students Shall Read* — issued jointly by the Association of American Publishers, the American Library Association, and the Association for Supervision and Curriculum Development — indicates a growing effort to censor what pupils read.

No responsible educators argue that all reading material is suitable for pupils of all ages. Most educators recognize as well that in this pluralistic society, some pupils (and their parents) will take offense at books and films that others consider classics.

Discretion and good judgment therefore must be used by instructors when selecting materials for required reading or viewing. Assigning an "X-rated" novel to a "born again" adolescent invites trouble.

At the same time, however, conservative parents and pupils ought not to be permitted to impose their narrow views on others by having materials they find offensive banned from school libraries and forbidding their assignment to pu-

pils who do not find them offensive.

If this pluralistic and heterogeneous society is to survive in freedom, there must be a tolerance of differing values. Fundamentalists must respect the freedom of others to read what they please; liberals must respect the fundamentalists' desire not to have their children compelled to read materials they find offensive.

In practice, maintaining this balance of rights and freedoms requires tact and sensitivity on a day-to-day basis at the classroom level. That is a much better place to settle such problems than in the emotion-charged atmosphere of a school board besieged by would-be book burners.

In the meantime, however, defenders of the right to read ought to begin thinking ahead to the school-board elections coming up in their jurisdictions this year and next. Emboldened by their success in ousting congressional liberals, the Far Right's book burners may set their sights next on gaining control of local school boards.

If they succeed, Americans might as well get ready to gather 'round the bonfires. They'll start by incinerating the works most often found on the hit lists of the far right — books by Ernest Hemingway, John Steinbeck, J.D. Salinger, and so on. What will really be going up in smoke, however, is the U.S. Constitution and its guarantees of freedom of thought, expression, and belief.

Cause of School Problems Labeled "Secular Humanism"

Declining educational standards, lax public morals, rebellious students—all these were the fault of a new philosophy, "secular humanism," which had taken over America, according to the "New Right." "Secular humanism" came to symbolize all that was wrong with society, from abortion to television. For Jerry Falwell, "secular humanism" meant "abortion-on-demand, recognition of homosexuals, free use of pornography, legalizing of prostitution and gambling and free use of drugs, among other things." One had to choose between "faith in God versus secular humanism," in the words of Sen. Jesse Helms (R, N.C.). The original definition of "humanism," which appeared in Western thought at the beginning of the Renaissance, was the study of Greek and Roman history, languages, art and literature. Humanists asserted the value of studying human activities at a time when most education was focused on the Catholic Church. Today, college students would recognize the "humanities" as liberal arts courses.

Whatever the original intentions of Renaissance humanists, the term as used by the "New Right" designated all that they opposed. "Secular humanism" in the public schools was blamed for subverting children away from religion and obedience to parents by teaching everything from Charles Darwin's theory of evolution to sex education. The tension between home and school is not new or unusual. Students are exposed to many influences in school from books, teachers and classmates. Many of the things they learn contradict what they are taught at home. Honest parents, troubled by the apparent decline in educational and moral standards, may agree with the "New Right" that the schools have gone too far in encouraging students to "make up their own minds." However, do the schools really have an obligation to reinforce the environment of the home?

The Idaho STATESMAN

Boise, Idaho, May 8, 1979

Author-educator Raymond Moore has come up with the interesting theory that sending children to school at age 6 or 7 is causing a general decline in civilization. In a recent talk in Salt Lake City, Moore attributed such behavior as homosexuality, abortions, drug abuse, learning disabilities and, in part, inflation, to the American tendency to send children to school at an early age. We're surprised he also didn't warn that it causes warts.

Moore's theory does contain a kernel of truth. Educators and parents must be sensitive to the development of an individual child's ability to absorb formal education. Boys particularly seem to be ready for school at a later age. But there seems, at least locally, to be ample evidence that educators are more, not less, sensitive to individual differences these days. Whereas holding a child back a grade or postponing entrance into school by a year were once rare occurrences, educators now are making such decisions quite often if the child's best interests so warrant.

As for the question of values, Moore's explanation for all these ills is too convenient and, to our mind, quite wrong. He theorizes that children lack adequate value systems because they spend too little time with their parents and too much time learning from their peers. That's not the problem. At home or at school our children are going to confront the complex moral questions of our age. We live, for better or worse, in a time of transition and upheaval in moral values. One thing you can always count on in such a period: the emergence of folk like Moore, who, out of pain and frustration, attempt to provide one nice, neat answer for all the world's difficulties. The only problem is, their answers never work.

Houston Chronicle

Houston, Texas, July 6, 1979

Officials of the National Education Association, the country's largest teachers' union, have apparently decided that one of the ways the NEA will take of coming to the defense of its constituents in the matter of competency tests for teachers and a return to the basics in student instruction is by blaming the "New Right" ("the same old conservatives," they call it) for their troubles.

NEA officials say the teachers are being isolated by the public demand for reform of teacher and method, that innovation in education is being inhibited and that the student is being denied the opportunity "to explore and develop his own personal talents and capabilities" by the new insistence on teaching the basics to avoid the functional illiteracy that even the NEA officials admit afflicts 15 percent of those students reaching the 12th grade.

If the NEA people really believe this, they're misreading, badly, the sentiments of the parents and those school administrators who are demanding a more thorough and rigorous training for their children and charges, not because they're members of the New Right, but because they have seen, first hand, the effects on the students of an educational approach that, in too many cases, hasn't been getting the job done. The parents have seen their children qualifying for every promotion, but the qualifications have failed to include a demonstrable ability to deal with such basic elements of education as being able to read and understand, to write clearly and to find their way through the simplest mathematical disciplines.

It seems to us that a desire for the enrichment of their children's education through innovative techniques is still in most parents' minds and would be welcomed. But what is also in their minds, and quite properly, is a desire that their children be instructed by competent teachers in the basic areas that make up the foundation for the refinements in education. Unfortunately, there has been a tendency to put the cart before the horse in education by emphasizing the enrichment and innovative programs before a knowledge of the basics was instilled; this has been perceived by many parents and they have taken exception to it, again quite properly.

The Union Leader

Manchester, N.H., July 8, 1981

There are encouraging and distinct signs this country is coming around to the realization that it cannot shut out God from its political considerations.

Tough-minded U.S. Senator Jesse Helms of North Carolina describes his brand of politico-religious conservatism as "faith in God versus secular humanism."

Certainly there is only one choice for those possessing religious beliefs. But the liberals of this country who have long pushed the steady secularization of American life are deeply worried.

Prayers were banished from the schools. The First Amendment was trotted out regularly to remind us of the gap between church and state and the liberals smiled.

But now these liberals are no longer smiling. They realize Jesse Helms has got something that just won't roll over and play dead.

This nation can ill afford to be neutral on the subject of God unless we are a country of atheists.

Helms' struggle to recreate an awareness of God in the deliberations of our political leadership is an honorable one.

We owe a vote of thanks to Jesse Helms.

WORCESTER TELEGRAM.

Worcester, Mass., August 10, 1981

The Moral Majority and some related groups want to redirect the United States along a course of fundamentalism. They have come out strongly against the teaching of evolution in schools and freedom of choice on abortions, among other things.

They are opposed to humanism, particularly secular humanism. It has become a rallying cry that covers almost every ill in American life.

Humanists, they feel, have rejected God, creation and morality.

The Rev. Tim LaHaye, chairman of Californians for Bibilical Morality, that state's arm of the Moral Majority, has warned his followers that "the battle for the mind is between atheistic, godless humanism and basic Christian consensus . . . moral values or anarchy, one or the other."

The religious fundamentalists are particularly shocked by the humanistic belief that man has the capacity for solving his own problems without divine intervention. They also find distasteful the idea that man has the capacity to measure human values himself.

LaHaye believes "Either God exists and has given man moral guidelines by which to live, or God is a myth and man is left to determine his own fate. Your response to either position will usually determine your attitude toward such issues as abortion, voluntary school prayer, pornography, homosexuality, capital punishment, the priority you place on traditional family life and many other social problems."

Not everyone will share such an interpretation of humanism by LaHaye and others of the religious right. As a philosophy, humanism has always prized man's shared cultural heritage, common values and pursuit of knowledge.

From the fifth century B. C., when Protagoras, the Greek philosopher, said "man is the measure of all things" until now, humanists have contributed much to intellectual advancement. They have championed free thought, human reason and the validity of the scientific method.

There is room in this country for all varieties of belief, ranging from humanism to fundamentalism.

America means freedom of religion and also freedom of thought. That is what makes it such a remarkable nation.

The Dispatch

Columbus, Ohio, May 12, 1979

IF THE SCHOOLS retreated from their tendency to emphasize social consciousness would they allow the family to re-emerge as the values-setting center it should be? One thoughtful advocate of academic basics thinks not.

In essence, he suspects the American family is becoming so "liberated" it is literally falling apart.

Writing in the *Bulletin of the Council on Basic Education*, Headmaster Clay Stites of the Friends Academy, Andover, Mass., expresses concern with the care and nurture of children in a time when adults are encouraged widely to be "single, fast, and unburdened by responsibilities to others." Also, he says, single-parent families are increasing, the divorce rate is rising, and the remarriage rate does not keep pace.

Americans, particularly younger adults, aspire to "the cool and detached". Many of today's slogans encourage them, such as "Have it your way," "You deserve a break," and "No hassles." And he sees children overprogrammed at home with outside activities, or entrusted to day care centers, the schools and summer camps.

Mr. Stites does not excuse these tendencies on the grounds single parents have to work, or that other families are affluent enough to afford a host of frenzied activities. The effects would be the same in any event.

He doubts these types of freedom bring personal happiness to many parents or that they prepare many children for a happy adulthood.

We hope Headmaster Stites keeps the faith and sticks to his evident belief that the sounder values learning lies with academic basics in the schools. For, as he observes, the values of the last generation are not always those of the next. But the next generation must have the right tools to do better.

TULSA WORLD

Tulsa, Okla., January 19, 1980

THAT OLD bugaboo Middle Class Morality has taken a beating in some education circles in recent years. But the trend toward permissiveness is by no means unanimous.

In a new book, Surviving And Other Essays, Dr. Bruno Bettelheim, author and educator, has the nerve to assert that it is a shortage of middle class values rather than an excess that is cheating many children out of a decent education.

"None of the learning our present schools expect to instill in their students can take place," Bettelheim declared, "can take place without what has been described as a puritanical, or a specifically middle class morality."

Bettelheim's departure from the chic, anti-middle class prejudice was brought to mind by a series in The Washington Star on four troubled elementary schools in the District of Columbia area.

The series' author, Pat Lewis, found disturbing explanations for poor performance by children.

One teacher, discussing student inattention, rationalized: "As a student, I used to sleep and daydream. If they are staring out the window, they may be doing something more important" than what is going on in class.

"Another teacher told Lewis: "I know some (students) have to be made to learn. But I don't want to force them."

This is partly a manifestation of the 1960s self-gratification, do-your-own-thing philosophy. Tolerance, of course, is a good thing. But it can be overdone.

The attitude has been erroneously called humanism. But, in its most extreme form, it is almost the opposite of humanism. It can more accurately be called a form of nihilism.

It would be an exaggeration to say that deliberate non-direction is widespread in public schools. Most teachers and administrators try very hard to teach children to reason and to assimilate useful knowledge. But even in limited amounts, phony humanism is disastrous.

Dr. Bettelheim does educators a favor by reminding them of the obvious: "It is absolutely necessary for (a student) to acquire a specific body of attitudes and a certain sum of knowledge and skills."

Arkansas Gazette.

Little Rock, Ark., June 19, 1981

Al Capone discovered a long time ago that he could "get further with a kind word and a gun than with a kind word alone."

The Moral Majority apparently has paraphrased the proverb to read: "You can get further with revealed truth and a law than with revealed truth alone." Consequently, the country's most pressing need at the moment is to canonize the theology of Reverend Jerry Falwell, enshrine the document in a new Ark of the Covenant, and require compliance with its provisions by all the citizens.

Three members of Congress teamed up to introduce the legislation in a bill called the Family Protection Act of 1981. Wanda Harding, a spokeswoman for the Moral Majority, said the measure represents "everything" the group had supported.

Sponsors of the bill are: Senator Paul Laxalt (Rep., Nev.), Senator Roger Jepsen (Rep., Ia.), and Congressman Albert Lee Smith (Rep., Ala.), all of whom are dedicated to the comprehensive principles embraced in Reaganism. Smith said the administration "conceptually" supports the measure.

President Reagan enjoyed the full support (spiritual and financial) of the Moral Majority during his campaign. Now that the group has wrapped all its objectives into a single bill, Mr. Reagan jollywell better give the package his "conceptual" support. Laxalt, having measured the mood of the country and the political power of the President, said: "I think we've got an excellent chance of passing it in this political climate."

Whatever the prospects, the measure has many titles, none of which are offensive until they are examined. Perusal reveals that all are objectionable. For example:

The legislation has 31 provisions with the stated aim of "reinforcing" the legal rights of parents to "direct the religious and moral upbringing of their children." The catch here is that parents have had, and still have, all those rights. One of the essential rules of good government is: If conditions do not demand the passage of a new law, they dictate that no new law should be passed.

The matter should end there, but it doesn't. In the process of directing the "religious and moral upbringing of their children," parents would be given the right to "review" textbooks used in schools. This seems a bit absurd since no law exists to prevent parents (or anyone else) from examining whatever happens to be in print. Since the Moral Majority is one of several organizations that favor censorship to some degree, the proposal to legalize a reading and reviewing right that already exists may seem a bit confusing. Surely there is more than meets the eye in this important title of the Family Protection Act of 1981.

Perhaps the sponsors of the bill have something else in mind. The right to "read" and "review" is innocent enough; it becomes intolerable if it is followed by a book burning ceremony in which those tomes that are weighed in the balances and found wanting are consigned to the bonfire.

Religious schools, of course, would be exempt from all government regulations — including, presumably, the "right" of parents to review the books. If sex and violence were considered reasons to burn the book, the Bible just might end up in the blaze. Consider the Song of Solomon (a more sensual poem is hard to find in the English literature) or the depredation that the Children of Israel visited on the people who happened to occupy the Promised Land. The Holocaust had its survivors; the City of Ai had none and dozens of other communities suffered the same fate. Before we condemn books because they record sex and violence, perhaps we should make exceptions.

The private schools presumably would be exempt from the implied censorship of books by parents. They also would be free from all government regulations such as quotas, guidelines, affirmative action, and any requirement to consider racial balance. This, too, is an existing right so long as the schools remain "private" in the true sense of the word.

Another section of the bill might make the exemption necessary. Seven provisions of the measure deal with taxes. One would qualify the private schools as tax exempt and, in interpretation, the parents who chose that route for the education of their children just might enjoy a profitable tax loophole or even an exemption from paying public school taxes. Now it is easy to see why the schools would have to be free from government regulations. They could get money — even government money — without having to abide by the rules that, presumably, equalize opportunities for all citizens.

Smith, speaking at a news conference, wrapped it all up when he said "we have certain laws and rules which, as Christians, we follow" but he left unsaid the requirement implied in the law that "all you people out there would be advised to follow them, too."

That is what it all comes down to: The paraphrase of the Capone proverb which says "you can get further with revealed truth and a law than with revealed truth alone."

The Washington Star
and Daily News

Washington, D.C., January 6, 1980

". . . We have an educational system resting on a morality that holds that if man is to survive in this world, it is absolutely necessary for him to acquire a specific body of attitudes and a certain sum of knowledge and skills. But how is today's educator going to reach a youth who is convinced that society owes him a living no matter what — either because of past injustices inflicted on him or because of the expansiveness of our modern affluent society?"

That formulation is from Bruno Bettelheim's new book, *Surviving and Other Essays* (Knopf). In one essay, excerpted in the *American Educator*, Dr. Bettelheim firmly asserts that "none of the learning our present schools expect to instill in their students can take place without what has been described as a puritanical, or a specifically middle-class, morality."

The essence of middle-class morality is the postponement of immediate pleasure to gain more lasting future satisfactions and to reach one's goals. "Before the age of reason conscience . . . operates on the irrational basis on which it was originally formed; it tells the child what he must do and must not do on the basis of fear (not of reason)," writes Dr. Bettelheim.

"Thus, while conscience originates in fear, any learning that is not immediately enjoyable depends on the prior formation of a conscience. It is true that too much fear interferes with learning, but for a long time any learning that entails serious application does not proceed well unless also motivated by some manageable fear."

Dr. Bettelheim's essay came to our attention at the same time Pat Lewis' four-part series, "High Schools Today," was appearing in *The Star*. In large part, unhappily, the mood, philosophy and practices she found in a detailed look at four secondary schools illustrated the distinguished educator's thesis of "widely divergent values" in collision.

Ms. Lewis sat in on an English class in which a teacher and students discussed whether the draft should be reinstated. The students were dismissive of military service. "Can it be there will be a Camelot revisited? If Edward Kennedy stands up and says: 'Ask not what your country can do for you, but what you can do for your country,' what will you say?" the teacher asked.

"I would want the country to do something for me first," answered one young man, while eight of his peers slept soundly through the discussion.

How do teachers respond to that sort of value vacuum? Another teacher reflects, "I know some (students) have to be made to learn. But I don't want to force them. I think they should want to learn. Teachers should try to make things interesting enough to want to learn — that's the challenge," he said. A third teacher, contemplating pervasive student ennui, rationalizes: "As a student I used to sleep and daydream," he said. "If they are staring out the window, they may be doing something more important" than what is going on in class.

We do not suggest that the examples from *The Star's* series are the norm in the high schools. But there is sufficient evidence that the intellectual torpor and philosophical fragmentation that Ms. Lewis found are not exceptional today — reflected in such indices as test scores, for one thing, and rampant teacher strikes.

The foundering that characterizes vast reaches of public education today can be attributed to the loss, or repudiation, of the notion that a strict moral standard is crucial to learning. "The fact is that so much of learning is not a pleasurable experience but hard work . . . The voice of reason is very soft; it is easily drowned out by the voice of our appetites. If our teaching is based on pleasing the emotions, the noisy clamor of emotions will drown out the quiet voice of reason any day of the week." So writes Dr. Bettelheim. It makes sense to us.

Roanoke Times & World-News

Roanoke, Va., March 16, 1980

The fuss over having the Bible in public schools is only one facet of a broader dispute. A significant number of parents see traditional religion-based values as having been banished from the public schools, supplanted by another value system they generally describe as humanism.

The schools, these parents contend, should not be taking their children and exposing them to ideas of morality contrary to the parents' belief. If religion should not be taught in public schools, they ask, then why teach humanism, which the U.S. Supreme Court has defined as a religion?

The reference here apparently is to a 1961 case, Torcaso v. Watkins, where the high court declared that the First Amendment gives the same protections to and sets the same limits on secular or humanistic religions as apply to theistic religions. Commenting on this in the winter, 1978 issue of the *Emory Law Journal,* Robert L. Toms and John W. Whitehead said: "It logically follows that the government is prohibited from establishing non-theistic or secular ideologies in the public schools, just as it is prohibited from establishing theistic practices."

The key word there is *establishing,* which echoes the terminology of the First Amendment. Under the Bill of Rights, government cannot prefer one religion over another. No group, then, can demand the right to have biblical values taught in the public schools unless it is prepared to grant similar opportunities to other religions.

Even fundamental Christians may not want to open that can of worms. But for concerned parents, that leaves the question of what is being taught in the public schools, and whether this can be called humanism in the religious sense.

An immediate problem is defining the term. As a historical movement during the Renaissance, humanism did emphasize attitudes and beliefs opposed to those of the Christian churches. It was, and remains today, man-centered. But as *World Book Encyclopedia* notes, there have been many varieties of humanism, both religious and non-religious. Almost any moral standard — including, probably, most of those set by God-centered religions — can be included under the heading of humanism.

The possibility of guilt by association is thus broadened. Those who would condemn the teaching of "humanism" in the public schools risk blacklisting many of their own beliefs, and could reduce those schools to fleeing from moral issues — quite the opposite of the objectors' intent.

This looks like a dilemma, but perhaps it should be seen instead as a gray area — which is not new in society, or in jurisprudence, when rights and claims of groups or individuals conflict. In the spirit of the Constitution, it would seem that what educators must do, when ethical issues arise in their courses, is to acknowledge the prevailing differences in viewpoint — without preferring one over another. What parents should do — rather than try to exile all unwelcome ideas from the schools — is make sure that children, at home, understand what the parents believe and why.

Some kind of truce is necessary to avoid turning schools into a battleground of creeds. In our time, surely the classrooms have experienced enough cultural clashes already.

Simple humanism

Some of our readers aren't interested in whether "humanism" (discussed in the editorial above) is a religion or not. They don't know, and may not care, whether humanism is taught in public schools. Here is how the situation stands:

The public schools are lawfully permitted to teach students to be: Trustworthy, Loyal, Helpful, Friendly, Courteous, Kind, Obedient, Cheerful, Thrifty, Brave and Clean.

Any school system which instills the above virtues will never be in trouble with a federal court. Any students who learn the virtues will never be in trouble with a juvenile court. So, relax: The list above is a "humanist" agenda.

It is the time-honored Boy Scouts code of honor—minus the last one, "Reverent." If the schools can help wholeheartedly with the first 11, church and family should be able to take care of the 12th without trying to shove that one, too, at the schools.

THE MILWAUKEE JOURNAL

Milwaukee, Wisc., May 25, 1981

A truly scary story in The New York Times reported on parent groups springing up across the country to rid schools of "secular humanism." The parents blame this "ism" for crime, drug abuse, sexual promiscuity and a decline in religious belief and American power in the world.

Not content just to ban certain books that they disagree with, the groups even attack such features of schooling as creative writing, open classrooms and "the new math." They want reading instruction to focus on phonics. They want history texts slanted to emphasize only the positive side of America's past.

Most of all, they apparently want schools to permit children no uncertainty about what is right and what is wrong. In short, children should not be encouraged to challenge, to think for themselves. And that, of course, would thwart a fundamental purpose of American public schooling.

These groups are winning some victories, and not only in banning books. They're also intimidating educators. In Plano, Tex., teachers no longer ask pupils to express opinions because that would tend to deny absolute right and wrong. One teacher there told The Times: "Is there anything controversial in this lesson plan? If there is, I won't use it. I won't use things where a kid has to make a judgment."

How sad.

It's difficult to understand what motivates such groups, but Paul Kurtz, a humanist philosopher at New York's State University at Buffalo, says: "I think secular humanism is a straw man. They are looking for someone to blame."

Perhaps he's right. Many of the activists of this type whom we have observed in Wisconsin seem bewildered and frightened at the realities of modern life, some of which can be ugly as well as uplifting. Apparently unable to apply their beliefs to life today, they want to do the impossible: Turn back the clock — to a serene era that may never really have existed (except now in their selective memories).

What is scariest about this movement is not its rigid, anti-thought philosophy. (America's strength lies partly in its diversity, and there should be room for people who wish to live their lives that way.) What we find most troubling is their determination to impose their narrow views on everyone else by turning public schooling into a vehicle for their philosophy alone.

That is a fundamental threat to the concept of education and to America itself. It must be resisted.

the Charleston Gazette

Charleston, W.Va., June 5, 1981

IN Piano, Texas, according to a *New York Times* report, teachers are forbidden to solicit the opinions of students — a standard technique for stimulating discussion — because to do so is to deny absolute right and wrong.

Whence this madness? The rule was imposed by the Piano regiment of the avenging army that was roused to action by the political successes of the Moral Majority. In French Lick, Ind., the classic dramatic work "Death of a Salesman" has been banned from a high school English course; in Onida, S.D., the word "evolution" may not be uttered in an advanced biology class.

To this curiosa we are compelled to add our home-grown favorites. During the school book unpleasantness here, Adm. Farragut's "damn" chilled the blood of True Believers who also denounced as "un-American writing" a textbook suggestion that the Yuma Indian language is more pleasing to the ear than English.

Part III: Lifestyles

"For the times, they are a-changin'...." ran the 1960s refrain. The reverberations of that strife-torn decade have yet to die down, even if former protesters are trading in beads and headbands for suits and ties. A great many sexual taboos were broken, and people have become more accustomed to, if not more tolerant of, different living arrangements. Television finally accepted the existence of controversy in prime time, although most of the innovation seems to have been reduced to more references to sex. The divorce rate continues to rise; young people are engaging in sexual relations much sooner than before, and there seem to be few limits on what can be shown on the screen. The women's movement, which gained new strength during the 1960s, made lasting impressions on male-female relationships. These developments are the source of the "New Right's" frustration, and reversing them is the goal of their political efforts.

Television, Movies Draw Ire of "New Right," Others

Television in America has long been criticized for inane programs, tasteless advertising and harmful effects on reading scores. The "New Right" was not alone in its desire to change television and in its distaste with current films. Both liberals and fundamentalists deplored TV and movie violence. The Moral Majority found an unexpected ally in women's groups in its denunciations of sexual content in TV shows and commercials and in its campaign against pornographic films. Despite the occasional agreement, the "New Right" was more likely than its philosophical opponents to seek a ban on the offending material. The first of these organized campaigns was mounted against the film *Monty Python's Life of Brian,* a satire set in Palestine during the time of Jesus. Both Christian and Jewish groups protested the release of the movie, which followed the imaginary exploits of a young man who was mistaken for the Messiah. The Roman Catholic Archdiocese of New York called the film "an act of blasphemy." Morality in Media, an interfaith organization, said the movie was an "outrage" and vowed to support "any and every effort" to keep it from "seeing the light of day." The campaign forced the withdrawal of *Monty Python's Life of Brian* from several cities, including Baton Rouge, La., Charlotte, N.C. and Columbia, S.C. However, most efforts to obtain court orders blocking the film were unsuccessful.

The Detroit News
Detroit, Mich., November 21, 1979

George Orwell's fable, "Animal Farm," has been widely interpreted as a critique of Stalinist Russia, where commissars replaced the nobility in an immutable pecking order of authority and privilege.

And while this reading is correct as far as it goes, the real moral energy of Mr. Orwell's tale is realized in a much broader indictment of the basic revolutionary process.

When Mr. Orwell's pig (commissar) announces to the assembled field animals that henceforth, "All animals are equal, but some animals are more equal than others," the reader knows that the human "oppressors" have been replaced by the porcine, and that "the revolution" has failed.

We thought of George Orwell the other day while watching a group of feminists and other outraged folk demonstrating against a television show called "Three's Company."

Mr. Orwell, more than most, would have appreciated the irony of all these angry people, some of whom long ago liberated themselves from "repressive" moral dogma, gathered together to protest a mindless game show that they deem "morally offensive."

When people did this 20 years ago they belonged to that most "repressive" of all censorship societies, the Legion of Decency. Today, apparently, it's enough to belong to the National Organization for Women.

Frankly, after precisely one viewing of the program in question, we were almost tempted to join the demonstration. Surely, even in that vast sea of drivel that is early evening television, there have been few shows as leeringly inane as "Three's Company." The point appears to be to make a man's secretary and wife haggle over which knows him more intimately.

But even granting the abysmal taste of this prodigiously stupid program, is it a good idea to pressure a local station or a network to withdraw it? Do we really want any interest group, however well-intentioned, to have veto power over television programing? Wouldn't it be wiser for each of us to turn off the tube when it offends, instead of pressing for moral or ethical standards that aren't necessarily shared by everyone in a diverse society?

Revolutions, including the sexual one, come and go. But, as George Orwell understood, even those who are most oppressed are capable of becoming oppressors when their fortunes improve and their own interests appear to be at stake.

DESERET NEWS
Salt Lake City, Utah, August 18, 1979

Want to know how to reduce violence on television?

Don't count on government for much help. Instead, let companies that advertise during particularly violent shows know by letter or in person how dissatisfied you are.

Such consumer pressure — and with it the possibility of the TV networks getting hit where it hurts most, in the pocketbook — gets results. That's the word this week from the National Citizens Committee on Broadcasting.

The group monitors the length and number of violent incidents in prime-time commercial TV shows. From an average of 190 such incidents each week in a four-week test period in 1976, violence declined to 168 such episodes a week by last May, the study shows. The study gives much of the credit to TV watchers who complained to advertisers on violent shows.

"There are fewer overall incidents of violence, their duration is shorter, and this year many programs have no definable incidents at all," says the report.

Interestingly, Chrysler Corporation was identified as No. 1 among the 10 advertisers whose commercials appeared on the most violent shows. Others in order were Hi C Fruit Drinks, Budweiser Beer, Duracell Batteries, Mennen Products, Borden Food Products, Wrangler Jeans, General Mills, Sealy Mattress, and Miller Products. Only Miller was a repeater from a similar list compiled in 1977.

And conversely, the 10 "least violent sponsors" were Nikon Cameras, Alberto Culver Products, Perrier Mineral Water, Timex Watches, Shulton Old Spice, Beneficial Finance, Ace Hardware, Lincoln Mercury Motors, Fruit of the Loom, and Breck Products.

Many companies do not particularly specify beyond a particular time frame where or when their ads should appear. Consequently, many are shocked when viewers complain of the violence of shows with which they're associated. And if the TV station runs out of advertisers for a particular show, it soon gets the message on TV violence.

THE BLADE

Toledo, Ohio, September 11, 1979

COMPLAINING that television portrays the average American worker as "Archie Bunker or worse," the president of the International Association of Machinists has joined the ranks of would-be censors of that already too-timid medium.

Of course, the word "censorship" never passes the lips of those who complain that television misrepresents this ethnic group or that sex; the fashionable term is "stereotype." To make sure that blue-collar workers are not "stereotyped" by television, the machinists union's outspoken president, William Winpisinger, says that 500 full-time union representatives will be trained in the rules and regulations of the broadcasting industry — the better, presumably, to bring pressure on television writers and producers who dare to present a character like Archie Bunker (who, as "All in the Family" viewers know, actually has evolved into a rather complex and sympathetic figure).

The main problem with such television truth squads is that they operate on the assumption that entertainment has only one purpose: to provide edifying "role models" for whatever group happens to be portrayed. But the creative arts (a category in which commercial television can be included only provisionally, thanks in part to the programmers' fear of offending segments of their audience) simply cannot remain creative if each and every character, situation, and flight of fancy must gain the approval of pressure groups who can be expected to take offense at any unfavorable depiction of one of their number.

What are called stereotypes often reflect reality as much as prejudice. One man's or woman's stereotype is another's permissible generalization — or conscious departure from the norm. As with all creative efforts, the proof of a television drama's authenticity is in its execution. But precious few ambitious, imaginative, or realistic programs will see the light of day if pressure groups like Mr. Winpisinger's truth squad succeed in their image-protecting mission.

WORCESTER TELEGRAM.

Worcester, Mass., May 24, 1979

Question: Are prime-time television situation comedies being used as agents for social change?

Unlikely as that may seem, Michael J. Robinson says it is. Underneath those bizarre contrivances, those labored gags he finds a consistent message: Liberal Chic.

"With few exceptions," he writes in Public Opinion, "prime time has become a plug for sexual openness and freedom. But the plug doesn't stop there. Entertainment television serves as a soft-core, progressive statement about love, marriage, drugs, blacks, women and gays."

Robinson doesn't say that's bad. In fact, he concedes that his own values support gay rights, feminism, integration and the rest of the package.

But he thinks it important to understand that TV sitcom is not ideologically neutral. It sends a message — a message that reflects the biases and convictions of its liberal, urban scriptwriters and producers.

Robinson names shows. "Taxi," "Just Friends," and "Fantasy Island" among others, promote the idea of open sex (what used to be called "illicit sex") without guilt.

"M.A.S.H." satirizes war, the military and U.S. foreign policy.

"One Day at a Time" "paints life as a socio-sexual odyssey in which mothers and daughters discuss their intimate lives as if they were the weather."

Shows like "Soap" "treat WASP values as if they were diseases." And perhaps the most influential show of all — "All in the Family" — pours ridicule on the conventional Archie Bunker and portrays "hookers . . . and homosexuals as heroes . . ."

Robinson thinks it no coincidence that polls over the years show the American people growing more tolerant of homosexuality, extramarital sex, interracial marriage, pot smoking, abortion and the like.

He makes no charge that the country is being subtly brainwashed by some sort of conspiracy in New York and Hollywood.

But he points out that the values held by urban coastal intellectuals are not necessarily those held in the American Midwest.

By contrast, Robinson thinks that TV news programs have a conservative effect on viewers. By constantly and dramatically pointing out blunders and rascality in Washington and in the statehouses, TV news undermines the old belief in the value of big government.

Robinson's theories won't be accepted by everyone. They certainly don't call for censorship or any more of the "equal time" nonsense. But perhaps they do call for some thought by the wheelers and dealers of TV networks. Are they giving the American people and traditional values an even break?

The State

Columbia, S.C., October 25, 1979

IT IS important that the controversial film *Life Of Brian* be shown in Columbia because of the significant issue raised by its cancellation last Friday.

General Cinema, the film's distributor, suspended showing the motion picture after a telephone call from U.S. Sen. Strom Thurmond. The senator's help had been asked by a local churchman who disapproved of it.

The issue here is not one of religious concerns. (In the opinion of some, the motion picture is a parody of the life of Christ, but the filmmakers and others deny that.) As much as we dislike saying so, even if the film were as blasphemous as alleged, individuals have a right to see it if they so choose.

Churchmen and protesters let their zeal carry them too far beyond moral persuasion when they embraced a form of censorship of something in the public domain. Like the rest of us, the critics of *Life Of Brian* have a right to their own opinions, but they have no right to deny others access to the film.

(We should add, even if it sounds somewhat contradictory, that any theater owner has a right not to show a particular film he considers tasteless or whatever. If there is enough demand, another theater will likely show it. In both cases, the moviemen are exercising their right of free choice.)

We are surprised that Senator Thurmond took a role in this chain of events on the strength of hearsay. He responded to a complaint from the churchman who expressed fear there would be a public upheaval if the film were shown in Columbia. The senator himself relayed that concern to a representative of the distributor, and the word was passed to close the film down in Columbia.

Surely the senator was mindful of his own influence and the impact of such a telephone call, or he would not have made the call himself. But, as a man of considerable influence, Mr. Thurmond should have been cautious about his involvement without a studied inquiry into the situation.

Indeed, the series of events which led to the closing of the motion picture in Columbia is an alarming illustration of critics not knowing what they were talking about. The word-of-mouth warnings about the film have been nationally widespread, but there is good evidence that misconceptions are equally widespread.

We agree with the opinions of this newspaper's religion writer, Barbara Stoops, in her Sunday column. She is a sensitive and knowledgeable reporter and observer. And with her, we wonder why there is such a "to do" over *Life Of Brian* when there have long been present in Columbia many unprotested examples of offenses against good taste and propriety.

The point here, however, is that well-meaning citizens — including a U.S. senator — have had a hand in censorship by coercion. Far more has been at stake here than a mere film.

EVENING EXPRESS

Portland, Maine, October 31, 1979

Should one person's precepts and prejudices dictate what another may see? Certainly not.

That's why we're concerned about the protests over the showing of "Monty Python's Life of Brian."

Demonstrators calling the movie "blasphemous" protested its showing at Cinema City in Westbrook. In Brunswick the owners of Cook's Corner Cinemas canceled it after five days when protesters threatened a "permanent boycott of this theater if they insist on showing this movie." And in Lewiston a theater owner refused to bid on the film because he was afraid of the controversy it might generate.

While respecting the right of persons to protest the film, we are bothered that they would deny others a freedom of choice. And that's just what the protesters in Brunswick did.

For those who feel they would be offended by the well-publicized movie, the solution is simple. Stay away from it. They, too, have that freedom of choice.

What is it that some find so upsetting about "The Life of Brian" made by Monty Python, a group noted for its biting parody and outrageous iconoclasm?

"It's supposed to be a comical spoof, but it's an insult to Christianity as far as I'm concerned and as far as a lot of other people are concerned," said a spokesman for the group that picketed in Westbrook.

The movie is more than insulting, according to one film critic who said it goes so far as to show "contempt for both taste and religion."

But what is wrong with a movie being insulting or contemptuous? Movies past and present have scorned the free enterprise system, the military establishment, the television industry and, yes, religion too. Movie-makers have that freedom of expression.

The same freedom belongs to those wishing to see the movies. That right should not be tampered with by others who would impose their values on the community as a whole.

The Boston Herald American

Boston, Mass., September 9, 1979

It is in no way a compliment to the Monty Python comedy troupe to note that with one unbelievably stupid swing they managed to hit for the cycle in the Bad Taste League.

They did so by making a movie satire that was so offensive that it was condemned by clergy of the Protestant, Catholic and Jewish faiths.

The comic climax, believe it or not, has to do with a crucifixion scene in which a fictional contemporary of Christ who has been mistaken for the Messiah is tied to a cross while someone sings "always look on the bright side of life — on the bright side of death."

Funny? Robert E.A. Lee of the Lutheran Council of the USA and Rev. Eugene Clark of the Catholic Archdiocese of New York didn't think so. They called the movie "blasphemy."

Nor did three rabbinical associations, which condemned it as a "crime against religion."

But if you believe Warner Brothers, which is distributing the mess, no harm was meant. "It was never our intention to offend anyone's beliefs and we certainly regret having done so," they said. "The film is a satire . . ."

Let's all hope Monty Python doesn't try to show us the funny side of the Holocaust. They might see it as a situation comedy.

Portland Press Herald

Portland, Maine, November 1, 1979

It's one thing to publicly protest the contents of a motion picture one finds offensive, and to try to convince people not to patronize the film. But it's quite another thing to interfere with the freedom of others to make their own choice whether or not to view such a movie.

That is what converts the current organized opposition to the movie, "Monty Python's Life of Brian," from an ordinary peaceful protest to an exercise in censorship.

Picketers at a Brunswick movie house showing the film forced the theater owners to withdraw the movie by threatening a "permanent boycott" of the place if they refused.

Other theater owners have reportedly been intimidated by the threat of a confrontation and refused to bid on the movie.

The picketers included a number of religious groups who feel that "Brian," a parody set in the time of Jesus Christ, is blasphemous.

We have no quarrel with devout Christians who may be outraged by such an irreverent portrayal. And we have no quarrel with those who wish to give expression to that outrage by carrying a picket sign outside a theater.

What we do object to is applying pressure upon theater owners in an effort to force them to deny availability of the film to those in the community who may wish to see it.

There's nothing wrong with trying to persuade theatergoers that a film is not worth seeing.

There's everything wrong with trying to prevent the film from being shown in the first place.

The Union Leader

Manchester, N.H., September 19, 1979

Thanks to the Monty Python BBC nitwits and Warner Brothers, the word "blasphemy" may once again come into popular usage. The prime definition of the word, which is being used widely to describe the Warner Brothers-Orion Pictures' presentation, "Life of Brian," is 'any contemptuous or profane act, utterance, or writing concerning God." To which some modern-day humorists have sought to append an amendment —"unless it's accomplished in the name of humor."

The storm of protest that has blown up nationwide over the the Monty Python group's crude caricature of the life of Jesus has left Warner Brothers sputtering that the public likes the film and, besides, "it was never our intention to offend anyone's beliefs and we certainly regret having done so."

The hell it wasn't and the hell they do.

The Monty Python blasphemers believe in anything-for-a-laugh. They admit it. But the sanctimonious Warner Brothers' credo has been shown to be anything-for-a buck.

The Warner Brothers disclaimer is meaningless since it is not accompanied by a declaration of plans to alter the distribution of the despicable film that has given such serious offense to both Christians and Jews and produced strong statements of protest from representatives of Protestant, Catholic and Jewish organizations.

And where is the equally sanctimonious Motion Picture Association of America on this issue? Why, MPAA has allowed the film to use its seal of approval (R rating—"restricted, under 17 requires accompanying parent or adult guardian") even though its former standards for production, revised but presumably not rescinded, specify that "religion shall not be demeaned."

If Christians and Jews are really offended by this blasphemous film, let them show their concern not only in verbal and written protests to Warner Brothers but also by withholding their patronage and their bucks at the box office. Apparently that's the only language Warner Brothers understands.

St. Louis Review

St. Louis, Mo., September 28, 1979

Everyone knows that the movies along with TV can present some pretty objectionable "entertainment" these days. Also the self-censorship that the movie industry employs is very lenient indeed.

But even so, it isn't often that a film comes along that is accused of bordering on blasphemy. A film entitled "The Life of Brian" has that dubious distinction.

Whether it is blasphemous or borders on it is difficult to say. But the vast majority of the reviewers agree that this movie is done in extremely poor taste. It constructs a situation that casts ridicule on the person of Jesus, on Jewish practices and consequently on Christian and Jewish beliefs.

We are living in an age of the crude satire. Other ages have done this before. We all remember the Liliputians. But anti-government satire is different from that which is anti-religious.

Religion and religious practices are too closely identified with the self-concept of persons. The religious personality is an extremely important dimension of the total personality.

Rightfully people feel attacked when their religious beliefs or when such an important personage as Jesus is exposed to ridicule or satire.

There is always a delicate line between that which is really funny and that which is in very poor taste and offensive.

"The Life of Brian" unquestionably crosses over that line and goes in the direction of blasphemy in the way it parodies the person of Christ and the Jewish situation at the time of Christ.

Jewish and Christian organizations agree on this point. In our own archdiocese the Archdiocesan Council of the Laity has asked Catholics to show their displeasure by avoiding the film. Nothing can be more effective in saying no to a film of this type than a box office failure.

Boycott of TV Advertisers Threatened by "New Right"

The Moral Majority and other fundamentalist groups announced a drive in 1980 to boycott the products that were advertised on "objectionable" television shows. The aim was to pressure as many sponsors as possible to withdraw from such popular programs as "Charlie's Angels," "Three's Company," and "Soap" and thus make the shows unprofitable to air. Advertisers were well known for their unwillingness to associate their products with controversial shows, and the "New Right" intended to take full advantage of the sponsors' hesitancy. The move was comparable to previous drives by parents' groups to eliminate or curtail the amount of advertising on children's television programs.

THE INDIANAPOLIS STAR

Indianapolis, Ind., December 15, 1980

"We believe we are facing a major struggle with these groups over the Bill of Rights," says Ira Glasser of the American Civil Liberties Union about religion-oriented boycotts against advertisers who sponsor the sex-and-violence flagship shows on the television networks.

Maybe so, and if so, the ACLU is riding for a fall.

The reason is that the Bill of Rights has nothing to do with the subject. Soapy decisions behind some murder attempt on the fictional life of a J.R. Ewing by a sister-in-law who also carries his child have as much to do with free speech as does the cost of the oil that fires the generator that furnishes the current that beams a television signal into the atmosphere.

The subject is power. The networks and big advertisers have it, and they do not want a group of fired-up church people to modify it. They are worried, Time magazine reports. Sales may go clunk for advertisers who sponsor certain video junk.

Individual tastes may vary but certainly in a free country we must stand by the rights of citizen consumers to complain and refuse to buy, even when they cause an advertiser to cancel. The ACLU is standing with the others, it seems. It may need more than luck if it goes to court.

The ACLU is confusing hucksterism with high purpose, as does Alfred Schneider of ABC when he protests, "If you lose advertisers, that is an indirect form of censorship."

What hypocrisy! The truth is that if you lose advertisers you lose some network executives, who are among other things censors, and in fact already spend a lot of time telling lemming-like captive production companies what the advertisers will and will not tolerate in story lines.

• Some things about the "religious right" bother a lot of people. But we have a strong suspicion that the preachers have a pretty clear focus on what their congregations consider intolerable as entertainment in the living rooms of America.

The TV sleaze merchants should be advised of an old American saying about free speech that the ACLU may have helped to popularize. The advice is "Aw, go hire a hall."

TULSA WORLD

Tulsa, Okla., October 20, 1980

SO YOU don't like the sex and immorality on "Charlie's Angels" or "Three's Company."

Maybe you object to the blood and guts spilling into your living room from popular movies that end up on tv.

And, after all, football and boxing aren't benign when it comes to pounding, thrashing, crunching and injuring opponents.

Even baseball's George Brett ended up with a pain in the tail from all this knocking around — a personal malady we've been hearing about at great length.

You don't have to boycott the advertisers of programs carrying sex and gore. It isn't necessary to pledge not to buy certain products, although when you hit 'em in the pocketbook it certainly is a bigger blow than a letter complaining about their morals and ethics.

Of course, it's fine if you want to support the Clean Up Tv church-sponsored movement aimed at the wallets of two companies which sponsor "objectionable" tv programs. It's your choice.

When you think about it, there are plenty more sponsors of other shows and events maybe worthy of wrath and this idea has the makings of a real whiz-bang epidemic.

But the tv has a button controlling on and off. If it's used, then the choice is up to you and content is not controlled by another person's opinion of what you should see.

Better to just turn it off. Better than turning on to another form of censorship.

The Charlotte Observer

Charlotte, N.C., November 19, 1980

The TV boycott threatened by the Moral Majority, the fundamentalist religious group, worries CBS executive Gene Mater. Mr. Mater says his network has "problems" with the boycott, implying the new crusade against TV sex and violence will be somehow un-American. Nonsense.

We often have disagreed with the Moral Majority over its narrow judgment of political candidates and its failure to acknowledge that compromise is an essential ingredient in governing people of divergent beliefs. But an honest boycott is in the best democratic tradition.

The fundamentalists object to shows using gratuitous violence and "jiggles" to snare viewers. While trying to gather large audiences and make money, the networks have a right to appeal to viewers' basest instincts. But people don't have to watch. And the Moral Majority is within its rights to try to get them not to, in an effort to dent the ratings of those shows they consider offensive.

Mr. Mater and other network executives can't hide behind cries of "censorship." The fundamentalists simply want to deliver a pocketbook message to the networks. If sex and violence turn enough people off, the networks' reliance on them will hurt television profit margins.

Otherwise, the boycott won't work, and the networks won't lose a penny. CBS and the other networks apparently are worried that the Moral Majority may be right.

Coalition for Better Television Drops Plans for TV Boycott

The Coalition for Better Television announced June 29 that it had canceled plans for a boycott of sponsors of television programs considered morally offensive. The widely publicized boycott had been scheduled to begin that day and already had influenced Proctor & Gamble Co. to drop its sponsorship of 50 individual prime-time TV programs in the 1980–81 season. Owen Butler, chairman of Proctor & Gamble, said June 16 that the Coalition for Better Television "is expressing very important and broadly held views about gratuitous sex, violence and profanity." He did not endorse the boycott directly, but he warned sponsors that they would have to accept responsibility for the content of the shows in which their advertisements appeared. Butler did not reveal which programs Proctor & Gamble had decided to drop.

Meanwhile, the Coalition for Better Television said it had canceled the boycott because advertisers had promised to "clean up" TV, in the words of coalition chairman Rev. Donald Wildmon. He charged that the national networks "belittled, mocked and insulted" American morals, and he praised Proctor & Gamble's action. The coalition claimed to represent 400 conservative groups and had been organized in February to keep track of sex and violence on TV. The networks denounced the group's tactics as an attempt to institute censorship. According to polls conducted by NBC and ABC, the boycott would have attracted little public support.

Sentinel Star
Orlando, Fla., June 20, 1981

PROCTER & Gamble Co., the nation's largest television advertiser, has withdrawn its sponsorship from more than 50 shows because it has decided that a large segment of the public finds the gratuitous sex and violence distasteful.

Chalk one up for the National Federation of Decency, a coalition of primarily religious groups, led by an articulate Mississippi pastor, the Rev. Donald Wildmon.

Procter & Gamble's action, announced in a speech to the Academy of Television Arts and Sciences, indicates that this one rural preacher has a better grasp of the public pulse than the national television networks.

The National Federation of Decency, carefully eschewing censorship, organized its members for a boycott of the products advertised on objectionable shows. It was a well-planned, free-market protest that accomplished its goal.

It is apparent that a large number of Americans are disgusted with sleaze on their home screens. The Rev. Wildmon realized it. Procter & Gamble, one of the most successful mass marketers in history, realized it. Before the summer is over, maybe the networks and other big advertisers will realize it, too.

The issue is taste, not censorship. As the Procter & Gamble spokesmen stressed, the key word is gratuitous — gratuitous sex and gratuitous violence, which serve no valid artistic purpose.

The networks, rather than admit fault, have tried to brand the protest as an assault against the First Amendment by resurrected Puritans. So far, this is a red herring. The coalition has been careful to limit its protest to matters of bad taste.

These people sought public pressure rather than government action to correct the problem. So long as they continue in this vein, they are working entirely within the constitutional framework and deserve the support of anyone who agrees with them.

The Courier-Journal
Louisville, Ky., June 24, 1981

PROCTER AND GAMBLE got a bum rap last week in a news story which erroneously reported the company to be cutting back sharply, seemingly in response to pressure from religious fundamentalists, in its sponsorship of sex on TV. But the truth of the matter isn't much more encouraging.

In a speech to the Academy of Television Arts and Sciences, the company's board chairman reaffirmed P & G's long-standing policy of not advertising on shows that it finds too sexy, profane or violent. He said he just wanted to remind his broadcaster audience that people are out there watching — and objecting.

Maybe so: a writer to *Readers' Views* today echoes his view. But a new Roper poll for NBC suggests that the objectors also are few in number. Even most religious fundamentalists seem to be more disturbed if a program is silly or boring than if it has too much sex. This makes one wonder whether the conservative Coalition for Better Television, which has called for an economic boycott unless offending advertisers drop such offending shows as *Dallas, Three's Company* and *The Love Boat,* will make much of a dent.

Even without the Roper poll, the broadcasters hardly needed reminding that the shows that draw the most complaints also have the most viewers. (They also are well aware that P & G, as television's biggest advertiser, isn't above working both sides of the street. Its afternoon soap operas are among the sexier shows on TV.)

The truth of the matter is that the economics of television has made it a medium that defines success almost entirely in terms of numbers, and thus of programming with "universal" (i.e., lowest-common-denominator) appeal.

There are *some* limits, to be sure: TV fears restrictive laws or license revocations if it abuses its franchise. Thus in 1975, in response to viewer complaints about violence in programming, the FCC forced broadcasters to do more self-policing. Their new "family viewing" code pledged more care in what was shown in early evening, when children are heavy viewers. It's possible that complaints now about too much sex in prime-time, even though they seem to come from a tiny minority, could force similar restraint.

Advertisers are sensitive to complaints and boycotts, especially over such sensitive issues as morality. And some actually prefer to sponsor quality programming, if it will appeal to even a fraction of those who might buy the product. In the long run, however, most advertisers will sponsor and all broadcasters will broadcast what most people want — or at least will tolerate.

So it's admittedly small consolation to be told that if we don't want objectionable programs in our homes we have merely to twist the dial. No parent can keep constant vigil over what his child watches; no family can be entirely happy at the prospect that something offensive will suddenly intrude as an unwanted visitor.

But if we set a standard acceptable to those viewers who are most easily offended, the result would be a television fare even more vacuous and unenlightening than what we've got now. It might be purer than P & G's Ivory Snow. But would *anybody* watch?

TULSA WORLD
Tulsa, Okla., June 19, 1981

THE COALITION for Better Television has found an effective way of pressuring the television networks to clean up programming — hit them in their pocketbooks.

The group has threatened a boycott of commercial advertisers sponsoring shows deemed too violent or sexually explicit. Procter & Gamble, tv's biggest spender, already has refused to advertise on 50 such shows.

Coalition members are doing what they can to influence the content of television programming. The networks are concerned about censorship.

The most difficult aspect of this controversy is defining the issue. When does a boycott threaten First Amendment values?

If a group protests CBS' documentary series on national defense, there is a clear threat to traditional First Amendment values. The case is much harder to make, however, when the network seeks protection for "Charlie's Angels."

Wrapping oneself in the First Amendment is not an adequate defense. Freedom of expression is not an unlimited right. The networks recognized that when they adopted the family viewing hour several years ago.

It's not enough to tell critics to turn off objectionable programming. Television's impact is too pervasive these days, particularly where children are concerned.

If the issue is truly a matter of censoring protected expression, then the networks have Constitutional protection. But there are limits when the right the networks are claiming is the right to maximize profits by broadcasting objectionable junk.

The Boston Globe
Boston, Mass., June 19, 1981

Procter and Gamble wants television to clean house. The manufacturer of Ivory soap, Tide and Cheer detergents, Sure and Secret deodorants, Head and Shoulders shampoo, Spic 'n Span and Mr. Clean, the company that spent $620 million on advertising last year acknowledged that it refused to sponsor at least 50 prime-time television network shows because they offended viewer sensibilities.

Owen Butler, chairman of the Cincinnati company, told television critics in Hollywood this week that there is too much sex and violence on television. "For sound commercial reasons," he said, "we are not going to let our advertising messages appear in an environment which we think many of our potential customers will find distasteful."

His contention certainly makes sense. There is too much sex and violence on television, too much that capitalizes on titillation and gore. Still, Procter and Gamble and other advertisers are hardly 99 and 44/100ths percent pure. They helped create the system, the "distasteful environment," by paying the networks to produce the mindless sleaze that passes for television entertainment. Sex and violence have always generated high ratings. High ratings have always led to high profits. The more people who watch a show, the more people who are likely to buy brands X, Y or Z. That's what television advertising is all about.

Butler's remarks come two weeks before the Coalition for Better Television, an organization with connections to the Moral Majority, plans to release a hit list of television shows whose sponsors will be targeted for a consumer boycott. Although Butler stopped short of endorsing that boycott, he said, "We are listening very carefully to what they [the coalition] say and I urge you to do the same."

There is a subtle and dangerous difference between cleaning television up because it needs it and sanitizing it on the advice of some self-appointed moralists. The Rev. Jerry Wildmon, a Mississippi preacher who heads the coalition, has said he is concerned about the value system depicted on television. So are many Ameri-

cans. The problem is Wildmon believes that his values should prevail. He believes that his organization is best qualified to make programming decisions for the rest of the country. He believes that threatening advertisers economically will force them to see the light.

Television capitulated too readily to single-minded pressure groups during the Fifties when "patriots" were busily tracking Communists, ferreting out subversion where there was none. A leading man was forced off the Molly Goldberg show because he had been a member of the "End Jim Crow in Baseball Committee." A cereal manufacturer withdrew support from a children's program because its star was alleged to have supported a congressional candidate who didn't meet the red, white and blue test. The president of the National Association of Supermarkets threatened to single out and display products whose manufacturers sponsored the "wrong" programs, while networks set up security forces and required loyalty oaths. There is little reason to believe that television will be any more courageous today. Controversy has never been good for business.

The Coalition for Better Television has already exonerated Procter and Gamble. None of its programs will appear on the hit list; none of its products will be targeted for boycott. At present the company has no plans to withdraw advertising from the highly profitable soap operas that trade on pre-marital sex, divorce, alcoholism, teenage pregnancy and extramarital escapades. Maybe such subject matter isn't as distasteful in the middle of the afternoon as it is after dark.

Of course, television brought this situation on itself by failing to respond to more moderate criticism in the past. Television should be better than it is. Advertisers and networks should take more responsibility for the programs produced under their corporate signatures. They should do so because they are accountable to the public, not because they fear economic reprisals from a group which has been invested with more influence than it undoubtedly has.

St. Louis Review
St. Louis, Mo., July 3, 1981

Television producers have been at fault for many years in their disdain for critics of the moral content of television programs. They have insisted on their right to exercise hegemony over what programs American will view. Increasingly, they have flaunted their support for life styles at variance with traditional, ethical and moral behavior. Television producers were scornful of the protest voiced over programs which featured and promoted the acceptablity of abortion. Television producers have tried to change accepted moral values by favorable presentation of pre-marital sex, homosexuality and the illegal use of narcotics.

A protest like that recently launched

by the Coalition for Better Television was inevitable. The group has made use of a typically American instrument for achieving its purposes — a threat to the pocketbook. They have contacted advertisers to threaten a boycott if they continued to support programs which the group regards as morally objectionable.

Something needed to be done and the tactics of the coalition are legitimate in our society. We might wonder whatever became of Catholic leadership in a campaign for moral values in our society. At one time, the Catholic Legion of Decency was a powerful voice for morality in our nation. It is disappointing that no effective

Catholic protest against the trashing of the air waves has been mounted. Have Catholics become so sophisticated that they do not believe there is a moral problem in present-day programming?

On the other hand, one wonders if the Coalition for Better Television will become the new arbiters of moral values for all of us. While their general thrust is good, it is not certain that this group is competent to judge the moral values which will be embodied in the future programming.

We are on the horns of a dilemma. Censorship is a very treacherous path to tread, while permissiveness is a road to disaster.

THE SAGINAW NEWS

Saginaw, Mich., June 19, 1981

The Procter & Gamble Co. has publicly disclosed a policy of reviewing sponsorship to make sure programming conforms to its own standards of decency.

During the current season, the firm said, it has pulled ads from 50 television shows it felt contained "excessive or gratuitous sex, violence, profanity or other offensive matter that may be demeaning to a particular race or religion."

Cheers quickly went up from the Rev. Jerry Falwell, founder of the Moral Majority, and others working to "clean up TV."

P&G, whose $486 million makes it the largest advertiser on TV, denied its actions were related to pressure from those groups.

We're glad to hear it. Any company has the right to decide where to spend its money, and to avoid material that may either offend its morals, image or per-share revenue.

"For sound, commercial reasons," said Owen B. Butler, P&G's new chairman, the firm doesn't want its advertising on programs that "we think many of our potential customers will find distasteful."

We believe him. The consumer-products firm said its policy doesn't apply to daytime soap operas. Some are considered much steamier, if not more violent, than anything on prime time, but air when the kids supposedly are not around.

But we would be disturbed if the decision were really made not by a business, for business reaons, but, by pressure groups seeking to determine what others may see and hear.

There is a difference. It is between an independent economic judgment, and a cave-in to self-appointed censors.

Butler's plea for higher quality programming is valid. But definitions of "quality" differ widely. To some, quality is only that which reflects and promotes Biblical fundamentalism. That, too, is their privilege. The problem is that if they had their way, the kind of "quality" reflected in, say, some of public TV's Masterpiece Theater would never be aired.

Ultimately, these decisions will be made by a marketplace made increasingly wider by the rapid growth of cable and pay TV. For Procter & Gamble and the Moral Majority, and those whose opinions of TV quality don't coincide with either, the selective use of the channel and off-on switches is the best guarantee of both one's own morality and everyone else's right to a decent choice.

The Hartford Courant

Hartford, Conn., July 3, 1981

Television networks received orders not only from the U.S. Supreme Court this week.

They and their advertisers apparently succumbed to a directive from the Coalition for Better Television, a Mississippi-based coalition of right-wing groups.

The directive came in the form of a threat — make programs more "wholesome," or prepare for a national boycott of products of companies that advertise most often in the programs.

The companies, in particular, agreed to abide by the standards set by this coalition. Threats by CBTV proved effective — more effective, probably, than an actual boycott would have been.

TV networks obviously are not paragons of virtue. The quality of programs ranges from excellent to terrible. Everyone, from parent-teacher associations to senior citizens, has pleaded, preached, cajoled and threatened the networks.

A private group has the right to boycott a commercial product, and the targeted concern should, of course, listen to critics and make improvements, wherever improvements are deemed justified.

But the networks and advertisers did not really promise to make improvements when they agreed to change programming to suit CBTV's tastes. They caved in to a well-organized, vocal group, which is more interested in "cleaning up" television than in improving it.

Just what does "cleaning up" mean? For feminists, say, it means portrayal of the New Woman, for the Gay Task Force, it means providing a positive image of homosexuals, and for the Moral Majority, it means "no excessive sex, violence and profanity."

That's why the networks put themselves in a dangerous situation when they abdicated programming responsibilities. The implications are disturbing, especially if boycotters begin demanding changes in news and current affairs presentations.

The public, by all accounts, is concerned about violence and sex on television. When it comes to specifics, however, surveys tell a different story. Most people want their favorite programs to say on the air, be it the vacuous "Dukes of Hazzard" or the suggestive "Charlie's Angels."

A good many members of the Moral Majority, we suspect, are fans of Sheriff Lobo and the wacky crew at WKRP in Cincinnati.

Advertisers were eager to please fundamentalist preachers in this case, and the networks gave in too easily.

Better to have accepted the challenge of a boycott and shown that a small, activist group cannot dictate national programming.

The Times-Picayune
The States-Item

New Orleans, La., June 23, 1981

America's ayatollahs — the self-ordained guardians of purity who have become increasingly vocal since last year's elections — have scored a victory, and the precedent is disturbing.

These men are the leaders of fundamentally oriented religious groups who have used their new clout to speak out against everything they deem ungodly. One of their targets has been prime-time television programming, which they have denounced as too violent, sexy and profane.

The logical response would be to turn off the set and to tell their followers to do likewise, thereby causing ratings drops that could kill objectionable shows. It's a perfectly acceptable response, and it's what anyone should do to indicate his disapproval of a particular broadcast since networks and advertisers should be responsive to the audience they serve.

But these religious groups are going further. In an attempt to drive off the air the programs they dislike, they are urging a boycott of products that sponsor shows to which they object.

This week, Procter & Gamble, one of the nation's most prominent sponsors, surrendered to such pressure by withdrawing its economic support from 50 shows because, according to a corporate spokesman, they did not meet the company's "program guidelines."

In the wake of this decision, the outlook is ominous because no one has bothered to determine the size of these religious coalitions or the breadth of support for them. Instead, as they did in the McCarthy years, big companies may figure it is easier — and better for their public image — to give in to such pressure groups.

But this is an abdication of a company's role to make its own decisions about programs to sponsor. And these religious leaders — as well as people who object to other types of programming — can use the Procter & Gamble victory like a club when they confront officials of other major corporations about programs they dislike.

What will the result be? Showing cast lists and scripts to these religious leaders for approval?

This time around, the outcome is hard to predict because television ratings show that many of the popular, revenue-producing programs are the offerings which religious leaders oppose. Also, given a choice, most viewers invariably reject the homey-type offerings which these religious groups say they like.

We wish to make clear that we are not endorsing gratuitous sex and violence on television. We do, however, object to tactics whose objective seems to be censorship.

If enough advertisers give in, there are disheartening prospects of blandness: television schedules bloated with mindless comedies and superficial stories which bear no relation to real life. Given such choices, an even greater switch to cable television, where no sponsors exist, is possible.

The Dallas Morning News

Dallas, Texas, July 5, 1981

AMERICA has always had a love-hate relationship with television.

It's been called "chewing gum for the eyes," a "vast wasteland," "a drug" and worse.

Yet surveys show that despite the criticism, wisecracks, competition and threatened boycotts, Americans still devote more of their time to TV — an average of over six hours a day — than to anything other than working and sleeping. They get much of their news from TV and say it is their primary leisure activity.

The problem with television is that too often TV executives have attempted to draw the widest possible audience by reaching for the lowest common denominator. The result has been either more vacuous, violent or titillating programming, which in turn has prompted more protests and threatened boycotts.

After several years of struggling, the protest groups have won a victory of sorts in recent weeks. Procter and Gamble Co., the nation's largest television advertiser, has withdrawn sponsorship from more than 50 shows because of what it considered excessive sex and violence. Last week, Smith Kline Corp., another major advertiser, said it also is becoming more concerned.

In response, one of the major protest groups, the Coalition for Better Television, now says it will call off its boycott of companies that sponsor objectionable TV programs.

Quite wisely, the coalition has realized that it is sometimes more judicious and effective to compromise rather than threaten. The protesters have made their point. They have caught the attention of the networks, advertisers and public. While the debate has been vitriolic at times, it has raised important issues about the direction of television programming and the role of the public.

The challenge is now for viewers to put their dials where their mouths are, so to speak. The fact is that people may not get the TV they deserve, but the TV they choose.

As the video boom of the 1980s develops, audiences will have the chance to choose from a multiplicity of offerings, so the burden of excellence is on the public. Their choices will shape the future of commercial TV, public TV, cable TV, videodiscs, videocassettes, etc.

Several decades ago, essayist E. B. White set some goals the public should consider when addressing the video panorama of the future. As he put it, " . . . television should be the visual counterpart of the literary essay, should arouse our dreams, satisfy our hunger for beauty, take us on journeys, enable us to participate in events, present great drama and music, explore the sea and the sky and the woods and the hills. It should be our Lyceum, or Chautauqua, our Minsky's and our Camelot. It should state and clarify the social dilemma and the political pickle. Once in a while it does, and you get a quick glimpse of its potential."

The recent controversy over TV, if anything, should remind viewers that this marvelous medium is worth fighting for. The debate over its potential may be rocky, but it should continue.

THE MILWAUKEE JOURNAL

Milwaukee, Wisc., June 21, 1981

Procter & Gamble's effort to keep its products from being associated with excessive violence and sleaze on television seems worthy of applause.

P & G's critics all too swiftly depict the company's decision as a sellout to the Moral Majority and other holier-than-thou pressure groups that have threatened a boycott of products sold by the sponsors of such TV shows. P & G's motivation can be debated, of course. But in the absence of any real evidence that the company did merely bow to such pressure — and little but speculation has been offered by the critics — P & G's explanation deserves to be taken at face value. Surely, it would be foolish to expect any company to continue associating its products with TV's excessive violence-and-sex trend, just to avoid an *appearance* of agreeing with the nation's noisier moral crusaders.

O. B. Butler, board chairman of P & G, well described the challenge. He said his company must be responsible for "the environment in which our commercials appear" without permitting any outside group — no matter how well-intentioned — to dictate "our program choices . . . by threats of boycott." P & G has not withheld sponsorship of all shows involving sex and violence, because these themes can serve a legitimate purpose in drama. But the company tries to steer clear of what Butler termed "purely gratuitous 'jiggle' and unnecessarily bloodthirsty violence."

Such TV shows obviously are popular, so the temptation to reach that audience with advertising must be great. But sponsorship of vulgarity helps perpetuate it, thereby diminishing the possibility of less sleazy shows. It's quite clear that in recent years the networks and programming syndicates themselves have done little to raise the overall taste and quality of prime-time TV entertainment.

It may seem awkward for The Journal or any other commercial medium of mass communication to applaud the sort of choice made by Procter & Gamble. Advertising revenue is what makes it possible for most print and broadcast media to exist at all.

Yet, how else is a society to express its judgment about the quality of the media's product? We can think of no better way than through the noncoerced choices of consumers, advertisers, viewers and readers in the marketplace. Surely no one should want the alternative — rigid censorship, imposed from the outside by government or some self-appointed body of critics.

As it turns out, Procter & Gamble is not the only sponsor that has pulled advertising dollars away from excessive TV violence and sex. And to the extent that those choices were reasonable and made independent of threats of boycott or other outside pressure, we applaud them, too.

The Chattanooga Times
Chattanooga, Tenn., June 19, 1981

Procter & Gamble's announcement this week that it will not sponsor television shows it says contain excessive sex, violence and profanity is a remarkable decision likely to have far-reaching effects on what you see on television this fall — assuming the writers' and directors' strikes are settled. P&G is television's largest advertiser — $125.2 million last year — and its decision could very well influence other companies to intensify their commitment to help "clean up" a medium that often seeks the lowest common denominator in entertainment.

Chairman Owen B. Butler said the P&G action is not a reaction to efforts by several groups to encourage boycotts of products of companies that sponsor "objectionable" programming. P&G simply decided, he said, to withdraw sponsorship for 50 network programs that did not meet the company's "program guidelines." But whether the groups' campaign was a factor or not is irrelevant. The key issue is P&G has decided that it has a responsibility to help improve, however it can, the content of what is beamed into millions of homes daily. For that, the company deserves commendation.

When such groups as the Moral Majority and the Coalition for Better TV (CBTV) began a nationwide effort to improve the quality of television fare by rating programs according to their content of sex and violence, especially the sex, the networks cried censorship. They warned darkly that a few people were trying to impose their cultural or moral values on the nation, and that if they were successful, television's creativity would be stifled. The arguments are unpersuasive.

In the first place, the networks practice "censorship" themselves through what are euphemistically called departments of "programming practices." NBC, for example, routinely "bleeps" comments by Tonight Show host Johnny Carson and some of his guests. And all the networks edit — butcher may be a better term — movies to excise violence, nudity and (some) profanity, not to mention trimming footage to make the not-made-for-TV movies fit a certain time slot.

Besides, censorship is the wrong word. Censorship is practiced by governments and, more often than not, involves the stifling of dissident political views, not reducing the amount of "jiggle" on a television show that specializes in banality and leers. A boycott, which is what several groups are advocating, is nothing more than an attempt to hold organizations, like corporations, accountable for their actions. And boycotts, after all, do have a rich historical tradition in this country.

The networks' claim that consumer boycotts of companies that sponsor objectionable shows will diminish television's "creativity" is laughable. If the networks consider shows like "Three's Company" and "Soap" examples of creativity, then the only logical response of even a slightly discerning viewer should be to cheer the pressure groups' efforts. What the networks are saying, in effect, is that shows without ample amounts of sex and violence will not survive. That claim, however, is rebutted by the track records of shows like "The Waltons" and "Little House on the Prairie."

It does have some validity, to the extent that an argument can be made that television reflects society as much as it influences it; in a way, it is another version of the old chicken-or-the-egg riddle. And it is true, unfortunately, that television has long been a hostage of the ratings. But viewers old enough to remember television's offerings in the 1950s and early 1960s — the so-called "golden age" of television — could argue persuasively that the networks, if they chose, could create powerful drama without gratuitous violence or adolescent views of sex. A spokeswoman for General Foods made the excellent point that "violence and sex are acceptable themes in adult programming. It is the treatment of those themes" that companies should judge in deciding whether to sponsor a particular show.

The proposed boycott's success is not guaranteed, obviously. But that does not mean that groups like CBTV have not raised an important issue. As Mr. Butler put it in a speech to the Academy of Television Arts and Sciences this week: "We think the coalition is expressing some very important and broadly held views about *gratuitous* (our emphasis) sex, violence and profanity . . . we are listening very carefully to what they say, and I urge you to do the same." The question is: Will they?

The Register
Santa Ana, Calif., June 24, 1981

For the life of us, we have a hard time figuring out why people are so upset about the campaign of the Moral Majority and the Coalition for Better Television to threaten to boycott sponsors of programs they find objectionable.

If these self-proclaimed guardians of morality were trying to institute government censorship or set up a panel of federal censors, we could understand the excitement, and we'd be right out there on the barricades fighting against government-decreed puritanism. But so far they have adhered to the idea of private pressure by private citizens acting in a voluntary manner. We may not agree with all their opinions about what shows constitute the clearest danger to the tender minds of American youth, but we would hardly deny them the right to express their opinions or work to change the nature of television through voluntary means.

There's plenty of overblown rhetoric on all sides of the issue, perhaps worked up to a lather because of the announcement by Proctor & Gamble, TV's heaviest advertiser, that it's refusing to advertise on 50 shows it considers too sexy or violent, and that it listens "very carefully" to conservative critics. Rev Donald Wildmon, leader of the Coalition for Better Television, predictably called Proctor & Gamble's position "socially responsible." The president of the company that makes "Dallas," however, likened the situation to the Big Bad Red Scares of the 1950s. Yawn.

What's the upshot? "Dallas," one of the chief targets of the critics, still hovers near the top of the ratings, only slightly deterred by being in repeats. "Charlie's Angels" was cancelled in February, but its problems started before the boycott picked up much steam. Some sponsors have said they'll look at shows more carefully, some have said they've always checked shows for taste and the boycotters are all wet, and some claim to pay no attention.

It's all part of the controversy that is a natural element of a relatively free and diverse society. The Moral Majority is by no means the first or only group to express concern about television programming. Organized groups of almost every ethnic minority have complained about stereotyping, and the complaints have sometimes had an effect. Others have complained about too many gunfights, so we got car chases instead. Network television has always been subject to numerous pressures from groups of diverse persuasions, and writers, advertisers and producers have walked a fine line, sometimes producing pap and occasionally developing shows with genuine quality.

As technology progresses, the whole flap may become moot. With the advent and increasing availability of cable and pay-TV, as well as the acceptance of home video recorders, people with specialized or minority tastes are finding entertainment more to their liking, with less reliance on network products geared to a mass audience. We'll soon be able to get everything from dirty movies to symphony concerts and operas, and the rationale for trying to gear everything to some sort of mythical average family will disappear.

Certain elements of the Moral Majority coalition do have some disturbing ideas. Some of the legislation proposed or supported by the so-called New Right Christians indicates an alarming tendency to want to turn rather narrow moral principles into the Law of the Land. We're opposed to such efforts, and we'll continue to pinpoint areas where we think the coalition is becoming dangerous or repressive.

But the campaign to clean up TV (or make it even more boring, depending on your perspective) has so far been conducted by means that are perfectly legitimate in a free society. Boycotts, pressure groups, petitions, convocations of outraged citizens — all of these are healthy expressions of opinion that do not threaten anybody's legitimate rights. Most pressure groups sooner or later slip into the old "There Oughta Be a Law" syndrome, and at the that point they should be opposed. Until it happens, we'll remain interested observers.

The Seattle Times

Seattle, Wash., June 19, 1981

MOST companies sponsoring TV programs have made it a practice for decades to monitor the content of their offerings so as to avoid offending large audiences (and in the process, prospective customers.)

Thus, this week's report that Procter & Gamble, TV's biggest advertiser ($125 million in one year), had withdrawn sponsorship of 50 programs it regarded as too violent or sexually explicit ordinarily would not have occasioned special notice.

What did raise eyebrows was the company's acknowledgment that its decisions were based partly on a judgment that a "large, serious and increasingly vocal segment of our population is objecting to sex and violence" and that the company listens "very carefully" to conservative critics in groups like the Moral Majority and the National Coalition on Television Violence.

(Among TV showings from which Procter & Gamble withdrew support, The Cincinnati Enquirer reported, were the movies "East of Eden" and "The Women's Room" and one episode of "Taxi.")

Many viewers, especially parents, would applaud any effort that might rid TV of some of its trashiest entertainment (though, ironically, none of the daytime soap operas sponsored by Procter & Gamble were affected by sponsorship changes.)

Even so, there ought to be mixed feelings about the announcement from top executives of the firm.

It is conceivable, for instance, that there could be a subtle but nonetheless inhibiting effect on the integrity of artistic expression among writers and producers of future TV shows.

Worse, it suggests that self-appointed groups seeking to set moral values in the nation, despite their minority status in terms of numbers, may be more influential than many citizens might suspect.

This week's announcement already has stirred conjecture among advertising executives that the Procter & Gamble action will permit the influence of such groups to grow even more.

WORCESTER TELEGRAM.

Worcester, Mass., June 21, 1981

In recent years, the television networks have been injecting lots of sex into their prime-time shows in their struggle for high viewer ratings.

But now, according to reports from within the TV industry, many of the sponsors have grown less enthusiastic about the technique. They are increasingly worried about the possibility of product boycotts by groups like Moral Majority, and they are standing in line to get their commercials on "clean" shows instead of programs considered in bad taste.

Procter & Gamble Co., television's biggest advertiser, has withdrawn sponsorship from more than 50 TV shows for reasons of taste.

Procter & Gamble products include Ivory soap, Tide and Cheer detergents, Sure and Secret deodorants, Folgers coffee, Duncan Hines cake mixes and Charmin toilet tissue. In most of its commercials, the company has sought a wholesome image. And now it is taking steps to see that none of its products are boycotted because the shows on which the commercials appear are seen as unwholesome.

Procter & Gamble chairman O.B. Butler said his company was also responding to correspondence and other contacts from a "large, serious and increasingly vocal segment of our population" that finds some shows "distasteful." Contributing to the timing, no doubt, was the fact that the Coalition for Better Television — made up of several hundred groups, including the Moral Majority — is expected to announce next week a boycott of sponsors of shows it deems most offensive.

The Procter & Gamble move reflects pressure from a variety of New Right and other groups. That may not sit well with fans of the shows in question or with those who believe broadcasters should be free of pressures like sponsor boycotts.

It would be much nicer, certainly, if large numbers of viewers would just stop watching tasteless shows. That would get such programming off the air faster than anything else. But that doesn't seem to happen. In fact, just the opposite.

Many responsible people believe that tastelessness and violence on TV are changing our society for the worse. Most of these people would not advocate that the government get involved any further than it is in deciding what should be broadcast. The networks spinelessly plead that they are only giving the viewers what they want. So where are people who care about the American moral climate to turn but to private pressure groups?

These measures themselves may be distasteful in some ways, and they surely won't accomplish everything that groups like Moral Majority would really like. But the networks have asked for it. And it's a little like poetic justice to see the makers of Ivory soap and all those detergents pressured into taking part in a clean-up of the TV screen along with the laundry and the dishes.

The Washington Post
Times Herald

Washington, D.C., June 30, 1981

JUST WHEN the wailing and hand-wringing on both sides was reaching absurd dimensions, the Coalition for Better Television has declared victory and called off a threatened boycott of sponsors of TV shows it considers offensive. It's quite a coup, really —coming as it does before any true ratings of the coalition's show might reveal less than meets the network eye in terms of serious economic muscle. The coalition, of which the Moral Majority is a key supporter, apparently is satisfied that enough sponsors are shaking in their socks at the prospect of a boycott that they're getting religion, so to speak, and steering clear of shows that seem to contain excessive sex and/or violence.

As they say in the industry, we'll see. But clearly the threat brought some results. Procter & Gamble, television's largest advertiser, has withdrawn sponsorship from 50 shows it believed contained excessive sex and violence; and coalition chairman Donald E. Wildmon claims that other advertisers have withdrawn support from TV shows, and that networks have been unable to get full advertising revenues for some shows because of sponsor withdrawals. Is this "censorship," as some network executives have termed it?

The idea that some group with ideas that other people consider bad, weird, prudish or otherwise off the mark could dictate what does or doesn't get on the air—or even that a sponsor could assume total control, say, of the content of network news shows— is disturbing, no question. But when is a situation ever that stark? To begin with, there is nothing anti-democratic or evil about a lawful, orderly, dignified call for a boycott.

Second, any network worth its initials should have the fortitude and integrity not to let every coalition that comes along with a gruff word dictate what goes or doesn't go on the home screens. Similarly, no sponsor should have line-by-line review of every script. Obviously a sponsor can drop its participation and thereby kill a program; but here again, advertising agencies and their clients should try to know what they're doing before caving in to every group-growl they hear.

We confess to more than a passing interest in advertisers, of course, and while we're at it, in television broadcasting. The balance of these interests, along with the likes and dislikes of readers and viewers, is at once fascinating and imperfect, since they are so interdependent. But the relationships do have a way of working—and if what you see is more to your liking, so much the better.

The Virginian-Pilot

Norfolk, Va., February 24, 1981

Having helped banish liberals from the citadel on the Potomac, the Moral Majority now aims to expel sinfulness from TV. One of the Reverend Jerry Falwell's expansive subordinates in Los Angeles even talks of buying one of the networks.

Wish dreaming? Not necessarily. With oil billionaires Nelson and Bunker Hunt and T. Cullen Davis backing them, it would not be out of the question, says a Merrill Lynch executive. "They could buy effective control of ABC for $150 million if the institutional holders went along—which they might if there was a lot of national heat for them not to fight the evangelicals."

Eliminating smut from TV would require massive house-cleaning. "A medium that once featured family-oriented programming now makes jokes about homosexuality, incest, wife-swapping, and depravity," notes a Falwell adviser without fear of contradiction.

Author Ben Stein, although wary of the political aims of the Christian right, acknowledges in Saturday Review that TV is vulnerable. It is guilty of indecent exposure in the American living room. Homosexuals are treated as acceptable jokes on "Too Close for Comfort," abortion and incest are commonplace on "Maude" and "Soap" respectively, extramarital sex is presented as cute on "Mary Hartman," "All's Fair," "Three's Company," "Dallas," and many other shows, and soap operas dote on sex and drug entanglements.

"Where Robert Young once wisely counseled his daughter about kindness to new girls in school, Ted Knight now screams at his daughter about working seminude in a bar—and the mother says it's fine," observes Mr. Stein.

Defenders of First Amendment rights may wax indignant over a tiny band of moralists censoring TV, but Mr. Stein says "the major flaw in this argument is that a narrow band of network executives and TV producers control American TV right now." Their look-alike programs reveal a parochial pandering state of mind.

One need not idealize Jerry Falwell to hope that his threatened boycott of products peddled on gutter-level shows will chasten producers who think smut sells. It also, as Mr. Stein reports, "has been shown to lower scholastic achievement, encourage violence, generate lassitude, and paint a wildly untrue and distorted picture of American life."

Awful as TV programs have become, "an ayatollah for TV would be far worse," he adds. The Moral Majority may, however, lend an influential voice to secular critics and upholders of good taste who think it is high time to detoxify the tube. The wasteland of the Sixties has degenerated into the sludge pit of the Eighties. It is polluting the airwaves and the minds of adolescents who find Mary Hartman and J.R. more attractive role models than Shirley Temple and John Boy Walton.

Those believing this to be progress might profitably recall the line from a sit-com by Shakespeare:

My Oberon! What visions have I seen!

Methought I was enamour'd of an ass.

Lincoln Journal

Lincoln, Neb., July 1, 1981

All the ingredients for a prime-time happy ending are there. Advertisers have rebelled against paying for trash on television. The networks have cleaned up their fall schedules. And the Coalition for Better Television has decided it won't, after all, launch a boycott of firms that sponsor shows featuring sleazy sex and violence.

Actually, the coalition doesn't need to proceed with its boycott. The simple threat of it so scared advertisers and networks alike that they underwent a miraculous conversion. Chalk up a win for the coalition.

The sponsors were good losers, the TV industry less so. It called the coalition of conservatives and religious groups a bunch of would-be censors. Obviously what the coalition was up to had little relation to censorship, since it was not an official body. Rather, it was serving as a conduit for the public to express its fed-upness with the abominable quality of TV programming.

Apparently the television establishment found the idea of an organized protest offensive. Well, it takes one to know one, as they say. Consider the vast power and resources of that TV establishment — ad agencies, publicity departments, multi-million-dollar promotional budgets, a virtual monopoly of the air waves in many communities — all directed toward making the American public believe it really wanted to see the kind of junk that the home screens were dumping into their living rooms. Now, *that's* an organized effort.

The coalition, with far less money but probably more belief in what it was doing, beat the TV industry at its own game.

Swallowing hard, an ABC vice president said: "Our new schedule reflects something important that is happening in the country right now. There's an evolving mood based on a renewal of traditional values — home and family, courage and honesty, respect for authority and teamwork."

Well! Bring the TV down from the attic.

the Charleston Gazette

Charleston, W.Va., June 29, 1981

AN ad hoc group calling itself the Coalition for Better Television, with headquarters in Tupelo, Miss., hopes to get the authority to decide what *you* watch on your television set.

Indirectly, that is. The coalition, a band of angels with cash flowing freely from the Moral Majority's bank account, is pointing a harsh finger at ABC, CBS, and NBC chiefs, telling them that a boycott of the companies that sponsor television shows with more sex, violence and profanity than the coalition approves is imminent. The ultimatum to the networks: either tidy up the programming schedule for the fall season — make it morally sound that is — or prepare for economic catastrophe. The coalition is using a computer to monitor companies that sponsor what it refers to as "objectionable" shows. Acknowledging the threat, Procter and Gamble, which sponsors many television shows, said it will be very careful in selecting the programs it sponsors this fall. Hmmm.

We do not stand to defend the quality of modern day television. It is not difficult to turn on your television set and see a show which is mundane, silly and devoid of intellectual stimulation. Only occasionally, we admit, does something of rare quality seep into view on the commercial channels.

Our main disagreement with the National Coalition for Better Television is echoed in Fred Silverman's statement. The NBC president said the coalition is launching a "sneak attack on the foundation of democracy." He simply means that some safeguards in the First Amendment are being chiseled at here.

We think the best way, and perhaps the only way, to ensure that quality television is watched in your home is to monitor what is offered — yourself. It is not difficult to turn the switch. This permits you to select what you regard as proper subject matter for your family without encroaching upon the liberties of your neighbor.

The Washington Star
and Daily News

Washington, D.C., July 5, 1981

The boycott of advertisers who affix their logos to television shows deemed sexually offensive or gratuitously violent is off, for the moment. The boycott proposed by the Coalition for Better Television was cancelled after the Rev. Donald Wildmon and his associates said their advocacy had led a number of corporations to re-examine or drop their sponsorship of TV shows.

The prospective boycotters, affiliated with the Moral Majority, are offended by what they consider the television networks' "arrogant" disdain of, or assault on, traditional values, with a relative handful of network executives making the decisions about what programs will be on the air. The networks and their defenders retort that the coalition and those of like mind would assert their code of beliefs over the public's variety of choice — censorship, in short.

The economics of network television are not crucial in this confrontation — unless, of course, you happen to be a corporation spending multiple millions every year to sell suds on TV. The basic issue is who is responsible for the content of programming and what values should that programming embody?

Reverend Wildmon and his troops, notwithstanding the reflexive dismissal the connections with the Moral Majority occasions in some quarters, are not altogether grasping at straws. The evolution of opinion — or, if you prefer, its degradation — about what is permissible reflects the turbulence and change of the past 30 years. The limits of restraint seem to widen almost daily, and that is offensive to many people — more, we suspect, that have signed on with the Coalition for Better Television.

The cutting edge of this expansion has been popular entertainment and the prime vehicle television and film. That is a historic division, of course — arts and letters defying or at least questioning prevalent values, and the traditional bastions of those values fearing an effort to destroy what they view as long-validated codes of behavior.

Television, in its vividly pervasive presence, has magnified that tension. "Somebody's value system is going to be in dominant control," Reverend Wildmon says. Robert Mulholland, president of the NBC Television Network, said, "We don't believe any group has the ability to limit the choices for the American public. If it's entertainment today, is it the news tomorrow? What's next — newspapers, libraries?"

There are the poles. But *what* public are we talking about? Is the same public that provides record audiences for the trashy-chic "Dallas" also the public offended by an alleged overdose of titillating anatomy and incessant mayhem? If not, is it possible to talk of a system of generally shared standards of behavior and outlook?

Such a value system exists, we think, even within extended contemporary boundaries. Has network television and its ubiquitous influence tended to trespass those boundaries? Fairly often and often casually. Note the comment of Grant Tinker, just named NBC's chief executive officer. "News and news-related things, sports and the early morning shows — beyond those things, there's nothing that would attract me to watching television. And that comes close to a national scandal." His observation implies a quality of moral judgment, if a good deal else as well.

Advertisers seem to have shown unusual sensitivity to the complaints voiced by Reverend Wildmon — a frightening amount to those who see the boycott threat as a precursor to censorship. Procter & Gamble, for instance, the largest corporate advertiser on television, intends to pay closer attention to the shows it sponsors. Sex and violence will not automatically be precluded, a corporation spokesman said, depending on context and dramatic integrity.

This is a troubling issue. It is possible to draw some encouragement from the fact that, amidst the thunder and rhetorical lightning, there has been a more reasonable level of discussion during this latest fuss about the nature of the dispute itself than in some past head-buttings. That is something.

Des Moines Tribune

Des Moines, Iowa, July 6, 1981

The television screen was not littered with victims of the new crusade after all. The threatened boycott by the Coalition for Better Television did not materialize, and TV bosses, sponsors and viewers were left to wonder what goes on.

Isn't TV the unholy mess people were led to believe by the dire rhetoric of coalition preachers? Had the coalition got cold feet at the prospect of going eyeball-to-eyeball with rich and influential corporations? Or had some big corporations quietly submitted to the coalition's demands for a clean-up of "offensive" shows?

Evidently a substantial number of sponsors had come to terms with the coalition. As the Rev. Donald Wildmon explained, "Advertisers have listened, and they share our concerns. Conversation, consultation and fair compromise are far more commendable than confrontation."

Fine, except that coalition leaders previously had given the impression that there would be no compromising with evil, in whatever form it was presented on TV. The hellfire-and-damnation talk of a few months ago took on a charitable tone as the day of reckoning arrived. That's fine, too.

Wildmon estimated that 20 percent to 40 percent of the nation's population would have taken part in a boycott. That's a wild guess, since even the best-organized boycotts seldom are that effective. Economic coercion is old stuff to media executives. What sets the coalition venture apart from most other efforts like it is the moralistic posturing that accompanied threats of economic reprisal.

Such tactics may have turned off as many churchgoers as they won over to the boycott approach. The advertisers who came to terms with the coalition undoubtedly were motivated more by a potential loss of profits rather than the fear of an angry God. Perhaps the coalition's most valuable contribution is proving that, in a business environment, a sizable cut in profits is worse than hell.

The Idaho STATESMAN

Boise, Idaho, May 5, 1981

The Statesman has consistently criticized the Moral Majority's politicking and its narrow-minded thinking on a variety of social issues. Oddly enough, though, we and the Moral Majority come down near each other on the issue of sex on television.

The followers of the Rev. Jerry Falwell say they are not only going to quit tuning in shows that exploit sexuality, but also are going to boycott the products of the companies that sponsor the shows. Though our reasoning is probably a bit different than Falwell's, we feel the idea has merit.

Our concern, unlike Falwell's, is not with the morality or immorality of sex. Our concern is with the way the media take sex and use it to attract viewers without regard for the possible long-term effect on the audience.

Sex, of course, sells. But what else does sex in the media do? How does it affect the way society at large thinks and functions? What happens when week after week, year after year millions of people are subjected to the subtle and not-so-subtle sexuality of such programs as *Three's Company* and *Charlie's Angels*?

We're not psychologists, but the answer seems obvious. The media have the power to change society — not in one fatal swoop, but an inch at a time. The nature of that change is not readily apparent, but our fear is that social evolution wrought haphazardly in the quest for profits will not be good.

Television, of course, is not the only culprit. Magazine ads are loaded with blatant sex as well as subliminal sexual messages. Many movies also exploit sex. So do recording studios, billboards, radio and even newspapers. The result is that American men, women and children are bombarded every day with sights and sounds carefully designed to titillate.

In the past, ideas of morality and physical beauty were instilled in the individual by family, church, school and friends. Generally speaking, each of these "forces" was guided by a sense of responsibility to contribute to the welfare of the individual.

Today, the media have usurped part of this role, but have shunned the responsibility. In general, the responsibility of any medium is to return a profit to its owner. As far as the owners are concerned, the effect on the individual and society is the problem of the individual and society. Sex in the media is a bull and we all populate the china shop through which it runs.

Falwell and his constituents have decided to try to head off the bull. Probably they will have a little success, but will fail to mold the media to their own rigid standards. Nor should they. We and a lot of other people wouldn't like it if the only fare available was that approved by fundamentalist Christians.

What is needed is for people from all walks of life to make their own examination of sex in the media, to decide whether it is good, bad or indifferent, then boycott what they find is bad.

If enough people do, the media will get the message sooner or later.

THE BISMARCK TRIBUNE

Bismarck, N.D., July 2, 1981

The Coalition for Better Television has announced it will not, after all, start a boycott of advertisers sponsoring TV programs that, in its opinion, are too sexy or violent.

But the coalition's chairman, Donald E. Wildmon, says a boycott will remain in the group's arsenal, ready for use at any time.

"Our emotions tell us to boycott. We are angry," Wildmon says.

There is something terribly frightening about such boycotts in general and, in this case, threatened boycotts against advertisers in a communications medium, be it TV, radio or even newspapers.

The boycott is a powerful weapon, and there are no rules for its use. The boycott is just there, ready to be dropped on an advertiser sponsoring or underwriting something that unidentified monitors find objectionable.

At the moment, we have TV sex and violence under attack by the coalition, but tomorrow, we may have new targets — say, news or commentary — chosen, again, by unidentified monitors.

Everett Parker, head of the United Church of Christ's office of communications, says, "I think it's a very dangerous precedent to say, 'We're going to put a company out of business because we disagree on a single issue.' You'll see, it won't just be one type of programming they'll oppose. If they're successful with violence, they'll go after other social issues and political issues."

Peggy Charren, head of Action for Children's Television, has started a national petition campaign to oppose a boycott. She said the coalition "is trying to dictate what the American public may or may not watch on television."

But that's not all.

Once the boycott — or the threat of boycott — is legitimatized as a weapon, it would be available to any group that wants something banned from a communications medium.

Almost any special interest group can push a boycott against advertisers associated with something the group dislikes.

Now we have the Coalition for Better Television, with its sights set on sex and violence. But is it possible, in an ironic twist, that tomorrow we may have the Coalition for Sexier/More Violent Television and its threatened boycott against the sponsors of, say, Little House on the Prairie?

And what do we finally end up with, given the unleashing of boycotts?

We are left with confusion, or pabulum, or blank screens. Or, more hopefully, we are left with groups boycotting themselves into oblivion because viewers can't keep track of all the target advertisers or because viewers will begin to recognize the folly of it all and ignore the calls for boycotts.

Aside from effects, however, the boycott talk is disturbing in another respect.

The coalition and its friends are not a disinterested third party in all of this, despite appearances.

One friend, for example, is the Rev. Jerry Falwell of the Moral Majority, and Mr. Falwell says his group would give at least $2 million to support a coalition boycott call.

Mr. Falwell, the Moral Majority and similar groups, it should be noted, have become heavy users of TV, and they, also, solicit funds from consumers — the same people who buy sponsor products.

Mr. Falwell has employed an advertising agency and a computer-consulting firm since 1973, and in 1979 he paid $9 million to broadcast his daily radio and weekly television programs all over the country.

His "Old-Time Gospel Hour" raised about $115 million through its appeals from fiscal 1977 through fiscal 1980. In 1980, his Thomas Road Baptist Church borrowed $3.5 million through a bond issue, and the church's ability to service the debt depended on Mr. Falwell's ability to bring in money, particularly through the "Gospel Hour" program.

It is possible that boycotts supported by the coalition and its followers could erode the economics of commercial television, resulting in cheaper air time, easier access to prime time slots and perhaps even larger contributions to Moral Majority causes, political and moral, as advertised on TV.

If such were the effect, we all would be the losers, because some fine but extremely expensive programming might be lost.

The boycott, then, as a weapon for altering the offerings of an entertainment and communications medium, is not the answer. But there are alternatives.

First, we must develop a clearer understanding of the power of the medium. In particular, we need a better understanding of what TV does to our society, our economy and even our political system. The networks should then act accordingly and recognize that they are invited guests in viewers' homes.

The public also has a role in controlling broadcasts: The public, if it desires better programming, must exercise its right to choose that better programming.

Such seems to be the case now, witness the success of "The Defense of the United States," a recent, excellent CBS News series. And witness the demise of some T&T programs that have been dropped because the ratings just weren't good enough.

But now we have Mr. Wildmon, Mr. Falwell and the coalition, and their attempt to undermine conventional economic forces within the medium by imposing their will over the general public's will.

We should resist the group's attempt to restrict our choices — be they program choices, economic choices or political choices.

For, when we allow any one minority group to dictate alternatives, we are, to use Mr. Parker's phrase, setting "a very dangerous precedent."

The Birmingham News

Birmingham, Ala., June 30, 1981

The Coalition for Better Television has responded quickly to pledges from some of the nation's largest firms to press for TV programming which contains less sex and violence by calling off plans for a proposed boycott of sponsors of the most objectionable shows.

Doubtless the agreements between sponsors and the coalition do not mean that neither sex nor violence can be an element of TV shows, for both may be legitimate themes for exploration in dramatic fare. But the agreement should mean that we will have less gratuitous sex and violence that serves no purpose other than to attract the prurient and that tend to preempt themes which deserve exploration.

The coalition's quick response in calling off boycott plans should reassure those who feared it was attempting to establish itself as a censor of all television fare at the expense of the television networks' freedom to treat formerly taboo subjects seriously.

And one would hope that less focus on frivolous sex — if that is the eventual outcome of the confrontation — that overall television programming will be improved both in terms of quality and in terms of variety of subject matter.

THE BLADE

Toledo, Ohio, July 5, 1981

ONE of the ideas the so-called Moral Majority would like to sell the American people is that it is very powerful. For that reason, the best tactic in its much-discussed boycott of television programs that contain excessive amounts of sex and violence is to to declare victory at the earliest opportunity and then make a strategic withdrawal.

Events played into the hands of the would-be boycotters. Procter & Gamble, one of the biggest television advertisers, withdrew its sponsorship of 50 shows that it said contained excessive sex and violence. Some other companies did the same, even though there was no indication as to whether the boycott could have been successful if it had been formally mounted.

A spokesman for the Moral Majority said the group was still angry because "our values, our principles, our morals . . . have been ridiculed, belittled, mocked, and insulted by the networks." But because advertisers had pledged to "clean up" television the coalition had decided not to press for action now.

More likely the explanation is that the group could not be sure of success in its boycott efforts. A survey for ABC concluded: "The number of public participants in any Moral Majority-led boycott appears to be minimal." A CBS survey discovered that some of the organizations said to be members of the boycott coalition were not members.

The group, demonstrating its propensity for bully tactics despite its proclaimed adherence to Christian ideals, plans to raise a war chest "to buy and assist others in buying full-page ads across the nation naming public enemy No. 1 or 2 or 3 or whoever they are and listing their products." This is apparently the moral equivalent of the political hit lists for which right-wing political and religious groups have a peculiar penchant.

It is likely that many Americans are offended by much that they see on the screen, just as many others tolerate programs or perhaps even enjoy them. But it does not require any organized group to solve the problem. For those offended by such programs, the solution is as close as the off button on the TV set. That solves the problem without dictating to those who are content to watch what the networks offer in the way of entertainment.

One suspects, though, that the Moral Majoritarians really do want the right to dictate what is on the tube. Distasteful as much of today's television programming is by esthetic and moral standards, censorship is more repugnant by any standards.

ARKANSAS DEMOCRAT

Little Rock, Ark., July 6, 1981

The Coalition for Better Television has called off a threatened boycott of those TV advertisers whose sponsored programs run to excessive violence, sex or profanity. CBT did it because the sponsors acknowledged their fears of a boycott and promised some degree of reform.

What it appeared to come to was that all feared that some among them might moderate the complained-of material more than others – and grab a lion's share of the market. The coalition played on that fear by singling out Hershey as having done a better reform job than others and urging the public to buy the company's chocolates.

The networks weren't nearly as frightened by the boycott threat. They cited First Amendment rights of free speech and deplored the coalition's efforts to impose its brand of morality on a prime communications medium. But then the networks would be sure in any case to get such advertising as is shown. To them, the question of which advertiser wins out with the coalition is largely irrelevant.

But should coalitions threaten boycotts based on moral demands? Many think so, many think not. But the boycott is a legal weapon in most respects and is protected by the same First Amendment that the networks appeal to. Few will deny, moreover, that there is an excess of violence, sex and profanity on TV. The sponsors acknowledge that implicitly in yielding to the coalition's pressure to reduce it.

The Des Moines Register

Des Moines, Iowa, July 16, 1981

The Coalition for Better Television was created with the idea of ridding the airwaves of morally offensive programs. Shows would be monitored and their sins of sex, violence and bad language would be charted for all to see. Then the right-thinking folk were to refuse to buy the products advertised on the offending shows.

But the boycott was called off, or at least postponed. Perhaps enough sponsors were shaken by the coalition's threats that economic reprisals were unnecessary. Perhaps the coalition itself got cold feet at the prospect of confronting some of the country's biggest and most influential corporations. Network executives, if their words can be believed, did not surrender.

Whatever, the coalition is off on another venture. This time, its leaders want to enlist the loyalists in a campaign to thwart congressional proposals to deregulate broadcasting. The Senate already has acted favorably on bills to lift many government controls on the industry, mainly by simplifying TV licensing procedures and granting indefinite radio licenses to do away with three-year renewals.

The coalition includes conservative organizations that echo the Reagan administration's theme about getting the government off the citizen's back and turning bureaucratic regulators out to pasture. Now, all of a sudden, the coalition comes out in favor of continued government regulation of radio and television.

What goes on here? Can the old enemy, the government regulators, be trusted to protect public morality and old-fashioned American values? What are the coalition's aims? More important, what are its principles?

Maybe the coalition has perceived this as a time — recalling an old legislator's words — "to rise above principle." Coalition leaders apparently have calculated that they carry more political clout in Washington than they have economic clout with the networks and sponsors. Government regulation isn't such a bad idea if you can control the regulators. Anyway, citizen action can be awfully slow and sometimes not very reliable.

OKLAHOMA CITY TIMES

Oklahoma City, Okla., June 26, 1981

THE battle for the American conscience via the air waves waxes hotter as a noted liberal television producer squares off against what he calls political and religious broadcasters from the extreme right.

Norman Lear says he will ask every station in the country to carry free TV spots, featuring well-known entertainers, to counter the "fundamental superstars of evangelistic religious broadcasting." Their message: the right of everyone to have and express his own opinion.

The spots were prepared by People for the American Way, a tax-exempt organization that Lear helped found with a $300,000 contribution.

The campaign apparently will not single out a particular group but is aimed in general at "right-wing groups and single-issue zealots who have joined with evangelistic broadcasters to attack the integrity of anyone disagreeing with them."

Obviously, it's a counterattack against the efforts of groups like the Moral Majority and Coalition for Better Television to persuade advertisers to withdraw sponsorship of TV programs deemed too violent or sexually explicit.

But Lear and his colleagues apparently do not realize that concern over the direction television has taken is not limited to "right-wing zealots." Producers and writers don't see the problem because they are, as a group, more socially liberal than the viewing public. Thus, they don't understand that many other people — perhaps conservative but not extremist — have expressed deep opposition to the liberal chic that has pervaded prime-time television to the point of sexual permissiveness and profanity.

These people don't identify with the self-righteousness of certain outspoken groups but, like them, they resent the seemingly concerted effort to destroy the traditional values of marriage, home and family.

THE INDIANAPOLIS NEWS
Indianapolis, Ind., November 12, 1981

Norman Lear is one of those people with great gifts and ability in one area — television production. But his expertise doesn't cover what he's trying to do these days.

His blasts at the Moral Majority, the Coalition for Better Television and other such groups continually miss the point. The issue is not censorship; nor is it some kind of competition over who is more religious or more moral.

The question put forth by Moral Majority, the National Federation for Decency and others is what kind of television programing is the American public prepared to support?

Raising that question, according to Lear, is apparently a threat to toleration, pluralism and the First Amendment. "The future of our pluralistic society is at stake," he contended in setting forth the agenda of his organization, People for the American Way.

The organization's television ads suggest that toleration of choice in egg preparation — scrambled vs. omelette — is a good example of pluralism. So shouldn't our tolerance for varieties in egg preparation be extended to all areas of life, including television programing? The subtle suggestion is that Moral Majority is soon going to be trying to tell us the moral way to eat eggs.

We doubt it. The Moral Majority platform has yet to address the egg issue. Furthermore, most of these groups have less clout than Lear and others seem to assume they have.

These groups thus far have protested what they see on the tube. They have threatened to boycott products that sponsor objectionable shows. Lear is not complaining about the boycott that Jesse Jackson threatened against Coca Cola in return for jobs for blacks.

Lear complains that Moral Majority and similar groups tend to claim to be better Christians, or more moral persons, according to the agenda of the particular organization. "Today, the self-styled Infallibles are known as the Religious New Right, or the Christian New Right," Lear has declared. "To disagree with their conclusions on numerous matters of morality and politics is to be labeled a poor Christian, or unpatriotic, or anti-family."

Heaven forbid. Lear has not complained when other groups have used the same tactic in the past on other issues. Would he censor the United Methodist Church for its chastisement of Rep. William Dickinson, R-Ala., for his failure to vote according to the church's pro-choice position on the abortion issue? Dickinson is a United Methodist but voted the wrong way for a "good" Methodist.

A letter from a church official, Charlotte Hendee, chastised him for voting in 1979 to exclude Medicaid funding for abortions. Hendee also issues a subtle warning that Dickinson might regret his votes on a future election day. "On behalf of all United Methodists, many of whom are voters in your district, I urge you, a United Methodist member of Congress, to evaluate your denomination's thoughtful position on this sensitive issue, keeping in mind the denomination's long-standing position for human rights for all persons, regardless of their economic status."

Lear, by the way, agrees with the United Methodist pro-choice position.

His complaints about tactics miss the real issues. Lear's organization would do better to directly address the agenda of Moral Majority and similar organizations. Let him defend the moral implications of current television programing.

The Kansas City Times
Kansas City, Mo., July 3, 1981

In calling off its threat to boycott products which sponsor TV shows with "gratuitous sex, violence and obscenity," the Coalition for Better Television has won a victory without really firing a shot. The self-appointed guardians of what is fit for everybody else to see have even managed to make themselves look magnanimous and forbearing.

Chances are, many of the shows the coalition finds objectionable are scheduled for oblivion anyway. Television is continually changing and shifting and killing formats on the basis of polls. For a while it has been jiggles and suggestive dialogue and endless car chases with everything bursting into flames. For years before, it was various families, lovable but with one or both parents hopelessly scatterbrained except for a primitive wisdom that would be revealed at the end. They were as unreal as the bouncing roommates and beautiful female detectives who employ karate.

Sooner or later the public becomes bored and everything changes quickly. Sin and greed in Texas no longer are diverting, or TV producers run out of stunt-driving brothers-in-law for all those chase episodes. Then the industry jumps on new bandwagons and the whole process begins again.

It is mostly light entertainment, little of it very good, and people have been turning off their sets in droves, which is what they can do if they find the stories morally objectionable. It's probably a good thing, too, to pay enough attention to your children to know what they're watching on TV.

But is it right to intimidate advertisers, networks, stations and the entertainers with threats of a boycott? Certainly it is an exercise of free speech to do so. But there is an inherent danger in it. If no one really worries much about pressure against "Three's Company," what about the same sort of thing directed against a production of "Romeo and Juliet"? Or a news program that somebody decides is not strictly objective? Or a talk show that presents an unpopular point of view?

Television already seems timid enough about everything except the constant presentation of inanities and trivia. The coalition seems likely to frighten it into total blandness.

In art, entertainment and literature, the best procedure for specific objectors is to tell their flocks or the general public not to attend, listen, or read, or to flip the switch. Those who do not get their way, who are not successful persuaders, turn to blacklists and threaten boycotts. In the end, this says that people are not intelligent or mature enough to make up their own minds, that someone else will decide what is fit for them to read or see, and shut it off at the source, that everybody must conform to someone's moral imperative. Is that what we want?

THE ARIZONA REPUBLIC
Phoenix, Ariz., July 2, 1981

THE Committee for Better Television claims to have won its fight against TV programs it finds offensive because they put too much emphasis on sex and violence.

No one can say for certain whether it did or not, because the committee never got around to revealing its "hit list."

However, there was the smell of victory the moment Owen Butler, chairman of Procter & Gamble, announced that his company would withdraw its sponsorship from programs the committee objected to.

P. & G spent a fat $486.3 million on TV advertising last year.

That's real money. It talks in a language anyone can understand, even TV networks.

So the prospect is that fewer busts will jiggle and fewer buttocks will wiggle-waggle on TV next season. Possibly a bit less blood will be spilled.

However, anyone who thinks TV programming will be any less inane has another think coming.

The intellectual level of TV is certain to remain in the cellar because the economics of the industry demand it.

The cost of a TV commercial is determined by the size of the audience. TV programmers, therefore, must seek the widest possible audience, which means the lowest common denominator.

The strategy the Committee for Better Television adopted has given the industry the jitters, and for good reason.

It could be used by some future group to censor network news shows and documentaries.

Claiming to represent 5 million families, the committee said it would ask its supporters not only to boycott the programs it found offensive but also to boycott the sponsors.

The threat of a boycott scares corporations which depend on a mass market. Even a slight drop in sales can mean a big drop in profits.

The nation isn't going to suffer any great loss when *Charlie's Angels* goes off the air. It could even survive the disappearance of the *Dukes of Hazzard*.

However, if some day a group organizes to boycott the sponsors of news shows and shows like *Sixty Minutes* and *20/20*, that will be serious, indeed.

THE RICHMOND NEWS LEADER
Richmond, Va., July 6, 1981

The complaint: Sex and violence permeate American television. Big TV's response: Hide behind the First Amendment, denounce the critics, and cry, "Censorship!" — but do not take a hard look at the product. And yet: Television's problem lies not in sex and violence, nor does it center on attempts at censorship. The problem is banality.

Viewers of television entertainment are treated to glorified soap operas called situation comedies, as well as to endless crime and quiz shows. The sex tends toward the *double entendre*, toward the jiggle rather than the blatant; the violence has become stylized although that presents a false picture to children who might start thinking car crashes or bullets really do not damage.

Critics of television associated with evangelical religious groups seek to improve television by cleaning it up; a better idea, we think, would be to improve television. Sex, violence, nudity, and profanity are, after all, parts of life and of art. They should offend adults only when used gratuitously to hype a program with a story line suffering from terminal weakness.

TV's response to its detractors has not been enlightening. Some examples: Fred Silverman, who resigned last week as NBC president, called the attempt by the Coalition for Better TV, which sought to organize a boycott of sponsors whose programs it deemed offensive, "a sneak attack on the foundations of democracy." Norman Lear, who shares with Silverman the blame for much of what we

see (or, with great determination, do not see), has organized something called People for the American Way — a group placing ads countering what Lear terms "the intolerant messages and anti-democratic actions of moral majoritarians."

These are gross overstatements. The Dukes of Hazzard or the Fonz or Charlie's Angels or Old Arch or whoever may be amusing a time or two to some, and in large doses to many. Their absence from the screen hardly constitutes an indictment of American democracy. Those who control television raise a false issue in their cry of censorship, real or implied. They continue presenting programs they believe will make money. Yet through their control of the medium — and the sameness of their programming — these moguls seek to impose their standards, their morality on viewers who might yearn for something different . . . or better.

The Coalition for Better Television, which recently called off its boycott, hoped to hit 'em in the pocketbook by putting pressure on sponsors. Big TV perceived this as a Great Wrong. But the Coalition and its allies in the evangelical movement arose in part as a counterpoise to the permissiveness many thoughtful Americans believe permeates the popular culture, including television (as well as the related political and social Liberalism of many mainline church hierarchies, which spend much of their time deploring the evangelicals).

American political debate can be explained as a constant battle between competing pressure groups. For one such group — the evangelicals — forcefully to transform its values into action remains well within the perimeter of that debate. The evangelicals caught it because they were effective. And television hardly rebuffs all pressure groups. *TV Guide,* for instance, reports that many scripts involving homosexuality regularly are cleared with homosexual activists. In televisionland, it seems, homosexuals have clout, while those seeking more wholesome fare do not.

There remains for the exasperated the ultimate act of censorship, or perhaps of good taste: watching television very selectively, or not watching at all. Yet television remains our most pervasive medium, a revolutionary device that has wrought more contemporary change than newspapers or books or movies or the theater. And children *will* watch television.

Television remains far too important to be left to the executives staffing the networks and to the advertisers; government's dead hand at the switch would be worse. Criticism emanating from the evangelicals seems to be bringing a modicum of needed reform. Big TV responds by criticizing its critics and defending its own excesses. Yet make no mistake: The issue does not revolve around censorship. The issue is the continued retailing of banality masquerading as social comment, a mirror of society existing only in the minds of the cloistered few who run TV.

St. Petersburg Times
St. Petersburg, Fla., July 1, 1981

There's a device on every television set that makes it easy for viewers to protest shows that offend them: the off button.

Turning off the TV or switching stations is a much more acceptable way to object to network programing than the approach threatened by the Coalition for Better Television. The ultra-conservative group, led by the Moral Majority and the National Federation for Decency, has vowed to clean up television by boycotting the products of advertisers who sponsor TV shows that it finds too sexy or violent. The groups wants to rid TV of such programs to make more air time available for shows that emphasize "traditional family values."

Donald E. Wildmon, the coalition's chairman, said Monday that the group would call off its boycott temporarily because of the "positive response" by TV advertisers to its criticism of programing. But Wildmon also said that a future boycott remained a "real possibility" and that the coalition would continue its pressure campaign.

THE NETWORKS, which are sensitive to public opinion, ought to listen to any group that wants to express its views about programing. However, an organized boycott of advertised products is going too far. It

smacks of censorship through economic pressure and threatens freedom of choice for viewers who might enjoy some of the shows that a particular minority group finds offensive.

Unfortunately, Procter & Gamble, the largest national television advertiser, appears to have crumpled at the mere suggestion of a boycott. The company, which spent almost $500-million on commercials last year to make its products household names, recently announced that it was withdrawing sponsorship from 50 shows that the company felt contained excessive sex, violence and profanity.

P&G downplayed the idea that pressure from Wildmon's extremist group influenced the decision. But it seems more than a coincidence that Owen B. Butler, P&G's new chairman, made the announcement just two weeks before the coalition was scheduled to name the companies that make the products it intended to boycott. The largest TV advertiser has set a bad precedent. If the big companies don't take a stand against extremist pressure groups, it's even less likely that smaller firms will.

Procter & Gamble, other TV advertisers and the networks ought to know better than to get caught in a censorship trap. Once a company agrees to pull its advertising support for some

shows, it is asking for never-ending demands from fringe groups to stop supporting all kinds of programs. Today it might be a silly soap opera, but tomorrow it could be the evening news (there's a lot of violence on the news, after all).

Many corporations already pre-screen TV shows before advertising on them to determine if the content meets their approval. That's a valid management decision, but it should not be influenced by economic pressure groups that represent a small minority of TV viewers.

WILDMON SAYS that the inspiration for the coalition's threatened boycott came one evening when he was watching television with his wife and four children. "On one channel there was sex," he says. "On another there was profanity, and on the third a guy was preparing to work someone over with a hammer."

Why not simply turn off the TV, Mr. Wildmon? Instead of sitting in front of a television, a family could use the time to revive the lost art of conversation, play games together and enjoy each other's company. That would do a lot more to preserve the American family than a boycott of TV advertisers.

Conference on Families Underlines "New Right" Split

A series of six conferences from June–October 1980 on the state of the American family brought the "New Right"— liberal split into sharp focus. Former President Jimmy Carter called the series to "look for creative, compassionate solutions to the problems of families and then consider who or what might best carry them out." Separate meetings were held in cities around the country, and a final report was released in October by the White House. From the start, the conferences were an intensely emotional issue. Even the question of defining the word "family" was fraught with implications. Conservative delegates favored defining the family as a group of persons united by blood, marriage or adoption. The liberals widened the definition to include homosexual households and other persons living together who were not married. Other issues that were a source of deep division were: abortion, the Equal Rights Amendment and prayer in the public schools. Conservatives staged walkouts at the first and second conferences in Baltimore, Md. and Minneapolis, Minn., respectively. The remaining conferences reserved the controversial portions until the end. Conservatives and liberals managed to agree on the need for more cooperation between parents and schools to upgrade education, more public attention to the needs of the handicapped, an end to the tax disadvantage for married couples and renewed efforts to limit pornography.

DESERET NEWS
Salt Lake City, Utah, October 24, 1980

Is marriage still the foundation supporting the whole of our social institutions? This week, the United States Supreme Court answered, "yes."

It was not a firm, resounding, unanimous "yes," but a "yes" reached by a six to three margin. The split is disturbing.

The court refused to hear an appeal of an Illinois divorcee that she was unjustly denied her rights, i.e., custody of three daughters, aged 10, 13, and 15, for the sole reason that she was living with a man to whom she is not married.

Her ex-husband, the father of the three girls, sued for and gained custody on the grounds that the mother's violation of the state law against fornication jeopardized the "moral and spiritual well-being" of the daughters.

The Illinois Supreme Court wisely upheld the ruling of the lower court, stating that the mother's violation of the fornication statute showed her "disregard for existing standards of conduct that instructs her children, by example, that they, too, may ignore them . . . and could well encourage the children to engage in similar activity in the future."

This week's action of the U.S. Supreme Court allows the lower court ruling to stand. However, three of the U.S. Supreme Court justices, Thurgood Marshall, William J. Brennan Jr., and Harry A. Blackmun, wanted to reconsider the case. Justice Brennan cited statistics showing that in 1978 there were 1.1 million households headed by unmarried couples, an indication that this is an important social issue. He expressed fear that the lower court rulings may indeed have violated the mother's rights.

The familiar rationalization that "everybody" is doing some particular act or another so it must be all right seems to be implied in Justice Brennan's concern. The fact that a large number of people enjoy some of the benefits of marriage without really committing themselves is no indication that such a condition should be encouraged in any way. If allowed to spread, it will be a serious threat to the family and to society.

The preservation of these vital institutions must continue to be the prime concern of the courts, schools, churches, and everyone concerned with the future of humankind.

The Charlotte Observer
Charlotte, N.C., July 17, 1980

News from last weekend's western meeting of the White House Conference on Families was a breath of fresh air in an otherwise muggy season. Despite dark headlines about ERA, abortion, divorce, drug abuse, gay rights and other signs of social unrest, it turns out that those are not the major concerns of most Americans.

The three-day regional conference, held in Los Angeles, was one of a series devoted to reviewing federal policies that affect life and attitudes within American families. After their review, the conferees adopted 57 resolutions about how those policies might be improved. The recommendations will be forwarded to President Carter and the Congress.

What was reassuring was the priority assigned to each of those resolutions. Legal abortions, for instance, ranked 56th among the 57 resolutions. A recommendation regarding gay rights came in 54th. Though it precipitated considerable controversy, the proposed Equal Rights Amendment scored no higher than 50th.

The major concerns of American families are still those that have preoccupied mothers and fathers for generations: How can we improve the health of our children? How can we better provide for their education? How can we help them overcome their handicaps? How can we improve their housing? Will there be jobs for them when they are grown?

The conference's top 10 resolutions had to do with improving education, providing help for the disabled and the handicapped, creating jobs and economic opportunites, providing housing and better health services. Tenth on the list was a resolution calling for fairer tax and inheritance laws.

That is not to say that such things as abortion, equal rights, divorce and drug abuse are not legitimate American concerns. They are, of course. But it was reassuring to hear that those issues have not usurped the traditional place of education, health and equal opportunity as touchstones of the American dream.

OKLAHOMA CITY TIMES

Oklahoma City, Okla., October 22, 1980

THE sanctity of the family has suffered immensely in recent years, battered by the practitioners of the so-called "new morality" and by those who have stretched the limits of good taste in the entertainment field.

The courts have not always been too helpful. Two weeks ago the U.S. Supreme Court left intact a lower court ruling that, in the minds of many people, would result in interference with the right of parents to raise their children in a way that they think proper.

The justices refused to overturn an appellate court opinion in a Michigan case that parents have no right to be notified before a county-run health center gives contraceptives to their teen-age children.

The parents' lawsuit had argued that distributing contraceptives to minors without parental consent "violates the fundamental rights of parents to the care, custody and nurture of their children, and their right, as parents, to inculcate in their own children moral standards, religious beliefs and elements of good citizenship."

This week, however, in a different case the high court took another tack, in which it upheld the principle of the traditional family. It declined to help an Illinois woman who lost custody of her children because she has a "live-in" boyfriend. It let stand an Illinois Supreme Court ruling that gave custody of the woman's three daughters to her former husband.

She had custody originally but, after the boyfriend moved in and lived with her out of wedlock, the former husband went to court and eventually won custody of the girls. The trial court ruled in 1977 that the live-in arrangement required the children's removal "for their moral and spirtual well-being."

The extent to which traditional concepts of morality, marriage and the family have been diluted in this country is indicated, not just by the court's split vote, 6-3, but by the reasoning of the dissenting justices. They said nothing in the record or logic supports the conclusion that divorced parents who fornicate, for that reason alone, are unfit or adversely affect the well-being of their children beyond what effect the divorce may already have had on them.

Roanoke Times & World-News

Roanoke, Va., October 12, 1980

Much controversy about the family these days turns simply on the point that the people involved are not talking about the same thing. People with traditional, conservative, or fundamental views profoundly disagree with the definition of "family" as now propounded by the American Humanist Association. Its definition is:

Any two people or group of people wishing to make a commitment to one another over time and to share resources, responsibilities, goals and values should be considered a family, if they so consider themselves, and receive those benefits accorded family by society. Blood kinship should not be a requirement of family members, nor should marriage. By the same token, marriage should not be denied a couple wishing to make a legal commitment to each other.

It was very gracious of the humanist association to include the last sentence; it would kindly permit what to the traditionalist is the essence, or beginning point, of the family definition.

Even so, the humanist definition is not far from a definition put forward (but not adopted) in the Virginia General Assembly last winter. Planned as part of the national rage to adopt a "family policy," Senate Bill 139 would have defined as follows:

For the purpose of this chapter, "family" means the basic unit of society consisting of two or more persons who are related by blood, marriage, adoption *or covenantal caring* which is not contrary to law or sound public morals. [Italics added].

As a practical matter, the humanist association's definition — if it were adopted as law for all purposes — would wreak havoc with current juvenile and domestic court law, with the administration of welfare, Social Security and other programs. But if people wish to think and act poetically and call family what is not family, that may be their prerogative and their own pleasure.

There is some surprising evidence — from zoning cases, negligence lawsuits, etc. — that the legal definitions of family are not uniform. A study of them suggests that no one get into an argument involving "family" until the discussants have defined the terms. No one now can be sure of what is meant by the announcement that Susan is "in a family way."

The Miami Herald

Miami, Fla., October 25, 1980

THE TYPICAL American family is not passionately devoted to any particular emotional issue such as the Equal Rights Amendment, abortion law, or the status of homosexuals. Rather, its top priority is the need to tread water amid the raging economic currents that threaten to engulf it.

Zealots of various political persuasions tried to turn the White House Conference on Families into a vehicle for their own narrow concerns. Fortunately, they were unsuccessful. The majority of the 2,000 delegates who participated in last summer's meetings persisted in identifying the major concerns that are common to most American families, the issues that surpass the narrow ideologies of gay rights or abortion.

The report issued by the White House a few days ago disappointed the partisans. The great mass of struggling American families, however, has reason to be heartened by the report's recommendations.

First, the conferees want more sensitivity in the workplace to the needs of families. Workers shouldn't be expected to marry the company that employs them. The needs of families for security of income, stability of location, and flexibility in scheduling deserve far more respect than they typically get.

The Government shouldn't intrude into family affairs, most Americans agree. Thus it follows logically that Federal tax laws should not penalize marriage. The so-called "marriage tax" has led to a spate of highly publicized divorces by working couples who felt they couldn't afford the higher tax rate. That unfair taxation is a wholly unacceptable intrusion. The conference rightly recommended its abolition.

The conference also touched an almost-universal concern when it called for Federal tax policies that would encourage, instead of discourage, the keeping at home of aged, ill, and handicapped family members. The Government shouldn't make it cheaper to put Grandma in a home than to keep her with the family. It should not be biased toward paying professional custodians for services that relatives would provide lovingly if they could afford the time.

These priority proposals, along with a fifth addressing the abuse of alcohol and other drugs, are genuinely pro-family. They seek to encourage families to stay together. They try to bolster American families in resisting the enormous divisive forces of Western industrial society.

The conference report is, in short, a welcome statement on behalf of the nation's most cherished social institution.

THE CHRISTIAN SCIENCE MONITOR

Boston, Mass., July 25, 1980

No institution is more vital to the stability of society than the family. It is therefore heartening that the many serious problems facing families have become the focus of increased public attention. As the series "A time for families" concluding in today's Monitor shows, interest in the state of the family has reached national proportions. With compassionate concern, church leaders, social scientists, family counselors, politicians, government officials, industry leaders, and families themselves are seeking to understand what is happening and exploring ways of invigorating family life.

Is the family in crisis? Judging by the conclusions of those who study family trends in an historical context, the word is inaccurate and overused. Through the centuries the family has always experienced cycles of change, and change brings new problems and stresses. These are grave and must not be minimized. But the mass media often fail to convey the underlying durability and resilience of the institution. There is more continuity than discontinuity. The remarkable thing, perhaps, is that despite the social turbulence of recent decades, families are holding together as well as they are.

A balanced perspective

Examining the changes in a representative Midwestern town from the 1920s to the 1970s, sociologist Theodore Caplow of the University of Virginia and other researchers found there is greater family solidarity, a smaller generation gap, better marital communication, more religion, and less mobility today. "With respect to the major features of family life, the trend of the past two generations has run in the opposite direction from the trend that nearly everyone perceives and talks about," Dr. Caplow writes in "Middletown Families," a book to be published by the University of Minnesota Press next year.

If these findings cannot be automatically applied to communities everywhere, they at least suggest that a more balanced perspective is warranted. Family patterns do seem to be changing, but trends are not inexorable and, in any case, need careful interpretation.

Because family issues are complex — and the Monitor series has dealt with only some of them — it is also well to avoid oversimplifications. It is as fallacious, for example, to say that mothers who work are neglecting their children as to say that women must have professional careers in order to "fulfill" themselves. It is equally fallacious to suggest that families have to have a certain configuration to be vital and strong. Few would deny that families with two working parents or with a single parent have special concerns and must make an added effort if children are to be nurtured properly. But all families, even those called traditional, have marital and other problems demanding both effort and wisdom to surmount.

Disturbing trends

The point is that, whatever the human situation, it can be successfully addressed if sufficient moral and spiritual commitment and prayerful effort are poured into it. Branding the family which does not conform to some fixed pattern, therefore, is unhelpful.

This is not to ignore those negative forces which tend to pull the family down and often destroy it. There can be no false confidence or apathy about current trends. Such phenomena as widespread divorce, desertion, spouse and child abuse, cohabitation outside marriage, infidelity, out-of-wedlock births, and drug and alcohol use not only debilitate the family; they weaken the nation's entire moral fabric. They are scourges which society must combat with all the religious vigor and social dedication it can muster.

Everyone has a responsibility in this collective task. The churches need to speak out with greater clarity on the fundamental teachings of the Bible. Government, which certainly does not deliberately set out to undermine the family, nonetheless needs to weigh the impact of laws and policies on family stability and independence. Schools need to work closely with parents in the education of children. Industry needs to reform working schedules and make other changes to accommodate the two-breadwinner family and enable working mothers and fathers to carry out their obligations in the home. The television industry needs to summon up a social conscience — to offer programs that enhance and edify family life rather than cater to people's worst instincts (or, conversely, portray life in a prettified way).

There are some signs that all this is beginning to happen, but much, much more will be required of all religious and social institutions to help turn the negative trends around.

On the deepest level, the whole moral and spiritual tone of society needs purifying. It has become fashionable to accept "moral pluralism" — do-it-yourself moral standards — as something positive and progressive. In some quarters the argument is made that every individual should be free to set his or her own values and that it is the situation which should dictate the ethical solution and not an ethical standard which should govern all action.

The Judeo-Christian code

Such thinking holds perils for the nation. Moral wishywashiness, including sexual laxity, have characterized many civilizations that have lost their influence and greatness, a fact which ought not to be forgotten in an age of such intensely materialistic concerns. The United States, which for more than three centuries has lived by the Judeo-Christian code of morality, has attained an unprecedented degree of political freedom, economic well-being, and religious liberty. Surely its people and its institutions should not lightly accept the subtle and insidious notion that this code is outdated and should now give way to all manner of free-wheeling norms. As one Harvard scholar remarked, "We've tested the Ten Commandments and they work. We don't know what will happen to society without them."

With them, and with the profound precepts of the Sermon on the Mount, society can be assured of going forward. For the very purpose of the Judeo-Christian law is to discipline thought and action, to turn the individual away from a selfish absorption with material self to an awareness of and interest in the welfare of others. Practicing honesty, charity, purity, forebearance and other virtues, refusing to take advantage of others — sexually or otherwise — the human being overcomes his animalistic nature, brings to light his higher, his true self and identity, and establishes his spiritual relationship to his creator. Humanity, too, is benefited. Is not this Christ teaching the recipe for rooting out the lingering selfishness of the "me" generation?

Thoughtful social critics, while they may not use religious terms, nonetheless recognize the importance of teaching children self-discipline, cultivating moral and spiritual ideals, and giving them a larger vision of humanity — above all through the force of parental example. Most parents do not need to be told by professionals that youngsters grow up happier and more responsible when they have chores and duties as well as rights, when they are made to feel their self-worth through what they contribute, not through the things they possess, when they have a purpose in life, when they learn to care about and for others, including the wider family of man. Perhaps one New England mother expressed it best when she commented at White House hearings on the family earlier this year:

"We believe it is imperative that our nation face the real crisis in our society today, that is that we don't know how to love. And I guess there's a great amount of tension created because we see so many people and families seeking self-fulfillment directly, rather than self-fulfillment as a result of loving."

Put in these simple terms, America's family problems should loom less formidable — for they are problems we can do something about.

TULSA WORLD

Tulsa, Okla., June 9, 1980

SELF-STYLED "pro-family" proponents have walked out of the White House Conference on Families. They say the agenda was stacked in favor of abortion, gay rights and other stands which they oppose.

They won't miss much.

The idea that the myriad problems of the American family can be solved, or even dented, by a gathering of well-intentioned individuals at the White House boggles the mind.

The trouble with the Conference is not that its agenda includes particular subjects. The trouble is there is no way an agenda could be written that would begin to touch on all of the woes of the family. The subject is simply too broad and too complex, and too controversial to be considered as a single target.

To suggest that a few people are going to get together and solve the "family problem" is to suggest that they are going to solve every major problem in the country. Every major shortcoming of society obviously affects the family.

Those grievances range from the failure of schools to the cheapening of culture to inflation and high energy costs. All of these things, and many other societal failures, are contributing to family breakdown. They demand more attention than they can possibly receive at a White House sideshow.

Let's call the White House Conference on Families what it really is: a political propaganda exercise. It confuses talk with action.

By trying to focus on all problems, the conference is guaranteed not to make headway against any problem.

Those who boycotted the meeting need not worry that they will miss anything of substance.

The Birmingham News

Birmingham, Ala., February 24, 1980

The White House Conference on Families has quite obviously run aground over differences between professionals, many with government connections, and those for whom the family conference was first proposed. Here in Alabama the matter surfaced when Gov. Fob James declined to have the state represented in the conference, reportedly, on the basis of Mrs. James' objections that the guidelines, mandating that "stereotypes"and "sexual orientation" be disregarded, are not based on traditional Judeo-Christian values concerning the family.

To some, the issue may seem to be a tempest in a teapot. But those who have been aware of changes in the cultural attitudes toward the family - are deeply concerned that the basic unit of civilization itself is under attack and in peril of being destroyed. They worry, and rightly so, that government endorsement of domestic arrangements contrary to traditional family groupings will erode and destroy the legitimacy of the family which will have fatal consequences for the nation and finally civilization itself.

Translated, this worry stems from orchestrated efforts to legitimize such bizarre innovations as abortion on demand (subsidized by government), households headed by unmarried, single parents, or unmarried parents, and homosexual marriages, all seen as threats to social stability.

The attacks on the traditional family today are unprecedented in history. Never before has the traditional family been assailed by such numbers with such determination and even venom. But why, one is impelled to ask? Is there any evidence that the traditional family has outlived its usefulness, that it no longer serves the needs of the individual, the community or civilization itself?

Such is not the case, of course. While most Americans have been aware of the revolution taking place in the country during the past 15 to 20 years, few — including the radicals themselves — have recognized the effects since they do not tally with the stated objectives of the so-called revolutionaries. On the surface the confrontations were seen as a struggle against capitalism and for changes in the basic economic system. But the real struggle was for social changes that would bring the most immediate gratification to the radicals themselves — that is, liberate themselves from the ancient, most basic, most intrusive, but most supportive and creative, of all human institutions, the human family.

And while the boys and girls were having a ball on the campus celebrating almost every kind of behavior that defied accepted family values — drugs, sloth, discourtesy, promiscuousness and vilification of all authority, and especial parental authority — another revolution was taking place throughout the country, a revolution that has given birth to what some commentators have designated as a new class, a new elite, of college-educated sons and daughters of white-collar and blue-collar, middle-income parents.

The radicals may have pointed the way, but it has been the new class which has toted the water. With a significant number of the new elite status oriented and in search of dogmas and values that will give it identity and legitimacy, a revolt against traditional institutions and especially against the authority of tradition they have targeted the family as worthwhile of destruction.

The struggle against the traditional family values has become even more complex as young government bureaucrats, technocrats, educators and many in the communications industry have seen the opportunity for advancing their values (or lack of same) and gaining new power by intervention in areas normally off-limits to government. But one cannot view the results of government policies over the past 10 years without realizing how destructive they have been of the family and the authority and responsibility formerly vested in it. Such destructiveness is arrogantly and blatantly evident in some areas of welfare and wherever the federal courts hold sway.

Certainly most members of Congress in passing statutes regarding welfare, education and personal rights have not acted with the intention of destroying the traditional family. But Congress has acted without reckoning on the interpretive powers of bureaucrats who have social axes to grind and who implement and enforce the statutes, and it has not properly assessed the opportunities for the accretion of this power by a new elite which the lawmakers hardly even recognize as existing.

The new elite is generally bright, idealistic and innovative. But idealism is not a value in itself and its effects depend largely on the idea that fuels it and innovation can be destructive as well as creative. And as history makes plain, idealism is also a marvelous mask for selfishness, hiding ulterior motives even for the idealists themselves. One should examine the values of the new elite in assessing its legitimacy and in questioning the propriety of surrendering power to it.

So it is important that those who recognize the vital part the traditional family plays in maintaining and advancing proven values should speak out in support of the family. And those who claim a better domestic arrangement and a better set of values should be made to prove their claim before society departs from tested pastures for those greener ones down the hill. One would have to agree substantially with Mrs. James: The Judeo-Christian idea of family and the values the family has handed down from generation to generation as served civilization well, and the record of so-called alternative arrangements thus far reveals very little to recommend them.

St. Louis Review

St. Louis, Mo., June 20, 1980

"Curiouser and curiouser" was Alice's comment about the remarkable world of Wonderland. "Curiouser and curiouser" also describes the White House Conference on Families — the latest proof that the federal government has a unique facility for botching the many projects it undertakes.

The Conference was apparently seen by President Carter as a harmless way to score some points with middle America by highlighting the role of the family in American society. But then the bureaucrats took over. Among other things, they failed to define a family in any reasonable terms, so that the Conference considers a colony of homosexual males as truly a family as mother, father and children in Peoria. In fact, the first chairperson of the Conference was a divorced woman. But where the bureaucrats really outdid themselves was in determining the mechanics of the Conference. As it became apparent that the Conference was heading for the rocks of controversy, the stagers decided to blunt its impact by really having several Conferences in various parts of the nation instead of just one. They also learned a lesson from the Women's Conference held in Houston some years ago. Delegates had been elected to that Conference in virtual secrecy. In some states, including Missouri, alert women realized that the Women's Conference was being dominated by pro-abortion, anti-family groups and mobilized to elect more representative slates. They were rudely shouted down at the Conference by the totally unrepresentative harradins making up the majority delegations.

But moderates too had learned from the debacle of the Women's Conference. When the White House Conference was announced, they began to organize and as a result large numbers of pro-life, pro-family delegates were elected in state conferences. This was not agreeable to the organizers and so large numbers of unelected delegates were named to the Conference to "balance" the delegations. No similar attempt, of course, had been made to "balance" the Women's Conference, but now elected pro-life, pro-family forces were "balanced" by representatives of other points of view.

The manipulation of the delegations is proved most conclusively by the fact that the Missouri delegation, representing one of the most strongly pro-life states in the nation, failed to include in its list of 10 priority issues the abortion issue.

The family does need study, especially do we need more information on the impact on families of pending federal legislation. We also recognize that non-traditional families, especially one-parent families, form an important part of family life. The White House Conference on Families, however, is proving to be a farce and another waste of time and money.

Richmond Times-Dispatch

Richmond, Va., June 12, 1980

"As are families, so is society," wrote the 19th century American author, William Makepeace Thayer. Society's philosophy of the last quarter of the 20th century — or at least the philosophy of a large liberal segment of that society — was demonstrated last week in some of the resolutions adopted in Baltimore at the White House Conference on Families.

The principle behind many of the resolutions was "Gimme." The conferees asked for vastly more money from the federal government for various purposes alleged to benefit the American family.

"A laundry list of liberalism," was the way *The Washington Post* characterized the resolutions. "If put into effect," the news account said, "they would cost billions annually."

A resolution endorsing, among other things, a guaranteed "adequate" income for all families was one which, if implemented, presumably could run to huge amounts. We say presumably, because "adequate" was not defined. Other potentially costly proposals included one for governmental child care programs so that parents could work.

It is not surprising that one conferee found it strange that "we say get the government off our backs but in our recommendations we ask for more government aid."

Some of the resolutions, however, including some that would involve governmental aid, were soundly based. Among these were proposals for increased education and training as to the use of alcohol and drugs, for assistance to allow certain disabled elderly persons to continue living at home instead of having to go to costly nursing homes or homes for the aged, to change income tax laws to eliminate the "marriage penalty" under which married couples sometimes have to pay more tax than unmarried people living together and having the same income, and to more equitably divide certain Social Security benefits between a husband and wife in order to recognize the wife's contribution to the marriage and the family economy through her maintenance of the home even though she may not have been gainfully employed in the traditional meaning of that phrase.

Finally, though their basic philosophy may have been valid, it is hard to see that any useful purpose was served by the 30-to-50 conservatives who departed in mid-conference in protest of what they saw as unfair liberal control of the meeting. If those persons who participated in the walkout engineered by certain Virginia delegates had stayed in their seats, they at least could have increased the conservative vote on various issues and could even have defeated one dealing with non-discrimination against homosexuals, which passed by a one-vote margin, 292-to-291.

The Washington Star

Washington, D.C., June 14, 1980

The maneuvers that have been going on in connection with the ongoing White House Conference on Families should inspire long thoughts on just about all the most piquant ambivalences bedeviling government of the people, by the people, for the people — in case anybody notices.

What, for example, is the measure of the common will? To what extent does leadership mean telling the public which way to go, and to what extent does it mean going where the most numerous and articulate groups want to go?

These ponderous imponderables come to mind with all the issues that promise to make the White House Conference on Families a particularly squirmy tin of vermicelli. Abortion. Homosexual marriage. Children's rights. That lot.

A key element in preparations for the conference has been choosing the 750 delegates. Each state worked out its own rules for selecting them — subject to Washington approval. In most states there was a combination of gubernatorial appointment, "random selection" and election at preliminary gatherings of interested people.

The National Advisory Committee and the Washington staff of the White House Conference on Families spent much of their energy trying to get around the tendency of the anti-abortion people to win landslides whenever there was an election for delegates. The Washington-appointed coordinators in each state monitor the "random selections" so they are anything but random. Application forms requiring information about religion, family size, organizational affiliations and other clues to people's viewpoints make it possible to shape the composition of the conference to meet prearranged standards of ethnic and ideological distribution.

This has been done in the name of "ensuring a balance" and keeping the conference from being "stacked" in favor of "special interest groups."

There is a good deal of semantic flimflam here. To begin with, the word "stacked" implies cheating; fixing the odds in a contest. It is at least an irony to apply it to arriving at a position of power by election rather than by appointment. In several states, including Maryland, the appointees include people who were turned down by voters in the elections.

The same goes for "special interest groups." You'll never hear the White House using that term on the troops fighting for the Equal Rights Amendment. Only on those who support traditional family values and oppose abortion.

To be sure, there are genuine philosophic quandaries in the picture. Democracy's head counts do not answer every important question about what "the people" want. They are notoriously poor at weighing the passions of the few against the mild inclinations of the many. They bypass the possibility that, as Anatole France put it, "Nonsense spoken by 50 million voices is nonsense still."

Single-issue politics, whether practiced by those who favor abortion or by those who are against it, by the National Rifle Association or by the people who write letters beginning "Dear Potential Hand-Gun Victim," does violence to the idea of rational popular government. Citizen rule presupposes that people will make decisions about their communities the way they make decisions about their own lives, deliberately or unconsciously balancing a multiplicity of needs and desires against each other. The chaos that results when they don't do that takes a little longer to show up in public affairs than in private life, but it is no less inevitable and destructive.

For all the talk of "balance" and "neutral representatives," the manipulations of the White House Conference on Families to lessen the influence of the anti-abortion forces offer no deliverance from the myopias of single-issue politics, however; they simply arm a different set of fanatics. And remind us yet again how firmly allied the Carter administration is to people promoting profound changes in the cultural norms of our society.

Caveat emptor.

Sunday Journal and Star

Lincoln, Neb., February 17, 1980

Sometimes you have to wonder if the American family will be able to withstand the forthcoming White House conference devoted to it.

Judging from delegates selected so far to attend the three summer sessions set for various parts of the country, it looks like the gatherings will be a prickly melange of "pro-family" representatives opposed to abortion, sex education and the Equal Rights Amendments, joined by a number of ardent feminists, and leavened by others classified as "moderates."

Alabama may boycott the conference and send nobody.

Controversy has beset the project from the start. In 1977 President Carter named Patricia Fleming, a black, divorced mother of three teen-agers, to head it. She quit after Roman Catholic groups asked for a co-director who was male and from a more "intact" family. Then plans for the conference were abandoned until the White House revived them last year.

Individuals and groups who might be described as conservative are eying the whole undertaking suspiciously. Many say they see no reason for the conference, or for Uncle Sam to poke into family matters. More liberal would-be participants, however, argue that a lot of what government does — in taxes, housing, Social Security, health services — affects families, and thus government needs to understand better their needs and problems.

So far there isn't even agreement on what constitutes a family. So-called pro-family groups want the definition limited to persons related by blood, marriage or adoption. Others think it should include anybody in loving or caring relationships, including possibly unmarried persons and homosexual couples. Fireworks, anyone?

In such an atmosphere of argument and indecision, one would almost have to bet the conference will have limited impact on the family. Government's performance on another front leads to this conclusion.

For years — lo, decades — politicians and public servants have talked about preserving the family farm. The consensus today almost surely is that they're not making much headway. A major reason, of course, is the lack of general agreement on exactly what *is* a family farm, and precisely what role it plays in the larger society.

By the same token, it's going to be hard to do much for the American family if there's continuing dispute over what the word means.

THE RICHMOND NEWS LEADER
Richmond, Va., June 16, 1980

One conclusion can be drawn from the White House Conference on Families held earlier this month in Baltimore: The family remains far too important a matter to be left to most of those who organize and attend family conferences. The Baltimore meeting — others will be held in Minneapolis and Los Angeles — reaffirmed some Liberal verities and even managed to produce some good ideas. Yet the conference, which had been designed to discuss how government can help strengthen the family, failed to consider how government instead weakens the family.

Few would cavil with tax breaks for legally married couples and those who care at home for elderly parents. Few would cavil with treatment programs for abusers of alcohol and other drugs. All were endorsed by the delegates. And yet: The conferees predictably approved such Leftist measures as abortion and homosexual rights, the so-called equal rights amendment, and annual income guaranteed by the federal government.

Rather than boutique items, a conference on families might do well to consider inflation — caused by government, curable by government, and manifestly the American family's bitterest enemy. And the Baltimore conclave failed even to define the family, a semantic exercise that should be the underpinning for any serious consideration of a legislative agenda. A precise definition of the family would have meant, for the conference-attending class, grappling with the issue of homosexuality and homosexual lifestyles — something Carter's conference shied away from.

As for the meeting's organization: Conservative spokesmen said organizing officials, who have tended to be arch-Leftists, weighted the session against them. The conservatives charged that information systematically was withheld from them, and the rules jiggered to guarantee Liberal victories. Some 100 conservatives walked out and have been criticized for so doing, yet they believed their walkout was the best possible way to call attention to their plight.

Carter's family policy, like his foreign policy, remains a fine example of good intentions gone wrong. Yet in this domestic issue, the damage can be contained. Carter sought to make human rights the cornerstone of his dealings with other nations. In foreign policy, the U.S. plays alone on a stage with real enemies and no friends — only nations whose interests coincide with those of the U.S. Policies that are erratic or ill-considered or wrong have real effects. No international consensus exists.

As to the family, among Americans a consensus *does* exist. Most Americans believe in the family, in its durable strengths and enduring virtues. The family *is* important — too important to be left to many of those who flit endlessly from meeting to meeting, championing homosexual marriage. If clambakes such as the White House conference are to help families, they should continue to toil on matters such as tax reform. Further, they should study other problems that afflict families and can be solved by governmental action — inflation, say — while saying No to kooky fads.

THE ARIZONA REPUBLIC
Phoenix, Ariz., June 10, 1980

THE WHITE HOUSE Conference on Families did the expected when it passed resolutions supporting abortion on demand, the Equal Rights Amendment, and gay rights.

It remains to be seen how any of those three causes will "strengthen the family structure," which was the goal set by President Carter when he referred to the family conference in this year's State of the Union speech.

Ironically, the pro-abortion resolution was carried by a vote of 292-291 taken in the absence of more than 50 anti-abortionists who decided to boycott the vote in order to express their opposition.

The liberal drift of the conference had been anticipated. Supporters of the welfare state were in complete command.

Other resolutions called for full employment, comprehensive health care, additional tax exemptions for families with natural or adopted children, tax credits for day care, for the handicapped and the elderly, and higher limits on the amount of money that can be earned by someone getting Social Security old-age payments.

Certainly there can be no objection to discussing these subjects at family conferences. There are, however, a good many other family problems that are far more fundamental.

How about some discussion on the effect of permissive moral standards on the American family?

Why not make an effort to determine whether private schools do a better job than public schools when it comes to strengthening bonds within a family?

Or wouldn't it be interesting to consider whether passage of the ERA would lead to a further loosening of the bonds that hold families together?

White House conferences are intended mainly as educational exercises. All too often they are turned into cheering sections for the attitudes espoused by whoever happens to be in the White House when they are held.

Two more White House Conferences on Families are planned for later this year, one in Minneapolis and one in Los Angeles.

Perhaps they will spend less time seeking a cure for all family problems and try to find the causes for the obvious disintegration of the American family.

Detroit Free Press
Detroit, Mich., April 11, 1980

WHEN PRESIDENT Carter first proposed the White House Conference on Families, it seemed about as controversial as scrambled eggs for breakfast. The conference would generate concern about the state of the nation's family life; participants would go home with an agenda for making institutions more aware of how their policies shape and alter families.

But something quite different has happened. The conference, which finally begins this summer after four years of wrangling, often has resembled a family feud. Its first director, a black divorcee, resigned. Joseph Califano, former secretary of health, education and welfare, was accused of ordering her to choose a white Catholic male from a traditional family as her co-director. Other controversies since have splintered or angered state delegations and groups.

Gov. Fob James of Alabama pulled the state out of the event after his wife charged it was not in accord with "Judeo-Christian values." Gov. Otis R. Bowen canceled the Indiana state convention, where delegates were to be chosen for the national conference. He was said to object because special interests were "fragmenting and undermining the problem-solving process."

What has made the upcoming conference such a hot potato? For one thing, the definition of a family is changing, with some forces arguing only for traditional husband-wife families while others say a family can be anything from a homosexual alliance to a commune. Disputes have raged over the process of selecting state delegates, and the issues they ought to emphasize.

Against this backdrop, plans proceed for the three White House conferences to be held in Baltimore (June 5-7), Minneapolis (June 19-21) and Los Angeles (July 10-12). Michigan will choose delegates to the Minneapolis conference at an April 19 convention in Lansing. Some 1,100 people have registered for a state meeting that is expected to be relatively tranquil. However, given the wide range of concerns expressed last December at public hearings in Detroit and Oak Park, disputes could break out among Michigan's delegates over welfare, taxes, homosexuality or other issues.

But the national conference clearly is an idea whose time has come. The record numbers of women who are working mandate a re-examination of institutional policies and their impact on family cohesion. The growth of the elderly population is another change calling for alterations in public policies. Should women be allowed to nurse children on the job? Should families with small children be subjected to repeated job transfers? Should Medicare pay for home care as it does for hospital care? Should parents with sick children be granted sick days by their employers?

These are just a few of the questions the national conference could tackle. The answers are too important to allow the differences and rivalries to stifle the debate.

Family Protection Act Sums Up "New Right's" Legislative Views

The Family Protection Act, which remained tied up in Senate and House committees during 1981, represented the essence of "New Right" thinking on social issues. Sponsored by Sens. Roger W. Jepsen (R, Iowa) and Paul Laxalt (R, Nev.) and Rep. Albert Lee Smith Jr. (R, Ala.), the bill called for a broader definition of parental rights in suspected child abuse cases and the curtailment of abortion and birth control counseling for unmarried minors. It would bar the government-funded Legal Services Corporation from taking on lawsuits that involved abortion, busing, divorce or homosexual rights. It would grant tax credits for the care of elderly and handicapped persons living with relatives and would provide tax exemptions for both natural and adopted children. It would give state and local governments more leeway in setting educational standards, including allowing school boards to prohibit the "intermingling" of the sexes in sports or other school activities, and would allow voluntary prayer in public schools. The bill also would limit federal regulation of church-run schools, foster homes and emergency shelters. A number of organizations opposed the measure, agreeing with the American Civil Liberties Union that, "Instead of being protection for the family, it represents more federal intrusion into decisions usually made by the family."

Detroit Free Press

Detroit, Mich., June 20, 1981

IT'S TIME to stop sniggering at congressional conservatives who want to wipe out women's rights. These people are serious. They have introduced a "Family Protection Bill" that could, among other things, scratch women's achievements from the history books, take a disinterested view of wife-beating and swell the number of teenage pregnancies. If that's protecting families, what would it take to hurt them?

Legislation introduced by Sen. Roger Jepsen of Iowa would bar the federal government from providing legal services in cases involving spouse abuse, gay rights, abortion, desegregation and the disciplining of children. It also would deny contraceptives and abortion information to teenagers without parental notification and withhold federal money from schools where parents disapprove of textbooks. According to Sen. Jepsen, and co-sponsors Sen. Paul Laxalt of Nevada and Rep. Albert Lee Smith Jr. of Alabama, the bill embodies good, old-fashioned family values. Not quite.

Shorn of its smug, flag-waving rhetoric, the bill endorses ignorance, historical inaccuracy and cruelty. Its approach to women in history is a good case in point. As a result of the feminist movement, the true story of the variety of roles played by women through the centuries is beginning to be told. Today, young people have a chance to learn about women's contributions to literature and the arts and sciences, about reformist heroines such as Jane Addams, Susan B. Anthony and Margaret Sanger, and about Mary Beard, wife of famed historian Charles Beard, who for a long time wasn't given credit for the seven books she co-authored with her husband.

Sen. Jepsen and his ilk would take us back to the days when women were portrayed only as wives and mothers. The bill would cut off federal funds to schools using books that offend parents, especially books "that denigrate the role of women as it has been historically understood." "We should appreciate the role of women as mother and homemaker," Sen. Jepsen says. Does that mean references to such women as Marie Curie, co-discoverer of polonium and radium, would be deleted from texts?

The hardest part of the bill to understand, though, is what it would do about battered spouses and children. Arch-conservatives say the government should get out of people's private lives. But if the government doesn't help protect those incapable of protecting themselves — two-year-olds, for instance, with parents bent on maiming them — who will? Perhaps future amendments to the bill will provide the answer.

What is happening in Congress is that a group of people angry about the effects of social change are trying to wipe them out. They include congressmen working to make abortions illegal and those who would deny minors contraceptive information. The New Right believes a return to chastity is the best way to curb illegitimacy. The steps these people are taking are far more likely to increase the number of illegitimate births and poverty among women.

During last year's Republican Convention, Sen. Jesse Helms, R-N.C., thundered against "the permissiveness, the pornography, the drugs, abortion, living together, divorce." Now he and other spokesmen for the New Right are attacking those targets by charting a moral blueprint for the country. Their efforts might be laughable in some circumstances. In today's climate of moral self-righteousness, they seem ill-informed and dangerous, a greater threat to individual and family liberty than any of the situations they want to correct.

The Miami Herald

Miami, Fla., June 23, 1981

FAMILIES are under extreme pressure and stress these days, no doubt about it. Peer pressure on teenagers, galloping materialism, economic hardship, and the erosion of confidence in major institutions all undermine family ties that ought to be nurtured.

It's hard to decipher, however, just how the proposed Family Protection Act of 1981 would bolster the typical American family. Rather, this darling of the Moral Majority seems designed to force upon the public a knothole view of what constitutes a healthy, desirable family life. That coercion can only *increase* the destructive pressure on households that either cannot afford or do not aspire to the supposed ideal of a working man, a stay-at-home wife, and 2.3 children.

Symptomatic of the punitive tone of the proposal is its implicit tolerance of wife-beating. This crime frequently is associated with excessive use of alcohol or other drugs and with other forms of illness whose treatment often is paid for with Federal funds. Sens. Paul Laxalt of Nevada and Roger Jepsen of Iowa and Rep. Albert Lee Smith of Alabama want the Federal Government to stop "interfering" with domestic violence.

The obvious presumption is that wife-beating is harmless, or natural, or both. Most Americans do not share that presumption.

In a similar vein, the bill would withhold Federal funds from public-school programs that "denigrate the role of women as it has been historically understood." The Republican sponsors do not offer examples of such denigration. It's hard to imagine that elected school-board members, unless they preside over a system populated solely by orphans, could so insult their constituents.

Even the National Organization for Women (NOW), that nemesis of the male supremacist, values the role of mother and housewife. The current national president of NOW, Eleanor Smeal, is herself a lifelong mother-homemaker. And Ms., the leading feminist journal, rarely fails to include articles on child-rearing in each issue.

This bill's sponsors read history very selectively. They don't want women to follow the historic example of Madame Curie, for example, nor of Harriet Tubman, who risked her own life many times to help slaves escape. Nor of Abigail Adams, who in 1774 warned her husband, John: "If particular care and attention is not paid to the ladies, we are determined to foment a rebellion and will not hold ourselves bound by any laws in which we have no voice or representation."

Women have many historic roles. Motherhood is one of the most important, but it is not — nor can it ever be — the only one. That is where the sponsors of the "family" act betray both their biases and their ignorance. Their proposal must not become law, because it denies both the history and the current reality of American families.

THE CHRISTIAN SCIENCE MONITOR

Boston, Mass., July 23, 1981

The proposed Family Protection Act of 1981 offers some improvements over the similar legislation that expired in committee during the last Congress. But it still contains enough dubious provisions to require enormous pruning and revision if it is not to warrant failure again. To take but one category, there are seemingly innocent items that open the door to evasion of the constitutional separation of church and state. Congress ought to resist any temptation to rubber stamp them in thoughtless deference to the "family" rubric, which deserves better than this, or to the increased prominence of the bill's far-right supporters since the last election.

There is every reason to pursue the stated aim of the legislation, which is to preserve the integrity of the American family. It is not too much to say that the integrity of the nation depends on the integrity of the family. Though this derives fundamentally from the principled conduct and devotion of individuals, it can be affected by government policy. The example is often given of welfare regulations that encourage fathers to stay away from home.

So a legislative effort to examine and reform federal policy on behalf of the family is welcome. And some proposals in the current bill look promising, such as tax relief to revive the home care for elderly dependents that used to be taken for granted. At least this kind of subsidy cannot be dismissed out of hand when subsidies are provided for tobacco and other less worthy causes.

But such items are overshadowed by ones that can hardly contribute to the security of the American family if, as it seems, they undermine hard-won constitutional or other legal guarantees. For example, the proposed "education savings accounts" would provide advantages for taxpayers setting aside money for children or other relatives to attend various educational institutions including private elementary and secondary schools. Since most of these schools in the United States are parochial schools, this appears to be a less obvious move toward the same ends as the tuition tax credit drive. The latter is under well-deserved attack not only on church-state grounds but as a threat to public education and an injustice to taxpayers who would have to make up the revenue lost through such credits.

Also in the church-state realm are provisions to exempt religious organizations such as schools and orphanages from certain federal regulations on employment and discrimination; to prevent any federal prohibition of released time from schools for "parenthood education" by churches; and, on the question of school prayer, to "reverse the last 19 years of Supreme Court decisions and subsequent case law regarding the constitutionality of state-sponsored religious exercises in the public schools."

Other aspects of the bill, too, seem designed to use federal policy for philosophical rather than strictly family objectives. Much has been made of the prohibition on federal funds for educational materials which "do not reflect a balance between the status role of men and women, do not reflect different ways in which women and men live, and do not contribute to the American way of life as it has been historically understood." Asked what this meant, Senator Jepsen, who introduced the bill, said: "We should appreciate the role of women as mother and homemaker . . . ."

America should and does appreciate this role of women, as well as all the additional roles they have distinguished through the years. But Congress may find the legislative means questionable even where it agrees with the philosophy.

Already omitted is a provision in the failed bill that would have made employment discrimination against homosexuals legal in all cases. But there remains a ban on the use of Legal Services funds in cases simply seeking to adjudicate homosexual rights. Indeed, no grants for any purposes could go to an organization whose activities include legal assistance in such cases. The same applies to cases relating to abortion and, as if it were somehow in the same category, divorce. Legal Services funds would also be withheld not only from litigation to *achieve* school desegregation, as at present, but from the currently permissible legal advice on a client's own legal rights and responsibilities in desegregation proceedings.

In further legal matters, such as juvenile delinquency, child abuse, and spouse abuse, the bill would insulate state statutes from federal action. Congress will have to decide whether states will act more responsibly on these tragic problems without federal involvement. Certainly it is in the direction of today's trend toward removing the federal hand. But in other provisions the Family Protection Act would bring federal influence more than ever into family decisionmaking.

For example, a taxpayer would get an additional $1,000 personal exemption in the year a child is born to or adopted by the taxpayer. There would be an extra $3,000 exemption if the adopted child is handicapped, of mixed race, or over the age of six. In the case of international adoption, expenses of more than $500 but not more than $4,500 would be deductible. Should federal policy be used for such specific goals in family building?

The list could go on. The challenge to Congress is not to hurry the bill through like some other recent legislation only to find out later that it might have acted differently if it had used more care.

ST. LOUIS POST-DISPATCH

St. Louis, Mo., August 2, 1981

A bill called the Family Protection Act of 1981 sounds innocuous enough, but the legislation, sponsored by Sen. Roger Jepsen of Iowa, is so riddled with bad proposals that it should meet a quick death in Congress. The few good provisions in the bill — tax relief for providing home care for elderly dependents or tax exemption to promote adoption of hard-to-place children — can and should be enacted in separate legislation.

Several features of the bill are questionable. It would grant tax advantages to persons setting up "education savings accounts" to be used to send children or other relatives to school, including private, parochial schools. Religious organizations would be exempt from certain federal employment and discrimination regulations. The bill would also "reverse the last 19 years of Supreme Court decisions and subsequent case law regarding the constitutionality of state-sponsored religious exercises in the public schools," the senator says. Thus it would allow states to mandate school prayers.

In his zeal to "protect the family," Mr. Jepsen is clearly talking only about his definition of the family. Federal funds could not be spent on educational materials that did not reflect "a balance between the status role of men and women" or the "different ways in which women and men live." Mr. Jepsen said this means, "We should appreciate the role of women as mother and homemaker..." Also no federal funds could go to an organization that provided legal assistance in homosexual rights, abortion or divorce cases. The bill, in short, would put into law one philosophy of society and would trample on the rights of those who do not conform. Such legislation does not even deserve serious consideration in Washington.

Minneapolis Tribune

Minneapolis, Minn., July 25, 1981

There's something contradictory about the "Family Protection" bill before Congress this session. It is sponsored by conservative congressmen generally opposed to broadening the federal government's role, and it is backed by an administration that pledged to "get the government off the backs of the people." Yet the bill would increase the government's involvement in family matters that have traditionally been private.

"I would characterize the bill as extremely paternalistic," said a professor of anthropology and family law. "The philosophy is that the state knows what is best for its citizens and may dictate to them accordingly." The bill is also an attempt to use federal funds and authority to promote a certain political and social philosophy, according to other critics.

One provision, for example, would prevent the Legal Services Corp. from using federal money to pay for poor clients' divorce cases, or for any case — including housing- or job-discrimination cases — involving a gay person's assertion of civil rights. Another would redefine "child abuse" to exclude "discipline or corporal punishment" administered by parents or persons designated by parents — this despite the violence perpetrated against children in the name of discipline.

Another provision — called "interventionist in really quite a radical way" by Republican Rep. Millicent Fenwick of New Jersey — would give parents broad authority to enter school classrooms and censor educational programs and material. Still another would deny federal funds to any educational program that doesn't portray women in traditional roles. ("It's preposterous," was Fenwick's comment on that proposal.) Other parts of the bill are probably unconstitutional; an example is a provision permitting school prayers.

Unfortunately, provisions like those outnumber sections with merit, such as those providing tax incentives for savings accounts for education, for housing elderly relatives and for corporate contributions to employer-employee day-care centers. Those provisions should be separated from the rest and considered along with other tax legislation. The rest of the bill doesn't deserve serious attention. The "Family Protection" bill wouldn't protect families; it would let the government mold them into what some congressmen think they should be.

"Chastity Program" Offered to Curb Teenage Pregnancies

The teenage pregnancy rate appears to be soaring, despite the increased availability of birth control information. Sen. Jeremiah Denton (R, Ala.) proposed a new way to combat the epidemic—a program to promote "self-discipline" among adolescents. His bill originally called for recommending "chastity" as a solution to "the problem of adolescent promiscuity," but that was dropped from the version passed by the Senate Labor and Human Resources Committee June 24. Nevertheless, the name "Chastity Act" was adopted with great glee by the public and the press. In heated debate in a House-Senate conference committee July 28, Rep. Toby Moffett (D, Conn.) declared, "We're going to be laughed out of every junior high school in America for being irrelevant." Denton's proposal was part of a $30-million measure funding counseling centers for pregnant teenagers. His bill would prohibit the centers from recommending abortions to pregnant teenage girls and would allow the centers to require parental consent before a pregnant teenager could participate in the centers' prenatal care, nutrition and other programs. The $30-million "adolescent family life" program, as Denton's bill was called, included $10 million for "scientific research on the causes and consequences of premarital adolescent sexual relations and pregnancy." A compromise version was adopted by the conference committee July 28, with Moffett casting the only dissenting vote. The compromise permitted the centers to supply information about abortion if the teenager and her parents requested it. However, the bill said the centers' major goal should be to "promote adoption as a positive option for adolescent parents."

ALBUQUERQUE JOURNAL
Albuquerque, N.M., September 26, 1981

There is a high aroma of hypocrisy in the almost clandestine passage by Congress of the teen-aged chastity bill.

From the Congress which meekly follows the leader committed to limiting the intrusion of government into the personal lives of Americans and big business, here is a $10 million research project to find the "causes and consequences of premarital adolescent sexual relations."

Most teenagers in America today could probably tell Congress the "causes and consequences" for considerably less than $10 million.

Another $20 million will be spent for "necessary services" for pregnant teenagers and teenaged parents. This from the same administration — and tacked onto the same budget reconciliation bill — that is cutting funds that provide lunches to children and milk to babies.

The dean of American conservatives, Sen. Barry Goldwater, R-Arizona, could have been speaking of this particular piece of legislation when he cautioned that narrow-issue, religion-oriented leaders are threatening the American system by "injecting religious issues into the affairs of state."

The "chastity bill" could be viewed differently if it had been openly debated in Congress, with all citizens hearing the attendant issues and seeing how their representatives voted.

Instead, the controversial act sneaked in the back door, hiding under the shirttails of the massive bill that detailed the budget cuts accompanying the Reagan tax cut. . .

"Lawmakers should not be bothered by single-issue lobbies when national security and economic survival at stake," said Goldwater.

And, perhaps even more importantly, lawmakers should not slip through single-issue lobby legislation while ostensibly wrestling with the grander issues of the day.

The moralists in the Reagan coalition lost their credibility with this bit of chicanery on the "chastity bill."

CHARLESTON EVENING POST
Charleston, S.C., September 22, 1981

Congress has passed the teen-age chastity bill, authorizing the expenditure of $30 million for "scientific research on the causes and consequences of premarital adolescent sexual relations." There's another $60 million in the bill to cover incidentals like executive travel and association dues.

Well, we could produce a paper, maybe even a book, on a subject like that. And while we don't know how scientific our work would be, we wager it would be at least as informative and useful as what the government is apt to produce with an army of Ph.D's and other assorted social workers. Ours would be a lot more readable, too. And it wouldn't cost the taxpayer any $30 million. Thirty dollars, maybe.

You know, the trouble with the world today is there are too many scientists, engineers and consultants dabbling in non-scientific and non-engineering fields. They're all trying to make something deep and mysterious out of something that isn't that at all. Our parents and our grandparents — maybe even you out there reading this, if you're a little long in the tooth — grew up knowing instinctively what your government is going to spend $30 million of your money trying to find out. Here's our assessment and we're giving it free:

The cause of teen-age pregnancy is kids fooling around. The consequences are apt to be babies. Some of this can never be prevented; it's the way of the world. A lot of it could, though, if parents spent more of their time consulting their kids, and kids spent less of theirs feeling neglected because they are.

The Idaho STATESMAN
Boise, Idaho, September 25, 1981

The so-called teen-age chastity bill is a monument to the unlikelihood that the federal government ever will get spending under control. Its passage, authorizing $10 million a year for three years to conduct "scientific research on the causes and consequences of premarital adolescent sexual relations," is eloquent testimony to the fact that Congress cannot tell the difference between necessary and unnecessary spending.

We doubt that there are many teen-agers or former teen-agers who could not tell the government the causes and consequences of adolescent sexuality. Most, we assume, would be happy to do it for far less than $10 million a year.

More depressing than the actual waste of money is the fact that the bill was sponsored by two men, freshman Sen. Jeremiah Denton, R-Ala., and Sen. Orrin G. Hatch, R-Utah, who are not at all shy in their lip service to President Reagan's efforts to balance the budget.

That laudable task will never be accomplished so long as its supposed proponents continue to whack at the top of the budget while adding their own political plums to the bottom.

DAYTON DAILY NEWS

Dayton, Ohio, May 8, 1981

The idea is stunningly unrealistic and so it stands a very good chance in the Washington of 1981: Sen. Jeremiah Denton, R-Ala., has introduced a bill that would convert into supposed chastity centers the federally aided counseling services that now give birth-control information to young people.

President Reagan's budget would end aid to the centers. Sen. Denton's bill would continue the aid but make it conditional on a "pro-family" emphasis in counseling. The Senate Human Resources Committee appears likely to approve the bill next week.

Denton

When it is casual, random, ignorantly undertaken or begun too young, teenage sex can be personally corrosive, even destructive. Its social consequences can be grave — unwanted pregnancies, sickly infants, marriages that almost always fall apart. Social attention to the issue is indeed needed. The place for intervention, however, is before, not after, sexual activity begins.

Sen. Denton's bill misunderstands the nature of the birth-control clinics and is unrealistic in its demands on them.

The clinics don't initiate teens into sex. Nearly all the kids who come to them already are sexually active. The history of human sexuality over the centuries shows that sexual activity, once begun, almost always continues, except for episodic time-outs. Only rarely can anyone be yelled back into lasting continence, though counseling at the centers does emphasize that abstinence should be respected and is the surest birth control.

If the Denton bill passes, the centers would not be allowed to give teens birth control information without their parents' consent, and they would be barred from telling teens about abortion. The centers would be required to give "self-discipline" and "pro-family" lectures to the youths who come to them.

This is a formula for setting up teenage sex counseling to which teens in need of sex counseling will not come. The predictable consequences are, not less teenage sex, but more teenage pregnancies, abortions and marriages.

THE COMMERCIAL APPEAL

Memphis, Tenn., May 28, 1981

OPPOSITES SELDOM attract in politics, at least, and Sens. Edward M. Kennedy and Jeremiah Denton are about as opposite as they come.

Kennedy is the veteran Massachusetts Democrat who's spent a lifetime in politics championing liberal causes. Denton, whose career was the military, is a newcomer to politics and a New Right Republican sent to Congress last year by the state of Alabama. Yet, despite basic differences between these two men, they reportedly have reached agreement on legislation to help pregnant teenagers, whose numbers have reached epidemic proportions.

Denton is concerned about American morality, and especially teenage sex. The senator, whose language is often as strong as his convictions, puts it simply: "Look, I don't care if they tickle where it itches — I'm talking about screwing." Thus, he's introduced legislation for an Adolescent Family Life program — his so-called antipromiscuity bill — to replace an expiring Kennedy program, which has provided adolescent pregnancy centers and family counseling.

Under a compromise the two have reached, $20 million would keep up the present program while another $10 million would go for what Denton wants: research on ways to discourage teenage pregnancies, on the social consequences of teenage sexual activity, and on the health risks of long-term Pill use and early-age abortions.

TO DEAL WITH the problem of teenage pregnancy both before and after the fact is a sensible approach. If Kennedy and Denton can get together on a crisis that's costing this nation's children dearly and the rest of us, as well, why can't state and local officials also agree on ways to help?

Chicago Defender

Chicago, Ill., July 18, 1981

A $30 million-dollar program to promote chastity among teenagers sounds like a blue note in an age where talks of sexual morality is adversely orchestrated. Parents who have been brought up under strict observance of sexual abstinence are deviating shockingly from their own training.

To curb the threat to the basic moral structure of our society, Senator Jeremiah A. Denton (R-Ala.) proposes a 30 million dollar program that would put a stop to adolescent promiscuity and its attendant emotional and moral damages.

His bill would write into law a new definition of promiscuity. And its purpose is to "promote self-discipline, and chastity and other positive family-centered approaches to the problems of adolescent promiscuity and pregnancy. This program deserves public support.

The Houston Post

Houston, Texas, November 25, 1981

Congress speaks of spending $30 million to encourage teen-agers to practice "self-discipline and responsibility in matters of human sexuality." The Department of Health and Human Services' new director of federal adolescent pregnancy programs, Marjory Mecklenburg, has announced a policy based on the principle that unmarried teen-agers be taught to say no. Few adults who have experienced parenthood, even in the best of circumstances, would challenge the goal of Congress or the department.

But it will take a transformation of our entire society to teach some future generation of teen-agers the rewards of continence and the advantages of gaining adulthood, an education and marriage before producing a family. A congressional appropriation of $30 million or a departmental policy will not quickly change youthful mores that have been in the making for 30 years.

Four in 10 teen-age girls now become pregnant, two in 10 give birth. Of the 554,000 teen-age girls who gave birth in 1978, more than half were unmarried. They have neither the moral nor financial support of a husband. Eleven thousand of these mothers were younger than 15, and 203,000 were between 15 and 17 — scarcely the age for maternal maturity. More than a million teen-age girls become pregnant every year. Sixty percent of the young mothers have not finished high school. Of 600,000 families headed by young mothers under the age of 25, two out of three are poor. And having had one child, the 14- or 16-year-old is more likely to have another than her childless counterpart still in high school.

The burden of teen-age pregnancy falls first on the girl's parents, if she has them. Ultimately, it falls on society. Teen-age parenthood is a direct burden on the city of Houston, the state of Texas, the people of the nation. It is society that must provide medical help, try to prevent child abuse, work to educate this new generation to a wiser and more substantial future than those who mothered it. With the federal government planning to withdraw from programs of preventing birth, Planned Parenthood and other non-profit agencies will have to try harder, to take on larger caseloads, to reach more children before they act to give birth to children. The United States has one of the highest teen-age birth rates of any country in the world. It is a record to be challenged, a trend to be reversed.

The State

Columbia, S.C., September 17, 1981

THE TRAGEDY of pregnancies among unwed teenagers is certainly a concern of American society, and the concern is now an official program of the United States government.

Thirty million dollars a year for the next three years, beginning in 1982, has been authorized by Congress to help to care for unwed mothers and fathers, and parents of both. The money will also fund programs to discourage premarital sexual relations among teenagers, and also to fund research on the causes and consequences of such activity.

The authors of this legislation have been on the side of the angels, almost unassailable for their high motives and concern. Such legislation, nevertheless, involves personal moral, religious and ethical concerns.

This is not the province of government, although it is clear many families, churches and other influential institutions of our society have failed many individual youngsters.

It is now the law of the land. Its results should be closely monitored to see if the assumptions of the authors are justified, that the government can do what society won't do or hasn't done for itself. The question is one of legislating morals, and we doubt that can ever be done.

Newsday

Long Island, N.Y., August 9, 1981

Not all conservatives want the government to stay out of people's private lives. Sen. Jeremiah Denton (R-Ala.), for instance, has actually persuaded Congress to spend money trying to teach teenagers to say no to sex. Regrettably, his program would also weaken government-sponsored efforts to help sexually active girls avoid pregnancies.

"We're going to be laughed out of every junior high school in America for being irrelevant," warned one congressional opponent, Rep. Toby Moffett (D-Conn.).

Denton's program replaces one instituted in 1978 to fund prenatal and postnatal care for teenage girls, along with counseling on nutrition and contraception. Under the new rules, a teenager who wants to know about contraception will need her parents' permission. Furthermore, counselors won't be permitted to discuss abortion as an option unless the girl and her parents request it. Instead, teenagers will be encouraged to have their babies and give them up for adoption.

Denton's measure, nicknamed "the teenage chastity act," also calls for spending as much as $10 million a year on "scientific research on the causes and consequences of premarital adolescent sex-ual relations and pregnancy." But the causes and consequences seem rather obvious; what's needed is more effort to prevent girls who are children themselves from becoming mothers.

Obviously there's nothing wrong with urging young girls to abstain from sex: Parents have been doing that since time immemorial. Just as obviously, it hasn't been altogether effective. And it's not very likely that the teenagers who are most in need of sex education or contraception would ask their parents' permission to seek it. After all, outside counseling wouldn't be necessary if the kids were getting the information they need at home.

Oregon Journal

Portland, Ore., August 12, 1981

A congressional dispute over family planning programs seems to have been ironed out. Compromises were made by both sides, and the bill approved by House-Senate conferees probably is as good as can be obtained, given a large number of enemies in Congress of family planning.

Family planning would continue as a separate categorical program run by the federal government instead of being included in block grant state appropriations.

Conservatives, generally the ones who have spent seven months complaining about federal spending, added $30 million for a new teenage sexuality program. One-third of of the money would be spent on "scientific research on the causes and consequences of premarital adolescent sexual relations and pregnancy." That sounds like a researcher's boondoggle, but it also was the price for getting the bill through conference committee.

Nearly half of the three-year, $30 million appropriation would be spent to continue the existing program for prenatal care, nutrition counseling and other services to pregnant teenagers.

The rest of the money would be spent on prevention services which now are provided by maternity homes, YWCAs and others groups that operate programs for pregnant teens.

Earlier legislation prohibited any reference to abortion during counseling sessions, but conferees softened that provision. Information about abortion can be provided if a pregnant teenager and her parents request it.

To receive counseling, a teenager would have to have parental consent, which could pose a hurdle to kids reluctant to tell a parent about pregnancy. However, the parents usually learn about it eventually. Permission wouldn't be needed for testing for pregnancy or venereal disease.

How the $10 million is spent for "scientific research" deserves scrutiny. Sen. Jeremiah Denton, R-Ala., who has support from anti-abortion groups, suggested spending for "outreach services to teenagers to tell them it's okay to say 'no'."

One conferee, Rep. Toby Moffett, D-Conn., called the approach "store-front chastity centers" and warned that, "We're going to be laughed out of every junior high school in America for being irrelevant."

Other funds are directed at low-income families, explaining different family planning alternatives. Despite some congressional restrictions, it appears family planning programs will continue much as before. They should be, on this crowded planet.

The Register

Santa Ana, Calif., July 5, 1981

Now that Republicans control the U.S. Senate, some of them seem determined to prove that they can dream up as many silly ways to waste taxpayers' money as the Democrats used to.

The most obvious recent case in point was the passage by the Labor and Human Resources Committee of a $30 million bill that would encourage teen-agers to practice "self-discipline and responsibility in matters of human sexuality" and also promote adoption as an alternative to adolescent parenthood.

This one is the special pet of Sen. Jeremiah Denton of Alabama, who emerged from captivity as a POW in Vietnam as something of a hero and parlayed it into a seat in the Senate. Denton is not really a villain, and his feelings on the importance of strong family ties as a key to adolescent responsibility are obviously sincere. His problem is that he shares the common misperception that the way to approach a problem is to throw federal money at it.

It's significant that at the same session the committee also approved bills to reauthorize the Legal Services program, Head Start, the Older Americans Act and the Domestic Volunteer Services act. These are all programs that embody worthy ideas, but end up employing bureaucrats and consultants and institutionalizing problems instead of solving them.

The whole committee decided to help Denton get his little pet passed, including Sens. Edward Kennedy, Thomas Eagleton and Orrin Hatch.

Committee chairman Hatch of Utah, who is being touted as future presidential timber by certain conservatives, noted that Denton has received a certain measure of lampooning and criticism for his sponsorship of this bill.

"It should send some message to the media and others that this bill was reported out of this committee without objection even though there are wide ideological differences on the panel," quoth Senator Hatch.

It certainly does send us a message, though it's doubtless not the one Hatch had in mind.

Nobody is minding the store, and the taxpayers are getting the shaft as usual.

The Courier-Journal
Louisville, Ky., August 14, 1981

AMONG the wiser congressional actions in the hectic budget cutting before the August recess was a decision to renew and slightly expand a fledgling program of adolescent pregnancy counseling. But concessions made to conservative, "pro-chastity" forces could imperil some of its effectiveness.

The rising problem of teen-age pregnancy led Congress three years ago to appropriate funds for regional centers (one of them at Elkhart, Indiana) to coordinate existing counseling and care services across the country. These include prenatal and postnatal care, venereal-disease screening, adoption counseling and helping pregnant adolescents to stay in school. Twenty-seven programs received a total of $6.4 million in fiscal 1980-81, the first full year of operation. Congress has now approved a three-year extension at $30 million annually.

That's the plus side. The minus is that Senator Kennedy, the program's prime sponsor, had to make substantial concessions to New Right demands for a divided emphasis that could seriously impair the program's effectiveness.

The easiest concession was the most publicized: about one-fifth of the money is to be spent for what critics dubbed "store-front chastity centers." The idea, pushed hardest by Alabama Republican Jeremiah Denton, is simple. The government would promote among teen-agers the notion that it's "okay to say no."

Whether that will have any impact on adolescents is problematical: one congressman said, "We're going to be laughed out of every junior high school in America for being irrelevant." But who knows? Anti-smoking and anti-drug campaigns seem to have helped in persuading some youngsters to shun those habits. If $6.6 million keeps a lot of unmarried teen-agers from bearing children at heavy cost to society, the cost could be a bargain.

More serious are new restrictions on counseling in the Adolescent Pregnancy Programs, which have been conducted by family planning organizations, schools, hospitals and YWCAs. To troubled, pregnant teen-agers they must now stress adoption, which appeals to senators with a middle-class mentality but is seldom a solution for the poor and for minorities. They can't mention abortion unless the youngster asks about it. And no youngster can be counseled or treated without parental permission, except in cases of pregnancy and venereal disease testing.

Ideally, teens could talk to their parents about such matters. Real life suggests that they probably won't. If they won't, it does not follow that they will foreswear sexual activity. It will just mean that they won't have the counseling they need. Ignorance in this realm is not bliss; the result will no doubt be more pregnancies and disease and their tragic by-product: side-tracked lives.

Senator Denton wanted the changes because he believed the government's provision of contraceptive services and counseling had been teaching teens to say "yes." But that's a simplistic view. As the president of Planned Parenthood Federation of America said last May in Louisville, most young people seek such services only after they become sexually active. Her organization and those involved in the teen program are mainly there to head off the disastrous effects.

Young people *should* be taught to say no — especially in a society where the message of movies, television, music and jeans ads is that it's more acceptable to say yes. If it makes Congress happy to spend money for such a purpose, fine. But what Senator Denton and his New Right allies have done is the equivalent of requiring that hospitals devote some of their precious staff time and money to educating the public on how to stay healthy. The result of giving an institution or agency such a mixed assignment is usually that both roles suffer.

Actually Senator Denton and his colleagues have been leaders in demanding that government get out of the lives of the people. It would be nice sometimes if they'd take their own advice.

The Oregonian
Portland, Ore., July 4, 1981

The U.S. Senate Labor and Resources Committee has approved a bill that it hopes will deal with the increasing number of sexually active adolescents, especially those who become pregnant. The problem is evident. The Senate committee's solution, though, is naive and simplistic.

The proposal, which opponents have nicknamed the chastity bill, encourages "self-discipline and responsibility in matters of human sexuality." No argument with that. The bill also has a strong and commendable commitment to family involvement in teen pregnancy.

Indeed, good parent-child rapport should make it easier for teen-agers to talk with parents about this problem. But the bill does not now do anything to foster conditions for such rapport.

Also, one of the bill's fantasies is that government counseling and support programs — not yet designed or debated by the Senate — somehow can succeed where parents, churches and non-profit secular groups have had only marginal success.

Presenting adoption as a positive option for pregnant adolescents is one of the most controversial objects of the bill, because abortion services, as well as counseling and referral for abortion, would be excluded from this bill's government support.

The bill could do some good in providing support services for adolescent mothers and stating "prevention of adolescent sexual activity and adolescent pregnancy depends primarily upon developing strong family values and close family ties."

However, taken as a whole, the bill wallows in wishful thinking, and the proposed $30 million appropriation would do little to alleviate teen-age sexual promiscuity.

Los Angeles Times
Los Angeles, Calif., May 11, 1981

Sen. Jeremiah Denton (R-Ala.) described far better than we ever could the objections to his bill to use federal money to "promote self-discipline and chastity" among teen-agers instead of giving them birth-control information. Said Denton: "You can have a great time with these bills. You can say we are going back to 1450. There is going to be a great pillorying about this."

As well there should be. It is indeed tempting to take a few funny shots at Denton and dismiss the whole thing as so much mumbo-jumbo. But that would be wrong.

In the first place, the bill is receiving a serious hearing in the U.S. Senate, and may pass the Senate Committee on Human Resources this week. In the second place, it would, if enacted, divert resources from curbing the epidemic of teen-age pregnancies to some vague "pro-family emphasis." And, in the third place, it distorts very legitimate parental concern for elements of their children's lives that seem to be slipping out of control.

Denton's bill would provide $30 million for the continued operation of 27 centers, but would bar them from referring pregnant teen-agers to abortion clinics. Teen-age girls would also be required to get their parents' permission before being provided with birth-control information or devices.

The centers, one of which is in Inglewood, are administered by the federal government's Office of Adolescent Pregnancy Programs. The programs try to help young women learn to care for their babies, return to school and find jobs. Counseling on how to avoid future pregnancies is included, but is not the program's main focus.

Ironically, Denton's bill represents one of the few proposed increases in federal spending this year. Health and Human Services Secretary Richard S. Schweiker had already expressed interest in reducing the federal role in promoting birth control and sex education, and the Reagan Administration planned to leave spending for these programs up to the states.

Yes, it is tempting to say that Denton would love to create a Federal Chastity Commission to go along with the Federal Bureau of Pregnancy Investigation to check that abortion has been stamped out. But it is no laughing matter. It is yet another case of attempting to impose legislatively one group's moral standards on every group.

Sex, Sen. Denton, is here to stay, and teen-agers know it. They also need to know how to deal with it realistically; this bill would hurt, not help.

Falwell Loses Bid to Halt *Penthouse* Interview

A bid by Moral Majority leader Jerry Falwell to halt the distribution of *Penthouse* magazine was defeated Feb. 2 by a judge in Lynchburg, Va. Falwell had brought suit to suspend the magazine and to obtain $50 million in damages upon learning that an interview he had given to two freelance journalists would appear in the March issue of the sex magazine. A preliminary injunction against *Penthouse* was issued Jan. 30, after 500,000 copies had been distributed nationwide. District Court Judge James C. Turk lifted the injunction three days later, saying the "proper relief is to seek compensatory damages after the fact, rather than prior restraint." It was the first time the Moral Majority had actively sought to block the dissemination of a publication. Falwell said the reporters had told him the article would appear in a book and a London newspaper and not in a sex-oriented publication. In the interview, the Moral Majority leader had expressed strong dislike of pornography and had criticized former President Jimmy Carter for giving an interview to *Playboy* in 1976. Falwell's embarrassment was not ruled sufficient to obtain damages, however. Judge Turk ruled in August that Falwell could not prove that the interview had invaded his privacy or defamed his character. Turk added that the First Amendment rights of *Penthouse's* publishers could not be modified because of Falwell's personal objections.

THE SACRAMENTO BEE

Sacramento, Calif., February 12, 1981

We're not surprised that the Rev. Jerry Falwell, head of Moral Majority, wanted to keep the March issue of Penthouse locked up in a warehouse. The magazine can hardly be regarded as one of his favorite publications, and one can therefore understand why he cried foul when it published an interview with him that he said was obtained under false pretenses. Falwell said he didn't want to be caught in such company — at least not under circumstances where his followers might assume he had willingly entered this journalistic den of iniquity. It is surprising, however, that U.S. District Court Judge James C. Turk granted a two-day restraining order prohibiting distribution of the magazine until a motion for a temporary injunction could be heard. Judge Turk refused to grant the injunction, fortunately, and the magazine is now being distributed while Falwell is free to pursue a $10 million damage suit that charges he was hoodwinked by the magazine's interviewers. Still, it's regrettable that the first order was granted at all. If it can be accomplished with Penthouse, there's no legal reason it can't be done to the New York Times, the Washinton Post or any other publication.

Arkansas Gazette.

Little Rock, Ark., February 3, 1981

The Rev. Jerry Falwell is learning that the road to righteousness is sometimes a bumpy one. Over the weekend, Mr. Falwell, leader of the Moral Majority, suffered two setbacks.

On Sunday the Rev. Billy Graham, in an interview in *Parade* magazine, challenged the Moral Majority's expanding role in national politics. Mr. Graham said to a *Parade* writer: "It would disturb me if there was a wedding between religious fundamentalists and the political right. The hard right has no interest in religion except to manipulate it." Billy Graham is the most famous evangelist in the world, one who has had his own painful experiences dabbling in politics and therefore speaks with some authority on the subject.

Then on Monday morning a U.S. district judge at Lynchburg, Va., dissolved an injunction he had granted, briefly, at Mr. Falwell's behest, against the distribution of the current issue of *Penthouse* magazine. The issue of *Penthouse* will be sold as usual, probably sold out, complete with a disputed article that is an interview with Jerry Falwell. For the benefit of the uninitiated, *Penthouse* is a girlie magazine that features all manner of scandalous carryings-on, and Mr. Falwell said that the controverted interview was gotten under false pretenses — i.e., without his knowledge that it was for publication in *Penthouse*.

It does seem unlikely that Mr. Falwell would have knowingly granted an interview to a magazine whose subject matter is as lurid as *Penthouse's*. Nevertheless, the idea of an injunction against distribution of any publication is violative of the First Amendment. The Supreme Court has been absolutely clear in its dictum against prior restraint of publication, at least in cases that don't involve national security. No one has contended, at least not yet, that the national interest and Jerry Falwell's are identical.

Mr. Falwell is entitled, of course, to seek redress in some kind of suit for damages, libel or whatever, and press his case for as many millions as he chooses. A TV evangelist of his following may not need the money but he has the right to sue. What he does not have the right to do is stop any publication from appearing. The U.S. system doesn't work that way.

Roanoke Times & World-News

Roanoke, Va., February 2, 1981

Whatever one thinks of Penthouse magazine or of the Rev. Jerry Falwell is beside the point. U. S. District Judge James C. Turk's temporary order Friday to halt distribution of the magazine, until a hearing today in federal court in Roanoke, is wrong. It is a prior restraint on speech and a clear violation of the First Amendment to the U. S. Constitution.

Falwell, angry because his interview with two free-lance journalists is to appear in the March issue of the publication, asked for the restraining order in connection with a $10 million suit against the magazine's publishers. The interviewers, Falwell claims, agreed not to sell the story to a magazine like Penthouse. Spokesmen for the magazine have been quoted as saying the journalists made no such promise.

As a practical matter, the injury to free speech may seem slight. So what if the March issue of Penthouse hits the stands a few days late? As a matter of principle, however, the injury is grave. Words and ideas are fragile, precious commodities; the idea of any government official holding them hostage is — or should be — abhorrent in an America devoted to freedom of speech.

One need not believe that free speech is an absolute right in order to see the danger of trampling on it. The chance that Jerry Falwell might be embarrassed hardly qualifies as the kind of clear, overriding danger to the national security over which the issue of prior restraint may be arguable. If Falwell has been, or is about to be, wronged, there is a remedy that does not require a judge to forget the Constitution. The Lynchburg evangelist can have his day in court, *after* publication; if he proves a breach of contract, or an actionable libel, he can collect damages.

By granting the request to block distribution of the magazine, Judge Turk fell into an absurd, tragic trap. It is absurd because, if the magazine is not distributed, Falwell has no reason to claim he has been damaged. It is ironically tragic because neither party, Falwell or the magazine, is losing much. For Falwell, the point is being made that publication of the interview in Penthouse is over his objections. The magazine's publishers can look forward to the likelihood of brisk sales when the ban is lifted, as seems inevitable. It is the First Amendment, which exists to protect all Americans, that has been dealt the serious blow.

Richmond Times-Dispatch

Richmond, Va., February 5, 1981

United States District Judge James Turk acted properly Monday in refusing to bar the distribution of a magazine carrying an allegedly deceptively obtained interview with the Rev. Jerry Falwell of Lynchburg. Mr. Falwell may have ample justification for complaining about the article, but his dispute with the magazine — *Penthouse* — and the writers is a civil matter that does not merit judicial injunctive action.

It is Mr. Falwell's contention that the two free-lance authors who conducted the interview assured him that they would not sell their article to any pornographic publication, including *Penthouse.* That the interview does appear in that magazine embarrasses Mr. Falwell, who is one of the nation's most prominent conservative religious leaders and the founder of Moral Majority. In fact, he argues, his reputation as an evangelist has been damaged.

This may be true. But as Judge Turk noted, Mr. Falwell's remedy is to seek redress in a civil suit against the magazine and the authors. Only in the face of extreme danger, such as immediate threats to national security, can courts justify the imposition of prior restraints on publications; and such conditions obviously did not prevail in this case.

The Seattle Times

Seattle, Wash., August 10, 1981

ALL that fuss between the Rev. Jerry Falwell, Moral Majority founder, and Penthouse magazine reaffirms a principle that shouldn't have needed reaffirming: First Amendment rights can't hinge on personal likes or dislikes.

In dismissing Falwell's $50 million damage suit against Penthouse, Federal Judge James Turk of Roanoke, Va., declared:

"The First Amendment freedoms of speech and press are too precious to be eroded or undermined by the likes and dislikes of persons who invite attention and publicity by their own voluntary actions."

At first, Falwell unsuccessfully sought to halt distribution of Penthouse's March issue, which carried an interview he had given to two free-lance writers. They sold it to Penthouse against his wishes. Falwell charged his privacy was invaded and he was defamed by having the interview appear in the sex-oriented magazine.

The judge said Falwell, at best, might have a breach-of-contract case against the two free-lancers, and might want to refile his suit as such.

The case was not a question of what we, the Moral Majority or anybody else might think of Penthouse. As the court made clear, it was a direct assault on the right of free speech and press.

It is a decision ensuring Falwell his right — derived from that same First Amendment — to speak out against the morality of Penthouse.

The Washington Post

Washington, D.C., February 3, 1981

IT IS EASY to imagine the joy that must have burst out in the offices of Penthouse magazine when its editors got a chance to buy an interview with the Rev. Jerry Falwell. By publishing it, the magazine could not only embarrass one of those who preaches against publications such as itself but could also continue as well the process of protecting itself against legal action by printing articles that—as distinct from its pictures—have what is called redeeming social value.

It is equally easy to imagine the chagrin that must have engulfed Rev. Falwell's headquarters last Thursday when it was learned that his words, name and picture were to appear tucked in among artwork neither he nor we would care to describe. Rev. Falwell was the preacher who had sharply criticized Jimmy Carter for granting an interview to Playboy, and he says he had believed his own interview was to be used in some publication on religion and politics.

Rev. Falwell did what most people do these days when they feel aggrieved. He called a lawyer. After failing in an attempt to enjoin the distribution of this particular issue of Penthouse, Rev. Falwell now says he will press his claim that his reputation has been damaged.

Perhaps he will be successful. But this is not likely unless he had a solid agreement about where that interview could be used. Free-lance journalists like to sell their work to publications that pay well, and Penthouse is reputed to be a magazine that does just that.

Whichever way the case goes, however, both Penthouse and Rev. Falwell have already won. The magazine has gotten jillions worth of publicity and Rev. Falwell has gotten front-page exposure once again for combating the forces of lasciviousness and related evil. His reputation is hardly likely to suffer with his followers on account of this. What better place to save the fallen than in the pages of Penthouse magazine?

St. Petersburg Times

St. Petersburg, Fla., October 6, 1981

SOME of the Moral Majority's leaders met in the Bahamas the other day and set the group's top priority for the year ahead: a nationwide campaign to stamp out pornography.

In South Florida, however, officials aren't waiting for the Rev. Jerry Falwell's flock to prod them. They're already acting. In Fort Lauderdale a few days ago, for example, city commissioners unanimously approved an ordinance that its backers say will shut down adult bookstores.

In Dade County, meanwhile, a criminal-justice system that is said to be seriously overloaded nonetheless found time to stage new raids against such stores and arrest 16 clerks.

Nobody really knows all of pornography's effects on society. Experts disagree. Presidential commissions have divided. Knowledgeable people can't even reach a consensus on the experience of nations such as Denmark, which years ago legalized pornography with no apparent ill effects.

There *is* a consensus, however, that organized crime is deeply involved in the sale and distribution of such materials in the United States. That's why Dade's Organized Crime Bureau has helped map strategy for local raids. Many lawmen believe that selling pornography and drugs helps bankroll the Mob's other activities.

As great a threat as organized crime is, however, there are also dangers that arise whenever government is given overly broad authority to determine what citizens of a free society may or may not read.

Most well-adjusted individuals might regard the reading matter available in most adult bookstores as tasteless or disgusting. Nonetheless, the crucial question remains: Once you let government set limits on what citizens may read, where do you stop?

There is abundant evidence that the Moral Majority's view of what is obscene would not stop with extreme examples. It could well extend to such established publications as *Playboy* and *Penthouse,* which contain social commentary as well as erotic photographs.

Moreover, once government decides to regulate reading material, who will determine what is permissible and what is not? Judges? Police? Prosecutors? Boards of censorship? Private groups?

These questions should give pause even to thoughtful and law-abiding citizens who wouldn't be caught dead entering an adult bookstore. Moreover, many taxpayers may well question the sense of priorities that leads to a considerable investment of time by police, prosecutors, and courts in order to arrest 16 clerks. Does this seriously hamper organized crime?

Weighing the costs and risks against the dubious benefits raises serious doubts about government crackdowns on pornography. A far better target for law enforcement's resources and the Moral Majority's fervor would be guns. They've hurt society much more than pornography has.

EVENING EXPRESS

Portland, Maine, February 4, 1981

There ought to be no quarreling with the decision of a U.S. district judge to refuse to halt the publication of an issue of Penthouse magazine because it contained an interview with Rev. Jerry Falwell, the founder of Moral Majority.

If Falwell is right in claiming the interview was obtained "surreptitiously and by deceit," he is free to proceed in court to recover damages. But that allegation can't be used as the basis for prior restraint of the press.

One of the underpinnings of the First Amendment is judicial acceptance of the principle that government may not forbid publication in advance. To do otherwise would be to savage free speech. That principle applies just as much to Falwell as it did to then President Nixon when he unsuccessfully sought to prevent publication of the so-called Pentagon Papers.

It is understandable that Falwell objects to having his interview published in a magazine he considers salacious. The interview is sandwiched between full-page photographs of nude women and a report on pimps. His embarrassment must be all the more acute since, in the interview, he is critical of Jimmy Carter consenting to a 1976 interview which appeared in Playboy magazine, a Penthouse rival.

Nonetheless, Falwell's assertion that the interviewers assured him the article would not appear in a magazine like Penthouse is not justification to prevent publication, particularly since the interviewers deny Falwell's claim.

Those claims and counterclaims must now be sorted out in a civil court suit, assuming Falwell cares to press his case. If he has been damaged or deceived, or both, and can prove it, then he may recover.

But what he cannot do, as the district judge rightly noted, is throw a monkey wrench into a printing press. To do so would render the First Amendment meaningless.

Post-Tribune

Gary, Ind., February 5, 1981

We are relieved that that Virginia federal judge has withdrawn his ban on distribution of the March issue of Penthouse magazine.

The relief is not linked to any particular urge to peruse much of its generally lewd content.

Neither is it based on the possibility the publication may embarrass the Rev. Jerry Falwell whose tendency to link religion and politics we admit irritates us.

It is rather that "prior restraint" of any publication amounts to an infringement on the First Amendment which we think is potentially dangerous to the rights it is designed to protect.

Falwell charges that the interview with him which appears in the magazine was obtained under false pretenses and that its inclusion in such a rag as Penthouse will do him damage. We understand his concern and still wonder if Jimmy Carter was more hurt or helped by the interview he gave the generally less offensive girlie-magazine Playboy (although that was in an election that he won.)

Still, we agree with the judge's later holding that suit to recover "compensatory damages" is the "proper relief" rather than banning distribution of the magazine as was first temporarily ordered. We regret that the First Amendment is used at at times to protect publication of considerable we regard as filth. Still, in a nation governed "by laws, not men," protection of the right of free speech must include protection of some we object to.

The Chattanooga Times

Chattanooga, Tenn., August 12, 1981

In dismissing evangelist Jerry Falwell's $60 million lawsuit against *Penthouse* magazine, U.S. District Judge James Turk has effectively turned back what he called a "broad-based attack" on two of this nation's most precious freedoms, the freedom of speech and press. Whatever your opinion of *Penthouse,* it is difficult to disagree with the judge's reasoning.

The case grew out of an interview published in the magazine last March. Mr. Falwell, a Baptist minister and head of the Moral Majority, claimed that when he gave the interviews last year to two free-lance writers, he told them they couldn't sell the stories to *Penthouse,* which he considers pornographic.

But although Judge Turk left Mr. Falwell the option of pursuing the matter as a contract dispute, he noted pointedly: "(Mr. Falwell) is trampling upon fundamental constitutional freedoms by seeking to convert what is essentially a private contractual dispute into a broad-based attack on those principles of freedom of speech and press which are essential to a free society."

Judge Turk's opinion knocked down one by one the claims cited in the Falwell lawsuit. The evangelist claimed, for instance, that his statements to the press are protected by a common law copyright. There is no such law, the judge wrote, adding that Mr. Falwell "cannot seriously contend that each of his responses (in the interview) is a product of his intellectual labors which should be recognized as a literary or even intellectual creation. There is nothing concrete which distinguishes his particular expression of ideas from the ordinary."

Further, there was nothing defamatory in the interview since even Mr. Falwell admitted the writers accurately reproduced his comments. And there was no merit in the claim that the writers and *Penthouse* conspired to injure Mr. Falwell because he produced no evidence that the defendants "acted for any more sinister purpose than to sell magazines." They certainly did that; *Penthouse* estimated that it sold more than 500,000 extra copies of the March issue as a result of the Falwell brouhaha. Finally, Judge Turk ruled, Mr. Falwell cannot claim that the interview represented an invasion of privacy since he "has aggressively nurtured the public spotlight to promote and disseminate his personal views."

Mr. Falwell's dislike for *Penthouse* is understandable. But if everyone could sue a publication merely because they disliked it, the First Amendment would become a nullity. As Judge Turk wrote, "The First Amendment freedoms of speech and press are too precious to be eroded or undermined by the likes and dislikes of persons who invite attention and publicity."

Maybe Mr. Falwell will pursue his case by focusing on the writers, but it's doubtful. There is obviously more publicity value in suing a well-known magazine instead of two unknown writers. The important factor in this case is that the First Amendment has emerged intact from a type of holy assault.

The Idaho STATESMAN

Boise, Idaho, February 6, 1981

There was good news and bad news in U.S. District Judge James C. Turk's decision to let *Penthouse* magazine distribute its current issue, which includes an interview with Moral Majority founder, the Rev. Jerry Falwell.

The good news is that Turk allowed sales of the magazine. To do otherwise would have violated the Constitution's prohibition against prior restraint. The First Amendment simply does not allow the government to stop publication of any material save under dire and severely restricted circumstances.

The bad news is that Turk stopped distribution of the magazine for three days before deciding it was in the public interest to allow distribution. He ordered the delay, he said, to give both sides a chance to be heard.

Anyone who is a federal judge should know better. The Constitution, as interpreted in an array of court decisions, says that prior restraint is not allowed except in rare cases, certainly not to prevent embarrassment for anyone, not even so celebrated a person as Falwell.

If Falwell has been defamed or otherwise misused (he claims his interviewers sold the piece to *Penthouse* without his permission), he has the same recourse as anyone else who has been wronged in print, a suit against those who allegedly victimized him.

It's easy to sympathize with the good reverend, who voiced fears that appearance of the interview in *Penthouse* could "damage irreparably our financial support." A man in his profession has little to gain from having his face and words appear in a sexually oriented magazine.

Still, that's no reason for a federal judge to violate the Constitution, even for three days.

Detroit Free Press

Detroit, Mich., February 7, 1981

THE NATION'S grief over the disappearance of Penthouse magazine from the news stands would be limited, but it was good that a federal judge did not finally prevent distribution of the current issue. The real question was not the interview with the Rev. Jerry Falwell but whether a court should engage in prior restraint of a publication.

U.S. District Judge James Turk of Lynchburg, Va., came to see that a bit late, but on Monday he said: "This is a First Amendment case. The proper relief is to seek compensatory damages after the fact rather than prior restraint." He dissolved a temporary order that would have prevented distribution of the March issue.

The temporary order was, though, another ominous precedent. It came as the magazine was on its way to distributors, and further delay in dissolving the order might have had the effect of blocking publication. This case, then, must be added to those of the New York Times, in the Pentagon Papers case, and the Progressive magazine, in the case of an article on building nuclear bombs, as historically significant interruptions of an American tradition against prior restraint of publication.

The Rev. Mr. Falwell now may sue Penthouse, and if he has a case he may collect some money. He contends he was interviewed under false pretenses, not knowing the result would be in Penthouse. It says something about Mr. Falwell that he would have happily suppressed publication rather than following the time-honored practice of seeking remedy after publication. We should not be surprised, given his religious rigidities that sometimes take little account of constitutional processes.

And it says something about Judge Turk that he would have engaged in prior restraint, for whatever reason but especially for such a flimsy reason. Would he have shut down a Virginia newspaper if Mr. Falwell had made a similiar claim against it? Prior restraint is a doctrine that conflicts fundamentally with freedom of the press in this country, and it matters not whether the publication is the Richmond Times-Dispatch, the New York Times or Penthouse.

Penthouse figures it will sell an additional half a million copies of the March issue because Mr. Falwell brought it to so many people's attention. Sandwiched between photos of naked ladies will be the evangelist's words on morality. We can hardly wait not to buy a copy.

THE BLADE

Toledo, Ohio, February 3, 1981

THE Rev. Jerry Falwell, founder of the so-called Moral Majority, is given to sermonizing on almost any topic.

In a current magazine interview, for example, Mr. Falwell who, as befits a man of the cloth, operates on a modest budget of more than $50 million a year, takes on a broad range of targets, including former President Jimmy Carter.

Asked to comment on Mr. Carter's celebrated observation in 1976 that he occasionally lusted after women, Mr. Falwell delivered this stern response:

My objection was not to what he said but to whom he said it. Giving an interview to Playboy magazine was lending the credence and the dignity of the highest office in the land to a salacious, vulgar magazine that did not even deserve the time of his day . . . He should have denied them the interview . . . I feel that he was pitching; he was campaigning to an audience that does't read the Baptist Sunday school quarterlies . . .

What sheer hypocrisy!

Mr. Falwell is entitled, of course, to his opinion of any magazine that drapes generous displays of nudity and worse around ostensibly serious articles, though one may wonder how such a pillar of virtue knows what is really in Playboy.

But before slapping at fellow Baptist Jimmy Carter for his interview, perhaps Mr. Falwell ought to have taken prayerful note of the moral tone and spiritual qualities of Penthouse magazine — the March issue of which touts on its cover, right next to a barebreasted cupcake, its "Exclusive Interview With Reverend Jerry Falwell."

Mr. Falwell now claims that he did not know where this lengthy interview was to appear, but it is difficult to believe that anyone as familiar with the operations of the media as he is would bare his soul to writers unless he was certain of the audience he was addressing.

If the reverend thinks that Playboy is salacious and vulgar, to use his terms, wait until he dips into Penthouse.

Index

J

JARVIS, Howard A.
    "Tax revolt" influence noted—2–3
JEWS—see JUDAISM
JEPSEN, Sen. Roger W. (R, Iowa)
    Sponsors Family Protection Act—
        203–204
JOHNSON, Sonia
    Mormons excommunicate—45–51
JUDAISM
    Hollings regrets anti-Semitic remark—
        131–139
    Monty Python movie opposed—180–
        813
JUKES, Dr. Thomas
    Vs Calif "creation science"—76–84
JUSTICE, Department of
    Senate bars from school prayer
        cases—131–139

K

KANAWHA County—see WEST Virginia
KEITH, State Sen. Bill (La.)
    "Creation Science" bill—88–90

L

LABOR—see EMPLOYMENT
LAXALT, Sen. Paul (R, Nev.)
    Sponsors Family Protection Act—
        203–204
LEGAL Services Corporation
    Family Protection Act seeks limits—
        203–204
LEGAL System—see also SUPREME
Court
    Mormon judge on ERA case scored—
        45–51
    Sex harassment protection asked—
        54–60
    Arkansas "creation science" on trial—
        91–109
LEGISLATION—see CONGRESS
LIBERALISM—see also POLITICS
    "New Right" reacts against—5–20
    NCPAC "hit list" scored—27–34
    TV violence opposed—180–183
    Conference on families—197–202
LIBRARIES
    Targets of book-banners—161–174
LITERATURE
    Growing censorship noted—161–174
LOBBY Groups
    Conservative action noted—2–3
    Evangelical Christians form—5–20
    Effect on politics noted—27–34
    Anti-abortion "hit list" scored—35–
        36
    Goldwater scores "New Right"—61–70
LOUISIANA
    Passes "creation science" law—88–
        90
    Baton Rouge bans Monty Python
        movie—180–183

M

MALAMUD, Bernard
    Target of book-banners—161–162,
        171–174
MARRIAGE—see FAMILY Issues
MARYLAND
    "Voluntary" prayer law—124–127
MASSACHUSETTS
    Cardinal warns voters vs candidates—
        5–20

"Voluntary" prayer law—124–127
MEDEIROS, Humberto Cardinal
    Warns voters vs candidates—5–20
MEDIA—see BROADCASTING, TELEVISION
MERCHANT of Venice, The (play)
    Parental opposition cited—167–170
METZENBAUM, Sen. Howard (D, Ohio)
    Hollings regrets anti-Semitic remark—
        131–139
MILITARY Issues—see DEFENSE
MINORITIES
    Opposition to literary works noted—
        167–170
MINORS—see FAMILY Issues, TEENAGERS
MISSISSIPPI
    "Voluntary" prayer law—124–127
MISSOURI, University of (Kansas City)
    Supreme Court OKs private prayer
        group—140–145
MOFFETT, Rep. Toby (D, Conn.)
    Scores "Chastity Act"—205–208
MONTY Python's Life of Brian (movie)
    Religious groups oppose—180–183
MORALITY
    Religious principles and—1
    Moral Majority accused of forcing standards—21–26
    Goldwater scores "New Right"—61–
        70
    Parents seek book bans—161–174
    "Secular humanism" blamed for social
        problems—175–178
MORALITY In Media (lobby group)
    Opposes Monty Python movie—180–
        183
MORAL MAJORITY, Inc.
    Growing influence noted—5–20
    Republican victory hailed—21–26
    Goldwater criticizes—61–70
    Yale president scores—71–72
    TV boycott planned—184–196
    Penthouse distribution ban rejected—
        209–212
MORMON Church (Church of Jesus
Christ of Latter-Day Saints)
    Feminist excommunicated, ERA judge
        opposed—45–51
MORRIS, Desmond
    Target of book-banners—171–174
MOVIES
    "New Right," others oppose violence,
        sex—180–183

N

NATIONAL Broadcasting Co. (NBC)
    Scores boycott plan—185–196
NATIONAL Conservative Political
Action Committee (NCPAC)
    Lobby influence grows—2–3
    "Hit list" criticized—27–34
NATIONAL Pro-Life Political Action
Committee (NPLPAC)
    Congressmen withdraw re "hit list"—
        25–26
NEVADA
    "Voluntary" prayer law—124–127
NEW Hampshire
    "Voluntary" prayer law—124–127
NEW Jersey
    "Voluntary" prayer law—124–127
NEWMAN, Judge Jon O.
    Orders Island Tree case to trial—171–
        174
"NEW Right"
    Growing influence noted—2–26
    Difference from "old right"—4

Vs ERA—52–53
    Goldwater criticizes—61–70
    Yale president criticizes—71–72
    Book-banning pressure grows—163–
        166, 171–174
    Vs "secular humanism"—175–178
    Scores TV shows, plans boycott—
        180–196
    Scores conference on families—197–
        202
    Family Protection Act backed—203–
        204
NEW York
    High school student prayer group rejected—140–145
    Book-banning case ordered to trial—
        171–174
NORTH Carolina
    Charlotte bans Monty Python movie—
        180–183
NORTON, Eleanor Holmes
    Testifies on sex harassment—54–60
NOW—see WOMEN, National Organization for

O

OFFICE for Intellectual Freedom—see
AMERICAN Library Association
O'HAIR, Madalyn Murray
    Sues vs school prayer—110–111
O'HAIR, William
    Repents school prayer role—110–111
"ORIGIN of Life" Controversy—see
CONCEPTION
OVERTON, Judge William Ray
    Rejects Arkansas "creation science"—
        98–109

P

PARENTAL Rights—see FAMILY Protection Act
PENNSYLVANIA
    1963 suit vs school prayer—110–111
PENTHOUSE (magazine)
    Falwell sues to block distribution—
        209–212
PERLUSS, Judge Irving
    Rules vs "creation science"—76–84
PICO v. Board of Education, Island
Trees
    Case ordered to trial—171–174
PLAYBOY (magazine)
    Falwell scores Carter interview—209–
        212
POLITICAL Action Committees
(PACs)—See LOBBY Groups
POLITICS—see also ELECTIONS,
LOBBY Groups
    Conservative trend noted—2–3
    Church-state conflicts begin—4
    "New Right," Moral Majority noted;
        Catholic cardinal & voters—5–20
    NCPAC "hit list" scored; lobby groups'
        growth noted—27–34
    Anti-abortion "hit list" scored—35–
        36
    Goldwater scores "New Right"—61–70
PORNOGRAPHY
    Graham scores Moral Majority—21–
        26
    Schoolbook controversy—161–174
    Falwell scores "secular humanism"—
        175–178
    "New Right," women oppose—180–
        183
    Conference on families debates—197–
        202